Christopher T. S. Ragan

McGill University

Richard G. Lipsey

Professor Emeritus, Simon Fraser University

Eleventh Canadian Edition

MACROECONOMICS

PEARSON

Addison
Wesley

Toronto

National Library of Canada Cataloguing in Publication

Ragan, Christopher
  Macroeconomics/Christopher T. S. Ragan, Richard G. Lipsey.—11th Canadian ed.

Includes index.
Authors' names in reverse order on Canadian 10th ed.
ISBN 0-321-24207-6

1. Macroeconomics—Textbooks. I. Lipsey, Richard G., 1928– II. Lipsey, Richard G., 1928– .
Microeconomics. III. Title.

HB172.5.R35 2005   339   C2003-905961-8

Vice President, Editorial Director: Michael J. Young
Senior Acquisitions Editor: Gary Bennett
Marketing Manager: Steve McGill
Developmental Editor: Maurice Esses
Production Editor: Marisa D'Andrea
Copy Editor: Laurel Sparrow
Proofreader: Catherine Haggert
Production Coordinator: Janette Lush
Permissions Research: Marnie Lamb
Photo Research: Alene McNeill
Page Layout: Nelson Gonzalez
Art Director: Mary Opper
Interior and Cover Design: Anthony Leung
Cover Image: Tom Szuba, MasterFile

Statistics Canada information is used with the permission of the Minister of Industry, as
Minister responsible for Statistics Canada. Information on the availability of the wide range
of data from Statistics Canada can be obtained from Statistics Canada's Regional Offices, its
World Wide Web site at http://www.statcan.ca, and its toll-free access number 1-800-263-1136.
The Statistics Canada CANSIM II database can be accessed at http://cansim2.statcan.ca/.

2 3 4 5   09 08 07 06 05

Printed and bound in the United States of America.

PEARSON

Addison
Wesley

Brief Contents

Contents

List of Boxes

Applying Economic Concepts

Extensions in Theory

Lessons From History

Additional Topics on the Companion Website (www.pearsoned.ca/ragan)

To the Instructor

Economics is a living discipline, changing and evolving in response to developments in the world economy and in response to the research of many thousands of economists throughout the world. Through eleven editions, *Economics* has evolved with the discipline. Our purpose in this edition, as in the previous ten, is to provide students with an introduction to the major issues facing the world's economies, to the methods that economists use to study those issues, and to the policy problems that those issues create. Our treatment is everywhere guided by three important principles:

1. Economics is *scientific,* in the sense that it progresses through the systematic confrontation of theory by evidence. Neither theory nor data alone can tell us much about the world, but combined they tell us a great deal.

2. Economics is *useful* and it should be seen by students to be so. An understanding of economic theory combined with knowledge about the economy produces many important insights about economic policy. Although we stress these insights, we are also careful to point out cases where too little is known to support strong statements about public policy. Appreciating what is not known is as important as learning what is known.

3. We strive always to be *honest* with our readers. Although we know that economics is not always easy, we do not approve of glossing over difficult bits of analysis without letting readers see what is happening and what has been assumed. We take whatever space is needed to explain why economists draw their conclusions, rather than just asserting the conclusions. We also take pains to avoid simplifying matters so much that students would have to unlearn what they have been taught if they continue their study beyond the introductory course. In short, we have tried to follow Albert Einstein's advice:

Everything should be made as simple as possible, but not simpler.

Current Economic Issues

In writing the eleventh edition of *Economics,* we have tried to reflect the major economic issues that we face in the early twenty-first century.

Living Standards and Economic Growth

One of the most fundamental economic issues is the determination of overall living standards. Adam Smith wondered why some countries become wealthy while others remain poor. Though we have learned much about this topic in the past 230 years since Adam Smith's landmark work, economists recognize that there is still much we do not know.

The importance of technological change in determining increases in overall living standards is a theme that permeates both the microeconomics and macroeconomics halves of this book. Chapter 8 explores how firms deal with technological change at the micro level, and how changes in their economic environment lead them to create new products and new production processes. Chapters 11 and 12 discuss how imperfectly competitive firms often compete through their innovative practices, and the importance for policymakers of designing competition policy to keep these practices as energetic as possible.

Technological change also plays a central role in our discussions of long-run economic growth in Chapters 25 and 26. We explore the traditional channels of saving, investment, and population growth, but also the more recent economic theories that emphasize the importance of increasing returns and endogenous growth.

We are convinced that no other introductory economics textbook places as much emphasis on technological change and economic growth as we do in this book. Given the importance of continuing growth in living standards and understanding where that growth comes from, we believe this emphasis is appropriate. We hope you agree.

Globalization

Enormous changes have occurred throughout the world over the last few decades. Flows of trade and investment between countries have risen so dramatically that it is now common to speak of the "globalization" of the world economy. Today it is no longer possible to study any economy without taking into account developments in the rest of the world.

What is true for most countries is also true for Canada. Economic relations between Canada and the rest of the world have a significant impact on most of the major "domestic" issues in the news.

For example, some observers believe that the difficulties faced by Canadian farmers in recent years are caused partly by subsidies that U.S. and European governments provide to their farmers. Students should know how subsidies to foreign farmers affect farmers in Canada. They should also be able to discuss the overall costs and benefits to Canada from agricultural income-support policies, whether they are subsidies or supply-management schemes. We address these issues in some detail in Chapter 5. In Chapter 34, we address why agricultural-support policies continue to be a source of friction in international trade negotiations, such as the current Doha round of the WTO talks that began in 2001.

In recent years, many Canadians have begun worrying about a possible "brain drain" to the United States. The fear is that Canada's "best and brightest" are leaving in increasing numbers, in pursuit of greater employment prospects, lower income taxes, and higher living standards available south of the border. How mobile is labour across international borders? Does such labour mobility imply that Canada's policies cannot diverge significantly from those in other countries? We explore these issues at various points throughout the book, especially in Chapters 13, 14, and 18.

With globalization and the international trade of goods and assets come fluctuations in exchange rates. In recent years there have been substantial changes in the Canada–U.S. exchange rate; a 15-percent depreciation followed the Asian economic crisis in 1997–98, but an even greater appreciation occurred in 2003. Such volatility in exchange rates complicates the conduct of economic policy. In Chapters 28 and 29 we explore how the exchange rate fits into the design and operation of Canada's monetary policy. In Chapter 35 we examine the debate between fixed and flexible exchange rates.

The forces of globalization are with us to stay. In this eleventh edition of *Economics*, we have done our best to ensure that students are made aware of the world outside Canada and of how events elsewhere in the world affect the Canadian economy.

The Role of Government

The political winds appear to have shifted in Canada, the United States, and many other countries over the past two decades. Political parties that once advocated a greater role for government in the economy now argue the benefits of proscribed government. But has the fundamental role of government really changed? In order to understand the role of government in the economy, students must understand the benefits of free markets as well as the situations that cause markets to fail. They must also understand that governments often intervene in the economy for reasons related more to equity than to efficiency.

In this eleventh edition of *Economics*, we continue to incorporate the discussion of government policy as often as possible. Here are but a few of the many examples that we explore:

- the effects of payroll taxes (in Chapter 4)
- fiscal policy (in Chapters 22 and 24)
- policies related to the economy's long-run growth rate (in Chapter 26)
- the importance of debt and deficits (in Chapter 32)
- monetary policy (in Chapters 28, 29, and 30)
- policies that affect the economy's long-run unemployment rate (in Chapter 31)
- trade policies (in Chapter 34)
- policies related to the exchange rate (in Chapter 35)

The Book

Economic growth, globalization, and the role of government are pressing issues of the day. Much of our study of economic principles and the Canadian economy has been shaped by these issues. In addition to specific coverage of growth and internationally oriented topics, growth and globalization appear naturally throughout the book in the treatment of many topics once thought to be entirely "domestic."

Most chapters of *Economics* contain some discussion of economic policy. We have two main goals in mind when we present these discussions:

1. We aim to give students practice in using economic theory, because applying theory is both a wonderfully effective teaching method and a reliable test of students' grasp of theory.

2. We want to introduce students to the major policy issues of the day and to let them discover that few policy debates are as "black and white" as they often appear in the press.

Both goals reflect our view that students should see economics as useful in helping us to understand and deal with the world around us.

Macroeconomics: Structure and Coverage

Our treatment of macroeconomics is divided into six parts. In this edition we have made a clear distinction between the economy in the short run and the economy in the long run, and we have brought forward the material on long-run economic growth. The result is that students will now be confronted with issues of long-run economic growth *before* they are introduced to issues of money and banking. Given the importance of economic growth in driving overall living standards, we feel this is an appropriate ordering of the material; but for those who prefer to discuss money before thinking about economic growth, the ordering can be easily switched without any loss of continuity.

The first macro chapter, Chapter 19, identifies economic growth and the level of potential national income as the major determinants of a society's material standard of living. The discussion of national income accounting in Chapter 20 provides a thorough treatment of the distinction between real and nominal GDP, the distinction between GDP and GNP, and a discussion of what measures of national income *do not measure*.

Part 8 develops the core short-run model of the macro economy, beginning with the fixed-price (Keynesian Cross) model in Chapters 21 and 22 and then moving on to the *AD/AS* model in Chapter 23. Chapter 21 uses a closed economy model with no government to explain the process of national-income determination and the nature of the multiplier. Chapter 22 extends the setting to include international trade and government spending and taxation. Chapter 23 rounds out our discussion of the short run with the *AD/AS* framework, discussing the importance of both aggregate demand and aggregate supply shocks. We place the Keynesian Cross before the *AD/AS* model to show that there is no mystery as to where the *AD* curve comes from and why it is downward sloping; the *AD* curve is derived directly from the Keynesian Cross model. In contrast, books that begin their analysis with the *AD/AS* model are inevitably less clear about where the model comes from. We lament the growing tendency to omit the Keynesian Cross from introductory macroeconomic textbooks; we believe the model has much to offer students in terms of economic insights.

Part 9 begins in Chapter 24 by showing how the short-run model evolves toward the long run through the adjustment of factor prices—what we often call the Phillips Curve. We introduce potential output as an "anchor" to which real GDP returns following *AD* or

AS shocks. This chapter also addresses issues in fiscal policy, including the important distinction between automatic stabilizers and discretionary fiscal stabilization policy. Chapter 25 is a short chapter that contrasts short-run macroeconomics with long-run macroeconomics, emphasizing the different typical causes of output changes over the two time spans. Using Canadian data, we show that long-run changes in GDP have their root causes in changes in factor supplies and productivity, whereas short-run changes in GDP are more closely associated with changes in the factor utilization rate. With this short-run/long-run distinction firmly in place, we are well positioned for the detailed discussion of long-run economic growth that appears in Chapter 26. Our treatment of long-run growth, which we regard as one of the most important issues facing Canada and the world today, goes well beyond the treatment in most introductory texts.

Part 10 focuses on the role of money and financial systems. Chapter 27 discusses the nature of money, various components of the money supply, the commercial banking system, and the Bank of Canada. In Chapter 28 we review the determinants of the demand for money. We then turn to a detailed discussion of the link between the money supply and other economic variables such as interest rates, the exchange rate, national income, and the price level. This chapter builds directly on the material in Chapters 23 and 24, with an emphasis on the distinction between short-run and long-run effects. In Chapter 29 we discuss the Bank of Canada's monetary policy including a detailed discussion of inflation targeting. The chapter ends with a review of Canadian monetary policy over the past 25 years. This provides some important historical context for policy discussions later in the book, as well as an opportunity to draw some general conclusions about the operation of monetary policy.

Part 11 deals with some of today's most pressing macroeconomic policy issues. It contains separate chapters on inflation, unemployment, and government budget deficits. Chapter 30 on inflation examines the central role of expectations in determining inflation, and the importance of credibility on the part of the central bank. Chapter 31 on unemployment examines the determinants of frictional and structural unemployment and discusses likely reasons for increases in the NAIRU over the past few decades. Chapter 32 on budget deficits stresses the effect of deficits on national saving and long-term economic growth.

Virtually every macroeconomic chapter contains at least some discussion of international issues. However, the final part of *Economics* focuses primarily on international economics. Chapter 33 gives the basic treatment of international trade, developing both the traditional theory of static comparative advantage and newer theories based on imperfect competition and dynamic comparative advantage. Chapter 34 discusses both the positive and normative aspects of trade policy, as well as the GATT and WTO and prospects for regional free-trade areas. There is also a detailed discussion of NAFTA and a box on Canada–U.S. trade disputes. Chapter 35 introduces the balance of payments and examines exchange-rate determination. Here we also discuss three important policy issues: the desirability of current-account deficits or surpluses, whether there is a "right" value for the Canadian exchange rate, and the costs and benefits of Canada's adopting a fixed exchange rate.

We hope you find this menu both attractive and challenging; we hope students find the material stimulating and enlightening. Many of the messages of economics are complex—if economic understanding were only a matter of common sense and simple observation, there would be no need for professional economists and no need for textbooks like this one. To understand economics, one must work hard. Working at this book should help readers gain a better understanding of the world around them and of the policy problems faced by all levels of government. Furthermore, in today's globalized world, the return to education is large. We like to think that we have contributed in some small part to the understanding that increased investment in human capital by the next generation is necessary to restore incomes to the rapid growth paths that so benefited our parents and our peers. Perhaps we may even contribute to some income-enhancing accumulation of human capital by some of our readers.

Substantive Changes to This Edition

We have done a major revision and update of the entire text with guidance from an extensive series of formal reviews and other feedback from both users and nonusers of the previous editions of this book. As always, we have strived very hard to improve the teachability and readability of the book. We have focused the discussions so that the major point is emphasized as clearly as possible, without the reader being distracted by non-essential points. We have removed some material from the textbook and placed it in the

Additional Topics section of the book's Companion Website (**www.pearsoned.ca/ragan**). The Companion Website also includes new material that has been written especially for this edition. (A complete listing of the *Additional Topics* on the Companion Website is provided following the Table of Contents.) As in recent editions, we have kept all core material in the main part of the text. The three boxes (Applying Economic Concepts, Lessons From History, and Extensions in Theory) are used to show examples or extensions that can be skipped without fear of missing an essential concept. But we think it would be a shame to skip too many of them, as there are many interesting examples and policy discussions in these boxes.

What follows is a brief listing of the main changes that we have made to the textbook.

Macroeconomics

We have modified the ordering of our macroeconomic coverage from the previous edition. Following the introductory part, which includes discussion of the national accounts, we include two main theoretical parts that deal with the real economy. The first develops a model of the economy in the short run; we begin with the fixed-price Keynesian Cross and then extend this to the *AD/AS* model with fixed factor prices. The second part begins with the simple *AD/AS* model and then allows the process of factor-price adjustment to return real GDP to potential GDP. A discussion on the long-run growth of potential output follows. In both of these key theoretical parts, fiscal policy makes an appearance, especially in Chapters 22 and 24.

After dealing with short-run fluctuations and long-run growth, the book then introduces money, banking, and monetary policy. The next part contains three chapters, each one directed at analyzing an important policy problem: inflation, unemployment, and budget deficits. Each of these chapters builds on the theory developed earlier. Finally, the book concludes with a three-chapter part on international economics, including the gains from trade, trade policy, and open-economy macroeconomics.

This sequencing of topics allows students to understand both the short run and the long run, and the key differences between them, before delving into the details of money. We feel that by delaying the treatment of money in this way, more attention will be paid to the topic of long-run economic growth, an aspect of macroeconomics that we feel deserves to be emphasized. However, for those instructors who prefer to discuss money early on and delay or perhaps skip altogether the treatment of long-run growth, the chapters are written so that money and monetary policy can be examined before any attention is paid to long-run growth. In this respect, the ordering of our macroeconomics treatment is amenable to different teaching preferences and styles.

Part Seven: An Introduction to Macroeconomics

Chapter 19 provides a quick overview of macroeconomics, including an introduction to the main macroeconomic variables. We have moved the "growth versus fluctuations" section to the end of the chapter, where it will be better appreciated following the discussion of the main macro variables. In addition, we have streamlined this chapter considerably; in several places, we have moved advanced material to later chapters where the topics are addressed in further detail.

Chapter 20 examines the measurement of national income and price indexes. We have reworked the box on value added, using a specific example to better illustrate the main point. The circular flow diagram has been moved here (from the previous chapter), where it better motivates the discussion of the income and expenditure approaches for measuring national income. Finally, we have reworked the discussion of aggregate output and overall well-being.

Part Eight: The Economy in the Short Run

Chapter 21 presents a very simple model of the economy, with a fixed price level and exogenous exchange rate and interest rate, that illustrates the Keynesian Cross and the multiplier. We have rewritten much of the discussion of the consumption function (and put some of the previous detail in a new box). Our discussion of what causes shifts in the consumption function is now more systematic. We have also rewritten the discussion of investment and included a new diagram. In our treatment of the multiplier, we have written a new section on realistic values for the multiplier in Canada. Finally, we have added a new final section on self-fulfilling prophesies and the importance of expectations in a demand-determined economy.

Chapter 22 introduces government and international trade to the simple macro model. We have reworked the discussion of the net tax function, and added separate diagrams for taxation and government purchases. We have also included quick summaries of how the addition of government and foreign trade affects the model—we hope this clarifies our overall treatment of the extended model. Our discussion of the AE function has been rewritten to provide a step-

by-step approach. We have added a new discussion of how taxes and imports affect the realistic value of the multiplier. Finally, we have used a new diagram to better illustrate the objectives of fiscal stabilization policy.

We develop the simple *AD/AS* model in Chapter 23, thereby introducing an endogenous price level. But we remain in the short run because wages are fixed. We have deleted the previous material on Ricardian Equivalence, and expanded our discussion of the slope of the *AD* curve. We now refer to the aggregate supply curve simply as the *AS* curve, rather than distinguishing between short-run and long-run curves. We think this simpler notation will lead to less confusion.

Part Nine: The Economy in the Long Run

Chapter 24 focuses on the adjustment process that takes the model from the short run, in which wages and other factor prices are constant, to the long run, in which factor prices have fully adjusted to output gaps. We have added a new discussion at the beginning of the chapter that lays out the various time spans in macroeconomics—the short run, the adjustment process, and the long run. We now introduce the concept of potential output as an "anchor" to which real GDP returns following demand or supply shocks. A diagram in the box on the Phillips Curve to better illustrate the connection between the Phillips Curve and the *AD/AS* diagram has been added, as well as new diagrams showing the time path of GDP following shocks. We have also reworked our discussion of long-run equilibrium. Finally, we have rewritten the section on automatic fiscal stabilizers and added considerably to our concluding discussion of fiscal policy and long-run growth, introducing the notion of "supply-side" macro policies.

Chapter 25 is a short chapter outlining the key differences between short-run and long-run macroeconomics. We have moved this chapter on short run vs. long run to a later position in the book so that students will be able to grasp its important ideas more easily. We focus on breaking down output changes into three component parts, some of which change primarily over the short run and others mostly in the long run. We have modified the chapter to reflect its new placement after the development of the *AD/AS* model.

Chapter 26 examines the process of long-run economic growth in more detail than in other introductory textbooks. This chapter on growth now appears earlier in the book. We have substantially rewritten the section on the connection between saving, investment, and growth, and have added new figures showing the market for loanable funds. We have made some clarifying changes to the discussion of Neoclassical growth theory, as well as changes to the sections on technological change and the limits to growth.

Part Ten: Money, Banking, and Monetary Policy

Our introduction to money and the institutional details of banking occurs in Chapter 27. We have moved the section on "two perspectives on money" to the next chapter where it fits more naturally in the discussion of money neutrality. We have reworked our treatments of excess reserves and deposit expansion, and we have trimmed the discussion of near money and money substitutes.

Chapter 28 examines the interaction of money demand and money supply, and develops in detail the workings of the monetary transmission mechanism. We have completely rewritten the opening section to more clearly present the concept of present value and the relationship between interest rates and bond prices. We have added a new box that illustrates the interpretation of bond prices. We have also rewritten and shortened the discussion of money demand, and reworked the discussion of the monetary transmission mechanism. In our discussion of the neutrality of money, we have added a diagram of the money market so that students can see its connection to the AD/AS diagram. The discussion of long-run money neutrality, including mention of the possibility of "hysteresis," has been rewritten.

The conduct of Canadian monetary policy is examined in Chapter 29, which has been substantially rewritten for this edition. In our discussion of open-market operations, we have simplified the example by assuming that the Bank of Canada transacts directly with commercial banks. We have reworked the box on contractionary monetary policy and added a figure to illustrate the main point. We have also made it very clear that the Bank of Canada conducts its policy by setting the bank rate, but we point out the connection between setting the interest rate and setting reserves in the banking system. We have rewritten the box on the bank rate and added a data figure showing the path of the bank rate and the overnight rate. We have entirely rewritten the section on policy instruments and policy targets. We now have a detailed discussion of inflation targeting as well as some of the related technical complications, including the role of exchange-rate movements and the need to control for volatile food and energy prices. Finally, we have reworked our discussion of "25 years of monetary policy"—it now includes a section on the costs of very

low inflation (brought forward from the following chapter).

Part Eleven: Macroeconomic Problems

Chapter 30 examines inflation and the costs associated with disinflation. We have added a new figure at the beginning of the chapter to show the path of Canadian inflation. We have created a new box that contains previous material on how private agents form their expectations of inflation. The discussion of a constant inflation in the AD/AS model has been reworked to improve clarity. The previous discussion of the "death of inflation" now appears as an optional box.

Unemployment is examined in detail in Chapter 31. We have added a data figure showing the path of Canadian unemployment at the beginning of the chapter, and included an analytical diagram explaining stocks and flows in the box on labour-market flows. The discussion of New Classical theories of unemployment has been reworked, and we have added a table summarizing the key differences between the New Classical and New Keynesian theories. Finally, we have added a short discussion of the effects of free trade to the section on structural unemployment.

Chapter 32 discusses the effects of government debt and budget deficits. We have clarified the notation by continuing with the earlier assumption that T is taxes net of transfers. The figures illustrating the cyclically adjusted deficit have been improved, as has the figure illustrating the concept of Ricardian Equivalence. Finally, we have updated the concluding discussion of what effects can be expected from the budget surpluses that are widely expected to occur over the next few years.

Part Twelve: Canada in the Global Economy

Chapter 33 examines the gains from international trade. We have substantially rewritten the section on absolute and comparative advantage. We have also added a new discussion of the terms of trade, together with a new figure showing how changes in the terms of trade lead to changes in consumption possibilities.

The theory and practice of trade policy is given a detailed treatment in Chapter 34. We have expanded our discussion of a large country using tariffs to alter its terms of trade. We have also clarified our treatment of tariffs and quotas, using separate figures to show the effects of each policy. We have added a new discussion of Canadian softwood lumber and how this example nicely illustrates the difference between tariffs and quotas. Finally, we have updated the discussion of the World Trade Organization, adding a brief analysis of the problems associated with the current Doha round of trade negotiations.

Chapter 35 examines exchange rates and the balance of payments. We have modified the box on fixed exchange rates to clarify the discussion. We have added a data figure showing the path of Canada's current account balance. To our discussion of purchasing power parity, we have added a data figure showing the divergence between the actual Canada–U.S. exchange rate and the PPP exchange rate. We have also modified our treatment of flexible exchange rates as a shock absorber.

Finally, we have removed the old Chapter 33 (Challenges Facing the Developing Countries) from the printed book and we have placed it as Chapter 36W on the Companion Website.

If you are moved to write to us (and we hope that you will be!), please do. You can send any comments or questions regarding the text (or any of the supplementary material, such as the *Study Guide*) to:

Christopher Ragan
Department of Economics
McGill University
855 Sherbrooke St. West
Montreal, Quebec
H3A 2T7

Or, if you prefer to communicate through e-mail, send your comments to:

christopher.ragan@mcgill.ca

To the Student

You must develop your own technique for studying, but the following suggestions may prove helpful. Begin by carefully considering the Learning Objectives at the beginning of a chapter. Read the chapter itself relatively quickly in order to get the general run of the argument. At this first reading, you may want to skip the boxes and any footnotes. Then, after reading the Chapter Summary and the Key Concepts (at the end of each chapter), reread the chapter more slowly, making sure that you understand each step of the argument.

With respect to the figures and tables, be sure you understand how the conclusions that are stated in boldface at the beginning of each caption have been reached. You must not skip the captions. They provide the core of economic reasoning. You should be prepared to spend time on difficult sections; occasionally, you may spend an hour on only a few pages. Paper and pencil are indispensable equipment in your reading. It is best to follow a difficult argument by building your own diagram while the argument unfolds rather than by relying on the finished diagram as it appears in the book.

The end-of-chapter Study Exercises require you to practise using some of the concepts that you learned in the chapter. These will be excellent preparation for your exams. To provide you with immediate feedback, we have posted Solutions to Selected Study Exercises on the Companion Website (**www.pearsoned.ca/ragan**). The end-of-chapter Discussion Questions require you to apply what you have studied. We advise you to outline answers to some of the questions. In short, you should seek to understand economics, not to memorize it.

The bracketed boldface numbers in the text itself refer to a series of mathematical notes that are found starting on page M-1 at the end of the book. For those of you who like mathematics or prefer mathematical argument to verbal or geometric exposition, these may prove useful. Others may disregard them.

A time line, which runs from the mid-1600s to the mid-1900s, follows the mathematical notes. Along this time line we have placed brief descriptions of the life and works of some great economists, most of whom you will encounter in the textbook. We hope this will improve your sense of history and your sense of what these great economists achieved.

In this edition of the book, we have incorporated many elements to help you review material and prepare for examinations. Pay special attention to the learning objectives, the important concepts highlighted in red, the key terms that are boldfaced and restated in the margins, the captions that accompany the features and tables, the lists of key concepts, and the chapter summaries. A brief description of all the features in this book is given in the separate section that follows.

We also think you will find the book's Companion Website (**www.pearsoned.ca/ragan**) very useful, and we encourage you to check it out early in your program of study. As we mentioned above, the Companion Website includes Solutions to Selected Study Exercises. This site also includes a set of self-testing multiple-choice questions for each chapter. You can try these questions, send your answers to the electronic grader, and receive instant feedback. You can use these questions to practise for your upcoming exams. The Companion Website also contains a Glossary of all the key terms in the book. Four Video Cases, along with the accompanying CBC video segments, are also provided to help enhance your understanding of how to apply economic principles to current events.

At many points in the book, you will be directed to the Companion Website to find discussions of *Additional Topics*—these represent material written especially for this textbook, and include many interesting theoretical, empirical, and policy discussions. You will also be directed to the Companion Website to find articles from *World Economic Affairs*. The articles (written by academic and professional economists) were chosen because they discuss issues with particular clarity, and therefore should be of value to students who are just getting their feet wet in economics. We hope you find them useful.

We strongly suggest you make use of the excellent *Study Guide* written expressly for this text. The *Study Guide* is closely integrated with the book. In fact, special references in the margins of the textbook will direct you to appropriate practice questions and exercises in the *Study Guide*. They will test and reinforce your understanding of the concepts and analytical techniques stressed in each chapter of the text and will help you prepare for your examinations. The ability to solve problems and to communicate and interpret your results are important goals in an introductory course in economics. The *Study Guide* can play an important role in your acquisition of these skills.

If you have any comments, please e-mail Christopher Ragan at: christopher.ragan@mcgill.ca.

Features of This Edition

We have made a careful effort with this edition to incorporate features that will facilitate the teaching and learning of economics.

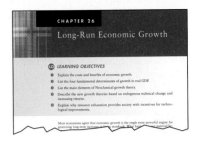

- A set of **Learning Objectives** at the beginning of each chapter clarifies the skills and knowledge to be learned in each chapter. These same learning objectives are used in the chapter summaries, as well as in the *Study Guide* and in the Testbank.

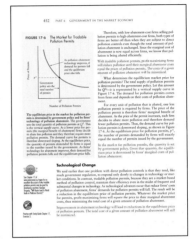

- **Major ideas** are highlighted in red in the text.
- **Key terms** are boldfaced where they are defined in the body of the text and they are restated with their definitions in the margins. In the index at the back of the book, each key term and its page reference to its definition are boldfaced.
- **Weblinks** to useful Internet addresses are given in the margins. Each weblink presents a URL address, along with a brief description of the material available there. Some links are to government home pages where much data can be obtained. Other links are to organizations such as OPEC, the UN, and the WTO. We have also included links to selected articles from *World Economic Affairs* that we have posted on the Companion Website for this textbook.
- **Study Guide** references in the margin direct students to appropriate questions in the *Study Guide* that reinforce the topic being discussed in the text.

- **Applying Economic Concepts** boxes demonstrate economics in action, providing examples of how theoretical material relates to issues of current interest.

- **Lessons From History** boxes contain discussions of a particular policy debate or empirical finding that takes place in a historical context.
- **Photographs with short captions** are now interspersed throughout the chapters to illustrate some of the arguments.

- **Extensions in Theory** boxes provide a deeper treatment of a theoretical topic that is discussed in the text.

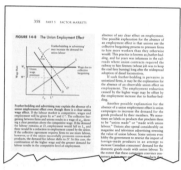

- **A caption for each Figure and Table** summarizes the underlying economic reasoning. Each caption begins with a boldfaced statement of the relevant economic conclusion.
- The **colour scheme for Figures** consistently uses the same colour for each type of curve. For example, all demand curves are blue, whereas all supply curves are red.

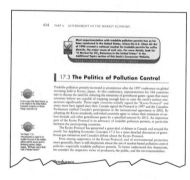

- **Additional Topics on the Companion Website** (www.pearsoned.ca/ragan) are referenced in special boxes inserted at the appropriate place in the body of the relevant chapter.

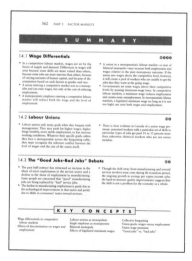

- **Chapter Summaries** are organized using the same numbered heading as found in the body of the chapter. The relevant learning objectives (LO) numbers are given in red next to each heading in the summary.
- **Key Concepts** are listed near the end of each chapter.

- A set of **Study Exercises** is provided for each chapter. These quantitative exercises require the student to analyze problems by means of computations or graphs.

- A set of **Discussion Questions** is also provided for each chapter. These questions require the student to synthesize and generalize. They are designed especially for discussion in class.

- A set of **Mathematical Notes** is presented in a separate section near the end of the book. Because mathematical notation and derivations are not necessary to understand the principles of economics but are more helpful in advanced work, this seems to be a sensible arrangement. References in the text to these mathematical notes are given by means of boldfaced numbers in square brackets.

- A **Time Line of Great Economists**, running from the mid-seventeenth century to the mid-twentieth century, is presented near the end of the book. Along this time line we have placed brief descriptions of the life and works of some great economists, most of whom the reader will encounter in the textbook. Along this time line we have also listed some major world events in order to give readers an appreciation for when these economists did their work.
- **Economists on Record**, given on the inside of the back cover, quotes some classic excerpts that are relevant to the study and practice of economics.
- For convenience, a list of the **Common Abbreviations Used in the Text** is given on the inside of the front cover.

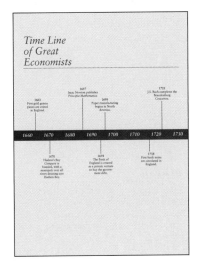

Supplements

A comprehensive set of supplements has been carefully prepared to assist students and instructors in using this new edition.

A thoroughly revised and expanded **Study Guide**, written by Paul T. Dickinson and E. Kenneth Grant, is designed for use either in the classroom or by students on their own. The *Study Guide* offers additional study support and reinforcement for each text chapter. It is closely integrated with the textbook. Special notes in the margins of the textbook direct students to appropriate practice exercises in the *Study Guide*. For each chapter, the *Study Guide* provides the following helpful material:

- Learning Objectives matching those in the textbook
- Chapter Overview
- Hints and Tips (newly added for this edition)
- Chapter Review consisting of multiple-choice questions, organized into sections matching the numbered sections in the textbook
- Short-Answer Questions
- Exercises
- Extension Exercises
- Additional Multiple-Choice Questions

The *Study Guide* is available as a cumulative volume or as split volumes for microeconomics and macroeconomics.

An **Instructor's Resource CD-ROM** has been specially prepared for this new edition. It contains the following items:

- An *Instructor's Manual* (in both Word and PDF format) written by Christopher Ragan. For each text chapter, it provides an overview with teaching suggestions, full solutions to all the Study Exercises, and suggested answers to all the Discussion Questions.
- *PowerPoint Slides* prepared by Christopher Ragan. Instructors can readily adapt these slides for lecture presentations.

- A special computerized testbank, known as **Pearson TestGen**, written by Gregory L. Flanagan and C. Michael Fellows. The testbank consists of more than 3000 multiple-choice questions. For each question, the authors have provided the correct answer, given the relevant page reference in the textbook, given the relevant numbered section in the textbook, given the relevant Learning Objective in the textbook, assigned a level of difficulty (easy, moderate, or challenging), identified the skill tested (recall or applied), noted whether the question is qualitative or quantitative, and noted whether the question involves a graph. *Pearson TestGen* enables instructors to search for questions according to any of these attributes and to sort questions into any order desired. With *Pearson TestGen*, instructors can easily edit existing questions, add questions, generate tests, and print the tests in a variety of formats. *Pearson TestGen* also allows instructors to administer tests on a local area network, have the tests graded electronically, and have the results prepared in electronic or printed reports.

A special **Companion Website** has been created for this book at **www.pearsoned.ca/ragan**. It includes a wealth of material, including the following:

- Self-Test Questions for each chapter. Students can send their answers to an electronic grader and receive instant feedback.
- Additional Topics (as listed following the Table of Contents). These topics, referenced prominently in the body of the book, enhance the coverage for interested instructors and students.
- A Glossary of all the key terms in the book.
- Solutions to Selected Study Exercises.
- Articles from *World Economic Affairs,* cited in the margins of the textbook.
- Hotlinks to the home pages of governments and other organizations that provide much current data.
- Video Cases, with the accompanying CBC video segments.
- A password-protected section from which instructors can download some of the text's supplements.

Acknowledgements

It would be impossible to acknowledge here by name all the teachers, colleagues, and students who contributed to the development and improvement of this book over its previous ten editions. Hundreds of users have written to us with specific suggestions, and much of the credit for the improvement of the book over the years belongs to them. We can no longer list them individually but we thank them all sincerely.

For the development of this eleventh edition, we are grateful to the many people who offered informal suggestions. We would also like to thank the following instructors who provided us with formal reviews of the textbook. Their observations and recommendations were extremely helpful.

- Ather H. Akbari (St. Mary's University)
- Constantine Angyridis (University of Toronto)
- Germain Belzile (Hautes Etudes Commerciales Montréal)
- Michael Benarroch (University of Winnipeg)
- Jeff Davidson (University of Lethbridge)
- Livio Di Mateo (Lakehead University)
- Curt Farrell (Grande Prairie Regional College)
- Tom Fulton (Langara College)
- Gregory Gagnon (University of Toronto)
- Hugh Grant (University of Winnipeg)
- David Gray (University of Ottawa)
- Mobinul Huq (University of Saskatchewan)
- Eric Kam (Ryerson University)
- Rafal Kosztirko (Mount Royal College)
- Nathasha Macdonald (College of the Rockies)
- Roberto Martínez-Espiñeira (St. Francis Xavier University)
- Paul Missios (Ryerson University)
- Ghada Mohamed (Lakehead University)
- Robin Neill (University of Prince Edward Island)
- D. Otchere (Concordia University)
- Donna Park (Langara College)
- Ian Parker (University of Toronto)
- Derek Pyne (Memorial University of Newfoundland)
- Donald Reddick (Kwantlen University College)
- Duane Rockerbie (University of Lethbridge)
- Francisco J. Santos-Arteaga (York University)
- Rob Scharff (Kwantlen University College)
- Jim Sentance (University of Prince Edward Island)
- Lance Shandler (Kwantlen University College)
- Faycal Régis Sinaceur (Concordia University)
- Peter Sinclair (Wilfrid Laurier University)
- Chieko Tanimura (Coquitlam College)
- Jane Waples (Memorial University of Newfoundland)

In addition, we would like to thank the following instructors for providing formal reviews for some of the supplements that accompany this eleventh edition.

- Paul T. Dickinson (McGill University)
- Linda Nielsen (Mount Royal College)
- Francisco J. Santos-Arteaga (York University)
- Rob Scharff (Kwantlen University College)
- Brian VanBlarcom (Acadia University)

We would like to acknowledge the work of Kit Pasula (Okanagan University College), who performed a technical review of the textbook.

We would also like to express our thanks to the many people at Pearson Education Canada who spent long hours managing, editing, and producing this text. In particular, Gary Bennett, Maurice Esses, and Marisa D'Andrea deserve much credit for doing an outstanding job.

Our special thanks go to Ingrid Kristjanson, who did a tremendous amount of editing and also carefully reviewed all changes made to this edition. Her comments led to many improvements. For her diligence and hard work we are especially grateful. This edition is dedicated to her.

A Great Way to Learn and Instruct Online

The Pearson Education Canada Companion Website is easy to navigate and is organized to correspond to the chapters in this textbook. Whether you are a student in the classroom or a distance learner you will discover helpful resources for in-depth study and research that empower you in your quest for greater knowledge and maximize your potential for success in the course.

[www.pearsoned.ca/ragan]

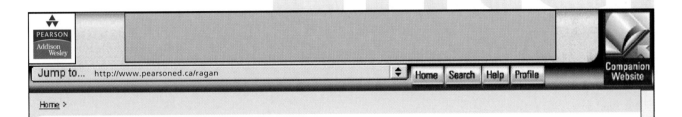

Jump to... | http://www.pearsoned.ca/ragan | Home | Search | Help | Profile

Home >

AW Companion Website

Economics, Eleventh Canadian Edition, by Ragan and Lipsey

Student Resources

The modules in this section provide students with tools for preparing for tests and enhancing their learning experience. These modules include:

- Solutions to Selected Study Exercises
- Quizzes
- Destinations
- Additional Topics cited in the book
- Articles from *World Economic Affairs*
- Glossary

In the quiz modules students can send answers to the grader and receive instant feedback on their progress through the Results Reporter. Coaching comments and references to the textbook may be available to ensure that students take advantage of all available resources to enhance their learning experience.

Instructor Resources

The modules in this password-protected section provide instructors with downloadable versions of the Instructor's Manual and the PowerPoint Slides.

PART ONE

What Is Economics?

Have you ever noticed that, when you go to a store to buy something, the product you seek is almost always available? Or, have you noticed that you rarely see either large numbers of people lined up waiting to buy goods or large amounts of unsold goods with nobody to buy them? What is it about a modern market economy that produces these remarkably coordinated outcomes in which the amount available of something is roughly equal to the amount that people want? What is the study of economics all about, and why will it help you to understand how today's economies function? How do economists do their job of analyzing and explaining economic outcomes? What are economic models, and why are some models more sensible than others? These are questions that you will be able to answer after reading the following two chapters.

Chapter 1 begins by talking about the self-organizing economy, and introduces Adam Smith's famous idea of an invisible hand. Here we see why markets made up of self-interested consumers and producers automatically produce the sort of coordination that we observe. We then examine the concepts of scarcity, choice, and opportunity cost, three ideas that are central to all economic systems. We then introduce the various decision makers in a typical market economy, including individual consumers, producers, and governments, and we see how their interactions can be represented by a circular flow of income and expenditure. Finally, we consider alternative economic systems, ranging from a pure market system to a centrally planned system in which a government planning authority makes all economic decisions. Canada, like all economies, is a mixed system, containing elements of both free markets and government intervention.

Chapter 2 discusses the study of economics itself. We examine positive and normative statements, a distinction upon which the progress of economics as a social science is based. We then examine the role of theory in economics, and why economists—like physicists or chemists—build models to help them think about the complex world they are trying to understand. Finally, we explain how economists test their theories by confronting the predictions of their theories with the available evidence. Here we also discuss graphing—a central tool for economists and one that is used extensively throughout this book—and you will see how different types of graphs can be used to present very different types of information.

Economic Issues and Concepts

L LEARNING OBJECTIVES

1. View the market economy as a self-organizing entity in which order emerges from a large number of decentralized decisions.

2. Describe the importance of scarcity, choice, and opportunity cost, and how all three concepts are illustrated by the production possibilities boundary.

3. Illustrate the circular flow of income and expenditure.

4. Comprehend that all actual economies are mixed economies, having elements of free markets, tradition, and government intervention.

If you want a litre of milk, you go to your local grocery store and buy it. It probably does not occur to you that farmers may have stopped producing milk or that dairies may have stopped delivering it to stores. When the grocer needs more milk, he orders it from the distributor, who in turn gets it from the dairy, which in its turn gets it from the dairy farmer. The dairy farmer buys cattle feed and electric milking machines, and gets power to run all his equipment by putting a plug into a wall outlet where the electricity is supplied as he needs it. The milking machines are made from parts manufactured in several different places in Canada, the United States, and overseas. The parts themselves are made from materials mined and smelted in a dozen or more different countries.

As it is with the milk you drink, so it is with everything else that you buy. When you go to the appropriate store, what you want is normally on the shelf. Those who make these products find that all the required components and materials are available when they need them—even though these things typically come from many different parts of the world and are made by people who have no direct dealings with each other.

1.1 The Complexity of the Modern Economy

Your own transactions are only a small part of the remarkably complex set of transactions that takes place every day in a modern society. Shipments arrive daily at our ports, railway terminals, and airports. These shipments include: raw materials, such as iron ore, logs and oil; parts, such as automobile engines, transistors, and circuit boards; tools, such as screwdrivers, lathes, and digging equipment; perishables, such as fresh flowers, coffee beans, and fruit; and all kinds of manufactured goods, such as washing machines, personal computers, and DVD players. Railways and trucking lines move these goods among thousands of different destinations within Canada. Some go directly to consumers. Others are used by local firms to manufacture their products—some of which will be sold domestically and some exported.

Most people who want to work can find work. They spend their working days engaging in the activities just described. In doing so, they earn incomes that they then spend on goods and services produced by others. Other people own firms that employ workers to assist in the many activities described above, such as importing, making, transporting, and selling things. They earn their incomes as profits from these enterprises.

An **economy** is a system, typically a very complex one, in which scarce resources—such as labour, land and machines—are allocated among competing uses. Decisions must be made about: which goods are produced, and which are not; who works where and at what wage; and who consumes which goods at what times. While each of these individual decisions may seem simple, the entire combination is remarkably complex, especially in modern societies.

economy A system in which scarce resources are allocated among competing uses.

The Self-Organizing Economy

Early in the development of modern economics, thoughtful observers wondered how such a complex set of dealings gets organized. Who coordinates the whole set of efforts? Who makes sure that all the activities fit together, providing jobs to produce the things that people want and delivering those things to where they are wanted? The answer is, surprisingly, no one!

The great insight of economists is that an economy based on free-market transactions is *self-organizing*.

By following their own self-interest, doing what seems best and most profitable for themselves, and responding to the incentives of prices determined in open markets, people produce a spontaneous economic order. In that order, literally thousands of millions of transactions and activities fit together to produce the things that people want within the constraints set by the resources that are available to the nation.

The great Scottish economist and political philosopher Adam Smith (1723–1790)[1], who was the first to develop this insight fully, put it this way:

> *It is not from the benevolence of the butcher, the brewer, or the baker, that we expect our dinner, but from their regard to their own interest. We address ourselves, not to their humanity but to their self-love, and never talk to them of our own necessities but of their advantages.*

Smith is not saying that benevolence is unimportant. Indeed, he praises it in many passages. He is saying, however, that the massive number of economic interactions that characterize a modern economy cannot all be motivated by benevolence. Although benevolence does motivate some of our actions, often the very dramatic ones, the vast majority of our everyday actions are motivated by self-interest. Self-interest, not benevolence, is therefore the foundation of economic order.

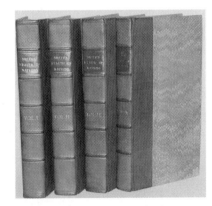

Adam Smith wrote An Inquiry into the Nature and Causes of the Wealth of Nations *in 1776. Now referred to by most people simply as* The Wealth of Nations, *it is considered to be the beginning of modern economics.*

---

[1] Throughout this book, we encounter many great economists from the past whose ideas shaped the discipline of economics. At the back of the book you will find a timeline, beginning in the 1600s, that contains brief discussions of many of these thinkers and places them in their historical context.

Efficient Organization

Another great insight, which was hinted at by Smith and fully developed over the next century and a half, was that this spontaneously generated economic order is relatively *efficient*. Loosely speaking, efficiency means that the resources available to a nation are organized in such a way as to produce the things that people want to buy and in the amounts that they want to purchase.

Using the words of Adam Smith, it can be said that an economy organized by free markets produces ordered behaviour that makes it appear as if people are guided by an *invisible hand*. This does not literally mean that a supernatural presence guides economic affairs. Instead, he referred to the amazing order that emerges out of so many independent decisions. The key to the explanation is that all individuals respond to the same set of prices, which are determined in markets that respond to overall conditions of national scarcity or plenty. Much of economics is devoted to a detailed elaboration of how this market order is generated.

A Planned Alternative

A century after Adam Smith, another great economist and political philosopher, Karl Marx (1818–1883), argued that although such a market system would produce high total output, it would distribute that output in such a way that, over time, the rich would get richer and the poor poorer. He went on to argue that when societies become rich enough, they should replace the unplanned but efficient economic order with a consciously planned system, called *communism*, in which the government plans all transactions and, in so doing, creates a more socially just distribution of the total output.

Beginning with the Soviet Union in the early 1920s, many nations listened to Marx and established systems in which conscious government *central planning* largely replaced the spontaneous order of the free market. For much of the twentieth century two systems, the centrally planned and the market, competed with each other for the favour of undecided governments. Then, within the last two decades of the century, governments of one communist country after another abandoned their central planning apparatus, largely because central planning was unsuccessful in generating economic growth and acceptable living standards. More and more economic transactions and activities were then left to be regulated by the self-organizing system of the market.

Lessons From History 1-1 elaborates on some of the reasons for the failure of the centrally planned economies. We hasten to add that Marx was right about many things, including the importance of technological change in raising living standards over the centuries (which is also a theme we discuss in this book). Where experience has shown him to be wrong, however, was in believing that central planning could successfully replace the market as a means of organizing all of a nation's economic activities.

In contrast to the failures of the command economies, the performance of the largely free-market economies is impressive. One theme of this book is *market success*—how free markets work to coordinate with relative efficiency the decentralized decisions made by private consumers and producers. However, doing things better does not necessarily mean doing things perfectly. Another theme of this book is *market failure*—how and why unfettered free markets sometimes fail to produce efficient results and fail to take account of social values that cannot be expressed through the marketplace.

Today, as in the time of Adam Smith, economists seek to understand the self-organizing forces of a market economy, how well they function, and how governments may intervene to improve their workings in specific situations.

CHAPTER 1   ECONOMIC ISSUES AND CONCEPTS   5

Main Characteristics of Market Economies

What, then, are the main characteristics of market economies that produce this spontaneous self-ordering?

Self-Interest.   Individuals pursue their own self-interest, buying and selling what seems best for themselves and their families.

Incentives.   People respond to incentives. Sellers usually want to sell more when prices are high; buyers usually want to buy more when prices are low.

Market Prices and Quantities.   Prices and quantities are determined in open markets in which would-be sellers compete to sell their products to would-be buyers.

Institutions.   All of these activities are governed by a set of institutions largely created by government. The most important are private property and freedom of contract. The natures of private property and contractual obligations are defined by legislature and enforced by the police and the courts.

1.2 Scarce Resources

All of the issues discussed so far would not matter much if we lived in an economy of such plenty that there was enough to satisfy all of everyone's wants. But such an economy is impossible. Why?

The short answer is, because we live in a world of scarcity. Compared to the known desires of individuals for such products as better food, clothing, housing, education, holidays, health care, and entertainment, the existing supplies of resources are clearly inadequate. They are sufficient to produce only a small fraction of the goods and services that people desire. This gives rise to the basic economic problem of choice under conditions of scarcity. If we cannot have everything we want, we must choose what we will and will not have.

One definition of *economics* comes from the great economist Alfred Marshall (1842–1924), whom we will encounter at several points in this book: "Economics is a study of mankind in the ordinary business of life." A more penetrating definition is the following:

Economics is the study of the use of scarce resources to satisfy unlimited human wants.

Scarcity is inevitable and is central to economic problems. What are society's resources? Why is scarcity inevitable? What are the consequences of scarcity?

Resources

A society's resources consist of: natural endowments such as land, forests, and minerals; human resources, both mental and physical; and manufactured aids to production such as tools, machinery, and buildings. Economists call such resources **factors of production** because they are used to produce the things that people desire. We divide these things into goods and services. **Goods** are tangible (e.g., cars and shoes), and **services** are intangible (e.g., haircuts and education).

factors of production Resources used to produce goods and services; frequently divided into the basic categories of land, labour, and capital.

goods Tangible commodities, such as cars or shoes.

services Intangible commodities, such as haircuts or medical care.

LESSONS FROM HISTORY 1-1

The Failure of Central Planning

The Bolshevik Revolution in 1917 in Russia brought the world its first example of a large-scale communist society. With the rise to power of Joseph Stalin and the creation of the Soviet Union in 1922, communism and central economic planning began their spread throughout Eastern and Central Europe. This spread of central planning was accelerated by the Soviet Union's role following the Second World War in "liberating" several countries from Nazi domination, thus creating the group of countries that became known as the Eastern Bloc or the Soviet Bloc.

Despite the successful geographic spread of communism, the Soviet system of central economic planning had many difficulties. By 1989, communism had collapsed throughout Central and Eastern Europe, and the economic systems of formerly communist countries began the difficult transition from centrally planned to market economies. Although political issues surely played a role in these events, the economic changes generally confirmed the superiority of a market-oriented price system over central planning as a method of organizing economic activity. The failure of central planning had many causes, but four were particularly significant.

Failure of Coordination

In the centrally planned economies, a body of planners attempted to coordinate all the economic decisions about production, investment, trade, and consumption that were likely

The fall of the Berlin Wall in November 1989 was the beginning of the end of the Soviet system of central planning.

---

production   The act of making goods or services.

consumption   The act of using goods or services to satisfy wants.

People use goods and services to satisfy many of their wants. The act of making them is called **production,** and the act of using them to satisfy wants is called **consumption.** Goods are valued for the services they provide. An automobile, for example, helps to satisfy its owner's desires for transportation, mobility, and possibly status.

Scarcity and Choice

For each of the world's six billion people, scarcity is real and ever present. As we said above, relative to people's desires, existing resources are inadequate; there are enough to produce only a fraction of the goods and services that are wanted.

But are not the advanced industrialized nations rich enough that scarcity is nearly banished? After all, they have been characterized as affluent societies. Whatever affluence may mean, however, it does not mean the end of the problem of scarcity. Most households that earn $100 000 per year (a princely amount by world standards) have no trouble spending it on things that seem useful to them and they would certainly have no trouble convincing you that their resources are scarce relative to their desires.

Because resources are scarce, all societies face the problem of deciding what to produce and how much each person will consume. Societies differ in who makes the to be made by producers and consumers throughout the country. Without the use of prices to signal relative scarcity and abundance, central planning generally proved impossible to do with any reasonable degree of success. Bottlenecks in production, shortages of some goods, and gluts of others plagued the Soviet economy for decades.

Failure of Quality Control

Central planners can monitor the number of units produced by any factory and reward plants that exceed their production targets and punish those that fall short. Factory managers operating under these conditions will meet their quotas by whatever means are available, and once the goods pass out of their factory, what happens to them is someone else's headache.

In market economies, poor quality is punished by low sales, and retailers soon give a signal to factory managers by shifting their purchases to other suppliers. The incentives that obviously flow from such private-sector purchasing discretion are generally absent from command economies, where purchases and sales are planned centrally and prices and profits are not used to signal customer satisfaction or dissatisfaction.

Misplaced Incentives

In market economies, relative wages and salaries provide incentives for labour to move from place to place, and the possibility of losing one's job provides an incentive to work diligently. This is a harsh mechanism that punishes job losers with loss of income (although social programs provide floors to the amount of economic punishment that can be suffered). In planned economies, workers usually have complete job security. Industrial unemployment is rare, and even when it does occur, new jobs are usually found for all who lose theirs. Although the high level of security is attractive to many people, it proved impossible to provide sufficient incentives for reasonably hard and efficient work under such conditions.

Environmental Degradation

Fulfilling production plans became the all-embracing goal in centrally planned economies, to the exclusion of most other considerations, including the environment. As a result, environmental degradation occurred in the Soviet Union and the countries of Eastern Europe on a scale unknown in advanced Western nations. A particularly disturbing example (only one of many) occurred in central Asia where high quotas for cotton output led to indiscriminate use of pesticides and irrigation. Birth defects are now very common, and the vast Aral Sea has been half-drained, causing major environmental effects.

This failure to protect the environment stemmed from the pressure to fulfill production plans and the absence of a "political marketplace" where citizens could express their preferences for the environment versus economic gain. Imperfect though the system may be in democratic market economies—and in some particular cases it has been quite poor—their record of environmental protection has been vastly better than that of the centrally planned economies.

---

choices and how they are made, but the need to choose is common to all. Just as scarcity implies the need for choice, so choice implies the existence of cost. A decision to have more of something requires a decision to have less of something else. The less of "something else" can be thought of as the cost of having the more of "something."

Scarcity implies that choices must be made, and making choices implies the existence of costs.

Opportunity Cost

To see how choice implies cost, we look first at a trivial example and then at one that vitally affects all of us; both examples involve precisely the same fundamental principles.

Consider the choice David faces on a Saturday night when he goes out for pizza and beer with his friends. Suppose that he has only $16 for the night and that each beer costs $4 and each slice of pizza costs $2. Since David is both hungry and thirsty, he would like to have four slices of pizza and three beers, but this would cost $20 and is therefore unattainable given David's scarce resources of $16. There are several combinations, however, that are attainable: 8 slices of pizza and 0 beers; 6 slices of pizza and

FIGURE 1-1 Choosing Between Pizza and Beer

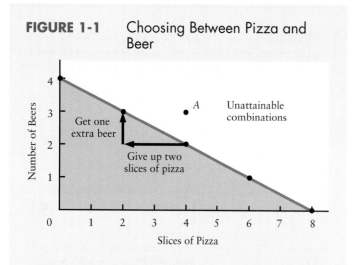

Limited resources force a choice among competing alternatives. Given a total of $16 to spend on $2 slices of pizza and $4 beers, some choices are unattainable, such as point A. All combinations on the line or in the green area are attainable. But even among attainable combinations, it is apparent that choice involves an opportunity cost. The opportunity cost of one extra slice of pizza is half of a beer; the opportunity cost of one extra beer is two slices of pizza.

1 beer; 4 slices of pizza and 2 beers; 2 slices of pizza and 3 beers; and 0 slices of pizza and 4 beers.

David's choices are illustrated in Figure 1-1, which graphs the combinations of beers and slices of pizza that David considers buying. The numbers of pieces of pizza are shown on the horizontal axis; the numbers of beers are shown on the vertical axis. The downward-sloping line shows the five possible combinations of beer and pizza that use up all of David's resources—$16. Notice that point A shows a combination—4 slices of pizza and 3 beers—that lies outside the line because its total cost is more than $16. Point A is *unattainable* to David. All points that lie on or inside the line are *attainable* combinations.

In this setting David can ask himself, "What is the cost of one beer?" One answer is that the cost is $4. An equivalent answer is that the cost of one beer is the two slices of pizza he must give up to get it. In fact, we say in this case that two slices of pizza is the *opportunity cost* of one beer since it is the opportunity David must give up to get one extra beer.

Every time a choice is made, opportunity costs are incurred.

Practise with Study Guide Chapter 1, Exercise 3.

opportunity cost
The cost of using resources for a certain purpose, measured by the benefit given up by not using them in their best alternative use.

The idea of opportunity cost is one of the central insights of economics. Here is a precise definition. The **opportunity cost** of using resources for a certain purpose is defined to be *the benefit given up by not using them in the best alternative way.* That is, it is the cost measured in terms of other goods and services that could have been obtained instead. If, for example, resources that could have produced 20 km of road are best used instead to produce one hospital, the opportunity cost of a hospital is 20 km of road; looked at the other way round, the opportunity cost of 1 km of road is one-twentieth of a hospital.

See *Applying Economic Concepts 1-1* for an example of opportunity cost that should seem quite familiar to you—the opportunity cost of getting a university degree.

Economists use graphs to illustrate theories and to show data. If you need a quick refresher about how to use graphs, look for "A Brief Introduction to Graphing" in the *Additional Topics* section of this book's Companion Website.

http://www.pearsoned.ca/ragan

Production Possibilities Boundary

Although David's choice between pizza and beer may seem to be a trivial consumption decision, the nature of the decision is the same whatever the choice being made. Consider, for example, the choice that any country must face between producing military and civilian goods.

APPLYING ECONOMIC CONCEPTS 1-1

The Opportunity Cost of Your University Degree

As discussed in the text, the opportunity cost of choosing one thing is what must be given up as the best alternative. Computing the opportunity cost of a college or university education is a good example to illustrate which factors are included in the computation of opportunity cost. You may also be surprised to learn how expensive your university degree really is!*

Suppose that a bachelor's degree requires four years of study and that each year you spend $4000 for tuition fees—approximately the average at Canadian universities in 2004—and a further $1500 per year for books and materials. Does this mean that the cost of a university education is only $22 000? Unfortunately not; the true cost of a university degree is much higher.

The key point is that the opportunity cost of a university education does not just include the out-of-pocket expenses on tuition and books. You must also take into consideration *what you are forced to give up* by choosing to attend university. Of course, if you were not studying you could have been doing any one of a number of things, but the relevant one is *the one you would have chosen instead*—your best alternative to attending university.

Suppose that your best alternative to attending university was to get a job. In this case, the opportunity cost of your university degree must include the earnings that you would have received had you taken that job. Suppose that your (after-tax) annual earnings would have been $20 000 per year, for a total of $80 000 if you had stayed at that job for four years. To the direct expenses of $22 000, we must therefore add $80 000 for the earnings that you gave up by not taking a job. This brings the true cost of your university degree—the opportunity cost—up to $102 000!

Notice that the cost of food, lodging, clothing, and other living expenses did not enter the calculation of the opportunity cost in this example. The living expenses must be incurred in either case—whether you attend university or get a job.

If the opportunity cost of a degree is so high, why do students choose to go to university? The simple answer is that they believe that they are better off by going to university than by not going (otherwise they would not go). Maybe the students simply enjoy learning, and thus are prepared to incur the high cost to be in the university environment. Or maybe they believe that a university degree will significantly increase their future earning potential. In this case, they are giving up four years of earnings at one salary so that they can invest in their own skills in the hope of enjoying many more years in the future at a considerably higher salary.

Whatever the case, the recognition that a university degree is very expensive should convince students to make the best use of their time while they are there. Read on!

The opportunity cost to an individual completing a university degree in Canada is large. It includes the direct cost of tuition and books as well as the earnings forgone while attending university.

* This box considers only the cost *to the student* of a university degree. For reasons that will be discussed in detail in Part Six of this book, provincial governments heavily subsidize post-secondary education in Canada. Because of this subsidy, the cost *to society* of a university degree is generally much higher than the cost to an individual student.

 Practise with Study Guide Chapter 1, Exercise 4.

If resources are fully and efficiently employed, it is not possible to have more of both. However, as the government cuts defence expenditures, resources needed to produce civilian goods will be freed up. The opportunity cost of increased civilian goods is therefore the forgone military output. Or, if we were considering an increase in military output, the opportunity cost of increased military output would be the forgone civilian goods.

The choice is illustrated in Figure 1-2. Because resources are limited, some combinations—those that would require more than the total available supply of resources for their production—cannot be attained. The negatively sloped curve on the graph divides the combinations that can be attained from those that cannot. Points above and to the right of this curve cannot be attained because there are not enough resources; points below and to the left of the curve can be attained without using all of the available resources; and points on the curve can just be attained if all the available resources are used efficiently. The curve is called the **production possibilities boundary**. (Sometimes the word "boundary" is replaced with "curve" or "frontier.") It has a negative slope because when all resources are being used efficiently, producing more of one kind of good requires producing less of the other kind.

A production possibilities boundary illustrates three concepts: scarcity, choice, and opportunity cost. Scarcity is indicated by the unattainable combinations outside the boundary; choice, by the need to choose among the alternative attainable points along the boundary; and opportunity cost, by the negative slope of the boundary.

The shape of the production possibilities boundary in Figure 1-2 implies that an increasing amount of civilian production must be given up to achieve equal successive increases in military production. This shape, referred to as *concave* to the origin, indicates that the opportunity cost of either good increases as we increase the amount of it that is produced. A straight-line boundary, as in Figure 1-1, indicates that the opportunity cost of one good in terms of the other stays constant, no matter how much of it is produced.

The concave shape in Figure 1-2 is the way in which economists usually draw a country's production possiblities boundary. The shape occurs because each factor of production is not equally useful in producing all goods. To see why differences among factors of production are so important, suppose we begin at point c in Figure 1-2, where most resources are devoted to the production of military goods, and then consider gradually shifting more and more resources toward the production of civilian goods. We might begin by shifting nutrient-rich land that is particularly well suited to growing wheat. This land may not be very useful for making military equipment, but it is very useful for making certain civilian goods (like bread). This shift of resources will therefore lead to a small reduction in military ouptut but a substantial increase in civilian output. Thus the opportunity cost of producing a few more units of civilian goods, which is equal to the forgone military output, is small. But as we shift more and more resources toward the production of civilian goods, and therefore move along the production possibilities boundary toward point a, we must shift more and more resources that are actually quite well suited to the production of military output, like aerospace engineers or the minerals needed to make gunpowder. As we produce more and more civilian goods (by having more and more resources devoted to producing

production possibilities boundary   A curve showing which alternative combinations of commodities can just be attained if all available resources are used efficiently; it is the boundary between attainable and unattainable output combinations.

Practise with Study Guide Chapter 1, Exercise 2.

FIGURE 1-2   A Production Possibilities Boundary

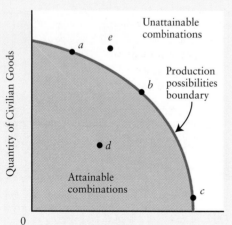

The negatively sloped boundary shows the combinations that are just attainable when all of the society's resources are efficiently used. The production possibilities boundary separates the attainable combinations of goods, such as *a, b, c,* and *d,* from unattainable combinations, such as *e.* Points *a, b,* and *c* represent full and efficient use of society's resources. Point *d* represents either inefficient use of resources or failure to use all the available resources.

them), the amount of military output that must be forgone to produce one *extra* unit of civilian goods rises. That is, the opportunity cost of producing one good rises as more of that good is produced.

Four Key Economic Problems

Modern economies involve thousands of complex production and consumption activities. Although this complexity is important, many of the basic kinds of decisions that must be made are not very different from those made in primitive economies in which people work with few tools and barter with their neighbours. Whatever the economic system, whether modern or primitive, or market or centrally planned, there are four key economic questions.

Practise with Study Guide Chapter 1, Exercise 1.

What Is Produced and How?

The allocation of scarce resources among alternative uses, called **resource allocation,** determines the quantities of various goods that are produced. What determines which goods get produced? Choosing to produce a particular combination of goods means choosing a particular allocation of resources among the industries or regions producing the goods.

Further, because resources are scarce, it is desirable that they be used efficiently. Hence it matters which of the available methods of production is used to produce each of the goods. What determines which methods of production get used and which ones do not?

resource allocation
The allocation of an economy's scarce resources of land, labour, and capital among alternative uses.

What Is Consumed and By Whom?

What is the relationship between an economy's production of goods and the consumption enjoyed by its citizens? Economists seek to understand what determines the distribution of a nation's total output among its people. Who gets a lot, who gets a little, and why?

If production takes place on the production possibilities boundary, then how about consumption? Will the economy consume exactly the same goods that it produces? Or will the country's ability to trade with other countries permit the economy to consume a different combination of goods?

Questions relating to what is produced and how, and what is consumed and by whom, fall within the realm of microeconomics. **Microeconomics** is the study of the allocation of resources as it is affected by the workings of the price system and government policies that seek to influence it.

microeconomics
The study of the allocation of resources as it is affected by the workings of the price system.

Why Are Resources Sometimes Idle?

When an economy is in a recession, many workers who would like to have jobs are unable to find employers to hire them. At the same time, the managers and owners of offices and factories would like to operate at a higher level of activity—that is, they would like to produce more goods and services. Similarly, during recessions raw materials are typically available in abundance. For some reason, however, these resources—labour, factories and equipment, and raw materials—are idle. Thus, in terms of Figure 1-2, the economy is operating within its production possibilities boundary.

Why are resources sometimes idle? Should governments worry about such idle resources, or is there some reason to believe that such occasional idleness is appropriate in a well-functioning economy? Is there anything that the government can do to reduce such idleness?

Is Productive Capacity Growing?

The capacity to produce goods and services grows rapidly in some countries, expands slowly in others, and actually declines in others. Growth in productive capacity can be represented by an outward shift of the production possibilities boundary, as shown in Figure 1-3. If an economy's capacity to produce goods and services is growing, combinations that are unattainable today will become attainable in the future. Growth makes it possible to have more of all goods. What are the determinants of growth? Can governments do anything to increase economic growth?

Questions relating to the idleness of resources during recessions, and the growth of productive capacity, fall within the realm of macroeconomics. **Macroeconomics** is the study of the determination of economic aggregates such as total output, total employment, the price level, and the rate of economic growth.

macroeconomics
The study of the determination of economic aggregates such as total output, the price level, employment, and growth.

1.3 Who Makes the Choices and How?

So choices have to be made, but who makes them and how are they made?

FIGURE 1-3 The Effect of Economic Growth on the Production Possibilities Boundary

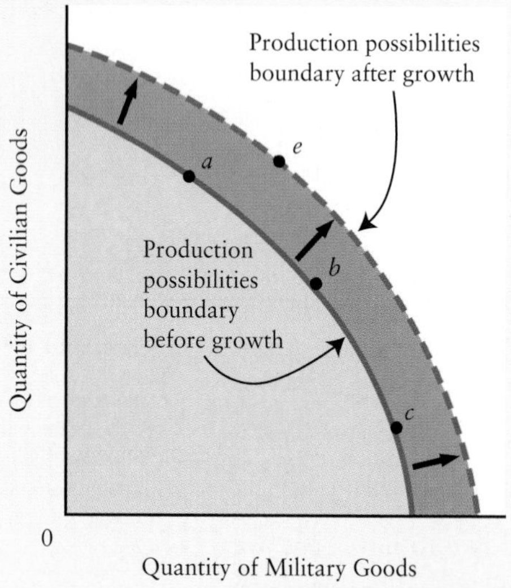

Economic growth shifts the boundary outward and makes it possible to produce more of all products. Before growth in productive capacity, points *a*, *b*, and *c* were on the production possibilities boundary and point *e* was an unattainable combination. After growth, as shown by the dark shaded band, point *e* and many other previously unattainable combinations are attainable.

The Flow of Income and Expenditure

Figure 1-4 shows the basic decision makers and the flows of income and expenditure that they set up. Individuals own factors of production. They sell the services of these factors to producers and receive payments in return. These are their incomes. Producers use the factor services that they buy to make goods and services. They sell these to individuals, receiving payments in return. These are the incomes of producers. These basic flows of income and expenditure pass through markets. Individuals sell the services of the factor that they own in what are collectively called *factor markets*. When you get a part-time job during university, you are participating in the factor market. Producers sell their outputs of goods and services in what are collectively called *goods markets*. When you purchase a haircut or a new pair of shoes, for example, you are participating in the goods market.

The prices that are determined in these markets determine the incomes that are earned and the purchasing power of those incomes. People who get high prices for their factor services earn high incomes; those who get low prices earn low incomes. The income each person earns expressed as a fraction of all incomes that are earned in the nation shows the share of total income that each person can command. The *distribution of income* refers to how the nation's total production is distributed among its citizens. This is largely determined by the price that each type of factor service can command in factor markets.

Maximizing Decisions

The basic decision makers in a market economy are individual consumers and producers. To these two groups we will shortly add a third, the government. The most important thing about how these two groups make their decisions is that everyone tries to do as well as possible for himself or herself. In the jargon of economics, people are *maximizers*. When individuals decide how many factor services to sell to producers and how many products to buy from them, they make choices designed to maximize their well-being, or *utility*. When producers decide how many factor services to buy from individuals and how many goods to produce and sell to them, they make choices designed to maximize their *profits*.

Marginal Decisions

The second key point is that when firms and consumers make an economic decision, they weigh the costs and benefits of that decision *at the margin*. For example, when you consider buying an additional CD, you know the *marginal cost* of the CD—that is, how much you must pay to get one extra CD—and you weigh it against the *marginal benefit* that you will derive from that CD. You will only buy that CD if you think the benefit to you in terms of extra utility exceeds the marginal cost.

Similarly, a producer considering whether to hire an extra worker must evaluate the *marginal cost* of the worker—the extra wages and benefits that must be paid—and weigh it against the *marginal benefit* of the worker—the increase in revenues that will be generated by the extra worker. A producer interested in maximizing its profit will only hire the extra worker if the benefit in terms of extra revenue exceeds the cost in terms of higher wages.

Consumers and producers who are maximizers are constantly making marginal decisions, whether to buy or sell a little bit more or less of the many things that they buy and sell.

Voting in an election is one of the few examples in which decisions are *not* made on a marginal basis. When you vote in a Canadian federal election, you have only one vote and you must support one party over the others. When you do, you vote for everything that party stands for, even though you may prefer to pick and choose elements from each party's political platform. You cannot say "I vote for the Liberals on issue A and for the Conservatives on issue B." You must make a total, rather than a marginal, decision.

The Complexity of Production

Producers decide what to produce and how to produce it. Production is a very complex process in any modern economy. A typical car manufacturer assembles a product out of thousands of individual parts. It makes some of these parts itself. Most are subcon-

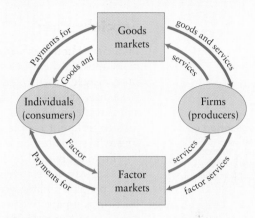

FIGURE 1-4 The Circular Flow of Income and Expenditure

The green line shows the flows of goods and services; the blue line shows the payments made to purchase these. Factor services flow from individuals who own the factors (including their own labour) through factor markets to firms that use them to make goods and services. These goods and services then flow through goods markets to those who consume them. Money payments flow from firms to individuals through factor markets. These payments become the income of individuals. When they spend this income buying goods and services, money flows through goods markets back to producers.

tracted to parts manufacturers, and many of the major parts manufacturers subcontract some of their work out to smaller firms. This kind of production displays two characteristics noted long ago by Adam Smith—*specialization* and the *division of labour*.

Specialization

In ancient hunter–gatherer societies, and in modern subsistence economies, most people make most of the things they need for themselves. However, from the time that people first engaged in settled agriculture and some of them began to live in towns, people have specialized in doing particular jobs. Artisan, soldier, priest, and government official were some of the earliest specialized occupations. Economists call this allocation of different jobs to different people the **specialization of labour**. There are two fundamental reasons why specialization is extraordinarily efficient compared with universal self-sufficiency.

First, individual abilities differ, and specialization allows each person to do what he or she can do relatively well while leaving everything else to be done by others. Even when people's abilities are unaffected by the act of specializing, the economy's total production is greater when people specialize than when they all try to be self-sufficient. This is true for individuals but it is also true for entire countries, and it is one of the most fundamental principles in economics: the principle of *comparative advantage*. A much fuller discussion of comparative advantage is found in Chapter 34, in which we discuss the gains from international trade.

The second reason that specialization is more efficient than self-sufficiency concerns changes in people's abilities that occur *because* they specialize. A person who concentrates on one activity becomes better at it than could a jack-of-all-trades. This is called *learning by doing*, and was a factor much stressed by early economists. Modern research into what are called *learning curves* shows that learning by doing is important in many modern industries.

The Division of Labour

Throughout most of history each artisan who specialized in making some product made the whole of that product. Over the last several hundred years, many technical advances in production methods have made it efficient to organize agriculture and manufacturing into large-scale firms organized around what is called the **division of labour**. This term refers to specialization *within* the production process of a particular product.

Mass Production.   In a mass-production factory, work is divided into highly specialized tasks using specialized machinery. Each individual repeatedly does one small task that is a small fraction of those necessary to produce any one product. This is an extreme case of the division of labour.

Artisans and Flexible Manufacturing.   Two very recent changes have significantly altered the degree of specialization found in many modern production processes. First, individual artisans have recently reappeared in some lines of production. They are responding to a revival in the demand for individually crafted, rather than mass-produced, products. Second, many manufacturing operations are being reorganized along new lines called "lean production" or "flexible manufacturing," which was pioneered by Japanese car manufacturers in the mid-1950s. It has led back to a more craft-based form of organization within the factory. In this technique, employees work as a team; each employee is able to do every team member's job rather than one very specialized task at one point on the assembly line.

specialization of labour
The specialization of individual workers in the production of particular goods or services.

division of labour
The breaking up of a production process into a series of specialized tasks, each done by a different worker.

Globalization

Market economies constantly change, largely as a result of the development of new technologies. Many of the recent changes are referred to as *globalization*, a term often used loosely to mean the increased importance of international trade. International trade is, however, an old phenomenon—it is at least as old as the ancient trading routes created largely by the spice trade. The usual pattern over most of the last 200 years was manufactured goods being sent from Europe and North America to the rest of the world, with raw materials and primary products being sent in return. What is new in the last few decades is the globalization of manufacturing. Assembly of a product may take place in North America but the hundreds of component parts are manufactured in dozens of different countries and delivered to the North American plant "just in time" for assembly.

A major cause of globalization is the rapid reduction in transportation costs and the revolution in information technology that has occurred in the past 50 years. The cost of moving products around the world has fallen greatly in recent decades owing to containerization and the increasing size of ships. Our ability to transmit and analyze data has been increasing even more dramatically, while the costs of doing so have been decreasing, equally dramatically. For example, today $2000 buys an ultra-slim laptop computer that has the same computing power as one that in 1970 cost $10 million and filled a large room. This revolution in information and communication technology has made it possible to coordinate economic transactions around the world in ways that were difficult and costly 50 years ago and quite impossible 100 years ago.

Globalization is as important for consumers as it is for producers. For example, as some tastes become universal to young people, spread by ever-increasing access to foreign television stations and global Internet chat lines, we can see the same clothes and hear the same music in virtually all big cities. And as tastes become more universal, many *corporations* are globalizing, as they become what economists call **transnational corporations (TNCs)**. McDonald's restaurants are as visible in Moscow or Beijing as in London, New York, Vancouver, or Montreal. Many other brands are also known around the world, such as Calvin Klein, Nike, Coca-Cola, Kelloggs, Heinz, Nestlé, Molson, Toyota, Rolls-Royce, Sony, and Mitsubishi.

transnational corporations (TNCs) Firms that have operations in more than one country. Also called *multinational enterprises (MNEs)*.

Through the ongoing process of globalization, national economies are ever more linked to the global economy, in which an increasing share of jobs and incomes is created.

The word *globalization* has recently become a focal point for an important and contentious set of policy debates and public protests. These debates are often very confusing to the observer. See *Applying Economic Concepts 1-2* for a brief outline of the key issues.

The revolution in computer technology has drastically reduced communication and transportation costs. This reduction in costs lies at the heart of globalization.

Markets and Money

People who specialize in doing only one thing must satisfy most of their wants by consuming things made by other people. In early societies the exchange of goods and services took place by simple mutual agreement among neighbours. In the course of time, however, trading became centred on particular gathering places called *markets*. For example, the French markets or trade fairs of Champagne were well-known throughout Europe

APPLYING ECONOMIC CONCEPTS 1-2

The Globalization Debate

In December 1999, the trade ministers from member countries of the World Trade Organization (WTO) met in Seattle to set the agenda for a new round of talks at which they would negotiate rules governing international trade. Thousands of angry protesters lined the streets of Seattle, throwing rocks and shouting slogans about the dangers of globalization and the undemocratic nature of the WTO talks. Thus the "Battle of Seattle" was joined. In the next few years, similar protests took place in Quebec City, Genoa, and several times in Washington, D.C. What are these protests about? What are the key issues?

The protesters, who generally refer to themselves as "anti-globalization activists," have two main arguments. First, they argue that increases in the flow of international trade and investment have been responsible for increasing global income inequality and worsening poverty in developing countries. Second, they argue that organizations such as the WTO, the World Bank, and the International Monetary Fund (IMF) operate in an undemocratic fashion and hold their meetings behind closed doors, out of view of and without critical input from the people whose lives their policies are so dramatically influencing. A related concern is that global economic agreements appear to give power to transnational corporations, taking power out of the hands of citizens. The anti-globalization activists are in favour of slowing down the process of globalization and dramatically reforming (if not eliminating) these international organizations.

On the other side of the barricades are the defenders of globalization and a rules-based approach to international trade. They argue that the process of globalization, far from being the cause of poverty in developing countries, is the best bet for reducing such poverty. They claim that freer trade between countries has been responsible for enormous advances in living standards over the past century, and that the developing countries of today will be much better off if trade is further liberalized. Indeed, some defenders of globalization argue that one of the problems has been the developed countries' unwillingness to permit genuinely free international trade with the developing countries—especially for products such as agricultural commodities and textiles in which the developing countries have a competitive advantage. According to this view, the biggest contributor to poverty in developing countries is too *little* trade, not too much.

Defenders of globalization also point out that the meetings held by the WTO and other international organizations are voluntary meetings held between the democratically elected leaders of the member countries, and that no agreements are legal until each of the member countries ratifies them in its parliament. Thus, the process is democratic.

Is there a middle ground in this debate? On the democratic issue, the defenders of globalization are probably correct, at least literally. The agreements do not come into force until they are passed by the respective parliaments. The political challenge for all countries involved is to improve communications so that these complicated international agreements—which often run to thousands of pages in length—are made clear enough that they can be effectively debated in the respective parliaments. With effective political debates within each member country, citizens will be more involved in the policy-making process.

The more subtle issue is the relationship between globalization and poverty. Most economists would argue, for reasons that we will explore in Chapters 34 and 35, that freer trade will lead to increases in *average* living standards within both developed and developing countries. A typical empirical finding is that an economy whose trade share increases from 20 percent to 40 percent of its GDP can expect to experience a 10-percent increase in per capita income. But there is no guarantee that, within any particular country, these gains in living standards will be shared among the various segments of society in a socially just way. One of the crucial challenges faced by governments negotiating international economic agreements is to ensure that the benefits from such agreements are spread throughout the population, thus increasing their public acceptability.

as early as the eleventh century AD. Even now, many small towns in Canada have regular market days. Today, however, the term *market* has a much broader meaning. We use the term *market economy* to refer to a society in which people specialize in productive activities and meet most of their material wants through voluntary exchanges with other people.

Specialization must be accompanied by trade. People who produce only one thing must trade most of it to obtain all of the other things they require.

Early trading was by means of **barter,** the trading of goods directly for other goods. But barter is costly in terms of time spent searching out satisfactory exchanges. If a farmer has wheat but wants a hammer, he must find someone who has a hammer and wants wheat. A successful barter transaction thus requires what is called a *double coincidence of wants.*

Money eliminates the cumbersome system of barter by separating the transactions involved in the exchange of products. If a farmer has wheat and wants a hammer, he merely has to find someone who wants wheat. The farmer takes money in exchange. Then he finds a person who wishes to sell a hammer and gives up the money for the hammer.

Money greatly facilitates specialization and trade.

barter An economic system in which goods and services are traded directly for other goods and services.

1.4 Is There an Alternative to the Market Economy?

The answer to the question in the above heading is no in one sense and yes in another. We answer no because the modern economy has no *practical* alternative to reliance on market determination. We answer yes because it is possible to identify other types of economic systems.

Types of Economic Systems

It is helpful to distinguish three pure types of economies, called *traditional, command,* and *market* economies. These economies differ in the way in which economic decisions are coordinated. But no actual economy fits neatly into one of these three categories—all real economies contain some elements of each type.

Traditional Economies

A **traditional economy** is one in which behaviour is based primarily on tradition, custom, and habit. Young men follow their fathers' occupations. Women do what their mothers did. There is little change in the pattern of goods produced from year to year, other than those imposed by the vagaries of nature. The techniques of production also follow traditional patterns, except when the effects of an occasional new invention are felt. Finally, production is allocated among the members according to long-established traditions.

Such a system works best in an unchanging environment. Under such static conditions, a system that does not continually require people to make choices can prove effective in meeting economic and social needs.

Traditional systems were common in earlier times. The feudal system, under which most people in medieval Europe lived, was a largely traditional society. Peasants, artisans, and most others living in villages inherited their positions in that society. They also usually inherited their specific jobs, which they handled in traditional ways.

traditional economy An economy in which behaviour is based mostly on tradition.

Command Economies

In command economies, economic behaviour is determined by some central authority, usually the government, which makes most of the necessary decisions on what to produce, how to produce it, and who gets it. Such economies are characterized by the *centralization* of decision making. Because centralized decision makers usually lay down elaborate and complex plans for the behaviour that they wish to impose, the terms **command economy** and *centrally planned economy* are usually used synonymously.

command economy
An economy in which most economic decisions are made by a central planning authority.

The sheer quantity of data required for the central planning of an entire economy is enormous, and the task of analyzing it to produce a fully integrated plan can hardly be exaggerated. Moreover, the plan must be continually modified to take account not only of current data but also of future trends in labour supplies, technological developments, and people's tastes for various goods and services. This is a notoriously difficult exercise, not least because of the unavailability of all essential, accurate, and up-to-date information.

Twenty years ago, more than one-third of the world's population lived in countries that relied heavily on central planning. Today, the number of such countries is small. Even in countries where central planning is the proclaimed system, as in Cuba, increasing amounts of market determination are being quietly permitted.

Free-Market Economies

In the third type of economic system, the decisions about resource allocation are made without any central direction. Instead, they result from innumerable independent decisions made by individual producers and consumers. Such a system is known as a **free-market economy** or, more simply, a *market economy*. In such an economy, decisions relating to the basic economic issues are *decentralized*. Despite the absence of a central plan, these many decentralized decisions are nonetheless coordinated. The main coordinating device is the set of market-determined prices—which is why free-market systems are often called *price systems*.

free-market economy
An economy in which most economic decisions are made by private households and firms.

In a pure market economy, all of these decisions, without exception, are made by buyers and sellers acting through unhindered markets. The state provides the background of defining property and protecting rights against foreign and domestic enemies but, beyond that, markets determine all resource allocation and income distribution.

Mixed Economies

Economies that are fully traditional or fully centrally planned or wholly free-market are pure types that are useful for studying basic principles. When we look in detail at any real economy, however, we discover that its economic behaviour is the result of some mixture of central control and market determination, with a certain amount of traditional behaviour as well.

mixed economy
An economy in which some economic decisions are made by firms and households and some by the government.

In practice, every economy is a **mixed economy** in the sense that it combines significant elements of all three systems in determining economic behaviour.

Furthermore, within any economy, the degree of the mix varies from sector to sector. For example, in some planned economies, the command principle was used more often to determine behaviour in heavy-goods industries, such as steel, than in agriculture. Farmers were often given substantial freedom to produce and sell what they wished in response to varying market prices.

When economists speak of a particular economy as being centrally planned, we mean only that the degree of the mix is weighted heavily toward the command principle. When we speak of one as being a market economy, we mean only that the degree of the mix is weighted heavily toward decentralized decision making.

Although no country offers an example of either system working alone, some economies, such as those of Canada, the United States, France, and Hong Kong, rely much more heavily on market decisions than others, such as the economies of China, North Korea, and Cuba. Yet even in Canada, the command principle has some sway. Crown corporations, legislated minimum wages, rules and regulations for environmental protection, quotas on some agricultural outputs, and restrictions on the import of some items are just a few examples.

See Chapter 1 of www.pearsoned.ca/ragan for an excellent discussion of Cuba's recent economic reforms: Archibald Ritter, "Is Cuba's Economic Reform Process Paralysed?"

The Great Debate

For over a century, a great debate raged on the relative merits of command economies versus market economies. The former Soviet Union, the countries of Eastern Europe, and China were command economies for much of the twentieth century. Canada, the United States, and most of the countries of Western Europe were, and still are, primarily market economies. The apparent successes of the Soviet Union and China in the 1950s and 1960s, including the ability to mobilize considerable resources into heavy industries, suggested to many observers that the command principle was at least as good for organizing economic behaviour as the market principle. Over the long run, however, planned economies proved to be a failure of such disastrous proportions that they seriously depressed the living standards of their citizens. (Some of the reasons for this failure were examined in *Lessons From History 1-1.*)

The failure of centrally planned economies suggests the superiority of decentralized markets over centrally planned ones as mechanisms for allocating an economy's scarce resources. Put another way, it demonstrates the superiority of mixed economies with substantial elements of market determination over fully planned command economies. However, it does *not* demonstrate, as some observers have asserted, the superiority of completely free-market economies over mixed economies.

There is no guarantee that completely free markets will, on their own, handle such urgent matters as controlling pollution or providing public goods (like national defence). Indeed, as we shall see in later chapters, much economic theory is devoted to explaining why free markets often *fail* to do these things. Mixed economies, with significant elements of government intervention, are needed to do these jobs.

Furthermore, acceptance of the free market over central planning does not provide an excuse to ignore a country's pressing social issues. Acceptance of the benefits of the free market still leaves plenty of scope to debate the most appropriate levels and types of government policies directed at achieving specific social goals. It follows that there is still considerable room for disagreement about the degree of the mix of market and government determination in any modern mixed economy—room enough to accommodate such divergent views as could be expressed by conservative, liberal, and modern social democratic parties.

So, the first answer to the question about the existence of an alternative to the market economy is no: There is no practical alternative to a mixed system with major reliance on markets but a substantial government presence in most aspects of the economy. The second answer is yes: Within the framework of a mixed economy there are substantial alternatives among many different and complex mixes of free-market and government determination of economic life.

The debate regarding the appropriate roles of governments and free markets figures prominently in discussions of how today's developing countries can best bring about improvements in their citizens' living standards. For a detailed discussion of the "Challenges Facing the Developing Countries," see the *Additional Topics* section of this book's Companion Website.

http://www.pearsoned.ca/ragan

Government in the Modern Mixed Economy

Market economies in today's advanced industrial countries are based primarily on voluntary transactions between individual buyers and sellers. Private individuals have the right to buy and sell what they wish, to accept or refuse work that is offered to them, and to move where they want when they want.

Key institutions are private property and freedom of contract, both of which must be maintained by active government policies. The government creates laws of ownership and contract and then provides the institutions to enforce these laws.

In modern mixed economies, governments go well beyond these important basic functions. They intervene in market transactions to correct what economists call *market failures*. These are well-defined situations in which free markets do not work well. Some products, called *public goods*, are not provided at all by markets because their use cannot be restricted to those who pay for them. Defence and police protection are examples of public goods. In other cases, private transactors impose costs called *externalities* on those who have no say in the transaction. This is the case when factories pollute the air and rivers. The public is harmed but plays no part in the transaction. These market failures explain why governments sometimes intervene to alter the allocation of resources.

Also, important equity issues arise from letting free markets determine people's incomes. Some people lose their jobs because firms are reorganizing to become more efficient in the face of new technologies. Others keep their jobs, but the market places so little value on their services that they face economic deprivation. The old and the chronically ill may suffer if their past circumstances did not allow them to save enough to support themselves. For many reasons of this sort, almost everyone accepts some government intervention to redistribute income. Care must be taken, however, not to kill the goose that lays the golden egg. By taking too much from higher-income people, we risk eliminating their incentive to work hard and produce income, some of which is to be redistributed to lower-income people.

These are some of the reasons all modern economies are mixed economies. Throughout most of the twentieth century in advanced industrial societies, the mix had been altering towards more and more government participation in decisions about the allocation of resources and the distribution of income. In the past three decades, however, there has been a worldwide movement to reduce the degree of government participation. The details of this shift in the market/government mix, and the reasons for it, are some of the major issues that will be studied in this book.

S U M M A R Y

1.1 The Complexity of the Modern Economy

- A market economy is self-organizing in the sense that when individual consumers and producers act independently to pursue their own self-interest, responding to prices determined in open markets, the collective outcome is coordinated and relatively efficient.

- An alternative economic system requires a central planning authority to make the decisions about who consumes and who produces which goods. The experience of those countries that adopted central planning was that such planning was extremely difficult and quite inefficient in allocating resources.

1.2 Scarce Resources

- Scarcity is a fundamental problem faced by all economies. Not enough resources are available to produce all the goods and services that people would like to consume. Scarcity makes it necessary to choose. All societies must have a mechanism for choosing what goods and services will be produced and in what quantities.

- The concept of opportunity cost emphasizes the problem of scarcity and choice by measuring the cost of obtaining a unit of one product in terms of the number of units of other products that could have been obtained instead.

- A production possibilities boundary shows all of the combinations of goods that can be produced by an economy whose resources are fully and efficiently employed. Movement from one point to another along the boundary requires a reallocation of resources.

- Four basic questions must be answered in all economies: What is produced and how? What is consumed and by whom? Why are resources sometimes idle? Is productive capacity growing?

1.3 Who Makes the Choices and How?

- The interaction of consumers and producers through goods and factor markets is illustrated by the circular flow of income and expenditure. Individual consumers sell factor services to producers and thereby earn their income. Similarly, producers earn their income by selling goods and services to individual consumers.

- Individual consumers make their decisions in an effort to maximize their well-being or utility. Producers' decisions are designed to maximize their profits.

- Modern economies are based on the specialization and division of labour, which necessitate the exchange (trade) of goods and services. Exchange takes place in markets and is facilitated by the use of money.

- Driven by the ongoing revolution in transportation and communications technology, the world economy is rapidly globalizing.

1.4 Is There an Alternative to the Market Economy?

- There are three pure types of economies: traditional, command, and free-market. In practice, all economies are mixed economies in that their economic behaviour responds to mixes of tradition, government command, and price incentives.

- In the late 1980s, events in Eastern Europe and the Soviet Union led to the general acceptance that the system of fully centrally planned economies had failed to produce mini-

mally acceptable living standards for its citizens. All of these countries are now moving toward greater market determination and less state command in their economies.

- Governments play an important role in modern mixed economies. They create and enforce important background institutions such as private property and freedom of contract. They intervene to correct market failures. They also redistribute income in the interests of equity.

KEY CONCEPTS

The self-organizing economy
Scarcity and the need for choice
Choice and opportunity cost
Production possibilities boundary

Resource allocation
Specialization
The division of labour
Globalization

Traditional economies
Command economies
Free-market economies
Mixed economies

STUDY EXERCISES

1. What is the difference between microeconomics and macroeconomics?

2. List the four main types of economic systems and their main attributes.

3. Explain the three economic concepts illustrated by the production possibilities boundary.

4. Consider an economy that produces only food and clothing. Its production possibilities boundary is shown below.

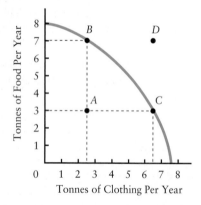

a. If the economy is at point A, how many tonnes of clothing and how many tonnes of food are being produced? At point B? At point C?
b. What do we know about the use of resources when the economy is at point A? At point B? At point C?
c. If the economy is at point B, what is the opportunity cost of producing one more tonne of food? What is the opportunity cost of producing one more tonne of clothing?
d. What do we know about the use of resources at point D? How would it be possible for the economy to produce at point D?

5. State and explain two reasons why the specialization of labour is more efficient than universal self-sufficiency.

6. Choiceland has 250 workers and produces only two goods, X and Y. Labour is the only factor of production, but some workers are better suited to producing X than Y (and vice versa). The table below shows the maximum levels of output of each good possible from various levels of labour input.

Number of Workers Producing X	Annual Production of X	Number of Workers Producing Y	Annual Production of Y
0	0	250	1300
50	20	200	1200
100	45	150	900
150	60	100	600
200	70	50	350
250	75	0	0

a. Draw the production possibilities boundary for Choiceland on a scale diagram.
b. Compute the opportunity cost of producing an extra 10 units of X if the economy is initially producing 60 units of X and 600 units of Y. How does this compare to the opportunity cost if the economy were initially producing 70 units of X?
c. Suppose now that the technology associated with producing good Y improves, so that the maximum level of Y that can be produced from any given level of labour input increases by 10 percent. Explain (or show in a diagram) what happens to the production possibilities curve.

7. Explain why a technological improvement in the production of one good means that a country can now produce more of *other* goods than it did previously. Hint: Draw a country's production possibilities boundary to help answer this question.

8. Consider your decision whether to go skiing for the weekend. Suppose that transportation, lift tickets, and accommodation for the weekend costs $300. Suppose also that restaurant food for the weekend will cost $75.

Finally, suppose that you have a weekend job that you will have to miss if you go skiing, which pays you $120 (after tax) for the one weekend day that you work. What is the opportunity cost of going skiing? Do you need any other information before computing the opportunity cost?

9. Suppose that you and a friend go wilderness camping for a week and must find your own food to survive. From past experience, you know that you and your friend have different abilities in fishing and hunting. If each of you were to work for one day either catching fish or trapping rabbits, the number of fish and rabbits that you could catch is given in the following table:

	Fish	Rabbits
You	6	3
Your friend	8	2

You and your friend decide that you should allocate the duties so that you get the most food for the least amount of effort. For simplicity, assume that one fish represents the same amount of food as one rabbit.

a. What is the opportunity cost for you to catch an additional rabbit? What is your friend's opportunity cost of catching an extra rabbit?
b. What allocation of tasks maximizes total output for the least amount of effort?
c. Suppose that you both decide to work for two days according to the allocation in part (b). What is the total amount of output? What would it have been had you chosen the reverse allocation of tasks?

DISCUSSION QUESTIONS

1. What is the difference between scarcity and poverty? If everyone in the world had enough to eat, could we say that food was no longer scarce?

2. Evidence accumulates that the use of chemical fertilizers, which increases agricultural production greatly, damages water quality. Analyze the choice between more food and cleaner water involved in using such fertilizers. Use a production possibilities curve with agricultural output on the vertical axis and water quality on the horizontal axis. In what ways does this production possibilities curve reflect scarcity, choice, and opportunity cost? How would an improved fertilizer that increased agricultural output without further worsening water quality affect the curve? Suppose that a pollution-free fertilizer were developed; would this mean that there would no longer be any opportunity cost in using it?

3. Discuss the following statement by a leading U.S. economist: "One of the mysteries of semantics is why the government-managed economies ever came to be called planned and the market economies unplanned. It is the former that are in chronic chaos, in which buyers stand in line hoping to buy some toilet paper or soap. It is the latter that are in reasonable equilibrium—where if you want a cake of soap or a steak or a shirt or a car, you can go to the store and find that the item is magically there for you to buy. It is the liberal economies that reflect a highly sophisticated planning system, and the government-managed economies that are primitive and unplanned."

4. Consider the market for physicians' services. In what way has this market taken advantage of the specialization of labour?

5. "It is not from the benevolence of the butcher, the brewer, or the baker, that we expect our dinner, but from their regard to their own interest. We address ourselves, not to their humanity but to their self-love, and never talk to them of our own necessities but of their advantages." Do you agree with this quotation from Adam Smith's classic, *The Wealth of Nations*? How are "our dinner" and "their self-interest" related to the price system? What does Smith assume to be the motives of firms and households?

6. In the chapter we used a simple idea of a production possibilities boundary to illustrate the concepts of scarcity, choice, and opportunity cost. We assumed there were only two goods—call them X and Y. But we all know that any economy produces many more than just two goods. Explain why the insights illustrated in Figure 1-2 are more general, and why the assumption of only two goods is a useful one.

CHAPTER 2

How Economists Work

LEARNING OBJECTIVES

1. Differentiate between positive and normative statements.

2. Illustrate how the use of models helps economists think about the economy.

3. Explain the interaction between economic theories and empirical observation.

4. Identify several types of economic data, including index numbers, time-series and cross-sectional data, and scatter diagrams.

5. Understand that the slope of a relation between X and Y is interpreted as the marginal response in Y to a unit change in X.

If you read a newspaper, watch television, or listen to the radio, you will often see or hear some economist's opinions being reported, perhaps about: unemployment, the exchange rate, or interest rates; some new tax; the case for privatization or regulation of an industry; or the possible reforms to Canada's health-care system. Where do economists' opinions come from? Are they supported by hard evidence, and if so, why do economists sometimes disagree with each other over important issues?

Economics is a social science. Unlike training in chemistry or physics, however, many economists would say that training in economics provides the student more with a "way of thinking" than with a collection of facts. This does not mean that facts are unimportant to the economist—quite the contrary. It means only that facts are typically harder to establish in economics than in the "hard" sciences and often economists do not know which facts are important without first having a way to organize their thinking.

Central to the economist's way of thinking is the distinction between *positive statements* and *normative statements*. Also crucial is the role of *theory* and, in particular, the use of economic *models* to provide a framework for thinking about complex issues. Such models can be used to generate *testable hypotheses*.

In this chapter, we explore what it means to be "scientific" in the study of economics. Along the way we will learn much about theories, data, testing and graphing.

2.1 Positive and Normative Advice

Economists give two broad types of advice, called *normative* and *positive*. They sometimes advise that the government ought to try harder to reduce unemployment or to preserve the environment. When they say such things they are giving normative advice.

They may be using their expert knowledge to come to conclusions about the costs of various unemployment-reducing or environment-saving schemes. When they say that the government *ought* to do something, however, they are making judgements about the value of the various things that the government could do with its limited resources. Advice that depends on a value judgement is normative—it tells others what they *ought* to do.

Another type of advice is illustrated by the statement, "If the government wants to reduce unemployment, reducing unemployment insurance benefits is an effective way of doing so." This is positive advice. It does not rely on a judgement about the value of reducing unemployment. Instead the expert is saying, "If this is what you want to do, here is a way to do it."

Normative statements depend on value judgements. They involve issues of personal opinion, which cannot be settled by recourse to facts. In contrast, **positive statements** do not involve value judgements. They are statements about what is, was, or will be—that is, statements that are about matters of fact.

The distinction between positive and normative is fundamental to any rational inquiry. Much of the success of modern science depends on the ability of scientists to separate their views on *what does happen* in the world from their views on *what they would like to happen*. For example, until the eighteenth century almost everyone believed that the Earth was only a few thousand years old. Evidence then began to accumulate that the Earth was billions of years old. This evidence was hard for most people to accept since it ran counter to a literal reading of many religious texts. Many did not want to believe the evidence. Nevertheless, scientists, many of whom were religious, continued their research because they refused to allow their feelings about what they wanted to believe to affect their scientific search for the truth. Eventually, all scientists came to accept that the Earth is about 4 billion years old.

Distinguishing what is true from what we would like to be, or what we feel ought to be, requires distinguishing between positive and normative statements.

Examples of both types of statements are given in Table 2-1. All four positive statements in the table are assertions about the nature of the world in which we live. In contrast, the four normative statements involve value judgements. Notice two things about the positive/normative distinction. First, positive statements need not be true. Statement C is almost certainly false. Yet it is positive, not normative. Second, the inclusion of a value judgement in a statement does not necessarily make the statement normative. Statement D is a positive statement about the value judgements that people hold. We could conduct a survey to check if people really do prefer low unemployment to

normative statement
A statement about what ought to be as opposed to what actually is.

positive statement
A statement about what actually is (was or will be), as opposed to what ought to be.

Practise with Study Guide Chapter 2, Short-Answer Question 1.

TABLE 2-1   Positive and Normative Statements

Positive	Normative
A Raising interest rates encourages people to save.	E People should be encouraged to save.
B High rates of income tax encourage people to evade paying taxes.	F Governments should arrange taxes so that people cannot avoid paying them.
C Lowering the price of tobacco leads people to smoke less.	G The government should raise the tax on tobacco to discourage people from smoking.
D The majority of the population would prefer a policy that reduced unemployment to one that reduced inflation.	H The government ought to be more concerned with reducing unemployment than inflation.

low inflation. We could ask them and we could observe how they voted. There is no need for the economist to rely on a value judgement in order to check the validity of the statement itself.

We leave you to analyze the remaining six statements to decide precisely why each is either positive or normative. Remember to apply the two tests. First, is the statement only about actual or alleged facts? If so, it is a positive one. Second, are value judgements necessary to assess the truth of the statement? If so, it is normative.

Disagreements Among Economists

Economists often disagree with each other in public discussions, frequently because of poor communication. The adversaries fail to define their terms or their points of reference clearly, and so they end up "arguing past" each other, with the only certain result being that the audience is left confused.

Another source of disagreement stems from economists' failure to acknowledge the full state of their ignorance. There are many things on which the evidence is far from conclusive. Informed judgements are then required in order to take a position on even a purely positive question. In such cases, a responsible economist will make clear the extent to which his or her view is based on judgement.

Perhaps the biggest source of public disagreement between economists is based on the positive/normative distinction. Different economists have different values, and these normative views play a large part in most discussions of public policy. Many economists stress the importance of individual responsibility and argue, for example, that lower employment insurance benefits would be desirable because people would have a greater incentive to search for a job. Other economists stress the need for a generous "social safety net" and argue that higher employment insurance benefits would be desirable because human hardship would be reduced. In such debates, and there are many in economics, it is the responsibility of the economist to state clearly what part of the proffered advice is normative and what part is positive.

Because the world is complex and because no issue can be settled beyond any doubt, economists rarely agree unanimously on an issue. Nevertheless, there is an impressive amount of agreement on many aspects of how the economy works and what happens when governments intervene to alter its workings. A survey published in the *American Economic Review*, perhaps the most influential economics journal, showed strong agreement among economists on many propositions, including: "Rent control leads to a housing shortage" (85 percent yes), "Tariffs usually reduce economic welfare" (93 percent yes), "Large government budget deficits have adverse effects on the economy" (83 percent yes), and "A minimum wage increases unemployment among young workers" (79 percent yes). Other examples of these areas of agreement will be found in many places throughout this book.

2.2 Economic Theories

Economists seek to understand the world by developing *theories* and *models* that explain some of the things that have been seen and to predict some of the things that will be seen. What is a theory and what is a model?

Theories

Theories are constructed to explain things. For example, what determines the number of eggs sold in Winnipeg on a particular day, and the price at which they are sold? As part of the answer to questions like these, economists have developed theories of demand and supply—theories that we will study in detail in the next three chapters. Any theory is distinguished by its definitions, assumptions, and predictions.

Definitions

The basic elements of any theory are its variables. A **variable** is a magnitude that can take on different possible values.

In our theory of the egg market, the variable *quantity of eggs* might be defined as the number of cartons of 12 Grade A large eggs. The variable *price of eggs* is the amount of money that must be given up to purchase each carton of eggs. The particular values taken on by those two variables might be: 2000 cartons at a price of $1.80 on July 1, 2002; 1800 cartons at a price of $1.95 on July 1, 2003; and 1950 cartons at a price of $1.85 on July 1, 2004.

There are two broad categories of variables that are important in any theory. An **endogenous variable** is one whose value is determined within the theory. An **exogenous variable** influences the endogenous variables but is itself determined outside the theory. To illustrate the difference, the price of eggs and the quantity of eggs are endogenous variables in our theory of the egg market—our theory is designed to explain them. The state of the weather, however, is an exogenous variable. It may well affect the number of eggs consumers demand or producers supply but we can safely assume that the state of the weather is not influenced by the market for eggs.

Assumptions

A theory's assumptions concern motives, physical relations, directions of causation, and the conditions under which the theory is meant to apply.

Motives.   The theories we study in this book make the fundamental assumption that everyone pursues his or her own self-interest when making economic decisions. People are assumed to know what they want, and to know how to go about getting it within the constraints set by the resources at their command.

Physical Relations.   If egg producers buy more chicks and use more labour, land, and chicken feed, they will produce more eggs. This is an example of one of the most important physical relations in economics. It concerns assumptions about how the amount of output is related to the quantities of factors of production used to produce it. This relation is called a *production function.*

Direction of Causation.   When economists assume that one variable is related to another, they are assuming some causal link between the two. For example, when the amount of eggs that producers want to supply is assumed to increase when the cost of their chicken feed falls, the causation runs from the price of chicken feed to the supply of eggs. Producers supply more eggs because the price of chicken feed has fallen; they do not get cheaper chicken feed because of their decision to supply more eggs.

Conditions of Application.   Assumptions are often used to specify the conditions under which a theory is meant to hold. For example, a theory that assumes there is "no

variable Any well-defined item, such as the price or quantity of a commodity, that can take on various specific values.

endogenous variable A variable that is explained within a theory. Sometimes called an *induced variable* or a *dependent variable.*

exogenous variable A variable that is determined outside the theory. Sometimes called an *autonomous variable* or an *independent variable.*

A key assumption in economics is that firms make decisions with the goal of maximizing their profits.

government" usually does not mean literally the absence of government, but only that the theory is meant to apply when governments are not significantly affecting the situation being studied.

Although assumptions are an essential part of all theories, students are often concerned about those that seem unrealistic. An example will illustrate some of the issues involved. Much of the theory that we are going to study in this book uses the assumption that owners of firms attempt to maximize their profits. The assumption of profit maximization allows economists to make predictions about the behaviour of firms, such as, "firms will supply more output if the market price increases."

Profit maximization may seem like a rather crude assumption. Surely, for example, the managers of firms sometimes choose to protect the environment rather than pursue certain highly polluting but profitable opportunities. Does this not discredit the assumption of profit maximization by showing it to be unrealistic?

The answer is no; to make successful predictions, the theory does not require that managers be solely and unwaveringly motivated by the desire to maximize profits. All that is required is that profits be a sufficiently important consideration that a theory based on the assumption of profit maximization will lead to explanations and predictions that are substantially correct.

It is not always appropriate to criticize a theory because its assumptions seem unrealistic. A good theory abstracts in a useful way; a poor theory does not. If a theory has ignored some genuinely important factors, its predictions will be contradicted by the evidence—at least where an ignored factor exerts an important influence on the outcome.

All theory is an abstraction from reality. If it were not, it would merely duplicate the world in all its complexity and would add little to our understanding of it.

Predictions

A theory's predictions are the propositions that can be deduced from it. They are often called *hypotheses*. For example, a prediction from our theory of the egg market is that, "if the price of chicken feed falls, producers will want to sell more eggs." Another prediction from the same theory is that, "if the price of eggs declines, consumers will want to purchase more eggs."

Models

economic model
A term used in several related ways: sometimes for an abstraction designed to illustrate some point but not designed to generate testable hypotheses, and sometimes as a synonym for theory.

Economists often use the term **economic model**. This term is used in two different but related ways.

First, a model may be an illustrative abstraction, not meant to be elaborate enough to generate testable hypotheses. The circular flow of income and expenditure in Chapter 1 is a model of this sort, as is the production possibilities boundary. Both models help us to organize our thinking and gain crucial economic insights, even though the real world is much more complex than the model. In some ways, a model of this sort is like a political caricature. Its value is in the insights it provides that help us to understand key features of a complex world.

Second, the term *model* is used as a synonym for a theory, as when economists speak of the Keynesian model of the determination of national income, or the demand-and-supply model of the Winnipeg egg market that we discussed earlier. In both cases, the word *model* could easily be replaced by the word *theory*. Sometimes, economists use *model* to refer to a specific quantitative version of a theory. In this case, specific numbers are attached to the mathematical relationships defined by the theory. The result is that the predictions are more precise. For example, rather than a prediction such as, "a decrease in the price of chicken feed will lead to an increase in the quantity of eggs supplied," the prediction from the more specific model might be, "a 10-percent reduction in the price of chicken feed will lead to an 8-percent increase in the number of chickens supplied."

2.3 **Testing Theories**

A theory is tested by confronting its predictions with evidence. Are events of the type contained in the theory followed by the consequences predicted by the theory? For example, is a decrease in the price of chicken feed followed by an increase in the amount of eggs producers want to sell? Generally, theories tend to be abandoned when they are no longer useful. A theory ceases to be useful when it cannot predict better than an alternative theory. When a theory consistently fails to predict better than an available alternative, it is either modified or replaced.

The old question, "Which came first: the chicken or the egg?", is often raised when discussing economic theories. In the first instance, it was observation that preceded economic theories. People were not born with economic theories embedded in their minds; instead, economic theories first arose when people observed the coordination of market behaviour and asked themselves how such coordination occurred. However, once economics was established, theories and evidence interacted with each other. It has now become impossible to say that one precedes the other. In some cases, empirical evidence may suggest inadequacies that require the development of better theories. In other cases, an inspired guess may lead to a theory that has little current empirical support but is subsequently found to explain many observations. This interaction between theory and empirical observation is illustrated in Figure 2-1.

The scientific approach is central to the study of economics: Empirical observation leads to the construction of theories, theories generate specific hypotheses, and the hypotheses are tested by more detailed empirical observation.

Rejection Versus Confirmation

An important part of the scientific approach consists of setting up a theory that will explain some observation. A theory designed to explain observation X will typically generate a hypothesis about some other observable variables, Y and Z. The hypothesis about Y and Z can be tested and may be *rejected* by the data. If the hypothesis is rejected, the value of the theory is brought into question.

The alternative to this approach is to set up a theory and then look for *confirming* evidence. Such an approach is hazardous because the world is sufficiently complex that some confirming evidence can be found for any theory, no matter how unlikely the theory may be. For example, flying saucers, the Loch Ness monster, fortune-telling, and astrology all have their devotees who can quote confirming evidence in spite of the failure of many attempts to discover systematic, objective evidence of these things.

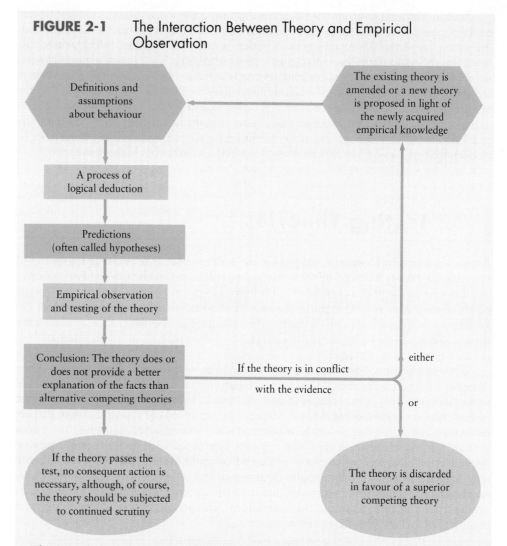

FIGURE 2-1   The Interaction Between Theory and Empirical Observation

Theory and observation are in continuous interaction. Starting (at the top left) with the assumptions of a theory and the definitions of relevant terms, the theorist deduces by logical analysis everything that is implied by the assumptions. These implications are the predictions or the hypotheses of the theory. The theory is then tested by confronting its predictions with evidence. If the theory is in conflict with facts, it will usually be amended to make it consistent with those facts (thereby making it a better theory), or it will be discarded, to be replaced by a superior theory. The process then begins again: The new or amended theory is subjected first to logical analysis and then to empirical testing.

Statistical Analysis

Most theories generate a hypothesis of the form, "if X increases, then Y will also increase." Statistical analysis is used to test such hypotheses and to estimate the numerical values of the function that describes the relationship. In practice, the same data can be used simultaneously to test whether a relationship exists and, if it does exist, to provide an estimate of the magnitude of that relationship.

Because economics is primarily a non-laboratory science, it lacks the controlled experiments central to sciences like physics and chemistry. Economics must therefore use millions of uncontrolled "experiments" that are going on every day in the marketplace. Households are deciding what to purchase given changing prices and incomes, firms are deciding what to produce and how, and governments are involved in the economy through their various taxes, subsidies, and regulations. Because all of these activities can be observed and recorded, a mass of data is continually being produced by the economy.

The variables that interest economists—such as the level of employment, the price of a DVD, and the output of automobiles—are generally influenced by many forces that vary simultaneously. If economists are to test their theories about relations among specific variables in the economy, they must use statistical techniques designed for situations in which other things *cannot* be held constant.

Fortunately, such techniques exist, although their application is usually neither simple nor straightforward. Later in this chapter we provide a discussion of some graphical techniques for describing data and displaying some of the more obvious relationships. Further examination of data involves techniques studied in elementary statistics courses. More advanced courses in econometrics deal with the array of techniques designed to test economic hypotheses and to measure economic relations in the complex circumstances in which economic evidence is often generated.

Correlation Versus Causation

Suppose you want to test your theory's hypothesis that "if X increases, Y will also increase." You are looking for a *causal* relationship from X to Y, because a change in X is predicted to *cause* a change in Y. When you look at the data, suppose you find that X and Y are positively correlated—that is, when X rises, Y also tends to rise. Is your theory supported? It might appear that way, but there is a potential problem.

A finding that X and Y are positively correlated means only that X and Y tend to move together. This is *not* the same as finding that movements in X *cause* movements in Y. The causality may be in the opposite direction—from Y to X. Or X and Y may have no direct causal connection but may instead be jointly caused by some third variable, Z.

Practise with Study Guide Chapter 2, Short-Answer Question 3.

Here is a concrete example. Suppose your theory predicts that individuals who get more education will earn higher incomes as a result—the causality runs from education to income. In the data, suppose we find education and income to be positively correlated. This positive correlation should not, however, be taken as support for the (causal) prediction. It may be true that individuals who grow up in higher-income households "buy" more education, just as they buy more clothes or entertainment. This is a case of "reverse causality": income causes education, rather than the other way around. Another possibility is that education and income are positively correlated because the personal characteristics that lead people to become more educated—ability and motivation—are the same characteristics that lead to high incomes. In this case, the *causal* relationship runs from personal characteristics to both income and education.

Most economic predictions involve causality. Economists must take care when testing predictions to distinguish between correlation and causality. This usually requires advanced statistical techniques.

Theories About Human Behaviour

So far we have talked about theories in general. But economic theories purport to explain and predict human behaviour. A scientific study of human behaviour is only possible if humans respond in predictable ways to things that affect them. Is it reasonable to expect such predictability? After all, we humans have free will and can behave in capricious ways if the spirit moves us.

Think, however, of what the world would be like if human behaviour were really unpredictable. Neither law, nor justice, nor airline timetables would be more reliable than the outcome of a single spin of a roulette wheel. A kind remark could as easily provoke fury as sympathy. Your landlady might evict you tomorrow or let you off rent-free. One cannot really imagine a society of human beings that could work like this. In fact, we live in a world that is a mixture of the predictable for "most of the people most of the time" with the haphazard or random.

How is it that human behaviour can show stable responses even though we can never be quite sure what any one individual will do? Successful predictions about the behaviour of large groups are made possible by the statistical "law" of large numbers. Very roughly, this "law" asserts that within a very large group of people the random actions of some individuals tend to offset the random actions of others.

For example, we might wonder if there is a relationship between highway speed limits and road accidents. When the speed limit is actually lowered, it will be almost impossible to predict in advance what changes will occur in any single individual's driving record. One individual whose record had been good may have a series of accidents after the speed limit is lowered because of deterioration in his physical or emotional health. Another person may have an improved accident record for reasons not associated with the change in the speed limit—for example, because she purchases a more reliable car. Yet others may have altered driving records for no reasons that we can discern—we may have to put it down to an exercise of unpredictable free will.

Because the unusual behaviour of one individual often offsets the unusual behaviour of someone else, it is much easier to accurately predict the average behaviour in large groups of people.

If we study only a few individuals, we will learn nothing about the effects of the altered speed limit, since we will not know the importance of all the other causes that are at work. But, if we observe 1000 individuals, the effects of the change in the speed limit—if such effects do exist—will tend to show up in the *average* responses. If a reduced speed limit does discourage accidents, the group as a whole will have fewer accidents even though some individuals have more. Individuals may do peculiar things that appear inexplicable, but the group's behaviour will nonetheless be predictable, precisely because the odd things that one individual does will tend to cancel out the odd things that some other individual does.

Testing theories about human behaviour requires studying large numbers of people—to take advantage of the "law" of large numbers.

Companion Website

Economists sometimes disagree about the usefulness of a theory or model. For a glimpse of one such debate between two Nobel Laureates, Milton Friedman and Ronald Coase, look for "How Economists Choose Their Theories" in the *Additional Topics* section of this book's Companion Website.

h t t p : / / w w w . p e a r s o n e d . c a / r a g a n

2.4 **Economic Data**

Economists seek to explain events that they see in the world. Why, for example, did the price of wheat rise last year even though the wheat crop increased? Explaining such observations typically requires an understanding of how the economy works, an understanding based in part on the insights economists derive from their theoretical models.

Economists also use real-world observations to test their theories. For example, did the amount that people saved last year rise—as the theory predicts it should have—when a large tax cut increased after-tax incomes? To test this prediction we need reliable data for people's incomes and their savings.

Political scientists, sociologists, anthropologists, and psychologists all tend to collect the data they use to formulate and test their theories. Economists are unusual among social scientists in mainly using data collected by others, often government statisticians. In economics there is a division of labour between collecting data and using it to generate and test theories. The advantage is that economists do not need to spend much of their scarce research time collecting the data they use. The disadvantage is that they are often not as well informed about the limitations of the data collected by others as they would be if they had collected the data themselves.

Once data are collected they can be displayed in various ways, many of which we will see later in this chapter. They can be laid out in tables. They can be displayed in various types of graphs. And where we are interested in relative movements rather than absolute ones, the data can be expressed in *index numbers*. We begin with a discussion of index numbers.

For data on the Canadian economy and many other quantifiable aspects of Canadian life, see Statistics Canada's website: www.statcan.ca.

index number
An average that measures change over time of such variables as the price level and industrial production; conventionally expressed as a percentage relative to a base period, which is assigned the value 100.

Index Numbers

Economists frequently look at data on prices or quantities and explore how specific variables change over time. For example, they may be interested in comparing the time paths of output in two industries: steel and newsprint. The problem is that it may be difficult to compare the time paths of the two different variables if we just look at the "raw" data.

Table 2-2 shows some hypothetical data for the volume of output in the steel and newsprint industries, and reveals that because the two variables are measured in different units, it is not immediately clear which of the two variables is more volatile or which, if either, has an upward or downward trend.

It is easier to compare the two paths if we focus on *relative* rather than *absolute* price changes. One way to do this is to construct some **index numbers**.

How to Build an Index Number

We start by taking the value of the variable at some point in time as the "base" to which the values of the variable in other periods will be compared. We call this the *base period*. In the present example, we choose 1992 as the

TABLE 2-2	Volume of Steel and Newsprint Output	
Year	Volume of Steel (thousands of tonnes)	Volume of Newsprint (thousands of rolls)
1992	200	3200
1993	210	3100
1994	225	3000
1995	215	3200
1996	250	3100
1997	220	3300
1998	265	3100
1999	225	3300
2000	255	3100
2001	230	3200
2002	245	3000

Comparing the time paths of two data series is difficult when absolute numbers are used. Since steel output and newsprint output are measured in different units and have quite different absolute numbers, it is difficult to detect which time series is more volatile.

base year for both series. We then take the output in each subsequent year, called the given year, and divide it by the output in the base year, and then multiply the result by 100. This gives us an index number for the output of steel and a separate index number for the output of newsprint. For each index number, the value of output in the base year is equal to 100. The details of the calculations are shown in Table 2-3.

An index number simply expresses the value of some series in any given year as a percentage of its value in the base year. For example, the 2002 index of steel output of 122.5 tells us that steel output in 2002 was 22.5 percent greater than in 1992. In contrast, the 2002 index for newsprint output of 93.8 tells us that newsprint output in 2002 was only 93.8 percent of the output in 1992—that is, output was 6.2 percent lower in 2002 than in 1992. The results in Table 2-3 allow us to compare the relative fluctuations in the two series. It is apparent from the values in the table that steel has shown significantly more percentage variability than has the output of newsprint. This is also clear in Figure 2-2.

The formula of any index number is:

$$\text{Value of index in any given period} = \frac{\text{Absolute value at given period}}{\text{Absolute value in base period}} \times 100$$

Care must be taken, however, when using index numbers. Note that when comparing an index number across non-base years, the percentage change in the index number is *not* given by the absolute difference in the values of the index number. For example, if you want to know how much steel output changed from 1996 to 1998, we know from Table 2-3 that the index number for steel output increased from 125.0 in 1996 to 132.5 in 1998. But this is not an increase of 7.5 percent. The *percentage* increase in steel output is computed as (132.5 − 125.0)/125.0 = 7.5/125.0 = 0.06, or 6 percent.

TABLE 2-3   Constructing Index Numbers

Year	Steel Procedure		Index	Newsprint Procedure		Index
1992	(200/200) × 100	=	100.0	(3200/3200) × 100	=	100.0
1993	(210/200) × 100	=	105.0	(3100/3200) × 100	=	96.9
1994	(225/200) × 100	=	112.5	(3000/3200) × 100	=	93.8
1995	(215/200) × 100	=	107.5	(3200/3200) × 100	=	100.0
1996	(250/200) × 100	=	125.0	(3100/3200) × 100	=	96.9
1997	(220/200) × 100	=	110.0	(3300/3200) × 100	=	103.1
1998	(265/200) × 100	=	132.5	(3100/3200) × 100	=	96.9
1999	(225/200) × 100	=	112.5	(3300/3200) × 100	=	103.1
2000	(255/200) × 100	=	127.5	(3100/3200) × 100	=	96.9
2001	(230/200) × 100	=	115.0	(3200/3200) × 100	=	100.0
2002	(245/200) × 100	=	122.5	(3000/3200) × 100	=	93.8

Index numbers are calculated by dividing the value in the given year by the value in the base year, and multiplying the result by 100. The 2002 index number for steel tells us that steel output in 2002 was 22.5 percent greater than in the base year, 1992. The 2002 index number for newsprint tells us that newsprint output in 2002 was 93.8 percent of the output in the base year, 1992.

FIGURE 2-2   Index Values for Steel and Newsprint Output

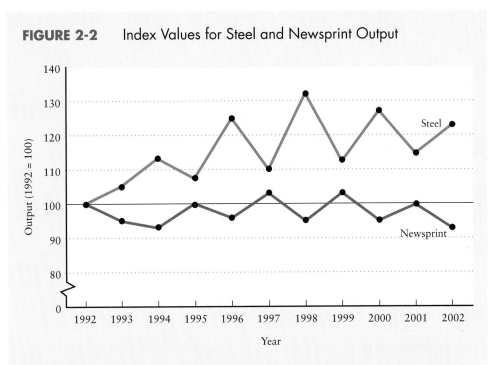

Comparing the time paths of two variables is much easier when index numbers are used. Since both index numbers are equal to 100 in the base year, relative volatility and trends become clear. Steel output is clearly more volatile in percentage terms than newsprint output. Steel output has an upward trend, whereas newsprint output appears to have little or no trend.

More Complex Index Numbers

Perhaps the most famous index number used by economists is the index of average prices—the consumer price index (CPI). This is a price index of the *average* price paid by consumers for the typical basket of goods that they buy. The inclusion of the word "average," however, makes the CPI a more complex index number than the ones we have constructed here.

With what you have just learned, you could construct separate index numbers for the price of beef, the price of coffee, and the price of orange juice. But in order to get the consumer price index we need to take the *average* of these separate price indexes (plus thousands of others for the goods and services we have ignored here). But it cannot be a simple average. Instead it must be a *weighted* average where the weight on each price index reflects the relative importance of that good in the typical consumer's basket of goods and services. For example, since the typical consumer spends a tiny fraction of income on sardines but a much larger fraction of income on housing, the weight on the "sardines" price index in the CPI will be very small and the weight on the "housing" price index will be very large. The result is that even huge swings in the price of sardines will have negligible effects on the CPI, whereas much more modest changes in the price of housing will have noticeable effects on the CPI.

We will spend much more time discussing the consumer price index when we study macroeconomics beginning in Chapter 19. For now, keep in mind the usefulness of the

Practise with Study Guide Chapter 2, Exercise 1.

simple index numbers we have constructed here. They allow us to compare the time paths of different variables.

Graphing Economic Data

A single economic variable such as unemployment, GDP, or the average price of a house can come in two basic forms.

Cross-Sectional and Time-Series Data

The first is called **cross-sectional data,** which means a number of different observations on one variable all taken in different places at the same point in time. Figure 2-3 shows an example. The variable in the figure is average housing price. It is shown for each of the ten Canadian provinces in March 2003.

The second type of data is called **time-series data.** It refers to observations taken on one variable at successive points in time. The data in Figure 2-4 show the unemployment rate for Canada from 1978 to 2003. (Note that the Canadian unemployment rate is simply a weighted average of the ten provincial unemployment rates, where the weight for each province is the size of that province's labour force expressed as a fraction of the total Canadian labour force.)

Scatter Diagrams

Another way in which data can be presented is in a **scatter diagram**. This type of chart is more analytical than those above. It is designed to show the relation between two different variables, such as the price of eggs and the quantity of eggs purchased. To plot a scatter diagram, values of one variable are measured on the horizontal axis and values of the second variable are measured on the vertical axis. Any point on the diagram relates a specific value of one variable to a corresponding specific value of the other.

The data plotted on a scatter diagram may be either cross-sectional data or time-series data. An example of a cross-sectional scatter diagram is a scatter of the price of eggs and the quantity sold in July 2003 at two dozen different places in Canada. Each dot refers to a price–quantity combination observed in a different place at the same time. An example of a scatter diagram using time-series data is the price and quantity of eggs sold in Thunder Bay for each month over the last ten years. Each of the 120 dots refers to a price–quantity combination observed at the same place in one particular month.

The table in Figure 2-5 shows data for the income and the saving of ten households in one particular year and these data are plotted

cross-sectional data
A set of measurements or observations made at the same time across several different units (such as households, firms, or countries).

time-series data
A set of measurements or observations made repeatedly at successive periods of time.

scatter diagram
A graph of statistical observations of paired values of two variables, one measured on the horizontal and the other on the vertical axis. Each point on the coordinate grid represents the values of the variables for a particular unit of observation.

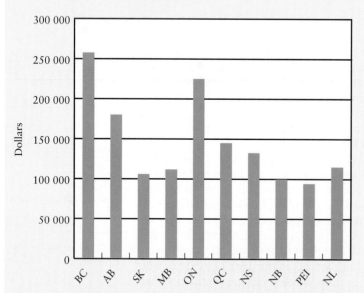

FIGURE 2-3   Average Housing Prices for Ten Canadian Provinces, March 2003

(*Source:* Canadian Real Estate Association (www.crea.ca). These data are available at www.crea.ca/public/news/mls_statistics.htm.)

FIGURE 2-4 Canadian Unemployment Rate, 1978–2003

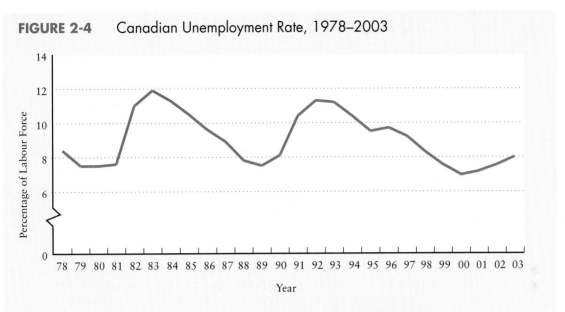

(*Source:* Annual average of monthly, seasonally adjusted data from Statistics Canada, CANSIM database, Series No. V2091177.)

FIGURE 2-5 A Scatter Diagram of Income and Saving

Household	Annual Income	Annual Saving
1	$ 70 000	$10 000
2	30 000	2 500
3	100 000	12 000
4	60 000	3 000
5	80 000	8 000
6	10 000	500
7	20 000	2 000
8	50 000	2 000
9	40 000	4 200
10	90 000	8 000

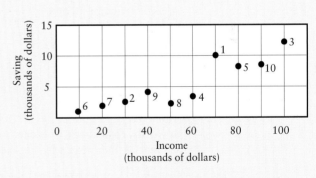

Saving tends to rise as income rises. The table shows the amount of income earned by ten selected households together with the amount they saved during the same year. The scatter diagram plots the income and saving for the ten households listed in the table. The number on each dot refers to the household in the corresponding row of the table.

on a scatter diagram. Each point in the figure represents one household, showing its income and its saving. The positive relation between the two stands out. The higher is the household's income, the higher its saving tends to be.

2.5 **Graphing Economic Theories**

Theories are built on assumptions about relationships between variables. For example, the quantity of eggs demanded is assumed to fall as the price of eggs rises. Or, the total amount an individual saves is assumed to rise as his or her income rises. How can such relations be expressed?

Functions

When one variable, X, is related to another variable, Y, in such a way that to every value of X there is only one possible value of Y, we say that Y is a *function* of X. When we write this relation down, we are expressing a *functional relation* between the two variables.

Here is a specific example. Consider the relation between a family's annual income, which we denote by the symbol Y, and the amount it spends on goods and services during that period, which we denote by the symbol C (for consumption). This relation between C and Y can be expressed several ways—in words, in a table or schedule, in a mathematical equation, or in a graph.

Verbal Statement.   When income is zero, the family will spend $800 a year (either by borrowing the money or by consuming past savings), and for every extra $1 of income that it obtains it will increase its expenditure by 80 cents.

Schedule.   This table shows selected values of the family's income and the amount it spends on consumption.

Annual Income	Consumption	Reference Letter
$ 0	$ 800	*p*
2 500	2 800	*q*
5 000	4 800	*r*
7 500	6 800	*s*
10 000	8 800	*t*

Mathematical Equation. $C = \$800 + 0.8Y$ is the equation of the relation just described in words. As a check, you can first see that when Y is zero, C is $800. Further, you can see that as Y increases by $1, the level of C increases by 0.8($1), which is 80 cents.

Graph.   Figure 2-6 shows the points from the preceding schedule and the line representing the equation given in the previous paragraph.

Comparison of the values on the graph with the values in the schedule, and with the values derived from the equation just stated, shows that these are alternative expressions of the same relation between C and Y. All four of these modes of expression refer to the same relation between consumption expenditure and income.

More Detail About Functions

Let us look in a little more detail at the mathematical expression of this relation between income and consumption. To state the expression in general form, detached from the specific numerical example above, we use a symbol to express the dependence of one variable on another. Using "f" for this purpose, we write

$$C = f(Y) \tag{2-1}$$

This is read, "C is a function of Y." Spelling this out more fully, we would say, "The amount of consumption expenditure depends upon the household's income."

The variable on the left-hand side is the dependent variable, since its value depends on the value of the variable on the right-hand side. The variable on the right-hand side is the independent variable, since it can take on any value. The letter "f" tells us that a functional relation is involved. This means that a knowledge of the value of the variable (or variables) within the parentheses on the right-hand side allows us to determine the value of the variable on the left-hand side. Although in this case we have used "f" (as a memory-aid for "function"), any convenient symbol can be used to denote the existence of a functional relation.

Functional notation can seem intimidating to those who are unfamiliar with it. But it is helpful. Since the functional concept is basic to all science, the notation is worth mastering.

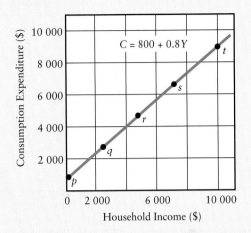

FIGURE 2-6   Income and Consumption

$$C = 800 + 0.8Y$$

Consumption expenditure rises as income rises. The figure graphs the schedule and the equation for the functional relation discussed in the text.

Functional Forms

The equation $C = f(Y)$ states that C is related to Y. It says nothing about the *form* that this relation takes. The term *functional form* refers to the specific nature of the relation between the variables in the function. The example above gave one specific functional form for this relation:

$$C = \$800 + 0.8Y \qquad (2\text{-}2)$$

Equation 2-1 expresses the general assumption that consumption expenditure depends on the consumer's income. Equation 2-2 expresses the more specific assumption that C is equal to $800 when Y is zero and rises by 80 cents for every $1 that Y rises. An alternative assumption would be $C = \$600 + 0.9Y$. You should be able to say in words the behaviour implied in this relation. There is no reason why either of these assumptions must be true; indeed, neither may be consistent with the facts. But that is a matter for testing. What we do have in each equation is a concise statement of a particular assumption.

Notice that Equation 2-2 also specifies a *linear* consumption function—the relationship between C and Y is shown as a straight line in Figure 2-6. This is a very special case. Another possibility is that the relationship between C and Y is *non-linear*—so that the consumption function when graphed is not a straight line. This possibility takes us to our next discussion, of linear and non-linear functions, and of how to measure and interpret the *slopes* of functions.

Graphing Functional Relations

Different functional forms have different graphs, and we will meet many of these in subsequent chapters. Figure 2-6 is an example of a relation in which the two variables move together. When income goes up, consumption goes up. In such a relation the two variables are *positively related* to each other.

Practise with Study Guide Chapter 2, Exercise 2.

FIGURE 2-7   Linear Pollution Reduction

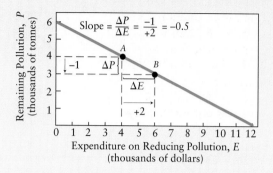

$$\text{Slope} = \frac{\Delta P}{\Delta E} = \frac{-1}{+2} = -0.5$$

Pollution as a linear function of clean-up expenditure. Between points A and B it costs $2000 to reduce pollution by 1000 tonnes. The cost of pollution abatement is the same elsewhere on the line. The slope of the line, -0.5, indicates that any $2000 expenditure on pollution clean-up reduces the amount of pollution by 1000 tonnes. The slope is constant, indicating that *every* $1 spent on clean-up leads to a reduction of pollution of 0.5 tonnes.

Figure 2-7 gives an example of variables that move in opposite directions. As the amount spent on reducing pollution goes up, the amount of remaining pollution goes down. In such a relation the two variables are *negatively related* to each other.

Both of these graphs are straight lines. In such cases the variables are *linearly related* to each other (either positively or negatively).

The Slope of a Straight Line

Slopes are important in economics. They show you how much one variable changes as the other changes. The slope is defined as the amount of change in the variable measured on the vertical or y-axis per unit change in the variable measured on the horizontal or x-axis. In the case of Figure 2-7 it tells us how many tonnes of pollution, symbolized by P, are removed per dollar spent on reducing pollution, symbolized by E. Consider moving from point A to point B in the figure. If we spend $2000 more on clean-up, we reduce pollution by 1000 tonnes. This is 0.5 tonnes per dollar spent. On the graph the extra $2000 is indicated by ΔE, the arrow indicating that E rises by 2000. The 1000 tonnes of pollution reduction is indicated by ΔP, the arrow showing that pollution falls by 1000. (The Greek uppercase letter delta, Δ, stands for a change in something.) To get the amount of pollution reduction per dollar of expenditure we merely divide one by the other. In symbols this is $\Delta P/\Delta E$.

If we let X stand for whatever variable is measured on the horizontal axis and Y for whatever variable is measured on the vertical axis, the slope of a straight line is $\Delta Y/\Delta X$. [1]

In Figure 2-6 the two variables change in the same direction, so both changes will always be either positive or negative. As a result their ratio, which is the slope of this line, is positive. In Figure 2-7 the two variables change in opposite directions; when one increases, the other decreases. So the two changes will always be of opposite sign. As a result their ratio, which is the slope of the line, is always negative.

Notice also that straight lines have the same slope no matter where on the line you measure that slope. This tells us what inspection of the diagram reveals: the change in one variable in response to a unit change in the other is the same anywhere on the line. We reduce pollution by 0.5 tonnes for every additional $1 that we spend no matter how much we are already spending.

Non-Linear Functions

Although it is sometimes convenient to simplify a real relation between two variables by assuming them to be linearly related, this is seldom the case over their whole range. Non-linear relations are much more common than linear ones. In the case of reducing pollution, it is usually quite cheap to eliminate the first units of pollution. Then, as

---

[1] Numbers in square brackets indicate mathematical notes that are found in a separate section at the back of the book.

the environment gets cleaner and cleaner, the cost of further clean-up tends to increase because more and more sophisticated and expensive methods need to be used. As a result, Figure 2-8 is more realistic than Figure 2-7. Inspection of Figure 2-8 shows that as more and more is spent, the amount of pollution reduction for an additional $1 of clean-up expenditure gets smaller and smaller. This is shown by the diminishing slope of the curve as we move rightward along it. For example, as we move from point A to point B, an increase in expenditure of $1000 is required to reduce pollution by 1000 tonnes. Thus, each tonne of pollution reduction costs $1. But as we move from point C (where we have already reduced pollution considerably) to point D, an extra $6000 must be spent in order to reduce pollution by 1000 tonnes. Each tonne of pollution reduction therefore costs $6.

Economists call the change in pollution when a bit more or a bit less is spent on clean-up the *marginal* change. The figure shows that the slope of the curve at each point measures this marginal change. It also shows that, in the type of curve illustrated, the marginal change per dollar spent is diminishing as we spend more on reducing pollution. There is always a payoff to more expenditure over the range shown in the figure, but the payoff diminishes as more is spent. This relation can be described as *diminishing marginal response*. We will meet such relations many times in what follows, so we emphasize now that diminishing marginal response does not mean that the *total* response is diminishing. In Figure 2-8, the total amount of pollution continues to fall as more and more is spent on clean-up. But diminishing marginal response does mean that the amount of pollution reduced per dollar of expenditure falls as our total expenditure rises.

FIGURE 2-8   Non-Linear Pollution Reduction

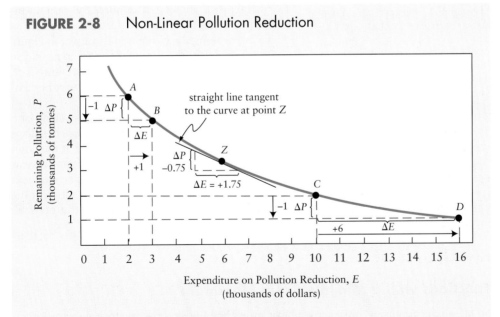

Pollution as a non-linear function of clean-up expenditure. The slope of the curve changes as we move along it. Between points A and B, it costs $1000 to reduce pollution by 1000 tonnes. Between points C and D, it costs $6000 to reduce pollution by 1000 tonnes. At point Z, the slope of the curve is equal to the slope of the straight line tangent to the curve at point Z. The slope of the tangent line is −0.75/1.75 = −0.43.

FIGURE 2-9   Increasing Production Costs

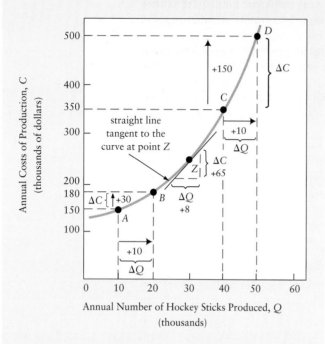

Annual Costs of Production, C (thousands of dollars)

Annual Number of Hockey Sticks Produced, Q (thousands)

Production costs increase at an increasing rate as annual output rises. From point *A* to point *B*, an extra annual output of 10 000 hockey sticks increases annual costs by $30 000. Each extra hockey stick costs $3. From point *C* to point *D*, an extra output of 10 000 hockey sticks increases annual costs by $150 000. Each extra hockey stick then costs $15. This is a case of increasing marginal cost. At point *Z*, the slope of the curve is equal to the slope of the straight line tangent to the curve at point *Z*. The slope of the tangent line is 65/8 = 8.1.

Figure 2-9 shows a graph where the marginal response is increasing. The graph shows the relationship between annual production costs and annual output for a firm that makes hockey sticks. Notice that the more hockey sticks produced annually, the higher the firm's costs. This is shown by the positive slope of the line. Notice also that as more and more hockey sticks are produced, the extra amount that the firm must pay to produce each extra hockey stick rises. For example, as the firm moves from point *A* to point *B*, annual costs rise by $30 000 in order to increase its annual output by 10 000 hockey sticks. Each extra hockey stick costs $3 ($30 000/10 000 = $3). But when the firm is producing many more hockey sticks, such as at point *C*, its factory is closer to its capacity and it becomes more costly to increase production. Moving from point *C* to point *D*, the firm's annual costs increase by $150 000 in order to increase its annual output by 10,000 hockey sticks. Each extra hockey stick then costs $15 ($150 000/10 000 = $15). This figure illustrates a case of *increasing marginal cost*, a characteristic of production that we will see often and learn more about later in this book.

Figures 2-8 and 2-9 show that with non-linear functions the slope of the curve changes as we move along the curve. For example, in Figure 2-8, the slope of the curve falls as the expenditure on pollution clean-up increases. In Figure 2-9, the slope of the curve increases as the volume of production increases.

How, exactly, do we measure the slope of a curved line? The answer is that we use the slope of a straight line *tangent to that curve* at the point that interests us. For example, in Figure 2-8, if we want to know the slope of the curve at point *Z*, we draw a straight line that touches the curve *only* at point *Z*; this is a tangent line. The slope of this line is –0.75/1.75 = –0.43. Similarly, in Figure 2-9, the slope of the curve at point *Z* is given by the slope of the straight line tangent to the curve at point *Z*.

For non-linear functions, the slope of the curve changes as X changes. Therefore, the marginal response of Y to a change in X depends on the value of X.

Functions with a Minimum or a Maximum

So far, all the graphs we have shown have had either a positive or negative slope over their entire range. But many relations change directions as the independent variable increases. For example, consider a firm that is attempting to maximize its profits and is trying to determine how much output to produce. The firm may find that its unit production costs are lower than the market price of the good, and so it can increase its profit by producing more. But as it increases its level of production, the firm's unit costs may be driven up because the capacity of the factory is being approached. Eventually, the firm may find that extra output will actually cost so much that its profits will be *reduced*. This is a relationship that we will study in detail in later chapters, and it is illustrated in Figure 2-10. Notice that when profits are maximized at point *A*, the slope of the curve is zero (because a tangent to the curve at point *A* is horizontal) and so the *marginal response* of profits to output is zero.

Now consider an example of a function with a minimum. You probably know that when you drive a car the fuel consumption per kilometre depends on your speed. Driving very slowly uses a lot of fuel per kilometre travelled. Driving very fast also uses a lot of fuel per kilometre travelled. The best fuel efficiency—the lowest fuel consumption per kilometre travelled—occurs at a speed of approximately 95 kilometres per hour. The relationship between speed and fuel consumption is shown in Figure 2-11 and illustrates a function with a minimum. Note that at point *A* the slope of the curve is zero (because a tangent to the curve at point *A* is horizontal) and so the *marginal response* of fuel consumption to speed is zero.

At either a minimum or a maximum of a function, the slope of the curve is zero. Therefore, at the minimum or maximum, the marginal response of *Y* to a change in *X* is zero.

FIGURE 2-10   Profits as a Function of Output

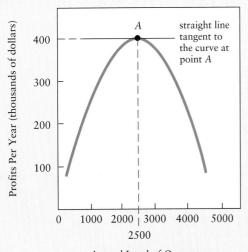

Profits rise and then eventually fall as output rises. When the firm is producing less than 2500 units annually, the marginal response of profit to output is positive—that is, an increase in output leads to an increase in profit. Beyond 2500 units annually, the marginal response is negative—an increase in output leads to a reduction in profit. At point *A*, profits are maximized and the marginal response of profit to output is zero. Because a tangent to the curve at point *A* is horizontal, the slope of the curve is zero at that point.

FIGURE 2-11   Average Fuel Consumption as a Function of Speed

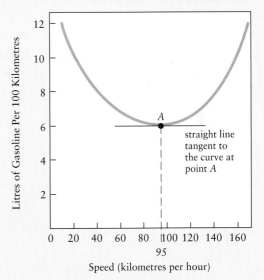

Average fuel consumption falls and then eventually rises as speed increases. Average fuel consumption in litres per kilometre travelled is minimized at point *A* at a speed of approximately 95 kilometres per hour (km/h). At speeds less than 95 km/h, the marginal response is negative—that is, an increase in speed reduces fuel consumption per kilometre. At speeds above 95 km/h, the marginal response is positive—an increase in speed increases fuel consumption per kilometre. At 95 km/h, the marginal response is zero and fuel consumption per kilometre is minimized. Because a tangent to the curve at point *A* is horizontal, the slope of the curve is zero at that point.

A Final Word

We have done much in this chapter. We have discussed why economists use theory and how they build economic models. We have discussed how they test their theories and how there is a continual back-and-forth process between empirical testing of predictions and refining the theoretical model. Finally, we have devoted considerable time and space to exploring the many ways that data can be displayed in graphs and how economists use graphs to illustrate their theories.

Many students find themselves intimidated when they are first confronted with all of the details about graphing. But try not to worry. You may not yet be a master of all the graphing techniques that we have discussed in this chapter, but you will be surprised at how quickly it all falls into place. And, as is true for most skills, there is no substitute for practice. In the next three chapters we will encounter many graphs. But we will start simply and then slowly attempt more complicated cases. We are confident that in the process of learning some basic economic theories you will get enough practice in graphing that you will very soon look back at this chapter and realize how straightforward it all is.

S U M M A R Y

2.1 Positive and Normative Advice

- A key to the success of scientific inquiry lies in separating positive questions about the way the world works from normative questions about how one would like the world to work.

2.2 Economic Theories

- Theories are designed to explain and predict what we see. A theory consists of a set of definitions of the variables to be employed, a set of assumptions about how things behave, and the conditions under which the theory is meant to apply.

- A theory provides conditional predictions of the type, "if one event occurs, then another event will also occur."
- The term "model" is often used as a synonym for theory. It is also used to describe an illustrative abstraction that is used to organize our thinking even though it may not generate testable hypotheses.

2.3 Testing Theories

- Theories are tested by checking their predictions against evidence. In some sciences, these tests can be conducted under laboratory conditions in which only one thing changes at a time. In economics, testing is almost always done using the data produced by the world of ordinary events.
- Economists make use of statistical analysis when testing their theories. They must take care to make the distinction between correlation and causation.

- The fact that people sometimes act strangely, even capriciously, does not destroy the possibility of scientific study of group behaviour. The odd and inexplicable things that one person does will tend to cancel out the odd and inexplicable things that another person does. The law of large numbers thus means that group behaviour is often easier to predict than individual behaviour.

- The progress of any science lies in finding better explanations of events than are now available. Thus in any developing science, one must expect to discard some existing theories and replace them with demonstrably superior alternatives.

2.4 **Economic Data**

- Index numbers express economic series in relative form. Values in each period are expressed in relation to the value in the base period, which is given a value of 100.
- Economic data may be graphed in three different ways. Cross-sectional graphs show observations taken at the same time. Time-series graphs show observations on one variable taken over time. Scatter diagrams show many points, each one of which refers to specific observations on two different variables.

2.5 **Graphing Economic Theories**

- A functional relation can be expressed in words, in a schedule giving specific values, in a mathematical equation, or in a graph.
- A graph of two variables has a positive slope when they both increase or decrease together and a negative slope when they move in opposite directions.
- The marginal response of a variable gives the amount it changes in response to a change in a second variable. When the variable is measured on the vertical axis of a diagram, its marginal response at a specific point on the curve is measured by the slope of the line at that point.
- Some functions have a maximum or minimum point. At such points, the marginal response is zero.

K E Y   C O N C E P T S

Positive and normative statements
Endogenous and exogenous variables
Theories and models
Variables, assumptions, and predictions

Economic data
Functional relations
Positive and negative relations between
  variables

Positively and negatively sloped curves
Marginal responses
Maximum and minimum values

S T U D Y   E X E R C I S E S

1. In the following examples, identify the exogenous (or independent) variable and the endogenous (or dependent) variable.

   a. The amount of rainfall on the Canadian prairies determines the amount of wheat produced in Canada.
   b. When the world price of coffee increases, there is a change in the price of your cup of coffee at the doughnut shop.
   c. If student loans were no longer available, there would be fewer students attending university.
   d. An increase in the tax on gasoline leads people to drive more fuel-efficient vehicles.

2. Use the appropriate graph—time-series, cross-sectional, or scatter diagram—to illustrate the economic data provided in each part below.

   a. Canada's prime interest rate in 2002:

January	3.75	July	4.50
February	3.75	August	4.50
March	3.75	September	4.50
April	4.00	October	4.50
May	4.00	November	4.50
June	4.25	December	4.50

b. A comparison of average household expenditures across provinces and territories in 2001.

Yukon Territory	$63 581
Nunavut	53 034
Northwest Territories	68 306
British Columbia	57 352
Alberta	65 767
Saskatchewan	48 516
Manitoba	51 845
Ontario	64 375
Quebec	50 170
New Brunswick	47 623
Nova Scotia	49 054
Prince Edward Island	47 015
Newfoundland and Labrador	46 646

c. Per capita growth rates of real GDP and investment rates for various countries, averaged over the period 1970–1990.

Country	Average Growth Rate (% per year)	Average Investment Rate (% of GDP)
Canada	2.6	22.0
Austria	2.6	25.5
Japan	3.6	31.0
United States	1.7	18.7
United Kingdom	2.1	18.2
Spain	2.5	23.0
Norway	3.2	28.2

3. Use the following figure to answer the questions below.

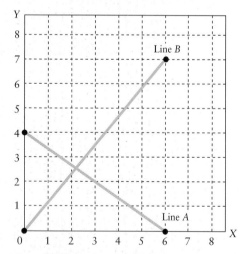

a. Is the slope of Line A positive or negative? Line B?
b. Calculate the slope of Line A. Write the equation describing the line in the form $Y = mX + b$ where m is the slope of the line and b is a constant term.

c. Calculate the slope of Line B. Write the equation describing the line in the form $Y = mX + b$ where m is the slope of the line and b is a constant term.

4. Suppose that the relationship between the government's tax revenue (T) and national income (Y) is represented by the following equation: $T = 10 + 0.25Y$. Plot this relationship on a scale diagram, with Y on the horizontal axis and T on the vertical axis. Interpret the equation.

5. Consider the following three specific functional forms for a functional relation between X and Y:
   i) $Y = 50 + 2X$
   ii) $Y = 50 + 2X + 0.05X^2$
   iii) $Y = 50 + 2X - 0.05X^2$

   a. For the values of X of 0, 10, 20, 30, 40, and 50, plot X and Y on a scale diagram for each specific functional form. Connect these points with a smooth line.
   b. For each functional form, state whether the slope of the line is constant, increasing or decreasing as the value of X increases.
   c. Describe for each functional form how the marginal change in Y depends on the value of X.

6. Suppose you want to create a price index for the price of pizza across several Canadian university campuses, as of March 1, 2004. The data are as follows:

University	Price Per Pizza
Dalhousie	$6.50
Laval	5.95
McGill	6.00
Queen's	8.00
Waterloo	7.50
Manitoba	5.50
Saskatchewan	5.75
Calgary	6.25
UBC	7.25
Victoria	7.00

a. Using Calgary as the "base university," construct the Canadian university pizza price index.
b. At which university is pizza the most expensive, and by what percentage is the price higher than in Calgary?
c. At which university is pizza the least expensive, and by what percentage is the price lower than in Calgary?
d. Are the data listed above time-series or cross-sectional data? Explain why.

7. For each of the functional relations listed below, plot the relations on a scale diagram (with X on the hori-

zontal axis and Y on the vertical axis) and compute the slope of the line.

i) $Y = 10 + 3X$
ii) $Y = 20 + 4X$
iii) $Y = 30 + 5X$
iv) $Y = 10 + 5X$

8. Suppose we divide Canada into three regions—the West, the Centre, and the East. Each region has an unemployment rate, defined as the number of people unemployed, expressed as a fraction of that region's labour force. The table that follows shows each region's unemployment rate and the size of its labour force.

Region	Unemployment Rate	Labour Force
West	5.5%	5.3 million
Centre	7.2%	8.4 million
East	12.5%	3.5 million

a. Compute an unemployment rate for Canada using a simple average of the rates in the three regions. Is this the "right" unemployment rate for Canada as a whole? Explain why or why not.
b. Now compute an unemployment rate for Canada using weights that reflect the size of that region's labour force as a proportion of the overall Canadian labour force. Explain the difference in this unemployment rate from the one in part (a). Is this a "better" measure of Canadian unemployment? Explain why.

9. Draw three graphs in which the dependent variable increases at an increasing rate, at a constant rate, and at a diminishing rate. Then draw three graphs in which it decreases at an increasing, constant, and diminishing rate. For each of these graphs state a real relation that might be described by it—other than the ones given in the text of this chapter.

DISCUSSION QUESTIONS

1. What are some of the positive and normative issues that lie behind the disagreements in the following cases?

   a. Economists disagree on whether the government of Canada should try to stimulate the economy in the next six months.
   b. European and North American negotiators disagree over the desirability of reducing European farm subsidies.
   c. Economists argue about the merits of a voucher system that allows parents to choose the schools their children will attend.
   d. Economists debate the use of a two-tier medical system in Canada (whereby health care continues to be publicly provided, but individuals are permitted to be treated by doctors who bill the patient directly—"extra billing").

2. Much recent public debate has centred on the pros and cons of permitting continued unrestricted sale of cigarettes. Proposals for the control of cigarettes range from increasing excise taxes to the mandatory use of plain packaging to an outright ban on their sale. Discuss the positive and normative assumptions that underlie the national mood to reduce the consumption of tobacco products.

3. Economists sometimes make each of the following assumptions when they construct models. Discuss some situations in which each of these assumptions might be a useful simplification in order to think about some aspect of the real world.

   a. The earth is flat.
   b. There are no differences between men and women.
   c. There is no tomorrow.
   d. There are only two periods—this year and next year.
   e. A country produces only two types of goods.
   f. People are wholly selfish.

4. What may at first appear to be untestable statements can often be reworded so that they can be tested by an appeal to evidence. How might you do this for each of the following assertions?

   a. Free-market economic systems are the best in the world.
   b. Unemployment insurance is eroding the work ethic and encouraging people to become wards of the state rather than productive workers.
   c. Robotics ought to be outlawed because it will destroy the future of working people.
   d. Laws requiring equal pay for work of equal value will make women better off.
   e. Free trade improves the welfare of a country's citizens.

5. There are hundreds of eyewitnesses to the existence of flying saucers and other UFOs. There are films and eyewitness accounts of Nessie, the Loch Ness monster. Are you convinced of their existence? If not, what would it take to persuade you? If you are already convinced, what would it take to make you change your mind?

PART TWO

An Introduction to Demand and Supply

What determines the prices of specific products? What determines whether there will be a lot produced or only a little? What are "black markets" and why are they often created when the government controls specific prices? Who benefits and who loses from a policy of rent controls? Why do Canadian governments have policies designed to assist farmers? These are the types of questions that you will be able to answer after reading the next three chapters.*

Chapter 3 introduces the basic concepts of demand and supply. We will see that the prices of goods in free markets are determined by the interaction of demand and supply. We will learn the meaning of equilibrium, and how equilibrium prices and quantities change in response to changes to either demand or supply.

Chapter 4 then introduces the important idea of elasticity—the sensitivity of one variable to a change in some other variable. This concept is central to an understanding of whether a change in the demand or supply of some commodity primarily affects quantity or price. As an application of the concept of elasticity, we will examine the important policy issue of who bears the burden of commodity taxes. Do firms pay such taxes, or do consumers, or do both? How does elasticity affect the answer?

In Chapter 5 you get some practice in using what you learned in Chapters 3 and 4. We start with a discussion of how various markets interact with each other, so that events in one market lead not only to changes in that market but to changes in other markets as well. We then go on to explore two examples of government-controlled prices. The first is rent controls—you will see that the policy of rent controls produces some unusual outcomes in the rental-housing markets of Toronto, New York, and many other cities. The second is agricultural price-support policies—you will see what effects such policies have, both on farmers' incomes and on the allocation of resources.

---

*Chapter 5 does not appear in *Macroeconomics*.

CHAPTER 3

Demand, Supply, and Price

(L) LEARNING OBJECTIVES

1 Explain what determines "quantity demanded," the amount of some product that consumers want to purchase.

2 Distinguish between a shift in a demand curve and a movement along a demand curve.

3 Explain what determines "quantity supplied," the amount of some product that producers want to sell.

4 Distinguish between a shift in a supply curve and a movement along a supply curve.

5 Distinguish the forces that drive market price to equilibrium.

6 State the four "laws" of demand and supply.

How do individual markets work? We are now ready to study this important question. The answer leads us to what are called the laws of supply and demand. And though there is much more to economics than just demand and supply (as many following chapters will illustrate), this is an essential starting point for understanding how a market, and thus a market economy, functions.

As a first step, we need to understand what determines the demand for and the supply of particular products. Then we can see how demand and supply together determine the prices of products and the quantities that are bought and sold. Finally, we examine how the price system allows the economy to respond to the many changes that impinge on it. Demand and supply help us to understand the price system's successes and failures, and the consequences of many government policies.

This chapter deals with the basic elements of demand, supply, and price. In the next two chapters we use the demand-and-supply apparatus to discuss such issues as cigarette taxes, legislated minimum wages, price controls on rental housing, the burden of payroll taxes, and agricultural income-support policies.

3.1 **Demand**

What determines the demand for any given product? How have Canadian consumers responded to the recent declines in the prices of personal computers and cellular telephones? How will they respond to the next sudden increase in the world price of oil, coffee, or wheat? We start by developing a theory designed to explain the demand for some typical product.

What Is "Quantity Demanded"?

The total amount of any particular good or service that consumers wish to purchase in some time period is called the **quantity demanded** of that product. It is important to notice two things about this concept.

> **quantity demanded**
> The amount of a good or service that consumers wish to purchase in some time period.

First, quantity demanded is a *desired* quantity. It is the amount that consumers wish to purchase when faced with a particular price of the product, other prices, their incomes, their tastes, and everything else that might matter. It may be different from the amount that consumers actually succeed in purchasing. If sufficient quantities are not available, the amount that consumers wish to purchase may exceed the amount that they actually purchase. (For example, think of standing in line to purchase tickets to a show, only to find out that the show is sold out before you get to the head of the line.) To distinguish these two concepts, the term *quantity demanded* is used to refer to desired purchases, and a phrase such as *quantity actually bought* or *quantity exchanged* is used to refer to actual purchases.

Second, quantity demanded refers to a *flow* of purchases. It must therefore be expressed as so much per period of time: 1 million units per day, 7 million per week, or 365 million per year. For example, being told that the quantity of new television sets demanded (at current prices) in Canada is 50 000 means nothing unless you are also told the period of time involved. Fifty thousand TVs demanded per day would be an enormous rate of demand; 50 000 per year would be a very small rate for a country as large as Canada. The important distinction between *stocks* and *flows* is discussed in *Extensions in Theory 3-1*.

The amount of some product that consumers wish to buy in a given time period is influenced by the following important variables: [2]

- Product's own price
- Average income
- Prices of other products
- Tastes
- Distribution of income
- Population
- Expectations about the future

We will discuss the separate effects of each of these variables later in the chapter. For now, we focus on the effects of changes in the product's own price. But how do we analyze the distinct effect of changes in one variable when all are likely to be changing at once? It is very difficult—in fact, so difficult that we don't do it. (If you go on to take advanced courses in econometrics you will learn how to estimate the effects of simultaneous changes in a number of variables.) Instead, we consider the influence of the variables one at a time. To do this, we hold all but one of them constant. Then we let the selected variable vary and study how its change affects quantity demanded. We can do the same for each of the other variables in turn, and in this way we can come to understand the importance of each. We can then combine the separate influences of the variables to discover what happens when several things change at the same time—as they often do.

Holding all other variables constant is often described by the expressions "other things being equal," "other things given," or the equivalent Latin phrase, *ceteris paribus*. When economists speak of the influence of the price of eggs on the quantity

EXTENSIONS IN THEORY 3-1

The Distinction Between Stocks and Flows

An important conceptual issue that arises frequently in economics is the distinction between stock and flow variables. Economic theories use both, and it takes a little practice to keep them straight.

As noted in the text, a flow variable has a time dimension—it is so much *per unit of time*. For example, the quantity of Grade A large eggs purchased in Edmonton is a flow variable. No useful information is conveyed if we are told that the number purchased was 2000 dozen eggs unless we are also told the period of time over which these purchases occurred. Two thousand dozen eggs per hour would indicate a much more active market in eggs than would 2000 dozen eggs per month.

In contrast, a stock variable is a variable whose value has meaning *at a point in time*. Thus the number of eggs in the egg producer's warehouse on a particular day—for example, 20 000 dozen eggs on September 3, 2003—is a stock variable. All those eggs are there at one time, and they remain there until something happens to change the stock held in the warehouse. The stock variable is just a number at a point in time, not a rate of flow of so much per unit of time.

The terminology of stocks and flows can be understood in terms of an analogy to a bathtub. At any moment, the tub holds so much water. This is the *stock,* and it can be measured in terms of the volume of water, say, 100 litres. There might also be water flowing into the tub from the tap; this *flow* is measured as so much water per unit time, say, 10 litres per minute.

The distinction between stocks and flows is important. Failure to keep them straight is a common source of confusion and even error. Note, for example, that because they have different dimensions, a stock variable and a flow variable cannot be added together without specify-

ing some time period for which the flow persists. We cannot add the stock of 100 litres of water in the tub to the flow of 10 litres per minute to get 110 litres. The new stock of water will depend on how long the flow persists; if it lasts for 20 minutes, the new stock will be 300 litres; if the flow persists for 60 minutes, the new stock will be 700 litres (or the tub will overflow!).

The amount of income earned is a flow; there is so much per year or per month or per hour. The amount of a consumer's expenditure is also a flow—so much spent per week or per month or per year. The amount of money in a bank account or a miser's hoard (earned, perhaps, in the past but unspent) is a stock—just so many thousands of dollars. The key test is always whether a time dimension is required to give the variable meaning.

The amount of water behind the dam at any time is the stock of water; the amount moving through the gate is the flow, which is measured per unit of time.

of eggs demanded, *ceteris paribus,* they refer to what a change in the price of eggs would do to the quantity of eggs demanded *if all other variables that influence the demand for eggs did not change.*

Quantity Demanded and Price

We are interested in studying the relationship between the quantity demanded of a product and that product's price. This requires that we hold all other influences constant and ask, "How will the quantity demanded of a product change as its price changes?"

A basic economic hypothesis is that the price of a product and the quantity demanded are related *negatively,* other things being equal. That is, the lower the price, the higher the quantity demanded; the higher the price, the lower the quantity demanded.

The British economist Alfred Marshall (1842–1924) called this fundamental relation the "law of demand." In Chapter 6, we will derive the law of demand as a prediction that follows from more basic assumptions about consumer behaviour. For now, let's simply explore why this relationship seems reasonable. Products are used to satisfy desires and needs, and there is almost always more than one product that will satisfy any desire or need. Hunger may be alleviated by meat or vegetables; a desire for green vegetables can be satisfied by broccoli or spinach. The desire for a vacation may be satisfied by a trip to the ocean or to the mountains; the need to get there may be satisfied by different airlines, a bus, a car, or a train. For any general desire or need, there are many different products that will satisfy it.

Now consider what happens if income, tastes, population, and the prices of all other products remain constant and the price of only one product changes. As the price goes up, that product becomes an increasingly expensive means of satisfying a desire. Some consumers will stop buying it altogether; others will buy smaller amounts; still others may continue to buy the same quantity. Because many consumers will switch wholly or partly to other products to satisfy the same desire, less will be demanded of the product whose price has risen. As meat becomes more expensive, for example, some consumers will switch to meat substitutes; others may forgo meat at some meals and eat less meat at others. Taken together as a group, consumers will want to buy less meat when its price rises.

Conversely, as the price goes down, the product becomes a cheaper method of satisfying a desire. Households will demand more of it. Consequently, they will buy less of similar products whose prices have not fallen and as a result have become expensive *relative* to the product in question. When the price of tomatoes falls, shoppers switch to tomatoes and cut their purchases of many other vegetables that now look relatively more expensive.

Demand Schedules and Demand Curves

A **demand schedule** is one way of showing the relationship between quantity demanded and the price of a product, other things being equal. It is a table showing the quantity demanded at various prices.

The table in Figure 3-1 shows a hypothetical demand schedule for carrots. It lists the quantity of carrots that would be demanded at various prices, given the assumption that all other variables are held constant. We should note in particular that average household income is assumed to be $50 000 per year because later we will want to see what happens when income changes. The table gives the quantities demanded for five selected prices, but in fact a separate quantity would be demanded at each possible price from 1 cent to several hundreds of dollars.

A second method of showing the relationship between quantity demanded and price is to draw a graph. The five price–quantity combinations shown in the table are plotted in Figure 3-1. Price is plotted on the vertical axis, and quantity is plotted on the horizontal axis.

The curve drawn through these points is called a **demand curve.** It shows the quantity that consumers would like to buy at each price. The negative slope of the curve indicates that the quantity demanded increases as the price falls. Each point on the demand curve indicates a single price–quantity combination. The demand curve as a whole shows something more.

demand schedule
A table showing the relationship between quantity demanded and the price of a commodity, other things being equal.

demand curve
The graphical representation of the relationship between quantity demanded and the price of a commodity, other things being equal.

FIGURE 3-1   The Demand for Carrots

A Demand Schedule for Carrots

Reference Point	Price Per Tonne ($)	Quantity Demanded When Average Household Income Is $50 000 Per Year (tonnes per year)
U	20	110
V	40	85
W	60	65
X	80	50
Y	100	40

A Demand Curve for Carrots

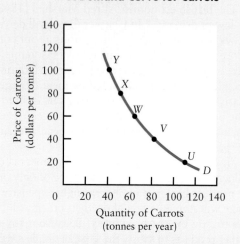

Both the table and the graph show the quantity of carrots that would be demanded at various prices, *ceteris paribus.* For example, row *W* indicates that if the price of carrots were $60 per tonne, consumers would desire to purchase 65 tonnes of carrots per year, given the values of the other variables that affect quantity demanded. The demand curve, labelled *D*, relates quantity of carrots demanded to the price of carrots; its negative slope indicates that quantity demanded increases as price falls.

The demand curve represents the relationship between quantity demanded and price, other things being equal.

When economists speak of demand in a particular market, they are referring not just to the particular quantity being demanded at the moment (i.e., not just to one point on the demand curve) but to the entire demand curve—to the relationship between desired purchases and all the possible prices of the product.

The term **demand** therefore refers to the entire relationship between the quantity demanded of a product and the price of that product. In contrast, a single point on a demand schedule or curve is the quantity demanded at that point. This distinction between "demand" and "quantity demanded" is an extremely important one and we will examine it more closely later in this chapter.

demand The entire relationship between the quantity of a commodity that buyers wish to purchase and the price of that commodity, other things being equal.

Shifts in the Demand Curve

The demand curve is drawn with the assumption that everything except the product's own price is being held constant. But what if other things change, as surely they do? For example, consider an increase in household income while price remains constant. If consumers increase their purchases of the product, the new quantity demanded cannot be represented by a point on the original demand curve. It must be represented on a new demand curve that is to the right of the old curve. Thus, the rise in income shifts the demand curve to the right, as shown in Figure 3-2. This shift illustrates the operation of an important general rule.

FIGURE 3-2   An Increase in the Demand for Carrots

Demand Schedules

Price Per Tonne ($) p	Quantity Demanded When Average Household Income Is $50 000 Per Year (tonnes per year) D_0		Quantity Demanded When Average Household Income Is $60 000 Per Year (tonnes per year) D_1	
20	110	U	140	U'
40	85	V	115	V'
60	65	W	95	W'
80	50	X	80	X'
100	40	Y	70	Y'

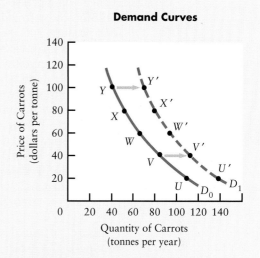

Demand Curves

An increase in average household income increases the quantity demanded at each price. This is shown by the rightward shift in the demand curve, from D_0 to D_1. When average income rises from $50 000 to $60 000 per year, quantity demanded at a price of $60 per tonne rises from 65 tonnes per year to 95 tonnes per year. A similar rise occurs at every other price.

A demand curve is drawn with the assumption that everything except the product's own price is held constant. A change in any of the variables previously held constant will shift the demand curve to a new position.

A demand curve can shift in two important ways. In the first case, more would be bought at each price—the demand curve shifts rightward so that each price corresponds to a higher quantity than it did before. In the second case, less would be bought at each price—the demand curve shifts leftward so that each price corresponds to a lower quantity than it did before.

We can assess the influence of changes in variables other than price by determining how changes in each variable shift the demand curve. Any change will shift the demand curve to the right if it increases the amount that households wish to buy, other things remaining equal. It will shift the demand curve to the left if it decreases the amount that households wish to buy, other things remaining equal.

1. Average Income.   If average income rises, consumers as a group can be expected to buy more of most products even if prices don't change at all. Goods for which the quantity demanded increases when income rises are called *normal goods*; goods for which the quantity demanded falls when income rises are called *inferior goods*. The term *normal goods* reflects economists' empirical finding that the demand for most goods rises when income rises. We therefore expect that a rise in average consumer income shifts the demand curve for most products to the right, indicating that more will be demanded at any given price. Such a shift is illustrated in Figure 3-2.

2. Prices of Other Goods.   We saw that the negative slope of a product's demand curve occurs because the lower its price, the cheaper the product becomes relative to other products that can satisfy the same needs or desires. These other products are called **substitutes.** Another way for the same change to come about is that the price of the

substitutes   Goods that can be used in place of another good to satisfy similar needs or desires.

substitute product rises. For example, carrots can become cheap relative to broccoli either because the price of carrots falls or because the price of broccoli rises. Either change will increase the amount of carrots that consumers wish to buy as consumers substitute away from broccoli and toward carrots. Thus a rise in the price of a substitute for a product shifts the demand curve for the product to the right. More will be demanded at each price. For example, Coke and Pepsi are substitutes. If the price of Pepsi increases, the demand curve for Coke will shift to the right.

Complements are products that tend to be used jointly. Cars and gasoline are complements; so are CD players and speakers, golf clubs and golf balls, electric stoves and electricity, and airplane flights to Calgary and ski-lift tickets in Banff. Because complements tend to be consumed together, a fall in the price of one will increase the quantity demanded of *both* products. Thus, a fall in the price of a complement for a product will shift that product's demand curve to the right. More will be demanded at each price. For example, a fall in the price of airplane trips to Calgary will lead to a rise in the demand for ski-lift tickets in Banff, even though the price of those lift tickets is unchanged. (So the demand curve for ski-lift tickets will shift to the right.)

complements Goods that tend to be used jointly.

3. Tastes.   Tastes have an effect on people's desired purchases. A change in tastes may be long-lasting, such as the shift from fountain pens to ballpoint pens or from typewriters to computers, or it may be a short-lived fad such as CB radios (a fad in the late 1970s and early 1980s) and many toys such as Pokémon cards and Beanie Babies. In either case, a change in tastes in favour of a product shifts the demand curve to the right. More will be demanded at each price. Of course, a change in tastes against some product has the opposite effect and shifts the demand curve to the left. The gradual but persistent reduction in demand for Camaro and Firebird cars recently led General Motors to close the plant at which those specific models were manufactured.

4. Distribution of Income.   A change in the distribution of income will cause an increase in the demand for products bought most by consumers whose incomes increase and a decrease in the demand for products bought most by consumers whose incomes decrease. If, for example, the government increases the child tax credit and at the same time raises basic tax rates, income will be transferred from households without children to households with children. Demands for products more heavily bought by childless persons will decline, while demands for products more heavily bought by households with children will increase.

5. Population.   Population growth does not create new demand unless the additional people have the means to purchase goods—that is, unless they have purchasing power. If there is an increase in population with purchasing power, the demands for all the products purchased by the new people will rise. Thus, we expect that an increase in population will shift the demand curves for most products to the right, indicating that more will be demanded at each price.

6. Expectations About the Future.   Our discussion has so far focused on how changes in the current value of variables may change demand. But it is also true that changes in people's *expectations about future values* of variables may change demand. For example, suppose that you are thinking about buying a house in a small town in Nova Scotia and you have learned that in the near future a large high-tech firm will be moving its head office and several hundred employees to this same small town. Since their future movement into your town will surely increase the demand for housing and thus will drive up the *future* price of houses, this expectation will lead you (and others like you) to increase your demand *today* so as to make the purchase before the price rises. Thus, the demand curve for houses will shift to the right today in anticipation of a future event.

Figure 3-3 summarizes the reasons that demand curves shift.

Movements Along the Curve Versus Shifts of the Whole Curve

Suppose that you read in today's newspaper that a sharp increase in the world price of coffee beans has been caused by an increased worldwide demand for coffee. Then tomorrow you read that the rising price of coffee is reducing the typical consumer's purchases of coffee, as shoppers switch to other beverages. The two stories appear to contradict each other. The first associates a rising price with rising demand; the second associates a rising price with declining demand. Can both statements be true? The answer is yes—because the two statements actually refer to different things. The first describes a shift in the demand curve; the second describes a movement along a demand curve in response to a change in price.

Consider first the statement that the increase in the price of coffee has been caused by an increased demand for coffee. This statement refers to a shift in the demand curve for coffee—in this case, a shift to the right, indicating more coffee demanded at each price. This shift, as we will see later in this chapter, will increase the price of coffee.

Now consider the second statement—that less coffee is being bought because of its rise in price. This refers to a movement along the new demand curve and reflects a change between two specific quantities demanded, one before the price increased and one afterward.

Possible explanations for the two stories are:

1. A change in tastes is shifting the demand curve for coffee to the right. This, in turn, raises the price of coffee (for reasons we will soon study in detail). This was the first newspaper story.

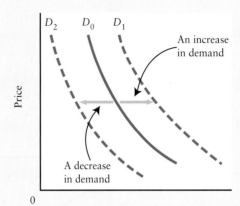

FIGURE 3-3   Shifts in the Demand Curve

A rightward shift in the demand curve from D_0 to D_1 indicates an increase in demand; a leftward shift from D_0 to D_2 indicates a decrease in demand. An increase in demand means that more is demanded at each price. Such a rightward shift can be caused by a rise in income, a rise in the price of a substitute, a fall in the price of a complement, a change in tastes that favours that product, an increase in population, a redistribution of income toward groups that favour the product, or the anticipation of a future event that will increase the price.

A decrease in demand means that less is demanded at each price. Such a leftward shift can be caused by a fall in income, a fall in the price of a substitute, a rise in the price of a complement, a change in tastes that disfavours the product, a decrease in population, a redistribution of income away from groups that favour the product, or the anticipation of a future event that will decrease the price.

2. The rising price of coffee is causing each individual household to cut back on its coffee purchases. The cutback is represented by an upward movement to the left along any particular demand curve for coffee. This was the second newspaper story.

To prevent the type of confusion caused by our two newspaper stories, economists use a specialized vocabulary to distinguish between shifts of curves and movements along curves.

We have seen that demand refers to the *entire* demand curve, whereas quantity demanded refers to the quantity that is demanded at a specific price, as indicated by a particular *point* on the demand curve. If we go back to our example of carrots in Figure 3-1, demand is given by the curve *D*; at a price of $40 per tonne, the quantity demanded is 85 tonnes, as indicated by the point *V*.

Economists reserve the term **change in demand** to describe a change in the quantity demanded at *every* price. That is, a change in demand refers to a shift of the entire demand curve. The term **change in quantity demanded** refers to a movement from one

change in demand A change in the quantity demanded at each possible price of the commodity, represented by a shift in the whole demand curve.

change in quantity demanded A change in the specific quantity of the good demanded, represented by a change from one point on a demand curve to another point, either on the original demand curve or on a new one.

FIGURE 3-4 Shifts Of and Movements Along the Demand Curve

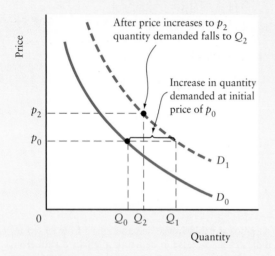

After price increases to p_2 quantity demanded falls to Q_2

Increase in quantity demanded at initial price of p_0

An increase in demand means that the demand curve shifts to the right, and hence quantity demanded will be higher at each price. A rise in price causes an upward movement to the left along the demand curve, and hence quantity demanded will fall. The demand curve is originally D_0 and price is p_0, which means that quantity demanded is Q_0. Suppose that demand increases to D_1, which means that at any particular price, there is a larger quantity demanded; for example, at p_0, quantity demanded is now Q_1. Now suppose that the price rises above p_0. This causes a movement up and to the left along D_1, and quantity demanded falls below Q_1. As the figure is drawn, the quantity demanded at the new price p_2 is less than Q_1 but greater than Q_0. So in this case the combined effect of the increase in demand and the rise in price is an increase in quantity demanded from Q_0 to Q_2.

point on a demand curve to another point, either on the same demand curve or on a new one.

A change in quantity demanded can result: from a shift in the demand curve with the price constant; from a movement along a given demand curve due to a change in the price; or from a combination of the two. [3]

We consider these three possibilities in turn.

An increase in demand means that the whole demand curve shifts to the right; a decrease in demand means that the whole demand curve shifts to the left. At a given price, an increase in demand causes an increase in quantity demanded, whereas a decrease in demand causes a decrease in quantity demanded. For example, in Figure 3-2, the shift in the demand curve from D_0 to D_1 represents an increase in demand, and at a price of $40 per tonne, quantity demanded increases from 85 tonnes to 115 tonnes, as indicated by the move from V to V'.

A movement down and to the right along a demand curve represents an increase in quantity demanded; a movement up and to the left along a demand curve represents a decrease in quantity demanded. For example, in Figure 3-2, with demand given by the curve D_1, an increase in price from $40 to $60 per tonne causes a movement along D_1 from V' to W', and quantity demanded decreases from 115 tonnes to 95 tonnes.

When there is a change in demand *and* a change in the price, the overall change in quantity demanded is the net effect of the shift in the demand curve and the movement along the new demand curve. Figure 3-4 shows the combined effect of an increase in demand, shown by a rightward shift in the whole demand curve, and an upward movement to the left along the new demand curve due to an increase in price. The increase in demand causes an increase in quantity demanded at the initial price, whereas the movement along the demand curve causes a decrease in the quantity demanded. Whether quantity demanded rises or falls overall depends on the relative magnitudes of these two changes.

3.2 Supply

What determines the supply of any given product? Why do Canadian oil producers extract and market more oil when the price of oil is high? Why do Canadian cattle ranchers sell more beef when the price of cattle-feed falls? We start by developing a theory designed to explain the supply of some typical product.

What Is "Quantity Supplied"?

The amount of a product that firms wish to sell in some time period is called the **quantity supplied** of that product. Quantity supplied is a flow; it is so much per unit of time. Note also that quantity supplied is the amount that firms are willing to offer for sale; it is not necessarily the amount that they succeed in selling, which is expressed by *quantity actually sold* or *quantity exchanged*.

The quantity supplied of a product is influenced by the following variables: [4]

- Product's own price
- Prices of inputs
- Technology
- Government taxes or subsidies
- Prices of other products
- Expectations about the future
- Number of suppliers

The situation with supply is the same as that with demand: There are several influencing variables, and we will not get far if we try to discover what happens when they all change at the same time. Again, we use the convenient *ceteris paribus* assumption to study the influence of the variables one at a time.

quantity supplied
The amount of a commodity that producers wish to sell in some time period.

Quantity Supplied and Price

We begin by holding all other influences constant and ask, "How do we expect the quantity of a product supplied to vary with its own price?"

A basic hypothesis of economics is that the price of the product and the quantity supplied are related *positively*, other things being equal. That is, the higher the product's own price, the more its producers will supply; the lower the price, the less its producers will supply.

In later chapters we will derive this hypothesis as a prediction from more basic assumptions about the behaviour of firms. But now we simply explore why this relationship seems reasonable. Firms will supply more because the profits that can be earned from producing a product will increase if the price of that product rises, whereas the costs of inputs used to produce it will remain unchanged. As a

A rise in the price of wheat, other things being equal, will lead farmers to plant less of other crops and plant more wheat.

result, firms, which are in business to earn profits, will wish to produce more of the product whose price has risen.

Supply Schedules and Supply Curves

The general relationship just discussed can be illustrated by a **supply schedule**, which shows the relationship between quantity supplied of a product and the price of the product, other things being equal. A supply schedule is analogous to a demand schedule; the former shows what producers would be willing to sell, whereas the latter shows what consumers would be willing to buy, at various prices of the product. The table in Figure 3-5 presents a hypothetical supply schedule for carrots.

supply schedule
A table showing the relationship between quantity supplied and the price of a commodity, other things being equal.

FIGURE 3-5   The Supply of Carrots

A Supply Schedule for Carrots

Reference Point	Price Per Tonne ($)	Quantity Supplied (tonnes per year)
u	20	20
v	40	45
w	60	65
x	80	80
y	100	95

A Supply Curve for Carrots

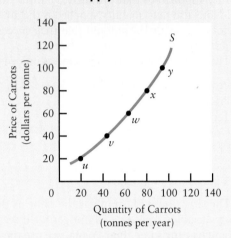

Both the table and the graph show the quantities that producers wish to sell at various prices, *ceteris paribus.* For example, row *w* indicates that if the price of carrots were $60 per tonne, producers would want to sell 65 tonnes per year. The supply curve, labelled *S*, relates quantity of carrots supplied to the price of carrots; its positive slope indicates that quantity supplied increases as price increases.

supply curve
The graphical representation of the relationship between quantity supplied and the price of a commodity, other things being equal.

A **supply curve,** the graphical representation of the supply schedule, is illustrated in Figure 3-5. Each point on the supply curve represents a specific price–quantity combination; however, the whole curve shows something more.

The supply curve represents the relationship between quantity supplied and price, other things being equal; its positive slope indicates that quantity supplied increases when price increases.

When economists make statements about the conditions of supply, they are not referring just to the particular quantity being supplied at the moment—that is, not to just one point on the supply curve. Instead, they are referring to the entire supply curve, to the complete relationship between desired sales and all possible prices of the product.

supply   The entire relationship between the quantity of some commodity that producers wish to sell and the price of that commodity, other things being equal.

Supply refers to the entire relationship between the quantity supplied of a product and the price of that product, other things being equal. A single point on the supply curve refers to the *quantity supplied* at that price.

Shifts in the Supply Curve

A shift in the supply curve means that at each price there is a change in the quantity supplied. An increase in the quantity supplied at each price is shown in Figure 3-6. This change appears as a rightward shift in the supply curve. In contrast, a decrease in the quantity supplied at each price appears as a leftward shift. For supply, as for demand, there is an important general rule:

A change in any of the variables (other than the product's own price) that affects the quantity supplied will shift the supply curve to a new position.

FIGURE 3-6   An Increase in the Supply of Carrots

Supply Schedules

Price Per Tonne ($) p	Quantity Supplied Before Cost-Saving Innovation (tonnes per year) S_0	Quantity Supplied After Innovation (tonnes per year) S_1
20	20 u	50 u'
40	45 v	75 v'
60	65 w	95 w'
80	80 x	110 x'
100	95 y	125 y'

Supply Curves

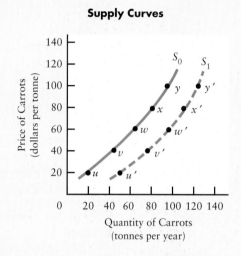

A cost-saving innovation increases the quantity supplied at each price. This is shown by the rightward shift in the supply curve, from S_0 to S_1. As a result of a cost-saving innovation, the quantity that is supplied at a price of $100 per tonne rises from 95 to 125 tonnes per year. A similar rise occurs at every price.

Let's consider the effect of changes in several variables.

1. Prices of Inputs.   All things that a firm uses to produce its outputs, such as materials, labour, and machines, are called the firm's *inputs*. Other things being equal, the higher the price of any input used to make a product, the less will be the profit from making that product. We expect, therefore, that the higher the price of any input used by a firm, the less the firm will produce and offer for sale at any given price of the product. A rise in the price of inputs therefore shifts the supply curve to the left, indicating that less will be supplied at any given price; a fall in the cost of inputs shifts the supply curve to the right.

2. Technology.   At any time, what is produced and how it is produced depend on what is known. Over time, knowledge changes. The enormous increase in production per worker that has been going on in industrial societies for about 200 years is due largely to improved methods of production. The Industrial Revolution is more than a historical event; it is a present reality. Discoveries in chemistry have led to lower costs of production for well-established products, such as paints, and to a large variety of new products made of plastics and synthetic fibres. Such inventions as silicon chips have radically changed products such as computers, televisions, and telephones, and the consequent development of smaller computers has revolutionized the production of countless other non-electronic products.

Any technological innovation that decreases production costs will increase the profits that can be earned at any given price of the product. Because increased profitability leads to increased willingness to produce, this change shifts the supply curve to the right.

3. Government Taxes or Subsidies.   We have just seen that anything increasing firms' costs will shift the supply curve to the left, and anything decreasing firms' costs will shift the supply curve to the right. As we will see in later chapters, governments often levy special taxes on the production of specific goods, such as gasoline, cigarettes, and alcohol. These taxes increase firms' costs and make the production of these goods less profitable. The result is that the supply curve shifts to the left.

For other goods, governments often subsidize producers—that is, they pay producers $X for each unit of the good produced. This often occurs for agricultural products, especially in the United States and the European Union. In such situations, the subsidy increases the profitability of production and shifts the supply curve to the right.

4. Prices of Other Products.   Changes in the price of one product may lead to changes in the supply of some other product because the two products are either *substitutes* or *complements* in the production process.

A prairie farmer, for example, can plant his field in wheat or oats. If the market price of oats falls, thus making oat production less profitable, the farmer will be more inclined to plant wheat. In this case, wheat and oats are said to be *substitutes* in production—for every extra acre planted in one crop, one fewer acre can be planted in the other. In this example, a reduction in the price of oats leads to an increase in the supply of wheat.

An excellent example in which two products are *complements* in production is oil and natural gas, which are often found together below the earth's surface. If the market price of natural gas rises, producers will do more drilling and increase their production of natural gas. But as more wells are drilled, the usual outcome is that more of *both* natural gas and oil are produced. Thus, the rise in the price of natural gas leads to an increase in the supply of the complementary product—oil.

5. Expectations About the Future.   As in our discussion of shifts in demand curves, expectations about the future can also play a role in shifting supply curves. This is especially important in agricultural markets in which producers (often farmers) must make planting and production decisions several months ahead of when the output will actually be sold. In such cases, it is the expectation of the future price, and not just the current price, which guides farmers' decisions. A canola farmer who expects prices to be high in the fall will plant a large crop, even though actual prices in the spring may be low. Thus, other things being equal, an increase in the expected future price of a product leads to an increase in the supply of the product.

6. Number of Suppliers.   For given prices and technology, the total amount of any product supplied depends on the number of firms producing that product and offering it for sale. If profits are being earned by current firms, then more firms will choose to enter this industry and begin producing. The effect of this increase in the number of suppliers is to shift the supply curve to the right. Similarly, if the existing firms are losing money, they will eventually leave the industry; such a reduction in the number of suppliers shifts the supply curve to the left.

Movements Along the Curve Versus Shifts of the Whole Curve

As with demand, it is important to distinguish movements along supply curves from shifts of the whole curve. Economists reserve the term **change in supply** to describe a shift of the whole supply curve—that is, a change in the quantity that will be supplied at every price. The term **change in quantity supplied** refers to a movement from one point on a supply curve to another point, either on the same supply curve or a new one. In other words, an increase in supply means that the whole supply curve has shifted to the right, so that the quantity supplied at any given price has increased; a movement up and to the

Practise with Study Guide Chapter 3, Exercise 4.

change in supply A change in the quantity supplied at each possible price of the commodity, represented by a shift in the whole supply curve.

change in quantity supplied A change in the specific quantity supplied, represented by a change from one point on a supply curve to another point, either on the original supply curve or on a new one.

right along a supply curve indicates an increase in the quantity supplied in response to an increase in the price of the product.

A change in quantity supplied can result from: a change in supply, with the price constant; a movement along a given supply curve due to a change in the price; or a combination of the two.

An exercise you might find useful is to construct a diagram similar to Figure 3-4, emphasizing the difference between a shift of the supply curve and a movement along the supply curve.

3.3 **The Determination of Price**

So far we have considered demand and supply separately. We now come to a key question: how do the two forces of demand and supply interact to determine price?

The Concept of a Market

Originally the term *market* designated a physical place where products were bought and sold. We still use the term this way to describe places such as Granville Island Market in Vancouver, Kensington Market in Toronto, or Jean Talon Market in Montreal. Once developed, however, theories of market behaviour were easily extended to cover products such as wheat or oil, which can be purchased anywhere in the world at a price that tends to be uniform the world over. Today we can also buy and sell items in markets that exist in cyberspace—consider the online auction services provided by eBay—thus extending our viewpoint well beyond the idea of a single place to which the consumer goes to buy something.

For present purposes, a **market** may be defined as existing in any situation (a physical place or an electronic medium) in which buyers and sellers negotiate the exchange of some product or related group of products. It must be possible, therefore, for buyers and sellers to communicate with each other and to make meaningful deals over the whole market.

Individual markets differ in the degree of *competition* among the various buyers and sellers. In the next few chapters we will confine ourselves to examining markets in which the number of buyers and sellers is sufficiently large that not one of them has any appreciable influence on the market price. This is a very rough definition of what economists call *perfectly competitive markets*. Starting in Chapter 10, we will consider the behaviour of markets in which there are small numbers of either sellers or buyers. But our initial theory of markets will actually be a very good description of the markets for such things as wheat, pork, newsprint, coffee, copper, and many other commodities.

eBay brings together buyers and sellers of thousands of different goods and services. It thus creates markets that exist only on the Internet.

market Any situation in which buyers and sellers can negotiate the exchange of goods or services.

Graphical Analysis of a Market

The table in Figure 3-7 brings together the demand and supply schedules from Figures 3-1 and 3-5. The quantities of carrots demanded and supplied at each price may now be compared.

There is only one price, $60 per tonne, at which the quantity of carrots demanded equals the quantity supplied. At prices less than $60 per tonne, there is a shortage of carrots because the quantity demanded exceeds the quantity supplied. This is a situation of **excess demand**. At prices greater than $60 per tonne, there is a surplus of carrots because the quantity supplied exceeds the quantity demanded. This is a situation of **excess supply**. This same story can also be told in graphical terms. The quantities demanded and supplied at any price can be read off the two curves; the excess supply or excess demand is shown by the horizontal distance between the curves at each price.

To examine the determination of market price, let's suppose first that the price is $100 per tonne. At this price, 95 tonnes are offered for sale, but only 40 tonnes are demanded. There is an excess supply of 55 tonnes per year. Sellers are then likely to cut their prices to get rid of this surplus. And purchasers, observing the stock of unsold carrots, will begin to offer less money for the product. In other words, *excess supply causes downward pressure on price.*

Now consider the price of $20 per tonne. At this price, there is excess demand. The 20 tonnes produced each year are snapped up quickly, and 90 tonnes of desired purchases cannot be made. Rivalry between would-be purchasers may lead them to offer more than the prevailing price to outbid other purchasers. Also, sellers may begin to ask a higher price for the quantities that they do have to sell. In other words, *excess demand causes upward pressure on price.*

excess demand
A situation in which, at the given price, quantity demanded exceeds quantity supplied.

excess supply
A situation in which, at the given price, quantity supplied exceeds quantity demanded.

Practise with Study Guide Chapter 3, Exercise 1.

FIGURE 3-7   Determination of the Equilibrium Price of Carrots

Demand and Supply Schedules

Price Per Tonne ($) p	Quantity Demanded (tonnes per year) D	Quantity Supplied (tonnes per year) S	Excess Demand (+) or Excess Supply (−) (tonnes per year) $D - S$
20	110	20	+90
40	85	45	+40
60	65	65	0
80	50	80	−30
100	40	95	−55

Demand and Supply Curves

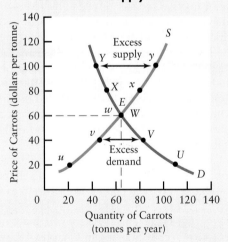

The equilibrium price corresponds to the intersection of the demand and supply curves. Equilibrium is indicated by E, which is point W on the demand curve and point w on the supply curve. At a price of $60, quantity demanded of 65 tonnes equals quantity supplied of 65 tonnes. At prices above equilibrium, there is excess supply and downward pressure on price. At prices below equilibrium, there is excess demand and upward pressure on price.

Finally, consider the price of $60. At this price, producers wish to sell 65 tonnes per year, and purchasers wish to buy that same quantity. There is neither a shortage nor a surplus of carrots. There are no unsatisfied buyers to bid the price up, nor are there unsatisfied sellers to force the price down. Once the price of $60 has been reached, therefore, there will be no tendency for it to change.

Equilibrium implies a state of rest, or balance, between opposing forces. The **equilibrium price** is the one toward which the actual market price will tend. It will persist, once established, unless it is disturbed by some change in market conditions which shifts the demand curve, the supply curve, or both.

The price at which the quantity demanded equals the quantity supplied is called the equilibrium price, or the market-clearing price. [5]

Any price at which the market does not "clear"—that is, quantity demanded does not equal quantity supplied—is called a **disequilibrium price.** Whenever there is either excess demand or excess supply in a market, that market is said to be in a state of **disequilibrium,** and the market price will be changing.

Figure 3-7 makes it clear that the equilibrium price occurs where the demand and supply curves intersect. Below that price, there is excess demand and hence upward pressure on the existing price. Above that price, there is excess supply and hence downward pressure on the existing price.[1]

Changes in Market Prices

Changes in any of the variables, other than price, that influence quantity demanded or supplied will cause a shift in the supply curve, the demand curve, or both. There are four possible shifts: an increase in demand (a rightward shift in the demand curve), a decrease in demand (a leftward shift in the demand curve), an increase in supply (a rightward shift in the supply curve), and a decrease in supply (a leftward shift in the supply curve).

To discover the effects of each of the possible curve shifts, we use the method known as **comparative statics.**[2] With this method, we derive predictions by analyzing the effect on the equilibrium of some change in which we are interested. More precisely, we derive predictions about how the *endogenous* variables (equilibrium price and quantity) will change following a change in some *exogenous* variable. We start from a position of equilibrium and then introduce the change to be studied. We then determine the new equilibrium position and compare it with the original one. The difference between the two positions of equilibrium must result from the change that was introduced because everything else has been held constant.

Each of the four possible curve shifts causes changes that are described by one of the four "laws" of demand and supply. Each of the laws summarizes what happens when an

equilibrium price
The price at which quantity demanded equals quantity supplied. Also called the market-clearing price.

disequilibrium price
A price at which quantity demanded does not equal quantity supplied.

disequilibrium
A situation in a market in which there is excess demand or excess supply.

comparative statics
The derivation of predictions by analyzing the effect of a change in some exogenous variable on the equilibrium.

---

[1] When economists graph a demand (or supply) curve, they put the variable to be explained (the dependent variable) on the horizontal axis and the explanatory variable (the independent variable) on the vertical axis. This is "backwards" to what is usually done in mathematics. The rational explanation of what is now economists' odd practice is buried in the history of economics and dates back to Alfred Marshall's *Principles of Economics* (1890) [6]. For better or worse, Marshall's scheme is now used by all economists, although mathematicians never fail to wonder at this example of the odd ways of economists.

[2] The term *static* is used because we are not concerned with the actual path by which the market goes from the first equilibrium position to the second or with the time taken to reach the second equilibrium. Analysis of these movements would be described as *dynamic analysis*.

initial position of equilibrium is disturbed by a shift in either the demand curve or the supply curve. By using the term "law" to describe what happens, economists do not mean that they are absolutely certain of the outcome. The term "law" in science is used to describe a theory that has stood up to substantial testing. The laws of demand and supply are thus hypotheses that predict certain kinds of behaviour in certain situations, and the predicted behaviour occurs sufficiently often that economists continue to have confidence in the underlying theory.

The four laws of demand and supply are derived in Figure 3-8. Study the figure carefully. Previously, we had given the axes specific labels, but because it is now intended to apply to any product, the horizontal axis is simply labelled "Quantity." This means quantity per period in whatever units output is measured. "Price," the vertical axis, means the price measured as dollars per unit of quantity for the same product.

The four laws of demand and supply are as follows:

1. An increase in demand causes an increase in both the equilibrium price and the equilibrium quantity exchanged.

2. A decrease in demand causes a decrease in both the equilibrium price and the equilibrium quantity exchanged.

3. An increase in supply causes a decrease in the equilibrium price and an increase in the equilibrium quantity exchanged.

4. A decrease in supply causes an increase in the equilibrium price and a decrease in the equilibrium quantity exchanged.

Demonstrations of these laws are given in the caption to Figure 3-8. The intuitive reasoning behind each is as follows:

1. **An increase in demand.** An increase in demand creates a shortage at the initial equilibrium price, and the unsatisfied buyers bid up the price. This rise in price causes a larger quantity to be supplied with the result that at the new equilibrium more is exchanged at a higher price.

2. **A decrease in demand.** A decrease in demand creates a surplus at the initial equilibrium price, and the unsuccessful sellers bid the price down. As a result, less of the product is supplied and offered for sale. At the new equilibrium, both price and quantity exchanged are lower than they were originally.

3. **An increase in supply.** An increase in supply creates a surplus at the initial equilibrium price, and the unsuccessful suppliers force the price down. This drop in price increases the quantity demanded, and the new equilibrium is at a lower price and a higher quantity exchanged.

4. **A decrease in supply.** A decrease in supply creates a shortage at the initial equilibrium price that causes the price to be bid up. This rise in price reduces the quantity demanded, and the new equilibrium is at a higher price and a lower quantity exchanged.

In this chapter, we have studied many forces that can cause demand or supply curves to shift. By combining this analysis with the four laws of demand and supply, we can link many real-world events that cause demand or supply curves to shift with changes in market prices and quantities. *Lessons From History 3-1* on page 70 shows how we can use demand-and-supply analysis to examine the effects of two real-world weather shocks: Brazil's 1994 frost and drought and Quebec's 1998 ice storm.

Practise with Study Guide Chapter 3, Exercise 3 and Short-Answer Question 4.

FIGURE 3-8   The Four "Laws" of Demand and Supply

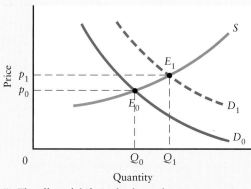

(i) The effect of shifts in the demand curve

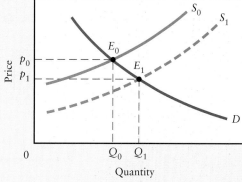

(ii) The effect of shifts in the supply curve

The effects on equilibrium price and quantity of shifts in either demand or supply are known as the laws of demand and supply.

An increase in demand. In part (i), suppose that the original demand and supply curves are D_0 and S, which intersect to produce equilibrium at E_0, with a price of p_0 and a quantity of Q_0. An increase in demand shifts the demand curve to D_1, taking the new equilibrium to E_1. Price rises to p_1 and quantity rises to Q_1.

A decrease in demand. In part (i), the original demand and supply curves are D_1 and S, which intersect to produce equilibrium at E_1, with a price of p_1 and a quantity of Q_1. A decrease in demand shifts the demand curve to D_0, taking the new equilibrium to E_0. Price falls to p_0, and quantity falls to Q_0.

An increase in supply. In part (ii), the original demand and supply curves are D and S_0, which intersect to produce equilibrium at E_0, with a price of p_0 and a quantity of Q_0. An increase in supply shifts the supply curve to S_1, taking the new equilibrium to E_1. Price falls to p_1, and quantity rises to Q_1.

A decrease in supply. In part (ii), the original demand and supply curves are D and S_1, which intersect to produce equilibrium at E_1, with a price of p_1 and a quantity of Q_1. A decrease in supply shifts the supply curve to S_0, taking the new equilibrium to E_0. Price rises to p_0, and quantity falls to Q_0.

Our discussion of demand, supply, and equilibrium has explained why equilibrium price and quantity are found at the intersection of the demand and supply curves. And we have shown diagrams (Figures 3-7 and 3-8) illustrating this in the general case. But we have not presented a specific example of demand and supply and "solved" precisely for the equilibrium price and quantity. This is a useful exercise but requires some algebra. See *Extensions in Theory 3-2* for an algebraic solution to a specific model of demand and supply.

Practise with Study Guide Chapter 3, Exercise 5 and Extension Exercise E1.

Economists often use data from market transactions to estimate demand and supply relationships. This is a difficult exercise, however, because the demand and supply curves in any given market are rarely stable. To learn more about what is needed to identify a demand or supply curve using real-world data, look for "Economic Data and the Identification Problem" in the *Additional Topics* section of this book's Companion Website.

http://www.pearsoned.ca/ragan

EXTENSIONS IN THEORY 3-2

The Algebra of Market Equilibrium

This box presents a specific model of demand and supply and the algebraic method for determining the equilibrium price and quantity. For simplicity, we assume that the demand and supply curves are linear relationships between price and quantity.

Consider the following demand and supply curves:

Demand: $Q^D = a - bp$
Supply: $Q^S = c + dp$

where p is the price, Q^D is quantity demanded, Q^S is quantity supplied, and a, b, c, and d are positive constants. Both curves are plotted in the accompanying figure.

What is the interpretation of the demand curve and how do we plot it? First, at a price of zero, consumers will buy a units—this is the horizontal intercept of the demand curve. Second, if the price rises to a/b, consumers will buy zero units, so a/b is the vertical intercept of the demand curve. Finally, the slope of the demand curve is $-1/b$; the quantity demanded increases by b units for every \$1 that price falls.

What is the interpretation of the supply curve, and how do we plot it? First, if the price is zero, suppliers will sell c units—this is the horizontal intercept of the supply curve. Second, for every \$1 increase in price, the quantity supplied

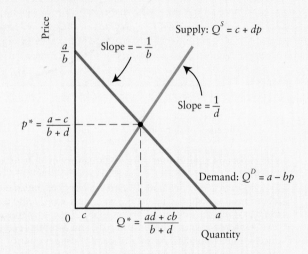

increases by d units. Thus the slope of the supply curve is $1/d$.

Given these demand and supply curves, the market equilibrium can be determined in two ways. The first is to construct a scale diagram and plot the two curves accurately. If

Prices and Inflation

The theory we have developed explains how individual prices are determined by the forces of demand and supply. To facilitate matters, we have made *ceteris paribus* assumptions. Specifically, we have assumed the constancy of all prices except the one we are studying. Does this mean that our theory is inapplicable to an inflationary world in which all prices are rising at the same time? Fortunately, the answer is no.

The price of a product is the amount of money that must be spent to acquire one unit of that product. This is called the **absolute price** or *money price*. A **relative price** is the ratio of two absolute prices; it expresses the price of one good in terms of (relative to) another.

We have been reminded several times that what matters for demand and supply is the price of the product in question *relative to the prices of other products*; that is, what matters is the relative price. For example, if the price of carrots rises while the prices of other vegetables are constant, we expect consumers to reduce their quantity demanded of carrots as they substitute toward the consumption of other vegetables. In this case, the *relative* price of carrots has increased. But if the prices of carrots and all other vegetables are rising at the same rate, the relative price of carrots is constant. In this case we expect no substitution to take place between carrots and other vegetables.

absolute price   The amount of money that must be spent to acquire one unit of a commodity. Also called *money price*.

relative price   The ratio of the money price of one commodity to the money price of another commodity; that is, a ratio of two absolute prices.

you do this carefully, you will be able to read the equilibrium price and quantity off the diagram. But your diagram will have to be very accurate for this to work!

A more precise method is to use algebra to solve for the equilibrium price and quantity. Here is how we do it. We know that in equilibrium quantity demanded equals quantity supplied, or $Q^D = Q^S$. We call the equilibrium quantity Q^*. But we also know that in equilibrium the price paid by the consumers will equal the price received by the producers—that is, there is only one equilibrium price, which we call p^*. Putting these two facts together we know that in equilibrium

Demand: $Q^* = a - bp^*$
Supply: $Q^* = c + dp^*$

We now have two equations and two unknown variables (p^* and Q^*) and can proceed to solve the system of equations. Since Q^* from the demand curve equals Q^* from the supply curve, it follows that

$$a - bp^* = c + dp^*$$

This implies

$$a - c = (b + d)p^*$$

which leads to

$$p^* = \frac{a - c}{b + d}$$

This is the solution for the equilibrium market price. By substituting this value of p^* back into *either* the demand curve or the supply curve (it doesn't matter which) we get the solution for Q^*:

$$Q^* = a - bp^* = a - b[(a - c)/(b + d)]$$

which can be simplified to be

$$Q^* = \frac{(ad + bc)}{b+d}$$

We now have the precise solutions for the equilibrium price and quantity in this market. Notice that the solutions for p^* and Q^* naturally depend on those (exogenous) variables that shift the demand and supply curves. For example, an increase in demand for the product would be reflected by an increase in a. This would shift the demand curve to the right, increasing both p^* and Q^*. A decrease in supply would have a different effect. It would be reflected by a decrease in c that would shift the supply curve to the left, leading to an increase in p^* and a reduction in Q^*.

Mastering the algebra of demand and supply takes a little practice, but is worth the effort. If you would like to practise, try the Study Exercises at the end of the chapter (and Chapters 4 and 5) that deal with the algebra of demand and supply.

In an inflationary world, we are often interested in the price of a given product as it relates to the average price of all other products. If, during a period when all prices were increasing by an average of 5 percent, the price of coffee increased by 30 percent, then the price of coffee increased relative to the prices of other goods as a whole. Coffee became *relatively* expensive. However, if coffee had increased in price by 30 percent when other prices increased by 40 percent, then the relative price of coffee would have fallen. Although the money price of coffee increased substantially, coffee became *relatively* cheap.

It has been convenient in this chapter to analyze changes in particular prices in the context of a constant price level. We can easily extend the analysis to an inflationary period by remembering that any force that raises the price of one product when other prices remain constant will, given general inflation, raise the price of that product faster than the price level is rising. For example, a change in tastes in favour of carrots that would raise their price by 5 percent when other prices were constant would raise their price by 8 percent if, at the same time, the general price level were rising by 3 percent. In each case, the price of carrots rises 5 percent *relative to the average of all prices.*

In microeconomics, whenever we refer to a change in the price of one product, we mean a change in that product's relative price; that is, a change in the price of that product relative to the prices of all other goods.

LESSONS FROM HISTORY 3-1

Ice Storms, Droughts, and Economics

Here are two simple examples of the demand and supply apparatus in action. Both examples show how the weather—something that changes in unpredictable and often dramatic ways—can have significant effects on either the demand or the supply of various products, with obvious implications for the observed market price.

The Weather and a Demand Shock

In January of 1998, Quebec, Eastern Ontario, and parts of the Northeastern United States were hit by a massive ice storm. So unprecedented was this storm in its magnitude that many electric power systems were devastated. Homes and businesses in the Montreal area went without power for as long as four weeks.

This electric power shortage had many economic effects, including lost factory production, damage to much capital stock, the death of farm livestock, and the displacement of thousands of people into shelters. Another effect of the power shortage, as soon as it became clear that it would last for more than just a few hours, was a sudden and substantial increase in the demand for portable gas-powered electric generators. Within just a few days, all stores in the greater Montreal area were sold out of such generators, and the prices for newly ordered units had increased.

Furthermore, the shortages and price increases for electric generators were not confined to the area directly hit by the ice storm. As it became clear that there was an excess demand for generators in Quebec, sellers in other parts of the country began to divert their supply toward Quebec. This reduction in supply caused shortages, and thus price increases, in other parts of the country, as far away as Edmonton.

The Weather and a Supply Shock

Brazil, which produces one-third of the world's coffee, experienced unusually severe weather in 1994. Two killing frosts in June and July and a period of drought thereafter severely damaged the next year's crop. Some experts estimated that the frosts and drought destroyed as much as 45 percent of Brazil's 1995 harvest.

This crop damage meant that the world's supply curve of coffee shifted to the left. Without a change in price, there would have been excess demand for coffee, with more people wanting to buy than wanting to sell. Predictably, the market forces reacted swiftly, and coffee prices soared by nearly 100 percent on the wholesale commodity market. Consumers also felt the impact of the supply shock, with retail prices climbing by about $5 per kilogram.

This severe weather hurt coffee growers in Brazil, reducing their incomes considerably. But coffee growers elsewhere—such as Colombia, Costa Rica and Kenya—actually benefited from Brazil's misfortune. They sold their normal-size crop at the elevated world price and thus enjoyed unusually high incomes.

The Quebec ice storm in January 1998 decimated the electricity distribution system. The demand for portable electricity generators (and many other emergency products) increased sharply as a result.

S U M M A R Y

3.1 **Demand**

- The amount of a product that consumers wish to purchase is called *quantity demanded*. It is a flow expressed as so much per period of time. It is determined by tastes, average household income, the product's own price, the prices of other products, the size of the population, the distribution of income among consumers, and expectations about the future.
- The relationship between quantity demanded and price is represented graphically by a demand curve that shows how much will be demanded at each market price. Quantity demanded is assumed to increase as the price of the product falls, other things held constant. Thus, demand curves are downward sloping.

- A shift in a demand curve represents a change in the quantity demanded at each price and is referred to as a *change in demand*.
- The demand curve shifts if:
  - average income changes
  - prices of other products change
  - consumers' tastes change
  - the distribution of income changes
  - population changes
  - expectations about the future are revised
- It is important to make the distinction between a movement along a demand curve (caused by a change in the product's price) and a shift of a demand curve (caused by a change in any of the other determinants of demand).

3.2 **Supply**

- The amount of a product that firms wish to sell is called *quantity supplied*. It is a flow expressed as so much per period of time. It depends on the product's own price, the costs of inputs, the number of suppliers, government taxes or subsidies, and the state of technology.
- The relationship between quantity supplied and price is represented graphically by a supply curve that shows how much will be supplied at each market price. Quantity supplied is assumed to increase as the price of the product increases, other things held constant. Thus, supply curves are upward sloping.
- A shift in the supply curve indicates a change in the quantity supplied at each price and is referred to as a *change in supply*.

- The supply curve shifts if:
  - the prices of inputs change
  - technology changes
  - the government imposes taxes or subsidies
  - the prices of other products change
  - expectations about the future are revised
  - the number of suppliers changes
- It is important to make the distinction between a movement along a supply curve (caused by a change in the product's price) and a shift of a supply curve (caused by a change in any of the other determinants of supply).

3.3 **The Determination of Price**

- The *equilibrium price* is the price at which the quantity demanded equals the quantity supplied. At any price below equilibrium, there will be excess demand; at any price above equilibrium, there will be excess supply. Graphically, equilibrium occurs where the demand and supply curves intersect.
- Price rises when there is excess demand and falls when there is excess supply. Thus the actual market price will be pushed toward the equilibrium price. When it is reached, there will be neither excess demand nor excess supply, and the price will not change until either the supply curve or the demand curve shifts.
- Using the method of *comparative statics*, we can determine

the effects of a shift in either demand or supply. An increase in demand raises both equilibrium price and equilibrium quantity; a decrease in demand lowers both. An increase in supply raises equilibrium quantity but lowers equilibrium price; a decrease in supply lowers equilibrium quantity but raises equilibrium price. These are called the laws of demand and supply.

- The absolute price of a product is its price in terms of money; its relative price is its price in relation to other products. In an inflationary period, a rise in the *relative price* of one product means that its absolute price rises by more than the price level; a fall in its relative price means that its absolute price rises by less than the price level.

KEY CONCEPTS

Ceteris paribus or "other things being equal"

Quantity demanded and quantity actually bought

Demand schedule and demand curve

Change in quantity demanded versus change in demand

Quantity supplied and quantity actually sold

Supply schedule and supply curve

Change in quantity supplied versus change in supply

Equilibrium, equilibrium price, and disequilibrium

Comparative statics

Laws of supply and demand

Relative price

STUDY EXERCISES

1. The following table shows hypothetical demand schedules for sugar for three separate months. To help make the distinction between changes in demand and changes in quantity demanded, choose the wording to make each of the following statements correct.

	Quantity Demanded for Sugar (in kilograms)		
Price/kg	October	November	December
$1.50	11 000	10 500	13 000
1.75	10 000	9 500	12 000
2.00	9 000	8 500	11 000
2.25	8 000	7 500	10 000
2.50	7 000	6 500	9 000
2.75	6 000	5 500	8 000
3.00	5 000	4 500	7 000
3.25	4 000	3 500	6 000
3.50	3 000	2 500	5 000

   a. When the price of sugar rises from $2.50 to $3.00 in the month of October there is a(n) (*increase/decrease*) in (*demand for/quantity demanded of*) sugar of 2000 kg.

   b. We can say that the demand curve for sugar in December shifted (*to the right/to the left*) of November's demand curve. This represents a(n) (*increase/decrease*) in demand for sugar.

   c. An increase in the demand for sugar means that quantity demanded at each price has (*increased /decreased*), while a decrease in demand for sugar means that quantity demanded at each price has (*increased/decreased*).

   d. In the month of December, a price change for sugar from $3.50 to $2.75 per kilogram would mean a change in (*demand for/quantity demanded of*) sugar of 3000 kg.

   e. Plot the three demand schedules on a graph and label each demand curve to indicate whether it is the demand for October, November, or December.

2. For each of the following statements, determine whether there has been a change in supply or a change in quantity supplied. Draw a demand and supply diagram for each situation to show either a movement along the supply curve or a shift of the supply curve.

   a. The price of Canadian-grown peaches skyrockets during an unusually cold summer that reduces the size of the peach harvest.

   b. An increase in income leads to an increase in the price of beef and also to an increase in beef sales.

   c. Technological improvements in the microchip lead to price reductions for personal computers and an increase in computer sales.

   d. Greater awareness of the health risks from smoking lead to a reduction in the price of cigarettes and to fewer cigarettes being sold.

3. The following diagram describes the hypothetical demand and supply for tuna in Canada in 2004.

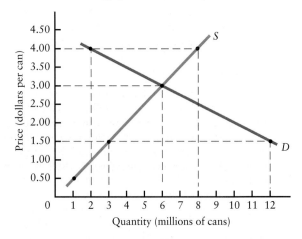

a. Suppose the price of a can of tuna is $4.00. What is the quantity demanded? What is the quantity supplied? At this price, is there a shortage or a surplus? By what amount?

b. Suppose the price of a can of tuna is $1.50. What is the quantity demanded? What is the quantity supplied? At this price, is there a shortage or a surplus? By what amount?

c. What is the equilibrium price and quantity in this market?

4. Consider households' demand for chicken meat. For each of the events listed below, state and explain the likely effect on the demand for chicken. How would each event be illustrated in a diagram?

a. A medical study reports that eating chicken meat reduces the likelihood of suffering from particular types of heart problems.

b. A widespread bovine disease leads to an increase in the price of beef.

c. An increase in average household income.

5. Consider the world market for a particular quality of coffee beans. The following table shows the demand and supply schedules for this market.

Price (per kilogram)	Quantity Demanded	Quantity Supplied
	(millions of kilograms per year)	
$2.00	28	10
$2.40	26	12
$3.10	22	13.5
$3.50	19.5	19.5
$3.90	17	22
$4.30	14.5	23.5

a. Plot the demand and supply schedules on a diagram.

b. Identify the amount of excess demand or supply associated with each price.

c. Identify the equilibrium price in this market.

d. Suppose that a collection of national governments were somehow able to set a minimum price for coffee equal to $3.90 per kilogram. Explain the outcome in the world coffee market.

6. Consider the supply for Grade A beef. As the price of beef rises, ranchers will tend to sell more cattle to the slaughterhouses. Yet, a central prediction from the supply-and-demand model of this chapter is that an increase in the supply of beef reduces the equilibrium price. Reconcile the apparent contradiction. Use a diagram to do so.

7. Consider the world market for wheat. Suppose there is a major failure in Russia's wheat crop due to a severe drought. Explain the likely effect on the equilibrium price and quantity in the world wheat market. Also explain why Canadian wheat farmers certainly benefit from Russia's drought. The diagrams below provide a starting point for your analysis.

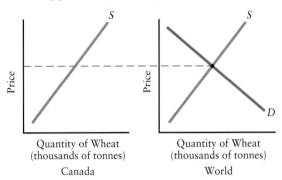

Quantity of Wheat (thousands of tonnes)

Canada

Quantity of Wheat (thousands of tonnes)

World

8. The *New York Times* recently stated:

While the world's appetite for chocolate grows more voracious each year, cocoa farms around the globe are failing, under siege from fungal and viral diseases and insects....Researchers predict a shortfall in beans from the cacao tree, the raw material from which chocolate is made, in as little as five to ten years.

Describe in terms of the supply-and-demand apparatus what is described in the quote. What is the implied prediction for the equilibrium price of chocolate? What is the implied prediction for the equilibrium quantity of chocolate?

9. This is a challenging question and is similar to the example shown in *Extensions in Theory 3-1*. It requires you to solve a supply-and-demand model as a system of *simultaneous equations* (meaning simply that both equations apply at the same time). Letting p be the price of the product, suppose the demand and supply functions for some product are given by

$$Q^D = 100 - 3p$$

$$Q^S = 10 + 2p$$

a. Plot both the demand curve and the supply curve.

b. What is the condition for equilibrium in this market?

c. By imposing the condition for equilibrium, solve for the equilibrium price.

d. Substitute the equilibrium price into either the demand or supply function to solve for the equilibrium quantity. Check to make sure you get the same answer whether you use the demand function or the supply function.

e. Now suppose there is an increase in demand so that the new demand function is given by

$$Q^D = 180 - 3p.$$

Compute the new equilibrium price and quantity. Is your result consistent with the "law" of demand?

f. Now suppose that, with the new demand curve in place, there is an increase in supply so that the new supply function is given by $Q^S = 90 + 2p$. Compute the new equilibrium price and quantity. Is your result consistent with the "law" of supply?

DISCUSSION QUESTIONS

1. Recently, a government economist predicted that this spring's excellent weather would result in larger crops of wheat and canola than farmers had expected. But the economist warned consumers not to expect prices to decrease because the cost of production was rising and foreign demand for Canadian crops was increasing. "The classic pattern of supply and demand won't work this time," the economist said. Discuss his observation.

2. What do you think would be the effect on the equilibrium price and quantity of marijuana if its sale and consumption were legalized?

3. Classify the effect of each of the following as (i) a decrease in the demand for fish or (ii) a decrease in the quantity of fish demanded. Illustrate each diagrammatically.

   a. The government of Canada closes the Atlantic cod fishery.
   b. People buy less fish because of a rise in fish prices.
   c. The Catholic Church relaxes its ban on eating meat on Fridays.
   d. The price of beef falls and, as a result, consumers buy more beef and less fish.

   e. Fears of mercury pollution lead locals to shun fish caught in nearby lakes.
   f. It is generally alleged that eating fish is better for one's health than eating meat.

4. Predict the effect on the price of at least one product of each of the following events:

   a. Winter snowfall is at a record high in the interior of British Columbia, but drought continues in Quebec ski areas.
   b. A recession decreases employment in Oshawa automobile factories.
   c. The French grape harvest is the smallest in 20 years.
   d. The province of Ontario cancels permission for citizens to cut firewood in provincial campgrounds.

5. Are the following two observations inconsistent?

   a. Rising demand for housing causes prices of new homes to soar.
   b. Many families refuse to buy homes as prices become prohibitive for them.

Elasticity

LEARNING OBJECTIVES

❶ Describe the measurement of price elasticity of demand, and know its determinants.

❷ Describe the measurement of price elasticity of supply, and know its determinants.

❸ Explain why the effect of a sales tax on price and quantity depends on relative demand and supply elasticities.

❹ Explain the effect of a change in income on quantity demanded, and how this elasticity defines normal and inferior goods.

❺ Differentiate between substitute and complement goods, and show how this difference relates to the cross elasticity of demand.

The laws of demand and supply predict the *direction* of changes in price and quantity in response to various shifts in demand and supply. However, it usually is not enough to know merely whether price and quantity rise or fall; it is also important to know by *how much* each changes.

In the previous chapter we discussed the coffee-crop failure in Brazil and how this drove up the world coffee price. But what did this crop failure do to the incomes of Brazilian coffee growers? If the price increased by more (in percentage terms) than their crop shrank, their incomes would have actually *increased;* that is, the crop failure actually would have made them, as a group, better off. On the other hand, if the price increased by less than the crop shrank, their incomes would have fallen.

Measuring and describing the extent of the responsiveness of quantities to changes in prices and other variables are often essential if we are to understand the significance of these changes. Such measurement is accomplished with the concept of *elasticity*.

4.1 **Price Elasticity of Demand**

Suppose there is a decrease in the supply of some farm crop—that is, a leftward shift in the supply curve. We saw in Figure 3-8 when we examined the laws of supply and demand that such a decrease in supply will cause the equilibrium price to rise and the equilibrium quantity to fall. But by how much will each change? The answer depends on what is called the *price elasticity of demand*.

Loosely speaking, demand is said to be *elastic* when quantity demanded is quite responsive to changes in price. When quantity demanded is quite unresponsive to changes in price, demand is said to be *inelastic*.

The meaning of elasticity is illustrated in the two parts of Figure 4-1. The two parts of the figure have the same initial equilibrium, and that equilibrium is disturbed by the same leftward shift in the supply curve. But the demand curves are different in the two parts of the figure, and so the sizes of the changes in equilibrium price and quantity are also different.

Part (i) of Figure 4-1 illustrates a case in which the quantity that consumers demand is relatively responsive to price changes—that is, demand is relatively *elastic*. The reduction in supply pushes up the price, but, because the quantity demanded is quite responsive, only a small change in price is necessary to restore equilibrium.

Part (ii) of Figure 4-1 shows a case in which the quantity demanded is relatively unresponsive to price changes—that is, demand is relatively *inelastic*. As before, the decrease in supply at the original price causes a shortage that increases the price. However, this time the quantity demanded by consumers does not fall much in response to the rise in price. The result is that equilibrium price rises more, and equilibrium quantity falls less, than in the first case.

In both of the cases shown in Figure 4-1, the shifts of the supply curve are identical. The sizes of the effects on the equilibrium price and quantity are different only because of the different elasticities of demand.

FIGURE 4-1   The Effect of the Shape of the Demand Curve

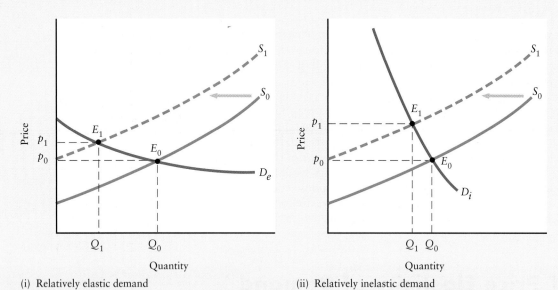

(i) Relatively elastic demand   (ii) Relatively inelastic demand

The more responsive the quantity demanded is to changes in price, the less the change in price and the greater the change in quantity resulting from any given shift in the supply curve. Both parts of the figure are drawn to the same scale. They show the same initial equilibrium, E_0, and the same shift in the supply curve, from S_0 to S_1. In each part, initial equilibrium is at price p_0 and output Q_0 and the new equilibrium, E_1, is at p_1 and Q_1. In part (i), the effect of the shift in supply from S_0 to S_1 is a slight rise in the price and a large decrease in quantity. In part (ii), the effect of the identical shift in the supply curve from S_0 to S_1 is a large increase in the price and a relatively small decrease in quantity.

The Measurement of Price Elasticity

In Figure 4-1, we were able to say that the demand curve in part (i) showed more responsiveness to price changes than the demand curve in part (ii) because two conditions were fulfilled. First, both curves were drawn on the same scale. Second, the initial equilibrium prices and quantities were the same in both parts of the figure. Let's see why these conditions matter.

First, by drawing both figures on the same scale, we saw that the demand curve that *looked* steeper actually did have the larger absolute slope. (The slope of a demand curve tells us the number of dollars by which price must change to cause a unit change in quantity demanded.) If we had drawn the two curves on different scales, we could have concluded nothing about which demand curve actually had the greater slope.

Second, because we started from the same price–quantity equilibrium in both parts of the figure, we did not need to distinguish between *percentage* changes and *absolute* changes. If the initial prices and quantities are the same in both cases, the larger absolute change is also the larger percentage change. However, when we wish to deal with different initial price–quantity equilibria, we need to decide whether we are interested in absolute or percentage changes.

To see why this matters, consider the changes in price and quantity demanded for three different products: cheese, T-shirts, and CD players. The information is shown in Table 4-1. Should we conclude that the demand for portable CD players is not as responsive to price changes as the demand for cheese? After all, price cuts of 40 cents cause quite a large increase in the quantity of cheese demanded, but only a small increase in the quantity demanded of CD players. It should be obvious that a 40-cent price reduction is a large price cut for a low-priced product and an insignificant price cut for a high-priced product. In Table 4-1, each price reduction is 40 cents, but they are clearly different proportions of the respective prices. It is usually more revealing to know the *percentage* change in the prices of the various products.

For similar reasons, knowing the quantity by which demand changes is not very revealing unless the initial level of demand is also known. An increase of 7500 kilograms is quite a significant change if the quantity formerly bought was 15 000 kilograms, but it is insignificant if the quantity formerly bought was 10 million kilograms.

Table 4-2 shows the original and new levels of price and quantity. Note that for both price and quantity, Table 4-2 also shows the *average* price and *average* quantity. These averages will be necessary for our computation of elasticity.

The **price elasticity of demand,** the measure of responsiveness of quantity of a product demanded to a change in that product's price, is symbolized by the Greek letter eta, η. It is defined as follows:

$$\eta = \frac{\text{Percentage change in quantity demanded}}{\text{Percentage change in price}}$$

This measure is called the price elasticity of demand, or simply *demand elasticity*. Because the variable causing the change in quantity demanded is the product's own price, the term *own-price elasticity of demand* is also used.

price elasticity of demand (η) A measure of the responsiveness of quantity demanded to a change in the commodity's own price.

TABLE 4-1 Price Reductions and Corresponding Increases in Quantity Demanded for Three Products

Commodity	Reduction in Price (cents)	Increase in Quantity Demanded (per month)
Cheese	40 per kilogram	7500 kilograms
T-shirts	40 per shirt	5000 shirts
CD players	40 per CD player	100 CD players

For each of the three products, the data show the change in quantity demanded resulting from the same absolute fall in price. The data are fairly uninformative about the responsiveness of quantity demanded to price because they do not tell us either the original price or the original quantity demanded.

TABLE 4-2   Price and Quantity Information Underlying Data of Table 4–1

Product	Unit	Original Price ($)	New Price ($)	Average Price ($)	Original Quantity	New Quantity	Average Quantity
Cheese	kilogram	3.40	3.00	3.20	116 250	123 750	120 000
T-shirts	shirt	16.20	15.80	16.00	197 500	202 500	200 000
CD players	player	80.20	79.80	80.00	9 950	10 050	10 000

These data provide the appropriate context for the data given in Table 4-1. The table relates the 40-cent-per-unit price reduction of each product to the actual prices and quantities demanded.

The Use of Average Price and Quantity in Computing Elasticity

Table 4-3 shows the percentage changes for price and quantity using the data from Table 4-2. The caption in Table 4-3 stresses that the demand elasticities are computed using changes in price and quantity measured in terms of the *average* values of each. Averages are used to avoid the ambiguity caused by the fact that when a price or quantity changes, the change is a different percentage of the original value than it is of the new value. For example, the 40-cent change in the price of cheese shown in Table 4-2 represents an 11.8 percent change in the original price of $3.40 but a 13.3 percent change in the new price of $3.00.

Using average values for price and quantity means that the measured elasticity of demand between any two points on the demand curve, call them A and B, is independent of whether the movement is from A to B or from B to A. In the example of cheese in Tables 4-2 and 4-3, the 40-cent change in the price of cheese is unambiguously 12.5 percent of the average price of $3.20, and that percentage applies to a price increase from $3.00 to $3.40 or to a price decrease from $3.40 to $3.00.

Once we have computed the average prices and quantities as in Table 4-2, the algebraic formula for price elasticity is straightforward. Suppose we have an initial price of p_0 and an initial quantity of Q_0. We then consider a new price of p_1 and a new quantity of Q_1 (both price-quantity combinations lie on the demand curve for the product). The formula for price elasticity is then

$$\eta = \frac{\Delta Q/\overline{Q}}{\Delta p/\overline{p}} = \frac{(Q_1 - Q_0)/\overline{Q}}{(p_1 - p_0)/\overline{p}}$$

where $\overline{p}$ is the average price and $\overline{Q}$ is the average quantity. In the case of cheese from Table 4-2, we have

$$\eta = \frac{7500/120\ 000}{0.40/3.20} = \frac{0.0625}{0.125} = 0.5$$

as shown in Table 4-3. Notice that elasticity is *unit free*—even though prices are measured in dollars and quantity of cheese is measured in kilograms, the elasticity of demand has no units.

Practise with Study Guide Chapter 4, Exercise 4.

TABLE 4-3   Calculation of Demand Elasticities

Product	(1) Percentage Decrease in Price	(2) Percentage Increase in Quantity	(3) Elasticity of Demand (2) ÷ (1)
Cheese	12.5	6.25	0.5
T-shirts	2.5	2.50	1.0
CD players	0.5	1.00	2.0

Elasticity of demand is the percentage change in quantity demanded divided by the percentage change in price. The percentage changes are based on average prices and quantities shown in Table 4-2. For example, the 40-cent-per-kilogram decrease in the price of cheese is 12.5 percent of $3.20. A 40-cent change in the price of CD players is only 0.5 percent of the average price per CD player of $80.00.

We leave it to you to use this formula to confirm the price elasticities for T-shirts and CD players shown in Table 4-3. The appendix to this chapter contains more information about computing price elasticity. [7]

Interpreting Numerical Elasticities

Because demand curves have negative slopes, an increase in price is associated with a decrease in quantity demanded, and vice versa. Because the percentage changes in price and quantity have opposite signs, demand elasticity is a negative number. However, we will follow the usual practice of ignoring the negative sign and speak of the measure as a positive number, as we have done in the illustrative calculations in Table 4-3. Thus the more responsive the quantity demanded to a change in price, the greater the elasticity and the larger is η.

The numerical value of demand elasticity can vary from zero to infinity. First consider the extreme cases. Elasticity is zero when a change in price leads to *no change* in quantity demanded. This is the case of a vertical demand curve, and is quite rare because it indicates that consumers do not alter their consumption at all when price changes. Elasticity is very large when even a very small change in price leads to an enormous change in quantity demanded. In these situations, which are also rare in the case of demands for individual commodities, the demand curve is very flat, almost horizontal. (In the limiting case, the demand curve is perfectly horizontal and elasticity is infinite.) Most of reality lies between the extremes of vertical and horizontal demand curves. We divide this "realistic" range of elasticities into two regions.

When the percentage change in quantity demanded is less than the percentage change in price (elasticity less than 1), there is said to be **inelastic demand.** When the percentage change in quantity is greater than the percentage change in price (elasticity greater than 1), there is said to be **elastic demand.** And when the percentage change in quantity demanded is exactly equal to the percentage change in price and so elasticity is equal to 1, we say that demand is *unit elastic.* This important terminology is summarized in part A of *Extensions in Theory 4-2*, which is found toward the end of the chapter.

A demand curve need not, and usually does not, have the same elasticity over every part of the curve. Figure 4-2 shows that a negatively sloped linear demand curve does not have a constant elasticity, even though it does have a constant slope. A linear demand curve has constant elasticity only when it is vertical or horizontal. Figure 4-3 illustrates these two cases, in addition to a third case of a particular *nonlinear* demand curve that also has a constant elasticity.

Practise with Study Guide Chapter 4, Exercise 1.

inelastic demand
Following a given percentage change in price, there is a smaller percentage change in quantity demanded; elasticity less than 1.

elastic demand
Following a given percentage change in price, there is a greater percentage change in quantity demanded; elasticity greater than 1.

What Determines Elasticity of Demand?

The main determinant of demand elasticity is the availability of substitutes. Some products, such as margarine, broccoli, lamb, and Toyota cars, have quite close substitutes—butter, other green vegetables, beef, and Mazda cars. A change in the prices of these products, *with the prices of the substitutes remaining constant,* can be expected to cause much substitution. A fall in price leads consumers to buy more of the product and less of the substitutes, and a rise in price leads consumers to buy less of the product and more of the substitutes. Products defined more broadly, such as *all* foods or *all* clothing or *all* methods of transportation, have many fewer satisfactory substitutes. A rise in their prices can be expected to cause a smaller fall in quantities demanded than would be the case if close substitutes were available.

FIGURE 4-2   Elasticity Along a Linear Demand Curve

Practise with Study Guide Chapter 4,
Exercises 3 and 6.

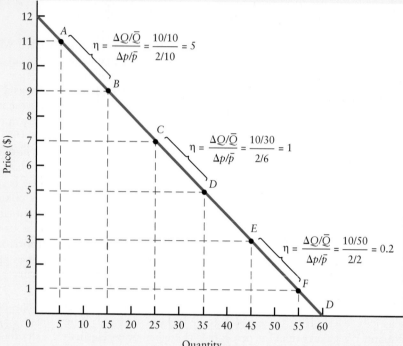

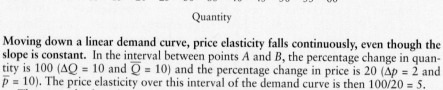

Moving down a linear demand curve, price elasticity falls continuously, even though the slope is constant. In the interval between points A and B, the percentage change in quantity is 100 ($\Delta Q = 10$ and $\overline{Q} = 10$) and the percentage change in price is 20 ($\Delta p = 2$ and $\overline{p} = 10$). The price elasticity over this interval of the demand curve is then 100/20 = 5.

The same *absolute* changes in price and quantity occur over the intervals CD and EF, but elasticity differs because these absolute changes represent different *percentage* changes. Between points C and D, price elasticity is equal to 1. Between points E and F, price elasticity is equal to 0.2. Note that elasticity approaches infinity as we get closer to where the demand curve intersects the vertical axis; elasticity approaches zero as we get closer to where the demand curve intersects the horizontal axis.

A product with close substitutes tends to have an elastic demand; a product with no close substitutes tends to have an inelastic demand.

Demand elasticity depends on the availability of substitutes. The availability of a product's substitutes, in turn, depends on how the product is defined and on the time period being considered. We explore these aspects next.

Definition of the Product

For food taken as a whole, demand is inelastic over a large price range. It does not follow, however, that any specific food, such as white bread or peanut butter, also has inelastic demand. Individual foods can have quite elastic demands, and they frequently do.

Clothing provides a similar example. Clothing as a whole has a less elastic demand than do individual kinds of clothes. For example, when the price of wool sweaters rises, many households may substitute away from wool sweaters and buy cotton sweaters or down vests instead. Thus, although purchases of wool sweaters fall, total purchases of clothing do not.

Any one of a group of related products will have a more elastic demand than the group as a whole.

Short Run and Long Run

Because it takes time to develop satisfactory substitutes, a demand that is inelastic in the short run may prove to be elastic when enough time has passed. A dramatic example of this principle occurred in 1973 when the Organization of Petroleum Exporting Countries (OPEC) shocked the world with its sudden and large increase in the price of oil. At that time, the short-run demand for oil proved to be highly inelastic. Large price increases were met in the short run by very small reductions in quantity demanded. In this case, the short run lasted for several years. Gradually, however, the high price of petroleum products led to such adjustments as the development of smaller, more fuel-efficient cars, economizing on heating oil by installing more efficient insulation, and replacement of fuel oil in many industrial processes with other power sources such as coal and hydroelectricity. The long-run elasticity of demand, relating the change in price to the change in quantity demanded after all adjustments were made, turned out to have an elasticity of well over 1, although the long-run adjustments took as much as a decade to work out.

The response to a price change, and thus the measured price elasticity of demand, will tend to be greater the longer the time span.

For such products as cornflakes and pillowcases, the full response to a price change occurs quickly, and there is little reason to make the distinction between short-run and long-run effects. But other products are typically used in connection with highly durable appliances or machines. A change in the price of, say, electricity and gasoline may not have its major effect until the stock of appliances and machines using these products has been adjusted. This adjustment may take several years to occur.

For products for which substitutes are developed over a period of time, it is helpful to identify two kinds of demand curves. A *short-run demand curve* shows the immediate response of quantity demanded to a change in price given the current stock of durable goods. The *long-run demand curve* shows the response of quantity demanded to a change in price after enough time has passed to change the stock of durable goods.

The long-run demand for a product is more elastic than the short-run demand.

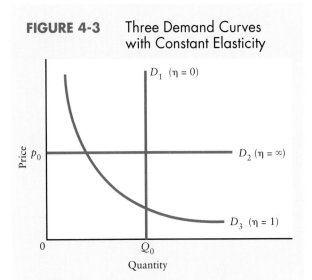

FIGURE 4-3 Three Demand Curves with Constant Elasticity

Each of these demand curves has a constant elasticity. D_1 has zero elasticity: The quantity demanded is equal to Q_0, independent of the price. D_2 has infinite elasticity at the price p_0: A small price increase from p_0 decreases quantity demanded from an indefinitely large amount to zero. D_3 has unit elasticity: A given percentage increase in price brings an equal percentage decrease in quantity demanded at all points on the curve; it is a rectangular hyperbola for which price times quantity demanded is a constant.

Because most people cannot easily or quickly change their method of transportation, the demand for gasoline is much less elastic in the short run than in the long run.

FIGURE 4-4   Short-Run and Long-Run Equilibrium Following an Increase in Supply

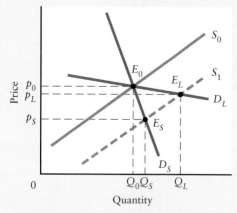

The magnitude of the changes in the equilibrium price and quantity following a shift in supply depends on the time allowed for demand to adjust. The initial equilibrium is at E_0, with price p_0 and quantity Q_0. Supply then increases and the supply curve shifts from S_0 to S_1.

Immediately following the increase in supply, the relevant demand curve is the short-run curve D_S, and the new equilibrium immediately following the supply shock is E_S. Price falls sharply to p_S, and quantity rises only to Q_S. In the long run, the demand curve is the more elastic one given by D_L, and equilibrium is at E_L. The long-run equilibrium price is p_L (greater than p_S), and quantity is Q_L (greater than Q_S).

Practise with Study Guide Chapter 4, Exercise 2 and Short-Answer Question 7.

Figure 4-4 shows the short-run and long-run effects of an increase in supply. In the short run, the supply increase leads to a movement down the relatively inelastic short-run demand curve; it thus causes a large fall in price but only a small increase in quantity. In the long run, demand is more elastic; thus long-run equilibrium has price and quantity above those that prevailed in short-run equilibrium.

This pattern is often referred to as *overshooting* of the price. The overshooting of price that is evident in the figure is the way in which markets clear when demand is less elastic in the short run than in the long run. Note also that there is *undershooting* of quantity—that is, the equilibrium quantity rises by less in the short run than in the long run.

Elasticity and Total Expenditure

We know that quantity demanded increases as price falls, but what happens to the total expenditure on that product? It turns out that the response of total expenditure depends on the price elasticity of demand.

To see the relationship between the elasticity of demand and total expenditure, we begin by noting that total expenditure at any point on the demand curve is equal to price times quantity:

$$\text{Total expenditure} = \text{Price} \times \text{Quantity}$$

Because price and quantity move in opposite directions along a demand curve, one falling when the other rises, the change in total expenditure appears to be ambiguous. It is easily shown, however, that the direction of change in total expenditure depends on the relative percentage changes in the price and quantity. If the percentage change in price exceeds the percentage change in quantity (elasticity less than 1), the price change will dominate, and total expenditure will change in the same direction as the price changes. If the percentage change in the price is less than the percentage change in the quantity demanded (elasticity greater than 1), the quantity change will dominate, and total expenditure will change in the same direction as quantity changes. If the two percentage changes are equal, total expenditure is unchanged—this is the case of unit elasticity.

Figure 4-5 illustrates the relationship between price elasticity and total expenditure; it is based on the linear demand curve in Figure 4-2. Total expenditure at each of a number of points on the demand curve is calculated in the table, and the general relationship between total expenditure and quantity demanded is shown by the plotted curve. In the figure we see that expenditure reaches its maximum when price elasticity is equal to 1. [8]

The following example uses this relationship between elasticity, price, and total expenditure. When a recent bumper potato crop sent prices down 50 percent (a rightward shift in the supply curve), the quantity purchased increased by only 15 percent. Demand

FIGURE 4-5   Total Expenditure and Quantity Demanded

Price ($)	Quantity Demanded	Expenditure ($)
12	0	0
10	10	100
8	20	160
6	30	180
4	40	160
2	50	100
0	60	0

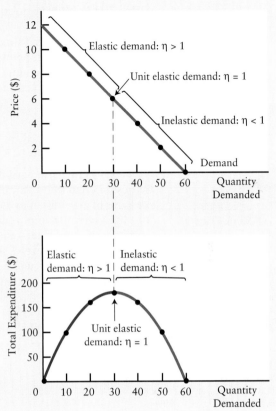

The change in total expenditure on a product in response to a change in price depends on the elasticity of demand. The table and graph are based on the demand curve shown in Figure 4-2. For quantities demanded that are less than 30, elasticity of demand is greater than 1, and hence any increase in quantity demanded will be proportionately larger than the fall in price that caused it. In that range, total expenditure is increasing. For quantities greater than 30, elasticity of demand is less than 1, and hence any increase in quantity demanded will be proportionately smaller than the fall in price that caused it. In that range, total expenditure is decreasing. The maximum of total expenditure occurs where the elasticity of demand equals 1.

was clearly inelastic, and the result of the bumper crop was that total expenditure on potatoes *fell* sharply. Potato farmers, therefore, experienced a sharp fall in income.

A second example relates to the OPEC oil shock in the early 1970s. As the OPEC countries acted together to restrict supply and push up the world price of oil, quantity demanded fell, but only by a small percentage—much smaller than the percentage increase in price. World demand for oil (at least in the short run) was very inelastic, and the result was that total expenditure on oil *increased* dramatically. The OPEC oil producers, therefore, experienced an enormous increase in income.

For information on OPEC and its activities, see www.opec.org.

4.2 **Price Elasticity of Supply**

The concept of elasticity can be applied to supply as well as to demand. **Price elasticity of supply** measures the responsiveness of the quantity supplied to a change in the product's price. It is denoted η_S and defined as follows:

$$\eta_S = \frac{\text{Percentage change in quantity supplied}}{\text{Percentage change in price}}$$

price elasticity of supply (η_S)
A measure of the responsiveness of quantity supplied to a change in the commodity's own price.

This is often called *supply elasticity*. The supply curves considered in this chapter all have positive slopes: An increase in price causes an increase in quantity supplied. Such supply curves all have positive elasticities because price and quantity change in the same direction.

Figure 4-6 shows a simple linear supply curve to illustrate the measurement of supply elasticity. Between points *A* and *B,* the change in price is $1.50 and the average price is $4.25. Between the same two points, the change in quantity supplied is 20 units and the average quantity is 40 units. The value of supply elasticity between points *A* and *B* is therefore

$$\eta_s = \frac{\Delta Q/\overline{Q}}{\Delta p/\overline{p}} = \frac{20/40}{1.50/4.25} = \frac{0.5}{0.353} = 1.42$$

Practise with Study Guide Chapter 4, Exercise 7.

As was the case with demand elasticity, care must be taken when computing elasticities. Keep in mind that even though the supply curve may have a constant slope, the measure of elasticity may be different at different places on the curve.

There are also important special cases of supply curves that should be noted. If the supply curve is vertical—the quantity supplied does not change as price changes—then elasticity of supply is zero. A horizontal supply curve has an infinite elasticity of supply: A small drop in price will reduce the quantity that producers are willing to supply from an indefinitely large amount to zero. Between these two extremes, elasticity of supply varies with the shape of the supply curve. Loosely speaking, steeper supply curves imply a smaller quantity response for a given change in price, and thus a lower elasticity.[1]

FIGURE 4-6 Computing Price Elasticity of Supply

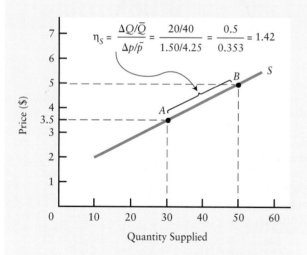

To compute supply elasticity, average price and quantity are used, just as in the computation of demand elasticity. Between points *A* and *B*, the elasticity of supply is 1.42. The same approach shown here can be used to compute elasticity between any two points on the supply curve.

Determinants of Supply Elasticity

Because much of the treatment of demand elasticity carries over to supply elasticity, we can cover the main points quickly.

Substitution and Production Costs

The ease of substitution can vary in production as well as in consumption. If the price of a product rises, how much more can be produced profitably? This depends in part on how easy it is for producers to shift from the production of other products to the one whose price has risen. If agricultural land and labour can be readily shifted from one crop to another, the supply of any one crop will be more elastic than if they cannot. Or, if machines used to produce coats can be easily modified to produce pants (and vice versa), then the supply of both pants and coats will be more elastic than if the machines cannot be so easily modified.

---

[1] Here is another special case that is often puzzling at first glance. Consider a linear supply curve that begins at the origin. It is easy to show that the elasticity of supply along such a curve is always 1—no matter how steep the supply curve is! See Study Exercise #8 to explore this further.

Supply elasticity also depends on how costs behave as output is varied. If the costs of producing a unit of output rise rapidly as output rises, then the stimulus to expand production in response to a rise in price will quickly be choked off by increases in costs. In this case, supply will tend to be rather inelastic. If, however, the costs of producing a unit of output rise only slowly as production increases, a rise in price that raises profits will elicit a large increase in quantity supplied before the rise in costs puts a halt to the expansion in output. In this case, supply will tend to be rather elastic.

Short Run and Long Run

As with demand, length of time for response is important. It may be difficult to change quantities supplied in response to a price increase in a matter of weeks or months, but easy to do so over a period of years. An obvious example is the planting cycle of crops. An increase in the price of wheat that occurs in mid-summer may lead wheat farmers to be more careful (and less wasteful) in their harvesting in the fall, but it occurs too late to influence how much wheat gets planted for this year's crop. If the high price persists, however, it will surely influence how much wheat gets planted the following spring. Also, new oil fields can be discovered, wells drilled, and pipelines built over a period of years but not in just a few months. Thus the elasticity of oil supply is much greater over five years than over one year.

As with demand, it is useful to make the distinction between the short-run and the long-run supply curves. The *short-run supply curve* shows the immediate response of quantity supplied to a change in price given producers' current capacity to produce the good. The *long-run supply curve* shows the response of quantity supplied to a change in price after enough time has passed to allow producers to adjust their productive capacity.

The long-run supply for a product is more elastic than the short-run supply.

Figure 4-7 illustrates the short-run and long-run effects of an increase in demand. The short-run overshooting of price and the undershooting of quantity that are evident in the figure are analogous to that shown in Figure 4-4 when we examined the short-run and long-run effects following a shift in supply. Here it arises following a shift in demand and is the market-clearing response when supply is less elastic in the short run than in the long run.

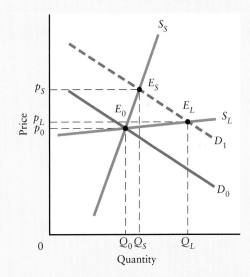

FIGURE 4-7   Short-Run and Long-Run Equilibrium Following an Increase in Demand

The size of the changes in the equilibrium price and quantity following a shift in demand depends on the time frame of the analysis. The initial equilibrium is at E_0, with price p_0 and quantity Q_0. Demand then increases such that the demand curve shifts from D_0 to D_1.

Immediately following the demand shift, the relevant supply curve is the short-run curve S_S, so that the new equilibrium immediately following the demand shock is at E_S. Price rises sharply to p_S, and quantity rises only to Q_S. In the long run, the supply curve is the more elastic one given by S_L. The long-run equilibrium is at E_L; price is p_L (less than p_S) and quantity is Q_L (greater than Q_S).

4.3 An Important Example Where Elasticity Matters

So far, this chapter has been fairly tough going. We have spent much time examining price elasticity (of both demand and supply) and how to measure it. But why should we care about this? In this section, we explore the important concept of *tax incidence* and show that elasticity is crucial to determining whether consumers or producers (or both) end up being harmed by excise taxes.

excise tax   A tax on the sale of a particular commodity.

The federal and provincial governments levy special sales taxes called **excise taxes** on many goods such as cigarettes, alcohol, and gasoline. At the point of sale of the product, the sellers collect the tax on behalf of the government and then periodically remit the tax collections.

When the sellers write their cheques to the government, these firms feel that they are the ones paying the tax. Consumers, however, argue that *they* are the ones who are shouldering the burden of the tax because the tax causes the price of the product to rise. Who actually bears the burden of the tax?

tax incidence   The location of the burden of a tax; that is, the identity of the ultimate bearer of the tax.

The question of who *bears the burden* of a tax is called the question of **tax incidence**. A straightforward application of demand-and-supply analysis will show that tax incidence has nothing to do with whether the government collects the tax directly from consumers or from firms.

The burden of a sales (or excise) tax is distributed between consumers and sellers in a manner that depends on the relative elasticities of supply and demand.

Let's consider a case where the government imposes an excise tax on cigarettes. The analysis begins in Figure 4-8. To simplify the problem, we analyze the case where there is initially no tax. The equilibrium without taxes is illustrated by the solid supply and demand curves. What happens when a tax of t per pack of cigarettes is introduced? A sales tax means that the price paid by the consumer, called the *consumer price,* and the price received by the seller, called the *seller price,* must now differ by the amount of the tax, t.

In terms of the figure, we can analyze the effect of the tax by considering a new supply curve S' that is above the original supply curve S by the amount of the tax, t. To understand this new curve, consider the situation faced by firms at the original equilibrium quantity Q_0. To supply that quantity, producers must receive p_0 per pack of cigarettes sold. However, for producers to receive p_0 when there is a tax on cigarettes, the consumer must pay a total price of $p_0 + t$: whether the consumer "pays the tax directly" by giving p_0 to the firm and t to the government, or whether the consumer pays the total $p_0 + t$ to the firm and the firm then remits the tax t to the government. Either way, the total amount that consumers must pay to obtain a given quantity from firms has increased by the amount of the tax, t.

FIGURE 4-8   The Effect of a Cigarette Excise Tax

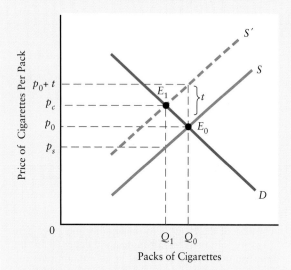

The burden of an excise tax is shared by consumers and producers. The original supply and demand curves for cigarettes are given by the solid lines S and D; equilibrium is at E_0 with price p_0 and quantity Q_0. When a sales tax of t per pack is imposed, the supply curve shifts up to the dashed line S', which lies above the original supply curve by the amount of the tax t. The new equilibrium is at E_1. The tax increases the consumer price and reduces the seller price. It also reduces the equilibrium quantity exchanged.

This upward shift in the supply curve for cigarettes is depicted in Figure 4-8 as the dashed curve, S'. This shift in the supply curve, caused by the tax, will cause a movement *along* the demand curve, reducing the equilibrium quantity.

Consider the situation at the consumer price of $p_0 + t$. Firms will still be willing to sell the original quantity, but households will demand less because the price has risen; there is excess supply and hence pressure for the consumer price to fall.

The new equilibrium after the imposition of the sales tax occurs at the intersection of the original demand curve D with the tax-shifted supply curve S'. At this new equilibrium, E_1, the consumer price rises to p_c (greater than p_0), the seller price falls to p_s (less than p_0), and the equilibrium quantity falls to Q_1.

Note that the quantity demanded *at the consumer price* is equal to the quantity supplied *at the seller price*, a condition that is required for equilibrium. As shown in the figure, compared to the original equilibrium, the consumer price is higher and the seller price is lower, although in each case the change in price is less than the full extent of the sales tax.

After the imposition of a sales tax, the difference between the consumer and seller prices is equal to the tax. In the new equilibrium, the quantity exchanged is less than that exchanged prior to the imposition of the tax.

The role of the relative elasticities of supply and demand in determining the incidence of the sales tax is illustrated in Figure 4-9. In part (i), demand is inelastic relative to supply; as a result, the fall in quantity is quite small, whereas the price paid by consumers rises by almost the full extent of the tax. Because neither the price received by

FIGURE 4-9   Elasticity and the Incidence of an Excise Tax

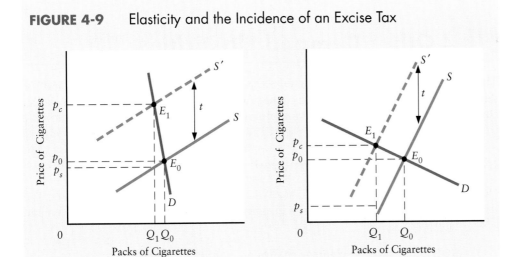

(i) Inelastic demand

(ii) Inelastic supply

The distribution of the burden of a sales tax between consumers and producers depends on the relative elasticities of supply and demand. In both parts of the figure, the initial supply and demand curves are given by S and D; the initial equilibrium is at E_0 with equilibrium price p_0 and quantity Q_0. A tax of t per pack of cigarettes is imposed, causing the supply curve to shift up by the amount of the tax to S'. The new equilibrium is at E_1. The consumer price rises to p_c, the seller price falls to p_s, and the quantity falls to Q_1. Sellers bear little of the burden of the tax in the first case (and consumers bear a lot), whereas consumers bear little of the burden in the second case (and sellers bear a lot).

sellers nor the quantity sold changes very much, sellers bear little of the burden of the tax. In part (ii), supply is inelastic relative to demand; in this case, consumers can more easily substitute away from cigarettes. There is little change in the price, and hence they bear little of the burden of the tax, which falls mostly on suppliers. Notice in Figure 4-9 that the size of the upward shift in supply is the same in the two cases, indicating the same tax in both cases.

When demand is inelastic relative to supply, consumers bear most of the burden of excise taxes. When supply is inelastic relative to demand, producers bear most of the burden.

Now we can examine who really pays for cigarette tax increases (or tax increases on gasoline and alcohol). The demand for cigarettes is inelastic both overall and relative to supply, suggesting that the burden of a cigarette tax is borne more by consumers than by producers. The demand for gasoline is also inelastic, but much more so in the short run than in the long run. (In the long run, drivers can change their driving habits and improve the efficiency of their vehicles, but in the short run such changes are very costly.) The supply of gasoline, given world trade in petroleum and petroleum products, is elastic relative to demand. The relatively inelastic demand and elastic supply imply that the burden of gasoline taxes falls mostly on consumers.

Applying Economic Concepts 4-1 discusses another important example of the issue of tax incidence—this time involving the burden of payroll taxes, such as the premiums that firms and workers pay for employment insurance and the Canada Pension Plan. *Extensions in Theory 4-1* shows how to work through the algebra of demand and supply in the presence of an excise or sales tax.

Practise with Study Guide Chapter 4, Exercise 8.

4.4 **Other Demand Elasticities**

The price of the product is not the only important variable determining demand for that product. Changes in income and changes in the prices of other products also lead to changes in demand, and elasticity is a useful concept in measuring their effects.

Income Elasticity of Demand

income elasticity of demand (η_Y) A measure of the responsiveness of quantity demanded to a change in income.

normal good A good for which quantity demanded rises as income rises—its income elasticity is positive.

inferior good A good for which quantity demanded falls as income rises—its income elasticity is negative.

One of the most important determinants of demand is the income of the customers. The responsiveness of demand to changes in income is termed the **income elasticity of demand** and is symbolized η_Y.

$$\eta_Y = \frac{\text{Percentage change in quantity demanded}}{\text{Percentage change in income}}$$

For most goods, increases in income lead to increases in demand—their income elasticity is positive. These are called **normal goods.** Goods for which demand decreases in response to a rise in income have negative income elasticities and are called **inferior goods.**

The income elasticity of normal goods can be greater than 1 (elastic) or less than 1 (inelastic), depending on whether the percentage change in quantity demanded is greater or less than the percentage change in income that brought it about. It is also common to use the terms *income-elastic* and *income-inelastic* to refer to income elas-

APPLYING ECONOMIC CONCEPTS 4-1
Who Really Pays for Payroll Taxes?

Some social programs in Canada are financed by **payroll taxes**—taxes collected from both firms and workers, computed as a proportion of workers' earnings. For example, the Employment Insurance program (formerly known as Unemployment Insurance) is financed by premiums paid by both firms and workers. The Canada Pension Plan is financed the same way. Who bears the burden of these payroll taxes?

The accompanying figure illustrates a model of the labour market. The figure shows a standard demand-and-supply apparatus except that the axes have been relabelled as "Employment" and "Hourly Wage Rate."* Firms represent the demand for labour services. As the wage falls, it is profitable for firms to hire more workers (and to produce more output). Thus the demand curve for labour is downward sloping. Workers represent the supply of labour services. As the wage rises, workers substitute away from other activities and supply more labour services. Thus the supply curve for labour is upward sloping. The supply curve is shown to be relatively inelastic, in keeping with a considerable amount of empirical evidence showing that the quantity of labour supplied to the economy is quite unresponsive to changes in the wage rate. In the absence of any payroll taxes, the equilibrium wage is w_0 and the equilibrium level of employment is E_0.

As in the analysis of excise taxes, the effect of the payroll tax is to drive a wedge between the wage paid by the firm (w_F) and the wage received by the worker (w_W). With a payroll tax of t dollars per hour, w_F rises above w_0 and w_W falls below w_0. Employment falls from E_0 to E_1. With the relatively inelastic supply curve shown in the figure, however, most of the burden of the tax falls on workers. The lower right-hand bracket shows the amount by which the workers' take-home wage falls. The upper right-hand bracket shows the amount by which the employers' total payment per worker rises. Together, these add up to the payroll tax, shown by the left-hand bracket. Were the supply curve *perfectly* inelastic, the entire burden of the tax would fall on workers.

The burden of payroll taxes would be shared more by firms if the supply of labour were more elastic (or if the demand were less elastic). But, as is the case with excise taxes that we discussed in the text, it is the shapes of the supply and demand curves that determine who bears the burden of payroll taxes.

Quite apart from how the burden of the tax is apportioned between workers and firms, the figure also shows why many economic commentators refer to payroll taxes as "job killers"—by increasing the total cost that firms must pay for each unit of labour services, payroll taxes naturally lead firms to hire fewer workers.

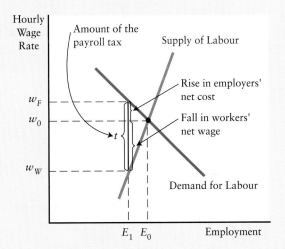

---

* This analysis assumes that the labour market is reasonably competitive—meaning that there are large numbers of both workers and firms, none of which have the power to influence the market wage. Though this is usually a good description of the labour market, there are some situations that are not well modelled by a simple supply-and-demand apparatus. We discuss the role of labour unions, for example, in Chapter 14.

ticities of greater or less than 1. (See *Extensions in Theory 4-2* for a summary of the different elasticity concepts.)

The reaction of demand to changes in income is extremely important. We know that in most Western countries during the twentieth century, economic growth caused the level of income to double every 20 to 30 years. This rise in income was shared to

EXTENSIONS IN THEORY 4-1

The Algebra of Tax Incidence

It is straightforward to show the burden of an excise tax using algebra to solve for the equilibrium price and quantity. Suppose the demand-and-supply model of the market is given by the following two linear equations.

(1) $Q^D = a - bp_c$ Demand curve

(2) $Q^S = c + dp_s$ Supply curve

where Q^D is quantity demanded at the consumer price, p_c, and Q^S is quantity supplied at the seller price, p_s. The presence of an excise tax of t dollars per unit implies that the price received by the seller, p_s, must be t dollars less than the price paid by the consumer, p_c:

(3) $p_s = p_c - t$

We can substitute equation (3) into (2) to express the supply curve in terms of the consumer price:

(4) $Q^S = c + d(p_c - t)$

or

(5) $Q^S = c - dt + dp_c$

When the market is in equilibrium, $Q^D = Q^S$, and so we can equate Q^D from equation (1) with Q^S from equation (5). This gives us

$$a - bp_c = c - dt + dp_c$$

This equation allows us to solve for the equilibrium consumer price, p_c^*.

$$p_c^* = \frac{a - c}{b + d} + \frac{d}{b + d}t$$

This solution for p_c^* can now be substituted back into the demand curve, equation (1), to solve for the equilibrium quantity, Q^*.

$$Q^* = a - bp_c^* = a - \frac{b(a - c + dt)}{b + d}$$

$$\rightarrow \quad Q^* = \frac{ad + bc}{b + d} - \frac{bd}{b + d}t$$

Now consider these solutions for p_c^* and Q^* in the case where there is no tax, $t = 0$. This exercise reveals

what we already know from Figures 4-8 and 4-9—that the excise tax increases the equilibrium consumer price and reduces the equilibrium quantity from the levels that we would observe in the absence of the excise tax.

Who bears the burden of the excise tax? To answer this question, we must examine both the equilibrium consumer and seller prices, p_c^* and p_s^*. We saw above that

(6) $p_c^* = \dfrac{a - c}{b + d} + \dfrac{d}{b + d}t$

and we also know that $p_c^* - t = p_s^*$. It follows that

(7) $p_s^* = \dfrac{a - c}{b + d} + \dfrac{d}{b + d}t - t$

$$= \frac{a - c}{b + d} - \frac{b}{b + d}t$$

Note that when $t = 0$, the equilibrium price in this model, for both consumers and sellers, is

$$p^* = \frac{a - c}{b + d}$$

We can therefore express the equilibrium consumer and seller prices in the presence of an excise tax in terms of p^*:

(8) $p_c^* = p^* + \dfrac{d}{b + d}t$

(9) $p_s^* = p^* - \dfrac{b}{b + d}t$

These solutions for p_c^* and p_s^* show how the burden of the excise tax depends on the slopes of the demand and supply curves. For example, consider a small value of d which reflects a relatively steep supply curve. The small value of d means that p_c^* is only a little above p^*, whereas p_s^* is considerably below p^*; thus, when the supply curve is relatively steep, sellers bear more of the burden of the tax. In contrast, consider a small value of b, which reflects a relatively steep demand curve. The small value of b means that p_s^* is only a little below p^*, but p_c^* is considerably above p^*; thus consumers bear more of the burden of the tax when the demand curve is relatively steep.

Practise with Study Guide Chapter 4, Extension Exercise E3.

some extent by most citizens. As they found their incomes increasing, they increased their demands for most products, but the demands for some products, such as food and basic clothing, did not increase as much as the demands for other products. In developing countries the demand for durable goods is increasing most rapidly as household incomes rise, while in North America and Western Europe, the demand for services has risen most rapidly. The uneven impact of the growth of income on the demands for different products has important economic effects, which are studied at several points in this book.

What Determines Income Elasticity of Demand?

The variations in income elasticities shown in Table 4-4 suggest that the more necessary a product, the lower its income elasticity. Food as a whole has an income elasticity of 0.2, consumer durables of 1.8. In Canada, starchy roots such as potatoes are inferior goods; their quantity demanded falls as income rises.

The more necessary is an item in the consumption pattern of consumers, the lower is its income elasticity.

Income elasticities for any one product also vary with the level of a consumer's income. When incomes are low, consumers may eat almost no green vegetables and consume lots of starchy foods such as bread and potatoes; when incomes are higher, they may eat cheap cuts of meat and more green vegetables along with their bread and potatoes; when incomes are higher still, they are likely to eat higher quality and prepared foods of a wide variety.

The distinction between luxuries and necessities helps to explain differences in income elasticities. The case of restaurant meals is one example. Such meals are almost always more expensive, calorie for calorie, than meals prepared at home. It would thus be expected that at lower incomes, restaurant meals would be regarded as an expensive luxury but that the demand for them would expand substantially as consumers became richer. This is actually what happens.

TABLE 4-4   Some Estimated Income Elasticities of Demand

Inferior goods (η_Y less than zero)	
Whole milk	−0.5
Pig products	−0.2
Starchy roots	−0.2
Inelastic normal goods (η_Y between zero and 1)	
Wine (France)	0.1
All food	0.2
Poultry	0.3
Elastic normal goods (η_Y greater than 1)	
Gasoline	1.1
Wine	1.4
Consumer durables	1.8
Poultry (Sri Lanka)	2.0
Restaurant meals (U.K.)	2.4

Income elasticities vary widely across commodities and sometimes across countries. The basic source of food estimates by country is the Food and Agriculture Organization of the United Nations, but many individual studies have been made. (For the United States except where noted.)

What is true of individual consumers is also true of countries. Empirical studies show that for different countries at comparable stages of economic development, income elasticities are similar. However, the countries of the world are at various stages of economic development and thus have widely different income elasticities for the same products. Notice in Table 4-4 the different income elasticities of poultry in the United States, where it is a standard item of consumption, and in Sri Lanka, where it is a luxury good.

Another example of the luxury–necessity distinction is shown in Table 4-4 by the different income elasticities for wine in France and the United States. In France, wine is a much more basic part of the meal than is the case in the United States, where wine is regarded as more of a luxury. As a result, increases in income lead to much smaller increases in the demand for wine in France than in the United States.

Cross Elasticity of Demand

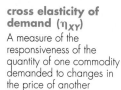

cross elasticity of demand (η_{XY})
A measure of the responsiveness of the quantity of one commodity demanded to changes in the price of another commodity.

The responsiveness of demand to changes in the price of *another* product is called the **cross elasticity of demand.** It is denoted η_{XY} and defined as follows:

$$\eta_{XY} = \frac{\text{Percentage change in quantity demanded of good } X}{\text{Percentage change in price of good } Y}$$

The change in the price of good Y causes the *demand curve* for good X to shift. If X and Y are substitutes, an increase in the price of Y leads to an increase in the demand for X. If X and Y are complements, an increase in the price of Y leads to a reduction in demand for X. In either case, we are holding the price of X constant. We therefore measure the change in the quantity demanded of X (at its unchanged price) by measuring the shift of the demand curve for X.

Cross elasticity can vary from minus infinity to plus infinity. Complementary products, such as cars and gasoline, have negative cross elasticities. A large rise in the price of gasoline will lead to a decline in the demand for cars, as some people

EXTENSIONS IN THEORY 4-2

The Terminology of Elasticity

Term	Numerical Measure of Elasticity	Verbal Description
A. Price elasticity of demand (supply)		
Perfectly or completely inelastic	Zero	Quantity demanded (supplied) does not change as price changes.
Inelastic	Between zero and 1	Quantity demanded (supplied) changes by a smaller percentage than does price.
Unit elastic	One	Quantity demanded (supplied) changes by exactly the same percentage as does price.
Elastic	Greater than 1, but less than infinity	Quantity demanded (supplied) changes by a larger percentage than does price.
Perfectly, completely, or infinitely elastic	Infinity	Purchasers (sellers) are prepared to buy (sell) all they can at some price and none at all at a higher (lower) price.
B. Income elasticity of demand		
Inferior good	Negative	Quantity demanded decreases as income increases.
Normal good	Positive	Quantity demanded increases as income increases:
Income-inelastic	Less than 1	Less than in proportion to income increase
Income-elastic	Greater than 1	More than in proportion to income increase
C. Cross elasticity of demand		
Substitute	Positive	Price increase of a substitute leads to an increase in quantity demanded of this good.
Complement	Negative	Price increase of a complement leads to a decrease in quantity demanded of this good.

decide to do without a car and others decide not to buy an additional car. Substitute products, such as cars and public transport, have positive cross elasticities. A large rise in the price of cars (relative to public transport) will lead to a rise in the demand for public transport as some people shift from cars to public transport. (See *Extensions in Theory 4-2* for a summary of elasticity terminology.)

The positive or negative signs of cross elasticities tell us whether goods are substitutes or complements.

Measures of cross elasticity sometimes prove helpful in defining whether producers of similar products are in competition with each other. For example, glass bottles and tin cans have a high cross elasticity of demand. The producer of bottles is thus in competition with the producer of cans. If the bottle company raises its price, it will lose substantial sales to the can producer. In contrast, men's shoes and women's shoes have a low cross elasticity and thus a producer of men's shoes is not in close competition with a producer of women's shoes. If the former raises its price, it will not lose many sales to the latter. Knowledge of cross elasticity can be important in matters of *competition policy* in which the issue is whether a firm in one industry is or is not competing with firms in another industry. We discuss competition policy in more detail in Chapter 12.

Substitute products have a positive cross elasticity; an increase in the price of one leads to an increase in demand for the other.

Practise with Study Guide Chapter 4, Extension Exercise E1.

S U M M A R Y

4.1 **Price Elasticity of Demand**

- *Price elasticity of demand* is a measure of the extent to which the quantity demanded of a product responds to a change in its price. Represented by the symbol η, it is defined as

$$\eta = \frac{\text{Percentage change in quantity demanded}}{\text{Percentage change in price}}$$

  The percentage changes are usually calculated as the change divided by the *average* value. Elasticity is defined to be a positive number, and it can vary from zero to infinity.

- When elasticity is less than 1, demand is *inelastic*—the percentage change in quantity demanded is less than the percentage change in price. When elasticity exceeds 1, demand is *elastic*—the percentage change in quantity demanded is greater than the percentage change in price.

- The main determinant of price elasticity of demand is the availability of substitutes for the product. Any one of a group of close substitutes will have a more elastic demand than will the group as a whole.

- Items that have few substitutes in the short run tend to develop many substitutes when consumers and producers have time to adapt. Therefore, demand is more elastic in the long run than in the short run.

- Elasticity and total expenditure are related in the following way: If elasticity is less than 1, total expenditure is positively related with price; if elasticity is greater than 1, total expenditure is negatively related with price; and if elasticity is 1, total expenditure does not change as price changes.

4.2 **Price Elasticity of Supply**

- *Elasticity of supply* measures the extent to which the quantity supplied of some product changes when the price of that product changes. Represented by the symbol η_S, it is defined as

$$\eta_S = \frac{\text{Percentage change in quantity supplied}}{\text{Percentage change in price}}$$

- Supply tends to be more elastic in the long run than in the short run because it usually takes time for producers to alter their productive capacity in response to price changes.

4.3 **An Important Example Where Elasticity Matters**   LO 3

- The distribution of the burden of a sales tax between consumers and producers depends on the relative elasticities of the supply of and the demand for the product.

- The less elastic that demand is relative to supply, the more of the burden of an excise tax falls on the consumers. The more elastic demand is relative to supply, the more of the burden of an excise tax falls on producers.

4.4 **Other Demand Elasticities**   LO 4 5

- *Income elasticity of demand* is a measure of the extent to which the quantity demanded of some product changes as income changes. Represented by the symbol η_Y, it is defined as

$$\eta_Y = \frac{\text{Percentage change in quantity demanded}}{\text{Percentage change in income}}$$

The income elasticity of demand for a product will usually change as income varies. For example, a product that has a high income elasticity at a low income (because increases in income bring it within reach of the typical household) may have a low or negative income elasticity at higher incomes.

- *Cross elasticity of demand* is a measure of the extent to which the quantity demanded of one product changes when the price of a different product changes. Represented by the symbol η_{XY}, it is defined as

$$\eta_{XY} = \frac{\text{Percentage change in quantity demanded of good } X}{\text{Percentage change in price of good } Y}$$

It is used to define products that are substitutes for one another (positive cross elasticity) and products that are complements for one another (negative cross elasticity).

K E Y   C O N C E P T S

Price elasticity of demand
Inelastic and perfectly inelastic demand
Elastic and infinitely elastic demand
Relationship between demand elasticity and total expenditure
Elasticity of supply

Short-run and long-run responses to shifts in demand and supply
The burden of a sales (or excise) tax
Consumer price and seller price
Income elasticity of demand

Income-elastic and income-inelastic demands
Normal goods and inferior goods
Cross elasticity of demand
Substitutes and complements

S T U D Y   E X E R C I S E S

1. Fill in the blanks to make the following statements correct.

   a. When a 10-percent change in the price of a good brings about a 20-percent change in its quantity demanded, the price elasticity of demand is _____. We can say that demand for this good is _____.

   b. When a 10-percent change in the price of a good brings about a 4-percent change in its quantity demanded, the price elasticity of demand is _____. We can say that demand for this good is _____.

   c. When a 10-percent change in the price of a good brings about a 10-percent change in its quantity demanded, the price elasticity of demand is _____. We can say that demand for this good is _____.

2. A hypothetical demand schedule for comic books in a small town is provided below.

   a. Fill in the table and calculate the price elasticity of demand over each price range. Be sure to use *average* prices and quantities when computing the percentage changes.

Demand Schedule for Comic Books

Price	Quantity Demanded	Total Expenditure	Percent Change in Price	Percent Change in Quantity Demanded	Elasticity of Demand
$11	1	_____			
9	3	_____	_____	_____	_____
7	5	_____	_____	_____	_____
5	7	_____	_____	_____	_____
3	9	_____	_____	_____	_____
1	11	_____	_____	_____	_____

b. Plot the demand curve and show the elasticities over the different ranges of the curve.

c. Explain why demand is more elastic at the higher prices.

3. Suppose that the market for frozen orange juice is in equilibrium at a price of $1.00 per can and a quantity of 4200 cans per month. Now suppose that at a price of $1.50 per can, quantity demanded falls to 3000 cans per month and quantity supplied increases to 4500 cans per month.

a. Draw the appropriate diagram for this market.

b. Calculate the price elasticity of demand for frozen orange juice between the prices of $1.00 and $1.50. Is the demand elastic or inelastic?

c. Calculate the elasticity of supply for frozen orange juice between the prices of $1.00 and $1.50. Is the supply elastic or inelastic?

d. Explain in general what factors would affect the elasticity of demand for frozen orange juice.

e. Explain in general what factors would affect the elasticity of supply of frozen orange juice.

4. What would you predict about the *relative* price elasticity of demand for each of the following items? Explain your reasoning.

a. food
b. vegetables
c. leafy vegetables
d. leafy vegetables sold at your local supermarket
e. leafy vegetables sold at your local supermarket on Wednesdays

5. Suppose a stamp collector buys the only two existing copies of a stamp at an auction. After the purchase, the collector goes to the front of the room and burns one of the stamps in front of the shocked audience. What must the collector believe in order for this to be a wealth-maximizing action? Explain with a demand-and-supply diagram.

6. For each of the following events, state the relevant elasticity concept. Then compute the measure of elasticity, using average prices and quantities in your calculations. In all cases, assume that these are *ceteris paribus* changes.

a. When the price of theatre tickets is reduced from $14.00 to $11.00, ticket sales increase from 1200 to 1350.

b. As average household income in Canada increases by 10 percent, annual sales of Toyota Camrys increase from 56 000 to 67 000.

c. After a major failure of Brazil's coffee crop sent coffee prices up from $3.00 per kilogram to $4.80 per kilogram, sales of tea in Canada increased from 7500 kg per month to 8000 kg per month.

d. An increase in the world demand for pulp (used in producing newsprint) increases the price by 14 percent. Annual Canadian production increases from 8 million tonnes to 11 million tonnes.

7. The following table shows the demand schedule for denim jeans.

	Price (per unit)	Quantity Demanded (per year)	Total Expenditure
A	$30	400 000	
B	35	380 000	
C	40	350 000	
D	45	320 000	
E	50	300 000	
F	55	260 000	
G	60	230 000	
H	65	190 000	

a. Compute total expenditure for each row in the table.

b. Plot the demand curve and the total expenditure curve.

c. Compute the price elasticities of demand between points A and B, B and C, C and D, and so on.

d. Over what range of prices is the demand for denim jeans elastic? Explain.

e. Over what range of prices is the demand for denim jeans inelastic? Explain.

8. Consider the following straight-line supply curves. In each case, p is the price (measured in dollars per unit) and Q^S is the quantity supplied of the product (measured in thousands of units per month).

i) $p = 2Q^S$
ii) $p = 4Q^S$
iii) $p = 5Q^S$
iv) $p = 10Q^S$

a. Plot each supply curve on a scale diagram. In each case, plot point *A* (which corresponds to price equal to $20) and point *B* (which corresponds to price equal to $40).

b. For each supply curve, compute the price elasticity of supply between points *A* and *B*.

c. Explain why the *slope* of a supply curve is not the same as the *elasticity* of supply.

9. This is a challenging question intended for those students who like mathematics. It will help you work through the issue of tax incidence. (See *Extensions in Theory 4-1* if you get stuck!)

Consider the market for gasoline. Suppose the market demand and supply curves are as given below. In each case, quantity refers to millions of litres of gasoline per month; price is the price per litre (in cents).

$$\text{Demand: } p = 80 - 5Q^D$$
$$\text{Supply: } p = 24 + 2Q^S$$

a. Plot the demand and supply curves on a scale diagram.

b. Compute the equilibrium price and quantity.

c. Now suppose the government imposes a tax of 14 cents per litre. Show how this affects the market equilibrium. What is the new "consumer price" and what is the new "producer price"?

d. Compute the total revenue raised by the gasoline tax. What share of this tax revenue is "paid" by consumers, and what share is "paid" by producers? (Hint: if the consumer price were unchanged from the pre-tax equilibrium, we would say that consumers pay none of the tax.)

DISCUSSION QUESTIONS

1. From the following quotations, what, if anything, can you conclude about elasticity of demand?

   a. "Good weather resulted in record wheat harvests and sent wheat prices tumbling. The result has been disastrous for many wheat farmers."

   b. "Ridership always went up when bus fares came down, but the increased patronage never was enough to prevent a decrease in overall revenue."

   c. "As the price of CD players fell, producers found their revenues soaring."

   d. "Coffee to me is an essential good—I've just gotta have it no matter what the price."

   e. "The soaring price of condominiums does little to curb the strong demand in Vancouver."

2. Home computers were a leader in sales appeal through much of the 1990s. But per capita sales are much lower in Mexico than in Canada, and lower in Newfoundland and Labrador than in Alberta. Manufacturers are puzzled by the big differences. Can you offer an explanation in terms of elasticity?

3. What elasticity measure or measures would be useful in answering the following questions?

   a. Will cheaper transport into the central city help to keep downtown shopping centres profitable?

   b. Will raising the bulk postage rate increase or decrease the revenues for Canada Post?

   c. Are producers of toothpaste and mouthwash in competition with each other?

   d. What effect will rising gasoline prices have on the sale of cars that use propane gas?

4. Interpret the following statements in terms of the relevant elasticity concept.

   a. "As fuel for tractors has become more expensive, many farmers have shifted from plowing their fields to no-till farming. No-till acreage increased dramatically in the past 20 years."

   a. "Fertilizer makers brace for dismal year as fertilizer prices soar."

   c. "When farmers are hurting, small towns feel the pain."

   d. "The development of the Hibernia oil field may bring temporary prosperity to Newfoundland and Labrador merchants."

5. When the New York City Opera faced a growing deficit, it cut its ticket prices by 20 percent, hoping to attract more customers. At the same time, the New York Transit Authority raised subway fares to reduce its growing deficit. Was one of these two opposite approaches to reducing a deficit necessarily wrong?

More Details About Demand Elasticity

The definition of elasticity used in the text may be written symbolically in the following form:[1]

$$\eta = \frac{\Delta Q}{\text{Average } Q} \div \frac{\Delta p}{\text{Average } p}$$

where the averages are over the range, or *arc*, of the demand curve being considered. Rearranging terms, we can write

$$\eta = \frac{\Delta Q}{\Delta p} \times \frac{\text{Average } p}{\text{Average } Q}$$

This is called *arc elasticity*, and it measures the average responsiveness of quantity to price over an interval of the demand curve.

Most theoretical treatments use a slightly different concept called *point elasticity*. This is the measure of responsiveness of quantity demanded to price *at a particular point* on the demand curve. The precise definition of point elasticity uses the concept of a derivative, which is drawn from differential calculus.

In this appendix, we first study arc elasticity, which we can regard as an approximation of point elasticity. Then we study point elasticity.

Before proceeding, we should note one further change. In the text of Chapter 4, we reported our price elasticities as positive values and thus implicitly multiplied all our calculations by −1. In theoretical work, it is more convenient to retain the concept's natural sign. Hence, normal demand elasticities have negative signs, and statements about "more" or "less" elasticity refer to the absolute, not the algebraic, value of demand elasticity.

---

[1]The following notation is used throughout this appendix.

$\eta \equiv$ elasticity of demand
$Q \equiv$ initial quantity
$\Delta Q \equiv$ change in quantity
$p \equiv$ initial price
$\Delta p \equiv$ change in price

4A.1 Arc Elasticity as an Approximation of Point Elasticity

Point elasticity is a precise measure of elasticity at a particular price–quantity point. Without using calculus, however, we can only approximate this point elasticity. We do this by measuring the responsiveness of quantity demanded to a change in price *over a small range* of the demand curve, starting from that price–quantity point. For example, in Figure 4A-1, we can measure the elasticity at point 1 by the responsiveness of quantity demanded to a change in price that takes price and quantity from point 1 to point 2. The algebraic formula for this elasticity concept is

$$\eta = \frac{\Delta Q}{\Delta p} \times \frac{p}{Q} \qquad (4A\text{-}1)$$

This is similar to the definition of arc elasticity above except that, because elasticity is being measured at a point, the p and Q corresponding to that point are used (rather than the average p and Q over an arc of the curve).

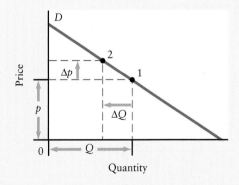

FIGURE 4A-1 A Straight-Line Demand Curve

Because p/Q varies with $\Delta Q/\Delta p$ constant, the elasticity varies along this demand curve; it is high at the left and low at the right.

Equation 4A-1 splits elasticity into two parts. The first part, $\Delta Q/\Delta p$, is related to the *slope* of the demand curve. In fact, it is the *reciprocal* of the slope. The second part, p/Q, is related to the *point* on the curve at which the measurment is made.

Although point elasticity of demand refers to a price–quantity point on the demand curve, the first term in Equation 4A-1 still refers to changes over an arc of the curve. This is the part of the formula that involves approximation, and, as we shall see, it has some unsatisfactory results. Nonetheless, we can derive some interesting results by using this formula as long as we confine ourselves to straight-line demand curves.

The elasticity of a downward-sloping straight-line demand curve varies from zero at the quantity axis to infinity at the price axis.

First, notice that because a straight line has a constant slope, the ratio $\Delta p/\Delta Q$ is the same everywhere on the line. Therefore, its reciprocal, $\Delta Q/\Delta p,$ must also be constant. The changes in η can now be inferred by inspecting the ratio p/Q. Where the line cuts the quantity axis, price is zero, so the ratio p/Q is zero; thus $\eta = 0$. Moving up the line, p rises and Q falls, so the ratio p/Q rises; thus elasticity rises. Approaching the top of the line, Q approaches zero, so the ratio becomes very large. Thus elasticity increases without limit as the price axis is approached.

Where there are two straight-line demand curves of the same slope, the one farther from the origin is less elastic at each price than the one closer to the origin.

Figure 4A-2 shows two parallel straight-line demand curves. Compare the elasticities of the two curves at any price, say, p_0. Because the curves are parallel, the ratio $\Delta Q/\Delta p$ is the same on both curves. Because elasticities at the same price are being compared on both curves, p is the same, and the only factor left to vary is Q. On the curve farther from the origin, quantity is larger (i.e., $Q_1 > Q_0$) and hence p_0/Q_1 is smaller than p_0/Q_0; thus η is smaller.

It follows that parallel shifts of a straight-line demand curve reduce elasticity (at each price) when the line shifts outward and increase elasticity when the line shifts inward.

For two intersecting straight-line demand curves, the steeper curve is the less elastic.

In Figure 4A-3, there are two intersecting curves. At the point of intersection, p and Q are common to both curves, and hence the ratio p/Q is the same. Therefore, η varies only with $\Delta Q/\Delta p$. On the steeper curve, $\Delta Q/\Delta p$ is smaller than on the flatter curve, so elasticity is lower.

FIGURE 4A-2   Two Parallel Straight-Line Demand Curves

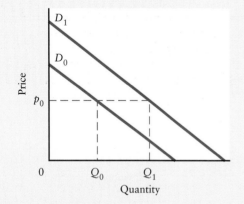

For any given price, the quantities are different on these two parallel curves; thus the elasticities are different, being higher on D_0 than on D_1.

FIGURE 4A-3   Two Intersecting Straight-Line Demand Curves

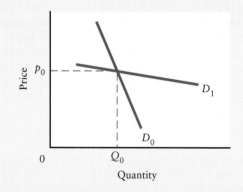

Elasticities are different at the point of intersection of these demand curves because the slopes are different, being higher on D_0 than on D_1. Therefore, D_1 is more elastic than D_0 at p_0.

FIGURE 4A-4   Two Straight-Line Demand Curves from the Same Price Intercept

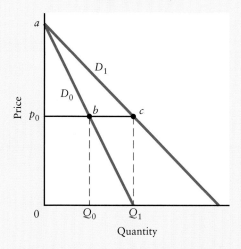

The elasticity is the same on D_0 and D_1 at any given price. This situation occurs because the steeper slope of D_0 is exactly offset by the smaller quantity demanded at any price.

FIGURE 4A-5   Point Elasticity of Demand Measured by the Approximate Formula

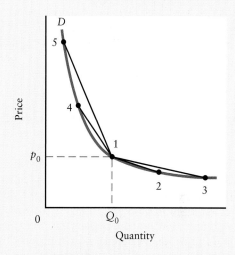

When the approximation of $\eta = (\Delta Q/\Delta p) \times (p/Q)$ is used, many elasticities are measured from point 1 because the slope of the chord between point 1 and every other point on the curve varies.

If the slope of a straight-line demand curve changes while the price intercept remains constant, elasticity at any given price is unchanged.

This case is interesting for at least two reasons. First, when more customers having similar tastes to those already in the market enter the market, the demand curve pivots outward in this way. Second, when more firms enter a market that is shared proportionally among all firms, each firm's demand curve shifts inward in this way.

Consider in Figure 4A-4 the elasticities at point b on demand curve D_0 and at point c on demand curve D_1. We shall focus on the two triangles abp_0 on D_0 and acp_0 on D_1 formed by the two straight-line demand curves emanating from point a and by the price p_0. The price p_0 is the line segment $0p_0$. The quantities Q_0 and Q_1 are the line segments p_0b and p_0c, respectively. The slope of D_0 is $\Delta p/\Delta Q = ap_0/p_0b$, and the slope of D_1 is $\Delta p/\Delta Q = ap_0/p_0c$. From Equation 4A-1 we can represent the elasticities of D_0 and D_1 at the points b and c, respectively, as

$$\eta \text{ at point } b = (p_0b/ap_0) \times (0p_0/p_0b) = (0p_0/ap_0)$$
$$\eta \text{ at point } c = (p_0c/ap_0) \times (0p_0/p_0c) = (0p_0/ap_0)$$

Because the distance corresponding to the quantity demanded at p_0 appears in both the numerator and the denominator and thus cancels out, the two values of the elasticity are the same. Put differently, if the straight-line demand curve D_0 is twice as steep as D_1, it has half the quantity demanded at p_0. Therefore, in Equation 4A-1 the steeper slope (a smaller ΔQ for the same Δp) is exactly offset by the smaller quantity demanded (a smaller Q for the same p).

The demand elasticity measured from any point, according to Equation 4A-1, depends on the direction and magnitude of the change in price and quantity.

Except for a straight line (for which the slope does not change), the ratio $\Delta Q/\Delta p$ will not be the same over different ranges of a curve. Figure 4A-5 shows a demand curve that is not a straight line. To measure the elasticity from point 1, the ratio $\Delta Q/\Delta p$—and thus η—will vary according to the size and the direction of the price change. This result is very inconvenient; we can avoid it by using the concept of point elasticity in its exact form.

4A.2 **The Precise Definition of Point Elasticity**

To measure the point elasticity *exactly*, it is necessary to know the reaction of quantity to a change in price *at that point*, not over a range of the curve.

The reaction of quantity to price change at a point is called dQ/dp, and this is defined as the reciprocal of the slope of the straight line tangent to the demand curve at the point in question. In Figure 4A-6, the elasticity of demand at point 1 is the ratio p/Q (as it has been in all previous measures), now multiplied by the ratio of $\Delta Q/\Delta p$ measured along the straight line T, tangent to the curve at point 1, that is, by dQ/dp. Thus the exact definition of point elasticity is

$$\eta = \frac{dQ}{dp} \times \frac{p}{Q} \qquad (4A\text{-}2)$$

The ratio dQ/dp, as defined, is in fact the differential calculus concept of the *derivative* of quantity with respect to price.

This definition of point elasticity is the one normally used in economic theory. Equation 4A-1 is mathematically only an approximation of this expression. In Figure 4A-6, the measure of arc elasticity will come closer to the measure of point elasticity as a smaller

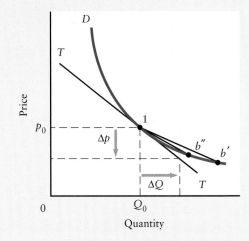

FIGURE 4A-6   Point Elasticity of Demand Measured by the Exact Formula

When the exact definition $\eta = (dQ/dp) \times (p/Q)$ is used, only one elasticity is measured from point 1 because there is only one tangent to the demand curve at that point.

price change is used to calculate the arc elasticity. The $\Delta Q/\Delta p$ in Equation 4A-1 is the reciprocal of the slope of the chord connecting the two points being compared. As the chord becomes shorter, its slope gets closer to that of the tangent T. (Compare the chords connecting point 1 to b' and b'' in Figure 4A-6.) Thus the error in using Equation 4A-1 as an approximation of Equation 4A-2 tends to diminish as the size of Δp diminishes.

An Introduction to Macroeconomics

What is macroeconomics all about? What do we mean when we talk about national income, and what is the difference (if any) between national income and national output? What is unemployment, and is it a problem? Is it just a coincidence that periods of high inflation are also periods of high interest rates? How is Canada's exchange rate related to Canada's trade balance with the rest of the world? These are some of the questions that dominate macroeconomics.

Chapter 19 is an overview chapter that introduces all of the major issues discussed in Chapters 21 through 35. One of the themes of this chapter (and of macroeconomics itself) is the distinction between trends and cycles. This reflects a difference between the short run—in which our focus is on the cyclical fluctuations in macroeconomic variables—and the long run—in which our primary focus is on the trends in those same variables.

Chapter 20 explains how Gross Domestic Product (GDP) measures the value of national income, national output and national expenditure. The important distinction between real and nominal national income helps to explain why measured national income can rise even though no more goods are being produced (the answer has something to do with inflation). Finally, we examine some of the things that national income does not measure. Illegal activities, non-market activities, and economic "bads" (such as pollution) are just some of the omissions from measures of national income.

What Macroeconomics Is All About

Ⓛ LEARNING OBJECTIVES

❶ Explain the meaning and importance of the key macroeconomic variables, including national income, unemployment, inflation, interest rates, exchange rates, and trade flows.

❷ View most macroeconomic issues as being about either long-run trends or short-run fluctuations, and see that government policy is relevant for both.

Turn on the evening news or read your local newspaper, and you will likely hear talk of unemployment, inflation, recession, changes in exchange rates, and productivity growth. Almost everyone cares about economic issues. Workers are anxious to avoid the unemployment that comes with recessions and to share in the rising income that is brought about by economic growth. Firms are concerned about how interest rates, recession, and foreign competition affect their profits. Consumers want to know how changes in interest rates affect mortgage payments and how changes in exchange rates affect the prices of the goods they purchase.

Macroeconomics is the study of how the economy behaves in broad outline without dwelling on much of its interesting but sometimes confusing detail. **Macroeconomics** is concerned with the behaviour of economic *aggregates*, such as total output, total investment, total exports, and the price level, and with how government policy may influence these aggregates. These aggregates result from activities in many different markets and from the combined behaviour of millions of different decision makers.

We know perfectly well that an economy producing a lot of wheat and few computers is different from one producing many computers but little wheat. We also know that an economy with cheap wheat and expensive computers is different from one with cheap computers and expensive wheat. Studying aggregates alone may cause us to miss these important differences, but it focuses our attention on some important issues for the economy as a whole.

In return for suppressing some valuable detail, studying economic aggregates allows us to view the big picture. When aggregate output rises, the output of many commodities and the incomes of many people rise with it. When the price level rises, many people in the economy are forced to make adjustments. When the unemployment rate rises, many workers suffer reductions in their incomes. Such movements in economic aggregates matter for most individuals because they influence the health of the industries in which they work and the prices of the goods that they purchase. This is why macroeconomic issues get airtime on the evening news, and it is one of the important reasons why we study macroeconomics.

macroeconomics
The study of the determination of economic aggregates, such as total output, total employment, the price level, and the rate of economic growth, and of how government policy may influence these aggregates.

It will become clear as we proceed through this chapter (and later ones) that macroeconomists have two different views of the economy. They think about the *short-run* behaviour of macroeconomic variables, such as output, employment, and inflation, and about how government policy can influence these variables. This is largely the study of *business cycles*. They also think about the *long-run* behaviour of the same variables, especially the long-run path of aggregate output. This is the study of *economic growth* and is concerned with explaining how technological change occurs and how our living standards continue to increase over long periods of time.

A full understanding of macroeconomics requires understanding the nature of business cycles as well as the nature of long-run economic growth.

▌ 19.1 Key Macroeconomic Variables

In this chapter, we discuss several important macroeconomic variables, with an emphasis on what they mean and why they matter for our well-being. Here and in Chapter 20 we also explain how the key macroeconomic variables are measured. The remainder of this book is about the causes and consequences of changes in each of these variables, the many ways in which they interact, and the effects they have on our well-being.

Output and Income

The most comprehensive measure of a nation's overall level of economic activity is the value of its total production of goods and services, called *national product.*

One of the most important ideas in economics is that the production of output generates income.

As a matter of convention, economists define their terms so that, for the nation as a whole, all of the value that is produced ultimately belongs to someone in the form of an income claim on that value. For example, if a firm produces $100 worth of ice cream, that $100 ultimately represents income for the firm's workers, the firm's suppliers of material inputs, or the firm's owners. Thus, the national product is *by definition* equal to national income.

There are several related measures of a nation's total output and total income. Their various definitions, and the relationships among them, are discussed in detail in the next chapter. In this chapter, we use the generic term *national income* to refer to both the value of total output and the value of the income claims generated by the production of that output.

Aggregating Total Output

To measure total output, quantities of many different goods are *aggregated*. To construct such totals, we add up the *values* of the different products. We cannot add tonnes of steel to loaves of bread, but we can add the money value of steel production to the money value of bread production. Hence by multiplying the physical output of a good by its price per unit and then summing this value for each good produced, we can calculate the quantity of total output *measured in dollars*.

This value of total output gives the money value of national output, usually called **nominal national income**. A change in this measure can be caused by a change in

nominal national income   Total national income measured in current dollars. Also called current-dollar national income.

either the physical quantities or the prices on which it is based. To determine the extent to which any change is due to quantities or to prices, economists calculate **real national income.** This measures the value of individual outputs not at current prices but at a set of prices that prevailed in some base period.

real national income
National income measured in constant (base-period) dollars. It changes only when quantities change.

Nominal national income is often referred to as *current-dollar national income.* Real national income is often called *constant-dollar national income.* Denoted by the symbol Y, real national income tells us the value of current output measured at constant prices—the sum of the quantities valued at prices that prevailed in the base period. Since prices are held constant when computing real national income, changes in real national income reflect *only* changes in quantities. Comparing real national incomes of different years therefore provides a measure of the change in real output that has occurred during the intervening period.

Since our interest is primarily the *real* output of goods and services, we shall use the terms national income and national output to refer to *real* national income unless otherwise specified.

To see the most recent values for most of the macroeconomic variables discussed in this chapter, go to Statistics Canada's website: www.statcan.ca. Click on "Canadian Statistics" and then "Latest Indicators."

National Income: Recent History

One of the most commonly used measures of national income is called *gross domestic product (GDP).* GDP can be measured in either real or nominal terms; we focus here on real GDP. The details of its calculation will be discussed in Chapter 20.

Part (i) of Figure 19-1 shows real national income produced by the Canadian economy over the past 40 years; part (ii) shows its annual percentage change for the same period. The GDP series in part (i) shows two kinds of movement. The major move-

FIGURE 19-1 Growth and Fluctuations in Real GDP, 1962–2002

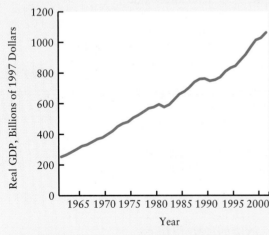

(i) Real GDP

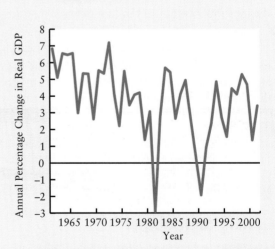

(ii) Annual growth rate of real GDP

Real GDP measures the quantity of total output produced by the nation's economy over the period of a year. Real GDP is plotted in part (i). It has risen steadily since 1962, with only a few interruptions. This demonstrates the long-term growth of the Canadian economy. Short-term fluctuations are obscured by the long-term trend in part (i) but are highlighted in part (ii). The growth rate fluctuates considerably from year to year. The long-term upward trend of real GDP shows up in part (i) because most of the observations in part (ii) are positive.

(*Source:* These data are from Statistics Canada's CANSIM database, Series V3862685. Current data are available at www.statcan.ca. Go to "Canadian Statistics" and click on "Economic conditions" and then "National accounts.")

ment is a positive trend that increased real output by approximately four times since 1962. This is what economists refer to as *long-term economic growth*.

A second feature of the real GDP series is short-term fluctuations around the trend, often described as *cyclical fluctuations*. Overall growth so dominates the real GDP series that the fluctuations are hardly visible in part (i) of Figure 19-1. However, as can be seen in part (ii), the growth of GDP has never been smooth. In most years, GDP increases, but in 1982 and 1991 GDP actually decreased, as shown by the negative rate of growth in the figure.

The **business cycle** refers to this continual ebb and flow of business activity that occurs around the long-term trend. For example, a single cycle will usually include an interval of quickly growing output, followed by an interval of slowly growing or even falling output. The entire cycle may last for several years. No two business cycles are exactly the same—variations occur in duration and magnitude. Some expansions are long and drawn out. Others come to an end before high employment and industrial capacity are reached. Nonetheless, fluctuations are systematic enough that it is useful to identify common factors in each of the four phases. These factors are outlined in *Applying Economic Concepts 19-1*.

Potential Output and the Output Gap

Actual national output represents what the economy *actually* produces. An important related concept is *potential* output, which measures what the economy would produce if all resources—land, labour, and productive capacity—were employed at their normal levels of utilization. This concept is usually referred to as **potential output** (but is sometimes called *full-employment output*).[1] Its symbol, Y^*, distinguishes it from actual output, indicated by Y. The **output gap** measures the difference between potential output and actual output. The gap is calculated by subtracting potential output from actual output ($Y - Y^*$).

When actual output is less than potential output, the gap measures the market value of goods and services that are not produced because the economy's resources are not fully employed. The goods and services that are not produced when the economy is operating below Y^* are permanently lost to the economy. When the economy is operating below its potential level of output—that is, when Y is less than Y^*—the output gap is called a **recessionary gap**.

In booms, actual output exceeds potential output. Actual output can exceed potential output because potential output is defined for a *normal* rate of utilization of factors of production, and there are many ways in which these normal rates can be exceeded temporarily. Labour may work longer hours than normal; factories may operate an extra shift or delay closing for routine repairs and maintenance. Although these expedients are only temporary, they are effective in the short term. When actual GDP exceeds potential GDP, there is often upward pressure on prices. Thus, when Y exceeds Y^*, we say the output gap is an **inflationary gap**.

Figure 19-2 shows potential GDP for the years since 1971. The upward trend reflects the growth in the productive capacity of the Canadian economy over this period, caused by increases in the labour force, capital stock, and the level of technological knowledge. The figure also shows actual GDP (reproduced from Figure 19-1), which has kept approximately in step with potential GDP. The distance between the two, which is the output gap,

business cycle
Fluctuations of national income around its trend value that follow a wavelike pattern.

potential output (Y^*)
The real gross domestic product that the economy would produce if its productive resources were employed at their normal levels of utilization. Also called *potential GDP*.

Practise with Study Guide Chapter 19, Exercise 2.

output gap   Actual national income minus potential national income, $Y-Y^*$.

recessionary gap
A situation in which actual output is less than potential output.

inflationary gap
A situation in which actual output exceeds potential output.

---

[1] The words *real* and *actual* have similar meanings in everyday usage. When national income is measured, however, their meanings are different. *Real* national income is distinguished from *nominal* national income; and *actual* national income is distinguished from *potential* national income. The latter both refer to *real* measures of national income.

APPLYING ECONOMIC CONCEPTS 19-1

The Terminology of Business Cycles

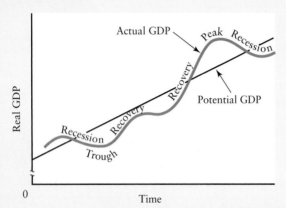

The accompanying figure shows a stylized business cycle, with real GDP fluctuating around a steadily rising level of potential GDP—the economy's normal capacity to produce output. We begin our discussion of terminology with a trough.

A *trough* is characterized by unemployed resources and a level of output that is low in relation to the economy's capacity to produce. There is thus a substantial amount of unused productive capacity. Business profits are low; for some individual companies, they are negative. Confidence about economic prospects in the immediate future is lacking, and, as a result, many firms are unwilling to risk making new investments.

The process of *recovery* moves the economy out of a trough. The characteristics of a recovery are many: run-down equipment is replaced; employment, income,

and consumer spending all begin to rise; and expectations become more favourable. Investments that once seemed risky may be undertaken as firms become more optimistic about future business prospects. Production can be increased with relative ease merely by re-employing the existing unused capacity and unemployed labour.

Eventually the recovery comes to a *peak* at the top of the cycle. At the peak, existing capacity is used to a high degree; labour shortages may develop, particularly in categories of key skills, and shortages of essential raw materials are likely. As shortages develop in more and more markets, a situation of general excess demand develops. Costs rise, but because prices rise also, business remains profitable.

Peaks are eventually followed by *recessions*. A **recession,** or contraction, is a downturn in economic activity. Common usage defines a recession as a fall in real GDP for two successive quarters. As output falls, so do employment and households' incomes. Profits drop, and some firms encounter financial difficulties. Investments that looked profitable with the expectation of continually rising income now appear unprofitable. It may not even be worth replacing capital goods as they wear out because unused capacity is increasing steadily. In historical discussions, a recession that is deep and long-lasting is often called a **depression**, such as the Great Depression in the early 1930s during which the level of economic activity fell so much that output fell by 30 percent and the unemployment rate increased to 20 percent!

These terms are non-technical but descriptive. The entire falling half of the cycle is often called a *slump,* and the entire rising half is often called a *boom.*

recession A downturn in the level of economic activity. Often defined precisely as two consecutive quarters in which real GDP falls.

depression A persistent period of very low economic activity with very high unemployment and high excess capacity.

is plotted in part (ii) of Figure 19-2. Fluctuations in economic activity are apparent from fluctuations in the size of the gap.

Why National Income Matters

National income is an important measure of economic performance. Short-run movements in the business cycle receive the most attention in politics and in the press, but most economists agree that long-term growth—as reflected by the growth of *potential GDP*—is in many ways the more important of the two.

Recessions are associated with unemployment and lost output. When actual GDP is below potential GDP, economic waste and human suffering result from the failure to use the economy's resources at their normal intensity of use. Booms, although associated

FIGURE 19-2   Potential GDP and the Output Gap, 1971–2002

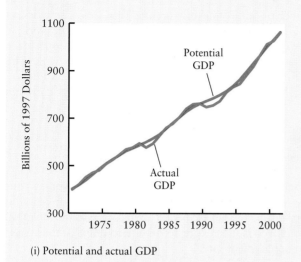

(i) Potential and actual GDP

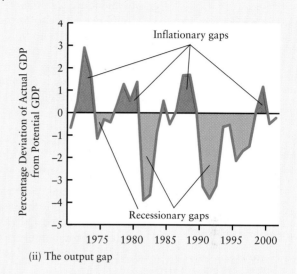

(ii) The output gap

Potential and actual GDP both display an upward trend. The output gap measures the difference between an economy's potential output and its actual output; the gap is expressed here as a percentage of potential output. Since 1971, potential and actual GDP have increased by almost three times. The distance between the two is the output gap, which shows clearly the cyclical behaviour. Shaded regions in part (ii) show inflationary and recessionary gaps.

(*Source:* Actual GDP: Statistics Canada, CANSIM database, Series V3862685. Potential output: *Bank of Canada Review*, Spring 2003.)

with high employment and high output, can bring problems of their own. When actual GDP exceeds potential GDP, inflationary pressure usually ensues, causing serious concern for any government that is committed to keeping the inflation rate low.

The long-run trend in real per capita national income is an important determinant of improvements in a society's overall standard of living. When income per person grows, each generation can expect, on average, to be better off than preceding ones. For example, if real per capita income grows at the relatively modest rate of 1.5 percent per year, the average person's lifetime income will be about *twice* that of his or her grandparents.

Although economic growth makes people better off *on average*, it does not necessarily make *every* individual better off—the benefits of growth do not typically fall evenly on all members of the population. For example, if growth involves significant changes in the structure of the economy, such as a shift away from agriculture and toward manufacturing (as happened in the first part of this century), then these changes will hurt some people for extended periods of time.

Employment, Unemployment, and the Labour Force

National income and employment are closely related. If more is to be produced, either more workers must be used in production, or existing workers must produce more. The first change means a rise in employment; the second means a rise in output per person employed, which, as we have seen, is a rise in productivity. In the short run, changes in

Practise with Study Guide Chapter 19, Exercise 4.

productivity tend to be very small; thus, most changes in output are accomplished by changes in employment. Over the long run, however, changes in both productivity and employment are significant.

employment
The number of persons 15 years of age and older who hold jobs.

unemployment
The number of persons 15 years of age and older who are not employed and are actively searching for a job.

labour force
The total number of persons employed in both civilian and military jobs, plus the number of persons who are unemployed.

unemployment rate
Unemployment expressed as a percentage of the labour force, denoted U.

Employment denotes the number of adult workers (defined in Canada as workers aged 15 and over) who hold jobs. **Unemployment** denotes the number of adult workers who are not employed but who are actively searching for a job. The **labour force** is the total number of people who are either employed or unemployed. The **unemployment rate** is equal to the number of unemployed people expressed as a fraction of the labour force—it represents the fraction of people wanting jobs who do not currently have one.

$$\text{Unemployment rate} = \frac{\text{Number of people unemployed}}{\text{Number of people in the labour force}} \times 100 \text{ percent}$$

The level of unemployment in Canada is estimated from the Labour Force Survey conducted each month by Statistics Canada. Persons who are currently without a job but who say they have searched actively for one during the sample period are recorded as unemployed. The estimated total number of unemployed is then expressed as a percentage of the labour force to obtain the figure for the unemployment rate.

Frictional, Structural, and Cyclical Unemployment

When the economy is at potential GDP, economists say there is *full employment*. But there will still be some unemployment even when the economy is at potential GDP. There are two reasons.

First, there is a constant turnover of individuals in given jobs and a constant change in job opportunities. New people enter the workforce; some people quit their jobs; others are fired. It may take some time for these people to find jobs. So at any point in time, there is unemployment due to the normal turnover of labour. Such unemployment is called *frictional unemployment*.

Second, because the economy is constantly changing and adapting, at any moment there will always be some mismatch between the characteristics of the labour force and the characteristics of the available jobs. This is a mismatch between the *structure* of the supplies of labour and the *structure* of the demands for labour. Such unemployment is called *structural unemployment*. The mismatch may occur, for example, because labour does not currently have the skills that are in demand or because labour is not in the part of the country where the demand is located.

Economists make the distinction between frictional, structural, and cyclical unemployment. But this distinction matters little to the individual who has difficulty finding an appropriate job.

Even when the economy is said to be at full employment, some unemployment exists due to natural turnover in the labour market and to mismatch between jobs and workers.

Full employment is said to occur when the only existing unemployment is frictional and structural. At full employment, factors of production are being used at their normal intensity, and the economy is at potential GDP. During recessions, unemployment rises above its full-employment level; during booms, unemployment falls below its full-employment level. Unemployment that is neither structural nor frictional is called *cyclical unemployment* because it changes with the ebb and flow of the business cycle.

Unemployment also has *seasonal* fluctuations. For example, workers employed in the fishing industry are often unemployed during the winter and ski instructors may be unemployed in the summer. Because these seasonal fluctuations are relatively regular and therefore easy to predict, Statistics Canada *seasonally adjusts* the unemployment statistics to remove these fluctuations, thus revealing more clearly the cyclical and trend movements in the data. For example, suppose that, on average, the Canadian unemployment rate increases by 0.3 percentage points in December. Statistics Canada would then adjust the December unemployment rate so that it shows an increase only if the increase in the *unadjusted* rate exceeds 0.3 percentage points. In this way, the (seasonally adjusted) December unemployment rate is reported to increase only if unemployment rises by more than its normal seasonal increase. All of the unemployment data shown in this book are seasonally adjusted.

Unemployment: Recent History

Figure 19-3 shows the trends in the labour force, employment, and unemployment since 1960. Despite booms and slumps, employment has grown roughly in line with the growth in the labour force. Although the long-term trend dominates the employment data, the figure also shows that the short-term fluctuations in the unemployment rate have been substantial. The unemployment rate has been as low as 3.4 percent in 1966 and as high as 12 percent in 1982. By 2000, after the economy had been growing steadily for several years, the unemployment rate was 6.8 percent, the lowest it had been in nearly 20 years. Part (ii) of Figure 19-3 also shows that there has been a modest upward trend in the unemployment rate over the past 40 years. In Chapter 30 we discuss how some structural changes in the economy can help explain this trend.

Why Unemployment Matters

The social and political significance of unemployment is enormous. The government is blamed when the rate is high and takes credit when it is low. Few macroeconomic policies are planned without some consideration of how they will affect unemployment. No other summary statistic carries such weight as a source of both formal and informal policy concern.

Unemployment involves economic waste and human suffering. Human effort is the least durable of economic commodities. If a fully employed economy has 17 million people who are willing to work, their services must either be used this year or wasted. When only 15.7 million people are actually employed, one year's potential output of 1.3 million workers is lost forever. In an economy in which there is not enough output to meet everyone's needs, such a waste of potential output is cause for concern.

The loss of income associated with unemployment is clearly harmful to individuals. In some cases, the loss of income pushes people into poverty. But this lost income does not capture the full cost of unemployment. A person's spirit can be broken by a long period of desiring work but being unable to find it. Research has shown that crime, mental illness, and general social unrest tend to be positively associated with long-term unemployment.

In the not-so-distant past, only personal savings, private charity, or help from friends and relatives stood between the unemployed and starvation. Today, welfare and employment insurance have created a safety net, particularly when unemployment is for short periods, as is most often the case in Canada. However, when an economic slump lasts long enough, as in the early 1980s and the early 1990s, some unfortunate people exhaust their employment insurance and lose part of that safety net.

FIGURE 19-3   Labour Force, Employment, and Unemployment, 1960–2003

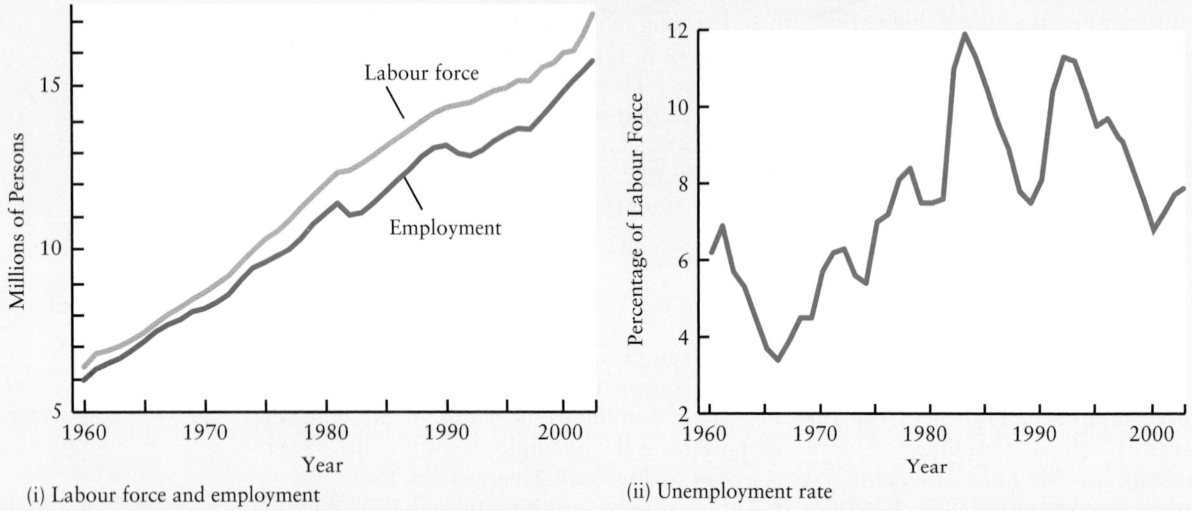

(i) Labour force and employment

(ii) Unemployment rate

The labour force and employment have grown since 1960 with only a few interruptions. The unemployment rate responds to the cyclical behaviour of the economy. The labour force and the level of employment in Canada have both almost tripled since 1960. Booms are associated with a low unemployment rate and slumps with a high unemployment rate.

(*Source:* These data are from Statistics Canada's CANSIM database. Labour force: Series V2091051. Employment: Series V2091072. Unemployment rate: Series V2091177. Current labour-force statistics are available on Statistics Canada's website at www.statcan.ca. Go to "Canadian Statistics" and click on "Labour, employment, and unemployment.")

Inflation and the Price Level

Inflation means that prices of goods and services are going up, *on average*. If you are a typical reader of this book, inflation has not been very noticeable during your lifetime. When your parents were your age, however, high inflation was a major economic problem. (Some countries have had their economies almost ruined by very high inflation, called *hyperinflation*. We will say more about this in Chapter 27.)

For studying inflation, there are two related but different concepts that are sometimes confused, and it is important to get them straight. The first is the **price level,** which refers to the average level of all prices in the economy and is given by the symbol, *P*. The second is the rate of **inflation,** which is the rate at which the price level is rising.

To measure the price level, economists construct a *price index*, which averages the prices of various commodities according to how important they are. The best-known price index in Canada is the **Consumer Price Index (CPI),** which measures the average price of the goods and services that are bought by the typical Canadian household. *Applying Economic Concepts 19-2* shows how a price index such as the CPI is constructed.

As we saw in Chapter 2, a price index is a pure number—it does not have any units. Yet as we all know, prices in Canada are expressed in dollars. When we construct a price index, the units (dollars) are eliminated because the price index shows the price of a basket of goods at some specific time *relative to the price of the same basket of goods in some base period*. For example, if we choose 1992 as the base year for the CPI, the price of the basket of goods is set to be 100 in 1992. If the CPI in 2002 is computed to

price level   The average level of all prices in the economy, expressed as an index number.

inflation   A rise in the average level of all prices.

Consumer Price Index (CPI)   An index of the average prices of goods and services commonly bought by households.

APPLYING ECONOMIC CONCEPTS 19-2

How the CPI Is Constructed

Although the details are somewhat more complicated, the basic idea behind the Consumer Price Index is straightforward, as is illustrated by the following hypothetical example.

Suppose we wish to discover what has happened to the overall cost of living for typical university students. A survey of student behaviour in 1994 shows that the average university student consumed only three goods—pizza, coffee, and photocopying—and spent a total of $200 a month on these items, as shown in Table 1.

TABLE 1   Expenditure Behaviour in 1994

Product	Price	Quantity per Month	Expenditure per Month
Photocopies	$0.10 per sheet	140 sheets	$14.00
Pizza	8.00 per pizza	15 pizzas	120.00
Coffee	0.75 per cup	88 cups	66.00
Total expenditure			$200.00

By 2004, the price of photocopying has fallen to 5 cents per copy, the price of pizza has increased to $8.50, and the price of coffee has increased to 80 cents. What has happened to the cost of living? In order to find out, we calculate the cost of purchasing the 1994 bundle of goods at the prices that prevailed in 2004, as shown in Table 2.

The total expenditure required to purchase the bundle of goods that cost $200.00 in 1994 has risen to $204.90. The increase in required expenditure is $4.90, which is a 2.45-percent increase over the original $200.00.

If we define 1994 as the *base year* for the "student price index" and assign an index value of 100 to the cost of the average student's expenditure in that year, the value of the index in 2004 is 102.45. Thus, goods and services that cost $100.00 in the base year cost $102.45 in 2004, exactly what is implied by Table 2.

The Consumer Price Index, as constructed by Statistics Canada, is built on exactly the same principles as the preceding example. In the case of the CPI, many

TABLE 2   1994 Expenditure Behaviour at 2004 Prices

Product	Price	Quantity per Month	Expenditure per Month
Photocopies	$0.05 per sheet	140 sheets	$7.00
Pizza	8.50 per pizza	15 pizzas	127.50
Coffee	0.80 per cup	88 cups	70.40
Total expenditure			$204.90

thousands of consumers are surveyed, and the prices of thousands of products are monitored, but the basic method is the same:

1. Survey the consumption behaviour of consumers.

2. Calculate the cost of the goods and services purchased by the average consumer in the year in which the original survey was done. Define this as the *base period* of the index.

3. Calculate the cost of purchasing the same bundle of goods and services in other years.

4. Divide the result of Step 3 (in each year) by the result of Step 2, and multiply by 100. The result is the value of the CPI for each year.

The CPI is not a perfect measure of the cost of living because it does not account for quality improvements or for changes in consumers' expenditure patterns. For example, the use of home computers is much more widespread today than it was 20 years ago, when they would have appropriately had a very small role in the CPI. Changes of this type require the underlying survey of consumer expenditure to be updated from time to time to make sure that the expenditure patterns in the survey approximately match consumers' actual expenditure patterns.

be 119, the meaning is that the price of the basket of goods is 19 percent higher in 2002 than in 1992.

Since the price level is measured with an index number, its value at any specific time only has meaning when it is compared to its value at some other time.

To compute the rate of inflation from any point in your lifetime to today, check out the "inflation calculator" at the Bank of Canada's website: www.bank-banque-canada.ca.

Practise with Study Guide Chapter 19, Extension Exercise E1.

By allowing us to compare the general price level at different times, a price index such as the CPI also allows us to measure the rate of inflation. For example, the value of the CPI in October 2003 was 122.4 and in October 2002 was 120.5. The *rate of inflation* during that one-year period, expressed in percentage terms, is equal to the change in the price level divided by the initial price level, times 100:

$$\text{Rate of inflation} = \frac{122.4 - 120.5}{120.5} \times 100 \text{ percent}$$

$$= 1.58 \text{ percent}$$

Inflation: Recent History

If you are a typical reader of this textbook (roughly 18–22 years old), inflation has probably not been an important part of your life experience, especially if you have lived in Canada for the past decade or so. Inflation in Canada is currently around 2 percent per year, and has been at that level for over a decade. But it has not always been so. There was a time—not so long ago—when inflation in Canada was both high and unpredictable from year to year.

Figure 19-4 shows the CPI and the inflation rate (measured by the annual rate of change in the CPI) from 1960 to 2003. What can we learn from this figure? First, we learn that the price level has not fallen at all since 1960 (in fact, the last time it fell was in 1953, and even then it fell only briefly). The cumulative effect of this sequence of repeated price increases is quite dramatic: By 2003, the price level was over six times higher than it was in 1960. In other words, you now pay over $6 for what cost $1 in 1960. The second thing we learn is that, although the price level appears in the figure to be smoothly increasing, the rate of inflation is actually quite volatile. The increases in the inflation rate into double-digit levels in 1974 and 1979 were associated with major increases in the world prices of oil and foodstuffs and with loose monetary policy. The declines in inflation that followed were delayed responses to major recessions.

Why Inflation Matters

Money is the universal yardstick in our economy. This does not mean that we care only about money—it means simply that we measure *economic values* in terms of money, and we use money to conduct our economic affairs. Things as diverse as wages, bank balances, the value of a house, and a university's endowment are all stated in terms of money. We value money, however, not for itself but for what we can purchase with it. The terms **purchasing power of money** and *real value of money* refer to the amount of goods and services that can be purchased with a given amount of money. The purchasing power of money is negatively related to the price level. For example, if the price level doubles, a dollar will buy only half as much, whereas if the price level halves, a dollar will buy twice as much.

Inflation also reduces the real value of anything else whose price is *fixed* in money terms. Thus, the real value of a money wage, a savings account, or the balance that is owed on a student loan is reduced by inflation.

purchasing power of money   The amount of goods and services that can be purchased with a unit of money.

Inflation means an increase in the price level and a reduction in the purchasing power of money. Inflation also reduces the real value of any sum fixed in nominal terms.

When analyzing the effects of inflation, economists usually make the distinction between *anticipated* and *unanticipated* inflation. If households and firms fully anticipate inflation over the coming year, they will be able to adjust many nominal prices and wages so as to maintain their real values. In this case, inflation will have fewer real effects on the economy than if it comes unexpectedly. For example, if workers and firms expect 5-percent inflation over the coming year, they can agree to increase nominal wages by 5 percent, thus leaving wages constant in real terms.

Unanticipated inflation, on the other hand, generally leads to changes in the real value of price and wages. Suppose workers and firms expect 5-percent inflation and they increase nominal wages accordingly. If actual inflation ends up being 10 percent, real wages will be reduced and the quantities of labour demanded by firms and supplied by workers will therefore be altered. As a result, the economy's allocation of resources will likely be affected.

Most economists agree that anticipated inflation has a smaller effect on the economy than unanticipated inflation.

In reality, inflation is rarely fully anticipated or fully unanticipated. Usually there is some inflation that is expected but also some that comes as a surprise. As a result, some adjustments in wages and prices get made by firms and workers and consumers, but not all the adjustments that would be required to leave the economy's allocation of resources unaffected. We will see later, in our discussions of monetary policy and inflation in Chapters 29 and 30, how the distinction between anticipated and unanticipated inflation helps us to understand the cost of *reducing* inflation.

Interest Rates

If a bank lends you money, it will charge you **interest** for the privilege of borrowing the money. If,

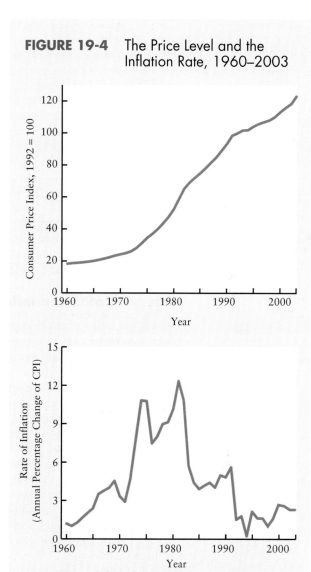

FIGURE 19-4   The Price Level and the Inflation Rate, 1960–2003

The trend in the price level has been upward over the past half-century. The rate of inflation has varied from almost 0 to over 12 percent since 1960.

(*Source:* These data are available on the Bank of Canada's website: www.bankofcanada.ca. The price level used is the seasonally adjusted consumer price index, PCPISA. Current data are also available from Statistics Canada, www.statcan.ca. Go to "Canadian Statistics" and click on "Economic conditions" and then "Prices.")

for example, you borrow $1000 today, repayable in one year's time, you may also be asked to pay $6.67 per month in interest. This makes $80 in interest over the year, which can be expressed as an interest rate of 8 percent per annum.

interest   The payment for the use of borrowed money.

interest rate
The price paid per dollar borrowed per period of time, expressed either as a proportion (e.g., 0.06) or as a percentage (e.g., 6 percent).

The **interest rate** is the price that is paid to borrow money for a stated period of time. It is expressed as a percentage amount per year per dollar borrowed. For example, an interest rate of 8 percent per year means that the borrower must pay 8 cents per year for every dollar that is borrowed.

There are many interest rates. A bank will lend money to an industrial customer at a lower rate than it will lend money to you—there is a lower risk of not being repaid. The rate charged on a loan that is not to be repaid for a long time will usually differ from the rate on a loan that is to be repaid quickly.

When economists speak of "the" interest rate, they mean a rate that is typical of all the various interest rates in the economy. Dealing with only one interest rate suppresses much interesting detail. However, because interest rates commonly move together, at least for major changes, following the movement of one rate allows us to consider changes in the general level of interest rates. The *prime interest rate,* the rate that banks charge to their best business customers, is an interest rate that attracts much attention because when the prime rate changes, most other rates change in the same direction. Another high-profile interest rate is the *bank rate,* the interest rate that the Bank of Canada (Canada's central bank) charges on short-term loans to commercial banks.

Interest Rates and Inflation

nominal interest rate
The price paid per dollar borrowed per period of time.

How does inflation affect interest rates? To begin developing an answer, imagine that your friend lends you $100 and that the loan is repayable in one year. The amount that you pay her for making this loan, measured in money terms, is determined by the **nominal interest rate.** If you pay her $108 in one year's time, $100 will be repayment of the amount of the loan (which is called the *principal*) and $8 will be payment of the interest. In this case, the nominal interest rate is 8 percent.

How much purchasing power has your friend gained or lost by making this loan? The answer depends on what happens to the price level during the year. The more the price level rises, the worse off your friend will be and the better the transaction will be for you. This result occurs because the more the price level rises, the less valuable are the dollars that you use to repay the loan. The **real interest rate** measures the *real* return on a loan, in terms of purchasing power.

real interest rate
The nominal rate of interest adjusted for the change in the purchasing power of money. Equal to the nominal interest rate minus the rate of inflation.

If the price level remains constant over the year, the real rate of interest that your friend earns would also be 8 percent, because she can buy 8 percent more goods and services with the $108 that you repay her than with the $100 that she lent you. However, if the price level rises by 8 percent, the real rate of interest would be zero because the $108 that you repay her buys the same quantity of goods as the $100 that she originally gave up. If she is unlucky enough to lend money at 8 percent in a year in which prices rise by 10 percent, the real rate of interest that she earns is −2 percent. The repayment of $108 will purchase 2 percent fewer goods and services than the original loan of $100.

The burden of borrowing depends on the real, not the nominal, rate of interest.

For example, a nominal interest rate of 8 percent combined with a 2-percent rate of inflation is a much greater real burden on borrowers than a nominal rate of 16 percent combined with a 14-percent rate of inflation. Figure 19-5 shows the nominal and real interest rates paid on short-term government borrowing since 1960.

Why Interest Rates Matter

Changes in real interest rates affect the standard of living of savers and borrowers. Many retirees, for example, rely on interest earnings from their stock of accumulated assets to provide much of their household income. In contrast, borrowers are made better off with low real interest rates. This point was dramatically illustrated during the 1970s when homeowners who had long-term fixed-rate mortgages benefited tremendously from several years of unanticipated inflation, which resulted in negative real interest rates.

Interest rates also matter for the economy as a whole. As we will see in Chapter 21, real interest rates are an important determinant of the level of investment by firms. Changes in real interest rates lead to changes in the cost of borrowing and thus to changes in firms' investment plans. Such changes in the level of desired investment have important consequences for the level of economic activity. We will see in Chapters 28 and 29 how the Bank of Canada influences interest rates as part of its objective of controlling inflation.

The International Economy

The two important indicators of the Canadian position in the international economy are the *exchange rate* and the *balance of payments*.

The Exchange Rate

If you are going on a holiday to France, you will need euros to pay for your purchases. Many of the larger banks, as well as any foreign-exchange office, will make the necessary exchange of currencies for you; they will sell you euros in return for your Canadian dollars. If you get 0.6 euros for each dollar that you give up, the two currencies are trading at a rate of 1 dollar = 0.6 euros or, expressed another way, 1 euro = 1.67 dollars.

As our example shows, the exchange rate can be defined either as dollars per euro or euros per dollar. In this book we adopt the convention of defining the **exchange rate** between the Canadian dollar and any foreign currency as the number of Canadian dollars required to purchase one unit of foreign currency. For example, on September 4, 2003, 1 Canadian dollar was worth 66.27 euro cents; expressed the other way, 1 euro was worth 1.51 Canadian dollars. The exchange rate on that day was therefore equal to 1.51, telling us that it took $1.51 (Canadian) to purchase 1 euro.

The exchange rate is the number of Canadian dollars required to purchase one unit of foreign currency.[2]

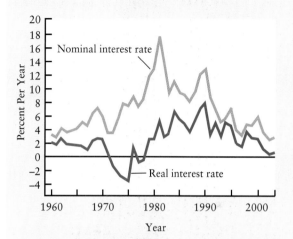

FIGURE 19-5   Real and Nominal Interest Rates, 1960–2003

Inflation over the past four decades has meant that the real interest rate has always been less than the nominal interest rate. The data for the nominal interest rate show the average rate on three-month treasury bills in each year since 1960. The real interest rate is calculated as the nominal interest rate minus the actual rate of inflation over the same period. The real interest rate has usually been below 4 percent for the past three decades. Through much of the 1970s, the real interest rate was negative, indicating that the inflation rate exceeded the nominal interest rate. The 1980s saw real interest rates rise as high as 8 percent. Since then, real rates have declined again to levels that are closer to the long-term historical average.

(*Source:* Nominal interest rate: 90-day treasury bill rate, Statistics Canada, CANSIM database, Series V122541. Real interest rate is based on authors' calculation of CPI inflation, using Series PCPISA from the Bank of Canada.)

exchange rate
The number of units of domestic currency required to purchase one unit of foreign currency.

---

[2] Some economists use a reverse definition of the exchange rate—the number of units of foreign currency that can be purchased by one Canadian dollar. It is up to the student, then, to examine carefully the definition that is being used by a particular writer or speaker. In this book the exchange rate is defined as the number of Canadian dollars required to purchase one unit of foreign currency because this measure emphasizes that foreign currency, like any other good or service, has a price in terms of Canadian dollars. In this case, the price has a special name—the exchange rate.

foreign exchange
Actual foreign currencies or various claims on them, such as bank balances or promises to pay, that are traded on the foreign-exchange market.

foreign-exchange market   The market where different national currencies, or claims to these currencies, are traded.

depreciation   A rise in the exchange rate—it takes more units of domestic currency to purchase one unit of foreign currency.

appreciation   A fall in the exchange rate—it takes fewer units of domestic currency to purchase one unit of foreign currency.

Practise with Study Guide Chapter 19, Exercise 5.

The term **foreign exchange** refers to foreign currencies or claims on foreign currencies, such as bank deposits, cheques, and promissory notes, that are payable in foreign money. The **foreign-exchange market** is the market where foreign exchange is traded—at a price expressed by the exchange rate.

Depreciation and Appreciation

A rise in the exchange rate means that it takes *more* Canadian dollars to purchase one unit of foreign currency—this is referred to as a **depreciation** of the Canadian dollar. Conversely, a fall in the exchange rate means that it takes *fewer* Canadian dollars to purchase one unit of foreign currency—this is referred to as an **appreciation** of the dollar.

A rise in the exchange rate reflects a depreciation of the Canadian dollar; a fall in the exchange rate reflects an appreciation of the Canadian dollar.

Figure 19-6 shows the path of the Canadian–U.S. exchange rate since 1970. Since over 80 percent of Canada's trade is with the United States, this is the exchange rate most often discussed and analyzed in Canada. In countries with trade more evenly spread across several trading partners, more attention is paid to what is called a *trade-weighted exchange rate*—this is a weighted-average exchange rate between the home country and its trading partners, where the weights reflect each partner's share in the home country's total trade. In Canada, the path of such a trade-weighted exchange rate is virtually identical to the Canadian–U.S. exchange rate shown in Figure 19-6; this merely reflects the very large proportion of total Canadian trade that is with the United States.

As we will see in later chapters, both domestic policy and external events have important effects on the Canadian exchange rate. For example, most economists believe that the appreciation of the Canadian dollar between 1986 and 1992 was caused in part by the Bank of Canada's efforts to reduce the rate of inflation. The Bank's policy was controversial at the time, not least because of the effect it had on the exchange rate and the many export-oriented firms that were harmed by Canada's strong dollar. We examine the link between monetary policy and exchange rates in detail in Chapters 28 and 29.

The depreciation of the Canadian dollar in the late 1990s is thought by most economists to have resulted from a nearly 30-percent decline in the world prices of commodities, many of which are important Canadian exports. The decline in commodity prices was partly caused by a significant recession that started in several Asian economies in the summer of 1997—economies that are large importers of Canadian commodities. Thus, events in faraway lands can have dramatic effects on the Canadian exchange rate. We examine the link between world commodity prices and the Canadian exchange rate in Chapter 35.

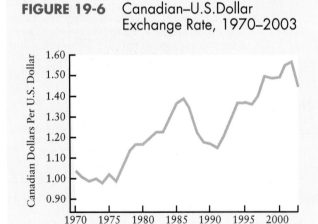

FIGURE 19-6   Canadian–U.S.Dollar Exchange Rate, 1970–2003

The Canadian dollar has depreciated significantly relative to the U.S. dollar since 1970. The Canadian-dollar price of one U.S. dollar increased from just over $1 in the early 1970s to over $1.40 in 2003.

(*Source:* Annual average of monthly data, Statistics Canada, CANSIM database, Series V37432.)

The Balance of Payments

To know what is happening to the course of international trade and international capital movements, governments keep an account of the transactions among countries, called the **balance-of-payments account.** These accounts record all international payments that are made for the buying and selling of both goods and services, as well as financial assets such as stocks and bonds.

Figure 19-7 shows one part of the balance of payments that is most often at the centre of controversy—the balance of trade. This balance, also called net exports, is the difference between the value of Canadian exports and the value of Canadian imports. As we can see from Figure 19-7, Canadian exports and imports have increased fairly closely in step with each other over the past 30 years. The trade balance has thus had mild fluctuations over the years, but has stayed at or near a roughly balanced position. Also apparent in Figure 19-7 is that Canadian trade flows (both imports and exports) began to grow more quickly after 1990. The increased importance of international trade is largely due to the Canada–U.S. Free Trade Agreement, which began in 1989, and to the North American Free Trade Agreement (which added Mexico), which began in 1993.

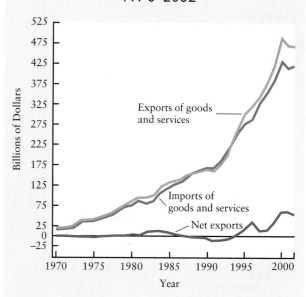

FIGURE 19-7 Canadian Imports, Exports, and Net Exports, 1970–2002

Though imports and exports have increased dramatically over the past 30 years, the trade balance has remained roughly in balance. The nominal values of imports and exports rose steadily over the past few decades, due to price increases and quantity increases. The growth of trade increased sharply after the early 1990s. The trade balance—net exports—is always close to zero.

(*Source:* Statistics Canada, CANSIM database. Exports: Series V499540. Imports: Series V499557.)

19.2 Growth Versus Fluctuations

balance-of-payments account A summary record of a country's transactions with the rest of the world, including the buying and selling of goods, services, and assets.

This chapter has provided a very quick tour through macroeconomics, and has introduced you to many complex and interesting issues about which macroeconomists think. If you take a few moments to flip again through the figures in this chapter, you will notice that most of the macroeconomic variables that we discussed are characterized by *long-run trends* and *short-run fluctuations*.

Figure 19-1, which shows the path of real GDP, provides an excellent example of both characteristics. The figure shows that real GDP has increased by over four times since 1962—this is substantial *economic growth*. The figure also shows considerable, and sometimes dramatic, year-to-year *fluctuations* in the growth rate of GDP.

An important theme in this book is that a full understanding of macroeconomics requires an understanding of both long-run growth and short-run fluctuations. As we proceed through this book, we will see that these two characteristics of modern economies have different sources and explanations. And broad macroeconomic policies have roles to play in both.

Long-Term Economic Growth

International trade is very important to the Canadian economy. Exports and imports of goods and services each represent about 40 percent of Canada's GDP.

Both total output and output per person have risen for many decades in most industrial countries. These long-term trends have meant rising average living standards. Although long-term growth gets less play on the evening news than current economic developments, it has considerably more importance for a society's living standards from decade to decade and from generation to generation.

There is considerable debate regarding the ability of government policy to influence the economy's long-run rate of growth. Most economists believe that a policy designed to keep inflation low and stable will contribute to the economy's growth. Some, however, believe there are dangers from having inflation too low—that a moderate inflation rate is more conducive to growth than a very low inflation rate. We examine this debate in Chapter 29.

Many economists also believe that when governments spend less than they raise in tax revenue—and thus have a budget surplus—the reduced need for borrowing drives down interest rates and stimulates investment by the private sector. Such increases in investment imply a higher stock of physical capital available for future production, and thus an increase in economic growth. Do government budget surpluses increase future growth? Or do budget surpluses have no effect at all on the economy's future ability to produce? We address this important debate in Chapter 31.

Short-Term Fluctuations

Short-run fluctuations in economic activity, like the ones shown in Figure 19-2, lead economists to wonder about the causes of *business cycles*. What caused the Great Depression in the 1930s, when almost one-fifth of the Canadian labour force was out of work and massive unemployment plagued all major industrial countries? Why did the Canadian economy begin a significant recession in 1990–91, from which recovery was initially very gradual? What explains why, a decade later, the Canadian unemployment rate was lower than it had been in almost 30 years?

Understanding business cycles requires an understanding of monetary policy. Most economists agree that the increase in inflation in the 1970s and early 1980s was related to monetary policy, though they also agree that other events were partly responsible. When the Bank of Canada implemented a policy in the early 1990s designed to reduce inflation, was it merely a coincidence that a significant recession followed? Most economists think not, though they also think that the slowdown in the U.S. economy was an important contributor to Canada's recession. Chapter 27 focuses on how the Bank of Canada uses its policy to influence the level of economic activity.

Government budget deficits and surpluses also enter the discussion of business cycles. Some economists think that, in recessionary years, the government ought to increase spending (and reduce taxes) in an effort to stimulate economic activity. Similarly, they believe that taxes should be raised to slow down a booming economy. Indeed, several government policies, from income taxation to unemployment insurance, are actually designed to mitigate the short-term fluctuations in national income. Other economists believe that the government cannot successfully "fine-tune" the economy by spending and taxing because our knowledge of how the economy works is imperfect and because such policies tend to be imprecise. We address these issues in Chapters 22 to 24.

What Lies Ahead?

There is much work to be done before any of these interesting policy debates can be thoroughly understood. Like firms that invest now to increase their production in the future, the next few chapters of this book will be an investment for you—an investment in understanding basic macro theory. The payoff will come when you are able to use a coherent model of the economy to analyze and debate some of the key macro issues of the day.

We begin in Chapter 20 by discussing the measurement of GDP. National income accounting is not exciting but is essential to a complete understanding of the chapters that follow. We then proceed to build a simple model of the economy to highlight some key macroeconomic relationships. As we proceed through the book, we modify the model, step by step, making it ever more complete and realistic. With each step we take, more of today's controversial policy issues come within the grasp of our understanding. We hope that by the time you get to the end of the book, you have developed some of the thrill for analyzing macroeconomic issues that we feel. Good luck, and enjoy the journey!

SUMMARY

19.1 Key Macroeconomic Variables

- The value of the total production of goods and services in a nation is called its national product. Because production of output generates income in the form of claims on that output, the total is also referred to as national income. One of the most commonly used measures of national income is gross domestic product (GDP).
- Potential output is the level of output produced when factors of production are employed at their normal intensity of use. The output gap is the difference between actual and potential output.
- Fluctuations of national income around its potential level are associated with the business cycle. Recoveries pass through peaks and turn into recessions that, in turn, pass through troughs to become recoveries.
- The unemployment rate is the percentage of the labour force not employed and actively searching for a job. The labour force and employment have both grown steadily for the past half-century. The unemployment rate fluctuates considerably from year to year. Unemployment

imposes serious costs on the economy in the form of economic waste and human suffering.
- The price level is measured by a price index, which measures the price of a set of goods in one year relative to their price in an (arbitrary) base year. The inflation rate measures the rate of change of the price level. Although it fluctuates considerably, the inflation rate has been consistently positive.
- The interest rate is the price that is paid to borrow money for a stated period and is expressed as a percentage amount per dollar borrowed. The nominal interest rate is this price expressed in money terms; the real interest rate is this price expressed in terms of goods or purchasing power.
- The exchange rate is the number of Canadian dollars needed to purchase one unit of foreign currency. The balance of payments is a record of all international transactions made by Canadian firms, households, and governments.

19.2 Growth Versus Fluctuations

- Most macroeconomic variables have both long-run trends and short-run fluctuations. The sources of the two types of movements are different.
- Important questions for macroeconomics involve the role of policy in influencing long-run growth as well as short-run fluctuations.

KEY CONCEPTS

National product and national income
Real and nominal national income
Potential and actual output
The output gap
Employment, unemployment, and the
 labour force

Full employment
Frictional, structural, and cyclical
 unemployment
The price level and the rate of inflation
Real and nominal interest rates

The exchange rate
Depreciation and appreciation of the
 Canadian dollar
The balance of payments

STUDY EXERCISES

1. Fill in the blanks to make the following statements correct.

   a. The value of total production of goods and services in Canada is called its _national product_. National _Income_ and national _GDP_ are equal because all production generates a claim on its value in the form of income.

   b. In measuring Canada's total output, it would be meaningless to add together all goods and services produced during one year (i.e., 50 000 trucks plus 14 million dozen eggs plus 100 million haircuts, etc.). Instead, total output is measured in _dollars_.

   c. The difference between nominal national income and real national income is that with the latter, _prices_ are held constant to enable us to see changes in _quantities_.

   d. If all of Canada's resources—its land, labour, and capital—are being employed at normal levels of utilization, then we say that Canada is producing its _potential national income_.

   e. The output gap measures the difference between _potential output_ and _actual output_. During booms, _actual income_ is greater than _potential income_ and during recessions _actual income_ is less than _potential income_.

2. Fill in the blanks to make the following statements correct.

   a. The labour force includes people who are _____ and people who are _____. The unemployment rate is expressed as the number of people who are _____ as a percentage of people in the _____.

   b. At any point in time, some people are unemployed because of the normal turnover of labour (new entrants to the labour force, job leavers, and job seekers). This unemployment is referred to as _____. Some people are said to be _____ unemployed because their skills do not match the skills necessary for the available jobs.

   c. Suppose 1992 is the base year in which the price of a basket of goods is set to be 100. If the price of the same basket of goods in 2003 is 137, then we can say that the price level is _____ and that the price of the basket of goods has increased by _____ percent between 1992 and 2003.

   d. Suppose Canada's CPI in May 2002 was 112.7 and in May 2003 was 113.4. The rate of inflation during that one-year period is _____ percent.

   e. The price that is paid to borrow money for a stated period of time is known as the _____.

   f. The real interest rate is equal to the nominal interest rate _____ the rate of inflation.

   g. The number of Canadian dollars required to purchase one unit of foreign currency is the _____ between the Canadian dollar and that foreign currency.

   h. A _____ in the exchange rate reflects a depreciation of the Canadian dollar; a _____ in the exchange rate reflects an appreciation of the Canadian dollar.

3. Consider the macroeconomic data shown below for a hypothetical country's economy.

Year	Real GDP Actual (billions of $)	Real GDP Potential (billions of $)	Output Gap (% of potential)	Unemployment Rate (% of labour force)
1996	768	788	—	11.1
1997	784	796	—	10.2
1998	797	805	—	9.1
1999	811	815	—	8.3
2000	825	825	—	7.6
2001	840	836	—	7.3
2002	853	847	—	7.1
2003	862	858	—	7.3
2004	870	870	—	7.6

a. Compute the output gap for each year.
b. Explain how GDP can exceed potential GDP.
c. Does real GDP ever fall in the time period shown? What do economists call such periods?
d. What is the unemployment rate when this economy is at "full employment"? What kind of unemployment exists at this time?

4. Consider the data shown below for the Canadian Consumer Price Index (CPI), drawn from the *Bank of Canada Review.*

a. Compute the missing data in the table.
b. Do average prices ever fall in the time period shown? In which year do prices come closest to being stable?
c. Across which two consecutive years is the rate of inflation closest to being stable?
d. In a diagram with the price level on the vertical axis and time on the horizontal axis, illustrate the difference between a situation in which the price level is stable and a situation in which the rate of inflation is stable.

Year	CPI (1992 = 100)	CPI Inflation (% change from previous year)
1987	81.5	4.35
1988	84.8	4.05
1989	89.0	——
1990	93.3	——
1991	98.5	5.57
1992	100.0	——
1993	101.8	——
1994	102.0	0.20
1995	104.2	2.16
1996	105.9	——
1997	107.6	——
1998	108.9	1.21

5. The data below show the nominal interest rate and the inflation rate for several developed economies.

Country	Nominal Interest Rate (on 10-year government bonds)	Inflation Rate (% change in CPI from previous year)	Real Interest Rate
Australia	5.61	1.6	—
Canada	5.25	0.6	—
France	4.13	0.2	—
Germany	4.03	0.2	—
Japan	1.79	0.2	—
Switzerland	2.50	0.3	—
U.K.	4.71	2.4	—
U.S.A.	5.19	1.7	—

a. Compute the real interest rate for each country, assuming that people expected the inflation rate at the time to persist.
b. If you were a lender, in which country would you have wanted to lend in March of 1999? Explain.
c. If you were a borrower, in which country would you have wanted to borrow in March of 1999? Explain.

6. Consider the following data drawn from *The Economist.* Recall that the Canadian exchange rate is the number of Canadian dollars needed to purchase one unit of some foreign currency.

Currency	Cdn Dollar Exchange Rate March 1999	March 1998
U.S. dollar	1.520	1.410
Japanese yen	0.01267	0.01093
British pound	2.492	2.311
Swedish krona	0.187	0.176
Brazilian real	0.694	1.248
Mexican peso	0.153	0.162

a. Which currencies appreciated relative to the Canadian dollar from March 1998 to March 1999?
b. Which currencies depreciated relative to the Canadian dollar from March 1998 to March 1999?
c. Using the information provided in the table, can you tell whether the Japanese yen depreciated or appreciated *against the U.S. dollar* from March 1998 to March 1999? Explain.

DISCUSSION QUESTIONS

1. Explain carefully what has happened to the CPI to justify each of the following newspaper headlines.

   a. "Prices on the rise again after a year of stability"
   b. "Inflation increases for three successive months"
   c. "Finance minister pleased at moderation in inflation rate"
   d. "Cost-of-living increases devastating pensioners"

2. Explain why during booms it is possible for the unemployment rate to increase even while total employment is rising.

3. Evaluate the following statements about unemployment.

   a. "Unemployment is a personal tragedy and a national waste."

   b. "No one needs to be unemployed these days; just look at the Help Wanted ads in the newspapers and the signs in the stores."
   c. Employment insurance is a boondoggle for the lazy and unnecessary for the industrious."

4. Consider a 10-year period over which output per worker falls, but GDP increases. How can this happen? Do you think this is likely to be good for the economy?

5. When the Canadian dollar depreciates in foreign-exchange markets, many people view this as "good" for the Canadian economy. Who is likely to be harmed by and who is likely to benefit from a depreciation of the Canadian dollar?

CHAPTER 20

The Measurement of National Income

LEARNING OBJECTIVES

1 Describe the problem of "double counting" and how the concept of value added solves this problem when measuring national income.

2 Explain the income approach and the expenditure approach to measuring national income.

3 Explain the difference between real and nominal GDP, and why GDP per person is a better measure of living standards than just GDP itself.

4 List some of the many things affecting overall well-being that are omitted from official measures of GDP.

This chapter provides a detailed look at the measurement of national income. Once we know more precisely what is being measured and how it is measured, we will be ready to build a macroeconomic model to explain the determination of national income. Understanding how national income is measured is an important part of understanding how and why it changes. Indeed, this is a general rule of all economics and all science: Before using any data, it is essential to understand how those data are developed and what they measure.

20.1 National Output and Value Added

The central topic of macroeconomics is the overall level of economic activity—aggregate output and the income that is generated by its production. We start by asking: What do we mean by output?

This question may seem odd. Surely the town bakery knows what it produces, and if General Motors or Bombardier do not know their own outputs, what do they know? If each firm knows the value of its total output, the national income statisticians simply have to add up each separate output value to get the nation's output—or is it really that simple?

The reason that obtaining a total for the nation's output is not quite that simple is that one firm's output is often another firm's input. The local baker uses flour that is the output of the flour milling company, and the flour milling company, in turn, uses wheat that is the farmer's output. What is true for bread is true for most goods and services.

Production occurs in stages: Some firms produce outputs that are used as inputs by other firms, and these other firms, in turn, produce outputs that are used as inputs by yet other firms.

If we merely added up the market values of all outputs of all firms, we would obtain a total greatly in excess of the value of the economy's actual output.

Consider the baker as a simple example. If we added the total value of the output of the wheat farmer, the flour mill, and the baker, we would be counting the value of the wheat three times, the value of the milled flour twice, and the value of the bread once.

The error that would arise in estimating the nation's output by adding all sales of all firms is called **double counting.** "Multiple counting" would actually be a better term because if we added up the values of all sales, the same output would be counted every time that it was sold by one firm to another.

The problem of double counting could in principle be solved by distinguishing between two types of output. **Intermediate goods** are outputs of some firms that are used as inputs by other firms. **Final goods** are products that are not used as inputs by other firms, at least not in the period of time under consideration. The term *final demand* refers to the purchase of final goods for consumption, for investment (including inventory accumulation), for use by governments, and for export.

If the sales of firms could be easily disaggregated into sales of final goods and sales of intermediate goods, then measuring total output would be straightforward. It would simply equal the value of all *final* goods produced by firms. However, when Stelco sells steel to the Ford Motor Company, it does not care, and usually does not know, whether the steel is for final use (say, construction of a warehouse that will not be sold by Ford) or for use as part of an automobile that will be sold again. Even in our earlier example of bread, a bakery cannot be sure that its sales are for final use, for the bread may be further "processed" by a restaurant prior to its final sale to a customer. In general, it is extremely difficult if not impossible to distinguish final from intermediate goods successfully. The problem of double counting must therefore be resolved in some other manner.

To avoid double counting, economists use the concept of **value added,** which is the amount of value that firms and workers add to their products over and above the costs of intermediate goods. An individual firm's value added is:

$$\text{Value added} = \text{Revenue} - \text{Cost of intermediate goods}$$

Consider an example of a steel mill. A steel mill's value added is the revenue it earns from selling the steel it produces minus the value of the ore that it buys from the mining company, the value of the electricity and fuel oil that it uses, and the values of all other inputs that it buys from other firms.

We have said that a firm's value added equals the value of its output minus the value of inputs *purchased from other firms.* Earnings by factors of production, such as labour income or profits, are not purchases from other firms, and hence are not subtracted from the value of output when computing value added. But since the total value of output (revenue) is the sum of the cost of material inputs and earnings by factors of production (including profits), it follows that value added is exactly equal to the sum of factor incomes.[1]

$$\text{Value added} = \text{Income to factors of production}$$

double counting
In national income accounting, adding up the total outputs of all the sectors in the economy so that the value of intermediate goods is counted in the sector that produces them as well as every time they are purchased as an input by another sector.

intermediate goods
All outputs that are used as inputs by other producers in a further stage of production.

final goods   Goods that are not used as inputs by other firms but are produced to be sold for consumption, investment, government, or exports during the period under consideration.

value added
The value of a firm's output minus the value of the inputs that it purchases from other firms.

Practise with Study Guide Chapter 20, Exercises 1 and 2.

---

[1] We are ignoring here the role of indirect taxes, such as provincial sales taxes or the Goods and Services Tax (GST). Such taxes are included in the market value of a firm's output, but these taxes are remitted to the government and do not represent a payment to a factor of production.

APPLYING ECONOMIC CONCEPTS 20-1

Value Added Through Stages of Production

Because the output of one firm often becomes the input of other firms, the total value of goods sold by all firms greatly exceeds the value of the output of final products. This general principle is illustrated by a simple example in which a mining company starts from scratch and produces iron ore valued at $1000; this firm's value added is $1000. The mining company then sells the iron ore to a different firm that produces steel valued at $1500. The steel producer's value added is $500 because the value of the goods is increased by $500 as a result of the firm's

activities. Finally, the steel producer sells the steel to a metal fabricator who transforms the steel into folding chairs valued at $1800; the metal fabricator's value added is $300. We find the value of the final goods, $1800, either by counting only the sales of the last firm or by taking the sum of the values added by each firm. This value is much smaller than the $4300 that we would obtain if we merely added up the market value of the commodities sold by each firm.

Transactions at Three Different Stages of Production

	Mining Company (produces iron ore)	Steel Producer	Metal Fabricator (produces chairs)	All Firms	
A. Purchases from other firms	$ 0	$1000	$1500	$2500	Total interfirm sales
B. Purchases of factors of production	1000	500	300	1800	Total value added
A + B = value of product	$1000	$1500	$1800	$4300	Total value of all sales

Value added is the correct measure of each firm's contribution to total output—the amount of market value that is produced by that firm.

The firm's value added is the *net value* of its output. It is this net value that is the firm's contribution to the nation's total output, representing the firm's own efforts that add to the value of what it takes in as inputs. The concept of value added is further illustrated in *Applying Economic Concepts 20-1*. In this simple example, as in all more complex cases, the value of the nation's total output is obtained by summing all the individual values added.

The sum of all values added in an economy is a measure of the economy's total output.

20.2 National Income Accounting: The Basics

The measures of national income and national product that are used in Canada derive from an accounting system called the National Income and Expenditure Accounts (NIEA). The accounts, which are produced by Statistics Canada, provide us with a framework for analyzing the generation of national income. The National Income and

Expenditure Accounts are not simply collections of economic data. They have a logical structure, based on the simple yet important idea of the circular flow of income, which you first saw in Chapter 1 and which is shown again in Figure 20-1. The figure shows the overall flows of national income and expenditure, and also how government, the financial system, and foreign countries enter the flows. The key point from the circular flow is:

The value of domestic output is equal to the value of the expenditure on that output, and is also equal to the total claims to income that are generated by producing that output.

The circular flow of income suggests three different ways of measuring national income. The first is simply to add up the value of all goods and services produced in the economy. This requires the concept of value added, which we discussed in the previous section. The remaining two approaches correspond to the two halves of the circular flow of income. One approach is to add up the total flow of expenditure on domestic out-

FIGURE 20-1   The Circular Flow of Expenditure and Income

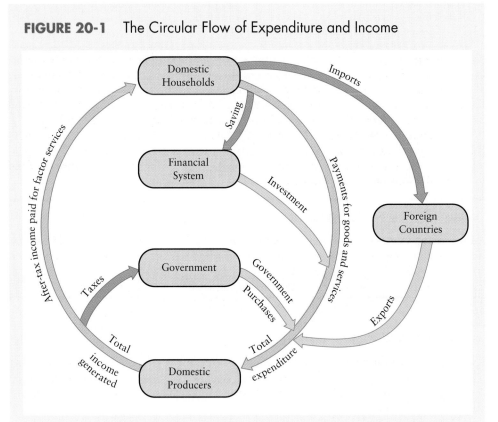

National income is equal to national product. Their flows are shown by the circular flow of income and expenditure. Consider first only the red lines. In this case, the flow would be a simple circle from households to producers and back to households. Now add the blue and green lines. The blue lines represent *injections* to the circular flow (exports, investment, and government purchases) while the green lines represent *withdrawals* from the circular flow (imports, saving, and taxes). Injections and withdrawals complicate the picture but do not change the basic relationship: Domestic production creates a claim on the value of that production. When all of the claims are added up, they must be equal to the value of all of the production.

put; the other is to add up the total flow of income generated by the flow of domestic production. All three measures yield the same total, which is called **gross domestic product** (**GDP**). When it is calculated by adding up the total value added in the economy, it is called *GDP by value added.* When it is calculated by adding up total expenditure for each of the main components of final output, the result is called *GDP on the expenditure side.* When it is calculated by adding up all the income claims generated by the act of production, it is called *GDP on the income side.*

The conventions of double-entry bookkeeping require that all value produced must be accounted for by a claim that someone has to that value. Thus the two values calculated from the income and the expenditure sides are identical conceptually and differ in practical measurements only because of errors of measurement. Any discrepancy arising from such errors is then reconciled so that one common total is given as *the* measure of GDP. Both calculations are of interest, however, because each gives a different and useful breakdown. Also, having two independent ways of measuring the same quantity provides a useful check on statistical procedures and on unavoidable errors in measurement.

GDP from the Expenditure Side

GDP for a given year is calculated from the expenditure side by adding up the expenditures needed to purchase the final output produced in that year. Total expenditure on final output is the sum of four broad categories of expenditure: consumption, investment, government, and net exports. In the following chapters, we will discuss in considerable detail the causes and consequences of movements in each of these four expenditure categories. Here we define what they are and how they are measured. Throughout, it is important to remember that these four categories of expenditure are exhaustive—they are *defined* in such a way that all expenditure on final output falls into one of the four categories.

1. Consumption Expenditure

Consumption expenditure includes expenditure on all goods and services sold to their final users during the year. It includes: services, such as haircuts, dental care, and legal advice; non-durable goods, such as fresh vegetables, clothing, cut flowers, and fresh meat; and durable goods, such as cars, television sets, and air conditioners. *Actual* measured consumption expenditure is denoted by the symbol C_a.

2. Investment Expenditure

Investment expenditure is expenditure on goods not for present consumption, including inventories, capital goods such as factories, machines and warehouses, and residential housing. Such goods are called *investment goods.* Let's examine these three categories in a little more detail.

Inventories.   Almost all firms hold stocks of their inputs and their own outputs. These stocks are called **inventories.** Inventories of inputs and unfinished materials allow firms to maintain a steady stream of production despite interruptions in the deliveries of inputs bought from other firms. Inventories of outputs allow firms to meet orders despite fluctuations in the rate of production.

The accumulation of inventories during any given year counts as current investment for that year because it represents goods produced but not used for current consumption. These goods are included in the national income accounts at market value, which includes the wages and other costs that the firm incurred in producing them and

gross domestic product (GDP)   The total value of goods and services produced in the economy during a given period.

consumption expenditure   Household expenditure on all goods and services. Represented by the symbol *C* as one of the four components of aggregate expenditure.

investment expenditure   Expenditure on the production of goods not for present consumption. Represented by the symbol *I.*

inventories   Stocks of raw materials, goods in process, and finished goods held by firms to mitigate the effect of short-term fluctuations in production or sales.

the profit that the firm will make when they are sold. Thus, in the case of inventories of a firm's own output, the expenditure approach measures what will have to be spent to purchase the inventories when they are sold rather than what has so far been spent to produce them.

The drawing down of inventories, often called *decumulation,* counts as disinvestment (negative investment) because it represents a reduction in the stock of finished goods that are available to be sold.

Plant and Equipment.   All production uses capital goods, which are manufactured aids to production, such as tools, machines, and factory buildings. The economy's total quantity of capital goods is called the **capital stock.** Creating new capital goods is an act of investment and is called *business fixed investment,* often shortened to **fixed investment.**

Residential Housing.   A house or an apartment building is a durable asset that yields its utility over a long period of time. Because such an asset meets the definition of investment that we gave earlier, housing construction—the building of a *new* house—is counted as investment expenditure rather than as consumption expenditure. However, when an individual purchases a house from a builder or from another individual, an existing asset is simply transferred, and the transaction is not part of national income. Only when a new house is built does it appear as residential investment in the national accounts.

Gross and Net Investment.   The total investment that occurs in the economy is called gross investment. Gross investment is divided into two parts: replacement investment and net investment. Replacement investment is the amount of investment that just maintains the level of existing capital stock; it is called the *capital consumption allowance* or simply **depreciation.** Net investment is equal to gross investment minus depreciation.

$$\text{Net investment} = \text{Gross investment} - \text{Depreciation}$$

When net investment is positive, the economy's capital stock is growing. If net investment is negative—which rarely happens—the economy's capital stock is shrinking.

All investment goods are part of the nation's total current output, and their production creates income whether the goods produced are a part of net investment or are merely replacement investment. Thus, all of gross investment is included in the calculation of national income. *Actual* total investment expenditure is denoted by the symbol I_a.

3. Government Purchases

When governments provide goods and services that households want, such as highways and libraries, they are adding to the sum total of valuable output in the economy. With other government activities, the case may not seem so clear. Should expenditures by the federal government to send peacekeepers overseas, or to pay a civil servant to refile papers from a now-defunct department, be regarded as contributions to national income?

National income statisticians do not speculate about such matters. Instead they include all **government purchases** of goods and services as part of national income. (Government expenditure on investment goods is included as government purchases rather than investment expenditure.) *Actual* government purchases of goods and services are denoted G_a.

capital stock
The aggregate quantity of capital goods.

fixed investment
The creation of new plant and equipment.

depreciation
The amount by which the capital stock is depleted through its contribution to current production. Also called *capital consumption allowance.*

government purchases
All government expenditure on currently produced goods and services, exclusive of government transfer payments. Represented by the symbol G.

Cost Versus Market Value.   Government output is typically valued at cost rather than at market value. In many cases, there is really no choice. What, for example, is the market value of the law courts? No one knows. But, since we do know what it costs the government to provide these services, we value them at their cost of production.

Although valuing at cost is the only possible way to measure many government activities, it does have one curious consequence. If, because of an increase in productivity, one civil servant now does what two used to do, and the displaced worker shifts to the private sector, the government's measured contribution to national income will fall (but the private sector's contribution will rise). Conversely, if two workers now do what one worker used to do, the government's contribution will rise. Both changes could occur even though what the government actually produces has not changed. This is an inevitable but curious consequence of measuring the value of the government's output by the cost of producing it.

Government Purchases Versus Government Expenditure.   Only government *purchases* of currently produced goods and services are included as part of GDP. A great deal of government expenditure does *not* count as part of GDP. For example, when the government makes payments to a retired person through the Canada Pension Plan, it is not purchasing any currently produced goods or services from the retiree. The payment itself does not add to total output. The same is true of payments for employment insurance, welfare, and interest on the national debt (which transfers income from taxpayers to holders of government bonds). These are examples of **transfer payments,** which are government expenditures that are not made in return for currently produced goods and services. They are not a part of expenditure on the nation's total output and are therefore not included in GDP. (Of course, the recipients of transfer payments often choose to spend their money on consumption goods. Such expenditure then counts in the same way as any other consumption expenditure.)

transfer payment
A payment to a private person or institution not made in exchange for a good or service.

4. Net Exports

The fourth category of aggregate expenditure arises from foreign trade. How do imports and exports influence national income? **Imports** are domestic expenditure on foreign-produced goods and services, whereas **exports** are foreign expenditure on domestically produced goods and services.

imports   The value of all goods and services purchased from firms, households, or governments in other countries.

exports   The value of all goods and services sold to firms, households, and governments in other countries.

Imports.   A country's national income is the total value of final commodities produced in that country. If you buy a car that was made in Japan, only a small part of that value will represent expenditure on Canadian production. Some of it represents payment for the services of the Canadian dealers and for transportation; the rest is expenditure on Japanese products. If you take your next vacation in Italy, much of your expenditure will be on goods and services produced in Italy and thus will contribute to Italian GDP rather than to Canadian GDP.

Similarly, when a Canadian firm makes an investment expenditure on a machine that was made partly with imported raw materials, only part of the expenditure is on Canadian production; the rest is expenditure on foreign production. The same is true for government expenditure on such things as roads and dams; some of the expenditure is for imported materials, and only part of it is for domestically produced goods and services.

Consumption, investment, and government expenditures all have an import content. To arrive at total expenditure *on Canadian products*, we need to subtract from total Canadian expenditure any expenditure on imports, which is given the symbol IM_a.

Exports.   If Canadian firms sell goods to German households, the goods are part of German consumption expenditure but also constitute expenditure on Canadian output. Indeed, all goods and services that are produced in Canada and sold to foreigners must be counted as part of Canadian production and income; they are produced in Canada, and they create incomes for the Canadian residents who produce them. They are not purchased by Canadian residents, however, so they are not included as part of C_a, I_a, or G_a. Therefore, to arrive at the total value of expenditure on *Canadian* output, it is necessary to add in the value of Canadian exports of goods and services. Actual exports are denoted X_a.

It is customary to group actual imports and actual exports together as **net exports**. Net exports are defined as total exports minus total imports ($X_a - IM_a$), which is also denoted NX_a. When the value of Canadian exports exceeds the value of Canadian imports, net exports are positive. When the value of imports exceeds the value of exports, net exports are negative.

net exports
The value of total exports minus the value of total imports. Represented by the symbol *NX*.

Practise with Study Guide Chapter 20, Short-Answer Question 1.

For the most recent data on national income, see Statistics Canada's website: www.statcan.ca.

Total Expenditures

Gross domestic product measured from the expenditure side is equal to the sum of the four expenditure categories that we have just discussed. In terms of a simple equation, we have

$$GDP = C_a + I_a + G_a + (X_a - IM_a)$$

GDP, calculated from the expenditure side, is the sum of consumption, investment, government, and net export expenditures.

These data are shown in Table 20-1 for Canada in 2002.

TABLE 20-1	GDP from the Expenditure Side, 2002	
Category	Billions of Dollars	Percent of GDP
Consumption	$651.2	57.0
Government purchases	243.4	21.3
Investment	200.2	17.5
Net exports	47.0	4.1
Statistical discrepancy	0.3	0.1
Total	$1142.1	100.0

GDP measured from the expenditure side of the national accounts gives the size of the major components of aggregate expenditure. Consumption was by far the largest expenditure category, equal to 57 percent of GDP.

(*Source:* These data are available at the website for Statistics Canada: www.statcan.ca. Go to "Canadian Statistics" and click on "Economic conditions" and then "National accounts.")

GDP from the Income Side

As we said earlier, the conventions of national income accounting are such that the production of a nation's output generates income *exactly* equal to the value of that production. Labour must be employed, land must be rented, and capital must be used. The calculation of GDP from the income side involves adding up factor incomes and other claims on the value of output until all of that value is accounted for.

1. Factor Incomes

National income accountants distinguish three main components of factor incomes: wages and salaries, interest, and business profits.

Wages and Salaries.   Wages and salaries are the payment for the services of labour. They include take-home pay, income taxes withheld, employment-insurance contributions, pension-fund contributions, and other fringe benefits. In total, wages and salaries represent the part of the value of production that is attributable to labour.

Interest.   Interest includes interest that is earned on bank deposits, interest that is earned on loans to firms, and miscellaneous other investment income (but excludes interest income earned from loans to Canadian governments).[2]

Business Profits.   Some profits are paid out as *dividends* to owners of firms; the rest are retained for use by firms and are called *retained earnings*. Both dividends and retained earnings are included in the calculation of GDP. For accounting purposes, total profits include corporate profits, incomes of unincorporated businesses (mainly small businesses, farmers, partnerships, and professionals), and profits of government business enterprises and Crown corporations (such as Canada Post).

Profits and interest together represent the payment for the use of capital—interest for borrowed capital and profits for capital contributed by the owners of firms.

Net Domestic Income.   The sum of wages and salaries, interest, and profits is called *net domestic income at factor cost*. It is "net" because it excludes the value of output that is used as replacement investment. It is "domestic income" because it is the income accruing to domestic factors of production. It is "at factor cost" because it represents only that part of the value of final output that accrues to factors in the form of payments due to them for their services. As we will see immediately, some part of the value of final output does not accrue to the factors at all.

2. Non-Factor Payments

Every time a consumer spends $10 on some item, less than $10 is generated as income for factors of production. This shortfall is due to the presence of indirect taxes and depreciation.

Indirect Taxes and Subsidies.   An important claim on the market value of output arises out of indirect taxes, which are taxes on the production and sale of goods and services. In Canada, the most important indirect taxes are provincial excise and retail sales taxes, which differ across provinces, and the federal Goods and Services Tax (GST), which is uniform across all provinces.

For example, if a good's market price of $10.00 includes 50 cents in provincial sales taxes and 70 cents in federal GST, only $8.80 is available as income to factors of production. Governments are claiming $1.20 of the $10.00 initial value of the good. Adding up income claims to determine GDP therefore necessitates including the portion of the total market value of output that is the governments' claims exercised through their taxes on goods and services.

It is also necessary to subtract government subsidies on goods and services, since these payments allow factor incomes to *exceed* the market value of output. Suppose that a municipal bus company spends $150 000 producing bus rides and covers its costs by selling $140 000 in fares and obtaining a $10 000 subsidy from the local government. The total income that the company will generate from its production is $150 000, but the total market value of its output is only $140 000, with the difference made up by the subsidy. To get from total income to the market value of its total output, we must subtract the amount of the subsidy.

---

[2] The treatment of interest in the national accounts is a little odd. Interest paid by the government is considered a transfer payment, whereas interest paid by private households or firms is treated as expenditure (and its receipt is counted as a factor payment). This is only one example of arbitrary decisions in national income accounting. Others are discussed in *Extensions in Theory 20-1.*

TABLE 20-2   GDP from the Income Side, 2002

Category	Billions of Dollars	Percent of GDP
Factor Incomes		
Wages, salaries and supplementary income	$ 595.3	52.1
Interest and miscellaneous investment income	49.7	4.4
Business profits (including net income of farmers and unincorporated businesses)	210.4	18.4
Net Domestic Income at factor cost	855.4	74.9
Non-Factor Payments		
Capital consumption allowance	149.6	13.1
Indirect taxes less subsidies	137.6	12.0
Statistical discrepancy	−0.3	−0.1
Total	$1142.1	100.0

GDP measured from the income side of the national accounts gives the sizes of the major components of the income that is generated by producing the nation's output. The largest category, equal to about 52 percent of income, is compensation to employees, which includes wages and salaries and other benefits.

(*Source:* These data are available at the website for Statistics Canada: www.statcan.ca. Go to "Canadian Statistics" and click on "Economic conditions" and then "National accounts.")

Depreciation.   Another claim on the value of final output is depreciation, or capital consumption allowance. Depreciation is the value of capital that has been used up in the process of producing final output. It is part of gross profits, but because it is needed to compensate for capital used up in the process of production, it is not part of net profits. Hence, depreciation is not income earned by any factor of production. Rather, it is value that must be reinvested just to maintain the existing stock of capital equipment.

Total Income

To measure GDP from the income side, we begin with total income to the factors of production and add total non-factor payments. That is, GDP equals factor income plus depreciation plus indirect taxes (net of subsidies).

From the income side, GDP is the sum of factor incomes *plus* indirect taxes (net of subsidies) *plus* depreciation.

The various components of the income side of the GDP in the Canadian economy in 2002 are shown in Table 20-2. Note that one of the terms in the table is called *statistical discrepancy*. This is a "fudge factor" to make sure that the independent measures of income and expenditure come to the same total. Statistical discrepancy is a clear indication that national income accounting is not error-free. Although national income and national expenditure are conceptually identical, in practice both are measured with slight error.

We have now seen the two methods for computing a country's national income. Both are correct and give us the same measure of GDP, but each gives us some different additional information. For some questions, such as what the likely future path of the nation's capital stock will be, it is useful to know the relative importance of consumption and investment. In this case, the expenditure approach for computing GDP provides some of the necessary information (Table 20-1). For other questions, such as what is happening to the distribution of income between labour and capital, we need information about the composition of factor incomes. In this case, a useful starting point would be to examine GDP on the income side (Table 20-2).

Measuring national income is not problem-free. As in any accounting exercise, many arbitrary rules are used. Some of them seem odd, but the important thing is to use these rules consistently over time. That way, comparisons of GDP over time will reflect genuine changes in economic activity, which is what we desire for the measure. *Extensions in Theory 20-1* discusses the issue of arbitrariness in national income accounting.

EXTENSIONS IN THEORY 20-1

Arbitrary Decisions in National Income Accounting

National income accounting practices contain many arbitrary decisions. For example, goods that are finished and held in inventories are valued at market value, thereby anticipating their sale, even though the actual selling price may not be known. In the case of a Ford in a dealer's showroom, this practice may be justified because the *value* of this Ford is perhaps virtually the same as that of an identical Ford that has just been sold to a customer. However, what is the correct market value of a half-finished house or an unfinished novel? Accountants arbitrarily treat goods in process at cost (rather than at market value) if the goods are being made by firms. They ignore completely the value of the unfinished novel. The arbitrary nature of these decisions is inevitable: Because people must arrive at some practical compromise between consistent definitions and measurable magnitudes, any decision will be somewhat arbitrary.

Such arbitrary decisions surely affect the size of measured GDP. But does it matter? The surprising answer,

for many purposes, is no. It is wrong to think that just because a statistical measure is imperfect (as all statistical measures are), it is useless. Simple measures often give estimates to the right order of magnitude, and substantial improvements in sophistication may make only trivial improvements in these estimates.

In 2002, for example, Canadian GDP was measured as $1142.1 billion. It is certain that the market value of all production in Canada in that year was neither $100 billion nor $2000 billion, but it might well have been $1100 billion or $1200 billion had different measures been defined with different arbitrary decisions built in. Similarly, Canadian per capita GDP is about three times the Spanish per capita GDP and is a little less than U.S. per capita GDP. Other measures might differ, but it is unlikely that any measure would reveal the Spanish per capita GDP to be higher than Canada's, or Canada's to be significantly above that of the United States.

20.3 National Income Accounting: Some Extra Issues

Now that we have examined the basics of national income accounting, we are ready to explore some more detailed issues. We discuss the distinction between GDP and the related concept of gross national product (GNP), the important difference between real and nominal GDP, and some simple measures of productivity.

GDP and GNP

A measure of national output closely related to GDP is **gross national product (GNP)**. The difference between GDP and GNP is the difference between *income produced* and *income received*. GDP measures the total output *produced in Canada* and the total income generated as a result of that production. GNP measures the total amount of income *received by Canadian residents*, no matter where that income was generated. How can GDP differ from GNP? Let's consider two examples.

For the first example, consider a Toyota factory located in Cambridge, Ontario. Suppose in 2004 that the value added generated by that factory is $100 million. Canadian GDP is therefore higher by $100 million as a result of that production. But suppose

gross national product (GNP) The value of total incomes earned by domestically based producers and factors of production.

Toyota cars produced in Canada contribute to Canada's GDP. But the portion of profits that returns to foreign shareholders is not part of Canada's GNP.

that $5 million of the profits (part of the value added) generated at that factory is remitted to foreign owners. Since only $95 million of the value added generates income *for Canadian residents*, Canadian GNP is higher by only $95 million.

The second example involves any Canadian-owned business located outside of Canada. The value added produced by that business contributes to the GDP in a foreign country, but not in Canada. But if there are profits remitted to the Canadian owners, those profits will be part of the income of Canadian residents and thus part of Canadian GNP.

GDP measures the value of all production located in Canada, no matter who receives the income from that production. GNP measures the income received by Canadian residents, no matter where the production occurred to generate that income.

The relative sizes of GDP and GNP depend on the balance between income from Canadian investments abroad and income from foreign investments in Canada. For most of Canada's history, Canada has been a *net debtor* country. Thus, the value of foreign-based assets owned by Canadian residents has been less than the value of Canadian-based assets owned by foreigners. As a result, the foreign-generated income received by Canadian residents is less than the Canadian-generated income going to foreigners. This makes Canadian GNP less than Canadian GDP. But the difference is small. In most years, GNP is only 3 or 4 percent lower than GDP.

Which Measure Is Better?

Given the difference between GDP and GNP, we are naturally led to ask if one measure is better than the other. The answer depends on what we want to measure.

GDP is superior to GNP as a measure of domestic economic activity. GNP is superior to GDP as a measure of the income of domestic residents.

If you want to know how easy it will be to find a job or whether factories are working double shifts or whether new buildings are going up right and left, look to changes in the GDP. By its definition, it is the GDP that tells us how much is being produced within a nation's borders. To know how much income is available to the residents of a country, however, one should look at the GNP, which counts income earned abroad and subtracts out income produced at home that accrues to residents of other nations. Thus, the GNP is a better measure of the income of a country's residents.

Disposable Personal Income

disposable personal income The part of national income that accrues to households and is available to spend or save.

Both GDP and GNP are important measures of overall economic activity and of national income. Most important to consumers, however, is **disposable personal income,** the part of national income that is available to households to spend or to save. The easiest way to calculate disposable personal income is to subtract from GNP the parts of the GNP that are not available to households. Hence, we must subtract all taxes (both income and sales taxes), capital consumption allowances, retained earnings, and interest paid to institutions. However, having subtracted taxes, we need to add back in transfer payments made to households. In recent years, disposable income has represented about 65 percent of GDP.

Real and Nominal GDP

In Chapter 19, we distinguished between real and nominal measures of aggregate output. When we add up money values of outputs, expenditures, or incomes, we end up with what are called *nominal values*. Nominal GDP increased by 68.0 percent between 1990 and 2002. If we want to compare *real* GDP in 2002 to that in 1990, we need to determine how much of that 68.0-percent nominal increase was due to increases in prices and how much was due to increases in quantities produced. Although there are many possible ways of doing this, the underlying principle is always the same: The value of output in each period is computed by using a common set of *base-period prices*. When this is done, economists say that real output is measured in *constant dollars*.

Total GDP valued at current prices is called *nominal national income*. GDP valued at base-period prices is called *real national income*.

Any change in nominal GDP reflects the combined effects of changes in quantities and changes in prices. However, when real income is measured over different periods by using a common set of base-period prices, changes in real income reflect only changes in quantities. Table 20-3 shows real and nominal GDP for selected years in Canada since 1980.

The GDP Deflator

If nominal and real GDP change by different amounts over a given time period, then prices must have changed over that period. For example, if nominal GDP has increased by 6 percent and real GDP has increased by only 4 percent over the same period, we know that average prices must have increased by 2 percent. Comparing what has happened to nominal and real GDP over the same period implies the existence of a price index measuring the change in prices over that period—"implies" because no explicit price index is used in calculating either real or nominal GDP. However, an index can be inferred by comparing these two values. The *GDP deflator* is defined as follows:

$$\text{GDP deflator} = \frac{\text{GDP at current prices}}{\text{GDP at base-period prices}} \times 100$$

The **GDP deflator** is the most comprehensive available index of the price level because it includes all the goods and services that are produced by the entire economy. It uses the current year's basket of production to compare the current year's prices with those prevailing in the base period. (Because it uses the current basket of goods and services, it does not run into the CPI's problem of sometimes being based on an out-of-date basket.) The GDP deflator was 7.5 percent higher in 2002 than in 2000

TABLE 20-3 Nominal and Real GDP in Canada: Selected Years (billions of dollars)

Year	Nominal GDP (current prices)	Real GDP (1997 prices)	GDP Deflator
1980	314.4	576.4	54.5
1985	485.7	660.3	73.6
1990	679.9	762.4	89.2
1995	810.4	832.1	97.4
1997	882.7	882.7	100.0
2000	1065.0	1013.1	105.1
2002	1142.1	1062.0	107.5

Nominal GDP tells us about the money value of output; real GDP tells us about the quantity of physical output. Nominal GDP gives the total value of output in any year, valued at the prices of that year. Real GDP gives the total value of output in any year, *valued at prices from some base year,* in this case 1997. The comparison of real and nominal GDP implicitly defines a price index, changes in which reveal changes in the (average) prices of goods produced domestically. Note that in 1997, nominal GDP equals real GDP (measured in 1997 prices) and thus the GDP deflator equals 100.

(*Source:* Statistics Canada, CANSIM database. Real GDP: Series V3862685. Nominal GDP: Series V646937.)

GDP deflator
An index number derived by dividing nominal GDP by real GDP. Its change measures the average change in price of all the items in the GDP.

(see Table 20-3). Thus, in 2002, it cost 7.5 percent more to produce the goods and services than it would have cost to produce the same goods and services in 2000. *Applying Economic Concepts 20-2* illustrates the calculation of real and nominal GDP and the GDP deflator for a simple hypothetical economy that produces only wheat and steel.

As we said above, a change in nominal national income can be split into a change due to prices and a change due to quantities. For example, from the data in Table 20-3 we see that in 2002, Canadian nominal GDP was 68.0 percent higher than in 1990. This increase was due to a 20.5-percent increase in prices and a 39.3-percent increase in real GDP.[3]

Output and Well-Being

The rise in real GDP during the last century has had two main causes:

1. An increase in the amounts of land, labour, and capital used in production; and,

2. An increase in the amount of output produced *per unit of input*.

In other words, more inputs have been used, and each input has become more productive.

Although it is useful to measure total output for some purposes, such as assessing the total size of a particular economy, for other purposes, such as studying the pace of technological improvement, it is better to measure the amount of output per unit of input—what economists call *productivity*. (The most common measure of labour productivity is GDP divided by the total number of hours worked.) For still other purposes, such as studying the change in overall living standards, it is probably best to examine output per person, or what economists call **per capita output** and often use as a measure of average income.

Despite the extent to which economists and policymakers tend to focus on changes in GDP, it is important to realize that over very long periods of time—say 50 years or more—changes in our overall well-being are not reflected very accurately in GDP statistics. *Lessons From History 20-1* illustrates that many of the benefits from the eighteenth- and nineteenth-century Industrial Revolution did not take the form of more output per person—they instead took the form of the development of *new products* that changed and improved the lives of millions of ordinary people. Many of these changes would be missed by the value of GDP, which captures the *amount* of output, but not its composition.

per capita output
GDP divided by total population.

See Chapter 20 of www.pearsoned.ca/ragan for an interesting discussion of why the computer revolution has not yet appeared in measurements of productivity growth: Jeremy Leonard, "Computers and Productivity in the Information Economy."

Canada and six other countries together form what is called the "G7" group of advanced industrialized nations. For a comparison of economic growth in the G7 countries over the past decade, look for "Growth in Canada and Other G7 Countries" in the *Additional Topics* section of this book's Companion Website.

h t t p : / / w w w . p e a r s o n e d . c a / r a g a n

---

[3] For large percentage changes in price and quantity, the nominal percentage change is not exactly equal to the sum of the price and the quantity changes; generally, the relationship is multiplicative. In this case, prices and quantities are respectively 1.205 and 1.393 times their original values. Thus, nominal GDP is $(1.205) \times (1.393) = 1.679$ times its original value, which is an increase of just under 68.0 percent. For small percentage changes, the sum is a very good approximation of the multiplicative change. If prices grow by 2 percent and quantities by 3 percent, the nominal change is $(1.02) \times (1.03) = 1.0506$, which is very close to 1.05.

APPLYING ECONOMIC CONCEPTS 20-2

Calculating Nominal and Real GDP

To see what is involved in calculating nominal GDP, real GDP, and the GDP deflator, an example may be helpful. Consider a simple hypothetical economy that produces only two commodities, wheat and steel. Table 1 gives the basic data for output and prices in the economy for two years.

TABLE 1   Data for a Hypothetical Economy

| | Quantity produced | | Prices | |
	Wheat (bushels)	Steel (tonne)	Wheat ($/bushel)	Steel ($/tonne)
Year 1	100	20	10	50
Year 2	110	16	12	55

Table 2 shows nominal GDP, calculated by adding the money values of wheat output and of steel output for each year. In year 1, the values of both wheat and steel production were $1000, so nominal GDP was $2000. In year 2, wheat output rose to $1320, and steel output fell to $880. Since the rise in the value of wheat was greater than the fall in the value of steel, nominal GDP rose by $200.

TABLE 2   Calculation of Nominal GDP

Year 1: $(100 \times \$10) + (20 \times \$50) = \$2000$
Year 2: $(110 \times \$12) + (16 \times \$55) = \$2200$

Table 3 shows real GDP, calculated by valuing output in each year *at year-2 prices;* that is, year 2 is used as the base year. In year 2, wheat output rose, but steel output fell. If we use year-2 prices, the fall in the value of steel output between years 1 and 2 exceeded the rise in the value of wheat output, and so real GDP fell.

TABLE 3   Calculation of Real GDP Using Year-2 Prices

Year 1: $(100 \times \$12) + (20 \times \$55) = \$2300$
Year 2: $(110 \times \$12) + (16 \times \$55) = \$2200$

In Table 4, the ratio of nominal to real GDP is calculated for each year and multiplied by 100. This ratio implicitly measures the change in prices over the period in question and is called the *GDP deflator.* The deflator shows that the price level increased by 15 percent between year 1 and year 2.

TABLE 4   Calculation of the GDP Deflator

Year 1: $(2000/2300) \times 100 = 86.96$
Year 2: $(2200/2200) \times 100 = 100.00$

Throughout this box we have used year 2 as the base year. But we could just as easily have used year 1. The changes we would have computed in real GDP and the deflator would have been very similar—but not identical—to the ones we did compute using year 2 as the base year. The choice of base year matters because of different *relative* prices in the different years (note that the price of steel relative to the price of wheat is lower in year 2 than in year 1). Put simply, with different relative prices in different years, the various output changes get weighted differently depending on which prices we use, and thus the *aggregate* measure of real GDP changes by different amounts. (If you want to understand this point in more detail, try doing Study Exercise #8 at the end of the chapter.)*

How do we choose the "right" base year? As with many other elements of national income accounting, there is some arbitrariness in the choice. There is no "right" year. The important thing is not which year to use—the important thing is to be clear about which year you are using and then, for a given set of comparisons, to be sure that you are consistent in your choice.

---

* In 2001, Statistics Canada adopted a new approach for computing real GDP that is less sensitive to changes in relative prices. The new *Fisher* approach essentially involves taking an average of different price indexes, each one using a different base year. For details, go to www.statcan.ca and search for "chain Fisher."

Practise with Study Guide Chapter 20, Extension Exercise E1.

LESSONS FROM HISTORY 20-1

Living Standards and Long-Run Economic Growth

GDP is not a very good indicator of the improvements in living standards that are generated by long-run economic growth. The reason is that so many of the major benefits that growth provides are imperfectly measured or not measured at all by GDP. This can be dramatically illustrated by looking at some of the most important changes that accompanied the first Industrial Revolution (1784–1870).

1. In early eighteenth-century Europe, average life expectancy was around 30 years; in France, one in five children were dead by the end of the first year of life, and 50 percent of registered children were dead by age 10. Life expectancy rose dramatically during the Industrial Revolution.

2. Industrialization reduced famine and hunger. Not only did the average food intake rise, but its year-to-year variation fell. It is of little consolation to a peasant that the average food consumption is above the subsistence level over the decades if fluctuations in harvests periodically drive it below the subsistence level, thus causing starvation.

3. Technological changes that accompanied the Industrial Revolution virtually eliminated many terrible diseases that had been common until that time, such as plague, tuberculosis, cholera, dysentery, smallpox, and leprosy.

4. The urbanization that accompanied industrialization increased literacy and education and broadened experience. Before then, poverty and a rural, peasant

existence, with little or no communication between the village and the outside world, tended to be associated with superstition and very narrow experience.

5. Privacy became possible when people moved from the peasant dwelling, where the entire family lived, ate, and slept in one room, to multiroom urban sites.

6. The introduction of a market economy greatly increased the mobility of persons among jobs. In the rural societies, there were few options for employment, and customary behaviour—doing what one's parents did—dominated job selection.

7. The Industrial Revolution was based on mass production of goods sold mainly to low- and middle-income people. These changed the quality of consumption. For example, instead of wooden clogs, people adopted leather shoes; instead of rough, homespun cloth, people had factory-made shirts and skirts; instead of mud floors and thatched roofs, people had wooden floors and rain-proof roofs; instead of all living in one room, parents had a room separate from their children. These things may seem trivial to us today, but they changed the way of life of ordinary people.

Throughout the late eighteenth century and all of the nineteenth century, a succession of new products continued to alter the way ordinary people lived until, by the mid-twentieth century, the ordinary working person had a structurally different way of life from his or her counterpart in the mid-eighteenth century. Statistics, however, are the same if a doubling of GDP takes the form of twice as much of the same, or of new things that enhance the quality of life. The effect on living standards is, however, much greater when new commodities replace older ones rather than just more of the same becoming available.

This box draws on material in: J. Blum, *Our Forgotten Past: Seven Centuries of Life on the Land* (London: Thames and Hudson, 1982); F. Braudel, *Structures of Everyday Life, 15th–18th Century* (New York: Harper and Row, 1981); and N. Rosenberg and L. E. Birdzell, Jr., *How the West Grew Rich* (New York: Basic Books, 1986).

Omissions from GDP

National income as measured in the National Income and Expenditure Accounts provides an excellent measure of the flow of economic activity in organized markets in a given year. But much economic activity takes place outside of the markets that the national income accountants survey. Although these activities are not typically included in the measure of GDP, they nevertheless use real resources and satisfy real wants and needs.

Illegal Activities

GDP does not measure illegal activities, even though many of them are ordinary business activities that produce goods and services sold in markets and that generate factor incomes. Many forms of illegal gambling, prostitution, and drug trade come into this category. To gain an accurate measure of the total demand for factors of production, of total marketable output, or of total incomes generated, we should include these activities, whether or not we as individuals approve of them. The omission of illegal activities is no trivial matter: The drug trade alone is a multibillion-dollar business.

Prostitution and other illegal activities involve genuine market transactions, but they are not included in official measures of national income.

Note that some illegal activities do get included in national income measures, although they are generally misclassified by industry. The income is included because people sometimes report their earnings from illicit activities as part of their earnings from legal activities. They do this to avoid the fate of Al Capone, the famous Chicago gangster in the 1920s and 1930s, who, having avoided conviction on many counts, was finally caught for income-tax evasion.

The Underground Economy

A significant omission from GDP is the so-called underground economy. The transactions that occur in the underground economy are perfectly legal in themselves; the only illegality involved is that such transactions are not reported for tax purposes. One example of this is the carpenter who repairs a leak in your roof and takes payment in cash (and does not report it as income) to avoid taxation. Because such transactions go unreported, they are omitted from GDP.

The growth of the underground economy is facilitated by the rising importance of services in the nation's total output. It is much easier for a carpenter to pass unnoticed by government authorities than it is for a manufacturing establishment. Estimates of the value of income earned in the underground economy run from 2 percent to 15 percent of GDP. In some countries, the figures are even higher. The Italian underground economy, for example, has been estimated at close to 25 percent of that country's GDP.

Home Production

If a homeowner hires a firm to do some landscaping, the value of the landscaping enters into GDP; if the homeowner does the landscaping herself, the value of the landscaping is omitted from GDP because there is no market transaction. Such production of goods and services in the home is called *home production*. Other non-market activities include voluntary work such as canvassing for a political party, helping to run a volunteer day-care centre, or leading a scout troop. Both home production and volunteer activities clearly add to economic well-being, and both use economic resources. Yet neither is included in official measures of national income.

Compared to developing countries, the non-market sector in most advanced industrial economies is relatively small, although much household maintenance, education, and child care are performed at home. The omissions become very misleading when national income measures are used to compare living standards in structurally different economies. Generally, the non-market sector of the economy is larger in rural than in urban settings and in less developed than in more developed economies. Be cautious, then, when interpreting data from a country with a very different climate and culture. When you hear that the per capita GDP of Nigeria is about $1200 per year (compared to about $26 000 in Canada), you should not imagine that living in Nigeria is like living in Canada with only $1200.

One extremely important non-market activity is leisure. If an attorney voluntarily chooses to reduce her time at work from 2400 hours to 2200 hours per year, measured national income will fall by the attorney's wage rate times 200 hours. Yet the value to the attorney of the 200 hours of new leisure enjoyed outside of the marketplace must exceed the lost wages (otherwise she would choose to work the extra 200 hours), so total economic welfare has increased even though measured GDP has fallen. Until recently, one of the most important ways in which economic growth benefited people was by permitting increased amounts of leisure. Because the time off is not marketed, its value does not show up in measures of national income.

Economic "Bads"

When an electric power plant sends sulfur dioxide into the atmosphere, leading to acid rain and environmental damage, the value of the electricity sold is included as part of GDP, but the value of the damage done by the acid rain is not deducted. Similarly, the gasoline that we use in our cars is part of national income when it is produced, but the damage done by burning that gasoline is not deducted. To the extent that economic growth brings with it increases in pollution, congestion, and other disamenities of modern living, measurements of national income will overstate the improvement in living standards. Such measures capture the increased output of goods and services, but they fail to account for the increased output of "bads" that generally accompany economic growth.

The extraction, refining, and transportation of oil are all included as goods and services in measures of GDP. But the environmental damage inflicted by an oil spill—an economic "bad"—is not included in any measure of GDP.

Do the Omissions Matter?

See Chapter 20 of www.pearsoned.ca/ragan for an excellent discussion of the role of per capita income in determining a country's overall "human development": William Watson, "If Canada Is Number One, Why Would Anyone Leave?"

GDP does a good job of measuring the flow of goods and services through the market sector of the economy. Usually, an increase in GDP implies greater opportunities for employment for households that sell their labour services in the market.

Unless the importance of unmeasured economic activity changes rapidly, *changes* in GDP will probably do a satisfactory job of measuring *changes* in economic opportunities.

However, when the task at hand is measurement of the overall flow of goods and services available to satisfy people's wants, regardless of the source of the goods and services, then the omissions that we have discussed become undesirable and potentially serious. Still, in the relatively short term, changes in GDP will usually be a good measure of the direction, if not the exact magnitude, of changes in economic well-being.

S U M M A R Y

20.1 National Output and Value Added ⓛⓞ①

- Each firm's contribution to total output is equal to its value added, which is the value of the firm's output minus the values of all intermediate goods and services—that is, the outputs of other firms—that it uses. The sum of all the values added produced in an economy is the economy's total output, which is called gross domestic product (GDP).

20.2 National Income Accounting: The Basics ⓛⓞ②

- From the circular flow of income, there are three ways to compute national income. One is to add up each firm's value added. The second is to add up total expenditure on domestic output. The third is to add up the total income generated by domestic production. By standard accounting conventions, these three aggregations define the same total.
- From the expenditure side of the national accounts,

$$GDP = C_a + I_a + G_a + (X_a - IM_a)$$

C_a comprises consumption expenditures of households. I_a is investment in plant and equipment, residential construction, and inventory accumulation. G_a is government purchases of goods and services. $(X_a - IM_a)$ represents net exports of goods and services.
- GDP measured from the income side adds up all claims to the market value of production. Wages, interest, profits, depreciation (or capital consumption allowance), and indirect taxes net of subsidies are the major categories.

20.3 National Income Accounting: Some Extra Issues ⓛⓞ③④

- GDP measures the value of all production located in Canada, no matter who receives the income from that production. GNP measures the income received by Canadian residents, no matter where the production occurred to generate that income. Because Canada is a net debtor, its GNP is usually 3 to 4 percent less than its GDP.
- Real measures of national income reflect changes in real quantities. Nominal measures of national income reflect changes in both prices and quantities. Any change in nominal income can be split into a change in quantities and a change in prices. Appropriate comparisons of nominal and real measures yield implicit deflators.
- Economists frequently use measures of GDP, GDP per capita, and various measures of labour productivity such as GDP per employed worker or GDP per hour worked.

Changes in overall living standards are better reflected by changes in productivity than by changes in GDP.
- GDP and related measures of national income must be interpreted with their limitations in mind. GDP excludes production resulting from activities that are illegal, that take place in the underground economy, or that do not pass through markets. Hence GDP does not measure everything that contributes to (or detracts from) human well-being.
- Notwithstanding its limitations, GDP remains a useful measure of the total economic activity that passes through the nation's markets. Recorded *changes* in GDP will generally do an accurate job of measuring *changes* in economic activity and economic opportunities.

KEY CONCEPTS

Intermediate and final goods
Value added
GDP as the sum of all values added
GDP from the expenditure side

GDP from the income side
GNP versus GDP
Disposable personal income
GDP deflator

Per capita GDP and labour
productivity
Omissions from GDP

STUDY EXERCISES

1. Fill in the blanks to make the following statements complete.

   a. If, when measuring Canada's national output, we add the market values of all firms' outputs in Canada, then we are committing the error of _____. Such an amount would greatly _____ the economy's actual output.

   b. Statisticians use the concept of _____ to avoid double counting in measuring national income. Each firm's _____ is the value of its output minus the costs of _____ that it purchases from other firms.

   c. If we measure GDP from the expenditure side, we are adding four broad categories of expenditure: _____, _____, _____, and _____. As an equation it is written as GDP = _____.

   d. If we measure GDP from the income side, we are adding three main components of factor incomes: _____, _____ and _____. To these items we must add nonfactor payments of _____ and _____.

2. Fill in the blanks to make the following statements correct.

   a. Comparing GDP and GNP, if we want the best measure of Canada's domestic economic activity, we should look at _____; if we want the best measure of the well-being of Canada's residents, then we should look at _____.

   b. If nominal GDP increases by 35 percent over a 10-year period, then it is unclear how much of this increase is due to increases in _____ and how much is due to increases in _____. To overcome this problem, we look at GDP valued at _____ prices and we refer to this measure as _____ national income.

   c. GDP divided by total population gives us a measure of _____.

   d. GDP divided by the number of employed persons in Canada gives us a measure of labour _____.

3. In measuring GDP from the expenditure side (GDP = $C_a + I_a + G_a + NX_a$), which of the following expenditures are included, and within which of the four categories?

   a. expenditures on automobiles by consumers
   b. expenditures on automobiles by firms
   c. expenditures on new machinery by Canadian-owned forest companies in Canada
   d. expenditures on new machinery by Canadian-owned forest companies in the United States
   e. expenditures on new machinery by U.S.-owned forest companies in Canada
   f. reductions in business inventories
   g. purchases of second-hand cars and trucks
   h. the hiring of economic consultants by the Manitoba government
   i. the purchase of Canadian-produced software by a firm in Japan

4. The list below provides some national income figures for the country of Econoland. All figures are in millions of dollars.

Wages and salaries	5000
Interest income	200
Personal consumption	3900
Personal saving	1100
Personal income taxes	200
Business profits	465
Indirect taxes	175
Subsidies	30
Government purchases	1000
Exports	350
Imports	390
Net private investment	950
Depreciation	150

   a. Using the expenditure approach, what is the value of GDP for Econoland?

b. Using the income approach, what is the value of GDP?

c. What is the value of net domestic income at factor cost?

5. The table below shows data for real and nominal GDP for a hypothetical economy over several years.

Year	Nominal GDP (billions of $)	Real GDP (billions of 2001 $)	GDP Deflator
1999	775.3	798.4	97.1
2000	814.1	838.6	97.1
2001	862.9	862.9	100
2002	901.5	882.5	102
2003	951.3	920.6	103.2
2004	998.8	950.5	105

a. Compute the GDP deflator for each year.

b. Compute the total percentage change in nominal GDP from 1999 to 2004. How much of this change was due to increases in prices and how much was due to changes in quantities?

6. Would inflation, as measured by the rate of change in the GDP deflator, ever be different from inflation as measured by the rate of change in the Consumer Price Index? Would it ever be the same? Explain.

7. For each of the following events, describe the likely effect on real GDP.

a. The Quebec ice storm of 1998 increases the demand for building materials to repair damage to homes.

b. The Quebec ice storm of 1998 damages many factories.

c. The building of a baseball stadium in Montreal increases the demand for Expos tickets by Montrealers.

d. The building of a baseball stadium in Montreal increases the demand for Expos tickets by residents of Vermont and New Hampshire.

8. Consider the following data for a hypothetical economy that produces two goods, milk and honey.

| | Quantity Produced | | Prices | |
	Milk (litres)	Honey (kg)	Milk ($/litre)	Honey ($/kg)
Year 1	100	40	2	6
Year 2	120	25	3	6

a. Compute nominal GDP for each year in this economy.

b. Using year 1 as the base year, compute real GDP for each year. What is the percentage change in real GDP from year 1 to year 2?

c. Using year 1 as the base year, compute the price deflator for each year. What is the percentage change in real GDP from year 1 to year 2?

d. Now compute the GDP deflator for each year, using year 1 as the base year.

e. Now compute the GDP deflator for each year, using year 2 as the base year.

f. Explain why the measures of real GDP growth (and growth in the deflator) depend on the choice of base year.

DISCUSSION QUESTIONS

1. Residents of some Canadian cities have recently become concerned about the growing proportion of their local real estate that is being bought up by foreign residents. What is the effect of this transfer of ownership on Canadian GDP and GNP?

2. What would be the effects of the following events on the measured value of Canada's real GDP? Speculate on the effects of each event on the true well-being of Canadians.

a. destruction of thousands of homes by flood water
b. destruction of hundreds of businesses by an ice storm
c. complete cessation of all imports from Europe
d. an increase in the amount of acid rain that falls

e. an increase in the amount of spending on devices that reduce pollution at a major hydroelectricity plant
f. reduction in the standard workweek from 37 hours to 30 hours
g. hiring of all welfare recipients as government employees
h. outbreak of hostilities in the Middle East in which Canadian troops became involved as peacekeepers

3. A recent United Nations study concluded that Canada is the best country in which to live—that Canada has the best "quality of life." In view of the fact that Canada does not have the highest per capita real GDP in the world, explain how it can be ranked as the "best."

4. One way of estimating the size of the underground economy is to see the amount of cash Canadians are carrying relative to the total value of GDP. Why would a rapid rise in the ratio of cash held by the public to GDP indicate a rise in the underground economy?

5. A company's wages and salaries are part of its value added. Suppose, however, that the cleaning and machinery maintenance that its own employees used to do are now contracted out to specialist firms who come in to do the same work more cheaply. What happens to the company's value added when a company follows this recent trend of "contracting out"? What happens to value added in the economy as a whole?

PART EIGHT

The Economy in the Short Run

What determines the level of economic activity over short periods of time? Sometimes, in the midst of a recession, the government attempts to increase national income by increasing its spending. Can such increased spending end a recession? Why do we hear so much about consumer and business "confidence" in the economy? How would a slowdown in economic activity in the United States affect the level of national income in Canada? This part of the book will address these sorts of questions.

Chapter 21 introduces the simplest possible model of the macro economy that we use to explain how national income is determined in the short run. We assume the price level, the interest rate, and the exchange rate are all held constant. You may be surprised that we can still have an interesting model of economic fluctuations when we hold constant three such important variables, but we will see that this very simple model generates important insights about how the economy works.

Chapter 22 extends this simple model by adding a government sector and international trade. This is your introduction to fiscal policy; it is also the first time we see the relationship between the exchange rate and a country's exports and imports. Surprisingly, this more complicated model works in exactly the same way as the simple one but it allows us to consider a more realistic setting.

Chapter 23 extends the model further by allowing the price level to vary. We make the distinction between the demand side and the supply side of the economy and examine the important concepts of aggregate demand and aggregate supply. We then examine what is called macroeconomic equilibrium—the simultaneous determination of the equilibrium level of national income and the equilibrium price level.

CHAPTER 21

The Simplest Short-Run Macro Model

LEARNING OBJECTIVES

1 Differentiate between desired expenditure and actual expenditure.

2 Explain the determinants of desired consumption and desired investment expenditures.

3 Define equilibrium national income.

4 Explain how a change in desired expenditure affects equilibrium income, and how this change is reflected by the multiplier.

In Chapters 19 and 20, we encountered a number of important macroeconomic variables. We considered how they are measured and how they have behaved over the past several decades. We now turn to a more detailed study of what *causes* these variables to behave as they do. In particular, we study the forces that determine real national income and the price level over short periods of time, say up to a few years. In particular, in this chapter and the next two we examine how the level of real GDP is determined and how it fluctuates around the level of potential GDP. For simplicity, we assume that potential GDP is constant; in later chapters we explore the long-run forces that explain the growth of potential GDP.

Real national income and the price level are determined simultaneously. It is, however, easier to study them one at a time. So, in this chapter and the next, we simplify matters by seeing how real national income is determined *under the assumption that the price level is constant*. The simplified analysis will be an important first step toward understanding how prices and incomes are determined together, which is the subject of Chapter 23.

Our ability to explain the behaviour of real national income depends on our understanding of what determines the amount that households and firms spend. So, we begin with an examination of the expenditure decisions of households and firms.

21.1 Desired Aggregate Expenditure

In Chapter 20, we discussed how national income statisticians divide *actual* GDP into its expenditure components: consumption, investment, government purchases, and net exports.

In this chapter and the next, we are concerned with a different concept. It is variously called *desired* or *planned* expenditure. Of course, all people would like to spend virtually unlimited amounts, if only they had the resources. Desired expenditure does not refer, however, to what people would like to do under imaginary circumstances; it refers to what people would like to spend out of the resources that are at their command. Recall from Chapter 20 that the *actual* values of the various categories of expenditure are indicated by C_a, I_a, G_a, and $(X_a - IM_a)$. Economists use the same letters without the subscript "*a*" to indicate the *desired* expenditure in the same categories: C, I, G, and $(X - IM)$.

Everyone makes expenditure decisions. Fortunately, it is unnecessary for our purposes to look at each of the millions of such individual decisions. Instead, it is sufficient to consider four main groups of decision makers: domestic households, firms, governments, and foreign purchasers of domestically produced commodities. The sum of their *desired* expenditures on domestically produced output is called **desired aggregate expenditure** (*AE*):

$$AE = C + I + G + (X - IM)$$

Desired expenditure need not equal actual expenditure, either in total or in any individual category. For example, firms might not plan to invest in inventory accumulation this year but might do so unintentionally if sales are unexpectedly low—the unsold goods that pile up on their shelves are undesired inventory accumulation. In this case, actual investment expenditure, I_a, will exceed desired investment expenditure, I.

National income accounts measure *actual* expenditures in each of the four expenditure categories. National income theory deals with *desired* expenditures in each of these four categories.

You are probably wondering why the distinction between desired and actual expenditure is so important. The answer will become clear in the next section where we discuss the concept of *equilibrium* national income, which involves the relationship between desired and actual expenditure. For now, however, the remainder of this section examines more fully the various components of desired expenditure.

Autonomous Versus Induced Expenditure. In what follows, it will be useful to distinguish between *autonomous* and *induced* expenditure. Components of aggregate expenditure that do *not* depend on national income are called **autonomous expenditures**. Autonomous expenditures can and do change, but such changes do not occur systematically in response to changes in national income. Components of aggregate expenditure that *do* change systematically in response to changes in national income are called **induced expenditures**. As we will see, the induced response of desired aggregate expenditure to a change in national income plays a key role in the determination of equilibrium national income.

Important Simplifications. Our goal in this chapter is to develop the simplest possible model of national-income determination. To do so, we focus on only two of the four components of desired aggregate expenditure—consumption and investment. Consumption is by far the largest component of aggregate expenditure; it also provides the most important link between desired aggregate expenditure and real national income. Investment is expenditure on new machines or factories or tools and adds to the stock of physical capital. It is much smaller than consumption but also much more volatile; understanding investment is therefore important for understanding fluctuations in real national income.

We begin by considering a **closed economy**—that is, one that does not trade with other countries. We also suppose there is no government and that the price level is constant. These assumptions are clearly extreme, but they serve a vital purpose. As we will

desired aggregate expenditure (*AE*) The sum of desired or planned spending on domestic output by households, firms, governments, and foreigners.

autonomous expenditure Elements of expenditure that do not change systematically with national income.

induced expenditure Any component of expenditure that is systematically related to national income.

closed economy An economy that has no foreign trade.

see in this chapter, the presence of government and foreign trade is *not* essential to understanding the basic principles of national-income determination. By simplifying the model as much as possible, we are better able to understand its structure and therefore how more complex versions of the model work. In following chapters we will complicate our simple macro model by adding a government and international trade and then by removing the assumption of a fixed price level. The result will be a much more complete model of the macro economy.

Desired Consumption Expenditure

Recall from Chapter 20 that *disposable income* is the amount of income households receive after deducting what they pay in taxes. In our simple model with no government and no taxation, disposable income, Y_D, is equal to national income, Y. We define **saving** as all disposable income that is not spent on consumption.

By definition, there are only two possible uses of disposable income—consumption and saving. When the household decides how much to put to one use, it has automatically decided how much to put to the other use.

What determines the division between the amount that households decide to consume and the amount they decide to save? The factors that influence this decision are summarized in the *consumption function* and the *saving function*.

The Consumption Function

The **consumption function** relates the total desired consumption expenditures of all households to the several factors that determine it. The key factors influencing desired consumption are:

- disposable income
- wealth
- interest rates
- expectations about the future.

In building our simple macro model, we emphasize the role of disposable income in influencing desired consumption; but as we will see, changes in the other variables are also important.

   It is not surprising that desired expenditure is related to disposable income. As income rises, households naturally want to spend more, both now and in the future. For example, if your monthly disposable income permanently increases from $1000 to $1500, your monthly consumption will also increase, but probably by less than the full $500 increase. The remainder will add to your monthly saving—money that will accumulate and help finance future vacations, education, home purchases, or even retirement.

Holding constant other determinants of desired consumption, an increase in disposable income leads to an increase in desired consumption.

   The consumption function has an interesting history in economics. *Extensions in Theory 21-1* discusses consumption behaviour in two hypothetical households, and illustrates the debate regarding the importance of *current* disposable income in determining consumption. As the discussion shows, however, our simple assumption that desired consumption is positively related to disposable income is a good approximation of the

---

saving   All disposable income that is not spent on consumption.

consumption function The relationship between desired consumption expenditure and all the variables that determine it; in the simplest case, the relationship between consumption expenditure and disposable income.

behaviour of the *average* household, and therefore is suitable for explaining aggregate behaviour.

Part (i) of Figure 21-1 illustrates a simple consumption function for a hypothetical economy. The first two columns of the table show the value of desired consumption (C) associated with each value of disposable income (Y_D). There is clearly a positive relationship. The figure plots these points and connects them with a smooth line. In this hypothetical economy, the equation of the consumption function is

$$C = 30 + 0.8Y_D$$

In words, this equation says that if disposable income is zero, desired aggregate consumption will be $30 billion, and that for every one-dollar increase in Y_D, desired consumption rises by 80 cents.

Practise with Study Guide Chapter 21, Exercise 1.

FIGURE 21-1   The Consumption and Saving Functions

Disposable Income (Y_D)	Desired Consumption (C)	Desired Saving (S)	$APC = C/Y_D$	ΔY_D	ΔC	$MPC = \Delta C/\Delta Y_D$
0	30	−30	—			
				30	24	0.8
30	54	−24	1.80			
				90	72	0.8
120	126	−6	1.05			
				30	24	0.8
150	150	0	1.00			
				150	120	0.8
300	270	30	0.90			
				150	120	0.8
450	390	60	0.87			
				75	60	0.8
525	450	75	0.86			
				75	60	0.8
600	510	90	0.85			

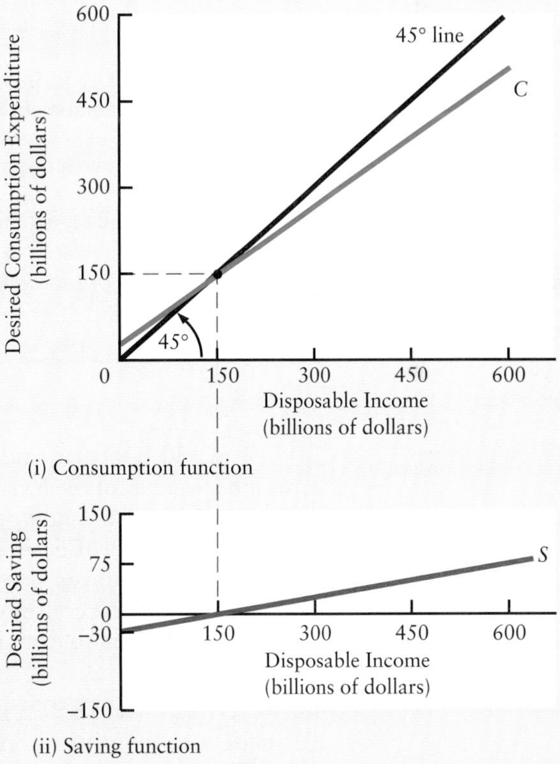

(i) Consumption function

(ii) Saving function

Both consumption and saving rise as disposable income rises. Line C in part (i) of the figure relates desired consumption expenditure to disposable income by plotting the data from the second column of the accompanying table. The consumption function cuts the 45° line at the break-even level of disposable income. Note that the level of autonomous consumption is $30 billion. The slope of the consumption function is equal to the marginal propensity to consume, which is shown in the table to be 0.8.

The relationship between desired saving and disposable income is shown in part (ii) by line S, which plots the data from the third column of the table. The vertical distance between C and the 45° line in part (i) is by definition the height of S in part (ii); that is, any given level of disposable income must be either consumed or saved. Note that the level of autonomous saving is −$30 billion.

EXTENSIONS IN THEORY 21-1

The Theory of the Consumption Function

Though it may seem natural to assume that a household's current consumption depends largely on its current disposable income, much debate and research has surrounded the issue of how to model consumption behaviour. To see what is involved, consider two quite different households.

The first household is short-sighted and spends everything it receives and puts nothing aside for a rainy day. When some overtime work results in a large paycheque, the members of the household go out and spend it. When it is hard to find work, the household's paycheque is small and its members reduce their expenditures. This household's monthly expenditure is therefore exactly equal to its current disposable income.

The second household is forward-looking. Its members think about the future as much as the present and make plans that stretch over their lifetimes. They put money aside for retirement and for the occasional rainy day when disposable income may fall temporarily. An unexpected windfall of income will be saved. An unexpected shortfall of income will be cushioned by spending some of the accumulated savings that were put aside for just such a rainy day. In short, this household's current expenditure will be closely related to its

expected *lifetime income*. Fluctuations in its *current income* will have little effect on its current consumption expenditure. Economists refer to this behaviour as *consumption smoothing*.

The figure shows the difference between our two sample households, short-sighted and forward-looking, and how their respective consumption expenditure is related to their

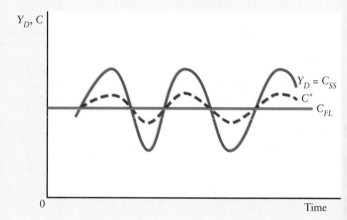

The \$30 billion is said to be *autonomous* consumption because it is autonomous (or independent) of the level of income. The $0.8Y_D$ is called *induced* consumption because it is induced (or brought about) by a change in income. In part (i) of Figure 21-1, the autonomous part of desired consumption is the vertical intercept of the consumption function. The induced part of consumption occurs as disposable income changes and we move along the consumption function.

We now go on to examine the properties of the consumption function in more detail.

Average and Marginal Propensities to Consume.   To discuss the consumption function concisely, economists use two technical expressions.

The **average propensity to consume** *(APC)* is total consumption expenditure divided by total disposable income:

$$APC = C/Y_D$$

The fourth column of the table in Figure 21-1 shows the APC calculated from the data in the table. Note that APC falls as disposable income rises.

The **marginal propensity to consume** *(MPC)* relates the *change* in desired consumption to the *change* in disposable income that brought it about. MPC is the change in desired consumption divided by the change in disposable income:

average propensity to consume (APC) The level of consumption divided by the level of disposable income.

marginal propensity to consume (MPC) The change in consumption divided by the change in disposable income that brought it about.

current disposable income. C_{SS} is the consumption path of the short-sighted household and is the same as the path of disposable income. C_{FL} is the consumption path for the forward-looking household and is flat.

John Maynard Keynes (1883–1946), the famous English economist who developed much of the basic theory of macroeconomics, inhabited his theory with households whose current consumption expenditure depended mostly on their current income. But these households are not as extreme as the short-sighted households we discussed above. Keynes did not assume that households *never* saved. He simply assumed that their current level of expenditure and saving depended on their *current* level of income. To this day, a consumption function based on this assumption is called a *Keynesian consumption function*.

During the 1950s, two U.S. economists, Franco Modigliani and Milton Friedman, both of whom were subsequently awarded Nobel Prizes in economics, analyzed the behaviour of forward-looking households. Their theories, which Modigliani called the *life-cycle theory* and Friedman called the *permanent-income theory*, explain some observed consumer behaviour that cannot be explained by the Keynesian consumption function.

The differences between the theories of Keynes, on the one hand, and Friedman and Modigliani, on the other, are not as great as it might seem at first sight. To see why this is so, let us return to our two imaginary households.

Even the extremely short-sighted household may be able to do some consumption smoothing in the face of income fluctuations. Most households have some money in the bank and some ability to borrow, even if it is just from friends and relatives. As a result, every change in income need not be matched by an equal change in consumption expenditures.

In contrast, although the forward-looking household wants to smooth its pattern of consumption completely, it may not have the borrowing capacity to do so. Its bank may not be willing to lend money for consumption when the security consists of nothing more than the *expectation* that the household's income will be much higher in later years. As a result, the household's consumption expenditure might fluctuate with its current income more than it would wish.

The foregoing discussion suggests that the consumption expenditure of both types of households will fluctuate to some extent with their current disposable incomes and to some extent with their expectations of future disposable income. Moreover, in any economy there will be households of both types, both spendthrifts and planners, and aggregate consumption will be determined by a mix of the two types. The consumption behaviour for the *average* household in such an economy is shown in the figure as the path C*. Consumption fluctuates in response to changes in disposable income, rising when income rises and falling when income falls.

$$MPC = \Delta C/\Delta Y_D,$$

where the Greek letter Δ, delta, means "a change in." The last column of the table in Figure 21-1 shows the *MPC* that corresponds to the data in the table. Note that in this simple example, the *MPC* is constant and equal to 0.8. [28]

The Slope of the Consumption Function.   The consumption function shown in Figure 21-1 has a slope of $\Delta C/\Delta Y_D$, which is, by definition, the marginal propensity to consume. The positive slope of the consumption function shows that the *MPC* is positive; increases in income lead to increases in desired consumption expenditure.

The 45° Line.   Figure 21-1(i) contains a line that is constructed by connecting all points where desired consumption (measured on the vertical axis) equals disposable income (measured on the horizontal axis). Because both axes are given in the same units, this line has a positive slope equal to 1; that is, it forms an angle of 45° with the axes. The line is therefore called the *45° line*.

The 45° line is a useful reference line. In part (i) of Figure 21-1, the consumption function cuts the 45° line at the break-even level of income—

Disposable income can either be saved or spent on consumption goods. Bank deposits are one important form of saving.

in this example, at $150 billion. When the consumption function is above the 45° line, desired consumption exceeds disposable income. In this case, desired saving must be negative; households are financing their consumption either by spending out of their accumulated saving or by borrowing funds. When the consumption function is below the 45° line, desired consumption is less than disposable income and so desired saving is positive; households are paying back debt or accumulating assets. At the break-even level of disposable income, desired consumption exactly equals disposable income and so desired saving is zero.

The Saving Function

Households decide how much to consume and how much to save. As we have said, this is only a single decision—how to divide disposable income between consumption and saving. Therefore, once we know the relationship between consumption and disposable income, we automatically know the relationship between saving and disposable income.

There are two saving concepts that are exactly parallel to the consumption concepts of APC and MPC. The **average propensity to save** *(APS)* is the proportion of disposable income that households want to save, computed by dividing total desired saving by total disposable income:

average propensity to save (APS) The proportion of disposable income devoted to saving; total saving divided by total disposable income.

$$APS = S/Y_D$$

The **marginal propensity to save** *(MPS)* relates the change in desired saving to the change in disposable income that brought it about:

marginal propensity to save (MPS) The change in total desired saving divided by the change in disposable income that brought it about.

$$MPS = \Delta S/\Delta Y_D$$

There is a simple relationship between the saving and the consumption propensities. APC and APS must sum to 1; and MPC and MPS must sum to 1. Because all disposable income is either spent or saved, it follows that the fractions of income consumed and saved must account for all income $(APC + APS = 1)$. It also follows that the fractions of any *increment* to income consumed and saved must account for all of that increment $(MPC + MPS = 1)$. [29]

Look back at the table in Figure 21-1 and calculate APC and APS for yourself by computing C/Y_D and S/Y_D for each row in the table. You will notice that the sum of APC and APS is *always* 1. Similarly, calculate MPC and MPS by computing $\Delta C/\Delta Y_D$ and $\Delta S/\Delta Y_D$ for each row in the table. You will also notice that MPC and MPS *always* add up to 1.

Part (ii) of Figure 21-1 shows the saving function. Notice that it is positively sloped, indicating that increases in disposable income lead to an increase in desired saving. Note also that the amount of desired saving is always equal to the vertical distance between the consumption function and the 45° line. When desired consumption exceeds income, desired saving is negative; when desired consumption is less than income, desired saving is positive.

Shifts of the Consumption Function

Earlier we said that desired consumption depended on four things—disposable income, wealth, interest rates, and households' expectations about the future. In Figure 21-1, we illustrate the most important relationship—between desired consumption and disposable income. In this diagram, changes in disposable income lead to *movements along* the consumption function. Changes in the other three factors will lead to *shifts of* the consumption function. Let's see why.

A Change in Wealth. Household wealth is the value of all accumulated assets minus accumulated debts. The most common types of household assets are savings accounts, mutual funds (portfolios of stocks or bonds), Registered Retirement Savings Plans (RRSPs), and the ownership of homes and cars. The most common household debts are home mortgages, car loans, and outstanding lines of credit from banks.

What happens to desired consumption if household wealth increases? Suppose, for example, that a rising stock market (often called a "bull" market) leads to an increase in aggregate household wealth. This increase in wealth implies that less current income needs to be saved for the future, and households will therefore tend to spend a larger fraction of their current income. The consumption function will shift up, and the saving function down, as shown in Figure 21-2. Current estimates suggest that an increase in aggregate wealth of $1 billion leads to an increase in desired aggregate consumption of approximately $50 million.

An increase in wealth shifts the consumption function up; a decrease in wealth shifts the consumption function down.

A Change in Interest Rates. Household consumption can be divided into consumption of *durable* and *non-durable* goods. Durable goods are goods that deliver benefits for several years, such as cars and household appliances. Non-durable goods are consumption goods that deliver benefits to households only for short periods of time, such as groceries, restaurant meals, and clothing. Since many durable goods are also expensive, many of them are purchased on credit—that is, households borrow in order to finance their purchases.

The cost of borrowing, as we discussed in Chapter 19, is the interest rate. A fall in the interest rate reduces the cost of borrowing and leads to an increase in desired consumption expenditure, especially of durable goods. That is, for any given level of disposable income, a fall in the interest rate leads to an increase in desired consumption; the consumption function shifts up and the saving function shifts down, as shown in Figure 21-2.

A fall in interest rates leads to an increase in desired consumption at any level of disposable income; the consumption function shifts up. A rise in interest rates shifts the consumption function down.

A Change in Expectations. Households' expectations about the future are important in determining their desired consumption. Suppose, for example, that large numbers of households become pessimistic about

Practise with Study Guide Chapter 21, Extension Exercise E2.

FIGURE 21-2 Shifts in the Consumption Function

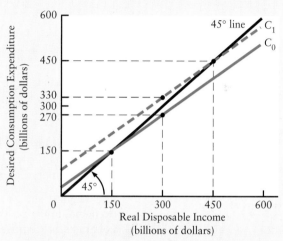

(i) The consumption function shifts upward with an increase in wealth, a decrease in interest rates, or an increase in optimism about the future

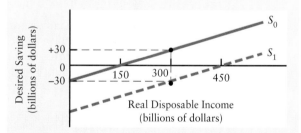

(ii) The saving function shifts downward

Changes in wealth, interest rates, or expectations about the future shift the consumption function. In part (i), line C_0 reproduces the consumption function from Figure 21-1(i). The consumption function then shifts up by $60 billion, so with disposable income of $300 billion, for example, desired consumption rises from $270 billion to $330 billion.

The saving function in part (ii) shifts down by $60 billion, from S_0 to S_1. Thus, for example, at a disposable income of $300 billion, desired saving falls from $30 billion to −$30 billion.

the future state of the economy and therefore pessimistic about their own employment prospects. In many cases, these fears will lead households to increase their current saving in anticipation of rough economic times (possibly unemployment) ahead. But increasing their current saving implies a reduction in current consumption (at the given level of disposable income). The result will be a downward shift in the consumption function.

The reverse is also true. Favourable expectations about the future state of the economy will lead many households to increase their current consumption, and reduce their current saving. The result will be an upward shift in the consumption function and a downward shift in the saving function.

Expectations about the future state of the economy influence desired consumption. Optimism leads to an upward shift in the consumption function; pessimism leads to a downward shift in the consumption function.

Summary

It is useful to summarize what we have learned so far about the consumption function. As you will soon see, it will play a crucial role in our model of national income determination. The main points are:

1. Desired consumption is positively related to disposable income. In a graph, this relationship is shown by the positive slope of the consumption function, which is equal to the marginal propensity to consume (*MPC*).

2. There are both *autonomous* and *induced* components of desired consumption. A movement along the consumption function shows changes in consumption induced by changes in disposable income. A shift of the consumption function shows autonomous changes in consumption.

3. An increase in household wealth, a fall in interest rates, or greater optimism about the future all lead to an increase in desired consumption and an upward shift of the consumption function.

4. By definition, all disposable income is either consumed or saved. Therefore, there is a saving function associated with the consumption function. Any event that causes the consumption function to shift must also cause the saving function to shift by an equal amount in the opposite direction.

Is the theory of the consumption function supported by empirical evidence? For a look at the Canadian data on aggregate consumption and disposable income, look for "The Consumption Function in Canada" in the *Additional Topics* section of this book's Companion Website.

http://www.pearsoned.ca/ragan

Desired Investment Expenditure

Our simple macroeconomic model has only consumption and investment. Having spent considerable time discussing consumption behaviour, we are now ready to examine the determinants of investment. Recall from Chapter 20 that there are three categories of investment:

- inventory investment

- residential investment
- new plant and equipment

Investment expenditure is the most volatile component of GDP, and changes in investment are strongly associated with economic fluctuations. As shown in Figure 21-3, total investment in Canada fluctuates around an average of about 17 percent of GDP. In each of the last two recessions (1982 and 1991) investment fell by over five percentage points. In contrast, consumption, government purchases, and net exports are much smoother over the business cycle, each typically changing by less than one percentage point. An important part of our understanding of business cycles will therefore rely on our understanding of the fluctuations in investment.

What explains such fluctuations in investment? Here we examine three important determinants of aggregate investment expenditure:

- the real interest rate
- changes in the level of sales
- business confidence

Let's now examine these in turn.

FIGURE 21-3   The Volatility of Investment, 1977–2002

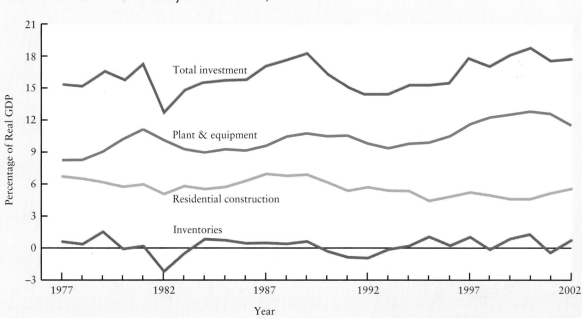

Total investment as a share of GDP fluctuates considerably. In percentage terms, changes in inventories are the most volatile component of investment.

(*Source: Bank of Canada Review,* various issues. The most recent data are also available at Statistics Canada's website: www. statcan.ca. Go to "Canadian Statistics" and click on "Economic conditions" and then "National accounts.")

Investment and the Real Interest Rate

The real interest rate represents the real cost of borrowing money for investment purposes. A rise in the real interest rate therefore reduces the amount of desired investment expenditure. This relationship is most easily seen if we separate investment into three components: inventories, residential construction, and new plant and equipment.

Inventories.   Changes in inventories represent only a small percentage of private investment in a typical year. As shown by the bottom line in Figure 21-3, inventory investment has always been between –2 percent and 2 percent of GDP over the past 20 years. (Inventory investment of –2 percent in a year means that inventories *fall* by 2 percent of GDP.) But the average size of such changes is not an adequate measure of their importance. Since they are one of the more volatile elements of total investment, they have an important influence on fluctuations in investment expenditure.

When a firm ties up funds in inventories, those same funds cannot be used elsewhere to earn income. As an alternative to holding inventories, the firm could lend the money out at the going rate of interest. Hence, the higher the real rate of interest, the higher the opportunity cost of holding an inventory of a given size; the higher the opportunity cost, the smaller the inventories that will be desired.

Residential Construction.   Expenditure on residential housing is also volatile. Most houses are purchased with money that is borrowed by means of mortgages. Interest on the borrowed money typically accounts for over one-half of the purchaser's annual mortgage payments; the remainder is repayment of the original loan, called the *principal.* Because interest payments are such a large part of mortgage payments, variations in interest rates exert a substantial effect on the demand for housing.

New Plant and Equipment.   The rate of interest is also a major determinant of investment in new plant and equipment. When interest rates are high, it is expensive for firms to borrow funds that can be used for fixed investment. At the same time, firms with cash on hand can earn high returns on interest-earning assets, again making investment in plant and equipment a less attractive alternative. Thus, high real interest rates lead to reduced investment in plant and equipment, and low real interest rates increase such investment.

The real interest rate reflects the opportunity cost associated with investment, whether it is investment in inventories, residential construction, or plant and equipment. The higher the real interest rate, the higher the opportunity cost of investment, and thus the lower the amount of desired investment.

Figure 21-3 shows these three components of investment over the past 25 years. Inventory investment is clearly the smallest of the three but in relative terms is the most volatile. Note that the three components move broadly together. They all fell in the 1981–82 recession, and again in the 1990–91 recession. There was also a decline in investment as a share of GDP, especially inventory investment, in 2001 when the Canadian economy slowed.

Investment and Changes in Sales

Firms hold inventories because of unexpected changes in sales and production, and they usually have a target level of inventories that depends on their normal level of sales. Because the size of

The largest part of investment by firms is in new plants and equipment, such as this expansion of a pulp mill in British Columbia.

inventories is related to the level of sales, the *change* in inventories (which is part of current investment) is related to the *change* in the level of sales.

For example, suppose a firm wants to hold inventories equal to 10 percent of its monthly sales. If normal monthly sales are $100 000, it will wish to hold inventories of $10 000. If monthly sales increase to $110 000, it will want to hold inventories of $11 000. Over the period during which its stock of inventories is being increased, there will be a total of $1000 of new inventory investment.

The higher the level of sales, the larger the desired stock of inventories. Changes in the rate of sales therefore cause temporary bouts of investment (or disinvestment) in inventories.

Changes in sales have similar effects on investment in plant and equipment. For example, if there is a general increase in consumers' demand for products that is expected to persist and that cannot be met by existing capacity, investment in new plant and equipment will be needed. Once the new plants have been built and put into operation, however, the rate of new investment will fall.

Investment and Business Confidence

Investment takes time. When a firm invests, it increases its future capacity to produce output. If it can sell the new output profitably, the investment will prove to be a good one. If the new output does not generate profits, the investment will have been a bad one. When it undertakes an investment, the firm does not know if it will turn out well or badly—it is betting on a favourable future that cannot be known with certainty.

When firms expect good times ahead, they will want to invest now so that they have a larger productive capacity in the future ready to satisfy the greater demand. When they expect bad times ahead, they will not invest because they expect no payoff from doing so.

Investment depends on firms' expectations about the future state of the economy. Optimism leads to more desired investment; pessimism leads to less desired investment.

The Conference Board of Canada publishes regular surveys of business and consumer confidence. Visit its website: www.conferenceboard.ca.

Investment as Autonomous Expenditure

We have seen that investment is influenced by many things, and a complete discussion of the determination of national income is not possible without including all of these factors.

For the moment, however, our goal is to build the *simplest* model of the aggregate economy in which we can examine the interaction of actual national income and desired aggregate expenditure. To build this simple model, we begin by treating investment as *autonomous*—that is, we assume it to be unaffected by changes in national income. Figure 21-4 shows the investment function as a horizontal line.

It is important not to confuse the assumption that investment is *autonomous* (which we are making) with the assumption that investment is *constant* (which we are not making). As we have said, investment is the most volatile component of aggregate expenditure, and we have explained why changes in interest rates and expectations about the future state of the economy have important influences on investment. Therefore, it will be important in our model that investment be able to change; shocks to firms' investment behaviour will end up being an important explanation for fluctuations in national income. Our assumption that investment is autonomous with respect to national income (and hence the *I* function in Figure 21-4 is horizontal) is mainly a simplifying one. But the assumption does reflect the fact that investment is an act undertaken by firms for

FIGURE 21-4   Desired Investment as Autonomous Expenditure

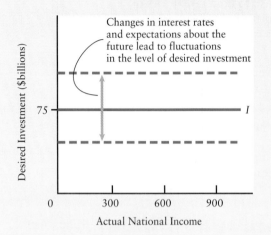

Desired investment is assumed to be autonomous with respect to current national income. In this example, the level of desired investment is $75 billion. However, changes in interest rates or business confidence will lead to upward or downward shifts in the investment function.

aggregate expenditure (AE) function   The function that relates desired aggregate expenditure to actual national income.

marginal propensity to spend   The change in desired aggregate expenditure on domestic output divided by the change in national income that brought it about.

future benefit, and thus the *current* level of GDP is unlikely to have a significant effect on desired investment.

The Aggregate Expenditure Function

The **aggregate expenditure** *(AE)* **function** relates the level of desired aggregate expenditure to the level of actual income. (In both cases we mean *real* as opposed to *nominal* variables.) In the simplified economy of this chapter, in which there is no government and no international trade, desired aggregate expenditure is just equal to desired consumption plus desired investment, $C + I$.

$$AE = C + I$$

The table in Figure 21-5 shows how the *AE* function can be calculated, given the consumption function from Figure 21-1 and the investment function from Figure 21-3. In this specific case, all of investment expenditure is autonomous, as is the $30 billion of consumption that would be desired if national income were equal to zero. Total autonomous expenditure is therefore $105 billion—induced expenditure is just equal to induced consumption, which is equal to the *MPC* times disposable income ($0.8 \times Y_D$). Furthermore, since our simple model has no government and no taxes, disposable income, Y_D, is equal to national income, Y. Hence, desired aggregate expenditure can be written as:

$$AE = \$105 \text{ billion} + (0.8)Y$$

The Marginal Propensity to Spend

The fraction of any increment to national income that people spend on purchasing domestic output is called the economy's **marginal propensity to spend.** The marginal propensity to spend is measured by the change in desired aggregate expenditure divided by the change in national income, or $\Delta AE/\Delta Y$, the slope of the aggregate expenditure function. In this book, the marginal propensity to spend is denoted by the symbol z, which is a number greater than zero and less than 1. For the example given in Figure 21-5, the marginal propensity to spend is 0.8. If national income increases by a dollar, 80 cents will go into increased expenditure; 20 cents will go into increased saving and will not be spent. The marginal propensity to spend should not be confused with the marginal propensity to consume.

The marginal propensity to spend is the amount of extra total expenditure induced when national income rises by $1, whereas the marginal propensity to consume is the amount of extra consumption expenditure induced when households' disposable income rises by $1.

FIGURE 21-5   The Aggregate Expenditure Function

National Income (Y)	Desired Consumption Expenditure ($C = 30 + 0.8 \times Y$)	Desired Investment Expenditure ($I = 75$)	Desired Aggregate Expenditure ($AE = C + I$)
30	54	75	129
120	126	75	201
150	150	75	225
300	270	75	345
450	390	75	465
525	450	75	525
600	510	75	585
900	750	75	825

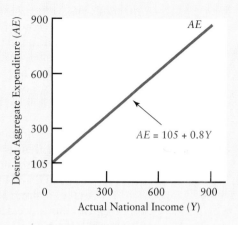

The aggregate expenditure function relates desired aggregate expenditure to actual national income. The curve AE in the figure plots the data from the first and last columns of the accompanying table. Its intercept, which in this case is $105 billion, shows the sum of autonomous consumption and autonomous investment. Its slope is equal to the marginal propensity to spend (which in this simple economy is just the marginal propensity to consume).

In the simple model of this chapter, the marginal propensity to spend is equal to the marginal propensity to consume. In later chapters, however, when we add government and international trade to the model, the marginal propensity to spend differs from the marginal propensity to consume. Both here and in later chapters, it is the more general measure—the marginal propensity to spend—that is important for determining equilibrium national income.

Practise with Study Guide Chapter 21, Exercise 3.

Summary

We have constructed an *AE* function that combines the spending plans of households and firms. The function shows, for any given level of *actual* national income, the level of *desired* aggregate spending. We are now ready to see what determines the *equilibrium* level of national income, and why the distinction between actual and desired expenditure is so important.

21.2 Equilibrium National Income

When something is in equilibrium, there is no tendency for it to change. Any conditions that are required for something to be in equilibrium are called *equilibrium conditions*. We will see that the distinction between desired and actual expenditure is central to the equilibrium conditions for national income.

Desired Expenditure and Actual Output

Table 21-1 illustrates the determination of equilibrium national income for our simple hypothetical economy. Suppose firms are producing a final output of $300 billion, and thus national income is $300 billion. According to the table, at this level of actual national income, desired aggregate expenditure is $345 billion. If firms persist in producing a current output of only $300 billion in the face of desired aggregate expenditure of $345 billion, one of two things will happen.

One possibility is that households and firms will be unable to spend the extra $45 billion that they would like to spend, so lines or waiting lists of unsatisfied customers will appear. These shortages will send a signal to firms that they can increase their sales if they increase their production. When the firms increase production, national income rises. Of course, the individual firms are interested only in their own sales and profits, but their individual actions have as their inevitable consequence an increase in GDP.

A more realistic possibility is that all spenders will spend everything that they wanted to spend. But since desired expenditure exceeds the actual amount of output, this is only possible if some sales come from the producers' accumulated inventories. In our example, the fulfillment of plans to purchase $345 billion worth of goods in the face of a current output of only $300 billion will reduce inventories by $45 billion. As long as inventories last, more goods can be sold than are currently being produced. But since firms want to maintain a certain level of inventories, they will eventually increase their production. Once again, the consequence of each individual firm's behaviour is an increase in national income. Thus, the final response to an excess of desired aggregate expenditure over actual output is a rise in national income.

For any level of national income at which desired aggregate expenditure exceeds actual income, there will be pressure for national income to rise.

TABLE 21-1   Equilibrium National Income

Actual National Income (Y)	Desired Aggregate Expenditure (AE = C + I)	Effect
30	129	
120	201	
150	225	Inventories are falling; firms increase output
300	345	
450	465	
525	525	Equilibrium income
600	585	Inventories are rising; firms reduce output
900	825	

National income is in equilibrium when desired aggregate expenditure equals actual national income. The data are from Figure 21-5.

Next consider the $900 billion level of actual national income in Table 21-1. At this level of output, desired expenditure on domestically produced goods is only $825 billion. If firms persist in producing $900 billion worth of goods, $75 billion worth must remain unsold. Therefore, inventories must rise. However, firms will not allow inventories of unsold goods to rise indefinitely; sooner or later, they will reduce the level of output to the level of sales. When they reduce their level of output, national income will fall.

For any level of income at which desired aggregate expenditure is less than actual income, there will be pressure for national income to fall.

Finally, look at the national income level of $525 billion in Table 21-1. At this level, and only at this level, desired aggregate expenditure is equal to actual national income. Purchasers can fulfill their spending plans without causing inventories to change. There is no incentive for firms to alter output. Because everyone wishes to purchase an amount equal to what is being produced, output and income will remain steady; they are in equilibrium.

The equilibrium level of national income occurs where desired aggregate expenditure equals actual national income.

Desired Saving and Desired Investment

We have just seen that equilibrium national income occurs where desired aggregate expenditure equals actual national income. The same equilibrium can also be described as the level of national income where *desired saving equals desired investment*.

The saving–investment formulation of the model is useful because it adds perspective on how equilibrium national income is determined. Later in this book, the saving–investment formulation will illuminate a key issue in economic policy—the possible influence of macroeconomic policy on long-run economic growth. Since investment adds to an economy's stock of productive resources, investment is often the only way for new and better technologies to be introduced to the workplace. In the long run, the level of a country's saving, through its effect on investment, can exert an important influence on economic growth. We are not yet ready to explore this important point, but when we are, the saving–investment balance will be an important part of the story. For now, our goal is to show that the equilibrium level of national income can be examined in terms of desired saving and desired investment.

Table 21-2 repeats data from Table 21-1, with three columns added: desired consumption, desired saving, and desired investment. Recall that in our simple model with no government and no taxes, desired saving is equal to actual income minus desired consumption, $S = Y - C$. Careful examination of this table reveals an important point: *The difference between desired investment and desired saving is exactly equal to the difference between desired aggregate expenditure and actual national income.* For example, if actual national income is $300 billion, desired aggregate expenditure is $345 billion—a difference of $45 billion. At the same time, desired saving is $30 billion while desired investment is $75 billion—also a difference of $45 billion.

TABLE 21-2 Equilibrium National Income and the Saving–Investment Balance

Actual National Income (Y)	Desired Aggregate Expenditure ($AE = C + I$)	Desired Consumption ($C = 30 + 0.8 \times Y$)	Desired Saving ($S = Y - C$)	Desired Investment (I)
30	129	54	−24	75
120	201	126	−6	75
300	345	270	30	75
525	525	450	75	75
600	585	510	90	75
900	825	750	150	75

National income is in equilibrium where desired saving is equal to desired investment. The data for Y, AE, and I are from Figure 21-5. At every level of national income, the difference between actual national income and desired aggregate expenditure is exactly equal to the difference between desired saving and desired investment.

This equality is no accident, but rather comes straight from the definition of desired aggregate expenditure. To see this, suppose the difference between desired saving and desired investment is equal to some number, W. Thus,

$$S - I = W$$

Practise with Study Guide Chapter 21, Exercise 3.

Now, recall that we use Y to denote actual national income, and that desired saving is just equal to actual national income minus desired consumption, $S = Y - C$. We can therefore rewrite the equation above to get

$$Y - C - I = W$$

But since desired aggregate expenditure is just the sum of desired consumption and desired investment, $AE = C + I$, we can rewrite the equation again to get

$$Y - (C + I) = W$$
$$\Rightarrow Y - AE = W$$

Thus, the difference between desired saving and desired investment is always equal to the difference between actual national income and desired aggregate expenditure.

In the simple model of this chapter, with no government and no international trade, the difference between desired saving and desired investment is exactly the same as the difference between actual national income and desired aggregate expenditure. Thus, the economy is in equilibrium when desired investment equals desired saving.

Equilibrium Illustrated

Figure 21-6 shows the determination of the equilibrium level of national income. The line labelled AE graphs the specific aggregate expenditure function that we have been working with throughout this chapter. The 45° line ($AE = Y$) graphs the equilibrium condition that desired aggregate expenditure equals actual national income. Anywhere along the 45° line, the value of desired aggregate expenditure, which is measured on the vertical axis, is equal to the value of actual national income, which is measured on the horizontal axis.

Graphically, equilibrium occurs at the level of income at which the AE line intersects the 45° line. This is the level of income where desired aggregate expenditure is just equal to actual national income. The equilibrium is also illustrated in part (ii) of the figure, but in terms of the saving–investment balance. The line labelled S is desired saving. The line labelled I is desired investment.

FIGURE 21-6   Equilibrium National Income

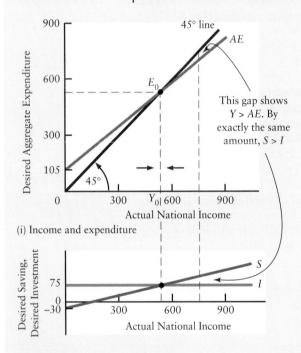

(i) Income and expenditure

(ii) Saving and investment

Equilibrium national income is that level of national income where desired aggregate expenditure equals actual national income. If actual national income is below Y_0 in part (i), desired aggregate expenditure will exceed national income, and output will rise. If national income is above Y_0, desired aggregate expenditure will be less than national income, and production will fall. Only when national income is equal to Y_0 will the economy be in equilibrium, as shown at E_0.

Part (ii) shows desired saving and desired investment on the same scale as part (i). Equilibrium national income occurs where desired saving equals desired investment. The vertical distance between saving and investment is exactly the same as the vertical distance in part (i) between AE and the 45° line.

Notice that the vertical distance between S and I is exactly equal to the distance between the 45° line and AE. When desired investment exceeds desired saving, desired aggregate expenditure exceeds actual national income by the same amount. When desired investment is less than desired saving, desired aggregate expenditure is less than actual national income by the same amount.

Now that we have explained the meaning of equilibrium national income, we will go on to examine the various forces that can *change* this equilibrium. We will then be well on our way to understanding some of the sources of short-run fluctuations in national income.

21.3 **Changes in Equilibrium National Income**

A glance at Figure 21-6 shows that the equilibrium level of national income (Y_0) occurs where the AE function intersects the 45° line. Through the adjustment in firms' inventories and production levels, the level of actual national income will adjust until this equilibrium level is achieved. Because the AE function plays a central role in determining equilibrium national income, you should not be surprised to hear that *shifts* in the AE function are central to explaining why national income changes.

Shifts of the *AE* Function

The AE function shifts when one of its components shifts—that is, when there is a shift in the consumption function or in the investment function. As we have already mentioned, both the consumption function and the investment function will shift if there is a change in interest rates or expectations of the future state of the economy. A change in household wealth is an additional reason for the consumption function to shift. Let's now consider what happens if there is an upward shift in the AE function.

Practise with Study Guide Chapter 21, Short-Answer Question 2.

Upward Shifts in the *AE* Function

Suppose households experience an increase in wealth and thus increase their desired levels of consumption spending at each level of disposable income. Or, suppose firms' expectations of higher future sales cause domestic auto makers to increase their planned investment. What is the effect of such events on national income?

Because any increase in autonomous expenditure shifts the entire AE function upward, the same analysis applies to each of the changes mentioned. Two types of shifts in AE can occur. First, if the same addition to expenditure occurs at all levels of income, the AE function shifts parallel to itself, as shown in part (i) of Figure 21-7. Second, if there is a change in the marginal propensity to spend, the slope of the AE function changes, as shown in part (ii) of Figure 21-7.

Figure 21-7 shows that an upward shift in the AE function increases equilibrium national income. After the shift in the AE curve, income is no longer in equilibrium at its original level because at that level desired aggregate expenditure exceeds actual national income. Given this excess demand, firms' inventories are being depleted and firms respond by increasing production. Equilibrium national income rises to the higher level indicated by the intersection of the new AE curve with the 45° line.

FIGURE 21-7   Shifts in the Aggregate Expenditure Function

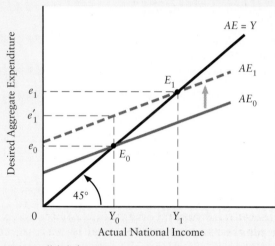

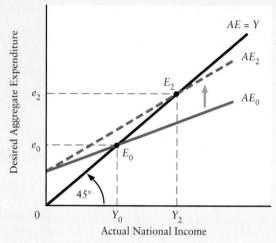

(i) A parallel shift in *AE*   (ii) A change in the slope of *AE*

Upward shifts in the *AE* function increase equilibrium income; downward shifts decrease equilibrium income. In parts (i) and (ii), the *AE* function is initially AE_0 with equilibrium national income equal to Y_0.

In part (i), a parallel upward shift in the *AE* curve from AE_0 to AE_1 reflects an increase in desired expenditure at each level of national income. For example, at Y_0, desired expenditure rises from e_0 to e_1' and therefore exceeds actual national income. Equilibrium is reached at E_1, where income is Y_1. The increase in desired expenditure from e_1' to e_1, represented by a movement along AE_1, is an induced response to the increase in income from Y_0 to Y_1.

In part (ii), a non-parallel upward shift in the *AE* curve from AE_0 to AE_2 reflects an increase in the marginal propensity to spend. This leads to an increase in equilibrium national income. Equilibrium is reached at E_2, where national income is equal to Y_2.

The Saving–Investment Balance.   We saw earlier that, in equilibrium, desired aggregate expenditure is equal to actual national income, and desired saving is equal to desired investment. When the *AE* function shifts and equilibrium income changes, the equality of desired saving and desired investment must still hold true at the new equilibrium.

Consider the case of a shift in the *AE* function that is caused by an increase in desired consumption at any level of income—that is, the consumption function shifts upward. As we discussed earlier (see Figure 21-1), when the consumption function shifts, the saving function shifts as well, and by an equal and opposite amount. This is true because consumption and saving always add up to disposable income. Hence, if the consumption function shifts up by some amount at every level of income, the saving function *must* shift down by exactly the same amount.

Figure 21-8 shows a downward shift in the saving function (corresponding to an upward shift in the consumption function). Equilibrium national income occurs where desired saving equals desired investment. With desired investment fixed, a downward shift in the saving function leads to an *increase* in equilibrium national income. This is just as it should be—a downward shift in the saving function implies an upward shift in the consumption and *AE* functions.

Another possibility is that the *AE* function shifts up because of an increase in autonomous investment rather than consumption. Draw a figure like Figure 21-8 yourself, but this time leave the saving function unchanged and let the investment function shift upward. You will see that equilibrium national income—where desired saving equals desired investment—increases.

Downward Shifts in the *AE* Function

What happens to national income if there is a decrease in the amount of consumption or investment expenditure desired at each level of income? These changes shift the *AE* function downward. A constant reduction in desired expenditure at all levels of income shifts *AE* parallel to itself. A fall in the marginal propensity to spend out of national income reduces the slope of the *AE* function. When we use the saving–investment relation, we must note that a downward shift in the consumption function implies an upward shift in the saving function, reducing the equilibrium level of income.

The Results Restated

We have derived two important general propositions from our simple model of national income determination.

1. A rise in the amount of desired aggregate expenditure at each level of national income will shift the *AE* curve upward and increase equilibrium national income.

2. A fall in the amount of desired aggregate expenditure at each level of national income will shift the *AE* curve downward and reduce equilibrium national income.

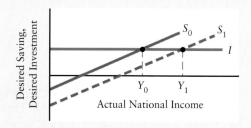

FIGURE 21-8   Shifts in Desired Saving

A downward shift in the saving function increases equilibrium national income. If the consumption function shifts up, the saving function must shift down by an equal amount, indicating a reduction in desired saving at every level of national income. Since equilibrium occurs where desired saving equals desired investment, the new equilibrium occurs at a higher national income—the economy moves from Y_0 to Y_1. The saving function has indeed shifted down, but the increase in equilibrium income has caused a movement *along* the new S_1 function and restored the level of saving to its previous level.

The Multiplier

We have learned whether specific changes in the *AE* function will cause equilibrium national income to rise or fall. We would now like to understand the *size* of these changes.

During a recession, the government sometimes takes measures to stimulate the economy. If these measures have a larger effect than estimated, demand may rise too much, and full employment may be reached while demand is still rising. As we will see in Chapter 24, this outcome will have an inflationary effect on the economy. On the other hand, if the government overestimates the impact of its measures, the recession will persist longer than necessary. In this case, there is a danger that the policy will be discredited as ineffective, even though the correct diagnosis is that too little of the right thing was done.

Defining the Multiplier

A measure of the magnitude of changes in national income is provided by the *multiplier*. We have seen that a shift in the *AE* curve will cause a change in equilibrium national income. A change in autonomous expenditure increases equilibrium national income by a *multiple* of the initial change in autonomous expenditure. That is, the change in national income is *larger than* the initial change in desired expenditure.

The multiplier is the change in equilibrium national income divided by the change in autonomous expenditure that brought it about. In the simple macro model, the multiplier is greater than 1.

To see why the multiplier is greater than 1, consider a simple example. Imagine what would happen to national income if Kimberley-Clark decided to spend $500 million per year on the construction of new paper mills. Initially, the construction of the paper mills would create $500 million worth of new national income and a corresponding amount of income for households and firms on which the initial $500 million is spent. But this is not the end of the story. The increase in national income of $500 million would cause an increase in disposable income, which would cause an induced increase in desired consumption.

Electricians, masons, and carpenters—who would gain new income directly from the building of the paper mills—would spend some of it on food, clothing, entertainment, cars, TVs, and other commodities. When output expanded to meet this demand, new incomes would be created for workers and firms in these industries. When they, in turn, spent their newly earned incomes, output would rise further. More income would be created, and more expenditure would be induced. Indeed, at this stage, we might wonder whether the increases in income would ever come to an end. To deal with this concern, we need to consider the multiplier in somewhat more precise terms.

Let autonomous expenditure be denoted by A. Now consider an increase in autonomous expenditure of ΔA, which in our example above was $500 million per year. Remember that ΔA stands for *any* increase in autonomous expenditure; this could be an increase in investment or in the autonomous component of consumption. The new autonomous expenditure shifts the AE function upward by that amount. National income is no longer in equilibrium because desired aggregate expenditure now exceeds actual income. Equilibrium is restored by a *movement along* the new AE curve.

The **simple multiplier** measures the change in equilibrium national income that occurs in response to a change in autonomous expenditure *at a constant price level*. We refer to it as "simple" because we have simplified the situation by assuming that the price level is fixed (an assumption we will remove in Chapter 23). Figure 21-9 illustrates the simple multiplier and makes clear that it is greater than 1. *Applying Economic Concepts 21-1* provides a numerical example.

simple multiplier
The ratio of the change in equilibrium national income to the change in autonomous expenditure that brought it about, calculated for a constant price level.

FIGURE 21-9   The Simple Multiplier

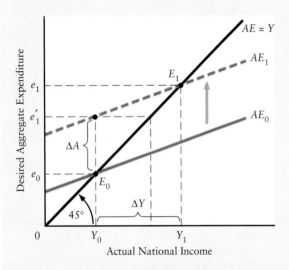

An increase in autonomous aggregate expenditure increases equilibrium national income by a multiple of the initial increase. The initial equilibrium is at E_0, where AE_0 intersects the 45° line. At this point, desired aggregate expenditure, e_0, is equal to actual national income, Y_0. An increase in autonomous expenditure of ΔA then shifts the AE function upward to AE_1.

Equilibrium occurs when income rises to Y_1. Here desired expenditure, e_1, equals national income, Y_1. The increase in desired expenditure from e_1' to e_1 represents the induced increase in expenditure that occurs as national income rises. Because ΔY is greater than ΔA, the simple multiplier is greater than 1 ($\Delta Y/\Delta A > 1$).

APPLYING ECONOMIC CONCEPTS 21-1

The Multiplier: A Numerical Example

Consider an economy that has a marginal propensity to spend out of national income of 0.80. Suppose an increase in business confidence leads many firms to increase their investment in new buildings and factories. Specifically, suppose desired investment increases by $1 billion per year. National income initially rises by $1 billion, but that is not the end of it. The factors of production that received the first $1 billion spend $800 million. This second round of spending generates $800 million of new income. This new income, in turn, induces $640 million of third-round spending, and so it continues, with each successive round of new income generating 80 percent as much in new expenditure. Each additional round of expenditure creates new income and yet another round of expenditure.

The table carries the process through 10 rounds. Students with sufficient patience (and no faith in mathematics) may compute as many rounds in the process as they wish; they will find that the sum of the rounds of expenditures approaches a limit of $5 billion, which is five times the initial increase in expenditure. [30]

Notice that most of the total change in national income occurs in the first few rounds. Of the total change

of $5 billion, 68 percent ($3.4 billion) occurs after only five rounds of activity. By the end of the tenth round, 89 percent ($4.5 billion) of the total change has taken place.

Round of Spending	Increase in Expenditure (millions of dollars)	Cumulative Total (millions of dollars)
1 (initial increase)	1000.0	1000.0
2	800.0	1800.0
3	640.0	2440.0
4	512.0	2952.0
5	409.6	3361.6
6	327.7	3689.3
7	262.1	3951.4
8	209.7	4161.1
9	167.8	4328.9
10	134.2	4463.1
11 to 20 combined	479.3	4942.4
All others	57.6	5000.0

The Size of the Simple Multiplier

The size of the simple multiplier depends on the slope of the *AE* function—that is, on the marginal propensity to spend, *z*.

As shown in Figure 21-10, a high marginal propensity to spend means a steep *AE* curve. The expenditure induced by any initial increase in income is large, with the result that the final rise in income is correspondingly large. By contrast, a low marginal propensity to spend means a relatively flat *AE* curve. The expenditure induced by the initial increase in income is small, and the final rise in income is not much larger than the initial rise in autonomous expenditure that brought it about.

The larger the marginal propensity to spend, the steeper the AE function and thus the larger the simple multiplier.

We can derive the precise value of the simple multiplier by using elementary algebra. (The formal derivation is given in *Extensions in Theory 21-2*.) The result is:

$$\text{Simple Multiplier} = \frac{\Delta Y}{\Delta A} = \frac{1}{1 - z}$$

FIGURE 21-10 The Size of the Simple Multiplier

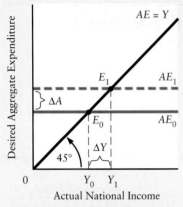 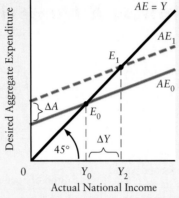 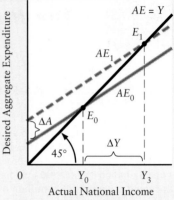

(i) Flat *AE*, multiplier equal to 1   (ii) Intermediate case   (iii) Steep *AE*, multiplier large

The larger the marginal propensity to spend out of national income (z), the steeper is the *AE* curve and the larger is the multiplier. In each part of the figure, the initial *AE* function is AE_0, equilibrium is at E_0, with income Y_0. The *AE* curve then shifts upward to AE_1 as a result of an increase in autonomous expenditure of ΔA. ΔA is the same in each part. The new equilibrium in each case is at E_1.

In part (i), the *AE* function is horizontal, indicating a marginal propensity to spend of zero ($z = 0$). The change in equilibrium income ΔY is only the increase in autonomous expenditure because there is no induced expenditure by the people who receive the initial increase in income. The simple multiplier is then equal to 1, its minimum possible value.

In part (ii), the *AE* curve slopes upward but is still relatively flat (z is low). The increase in equilibrium national income to Y_2 is only slightly greater than the increase in autonomous expenditure that brought it about. The simple multiplier is slightly greater than 1.

In part (iii), the *AE* function is quite steep (z is high). Now the increase in equilibrium income to Y_3 is much larger than the increase in autonomous expenditure that brought it about. The simple multiplier is much larger than 1.

Recall that z is the marginal propensity to spend out of national income and is between zero and 1. The *smallest* simple multiplier occurs when z equals zero. In this case, $(1 - z)$ equals 1 and so the multiplier equals 1. On the other hand, if z is very close to 1, $(1 - z)$ is close to zero and so the multiplier becomes very large. The relationship between z, the slope of the *AE* function, and the size of the multiplier is shown in Figure 21-10.

A Realistic Estimate for the Multiplier

To estimate the size of the multiplier in an actual economy, we need to estimate the value of the marginal propensity to spend out of national income in that economy. Evidence suggests that the Canadian value is much smaller than the 0.8 that we used in our example, in large part because there are a number of withdrawals from the circular flow of income that we have not yet included in our model of the economy. In addition to saving, which we have discussed, these withdrawals include income taxes and import expenditures. For the current Canadian economy these adjustments lead to a realistic estimate of around 0.2 for z. Hence, a realistic estimate of the simple multiplier in Canada is approximately $1/(1 - 0.2) = 1/0.8 = 1.25$.

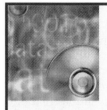

EXTENSIONS IN THEORY 21-2

The Algebra of the Simple Multiplier

Basic algebra is all that is needed to derive the exact expression for the multiplier. Readers who feel at home with algebra may want to follow this derivation. Others can skip it and rely on the graphical and numerical arguments that have been given in the text.

First, we derive the equation for the *AE* curve. Desired aggregate expenditure comprises autonomous expenditure and induced expenditure. In the simple model of this chapter, autonomous expenditure is equal to investment plus autonomous consumption. Induced expenditure is equal to induced consumption.

Hence, we can write

$$AE = zY + A \qquad [1]$$

where *A* is autonomous expenditure and zY is induced expenditure, *z* being the marginal propensity to spend out of national income. In the simple model of this chapter, with no government and no international trade, *z* is equal to the marginal propensity to consume.

Now we write the equation of the 45° line,

$$AE = Y \qquad [2]$$

which states the equilibrium condition that desired aggregate expenditure equals actual national income. Equations 1 and 2 are two equations with two unknowns, *AE* and

Y. To solve them, we substitute Equation 1 into Equation 2 to obtain

$$Y = zY + A \qquad [3]$$

Equation 3 can be easily solved to get *Y* expressed in terms of *A* and *z*. The solution is

$$Y = \frac{A}{1 - z} \qquad [4]$$

Equation 4 tells us the equilibrium value of *Y* in terms of autonomous expenditures and the marginal propensity to spend out of national income. Now consider a \$1 increase in *A*. The expression $Y = A/(1 - z)$ tells us that if *A* changes by one dollar, the change in *Y* will be $1/(1 - z)$ dollars. Generally, for a change in autonomous spending of ΔA, the change in *Y* will be

$$\Delta Y = \frac{\Delta A}{1 - z} \qquad [5]$$

Dividing through by ΔA gives the value of the multiplier:

$$\text{Simple Multiplier} = \frac{\Delta Y}{\Delta A} = \frac{1}{1 - z} \qquad [6]$$

Economic Fluctuations as Self-Fulfilling Prophecies

Expectations about the future play an important role in macroeconomics. We said earlier that households' and firms' expectations about the future state of the economy influence desired consumption and desired investment. But as we have just seen, changes in desired aggregate expenditure will, through the multiplier process, lead to changes in national income. This link between expectations and national income suggests that expectations about a healthy economy can actually produce a healthy economy—what economists call a self-fulfilling prophecy.

Imagine a situation in which many firms begin to feel optimistic about future economic prospects. This optimism will lead them to increase their desired investment, thus shifting up the economy's *AE* function. As we have seen, however, such an upward shift in the *AE* function will lead to an increase in national income. Such "good" economic times will then be seen by firms to have justified their initial optimism. Many firms in such a situation may take pride in their ability to predict the future—but this would be misplaced pride. The truth of the matter is that if enough firms are optimistic and take actions based on that optimism, their actions will *create* the economic situation that they expected.

Now imagine the opposite situation in which many firms begin to feel pessimistic about future economic conditions. This pessimism may lead them to scale down or cancel planned investment projects. Such a decline in planned investment would shift the *AE* function down and lead to a decrease in national income. The "bad" economic times will then be seen by the firms as justification for their initial pessimism, and many will take pride in their predictive powers. But again their pride would be misplaced; the truth is that sufficient pessimism on the part of firms will tend to *create* the conditions that they expected.

> Politicians in Canada and elsewhere are often heard "talking up" their national economies. This can be understood by examining the role that expectations play in booms and recessions. For more on this topic, look for "Recessions and Booms As Self-Fulfilling Prophecies" in the *Additional Topics* section of this book's Companion Website.
>
> http://www.pearsoned.ca/ragan

S U M M A R Y

21.1 Desired Aggregate Expenditure

- Desired aggregate expenditure *(AE)* is equal to desired consumption plus desired investment plus desired government purchases plus desired net exports. It is the amount that economic agents want to spend on purchasing the national product.

$$AE = C + I + G + X - IM$$

- The relationship between disposable income and consumption is called the consumption function. The constant term in the consumption function is autonomous expenditure. The part of consumption that responds to income is called induced expenditure.

$$C = a + bY_D$$

- A change in disposable income leads to a change in desired consumption and desired saving. The responsiveness of these changes is measured by the marginal propensity to consume *(MPC)* and the marginal propensity to save *(MPS)*, both of which are positive, and which sum to 1, indicating that all disposable income is either consumed or saved.

- Changes in wealth, interest rates, or expectations about the future lead to a change in autonomous consumption. As a result, the consumption function shifts.

- Firms' desired investment depends, among other things, on real interest rates, changes in sales, and business confidence. In our simplest model of the economy, investment is treated as an autonomous expenditure.

21.2 Equilibrium National Income

- Equilibrium national income is defined as that level of national income where desired aggregate expenditure equals actual national income. At incomes above equilibrium, desired expenditure is less than national income. In this case, inventories accumulate and firms will eventually reduce output. At incomes below equilibrium, desired expenditure exceeds national income. In this case, inventories are depleted and firms will eventually increase output.

- In a closed economy with no government, an alternative definition of equilibrium national income is that level of national income where desired saving equals desired investment.

- Equilibrium national income is represented graphically by the point at which the aggregate expenditure curve cuts the 45° line—that is, where desired aggregate expenditure equals actual national income. This is the same level of income at which the saving function intersects the investment function.

21.3 **Changes in Equilibrium National Income**   🔵④

- Equilibrium national income is increased by a rise in either autonomous consumption or autonomous investment expenditure. Equilibrium national income is reduced by a fall in these desired expenditures.
- The magnitude of the effect on national income of shifts in autonomous expenditure is given by the multiplier. It is defined as $\Delta Y/\Delta A$, where ΔA is the change in autonomous expenditure.
- The simple multiplier is the multiplier when the price level is constant. The simple multiplier = $\Delta Y/\Delta A$ = $1/(1 - z)$, where z is the marginal propensity to spend out of national income. The larger is z, the larger is the multiplier.

- It is a basic prediction of our simple macro model that the simple multiplier, relating an increase in spending on domestic output to the resulting increase in national income, is greater than 1.
- Expectations play an important role in the determination of national income. Optimism can lead households and firms to increase expenditure, which, through the multiplier process, leads to increases in national income. Pessimism can similarly lead to decreases in expenditure and national income.

K E Y   C O N C E P T S

Desired versus actual expenditure
The consumption function
Average and marginal propensities to consume
Average and marginal propensities to save

The aggregate expenditure *(AE)* function
Marginal propensity to spend
Equilibrium national income

Effect on national income of shifts in the *AE* curve
The simple multiplier
The size of the multiplier and slope of the *AE* curve

S T U D Y   E X E R C I S E S

1. Fill in the blanks to make the following statements correct.

   a. The equation for *actual* national income from the expenditure side is written as: GDP = _____.

   b. The equation for *desired* aggregate expenditure is written as: AE = _____.

   c. National income accounts measure _____ expenditures in four broad categories. National income theory deals with_____ expenditure in the same four categories.

   d. The equation for a simple consumption function is written as $C = a + bY$. The letter a represents the _____ part of consumption. The letters bY represent the _____ part of consumption. When graphing a consumption function, the vertical intercept is given by the letter _____, and the slope of the function is given by the letter _____.

   e. In the simple macro model of this chapter, all investment is treated as _____ expenditure, meaning that it is unaffected by changes in national income.

   f. The aggregate expenditure function in the simple macro model of this chapter is written as AE = _____, and is graphed with _____ on the vertical axis and _____ on the horizontal axis.

   g. An example of an aggregate expenditure function is $AE = \$47$ billion $+ 0.92Y$. Autonomous expenditure is _____ and the marginal propensity to spend out of national income is _____. In the simple model in this chapter, the marginal propensity to spend is the same as the marginal propensity to consume because _____.

2. Fill in the blanks to make the following statements correct.

   a. If actual national income is $200 billion and desired aggregate expenditure is $180 billion, inventories will begin to _____, firms will _____ the level of output, and national income will _____.

b. If actual national income is $200 billion and desired aggregate expenditure is $214 billion, inventories will begin to _____, firms will _____ the level of output, and national income will _____.

c. When actual national income and desired aggregate expenditure are equal, desired saving must equal desired _____.

d. If households experience an increase in wealth that leads to an increase in desired consumption, the *AE* curve will shift _____. Equilibrium national income will _____ to the level indicated by the intersection of the *AE* curve with the _____ line.

e. When autonomous desired expenditure increases by $10 billion, national income will increase by _____ than $10 billion. The magnitude of the change in national income is measured by the _____.

f. The larger is the marginal propensity to spend, the _____ is the multiplier. Where z is the marginal propensity to spend, the multiplier is equal to _____.

3. Consider the following table for a household's consumption expenditures and disposable income. All values are expressed in real 1997 dollars.

Disposable Income (Y_D)	Desired Consumption (C)	APC = C/Y_D	MPC = $\Delta C/\Delta Y_D$
0	150	—	
100	225	2.25	.75
200	300	1.5	.75
300	375	1.25	.75
400	450	1.13	.75
500	525	1.05	.75
600	600	1	.75
700	675	.96	.75
800	750	.94	.75

a. Compute the average propensity to consume for each level of income and fill in the table.

b. Compute the marginal propensity to consume for each successive change in income and fill in the table.

c. Plot the consumption function on a scale diagram. What is its slope?

4. This question relates to desired saving, and is based on the table from Question 3.

a. Compute desired saving at each level of disposable income. Plot the saving function on a scale diagram. What is its slope?

b. Show that the average propensity to save plus the average propensity to consume must equal 1.

5. In the chapter we explained at length the difference between *desired* expenditures and *actual* expenditures.

a. Is national income accounting based on desired or actual expenditures? Explain.

b. Suppose there were a sudden decrease in desired consumption expenditure. Explain why this would lead to an equally sudden increase in *actual* investment expenditure. Which type of investment would rise?

c. Illustrate the event from part (b) in a 45° line diagram. Illustrate the increase in actual investment.

6. Consider the following diagram of the *AE* function and the 45° line.

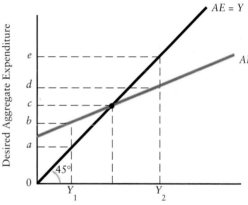

a. Suppose the level of actual national income is Y_1. What is the level of desired aggregate expenditure? Is it greater or less than actual output? Are inventories being depleted or accumulated?

b. If actual income is Y_1, explain the process by which national income changes toward equilibrium.

c. Suppose the level of actual national income is Y_2. What is the level of desired aggregate expenditure? Is it greater or less than actual output? Are inventories being depleted or accumulated?

d. If actual income is Y_2, explain the process by which national income changes toward equilibrium.

7. Consider a simple model like the one developed in this chapter. The following equations show the levels of desired consumption and investment:

$$C = 500 + 0.9Y$$
$$I = 100$$

Y	C	I	AE
0			
2 000			
4 000			
6 000			
8 000			
10 000			

a. Complete the table above.
b. What is the equilibrium level of national income in this model? Why?
c. What is the level of desired saving at the equilibrium level of national income? Explain why desired saving equals desired investment at the equilibrium level of income.

8. Suppose you are given the following information for an economy without government spending, exports, or imports. C is desired consumption, I is desired investment, and Y is income. C and I are given by:

$$C = 1400 + 0.8Y$$
$$I = 400$$

a. What is the equation for the aggregate expenditure (AE) function?
b. Applying the equilibrium condition that $Y = AE$, determine the level of equilibrium national income.
c. Using your answer from part (b), determine the values of consumption, saving, and investment when the economy is in equilibrium.

9. Consider an economy characterized by the following equations:

$$C = 500 + 0.75Y + 0.05W$$
$$I = 150$$

where C is desired consumption, I is desired investment, W is household wealth, and Y is national income.

a. Suppose $W = 10\,000$. Draw the aggregate expenditure function on a scale diagram along with the 45° line. What is the equilibrium level of national income?
b. The marginal propensity to spend in this economy is 0.75. What is the value of the multiplier?
c. Using your answer from part (b), what would be the change in equilibrium national income if desired investment increased to 250? Can you show this in your diagram?
d. Now suppose household wealth increases from 10 000 to 15 000. What happens to the AE function and by how much does national income change?

10. The "Paradox of Thrift" is a famous idea in macroeconomics—one that we will discuss in later chapters. The basic idea is that if every household in the economy tries to increase its level of desired saving, the level of national income will fall and they will end up saving no more than they were initially. Use the model and diagrams of this chapter to show how an (autonomous) increase in desired saving would reduce equilibrium income and lead to no change in aggregate saving.

DISCUSSION QUESTIONS

1. Relate the following newspaper headlines to shifts in the C, S, I, and AE functions and to changes in equilibrium national income.

a. "Revival of consumer confidence leads to increased spending."
b. "High mortgage rates discourage new house purchases."
c. "Concern over future leads to a reduction in inventories."
d. "Accelerated depreciation allowances in the new federal budget sets off boom on equipment purchases."
e. "Consumers spend as stock market soars."

2. Why might an individual's marginal propensity to consume be higher in the long run than in the short run? Why might it be lower? Is it possible for an individual's average propensity to consume to be greater than 1 in the short run? In the long run? Can a country's average propensity to consume be greater than 1 in the short run? In the long run?

3. Explain why a sudden, unexpected fall in consumer expenditure would initially cause an increase in actual investment expenditure by firms.

4. In the simple model of this chapter, aggregate investment was assumed to be autonomous. The simple multiplier was $1/(1 - z)$, where z was the marginal propensity to spend. With autonomous investment, the marginal propensity to spend is simply the marginal propensity to consume. Now suppose that investment is *not* completely autonomous. That is, suppose that $I = \bar{I} + mY$, where $\bar{I}$ is autonomous investment and m is the "marginal propensity to invest" ($m > 0$). Explain how this modification to the simple model changes the simple multiplier.

CHAPTER 22

Adding Government and Trade to the Simple Macro Model

LEARNING OBJECTIVES

1. Describe how the government budget surplus is related to national income.

2. Explain how net exports are related to national income.

3. Distinguish between the marginal propensity to consume and the marginal propensity to spend.

4. Explain why the presence of government and foreign trade reduces the value of the simple multiplier.

5. Explain how government can use fiscal policy to influence the level of national income.

In Chapter 21, we developed a simplified short-run model of national income determination in a closed economy with fixed prices. In this chapter, we add a government and a foreign sector to that model. In Chapter 23, we will expand the model further to explain the determination of the price level.

Adding government to the model allows us to study *fiscal policy,* the government's use of its taxing and spending powers to affect the level of national income. Adding foreign trade allows us to examine how external events affect the Canadian economy. Fortunately, the key elements of last chapter's theory of income determination are unchanged even after government and the foreign sector are incorporated.

22.1 Introducing Government

fiscal policy The use of the government's tax and spending policies in an effort to influence the level of GDP.

A government's **fiscal policy** is defined by its plans for taxes and spending. These influence the size of national income in both the short and the long run. Our discussion of fiscal policy begins in this chapter; we go into more detail in Chapter 24 and again in Chapter 32.

Government Spending

In Chapter 20, we distinguished between government *purchases of goods and services* and government *transfer payments*. The distinction bears repeating here. Government purchases are part of GDP. When the government hires a bureaucrat, buys a paper clip, or purchases fuel for the armed forces, it is adding directly to the demands for the economy's current output of goods and services. Hence, desired government purchases, G, are part of aggregate desired expenditure.

The other part of government spending, transfer payments, also affects desired aggregate expenditure, but only indirectly. Consider welfare or employment-insurance benefits, for example. These government expenditures place no demand on the nation's production of goods and services. However, when recipients spend some of these payments on consumption, their expenditure is part of aggregate expenditure. Thus, government transfer payments do affect aggregate expenditure but only through the effect these payments have on households' *disposable* income.

Tax Revenues

Taxes reduce households' disposable income relative to national income. In contrast, transfer payments raise disposable income relative to national income. For the purpose of calculating the effect of government policy on desired consumption expenditure, it is the net effect of the two that matters.

Net taxes are defined as total tax revenue received by the government minus total transfer payments made by the government, and it is denoted as T. (For convenience, the term "taxes" means "net taxes" unless explicitly stated otherwise.) Because transfer payments are smaller than total tax revenues, net tax revenues are positive. Disposable income is therefore substantially less than national income. (It was about two-thirds of GDP in 2003.)

net taxes   Total tax revenue minus transfer payments, denoted T.

The Budget Balance

The *budget balance* is the difference between total government revenue and total government expenditure; equivalently, it equals net tax revenue minus government purchases, $T - G$. When revenues exceed expenditures, the government has a **budget surplus.** When expenditures exceed revenues, the government has a **budget deficit.**[1] When the two amounts are equal, the government has a *balanced budget.*

In the simple model of Chapter 21, all saving was private since we had no government in the model. But now we must make a distinction between *private saving* and *public saving.* **Private saving** is the difference between disposable income and consumption expenditure, or the amount that households choose to save. **Public saving** is the difference between the government's tax revenues and its expenditures. Public saving is therefore equal to the budget surplus, $T - G$.

When government has a budget surplus, public saving is positive; when government has a budget deficit, public saving is negative.

budget surplus   Any excess of current revenue over current expenditure.

budget deficit   Any shortfall of current revenue below current expenditure.

private saving   Saving on the part of households—the part of disposable income that is not spent on current consumption.

public saving   Saving on the part of governments equal to the government budget surplus.

---

[1] When the government runs a budget deficit, it must borrow the excess of spending over revenues. It does this by issuing and selling *government bonds*. When the government runs a surplus, it uses the excess revenue to purchase outstanding government bonds. The stock of outstanding bonds is called the *national debt*. Deficits and the national debt are the principal topics of Chapter 32.

The Public Saving Function

In this chapter, government purchases of goods and services are treated as autonomous—that is, the level of government purchases *(G)* does not depend on the level of national income. We also treat *tax rates* as autonomous. This, however, implies that *tax revenues* are induced. As national income rises, a tax system with given tax rates will yield more revenue. For example, when income rises, people will pay more income tax in total even though the tax *rates* are unchanged. For the model in this chapter, we will use the following simple form for government tax revenues, *T*:

$$T = tY$$

net tax rate   The increase in net tax revenue generated when national income rises by one dollar. Also called the *marginal propensity to tax*.

The federal Department of Finance designs and implements Canada's fiscal policy. See its website: www.fin.gc.ca.

Practise with Study Guide Chapter 22, Exercise 1.

where *t* is the **net tax rate** or the *marginal propensity to tax*—the increase in net tax revenue generated when national income increases by $1. It may be tempting to think of *t* as the income tax rate, but note that we are trying to represent in a simple way what in reality is a complex tax structure that includes the taxation of personal income, corporate income, overall expenditures, the value of property, and expenditure on specific products. For that reason, we avoid associating *t* with any specific type of tax. Instead, in what follows we simply refer to *t* as the *net tax rate*.

Figure 22-1 illustrates these assumptions with a specific example using hypothetical data. It shows public saving when government purchases *(G)* are constant at $51 billion and net taxes are equal to 10 percent of national income (*t* = 0.1). Notice that public saving (the government budget surplus) increases with national income. This relationship occurs because net tax revenues rise with income but, by assumption, government purchases do not. The slope of the public saving function shows how much tax revenue rises when national income rises—this is the net tax rate, *t*. The position of the public saving function is determined by fiscal policy; that is, changes in the government's taxing and spending policies will cause the public saving function to shift. We will discuss this in detail later in the chapter.

Provincial and Municipal Governments

Many people are surprised to learn that the Canadian provincial and municipal governments account for *more* purchases of goods and services than does the federal government. The federal government raises about the same amount of tax revenue as do the provincial and municipal governments combined, but spends much more of its revenues on transfer payments to the provinces.

When measuring the overall contribution of government to desired aggregate expenditure and to public saving, all levels of government must be included.

As we proceed through this chapter discussing the role of government in the determination of national income, think of "the government" as the combination of all levels of government—federal, provincial, and municipal.

FIGURE 22-1   The Public Saving Function

Actual National Income (Y)	Government Purchases (G)	Net Tax Revenue $(T = 0.1 \times Y)$	Public Saving $(T - G)$
150	51	15	−36
300	51	30	−21
525	51	52.5	1.5
600	51	60	9
900	51	90	39

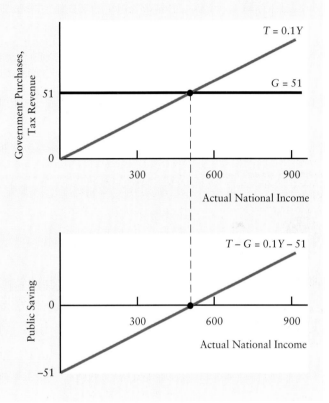

Public saving, which is equal to the government budget surplus, rises with national income. The slope of the public saving function is equal to the net tax rate, 0.1. As national income rises, public saving rises by the net tax rate times the change in national income. Thus, when national income rises by $300 billion, public saving rises by $30 billion.

Summary

Before introducing foreign trade, let's summarize how the presence of government affects our simple model.

1. All levels of government add directly to desired aggregate expenditure through their purchases of goods and services, G. Later in this chapter when we are constructing the aggregate expenditure (AE) function for our expanded model, we will have to include G, and we will treat it as autonomous expenditure.

2. Governments also collect tax revenue and make transfer payments. Net tax revenues are denoted T and are positively related to national income. Since T does not represent any expenditure on goods and services, it is not included directly in the economy's AE function. T will enter the AE function *indirectly*, however, through its effect on disposable income (Y_D) and consumption. Recall that $Y_D = Y - T$.

3. Government purchases and taxation, taken together, imply a public saving function, $T - G$. The public saving function is not used directly to construct the economy's AE function, but when we use the saving–investment approach to discuss equilibrium, it will enter the story as part of the economy's total saving.

22.2 **Introducing Foreign Trade**

Of all the goods and services produced in Canada in a given year, roughly 40 percent are exported. A similar value of goods and services is imported into Canada every year. Thus, while *net* exports may not contribute much to Canada's GDP (about 1 percent in a typical year), trade is tremendously important to Canada's economy.

Canada imports all kinds of goods and services, from French wine and Peruvian anchovies to Swiss financial and American architectural services. Canada also exports a variety of goods and services, including timber, nickel, automobiles, engineering services, computer software, flight simulators, and commuter jets. U.S.–Canadian trade is the largest two-way flow of trade between any two countries in the world today.

The Net Export Function

Practise with Study Guide Chapter 22, Exercise 3.

Exports depend on spending decisions made by foreign households and firms that purchase Canadian products. Typically, exports will not change as a result of changes in Canadian national income. We therefore treat exports as autonomous expenditure.

Imports, however, depend on the spending decisions of Canadian households and firms. Almost all consumption goods have an import content. Canadian-made cars, for example, use large quantities of imported components in their manufacture. Canadian-made clothes most often use imported cotton or wool. And most restaurant meals contain some imported fruits, vegetables, or meats. Hence, as consumption rises, imports will also increase. Because consumption rises with national income, we also get a positive relationship between imports and national income. In this chapter, we use the following simple form for imports:

$$IM = mY$$

marginal propensity to import   The increase in import expenditures induced by a $1 increase in national income. Denoted by *m*.

where *m* is the **marginal propensity to import**, the amount that desired imports rise when national income rises by $1.

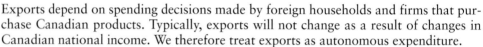

There is a positive relationship between desired imports and domestic national income. Since exports are autonomous with respect to domestic national income, desired net exports (exports minus imports) are negatively related to national income.

This negative relationship between net exports and national income is called the *net export function*. Data for a hypothetical economy with autonomous exports and with imports that are 10 percent of national income (*m* = 0.1) are illustrated in Figure 22-2. In this example, exports form the autonomous component and imports the induced component of the desired net export function.

Shifts in the Net Export Function

The net export function relates net exports (*NX*) to national income. It is drawn under the assumption that everything affecting net exports, except domestic national income, remains constant. The major factors that must be held constant are foreign national income, domestic and foreign prices, and the exchange rate. A change in any of these factors will shift the net export function. Notice that anything affecting Canadian exports will shift the net export function parallel to itself, upward if exports increase and downward if exports decrease. Also notice that anything affecting the *proportion of income* that Canadian consumers wish to spend on imports will change the *slope* of the net export function. Let's now explore some of these changes in detail.

FIGURE 22-2   The Net Export Function

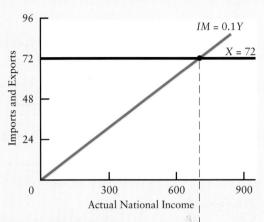

Actual National Income (Y)	Exports (X)	Imports (IM = 0.1 × Y)	Net Exports (NX = X − IM)
0	72	0	72
300	72	30	42
600	72	60	12
720	72	72	0
900	72	90	−18

(i) Export and import functions

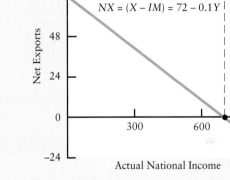

(ii) Net export function

Net exports fall as income rises. The data are hypothetical. They assume that exports are constant and that imports are 10 percent of national income. In part (i), exports are constant at \$72 billion while imports rise with national income. Therefore, net exports, shown in part (ii), decline with national income. The slope of the import function in part (i) is equal to the marginal propensity to import. The slope of the net export function in part (ii) is the negative of the marginal propensity to import.

Changes in Foreign Income

An increase in foreign income, other things being equal, will lead to an increase in the quantity of Canadian goods demanded by foreign countries—that is, to an increase in Canadian exports. This change causes the net export function to shift upward, parallel to its original position. A fall in foreign income leads to a reduction in Canadian exports and thus to a parallel downward shift in the net export function.

Changes in Relative International Prices

Any change in the prices of Canadian goods relative to those of foreign goods will cause both imports and exports to change. These changes will shift the net export function.

Consider what happens with a rise in Canadian prices relative to those in foreign countries. The increase in Canadian prices means that foreigners now see Canadian goods as more expensive relative both to goods produced in their own country and to goods

FIGURE 22-3   Shifts in the Net Export Function

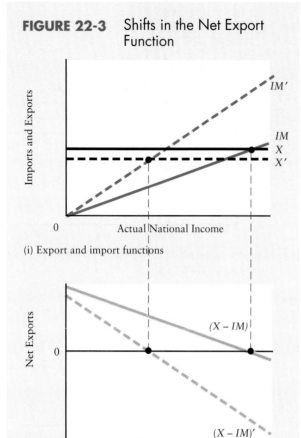

(i) Export and import functions

(ii) Net export function

Changes in relative international prices shift the NX function. A rise in Canadian prices relative to foreign prices lowers exports from X to X' and raises the import function from IM to IM'. This shifts the net export function downward from $(X - IM)$ to $(X - IM)'$. A fall in Canadian prices has the opposite effect.

imported from countries other than Canada. As a result, the value of Canadian exports will fall.[2] The X curve shifts down in Figure 22-3. Similarly, Canadians will see imports from foreign countries become cheaper relative to the prices of Canadian-made goods. As a result, they will shift their expenditures toward foreign goods and away from Canadian goods. That is, Canadians will spend a higher fraction of national income on imports—the IM curve in Figure 22-3 will rotate up. The combination of these two effects is that the net export function shifts downward and becomes steeper. A fall in Canadian prices relative to foreign prices would have the opposite effect, shifting the X function up and the IM function down, and thus shifting the NX function up.

A rise in Canadian prices relative to those in other countries reduces Canadian net exports at any level of national income. A fall in Canadian prices increases net exports at any level of national income.

The most important cause of a change in international relative prices is a change in the exchange rate. A *depreciation* of the Canadian dollar means that foreigners must pay less of their money to buy one Canadian dollar, and Canadian residents must pay more Canadian dollars to buy a unit of any foreign currency. As a result, the price of foreign goods in terms of Canadian dollars rises, and the price of Canadian goods in terms of foreign currency falls. This reduction in the relative price of Canadian goods will cause a shift in expenditure away from foreign goods and toward Canadian goods. Canadian residents will import less at each level of Canadian national income, and foreigners will buy more Canadian exports. The net export function thus shifts upward.

An example may help to clarify the argument. Suppose something causes the Canadian dollar to depreciate relative to the euro (the common currency in the European Union). The depreciation of the Canadian dollar leads Canadians to switch away from French wines and German cars, purchasing instead more B.C. wine and Ontario-made cars. This reduction in imports is reflected by the downward rotation of the IM curve. The depreciation of the Canadian dollar relative to the euro also stimulates Canadian exports. Quebec furniture and Maritime vacations now appear cheaper to Europeans than previously, and so their expenditure on such Canadian goods increases. This increase in Canadian exports is

---

[2] The rise in Canadian prices clearly leads to a reduction in the demand for Canadian goods by foreigners. But in order for the *value* of Canadian exports to fall, the price elasticity of demand for Canadian exports must exceed 1 (so that the quantity reduction dominates the price increase). Throughout this book, we make this assumption, which is generally believed to be true.

reflected by the upward shift in the X curve. The overall effect is that the net export function shifts up and becomes flatter.

One final word of caution regarding prices, exchange rates, and net exports. It is important to keep in mind that the simple model in this chapter treats prices and exchange rates as *exogenous* variables. That is, though we can discuss what happens if they change, we do not yet *explain* where these changes come from. Of course, in the actual economy the price level and the exchange rate are key macroeconomic variables that we wish to understand. In the next chapter, the price level becomes *endogenous* in our model and we therefore consider why it changes. In Chapter 35, the exchange rate becomes endogenous. For now, however, keep in mind that the price level and the exchange rate are exogenous variables—we can explain what happens in our model *if* they change but we cannot use our present model to explain *why* they change.

Summary

How does the presence of foreign trade modify our basic model? Let's summarize.

1. Foreign firms and households purchase Canadian-made goods. Changes in foreign income and relative prices (including exchange rates) will affect Canadian exports (X), but we assume that X is autonomous with respect to Canadian national income. When we construct the economy's aggregate expenditure (AE) function we will include X since it represents expenditure on domestic goods.

2. All components of domestic expenditure (C, I, and G) include some import content. Since C is positively related to national income, imports (IM) are also related positively to national income. When we construct the economy's AE function, which shows the desired aggregate expenditure on *domestic* products, we will *subtract IM* because these expenditures are on foreign goods.

3. When we use the saving–investment approach to consider equilibrium in our expanded model, net exports (NX) will play a role similar to investment in the closed-economy model. This will be explained in detail later.

22.3 Equilibrium National Income

As in Chapter 21, equilibrium national income is the level of income where desired aggregate expenditure equals actual national income. The addition of government and net exports changes the calculations that we must make but does not alter the basic workings of the model.

Desired Consumption and National Income

When there are taxes, disposable income (Y_D) is less than national income (Y). The relationship between consumption and national income involves both the relationship between consumption and disposable income and the relationship, via taxes, between disposable income and national income.

Continuing the example from Figure 22-1, let's look at the following steps for determining the consumption function in the presence of income taxes.

1. Net taxes (T) are 10 percent of national income:

$$T = (0.1)Y$$

2. Disposable income must therefore be 90 percent of national income:

$$Y_D = (0.9)Y$$

3. The consumption function is given as:

$$C = 30 + (0.8)Y_D$$

which tells us that the *MPC* out of disposable income is 0.8.

4. We can now substitute $(0.9)Y$ for Y_D in the consumption function. By doing so, we get:

$$C = 30 + (0.8)(0.9)Y$$

Therefore, $C = 30 + (0.72)Y$

Practise with Study Guide Chapter 22, Exercise 2.

We can therefore express desired consumption as a function of Y_D or as a *different* function of Y. In this example, 0.72 is equal to the *MPC* times $(1 - t)$, where t is the net tax rate. So, whereas 0.8 is the marginal propensity to consume out of *disposable* income, 0.72 is the marginal propensity to consume out of *national* income.

In the presence of taxes, the marginal propensity to consume out of national income is less than the marginal propensity to consume out of disposable income.

The *AE* Function

In Chapter 21, the only components of desired aggregate expenditure were consumption and investment. We now add government purchases and net exports. The separate components in their general form are:

$C = a + bY_D$	consumption
I	autonomous investment
G	autonomous government purchases
$T = tY$	net tax revenues
X	autonomous exports
$IM = mY$	imports

Our first step is to express desired consumption in terms of national income, by taking income taxes into account. We recognize that $Y_D = Y - T$ and therefore rewrite the consumption function as:

$$C = a + b(1 - t)Y$$

Now, we sum up the four components of desired aggregate expenditure:

$$AE = C + I + G + (X - IM)$$
$$= a + b(1 - t)Y + I + G + (X - mY)$$
$$AE = \underbrace{[a + I + G + X]}_{\substack{\text{Autonomous} \\ \text{expenditure}}} + \underbrace{[b(1 - t) - m]Y}_{\substack{\text{Induced} \\ \text{expenditure}}}$$

In this last equation, we can see the division between autonomous aggregate expenditure and induced aggregate expenditure. The first set of square brackets brings together all of the autonomous parts of expenditure—consumption, investment, government purchases, and exports. The second set of square brackets brings together all of the induced parts of expenditure, those that change when national income changes—consumption and imports.

Figure 22-4 graphs the AE function for our hypothetical economy. Notice that the slope of the AE function measures the change in desired aggregate expenditure (AE) that comes about from a $1 increase in national income (Y). From the last equation above, we can see that the slope of the AE function is $b(1 - t) - m$. This is the marginal propensity to spend out of national income.

Practise with Study Guide Chapter 22, Exercise 4.

FIGURE 22-4   The Aggregate Expenditure Function

The aggregate expenditure function is the sum of desired consumption, investment, government purchases, and net export expenditures. The autonomous components of desired aggregate expenditure are desired investment, desired government purchases, desired export expenditures, and the constant term in desired consumption expenditure. These sum to $228 billion in the given example and this sum is the vertical intercept of the AE curve. The induced components are the second terms in desired consumption expenditure ($0.72\,Y$) and desired imports ($-0.1\,Y$).

Bringing the autonomous elements together, and the induced elements together, the equation for the AE function is $AE = 228 + 0.62Y$. The slope of the AE function, $\Delta AE/\Delta Y$, is 0.62, indicating that a $1 increase in Y leads to a 62-cent increase in desired expenditure. This is the marginal propensity to spend on domestic output.

The equilibrium level of national income is $600 billion, the level of Y where the AE function intersects the 45° line. If national income is less than $600 billion, AE exceeds Y and inventories are running down; this leads firms to increase output, and national income will rise. If national income exceeds $600 billion, AE is less than Y and inventories are accumulating; this leads firms to reduce output, and national income will fall.

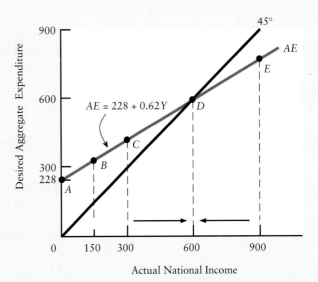

Point	Actual National Income (Y)	Desired Consumption Expenditure (C = 30 + 0.72 Y)	Desired Investment Expenditure (I = 75)	Desired Government Expenditure (G = 51)	Desired Net Export Expenditure (X − IM = 72 − 0.1 Y)	Desired Aggregate Expenditure (AE = C + I + G + X − IM)
A	0	30	75	51	72	228
B	150	138	75	51	57	321
C	300	246	75	51	42	414
D	600	462	75	51	12	600
E	900	678	75	51	−18	786

As in Chapter 21, the slope of the *AE* function is the *marginal propensity to spend* out of national income (z). With the addition of net taxes and net exports, however, the marginal propensity to spend is no longer simply equal to the marginal propensity to consume.

Suppose that the economy produces $1 of extra national income and that the response to this is governed by the relationships in Figure 22-4. Because 10 cents is collected by the government as net taxes, 90 cents becomes disposable income, and 80 percent of this amount (72 cents) is spent on consumption. However, 10 cents of all expenditure goes to imports, so expenditure on domestic goods rises by only 62 cents (72 − 10). Hence, z, the marginal propensity to spend, is 0.62. In algebraic terms,

$$z = b(1 - t) - m$$
$$= (0.8)(1 - 0.1) - 0.1$$
$$= 0.72 - 0.1$$
$$= 0.62$$

Equilibrium National Income

As in Chapter 21, the equilibrium level of national income is that level of national income where desired aggregate expenditure (along the *AE* function) equals the actual level of national income. As also was true in Chapter 21, the 45° line shows the *equilibrium condition*—the collection of points where $Y = AE$. Thus, the equilibrium level of national income in Figure 22-4 is at point *D*, where the *AE* function intersects the 45° line.

Suppose that national income is less than its equilibrium amount. The forces leading back to equilibrium are exactly the same as those described in Chapter 21. When households, firms, foreign demanders, and governments try to spend at their desired amounts, they will try to purchase more goods and services than the economy is currently producing. Hence, some of the desired expenditure must either be frustrated or take the form of purchases of inventories of goods that were produced in the past. As firms see their inventories being depleted, they will increase production, thereby increasing the level of national income.

The opposite sequence of events occurs when national income is greater than desired aggregate expenditure. Now the total of desired household consumption, business investment, government purchases, and net foreign demand on the economy's production is less than national output. Firms will notice that they are unable to sell all of their output. Their inventories will be rising, and sooner or later they will seek to reduce the level of output until it equals the level of sales. When they do, national income will fall.

Finally, when national income is equal to desired aggregate expenditure ($600 billion in Figure 22-4), there is no pressure for output to change. Desired consumption, investment, government purchases, and net exports just add up to national output.

The Saving–Investment Approach

In the closed-economy model of Chapter 21, we saw an alternative way of stating the equilibrium condition for national income: At the equilibrium level of income, desired saving equals desired investment. Adding government and international trade changes the precise form that this condition takes, but not the central underlying principle. Now, instead of describing equilibrium as desired saving being equal to desired investment, equilibrium will be characterized by desired *national* saving being equal to desired *national asset formation*. We define these new terms in turn.

National Saving

National saving is the sum of private and public saving, $S + (T - G)$. Private saving (S) is the part of disposable income that is not used for current consumption. Public saving ($T - G$) is the part of government revenue that is not spent by governments.

national saving
The sum of public saving $(T - G)$ and private saving (S).

The national saving function is illustrated in Figure 22-5. The slope of this function is the sum of the slopes of its two parts, private saving and public saving. In the example that we have been using throughout this chapter, the income tax rate, t, is 0.1. Thus, when national income rises by $1, public saving ($T - G$) rises by 10 cents. (Recall that G is assumed to be autonomous and so does not change when national income changes.) The remaining 90 cents is added to disposable income. From this 90-cent increase in disposable income, households increase their consumption by 72 cents ($MPC = 0.8$) and their saving by 18 cents ($MPS = 0.2$). The total increase in saving per marginal dollar of national income is therefore $t + MPS(1 - t)$, or $0.1 + (0.2)(0.9) = 0.28$. This is the slope of the national saving function.

National Asset Formation

In Chapter 21, all of national output was either consumption or investment goods. In addition, all income that was received by households was either consumed or saved. So the saving of households was the counterpart of the economy's investment. In the closed economy of Chapter 21—and indeed in any closed economy—the only way to

---

FIGURE 22-5 National Saving and National Asset Formation

The economy is in equilibrium when desired national saving, $(S + T - G)$, equals desired national asset formation, $(I + X - IM)$. The figure graphs the function from the second and third columns of the accompanying table; equilibrium national income is equal to $600 billion. When national income is less than $600 billion, desired national asset formation exceeds desired national saving and desired aggregate expenditure exceeds national income. Firms will respond to the imbalance by producing more, moving the economy toward equilibrium. When national income is above $600 billion, desired national asset formation is less than desired national saving, and desired aggregate expenditure is less than national income. Firms will reduce output to avoid accumulating excess inventories, and the economy will move toward equilibrium.

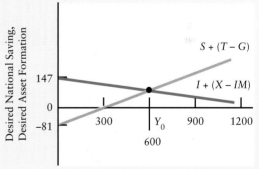

Actual National Income (Y)	Desired National Saving ($S + T - G$)	Desired National Asset Formation ($I + X - IM$)	Saving Minus Asset Formation ($S + T - G) - (I + X - IM$)
0	−81	147	−228
300	3	117	−114
600	87	87	0
900	171	57	114
1200	255	27	228

accumulate assets for future use is to devote some part of national output to investment, and that investment must be financed by saving. In an open economy, however, it is possible to accumulate assets in a different form—as net claims on foreigners, which could be foreign bonds, foreign bank deposits, or ownership of foreign factories or land. Net exports are central to determining the rate at which a country acquires such claims on foreigners.

Investment and net exports thus have a great deal in common: They are the two ways that current output can be used to accumulate assets. Investment, by definition, is production that will yield services in the future rather than in the present. Clearly, an economy that invests is adding to its assets.

To demonstrate that net exports also lead to asset accumulation, we must go through a number of steps. First, we note that net exports are the difference between what an economy produces and what it uses for consumption, investment, and government. An economy whose net exports are positive is producing more than it is using, with the difference sold abroad. Similarly, an economy that has negative net exports is using more than it is producing, with the difference purchased from abroad.

What happens when a country has positive or negative net exports? Here, the analogy to an individual is instructive. Suppose that you spend more than you earn and that you borrow money to cover the difference. You consequently go into debt. Now suppose that you earn more than you spend. As a result, you acquire assets (or reduce your debts). Spending more than you earn reduces your net asset position, and earning more than you spend increases your net asset position.

This simple idea can be extended to the national level because a nation's balances between expenditure and income are simply the total of what individual citizens do. If Canada's firms, households, and governments sell more to other countries than they buy from them (X exceeds IM), Canadians must accumulate foreign assets. These assets could be in the form of foreign currency, balances in foreign banks, foreign stocks and bonds, or even foreign lands and factories.

Conversely, if Canada's firms, households, and governments spend more abroad than they earn by selling abroad (IM exceeds X), Canadians must incur foreign liabilities (or run down foreign assets.) To finance the excess of imports over exports, funds must come from somewhere. Since they are not earned by selling current output, they must be raised by selling assets to foreigners. As a result, a new liability is generated domestically, in the form of domestic assets held by foreigners. Again, these could be bank balances, stocks and bonds, or titles to factories and farms.

Net exports result in the accumulation of assets for the exporting country. Hence, net exports are like investment in the sense that they generate future income for the exporting country.

national asset formation   The sum of investment and net exports. The extent to which the domestic economy is accumulating (domestic and foreign) assets.

To summarize, in a closed economy, **national asset formation** is just equal to investment. In an open economy, however, we must add net assets accumulated abroad (equal to positive net exports) or subtract net domestic assets accumulated by foreigners (equal to negative net exports) in order to calculate the extent to which the domestic economy is accumulating assets worldwide.

Figure 22-5 shows the national asset formation function, $I + (X - IM)$. Recall that I and X are both autonomous, whereas IM rises as national income rises. The result is a negative relationship between national income and national asset formation.

Equilibrium

Figure 22-5 shows both the national saving function and the national asset formation function. With the two relationships together, we can determine the equilibrium level of national income. National income will be at its equilibrium level when the following condition holds:

$$\underbrace{S + (T - G)}_{\substack{\text{Desired}\\\text{national}\\\text{saving}}} = \underbrace{I + (X - IM)}_{\substack{\text{Desired}\\\text{national}\\\text{asset formation}}}$$

When desired national saving is equal to desired national asset formation, national income is at its equilibrium level. [3]

To see why equilibrium occurs when desired national saving equals desired national asset formation, it is crucial to recognize that the vertical distance between the two curves in Figure 22-5 is exactly the same as the distance between the AE curve and the 45° line in Figure 22-4. Indeed, by picking any level of national income and comparing the tables in these two figures, you will see that the difference between actual national income and desired aggregate expenditure is *always* equal to the difference between desired national saving and desired national asset formation.

Let's use a little algebra to see why this must be the case. Suppose the difference between desired national saving, $(S + T - G)$, and desired national asset formation, $(I + X - IM)$, is equal to some number, which we call W. In symbols, this is

$$(S + T - G) - (I + X - IM) = W$$

Now, recall that disposable income is equal to actual income minus taxes, $Y - T$. Further, note that all of disposable income must be used up by consumption and saving. That is,

$$Y - T = C + S$$

which implies

$$S = Y - T - C$$

Now, this last equation can be substituted into our first equation above and, after a little rearranging of terms, we get

$$Y - [C + G + I + (X - IM)] = W$$

Finally, note that the expression in parentheses is simply desired aggregate expenditure, AE, and so the equation can be rewritten to be

$$Y - AE = W$$

---

[3] Some readers may have noticed in our analysis that government saving only takes the form of repaying debt, and is not used to finance public investment in items such as bridges, dams, or highways. This is a simplifying assumption only, for actual governments clearly do invest in such physical assets. Interestingly, however, our simplification does not alter the equilibrium condition. To see this, divide total government purchases of goods and services, G, into its two components: G_C is government consumption and G_I is government investment. The government's saving is now equal to $T - G_C$ and so the equilibrium condition becomes:

$$S + (T - G_C) = I + G_I + (X - IM)$$

But if we rearrange terms by moving G_I to the left-hand side of the equation, and note that $G = G_C + G_I$, we get back to the equilibrium condition shown in the text. The conclusion is as follows. When governments save by acquiring physical assets, they contribute equally to the saving and investment sides of the equation. Thus, our simplifying assumption (that governments do not invest in physical assets) does not alter the level of national income determined by the equilibrium condition.

We have just shown that the difference between desired national saving and desired national asset formation, which we called W, is exactly the same as the difference between actual national income and desired aggregate expenditure. It immediately follows that the equilibrium illustrated in Figure 22-5 is just another way of looking at the same equilibrium shown in Figure 22-4.

22.4 Changes in Equilibrium National Income

Changes in any of the components of desired aggregate expenditure will cause changes in equilibrium national income. In Chapter 21, we investigated the consequences of shifts in the consumption function and in the investment function. Here we take a first look at fiscal policy—the effects of government spending and taxation. We also consider shifts in the net export function. First, we explain why the simple multiplier is reduced by the presence of taxes and imports.

The Multiplier with Taxes and Imports

In Chapter 21, we saw that the *simple multiplier,* the amount by which equilibrium national income changes when autonomous expenditure changes by one dollar, was equal to $1/(1 - z)$, where z is the marginal propensity to spend out of national income. In the simple model of Chapter 21, with no government and no international trade, z is simply the marginal propensity to consume out of disposable income. But in the more complex model of this chapter, which contains both government and foreign trade, we have seen that the marginal propensity to spend out of national income is slightly more complicated.

The presence of imports and taxes reduces the marginal propensity to spend out of national income and thus reduces the value of the simple multiplier.

Let's be more specific. In Chapter 21, the marginal propensity to spend, z, was just equal to the marginal propensity to consume. That is,

Without Government and Foreign Trade:

$$z = MPC$$
$$\text{Simple multiplier} = 1/(1 - z)$$
$$= 1/(1 - MPC)$$

In our example, the MPC was 0.8 and so the simple multiplier was equal to 5.

$$\text{Simple multiplier}$$
$$= 1/(1 - 0.8) = 1/0.2 = 5$$

In our expanded model with government and foreign trade, the marginal propensity to spend out of national income must take account of the presence of net taxes and imports, both of which reduce the value of z.

> **With Government and Foreign Trade:**
> $$z = MPC(1 - t) - m$$
> Simple multiplier $= 1/(1 - z)$
> $$= 1/\{1 - [MPC(1 - t) - m]\}$$

In our example, $t = 0.1$ and $m = 0.1$. This makes the simple multiplier equal to 2.63.

$$\text{Simple multiplier} = 1/\{1 - [0.8(1 - 0.1) - 0.1]\} = 1/[1 - (0.72 - 0.1)\}$$
$$= 1/(1 - 0.62) = 2.63$$

What is the central point here? With taxes and imports both increasing in response to an increase in national income, every increase in national income generates more leakages from the flow of expenditure than would be the case in the simpler world with no taxes and no imports. Thus, as national income increases, there is less induced expenditure *on domestically produced goods* and therefore the overall change in equilibrium national income is lower.

The higher is the marginal propensity to import, the lower is the simple multiplier. The higher is the net tax rate, the lower is the simple multiplier.

A Realistic Value for the Multiplier

The lower value of the simple multiplier in our expanded model tells us that changes in autonomous expenditure bring about *smaller* changes in equilibrium national income. For example, suppose the level of desired investment increases by $5 billion. In Chapter 21, without government and foreign trade, the simple multiplier is equal to 5 and so the level of equilibrium national income will increase by $25 billion. But in our more complete model that includes government and trade, the multiplier is only 2.63 and so the same increase in investment by $5 billion will increase equilibrium national income by only $13 billion.

So far, we have built our model using values for key parameters that are simple to work with but not necessarily realistic. In particular, we assumed values of t and m that are well below their actual values. To find a realistic estimate for the multiplier in Canada, we need to use more realistic values for the net tax rate (t) and the marginal propensity to import (m). In Canada, a reasonable value for t is 0.30, the approximate share of combined government net taxation in GDP. Imports into Canada are close to 40 percent of GDP and so $m = 0.40$ is a reasonable value. If we use these more realistic values for t and m, and continue the reasonable assumption that the marginal propensity to consume out of disposable income is 0.8, the implied value of z is:

$$z = MPC(1 - t) - m$$
$$= 0.8(1 - 0.3) - 0.4 = 0.16$$

and so the implied value of the simple multiplier is

$$\text{Simple multiplier} = 1/(1 - z) = 1/0.84 = 1.19$$

There are two main lessons from this analysis:

1. Net taxes and imports reduce the size of the simple multiplier.

2. Realistic values of t and m in Canada suggest a simple multiplier that is much closer to 1 than to 2, and certainly far below the value of 5 that we used in the very simple model of Chapter 21.

Net Exports

Earlier in this chapter, we discussed the determinants of net exports and of shifts in the net export function. As with the other elements of desired aggregate expenditure, if the net export function shifts upward, equilibrium national income will rise; if the net export function shifts downward, equilibrium national income will fall.

Generally, exports themselves are autonomous with respect to domestic national income. Foreign demand for Canadian goods and services depends on foreign income, on foreign and Canadian prices, and on the exchange rate, but it does not depend on Canadian income. Export demand could also change because of a change in tastes. Suppose that foreign consumers develop a taste for Canadian-made furniture and desire to consume $1 billion more per year of these goods than they had in the past. The net export function (and the aggregate expenditure function) will shift up by $1 billion, and equilibrium national income will increase by $1 billion times the simple multiplier.

Fiscal Policy

Fiscal policy involves the use of government spending and taxation to influence total desired expenditure so as to change the equilibrium level of national income. Because government purchases increase desired aggregate expenditure and taxation decreases it, the *directions* of the required changes in spending and taxation are generally easy to determine once we know the direction in which the government wishes to change national income. But the *timing* and *magnitude* of the changes are more difficult issues.

Any policy that attempts to stabilize national income at or near any particular level (usually potential national income) is called **stabilization policy.** Here we introduce the idea of stabilization through fiscal policy. In Chapters 24 and 32, we examine various issues of fiscal policy in more detail, including why the practice of fiscal policy is more complicated than our simple theory suggests.

The basic idea of stabilization policy follows from what we have already learned. A reduction in tax rates or an increase in government purchases shifts the *AE* curve upward, setting in motion the multiplier process and increasing equilibrium national income. An increase in tax rates or a decrease in government purchases shifts the *AE* curve downward, causing a decrease in equilibrium income.

If the government has some target level of national income, it can use its taxes and expenditures in an attempt to push the economy toward that target. First, suppose that national income is well below the level of potential national income. In this case, the government would like to increase national income. The appropriate fiscal tools are to raise expenditures or to lower tax rates (or both). Second, suppose that the economy is "overheated," meaning that national income is above potential. What can the government do? The fiscal tools at its command are to reduce government expenditure and to raise tax rates, both of which have a depressing effect on national income.

Figure 22-6 illustrates the two situations: one in which the government's objective is to increase the level of national income, and the other in which the government's objective is to reduce the level of national income. In both cases, the "target" level of national income is the level of potential national income, Y^*, at which there is full employment. Let's now examine these two fiscal tools—government purchases and taxation—in a little more detail.[4]

stabilization policy Any policy designed to reduce the economy's cyclical fluctuations and thereby stabilize national income.

[4] The government would probably never attempt to *reduce* the level of GDP. But in a situation where real GDP is above potential output and also growing more quickly, it may try to reduce the growth rate of GDP, thus closing the gap between real GDP and potential output.

FIGURE 22-6   The Objective of Stabilization Policy

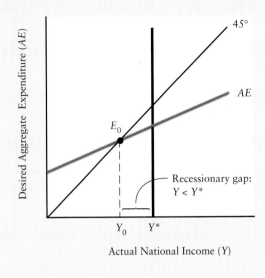

(i) Equilibrium $Y < Y^*$

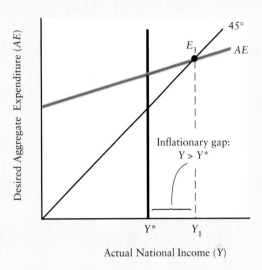

(ii) Equilibrium $Y > Y^*$

Stabilization policy is intended to bring national income closer to the level of potential national income, Y^*. In parts (i) and (ii), Y^* is the level of potential national income, where all factors of production are fully employed. In part (i), equilibrium national income is Y_0, which is less than Y^*; this is a recessionary gap. The government could either increase G or reduce t to increase equilibrium national income. In part (ii), equilibrium national income is Y_1, which is greater than Y^*; this is an inflationary gap. The government could either reduce G or increase t to reduce equilibrium national income.

Changes in Government Purchases

Suppose the government decides to reduce its purchases of all consulting services, saving $100 million per year in spending. Planned government purchases (G) would fall by $100 million, shifting AE downward by the same amount. How much would equilibrium income change? This amount can be calculated by using the simple multiplier. Government purchases are part of autonomous expenditure, so a *change* in government purchases of ΔG will lead to a *change* in equilibrium national income equal to the simple multiplier times ΔG. In this example, equilibrium income will fall by $100 million times the simple multiplier. Earlier we argued that a realistic value for the simple multiplier in Canada is about 1.2. Using this value in our example, the effect of the $100 million reduction in G is to reduce equilibrium national income by $120 million.

Changes in government purchases and tax rates can have significant effects on desired aggregate expenditure and thus on equilibrium national income.

Increases in government purchases would have the opposite effect. If the government increases its spending by $1 billion on new highways, equilibrium national income will rise by $1 billion times the simple multiplier.

FIGURE 22-7 The Effect of Changing the Tax Rate

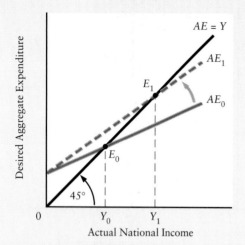

Changing the tax rate changes equilibrium income by shifting (and changing the slope of) the *AE* curve. A reduction in tax rates rotates the *AE* curve from AE_0 to AE_1. The new curve has a steeper slope because the lower tax rate withdraws a smaller amount of national income from the desired consumption flow. Equilibrium income rises from Y_0 to Y_1.

Changes in Tax Rates

If tax rates change, the relationship between disposable income and national income changes. As a result, the relationship between desired consumption and national income also changes. Consequently, a change in tax rates will cause a change in *z*, the marginal propensity to spend out of national income.

Consider first a decrease in tax rates. If the government decreases its net tax rate so that it collects 5 cents less out of every dollar of national income, disposable income rises in relation to national income. Hence, consumption also rises at every level of national income. This increase in consumption results in a (non-parallel) upward shift of the *AE* curve, that is, an increase in the slope of the curve, as shown in Figure 22-7. The result of this shift will be an increase in equilibrium national income.

A rise in tax rates has the opposite effect. A rise in tax rates causes a decrease in disposable income, and hence consumption expenditure, at each level of national income. This results in a (non-parallel) downward shift of the *AE* curve and decreases the level of equilibrium national income.

Governments can also combine an increase in government purchases with an increase in tax revenues in such a way that the budget is left unchanged. How do such *balanced budget changes* affect the level of national income? To see more details on this type of fiscal policy, look for "What Is the Balanced Budget Multiplier?" in the *Additional Topics* section of this book's Companion Website.

http://www.pearsoned.ca/ragan

| 22.5 **Demand-Determined Output**

In this and the preceding chapter, we have discussed the determination of the four categories of aggregate expenditure and have seen how they simultaneously determine equilibrium national income in the short run. An algebraic exposition of the model is presented in the appendix to this chapter.

Our macro model is based on three central concepts, and it is worth reviewing them.

Equilibrium National Income

The equilibrium level of national income is that level where *desired* aggregate expenditure equals *actual* national income. If actual national income exceeds desired expenditure, firms will eventually reduce production—national income falls. If actual national income is less than desired expenditure, firms will eventually increase production—national income rises.

The Multiplier

The multiplier measures the change in equilibrium national income that results from a change in the *autonomous* part of desired aggregate expenditure. The simple multiplier is equal to $1/(1 - z)$, where z is the marginal propensity to spend out of national income. In the model of Chapter 21, in which there is no government and no international trade, z is simply the marginal propensity to consume out of disposable income. In our expanded model that contains both government and foreign trade, z is reduced by the presence of net taxes and imports. To review:

$$\text{Simple multiplier} = 1/(1 - z)$$

Closed economy with no government:	$z = MPC$
Open economy with government:	$z = MPC(1 - t) - m$

Demand-Determined Output

The model that we have examined is constructed *for a given price level*—that is, the price level is assumed to be constant. This assumption of a given price level is related to another assumption that we have been (implicitly) making. We have implicitly assumed that firms are able and willing to produce any amount of output that is demanded without requiring any change in prices. When this is true, national income depends only on how much is demanded—that is, national income is *demand determined*. Things get more complicated if firms are either unable or unwilling to produce enough to meet all demands without requiring a change in prices. We deal with this possibility in Chapter 23 when we consider *supply-side* influences on national income.

There are two situations in which we might expect national income to be demand determined. First, when there are unemployed resources and firms have excess capacity, firms will be prepared to provide whatever is demanded from them at unchanged prices. In contrast, if the economy's resources are fully employed and firms have no excess capacity, increases in output may only be possible with higher unit costs, and these cost increases may lead to price increases.

The second situation is where firms are *price setters*. Readers who have studied some microeconomics will recognize this term. It means that the firm has the ability to influence the price of its product, either because it is large relative to the market or, more usually, because it sells a product that is *differentiated* to some extent from the products of its competitors. Firms that are price setters often respond to changes in demand by altering their production and sales, at least initially, rather than by adjusting their prices. Only after some time has passed, and the change in demand has persisted, do such firms adjust their prices. This type of behaviour corresponds well to our short-run macro model in which changes in demand lead to changes in output (for a given price level).

Our simple model of national income determination assumes a constant price level. In this model, national income is demand determined.

In the following chapters, we expand the model by making the price level an *endogenous* variable—that is, movements in the price level get explained within the model. We do this by considering the *supply side* of the economy—that is, those things that influence firms' abilities to produce output, such as technology and factor prices. When we consider the demand side and the supply side of the economy simultaneously, we will see that changes in desired aggregate expenditure usually cause both prices and real national income to change.

S U M M A R Y

22.1 Introducing Government   (LO) 1

- Government purchases, G, are part of autonomous aggregate expenditure. Taxes minus transfer payments are called net taxes and affect aggregate expenditure indirectly through households' disposable income. Taxes reduce disposable income, whereas transfers increase disposable income.

- The budget balance is defined as net tax revenues minus government purchases, $(T - G)$. When $(T - G)$ is positive, there is a budget surplus; when $(T - G)$ is negative, there is a budget deficit.
- When there is a budget surplus, there is positive public saving.

22.2 Introducing Foreign Trade   (LO) 2

- Exports are foreign purchases of Canadian goods, and do not depend on Canadian national income. Desired imports increase as national income increases. Hence, net exports decrease as national income increases.
- Changes in international relative prices lead to shifts in the net export function. A rise in the exchange rate (a

depreciation of the Canadian dollar) implies that Canadian goods are now cheaper relative to foreign goods. This leads to a rise in exports and a fall in imports, shifting the net export function up. A fall in the exchange rate (an appreciation of the Canadian dollar) has the opposite effect.

22.3 Equilibrium National Income   (LO) 3

- As in Chapter 21, national income is in equilibrium when desired aggregate expenditure equals actual national income. The equilibrium condition is

$$Y = AE, \quad \text{where } AE = C + I + G + (X - IM)$$

- The sum of investment and net exports is called *national asset formation* because investment and net exports represent the two ways in which national income that is not used in the current year can be used to generate future national income. At the equilibrium level of national

income, desired national saving is equal to desired national asset formation:

$$S + (T - G) = I + (X - IM)$$

- The slope of the AE function in the model with government and foreign trade is $z = MPC (1 - t) - m$, where MPC is the marginal propensity to consume out of disposable income, t is the net tax rate, and m is the marginal propensity to import.

22.4 **Changes in Equilibrium National Income**

- The presence of taxes and net exports reduces the value of the simple multiplier. With taxes and imports both increasing in response to an increase in national income, every increase in national income generates more leakages from the flow of expenditure.
- An increase in government purchases shifts up the *AE* function and thus increases the equilibrium level of national income. A decrease in the net tax rate makes

the *AE* function rotate upward and increases the equilibrium level of national income.
- An increase in exports can be caused by an increase in foreign demand for Canadian goods, a fall in the Canadian price level, or a depreciation of the Canadian dollar. An increase in exports shifts the *AE* function up and increases the equilibrium level of national income.

22.5 **Demand-Determined Output**

- Our simple model of national income determination is constructed for a given price level. That prices are assumed not to change in response to an increase in desired expenditure reflects a related assumption that output is demand determined.
- Output would be demand determined in two situations: if there are unemployed resources, or if firms are price setters.

- In later chapters when we consider the demand side and the supply side of the economy simultaneously, we will see that changes in desired aggregate expenditure usually cause both prices and real national income to change.

K E Y   C O N C E P T S

Taxes, transfers, and net taxes
The budget balance
The public saving function
The net export function

National saving
National asset formation
Calculation of the simple multiplier in an open economy with government

Fiscal policy and equilibrium income
Demand-determined output

S T U D Y   E X E R C I S E S

1. Consider the following table showing national income and government tax revenues in billions of dollars. Assume that the level of government purchases is $155 billion.

Actual National Income (Y)	Net Tax Revenues (T)	Public Saving ($T - G$)
100	45	—
200	70	—
300	95	—
400	120	—
500	145	—
600	170	—
700	195	—
800	220	—

a. Compute the level of public saving (the government budget surplus) for each level of national income and fill in the table.
b. Plot the public saving function on a scale diagram. Explain why it is upward sloping.
c. What is the net tax rate? Explain.
d. Suppose the government decides to increase the level of its purchases of goods and services by $15 billion. Show in your diagram what happens to the public saving function.

2. Consider the following table showing national income and imports in billions of dollars. Assume that the level of exports is $300 billion.

Actual National Income (Y)	Imports (IM)	Net Exports (X − IM)
100	85	—
200	120	—
300	155	—
400	190	—
500	225	—
600	260	—
700	295	—
800	330	—

a. Compute the level of net exports for each level of national income and fill in the table.
b. Plot the net export function on a scale diagram. Explain why it is downward sloping.
c. What is the marginal propensity to import? Explain.
d. Suppose one of Canada's major trading partners experiences a significant recession. Explain how this affects the net export function in your diagram.

3. Each of the following headlines describes an event that will have an effect on desired aggregate expenditure. What will be the effect on equilibrium national income? In each case, describe how the event would be illustrated in the 45° line diagram.

a. "Minister takes an axe to the armed forces."
b. "Russia agrees to buy more Canadian wheat."
c. "High-tech firms to cut capital outlays."
d. "Finance minister pledges to cut income-tax rates."
e. "U.S. imposes import restrictions on Canadian lumber."
f. "Asian slump means smaller market for B.C. lumber."
g. "Weak dollar spurs exports from Ontario manufacturers."

4. The following diagram shows desired aggregate expenditure for the economy of Sunset Island. The AE curve assumes a net tax rate (t) of 10 percent, autonomous exports of $25 billion, and a marginal propensity to import (m) of 15 percent.

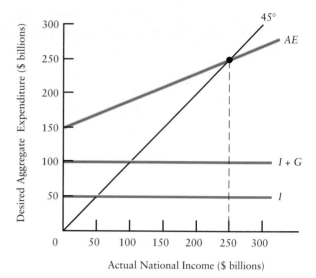

a. What is the level of desired investment expenditure (I)?
b. What is the level of government purchases (G)?
c. What is the autonomous portion of consumption?
d. What is total autonomous expenditure?
e. Starting from equilibrium national income of $250 billion, suppose government purchases decreased by $25 billion. Describe the effect on the AE curve and on equilibrium national income.
f. Starting from equilibrium national income of $250 billion, suppose the net tax rate increased from 10 percent to 30 percent of national income. Describe the effect on the AE curve and on equilibrium national income.
g. Starting from equilibrium national income of $250 billion, suppose investment increased by $50 billion. Describe the effect on the AE curve and on equilibrium national income.
h. Starting from equilibrium national income of $250 billion, suppose the marginal propensity to import fell from 15 percent to 5 percent of national income. Describe the effect on the AE curve and on equilibrium national income.

5. The economy of Sunrise Island has the following features:

- fixed price level
- no foreign trade
- autonomous desired investment (I) of $20 billion
- autonomous government purchases (G) of $30 billion
- autonomous desired consumption (C) of $15 billion
- marginal propensity to consume out of disposable income of 0.75
- net tax rate of 0.20 of national income

a. Write an equation expressing consumption as a function of disposable income.
b. Write an equation expressing net tax revenues as a function of national income.
c. Write an equation expressing disposable income as a function of national income.
d. Write an equation expressing consumption as a function of national income.
e. What is the marginal propensity to spend out of national income?
f. Calculate the simple multiplier for Sunrise Island.

6. The following table shows alternative hypothetical economies and the relevant values for the marginal propensity to consume out of disposable income (MPC), the net tax rate (t), and the marginal propensity to import, m.

Economy	MPC	t	m	z	Multiplier $1/(1 - z)$
A	0.75	0.2	0.15	—	—
B	0.75	0.2	0.30	—	—
C	0.75	0.4	0.30	—	—
D	0.90	0.4	0.30	—	—

a. Recall that z, the marginal propensity to spend out of national income, is given by the simple expression $z = MPC(1 - t) - m$. Using this expression, compute z for each of the economies and fill in the table.
b. Compare Economies A and B (they differ only by the value of m). Which one has the larger multiplier? Explain why the size of the multiplier depends on m.
c. Compare Economies B and C (they differ only by the value of t). Which one has the larger multiplier? Explain why the size of the multiplier depends on t.
d. Compare Economies C and D (they differ only by the value of MPC). Which one has the larger multiplier? Explain why the size of the multiplier depends on MPC.

7. Consider the diagram below showing the national saving function and the national asset formation function.

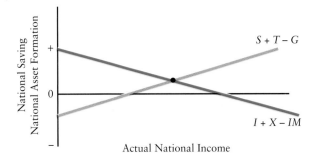

a. Explain why the national asset formation function is downward sloping. What determines its slope?
b. Explain why the national saving function is upward sloping. What determines its slope?
c. Suppose the government decided to increase its level of purchases. How would this policy change be illustrated in the diagram? What would happen to national income?
d. Suppose domestic firms decided to increase their desired investment. How would this change be illustrated in the diagram? What would happen to national income?
e. Suppose the Canadian government reduced net-tax rates. How would this change be illustrated in the diagram? What would happen to national income?

8. This question requires you to solve a macro model algebraically. Reading the appendix to this chapter will help you to answer this question. But, just in case, we lead you through it step by step. The equations for the model are as follows:

i) $C = a + bY_D$ Consumption
ii) $I = I_0$ Investment (autonomous)
iii) $G = G_0$ Government purchases (autonomous)
iv) $T = tY$ Tax revenue
v) $X = X_0$ Exports (autonomous)
vi) $IM = mY$ Imports

a. Step 1: Recall that $Y_D = Y - T$. Using this fact, substitute the tax function into the consumption function and derive the relationship between desired consumption and national income.
b. Step 2: Sum the four components of desired aggregate expenditure (C, I, G, NX). This is the aggregate expenditure (AE) function.
c. Step 3: Recall the equilibrium condition, $Y = AE$. Form the equation $Y = AE$, where AE is your expression for the AE function from part (b).
d. Step 4: Now collect terms and solve for Y. This is the equilibrium value of national income.
e. Step 5: Suppose the level of autonomous expenditure, which we could call A, rises by ΔA. What is the effect on the level of equilibrium national income?

9. This question repeats the exercise of Question 8, but for specific numerical values. The equations of the model are:

$C = 50 + 0.7Y_D$ $T = (0.2)Y$
$I = 75$ $X = 50$
$G = 100$ $IM = (0.15)Y$

a. Compute the AE function and plot it in a diagram. What is total autonomous expenditure?
b. What is the slope of the AE function?

c. Compute the equilibrium level of national income.

d. Suppose X rises from 50 to 100. How does this affect the level of national income?

e. What is the simple multiplier in this model?

DISCUSSION QUESTIONS

1. The countries of the European Union agreed in the Maastricht Treaty of 1991 to reduce their budget deficits to below 3 percent of GDP. What fiscal measures would reduce their deficits? Why might a reduction of 10 percent in government expenditure accomplish much less than a 10-percent decrease in the deficit, at least in the first instance?

2. It is typical for the federal government's forecasts of its own budget deficit to be less than the forecasts made by private-sector economists. Much of the discrepancy seems to be accounted for by assumptions about the state of the economy over the coming year. How do assumptions about the economy affect estimates of the budget deficit?

3. Classify each of the following government activities as either government purchases or transfers.

   a. Welfare payments for the poor
   b. Payments to teachers in public schools
   c. Payments to teachers at military colleges
   d. Payments on account of hospital and medical care
   e. Public Health Service vaccination programs

4. The trade deficit that the United States has with Japan has received much attention over the last 20 years. Given an economy in equilibrium, what is the relationship between saving and investment if the government budget remains balanced but there exists a trade deficit? What additional role must foreigners play in this situation? Can you explain why this situation is viewed by many Americans as troublesome? Do you agree with them?

5. In Chapter 20 we examined how national income was *measured*. Using the expenditure approach, we showed that GDP is always equal to the sum of consumption, investment, government purchases, and net exports. In Chapters 21 and 22 we examined the *determination* of national income. We showed that equilibrium national income occurs when actual national income equals the sum of desired consumption, investment, government purchases, and net exports. Does this mean that national income is always at its equilibrium level? Explain the important difference between "actual" and "desired" expenditures.

An Algebraic Exposition of the Simple Macro Model

We start with the definition of desired aggregate expenditure:

$$AE = C + I + G + (X - IM) \qquad [1]$$

For each component of AE, we write down a behavioural function.

$$C = a + bY_D \quad \text{(consumption function)} \qquad [2]$$

$$I = I_0 \quad \text{(autonomous investment)} \qquad [3]$$

$$G = G_0 \quad \text{(autonomous government purchases)} \qquad [4]$$

$$X = X_0 \quad \text{(autonomous exports)} \qquad [5]$$

$$IM = mY \quad \text{(imports)} \qquad [6]$$

where a is autonomous consumption spending, b is the marginal propensity to consume, and m is the marginal propensity to import. Obviously, the "behavioural" functions for investment, government purchases, and exports are very simple: These are all assumed to be independent of the level of national income.

Before deriving aggregate expenditure, we need to determine the relationship between national income (Y) and disposable income (Y_D), because it is Y_D that determines desired consumption expenditure. Y_D is defined as income after net taxes. In Chapter 22 we examined a very simple linear tax of the form

$$T = tY \qquad [7]$$

Taxes must be subtracted from national income to obtain disposable income:

$$Y_D = Y - tY = Y(1 - t) \qquad [8]$$

Substituting Equation 8 into the consumption function allows us to write consumption as a function of national income.

$$C = a + b(1 - t)Y \qquad [9]$$

Now we can add up all of the components of desired aggregate expenditure, substituting Equations 3, 4, 5, 6, and 9 into Equation 1:

$$AE = a + b(1 - t)Y + I_0 + G_0 + X_0 - mY \qquad [10]$$

Equation 10 is the AE function, which shows desired aggregate expenditure as a function of actual national income.

In equilibrium, desired aggregate expenditure must equal actual national income:

$$AE = Y \qquad [11]$$

Equation 11 is the equilibrium condition for our model. It is the equation of the 45° line in the figures in this chapter.

To solve for the equilibrium level of national income, we want to solve for the level of Y that satisfies both Equations 10 and 11. That is, solve for the level of Y that is determined by the intersection of the AE curve and the 45° line. Substitute Equation 11 into Equation 10:

$$Y = a + b(1 - t)Y + I_0 + G_0 + X_0 - mY \qquad [12]$$

Group all the terms in Y on the right-hand side, and subtract them from both sides:

$$Y = Y[b(1 - t) - m] + a + I_0 + G_0 + X_0 \qquad [13]$$

$$Y - Y[b(1 - t) - m] = a + I_0 + G_0 + X_0 \qquad [14]$$

Notice that $[b(1 - t) - m]$ is exactly the marginal propensity to spend out of national income, defined earlier as z. When national income goes up by one dollar, only $1 - t$ dollars go into disposable income, and only b of that gets spent on consumption. Additionally, m gets spent on imports, which are not expenditure on domestic national income. Hence $[b(1 - t) - m]$ gets spent on domestic output.

Substituting z for $[b(1 - t) - m]$ and solving Equation 14 for equilibrium Y yields

$$Y = \frac{a + I_0 + G_0 + X_0}{1 - z} \qquad [15]$$

Notice that the numerator of Equation 15 is total autonomous expenditure, which we call A. Hence, Equation 15 can be rewritten as

$$Y = \frac{A}{1 - z} \qquad [16]$$

Notice also that if autonomous expenditure rises by some amount ΔA, Y will rise by $\Delta A/(1 - z)$. So, the simple multiplier is $1/(1 - z)$.

The Algebra Illustrated

The numerical example that was carried through Chapters 21 and 22 can be used to illustrate the preceding exposition. In that example, the behavioural equations are:

$$C = 30 + 0.8Y_D \qquad [17]$$

$$I = 75 \qquad [18]$$

$$G = 51 \qquad [19]$$

$$X - IM = 72 - 0.1Y \qquad [20]$$

$$T = 0.1Y \qquad [21]$$

From Equation 8, disposable income is given by $Y(1 - t) = 0.9Y$. Substituting this into Equation 17 yields

$$C = 30 + 0.72Y$$

as in Equation 9.

Now, recalling that in equilibrium $AE = Y$, we add up all of the components of AE and set the sum equal to Y, as in Equation 12:

$$Y = 30 + 0.72Y + 75 + 51 + 72 - 0.1Y \quad [22]$$

Collecting terms yields

$$Y = 228 + 0.62Y$$

Subtracting $0.62Y$ from both sides gives

$$0.38Y = 228$$

and dividing through by 0.38, we have

$$Y = \frac{228}{0.38} = 600$$

This can also be derived by using Equation 16. Autonomous expenditure is 228, and z, the marginal propensity to spend out of national income, is 0.62. Thus, from Equation 16, equilibrium income is $228/(1 - 0.62) = 600$, which is exactly the equilibrium we obtained in Figure 22-4.

Output and Prices
in the Short Run

In Chapters 21 and 22, we developed a simple model of income determination. We saw that changes in wealth, interest rates, the government's fiscal policies, or expectations about the future lead to changes in desired aggregate expenditure. Through the multiplier process, such changes in desired expenditure caused equilibrium national income to change.

The simple model in Chapters 21 and 22 had a constant price level. We assumed that firms were prepared to provide more output when it was demanded without requiring an increase in prices. In this sense, we said that output was *demand determined*.

The actual economy, however, does not have a constant price level. Rather than assuming it is constant, we would like to understand what causes it to change. In other words, we would now like to expand our model to make the price level an *endogenous* variable—that is, one that is explained within the model.

We make the transition to a variable price level in three steps. First, we study the consequences for national income of *exogenous* changes in the price level—changes that happen for reasons that are not explained by our model of the economy. We ask how changes in the price level affect desired aggregate expenditure. That is, we examine the *demand side* of the economy. Second, we examine the *supply side* by exploring the relationship between the price level, the prices of factor inputs, and the level of output firms would like to supply. Finally, we examine the concept of *macroeconomic equilibrium* that combines both the demand and supply sides to determine the price level and real national income simultaneously.

23.1 **The Demand Side of the Economy**

Consider the macro model in Chapter 22. What happens to equilibrium GDP when the price level changes for some exogenous reason? To find out, we need to understand how the change affects desired aggregate expenditure.

Shifts in the *AE* Curve

The *AE* curve shifts in response to a change in the price level. This shift occurs because a change in the price level affects desired consumption expenditures and desired net exports. These are the changes on which we will focus in this chapter. (In later chapters, we will see that changes in the price level will change interest rates and shift the *AE* curve for an additional reason.)

Changes in the price level cause changes in the real value of cash held by the private sector. This change in wealth leads to changes in the amount of desired consumption expenditure.

Changes in Consumption

A change in the price level leads to a change in household wealth and thus to a change in desired consumption expenditure. Let's see how and why this occurs.

Much of the private sector's total wealth is held in the form of assets with a fixed nominal value. The most obvious example is money itself. We will discuss money in considerable detail in Chapters 27 and 28, but for now just note that most individuals and businesses hold money in their wallets, in their cash registers, or in their chequing accounts. What this money can buy—its real value—depends on the price level. The higher the price level, the less a given amount of money can purchase. For this reason, a rise in the domestic price level lowers the real value of money holdings. Similarly, a reduction in the price level raises the real value of money holdings.

A rise in the price level lowers the real value of money held by the private sector. A fall in the price level raises the real value of money held by the private sector.

Other examples of assets that have fixed nominal values include government and corporate bonds. The bondholder has lent money to the issuer of the bond and receives a repayment from the issuer when the bond matures. What happens when there is a change in the price level in the intervening period? A rise in the price level means that the repayment to the bondholder is lower in real value. This is a decline in wealth for the bondholder. However, the issuer of the bond, having made a repayment of lower real value because of the increase in the price level, has experienced an increase in wealth. In dollar terms, the bondholder's reduction in wealth is exactly offset by the issuer's increase in wealth.

Changes in the price level change the wealth of bondholders and bond issuers, but because the changes offset each other there is no change in aggregate wealth.[1]

---

[1] Some economists argue that in the case of *government* bonds, there *will* be a change in aggregate wealth when the price level changes. The argument relies on changes in the wealth of the bond issuers (governments) not being recognized by taxpayers, the individuals who are ultimately responsible to repay government debt. We will discuss this debate in Chapter 32.

In summary, a rise in the price level leads to a reduction in the real value of the private sector's wealth. As we saw in Chapter 21, a reduction in wealth leads to a decrease in autonomous consumption and thus to a downward shift in the AE function.

A rise in the domestic price level reduces private-sector wealth; this leads to a fall in desired consumption, and thus a downward shift in the AE curve. A fall in the domestic price level leads to a rise in wealth and desired consumption and thus to an upward shift in the AE curve.

Changes in Net Exports

When the domestic price level rises, Canadian goods become more expensive relative to foreign goods. As we saw in Chapter 22, this change in relative prices causes Canadian consumers to reduce their purchases of Canadian-made goods, which have now become relatively more expensive, and to increase their purchases of foreign goods, which have now become relatively less expensive. At the same time, consumers in other countries reduce their purchases of the now relatively more expensive Canadian-made goods. We saw in Chapter 22 that these changes cause a downward shift in the net export function.

A rise in the domestic price level shifts the net export function downward, which causes a downward shift in the AE curve. A fall in the domestic price level shifts the net export function and hence the AE curve upward.

Changes in Equilibrium GDP

Because it causes downward shifts in both the net export function and the consumption function, an exogenous rise in the price level causes a downward shift in the AE curve, as shown in Figure 23-1. When the AE curve shifts downward, the equilibrium level of real GDP falls.

Now suppose there is a fall in the price level. Canadian goods become relatively cheaper internationally, so net exports rise. Also, the purchasing power of assets denominated in money terms is increased, so households spend more. The resulting increase in desired expenditure on Canadian goods causes the AE curve to shift upward. The equilibrium level of real GDP therefore rises.

A Change of Labels.   In Chapters 21 and 22 the horizontal axis was labelled "Actual National Income." Notice in Figure 23-1, however, that we have labelled the horizontal axis "Real GDP." We use GDP rather than *national income* but the two are clearly the same. It is still *actual*, as opposed to *desired*, but we leave that off, also for simplicity. Finally, we add *real* because from this chapter onward the price level will be changing and thus it is necessary to distinguish changes in nominal GDP from changes in real GDP.

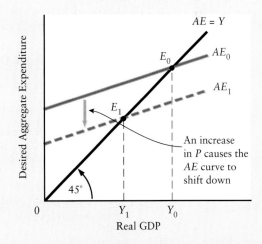

FIGURE 23-1   Desired Aggregate Expenditure and the Price Level

An exogenous change in the price level causes the AE curve to shift and thus causes equilibrium GDP to change. At the initial price level, the AE curve is given by the solid line AE_0, and hence equilibrium is at E_0 with real GDP equal to Y_0. An increase in the price level reduces desired aggregate expenditure and thus causes the AE curve to shift downward to the dashed line, AE_1. As a result, equilibrium GDP falls to Y_1.

The Aggregate Demand Curve

We now know from the behaviour underlying the *AE* function that the price level and real equilibrium GDP are negatively related to each other. This negative relationship can be shown in an important new concept, the *aggregate demand curve*.

Recall that the *AE* curve is drawn with real GDP on the horizontal axis and desired aggregate expenditure on the vertical axis, and that it is plotted for a *given* price level. We are now going to let the price level vary and keep track of the various equilibrium points that occur as the *AE* function shifts. This will give us an **aggregate demand (*AD*) curve** that shows the relationship between the price level and the equilibrium level of real GDP. It will be plotted with the price level on the vertical axis and real GDP on the horizontal axis. Because the horizontal axes of both the *AE* and *AD* curves measure real GDP, the two curves can be placed one above the other so that the levels of GDP on both can be compared directly. This is shown in Figure 23-2.

Now let us see how the *AD* curve is derived. Given a value of the price level, P_0, equilibrium GDP is determined in part (i) of Figure 23-2 at the point where the AE_0 curve crosses the 45° line. The equilibrium level of real GDP is Y_0. Part (ii) of the figure shows the same equilibrium level of GDP, Y_0, plotted against the price level P_0. The equilibrium point in part (i), E_0, corresponds to point E_0 on the *AD* curve in part (ii).

As we have seen, the *AE* curve shifts when the price level changes. As the price level rises to P_1, the *AE* curve becomes AE_1 and the equilibrium level of real GDP falls to Y_1. This determines a second point on the *AD* curve, E_1. By joining these points, we trace out the *AD* curve.

For any given price level, the *AD* curve shows the level of real GDP for which desired aggregate expenditure equals actual GDP.

Note that because the *AD* curve relates equilibrium GDP to the price level, changes in the price level that cause *shifts in* the *AE* curve cause *movements along* the *AD* curve. A movement along the *AD* curve thus traces out the response of equilibrium GDP to a change in the price level.

The Slope of the *AD* Curve

Figure 23-2 provides us with sufficient information to establish that the *AD* curve is negatively sloped.

1. A rise in the price level causes the *AE* curve to shift downward and hence leads to a movement upward and to the left along the *AD* curve, reflecting a fall in the equilibrium level of GDP.

2. A fall in the price level causes the *AE* curve to shift upward and hence leads to a movement downward and to the right along the *AD* curve, reflecting a rise in the equilibrium level of GDP.

In Chapter 3, we saw that demand curves for individual goods such as coffee, CD players, and automobiles are downward sloping. However, the reasons for the negative slope of the *AD* curve are different from the reasons for the negative slope of individual demand curves used in microeconomics. Why is this the case?

An individual demand curve describes a situation in which the price of one commodity changes *while the prices of all other commodities and consumers' money incomes are constant*. Such an individual demand curve is downward sloping for two reasons. First, as the price of the commodity rises, the purchasing power of each consumer's money

aggregate demand (*AD*) curve A curve showing combinations of real GDP and the price level that make desired aggregate expenditure equal to actual national income.

Practise with Study Guide Chapter 23, Exercise 1.

income will fall, and this fall in real income will lead to fewer units of the good being purchased. Second, as the price of the commodity rises, consumers buy less of that commodity and more of the now relatively cheaper substitutes.

The first reason has no application to the *AD* curve, which relates the total demand for all output to the *price level* rather than to any particular (relative) price. All prices and total output are changing as we move along the *AD* curve. Because the value of output determines income, consumers' money incomes will also be changing along this curve.

The second reason does apply to the aggregate demand curve, but only in a limited way. A rise in the price level entails a rise in *all* domestic commodity prices. Hence, there is no incentive to substitute among domestic commodities whose prices do not change relative to each other. However, it does give rise, as we saw earlier in this chapter, to some substitution between domestic and foreign products. Domestic goods rise in price relative to imported goods, and the switch in expenditure will reduce desired aggregate expenditure on domestic output and hence will reduce equilibrium national income.

So, what is the central reason that the *AD* curve is downward sloping? As we saw earlier, the key relationship is that between the price level and private-sector wealth. An increase in the price level reduces the real value of the private sector's holdings of money and therefore reduces wealth. As wealth falls, desired aggregate expenditure also falls. The *AE* function shifts downward and equilibrium national income declines. A higher price level is therefore associated with a lower value of real GDP.

(In later chapters we will see another, more important reason for a negatively sloped *AD* curve that involves interest rates and investment, but we will have to wait a few chapters before we see this in detail.)

Shifts in the *AD* Curve

What can cause the *AD* curve to shift? For a given price level, any change in an *autonomous* component of aggregate expenditure will cause the *AD* curve to shift. The change in autonomous expenditure could be the result of a change in government policy, such as the level of government purchases or taxation (or, as we will see later, a policy-induced change in interest rates). Or the change in autonomous expenditure could be caused by

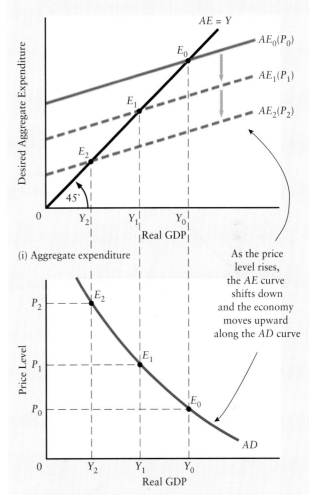

FIGURE 23-2 Derivation of the *AD* Curve

(i) Aggregate expenditure

(ii) Aggregate demand

As the price level rises, the *AE* curve shifts down and the economy moves upward along the *AD* curve

Equilibrium GDP is determined by the *AE* curve for each given price level; the level of equilibrium GDP and its associated price level are then plotted to yield a point on the *AD* curve. When the price level is P_0, the *AE* curve is AE_0, and hence equilibrium GDP is Y_0, as shown in part (i). Plotting Y_0 against P_0 yields the point E_0 on the *AD* curve in part (ii).

An increase in the price level to P_1 causes the *AE* curve to shift downward to AE_1 and causes equilibrium GDP to fall to Y_1. Plotting this new level of GDP against the higher price level yields a second point, E_1, on the *AD* curve. A further increase in the price level to P_2 causes the *AE* curve to shift downward to AE_2, and thus causes equilibrium GDP to fall to Y_2. Plotting P_2 and Y_2 yields a third point, E_2, on the *AD* curve.

A change in the price level causes a shift in the *AE* curve but a movement along the *AD* curve.

aggregate demand shock Any event that causes a shift in the aggregate demand curve.

something beyond the government's control, such as a change in households' consumption expenditure, firms' investment behaviour, or a change in foreigners' demand for Canadian exports.

Figure 23-3 shows a shift in the AD curve. Because the AD curve plots equilibrium GDP as a function of the price level, anything that alters equilibrium GDP *at a given price level* must shift the AD curve. In other words, any change—other than a change in the price level—that causes the AE curve to shift will also cause the AD curve to shift. Such a shift is called an **aggregate demand shock**.

For example, in the late 1990s, the U.S. economy was growing quickly. The U.S. economic boom led to an increase in America's demand for Canadian products, which caused an upward shift in Canada's net export function. This event, taken by itself, would shift Canada's AE function upward and thus would shift Canada's AD curve to the right.

For a given price level, an increase in autonomous aggregate expenditure shifts the AE curve upward and the AD curve to the right. A fall in autonomous aggregate expenditure shifts the AE curve downward and the AD curve to the left.

Remember the following important point. In order to shift the AD curve, the change in autonomous expenditure must be caused by something other than a change in the domestic price level. As we saw earlier in this chapter, a change in aggregate expenditure caused by a change in the domestic price level leads to a movement along (not a shift of) the AD curve.

The Simple Multiplier and the *AD* Curve

We saw in Chapters 21 and 22 that the simple multiplier measures the magnitude of the change in equilibrium national income in response to a change in autonomous expenditure *when the price level is held constant*. It follows that this multiplier gives the magnitude of the *horizontal shift* in the AD curve in response to a change in autonomous expenditure, as illustrated in Figure 23-3.

The simple multiplier measures the horizontal shift in the AD curve in response to a change in autonomous expenditure.

If the price level remains constant and firms are willing to supply everything that is demanded at that price level, the simple multiplier will also show the change in equilibrium income that will occur in response to a change in autonomous expenditure. This mention of firms' willingness to supply output brings us to a discussion of the *supply side* of the economy.

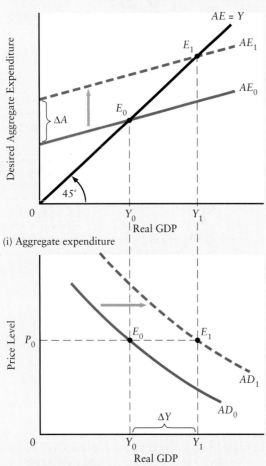

FIGURE 23-3   The Simple Multiplier and Shifts in the *AD* Curve

(i) Aggregate expenditure

(ii) Aggregate demand

A change in autonomous expenditure changes equilibrium GDP for any given price level. The simple multiplier measures the resulting horizontal shift in the *AD* curve. The original AE curve is AE_0 in part (i). Equilibrium is at E_0, with GDP of Y_0 at price level P_0. This yields point E_0 on the curve AD_0 in part (ii).

The AE curve in part (i) then shifts upward from AE_0 to AE_1, due to an increase in autonomous expenditure of ΔA. Equilibrium GDP now rises to Y_1, with the price level still constant at P_0. Thus, the AD curve in part (ii) shifts to the right to point E_1, indicating the higher equilibrium GDP of Y_1 associated with the same price level P_0. The magnitude of the shift, ΔY, is equal to the simple multiplier times ΔA.

23.2 **The Supply Side of the Economy**

So far, we have explained how the equilibrium level of GDP is determined *when the price level is taken as given* and how that equilibrium changes as the price level is changed exogenously. We are now ready to take the important next step: adding an *explanation* for the behaviour of the price level. To do this, we need to take account of the supply decisions of firms.

The Aggregate Supply Curve

Aggregate supply refers to the total output of goods and services that firms would like to produce. The **aggregate supply *(AS)* curve** relates the price level to the quantity of output that firms would like to produce and sell *on the assumption that technology and the prices of all factors of production remain constant.* What macroeconomists mean by the *short run* is the time period over which technology and the prices of all factors of production are constant. In the next few chapters, we will see how the economy behaves over longer periods of time when technology changes and when factor prices have had time to adjust to excess demands or supplies in factor markets. For now, however, remember that:

> The aggregate supply *(AS)* curve is drawn with the assumption that technology and factor prices are held constant.

aggregate supply (*AS*) curve   A curve showing the relation between the price level and the quantity of aggregate output supplied on the assumption that technology and all factor prices are held constant.

The Slope of the *AS* Curve

To study the slope of the *AS* curve, we need to see how costs are related to output and then how prices are related to output.

Costs and Output.   Suppose firms wish to increase their output above current levels. What will this do to their costs per unit of output—usually called their **unit costs?** The aggregate supply curve is drawn on the assumption that technology and the prices of all factors of production remain constant. This does not, however, mean that unit costs will be constant. As output increases, less efficient standby plants may have to be used, and less efficient workers may have to be hired, while existing workers may have to be paid overtime rates for additional work. For these and other similar reasons, unit costs will tend to rise as output rises, even when technology and input prices are constant. (Readers who have studied microeconomics will recognize the *law of diminishing returns* as one reason why costs rise in the short run as firms squeeze more output out of a fixed quantity of capital equipment.)

unit cost   Cost per unit of output, equal to total cost divided by total output.

Prices and Output.   To consider the relationship between price and output, we need to consider firms that sell in two distinct types of markets: those in which firms are *price takers* and those in which firms are *price setters.*

Some industries, especially those that produce raw materials, contain many individual firms. In these cases, each firm is too small to influence the market price, which is set by the overall forces of demand and supply. Each firm must accept whatever price is set by the market. Such firms are said to be *price takers.* When the market price changes, these firms will react by altering their level of production.

Because their unit costs rise with output, price-taking firms will produce more only if price increases and will produce less if price falls.

FIGURE 23-4   The Aggregate Supply Curve

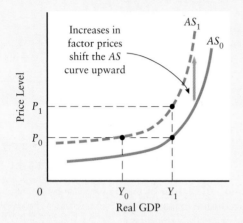

The *AS* curve is positively sloped, indicating that firms will provide more aggregate output only at a higher price level. The *AS* curve is drawn for a given level of technology and factor prices. Any change in technology or factor prices will shift the *AS* curve.

A shift up and to the left reflects a decrease in supply; a shift down and to the right reflects an increase in supply. Starting from (P_0, Y_1) on AS_0, suppose there is an increase in input prices. At price level P_0, only Y_0 would be produced. Alternatively, to get output Y_1 would require a rise to price level P_1. The new supply curve is AS_1, which may be viewed as being above and to the left of AS_0. An increase in supply, caused by a decrease in input prices or an improvement in technology, would shift the *AS* curve downward and to the right, from AS_1 to AS_0.

Many other industries, including most of those that produce manufactured products, contain few enough firms that each can influence the market price of its product. Most such firms sell products that differ from one another, although all are similar enough to be thought of as a single product produced by one industry. For example, no two kinds of automobiles are the same, but all automobiles are sufficiently alike that we have no trouble talking about the automobile industry and its product, automobiles. In such cases, each firm must quote a price at which it is prepared to sell each of its products; that is, the firm is a *price setter*. If the demand for the output of price-setting firms increases sufficiently to take their outputs into the range in which their unit costs rise, these firms will not increase their outputs unless they can pass at least some of these extra costs on through higher prices. When demand falls, they will reduce output, and competition among them will tend to cause a reduction in prices whenever their unit costs fall.

Price-setting firms will increase their prices when they expand output into the range in which unit costs are rising.

This is the basic behaviour of firms in response to the changes in demand and prices when technology and factor prices are constant, and it explains the slope of the *AS* curve, such as the one shown in Figure 23-4.

The actions of both price-taking and price-setting firms cause the price level and the supply of output to be positively related—the aggregate supply (*AS*) curve is upward sloping.

The Increasing Slope of the *AS* Curve

In Figure 23-4 we see that the *AS* curve not only slopes up but also gets steeper as real GDP increases. That is, at low levels of GDP the *AS* curve is relatively flat, but as GDP rises the *AS* curve gets progressively steeper. What explains this shape?

When output is low (below potential output), firms typically have excess capacity—some plant and equipment are idle. When firms have excess capacity, only a small increase in the price of their output may be needed to induce them to expand production. Once output is pushed above normal capacity, however, unit costs tend to rise quite rapidly. Many higher-cost production methods may have to be adopted—such as standby capacity, overtime, and extra shifts. These higher-cost methods will not be used unless the selling price of the output has risen enough to cover them. The more output is expanded beyond normal capacity, the more that unit costs rise and hence the larger is the rise in price that is necessary to induce firms to increase output. This increasing slope of the *AS* curve is sometimes called the *first asymmetry* in the behaviour of aggregate supply. (The second, *sticky wages*, will be discussed in the next chapter.)

As we will see later in this chapter, the shape of the *AS* curve is crucial for determining how the effect of an aggregate demand shock is divided between a change in the price level and a change in real GDP.

Shifts in the Aggregate Supply Curve

Shifts in the *AS* curve, which are shown in Figure 23-4, are called **aggregate supply shocks.** Two sources of aggregate supply shocks are of particular importance: changes in the prices of inputs and changes in productivity.

aggregate supply shock   Any event that causes a shift in the aggregate supply (*AS*) curve.

Changes in Input Prices

Factor prices are held constant along the *AS* curve, and when they change, the curve shifts. If factor prices rise, firms will find the profitability of their current production reduced. For any given level of output to be produced, an increase in the price level will be required. If prices do not rise, firms will react by decreasing production. For the economy as a whole, there will be less output supplied at each price level than before the increase in factor prices. Or, to put it another way, there will be a higher price level for each level of output than before the increase in factor prices. Thus, if factor prices rise, the *AS* curve shifts upward (or to the left). This is a decrease in aggregate supply.

Changes in the prices of raw materials—such as the lumber shown here—lead to changes in firms' production costs. Such changes cause shifts in the AS curve.

Similarly, a fall in factor prices causes the *AS* curve to shift downward (or to the right). There will be more output supplied at each price level. Or, to put it differently, the same amount of output will be supplied at a lower price level. This is an increase in aggregate supply. A dramatic example of such a reduction in factor prices occurred in 1997 and 1998 when the world prices of raw materials fell by an average of 30 percent. In the many countries that use raw materials as inputs in manufacturing, the *AS* curves shifted to the right.

Changes in Productivity

If labour productivity rises—that is, each worker can produce more with a given amount of effort—the unit costs of production will fall. Lower costs typically lead to lower prices, as competing firms cut prices in attempts to raise their market shares. That the same output is sold at a lower price causes a shift in the *AS* curve downward and to the right. This shift is an increase in aggregate supply, as illustrated in Figure 23-4.

A change in either factor prices or productivity will shift the *AS* curve because any given output will be supplied at a different price level than previously. An increase in factor prices or a decrease in productivity shifts the *AS* curve to the left; an increase in productivity or a decrease in factor prices shifts the *AS* curve to the right.

23.3 **Macroeconomic Equilibrium**

Practise with Study Guide Chapter 23, Exercise 2.

We have now reached our objective: We are ready to see how both real GDP and the price level are simultaneously determined by the interaction of aggregate demand and aggregate supply. Since our analysis is of *short-run* macroeconomic equilibrium, remember that factor prices and technology are assumed to be constant.

The equilibrium values of real GDP and the price level occur at the intersection of the *AD* and *AS* curves, as shown by the pair Y_0 and P_0 that arises at point E_0 in Figure 23-5. The combination of real GDP and price level that is on both the *AD* and *AS* curves is called a *macroeconomic equilibrium*.

FIGURE 23-5   Short-Run Macroeconomic Equilibrium

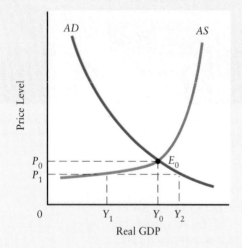

Macroeconomic equilibrium occurs at the intersection of the *AD* and *AS* curves and determines the equilibrium values for real GDP and the price level. Given the *AD* and *AS* curves in the figure, macroeconomic equilibrium occurs at E_0.

If the price level were equal to P_1, the desired output of firms would be Y_1. However, at P_1, the level of output that is consistent with expenditure decisions would be Y_2. Hence, when the price level is less than P_0, the desired output of firms will be less than the level of real GDP that is consistent with expenditure decisions. For any price level above P_0, the desired output of firms exceeds the level of output that is consistent with expenditure decisions.

The only price level where the supply decisions of firms are consistent with desired expenditure is P_0. At P_0, firms wish to produce Y_0. When they do so, they generate a real GDP of Y_0; when real GDP is Y_0, decision makers wish to spend exactly Y_0, thereby purchasing the nation's output. Hence, all decisions are consistent with each other.

To see why the point (Y_0, P_0) is the only macroeconomic equilibrium, first consider what Figure 23-5 shows would happen if the price level were below P_0. At this lower price level, the desired output of firms, as given by the *AS* curve, is less than desired aggregate expenditure—there is an excess demand for goods. Conversely, at a price level above P_0, the desired output by firms exceeds desired aggregate expenditure—there is an excess supply of goods.

Only at the combination of real GDP and price level given by the intersection of the *AS* and *AD* curves are demand behaviour and supply behaviour consistent.

Macroeconomic equilibrium thus requires that two conditions be satisfied. The first is familiar to us because it comes from Chapters 21 and 22. At the prevailing price level, desired aggregate expenditure must be equal to actual GDP—that is, households are just willing to buy all that is produced. The *AD* curve is constructed in such a way that this condition holds everywhere along it. The second requirement for equilibrium is introduced by consideration of aggregate supply. At the prevailing price level, firms must wish to produce the prevailing level of GDP, no more and no less. This condition is fulfilled everywhere along the *AS* curve. Only where the two curves intersect are both conditions fulfilled simultaneously.

Changes in the Macroeconomic Equilibrium

The aggregate demand and aggregate supply curves can now be used to understand how various shocks to the economy change both real GDP and the price level in the short run.

As indicated earlier, a shift in the *AD* curve is called an aggregate demand shock. A rightward shift in the *AD* curve is an increase in aggregate demand; it means that at all price levels, expenditure decisions will now be consistent with a higher level of real GDP. This is called a *positive* or *expansionary* shock. Similarly, a leftward shift in the *AD* curve is a decrease in aggregate demand—that is, at all price levels, expenditure decisions will now be consistent with a lower level of real GDP. This is called a *negative* or *contractionary* shock.

Also as indicated earlier, a shift in the *AS* curve is called an aggregate supply shock. A rightward shift in the *AS* curve is an increase in aggregate supply; at any given price level, more real GDP will be supplied. This is a *positive* shock. A leftward shift in the *AS* curve is a decrease in aggregate supply; at any given price level, less real GDP will be supplied. This is a *negative* shock.

Aggregate demand and supply shocks are labelled according to their effect on real GDP. Positive shocks increase equilibrium GDP; negative shocks reduce equilibrium GDP.

Let's now examine aggregate demand and supply shocks in detail.

Aggregate Demand Shocks

Figure 23-6 shows the effects of an increase in aggregate demand. This increase could have occurred because of, say, increased investment or government purchases, an increase in foreigners' demand for Canadian goods, or an increase in household consumption resulting from a reduction in personal income taxes. Whatever the cause, the increase in aggregate demand means that more domestic output is demanded at any given price level. As is shown in the figure, the increase in aggregate demand causes both the price level and real GDP to rise. Conversely, a decrease in demand causes both the price level and real GDP to fall.

Aggregate demand shocks cause the price level and real GDP to change in the same direction; both rise with an increase in aggregate demand, and both fall with a decrease in aggregate demand.

The Multiplier When the Price Level Varies

We saw earlier in this chapter that the simple multiplier gives the extent of the horizontal shift in the *AD* curve in response to a change in autonomous expenditure. If the price level remains constant and firms are willing to supply all that is demanded at the existing price level (as would be the case with a horizontal *AS* curve), the simple multiplier gives the increase in equilibrium national income.

But what happens in the more usual case in which the *AS* curve slopes upward? As can be seen in Figure 23-6, when the *AS* curve is positively sloped, the change in real GDP caused by a change in autonomous expenditure is no longer equal to the size of the horizontal shift in the *AD* curve. Part of the expansionary impact of an increase in demand is dissipated by a rise in the price level, and only part is transmitted to a rise in real GDP. Of course, an increase in output does occur; thus,

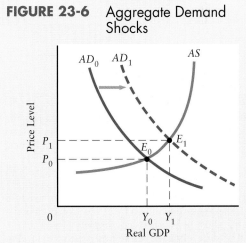

FIGURE 23-6   Aggregate Demand Shocks

Shifts in aggregate demand cause the price level and real GDP to move in the same direction. An increase in aggregate demand shifts the *AD* curve to the right, from AD_0 to AD_1. Macroeconomic equilibrium moves from E_0 to E_1. The price level rises from P_0 to P_1, and real GDP rises from Y_0 to Y_1, reflecting a movement along the *AS* curve.

FIGURE 23-7   The Multiplier When the Price Level Varies

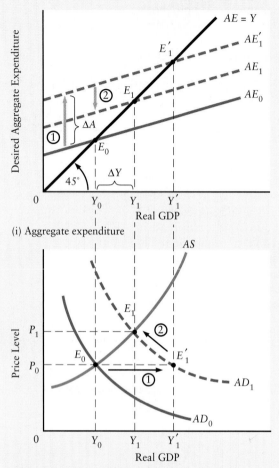

(i) Aggregate expenditure

(ii) Aggregate demand and supply

An increase in autonomous expenditure causes the *AE* curve to shift upward, but the rise in the price level causes it to shift part of the way down again. Hence, the multiplier is smaller than when the price level is constant. Originally, equilibrium is at point E_0 in both part (i) and part (ii). Desired aggregate expenditure then shifts by ΔA to AE_1', shifting the *AD* curve to AD_1. These shifts are shown by arrow ① in both parts. But the adjustment is not yet complete.

The shift in the *AD* curve raises the price level to P_1 because the *AS* curve is positively sloped. The rise in the price level shifts the *AE* curve down to AE_1, as shown by arrow ② in part (i). This is shown as a *movement along* the new *AD* curve, as indicated by arrow ② in part (ii). The new equilibrium is thus at E_1. The amount Y_0Y_1 is ΔY, the actual increase in real GDP. The multiplier, adjusted for the effect of the price increase, is the ratio $\Delta Y/\Delta A$ in part (i).

a multiplier may still be calculated, but its value is not the same as that of the *simple* multiplier.

When the *AS* curve is upward sloping, an aggregate demand shock leads to a change in the price level. As a result, the multiplier is smaller than the simple multiplier.

Why is the multiplier smaller when the *AS* curve is positively sloped? The answer lies in the behaviour that is summarized by the *AE* curve. To understand this, it is useful to think of the final change in real GDP as occurring in two stages, as shown in Figure 23-7.

First, with prices remaining constant, an increase in autonomous expenditure shifts the *AE* curve upward (from AE_0 to AE_1'). This increase in autonomous expenditure is shown in part (ii) by a shift to the right of the *AD* curve. The movement marked ① is the end of the first stage, but is not the end of the whole story.

In the second stage we must take account of the rise in the price level that occurs because of the positive slope of the *AS* curve. As we saw earlier in this chapter, a rise in the price level, via its effect on net exports and on wealth, leads to a downward shift in the *AE* curve (from AE_1' to AE_1). This second shift of the *AE* curve partly counteracts the initial rise in real GDP and so reduces the size of the multiplier. The second stage shows up as a downward shift of the *AE* curve in part (i) of Figure 23-7 and a movement upward and to the left along the new *AD* curve, as shown by arrow ②.

The Importance of the Shape of the AS Curve

We have now seen that the shape of the *AS* curve has important implications for how the effects of an aggregate demand shock are divided between changes in real GDP and changes in the price level. Figure 23-8 highlights the price level and GDP effects of aggregate demand shocks by considering *AD* shocks in the presence of an *AS* curve that exhibits three distinct ranges.

Over the *flat* range, any change in aggregate demand leads to no change in prices and, as seen earlier, a response of output equal to that predicted by the simple multiplier.

Over the *intermediate* range, along which the *AS* curve is positively sloped, a shift in the *AD* curve gives rise to appreciable changes in both real GDP and the price level. Because of the increase in the price level, the multiplier in this case is positive, but smaller than the simple multiplier.

Over the *steep* range, very little more can be produced, no matter how large the increase in demand. This range deals with an economy near its capacity constraints. Any change in aggregate demand leads to a sharp change in the price level and to little or no change in real GDP. The multiplier in this case is nearly zero.

The effect of any given shift in aggregate demand will be divided between a change in real output and a change in the price level, depending on the conditions of aggregate supply. The steeper the *AS* curve, the greater the price effect and the smaller the output effect.

Extensions in Theory 23-1 deals with the special case of a horizontal *AS* curve—sometimes called a *Keynesian AS* curve. In that case, the aggregate supply curve determines the price level, and the *AD* curve determines real GDP.

Reconciliation with Previous Analysis

One of the central points of this chapter is that aggregate demand shocks typically lead to changes in *both* the price level and the level of real GDP. Furthermore, with a steep enough *AS* curve, such aggregate demand shocks will result in no change in real GDP, but only a change in the price level. How do we reconcile this possibility with the analysis of Chapters 21 and 22, where shifts in *AE always* change real GDP? The answer is that each *AE* curve is drawn on the assumption that there is a constant price level. An upward shift in the *AE* curve shifts the *AD* curve to the right. However, a steep *AS* curve means that the price level rises significantly, and this rise shifts the *AE* curve back down, offsetting some of its initial rise.

We can see this interaction most easily if we study the extreme case, shown in Figure 23-9, in which the *AS* curve is vertical. An increase in autonomous expenditure shifts the *AE* curve upward, thus raising the amount demanded. However, a vertical *AS* curve means that output cannot be expanded to satisfy the increased demand. Instead, the extra demand merely forces prices up, and as prices rise, the *AE* curve shifts down again. The rise in prices continues until the *AE* curve is back to where it started. Thus, the rise in prices offsets the expansionary effect of the original shift and consequently leaves both real aggregate expenditure and equilibrium real GDP unchanged.

A vertical *AS* curve, however, is quite unrealistic. Most economists agree that the *AS* curve is shaped something like the one shown in Figure 23-8—that is, relatively flat for low levels of GDP and becoming steeper as GDP rises.

We now complete our discussion of changes in the short-run macroeconomic equilibrium by discussing supply shocks.

Practise with Study Guide Chapter 23, Extension Exercise E1.

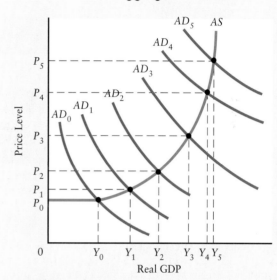

FIGURE 23-8 The Effects of Increases in Aggregate Demand

The effect of increases in aggregate demand is divided between increases in real GDP and increases in prices, depending on the slope of the *AS* curve. Because of the increasing slope of the *AS* curve, increases in aggregate demand up to AD_0 have virtually no impact on the price level. Successive further increases bring larger price increases and relatively smaller output increases. By the time aggregate demand is at AD_4 or AD_5, virtually all of the effect is on the price level.

Practise with Study Guide Chapter 23, Exercise 6.

EXTENSIONS IN THEORY 23-1

The Keynesian *AS* Curve

In this box, we consider an extreme version of the *AS* curve that is horizontal over some range of real GDP. It is called the *Keynesian aggregate supply curve*, after John Maynard Keynes (1883–1946), who in his famous book *The General Theory of Employment, Interest and Money* (1936) pioneered the study of the behaviour of economies under conditions of high unemployment. Despite its name, this curve does not describe Keynes' own views on the behaviour of the price level. It is instead the version of aggregate supply used by many of Keynes' followers in their early attempts to express Keynes' work in a formal model—something Keynes himself did not do.

The behaviour that gives rise to the Keynesian *AS* curve can be described as follows. When real GDP is below potential GDP, individual firms are operating with excess capacity. They then respond to changes in demand by altering output while keeping prices constant. In other words, they will supply whatever they can sell at their existing prices as long as they are producing below their normal capacity.*

Under these circumstances, the economy has a horizontal *AS* curve, indicating that any output up to potential output will be supplied at the going price level. The amount that is actually produced is then de-

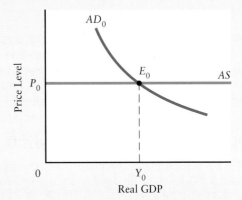

termined by the position of the *AD* curve, as shown in the figure. Thus, real GDP is said to be *demand determined*. If demand rises enough so that firms are trying to squeeze more than normal output out of their plants, their costs will rise, and so will their prices. Hence, the horizontal Keynesian *AS* curve applies only to levels of GDP below potential GDP.

This special case of a horizontal *AS* curve corresponds to the macro model that we developed in Chapters 21 and 22. Recall that in that simple model we assumed a constant price level. In other words, if the *AS* curve is horizontal, our macro model in this chapter is *exactly the same* as the simple version in Chapters 21 and 22. In this case, a change in autonomous expenditure, ΔA, will lead to increases in equilibrium GDP equal to ΔA times the simple multiplier. (In Figure 23-3 this is exactly the distance of the horizontal shift in the *AD* curve in response to any given ΔA.)

---

*There is considerable evidence that many firms do behave like this in the short run. One possible explanation for this is that changing prices frequently is too costly, so firms set the best possible (profit-maximizing) prices when output is at normal capacity and then do not change prices in the face of short-term fluctuations in demand.

Aggregate Supply Shocks

A negative aggregate supply shock, shown by a shift to the left in the *AS* curve, means that less real output will be supplied at any given price level. A positive aggregate supply shock, shown by a shift to the right in the *AS* curve, means that more real output will be supplied at any given price level.

Figure 23-10 illustrates the effects on the price level and real GDP of a negative aggregate supply shock. This could have occurred because of, say, an increase in the world price of important inputs, such as oil, copper or iron ore. As can be seen from the figure, following the decrease in aggregate supply, the price level rises and real GDP falls. This combination of events is called *stagflation*, a term derived by combining *stagnation* (sometimes used to mean less than full employment) and *inflation*. Conversely, an increase in aggregate supply leads to an increase in real GDP and a decrease in the price level.

Aggregate supply shocks cause the price level and real GDP to change in opposite directions. With an increase in supply, the price level falls and GDP rises; with a decrease in supply, the price level rises and GDP falls.

Oil-price increases have provided two major examples of negative aggregate supply shocks in recent decades. The economy is especially responsive to changes in the price for oil because, in addition to being used to produce energy, oil is an input into plastics and many other materials that are widely used in manufacturing. Massive increases in oil prices occurred during 1973–1974 and 1979–1980, caused by the successful efforts of the OPEC countries to form a cartel and restrict the output of oil. These increases in the price of oil caused leftward shifts in the *AS* curve in most countries. Real GDP fell while the price level rose—stagflation. (In subsequent years the price of oil fell, shifting the *AS* curve back to the right, but the declines were more gradual and thus less dramatic than the initial increases.)

Commodity prices have provided an important recent example of a positive aggregate supply shock. The Southeast Asian countries of Indonesia, Malaysia, Thailand, and South Korea are all significant users of raw materials. When their economies plunged into a major recession in 1997 and 1998, the world demand for raw materials fell, and the prices of such goods fell as a result. From the summer of 1997 to the end of 1998, the average price of raw materials fell by approximately 30 percent.

Though these were clearly bad economic times for much of Southeast Asia, the reduction in raw materials prices was a *positive* aggregate supply shock for countries that used raw materials as inputs for production. In countries like Canada, the United States, and most of Western Europe, the *AS* curves shifted to the right. The effect was to increase real GDP and reduce the price level.[2]

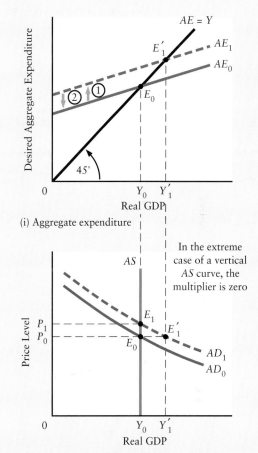

FIGURE 23-9   Demand Shocks When the *AS* Curve Is Vertical

(i) Aggregate expenditure

(ii) Aggregate demand and supply

In the extreme case where the *AS* curve is vertical, the effect of an increase in autonomous expenditure is solely to increase price level. An increase in autonomous expenditure shifts the *AE* curve upward from AE_0 to AE_1, as shown by arrow ① in part (i). Given the initial price level P_0, equilibrium would shift from E_0 to E_1' and real GDP would rise from Y_0 to Y_1'. However, the price level does not remain constant. This is shown by the *AS* curve in part (ii). Instead, the price level rises to P_1. This causes the *AE* curve to shift back down all the way to AE_0, as shown by arrow ② in part (i), and equilibrium GDP stays at Y_0. In part (ii), the new equilibrium is at E_1 with GDP at Y_0 and the price level at P_1. The multiplier is zero.

---

[2] Actually, it is more correct to say that the shock reduced the price level *compared to what it otherwise would have been*. Due to ongoing inflation, the causes of which we will discuss in Chapters 29 and 30, the price level in Canada rarely falls. But we have been assuming throughout this chapter that there is no ongoing inflation, and in that setting a positive *AS* shock like the one described in the text would indeed cause the price level to fall.

For information on OPEC, see its website: www.opec.org

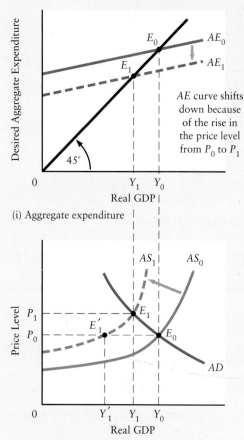

FIGURE 23-10 A Negative Aggregate Supply Shock

(i) Aggregate expenditure

(ii) Aggregate demand and supply

Aggregate supply shocks cause the price level and real GDP to move in opposite directions. The original equilibrium is at E_0, with GDP of Y_0 appearing in both parts of the figure. The price level is P_0 in part (ii), and at that price level, the desired aggregate expenditure curve is AE_0 in part (i).

A negative aggregate supply shock now shifts the AS curve in part (ii) to AS_1. At the original price level of P_0, firms are now only willing to supply Y_1'. The fall in supply causes a rise in the price level. The new equilibrium is reached at E_1, where the AD curve intersects AS_1. At the new and higher equilibrium price level of P_1, the AE curve has fallen to AE_1, as shown in part (i).

For interesting information on the Asian crisis, see Nouriel Roubini's website at www.stern.nyu.edu/~nroubini or Paul Krugman's website at www.princeton.edu/~pkrugman.

A Word of Warning

We have discussed the effects of aggregate demand and aggregate supply shocks on the economy's price level and real GDP. Students are sometimes puzzled, however, because some events would appear to be *both* demand and supply shocks. How do we analyze such complicated shocks? For example, when OPEC restricted the supply of oil and thus drove up the world price of oil, this was clearly a *negative supply shock*. After all, oil is a very important input to production for so many firms and so many industries. But for Canada, which produces and exports oil, doesn't the increase in the world price of oil also imply an increase in export revenue? And doesn't this imply a *positive demand shock?*

The answer to both questions is yes. The OPEC oil shock was indeed a negative aggregate supply shock to any country that uses oil as an input (which means most countries). But for those countries that also produce and export oil—like Canada—the OPEC oil shock was also a positive aggregate demand shock. The rise in the price of oil generated an increase in income to Canadian oil producers—it is no surprise that Alberta's economy was booming throughout the 1970s.

For such countries, a complete analysis of the OPEC oil shocks involves both a leftward shift of the AS curve and a rightward shift of the AD curve. In this case, the equilibrium price level clearly rises. The overall effect on real GDP, however, then depends on the relative importance of the supply and demand effects. For example, the United States and Canada both use oil as an important input to production, and so the AS shifts were similar in the two countries. As a share of its economy, however, the United States produces much less oil than does Canada, and so the rightward AD shift in Canada was larger than in the United States. The overall effect was that the United States suffered a larger reduction in real GDP than did Canada as a result of the OPEC oil shock.

The important message here is a simple one:

Many economic events—especially changes in the world prices of raw materials—cause both aggregate demand and aggregate supply shocks. The overall effect on the economy depends on the relative importance of the two separate effects.

Applying Economic Concepts 23-1 discusses the effect of the 1997–98 Asian economic crisis on the Canadian economy. The Asian crisis represented both a negative demand shock and a positive supply shock to Canada.

APPLYING ECONOMIC CONCEPTS 23-1

The Asian Crisis and the Canadian Economy

In the summer of 1997, the currencies of several countries in Southeast Asia plummeted (relative to the U.S. and Canadian dollars) as their central banks were no longer able to "peg" their exchange rates. We will discuss how such pegged exchange rates operate in Chapter 35. For now, the important point is that, for various reasons, banks, firms, and households in these countries had accumulated a large stock of debt denominated in foreign currencies, especially U.S. dollars. The sudden depreciations of their currencies—in some cases by 70 percent in just a few days—led to dramatic increases in the amount of domestic income required to pay the interest on this debt. Manufacturing firms and financial institutions went bankrupt, workers were laid off, and economic output fell sharply. By late in 1997, the economies of Malaysia, Indonesia, Thailand, South Korea, and the Philippines were suffering major recessions.

How did this Asian crisis affect Canada? It had offsetting positive and negative effects on the level of economic activity in Canada. The events in Asia generated both a *negative* aggregate demand shock and a *positive* aggregate supply shock for Canada.

To understand the demand side of the story, we must recognize that these Asian economies are important users of raw materials. When their level of economic activity declined sharply, so, too, did their demand for raw materials. Indeed, average raw materials prices fell by roughly 30 percent between 1997 and 1998. But raw materials are an important export for Canada. The decline in the world's demand for raw materials implied a reduction in demand for Canadian goods. As a result, Canadian producers of copper, pork, newsprint, lumber, iron ore, and many other raw materials suffered significantly. In terms of the simple diagram we have been using in this chapter, the demand part of the Asian crisis is represented as a leftward shift of the Canadian AD curve.

But the story does not end there. Also important to Canada is the fact that many Canadian manufacturing firms use those same raw materials as inputs for their production of car parts, pre-fabricated houses and trail-

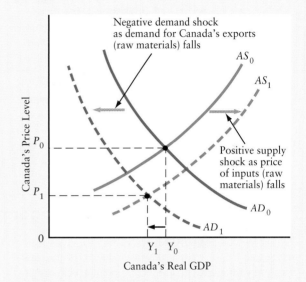

ers, electrical equipment, and so on. A dramatic reduction in the prices of raw materials implies a reduction in costs for manufacturing firms. This is a positive aggregate supply shock, and is illustrated by a rightward shift of the Canadian AS curve.

What is the overall effect on the Canadian economy? The effect of each shock taken separately is to reduce the price level—so the overall effect is unambiguously a lower price level.* In contrast, the effect on real GDP would appear to be ambiguous since the AD shock reduces GDP whereas the AS shock increases it. But this is not quite right. Since Canada is a net exporter of raw materials (it exports more raw materials than it imports), it must experience a decrease in national income when these prices fall. In other words, the net effect of the negative demand shock and the positive supply shock is to reduce Canadian GDP. The figure is therefore drawn with the AD shock being larger than the AS shock and so the new equilibrium level of GDP, Y_1, is lower than in the initial equilibrium, Y_0.

*Recall footnote 2 on page 587. We are assuming in this analysis that there is no ongoing inflation, so a positive AS shock or a negative AD shock reduces the price level. A more accurate description for the Canadian economy in 1998, with some ongoing inflation, is that the price level fell below what it otherwise would have been. This appears as a reduction in the rate of inflation.

S U M M A R Y

23.1 The Demand Side of the Economy

- The *AE* curve shows desired aggregate expenditure for each level of GDP at a particular price level. Its intersection with the 45° line determines equilibrium GDP for that price level. Equilibrium GDP thus occurs where desired aggregate expenditure equals actual GDP. A change in the price level changes private-sector wealth and thus causes a shift in the *AE* curve: upward when the price level falls, and downward when the price level rises. This leads to a new equilibrium level of real GDP.
- The *AD* curve plots the equilibrium level of GDP that corresponds to each possible price level. A change in equilibrium GDP following a change in the price level is shown by a movement along the *AD* curve.
- A rise in the price level lowers exports and lowers autonomous consumption expenditure (because it decreases wealth). Both of these changes reduce equilibrium GDP and cause the *AD* curve to have a negative slope.
- The *AD* curve shifts horizontally when any element of autonomous expenditure changes, and the simple multiplier measures the magnitude of the shift.

23.2 The Supply Side of the Economy

- The aggregate supply *(AS)* curve, drawn for given technology and factor prices, is positively sloped because unit costs rise with increasing output and because rising product prices make it profitable to increase output.
- An increase in productivity or a decrease in factor prices shifts the *AS* curve to the right. This is an increase in aggregate supply. A decrease in productivity or an increase in factor prices shifts the *AS* curve to the left. This is a decrease in aggregate supply.

23.3 Macroeconomic Equilibrium

- Short-run macroeconomic equilibrium refers to equilibrium values of real GDP and the price level, as determined by the intersection of the *AD* and *AS* curves. Shifts in the *AD* and *AS* curves, called aggregate demand and aggregate supply shocks, change the equilibrium values of real GDP and the price level.
- When the *AS* curve is upward sloping, an aggregate demand shock causes the price level and real GDP to move in the same direction. The division of the effects between a change in real GDP and a change in the price level depends on the shape of the *AS* curve. When the *AS* curve is flat, shifts in the *AD* curve primarily affect real GDP. When the *AS* curve is steep, shifts in the *AD* curve primarily affect the price level.
- In the usual case with an upward sloping *AS* curve, a demand shock leads to a change in the price level. As a result, the multiplier is smaller than the simple multiplier in Chapter 22.
- An aggregate supply shock moves equilibrium GDP along the *AD* curve, causing the price level and real GDP to move in opposite directions. A leftward shift in the *AS* curve causes stagflation—rising prices and falling real GDP. A rightward shift causes an increase in real GDP and a fall in the price level.
- Some events are both aggregate supply and aggregate demand shocks. Changes in the world prices of raw materials, for example, shift the *AS* curve. If the country (like Canada) is also a producer of such raw materials, there will also be a shift in the *AD* curve. The overall effect then depends on the relative sizes of the separate effects.

KEY CONCEPTS

Effects of an exogenous change in the price level
Relationship between the *AE* and *AD* curves

Negative slope of the *AD* curve
Positive slope of the *AS* curve
Macroeconomic equilibrium
Aggregate demand shocks

The multiplier when the price level varies
Aggregate supply shocks

STUDY EXERCISES

1. Fill in the blanks to make the following statements correct.

   a. In the simple macro model of the previous two chapters, the price level was _____. In the macro model of this chapter, the price level is _____.
   b. A change in the price level shifts the *AE* curve because the price level change affects desired _____ and desired _____.
   c A rise in the price level causes a(n) _____ in households' wealth, which leads to a _____ in desired consumption, which causes the *AE* curve to shift _____. A fall in the price level causes a(n) _____ in households' wealth, which leads to a _____ in desired consumption, which causes the *AE* curve to shift _____.
   d. A rise in the domestic price level causes net exports to _____, which causes the *AE* curve to shift _____. A fall in the domestic price level causes net exports to _____, which causes the *AE* curve to shift _____.
   e. Equilibrium GDP is determined by the position of the *AE* function for each given price level. An equilibrium point for a particular price level corresponds to one point on the _____ curve.
   f. A rise in the price level causes a downward shift of the _____ curve and a movement upward along the _____ curve.
   g. An increase in autonomous expenditure, with no change in the price level, causes the *AE* curve to _____ and causes the *AD* curve to _____.

2. Fill in the blanks to make the following statements correct.

   a. The _____ curve relates the price level to the quantity of output that firms would like to produce and sell.
   b. The analysis of the aggregate supply curve in this chapter is short-run, which tells us that _____ and _____ remain constant.

   c. The aggregate supply curve is upward sloping because firms will produce more output only if price _____ to offset higher unit costs.
   d. The aggregate supply curve is relatively flat when GDP is below potential output because firms typically have _____ and are able to expand production without much increase in unit costs.
   e. The aggregate supply curve is relatively steep when GDP is above potential output because firms are operating above _____ and _____ are rising rapidly.
   f. The aggregate supply curve shifts in response to changes in _____ and changes in _____. These are known as supply _____.

3. Fill in the blanks to make the following statements correct.

   a. Short-run macro equilibrium occurs at the intersection of _____ and _____, and determines equilibrium levels of _____ and _____.
   b. A positive *AD* shock will cause the price level to _____ and real GDP to _____. A negative *AD* shock will cause the price level to _____ and real GDP to _____.
   c. A positive *AS* shock will cause the price level to _____ and real GDP to _____. A negative *AS* shock will cause the price level to _____ and real GDP to _____.
   d. In previous chapters, the simple multiplier measured the change in real GDP in response to a change in autonomous expenditure when the price level was constant. When the price level varies, the multiplier is _____ than the simple multiplier.
   e. An increase in autonomous government spending is a _____ *AD* shock, which will initially cause a(n) _____ shift of the *AE* curve and a(n) _____ shift of the *AD* curve. Given an upward-sloping aggregate supply curve, there will be a _____ in the price level, which leads to a partial _____ shift of the *AE* curve.

4. Consider the effects of an exogenous increase in the domestic price level. For each of the assets listed, explain how the change in the price level would affect the wealth of the asset holder. Then explain the effect on *aggregate* (private sector) wealth.

   a. Cash holdings
   b. Deposits in a bank account
   c. A household mortgage
   d. A corporate bond that promises to pay the bond-holder $10 000 on January 1, 2008
   e. A government bond that promises to pay the holder $10 000 on January 1, 2008

5. Consider the following simplified AE function:

$$AE = 350 + 0.8Y + 0.1(M/P)$$

   where AE is desired aggregate expenditure, Y is real GDP, M is the private sector's *nominal wealth*, and P is the price level. Suppose that M is constant and equal to 6000.

   a. Explain why the expression for AE above makes sense. Why do M and P enter the AE function?
   b. Fill in the table below:

P	M/P	AE
1	—	—
2	—	—
3	—	—
4	—	—
5	—	—
6	—	—

   c. Plot each of the AE functions—one for each price level—on the same scale 45° line diagram.
   d. Compute the level of equilibrium national income for each of the values of P.
   e. Plot the pairs of price level and equilibrium national income on a scale diagram with P on the vertical axis and Y on the horizontal axis.

6. Consider the following diagrams showing the AD curves in two economies. Economy A is Autarkland—it does not trade with the rest of the world (*autarky* is a situation in which a country does not trade with other countries). Economy B is Openland—it exports to and imports from the rest of the world.

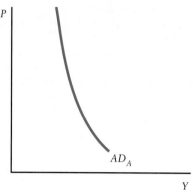

Economy A

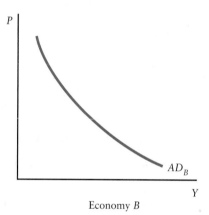

Economy B

   a. Explain why an increase in the domestic price level (for a given exchange rate) reduces net exports in Openland. How would you illustrate this with the AE curve in the 45° line diagram?
   b. Explain why the AD curve is steeper in Autarkland than in Openland.
   c. If there are never any net exports in Autarkland, why isn't the AD curve vertical? Explain what other aspect of the economy generates a downward-sloping AD curve.

7. The economy of Neverland has the following AD and AS schedules. Denote Y_{AD} as the level of real GDP along the AD curve; let Y_{AS} be the level of real GDP along the AS curve. GDP is shown in billions of 1997 dollars.

Price Level	Y_{AD}	Y_{AS}
90	1100	750
100	1000	825
110	900	900
120	800	975
130	700	1050
140	600	1125

a. Plot the *AD* and *AS* curves on a scale diagram.
b. What is the price level and level of real GDP in Neverland's macroeconomic equilibrium?
c. Suppose the level of potential output in Neverland is $950 billion. Is the current equilibrium level of real GDP greater than or less than potential?

8. Each of the following events is either a *cause* or a *consequence* of a shift in the *AD* or *AS* curve in Canada. Identify which it is and, if it is a cause, describe the effect on equilibrium real GDP and the price level.

a. OPEC's actions significantly increased the world price of oil in 1979–80.
b. During 1996–2001, Canadian real GDP was growing at a healthy pace but inflation showed no signs of rising.
c. World commodity prices declined sharply in 1997–98. Many of these commodities are both produced in Canada and used as important inputs for Canadian firms.
d. The end of the Cold War led to large declines in defence spending in many countries (including Canada).
e. Several provinces lowered their personal income tax rates in the late 1990s.
f. The federal government reduced its level of government purchases (*G*) in the late 1990s.

9. The diagrams below show the *AD* and *AS* curves in two different economies.

a. Explain what aspect of firms' behaviour might give rise to the horizontal *AS* curve in Economy A.

b. Explain what aspect of firms' behaviour gives rise to the upward-sloping *AS* curve in Economy B.
c. In which economy is output demand determined? Explain.
d. Consider the effects of an increase in autonomous expenditure. Which economy has the larger multiplier? Explain your reasoning.

10. This is a challenging question and involves algebraically solving the system of two equations given by the *AD* and *AS* curves. The equations for the curves are given by:

AD: $\quad Y_{AD} = 710 - 30P + 5G$

AS: $\quad Y_{AS} = 10 + 5P - 2P_{OIL}$

where Y is real GDP, P is the price level, G is the level of government purchases, and P_{OIL} is the world price of oil.

a. Explain the various terms in the *AD* curve. What is the value of the simple multiplier? (Hint: the simple multiplier is the change in equilibrium real GDP when some autonomous component of expenditure, like *G*, changes by $1.)
b. Explain the various terms in the *AS* curve. Explain why the price of oil enters negatively.
c. Solve for the equilibrium value of real GDP and the price level.
d. Using your solution to part (c), what is the effect of a change in *G* on equilibrium *Y* and *P*?
e. Using your solution to part (c), what is the effect of a change in P_{OIL} on equilibrium *Y* and *P*?

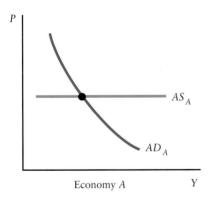

Economy A

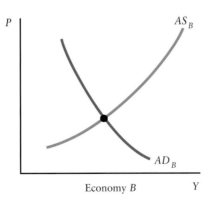

Economy B

DISCUSSION QUESTIONS

1. In 1979 and 1980, the British government greatly reduced income taxes but restored the lost government revenue by raising excise and sales taxes. These actions led to a sharp increase in the price level and a fall in output. Explain these events in terms of shifts in the aggregate demand or aggregate supply curves (or both).

2. This chapter discussed the meaning of aggregate demand and aggregate supply shocks, and several examples were given of each. But some shocks can be both demand-side shocks and supply-side shocks. Consider the prices of many commodities, such as lumber, newsprint, oil, copper, grains, and iron ore. The prices of such commodities are determined in world markets, and are subject to significant fluctuations from year to year. For example, in 1997–98, there was a significant decline in the prices of many such commodities. Explain how such a decline in commodity prices can lead to both a decline in Canadian aggregate demand and an increase in Canadian aggregate supply. How would you determine the net effect on real GDP and the price level?

3. Show the effects on the price level and real GDP of a major union wage settlement that significantly increases wages. Is this a supply shock, a demand shock, or both?

4. Following are the combinations of output and price level given by real GDP and the CPI, respectively, for some recent years. Treat each pair as if it is the intersection of an *AD* and an *AS* curve. Plot these data. Then think about the possible shifts in the *AD* or *AS* curves that could have caused them. Is it possible to know what the underlying shifts are? Why or why not?

Year	CPI (1992 = 100)	GDP (billions of 1997 dollars)
1994	102.0	810.0
1995	104.2	832.1
1996	105.9	845.2
1997	107.6	882.7
1998	108.9	919.0
1999	110.5	967.6
2000	113.5	1013.1
2001	116.4	1026.9
2002	119.0	1062.0

5. Consider a government policy to reduce both personal and corporate income tax rates. Explain the effects of such a policy on the short-run macroeconomic equilibrium. Is this a demand-side or a supply-side policy? Explain.

PART NINE

The Economy in the Long Run

What is the economy's level of potential output, and what happens if actual output is above potential? Why do wages and other factor prices rise when output is above potential, and how does this wage adjustment affect the equilibrium level of GDP? Are the short-run effects of a fiscal expansion the same as the long-run effects? What explains increases in per-capita GDP that take place over many years? Why is technological progress central to rising living standards? These and related questions are addressed in this part of the book.

Chapter 24 recalls the concept of potential output, and explains why wages and other factor prices tend to change when actual GDP differs from potential output. These changes in factor prices lead to changes in firms' costs and thus to shifts of the *AS* curve. The bottom line in this chapter is that, following aggregate demand or aggregate supply shocks, GDP eventually returns to the level of potential output. This implies different short-run and long-run effects of fiscal policies.

Chapter 25 explores the difference between the short run and the long run. A complete understanding of macroeconomics requires thinking differently about changes in GDP over a few months or years (the short run) and changes in GDP over many years or decades (the long run). We will see that short-run changes in GDP are determined by *AD* and *AS* shocks, whereas long-run changes in GDP are determined by changes in potential output.

Chapter 26 examines what we call long-run economic growth—the steady rise of potential output that occurs over many years. We examine several theories that seek to explain such growth, established theories as well as more modern theoretical approaches. The relationship between saving, investment, and growth is highlighted, as is the importance of technological change and productivity improvements.

CHAPTER 24

From the Short Run to the Long Run: The Adjustment of Factor Prices

LEARNING OBJECTIVES

❶ Explain why wages and other factor prices change when there is an output gap.

❷ Explain how induced changes in factor prices affect firms' costs and shift the *AS* curve.

❸ Explain why output gradually returns to potential output following an aggregate demand or supply shock.

❹ Recognize how lags and uncertainty place limitations on the use of fiscal policy.

In the previous three chapters, we developed in stages a model of the *short-run* determination of real GDP and the price level. In this chapter, we discuss how the short-run macroeconomic equilibrium evolves, through an adjustment process where wages and other factor prices change, into a *long-run* equilibrium, in which real GDP is equal to potential output, Y^*. In the next two chapters we will examine how Y^* increases over many years—what we call *long-run economic growth*. Before we proceed, however, we will define carefully our assumptions regarding the short run, the adjustment process, and the long run.

The Short Run in Macroeconomics

The defining characteristics of the *short run* in our macroeconomic model are:

- factor prices are assumed to be constant
- technology and factor supplies are assumed to be constant (and therefore Y^* is constant)

With these assumptions, the short-run macroeconomic equilibrium is determined by the intersection of the *AD* and *AS* curves, both of which are subject to shocks of various kinds. The level of real GDP therefore fluctuates around a *constant* level of potential output, Y^*. This version of our macroeconomic model is convenient to use when analyzing the economy over short periods. Even though factor prices, technology, and factor supplies are rarely constant, even over short periods of time, by making the simplifying assumption that they are constant in our short-run model we can focus on the most important changes over this time span: the fluctuations of real GDP relative to the level of potential output—what economists call *business cycles*.

The Adjustment of Factor Prices

As we will see in detail in this chapter, our theory of the *adjustment process* that takes the economy from the short run to the long run is based on the following assumptions:

- factor prices are assumed to be flexible
- technology and factor supplies are assumed to be constant (and therefore Y^* is constant)

This chapter will explain how the short-run deviations of real GDP from potential output cause wages and other factor prices to adjust, and how this adjustment is central to the economy's evolution from its short-run equilibrium to its long-run equilibrium. Note that, as in the short-run version of the model, the adjustment process is assumed to take place with a constant level of potential output.

Our theory of the macroeconomic adjustment process is useful for examining how the effects of shocks or policies differ in the short and long runs. As we will see, the assumption that potential output is constant leads to the prediction that AD or AS shocks have no long-run effect on real GDP; output eventually returns to Y^*.

In reality, neither technology nor factor supplies are constant over time; the level of potential output is continually changing. Our assumption throughout this chapter of a constant value for Y^* is a simplifying one, allowing us to focus on the *adjustment process* that brings the level of real GDP back to potential output.

The Long Run in Macroeconomics

As we will see in Chapters 25 and 26, the defining characteristics of the *long run* in our macro model are:

- factor prices are assumed to have fully adjusted
- technology and factor supplies are assumed to be changing

A central message of the current chapter is that, after factor prices have fully adjusted, real GDP will return to the level of potential output. The second assumption above implies that the level of potential output is changing (and typically growing). Thus, in the long-run version of our macroeconomic model, our focus is not on the nature of business cycles but rather on the nature of *economic growth*—where technological change and the growth of factor supplies play key roles.

The economy is probably never "in" the long run in the sense that AD or AS shocks would not cause real GDP to deviate from Y^*. But the long-run version of our model is still useful for examining some issues. For example, if we want to understand why our children's standard of living will be significantly greater than our grandparents', we should not focus on short-run issues of AD or AS shocks and stabilization policies; these effects will disappear after a few years. Instead, we will gain more understanding if we abstract from short-run issues and focus on why Y^* increases dramatically over periods of several decades.

Summary

The three time spans that are central to macroeconomic analysis are summarized in Table 24-1. Note for each time span the assumptions made regarding factor prices and the level of potential output, and also the implied causes of output changes. As we proceed through this chapter and the next two, you may find it useful to refer back to this table.

TABLE 24-1   Time Spans in Macroeconomic Analysis

Variables	The Short Run	The Adjustment Process	The Long Run
	Assumptions Regarding:		
Factor prices	Constant	Flexible	Fully adjusted
Technology and factor supplies (and therefore Y^*)	Constant	Constant	Changing
	Implied Causes of Output Changes:		
	AD/AS shocks cause Y to fluctuate around constant Y^*	Following AD or AS shocks, Y returns to Y^*	Changes in Y^* determine changes in Y

You already know from Chapter 23 how the short-run version of our macro model works. And now that you have a sketch of what economists mean by the adjustment process and the long run, we are ready to fill in the details. In this chapter we will see how this adjustment process takes the economy from its short-run equilibrium to its long-run equilibrium. To repeat, we make the following important assumptions for our theory of the macroeconomic adjustment process:

- factor prices are assumed to be flexible
- technology and factor supplies are assumed to be constant (and therefore Y^* is constant)

To understand what economic conditions cause factor prices to adjust, we need to examine the relationship between output gaps, factor markets, and factor prices. This is our starting point.

24.1 Output Gaps and Factor Prices

We begin by reconsidering two key concepts that we first encountered in Chapter 19—potential output and the output gap.

Potential Output and the Output Gap

Recall that *potential output* is the total output that can be produced when all productive resources—land, labour, and capital—are being used at their *normal rates of utilization.* When a nation's actual output diverges from its potential output, the difference is called the output gap.

Although growth in potential output has powerful effects from one decade to the next, its change from one *year* to the next is small enough to be ignored when studying the year-to-year behaviour of real GDP and the price level. In this chapter, therefore, we view variations in the output gap as determined solely by variations in *actual* GDP around a constant level of *potential* GDP. (In Chapter 26 we will examine why potential output changes over periods of several years.)

Figure 24-1 shows real GDP being determined in the short run by the intersection of the *AD* and *AS* curves. Potential output is constant, and it is shown by identical vertical lines in the two parts of the figure. In part (i), the *AD* and *AS* curves intersect to produce an equilibrium real GDP less than potential output. The result, as we saw in Chapter 19, is called a *recessionary output gap* because recessions are often characterized as having GDP below potential output. In part (ii), the *AD* and *AS* curves intersect to produce an equilibrium real GDP above potential output, resulting in what is called an *inflationary output gap*. The way in which an inflationary output gap puts upward pressure on prices will become clear in the ensuing discussion.

Factor Prices and the Output Gap

The output gap provides a convenient measure of the pressure on factor prices to change. When real GDP is above potential output, demand for factors will be high and there will be pressure on factor prices to rise. When real GDP is below potential output, demand for factors will be low and there will be pressure on factor prices to fall. This relationship holds for all factors of production, including labour, land, and capital equipment.

When there is an inflationary gap, actual GDP exceeds potential GDP, and the demand for factor services will be relatively high. When there is a recessionary gap, actual GDP is below potential GDP, and the demand for factor services will be relatively low.

FIGURE 24-1   Output Gaps in the Short Run

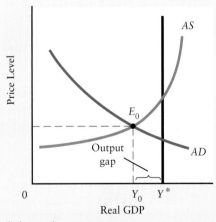 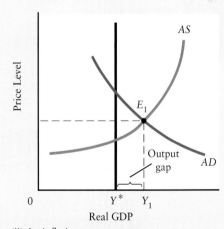

(i) A recessionary output gap   (ii) An inflationary output gap

The output gap is the difference between potential GDP, Y^*, and actual GDP, Y. Potential output is shown by the vertical line at Y^*. A recessionary gap, shown in panel (i), occurs when potential output is greater than real GDP. An inflationary gap, shown in panel (ii), occurs when real GDP is greater than potential output.

Before we examine the effects of output gaps in more detail, it is worth noting that even in the absence of an output gap, the presence of ongoing inflation influences factor prices, especially wages. Wage contracts often allow for changes in the price level that are expected to occur during the life of the contract. For the discussion in this chapter we make the simplifying assumption that the price level is expected to be constant (and therefore inflation is expected to be zero); hence changes in money wages are also expected to be changes in real wages. We will discuss inflation in considerable detail in Chapters 29 and 30.

Output Above Potential

Sometimes the *AD* and *AS* curves intersect where actual output exceeds potential, as illustrated in part (ii) of Figure 24-1. Because firms are producing beyond their normal capacity output, there is an unusually large demand for all factor inputs, including labour. Labour shortages will emerge in some industries and among many groups of workers. Firms will try to bid workers away from other firms in order to maintain the high levels of output and sales made possible by the boom conditions.

As a result of these tight labour-market conditions, workers will find that they have considerable bargaining power with their employers, and they will put upward pressure on wages. Firms, recognizing that demand for their goods is strong, will be anxious to maintain a high level of output. To prevent their workers from either striking or quitting and moving to other employers, firms will be willing to accede to some of these upward pressures.

When output is above potential, the excess demand for labour tends to push up wages.

The boom that is associated with an inflationary gap generates a set of conditions—high profits for firms and unusually large demand for labour—that causes wages (and other factor prices) to rise.

This increase in factor prices will increase firms' unit costs. As unit costs increase, firms will require higher prices in order to supply any given level of output, and the *AS* curve will therefore shift up. This shift has the effect of reducing equilibrium real GDP and raising the price level. Real GDP moves back toward potential and the inflationary gap begins to close.

Even as output moves back toward potential, factor prices will continue to rise as long as some inflationary gap remains. Indeed, wages and other factor prices will continue rising until the *AS* curve shifts up to the point where the equilibrium level of GDP is equal to potential GDP. At this point, there is no more pressure for factor prices to rise, firms' costs are stable, and the *AS* curve stops shifting.

Output Below Potential

Sometimes the *AD* and *AS* curves intersect where actual output is less than potential, as illustrated in part (i) of Figure 24-1. Because firms are producing below their normal-capacity output, there is an unusually low demand for all factor inputs, including labour. There will be labour surpluses in some industries and among some groups of workers. Firms will have below-normal sales and not only will resist upward pressures on wages but will seek reductions in wages.

The slump that is associated with a recessionary gap generates a set of conditions—low profits for firms and low demand for labour—that causes wages (and other factor prices) to fall.[1]

This reduction in factor prices will reduce firms' unit costs. As unit costs fall, firms require a lower price in order to supply any given level of output, and the *AS* curve therefore shifts down. This shift has the effect of increasing equilibrium real GDP and reducing the price level. Real GDP moves back toward potential and the recessionary gap begins to close.

Wages and other factor prices will continue to fall as long as some recessionary gap remains. As factor prices fall, the *AS* curve shifts down, and this process continues until the equilibrium level of GDP is equal to potential output. At this point, there is no longer pressure for factor prices to fall, firms' unit costs are stable, and the *AS* curve stops shifting.

Adjustment Asymmetry

At this stage, we encounter an important asymmetry in the economy's aggregate supply behaviour. Boom conditions (an inflationary gap), along with labour shortages, cause wages and unit costs to rise. The experience of many developed economies, however, suggests that the downward pressures on wages during slumps (recessionary gaps) often do not operate as quickly as the upward pressures during booms. Even when wages fall, they tend to fall more slowly than they would rise in an equally sized inflationary gap. This *wage stickiness* implies that the downward shift in the *AS* curve and the downward pressure on the price level are correspondingly slight.[2]

Both upward and downward adjustments to wages and unit costs do occur, but there are differences in the speed at which they typically operate. Booms can cause wages to rise very rapidly; recessions usually cause wages to fall only slowly.

Potential Output as an "Anchor"

We have just seen how wages and other factor prices change when output is above or below potential. These changes in factor prices lead to changes in firms' unit costs that shift the *AS* curve and change the equilibrium level of GDP. Moreover, we saw that this process of factor-price adjustment will continue as long as some output gap remains, coming to a halt only when the equilibrium level of GDP is equal to potential GDP, Y^*. This leads to an important prediction from our macroeconomic model regarding the distinction between the short-run and long-run effects of aggregate demand and supply shocks.

Potential output acts like an anchor for the level of real GDP. Following aggregate demand or supply shocks that push real GDP below or above potential, the adjustment of factor prices brings real GDP back to potential output.

---

[1] Due to ongoing inflation and productivity growth, nominal wages rarely fall, even when there is a low demand for labour. But remember that in this chapter, to allow us to focus on the adjustment process, we are assuming that technology is constant and expected inflation is zero. Thus nominal (and real) wages and other factor prices are assumed to fall when real GDP is below potential output.

[2] This is the second asymmetry in aggregate supply that we have encountered. The first involves the changing slope of the *AS* curve, discussed in Chapter 23.

Following an aggregate demand or supply shock, the short-run equilibrium level of output may be different than potential output. Any output gap will lead wages and other factor prices to adjust, eventually bringing the equilibrium level of output back to potential. The level of potential output therefore acts like an "anchor" for the economy.

Later in this chapter we will examine this factor-price adjustment process in greater detail, illustrating it for the cases of positive and negative shocks to aggregate demand and supply. We will also see this factor-price adjustment process following changes in fiscal policy. The idea that Y^* acts as an "anchor" for the economy will become clear: Shocks of various kinds may cause output to rise above or fall below Y^* in the short run, but the adjustment of factor prices to output gaps ensures that output eventually returns to Y^*.

Phillips curve
Originally, a relationship between the unemployment rate and the rate of change of money wages. Now often drawn as a relationship between GDP and the rate of change of money wages.

EXTENSIONS IN THEORY 24-1
The Phillips Curve and the Adjustment Process

In the 1950s, Professor A.W. Phillips of the London School of Economics was conducting pioneering research on macroeconomic policy. In his early models, he related the rate of inflation to the difference between actual and potential output. Later he investigated the empirical underpinnings of this equation by studying the relationship between the rate of increase of wages and the level of unemployment. He studied these variables because unemployment data were available as far back as the mid-nineteenth century, whereas very few data on output gaps were available when he did his empirical work. In 1958, he reported that a stable relationship had existed between these two variables for 100 years in the United Kingdom. This relationship came to be known as the Phillips curve. The **Phillips curve** provided an explanation, rooted in empirical observation, of the speed with which wage changes shifted the AS curve by changing firms' unit costs.

In the form in which it became famous, the Phillips curve related wage changes to the level of unemployment. But we can express the same information in a slightly different way. Note that unemployment and output gaps are negatively related—a recessionary gap is associated with high unemployment, and an inflationary gap is associated with low unemployment. We can therefore create another Phillips curve that plots wage changes against output (rather than against unemployment). Both figures show the same information.

Recall from Chapter 19 that when output equals Y^* the corresponding unemployment rate is called the *natural rate of unemployment*, and is denoted U^*. Inflationary gaps (when $Y>Y^*$ and $U<U^*$) are associated with *increases* in wages.

Recessionary gaps (when $Y<Y^*$ and $U>U^*$) are associated with *decreases* in wages.* Thus, a Phillips curve that plots wage changes against real GDP is upward sloping, whereas a Phillips curve that plots wage changes against the unemployment rate is downward sloping. Both versions of the Phillips curve are shown in the accompanying figure.

When output is at potential, all factors are being used at their normal rates of utilization. There is neither upward nor downward pressure on wages (or other factor prices) because there is neither an excess demand nor an excess supply of labour. Hence, the Phillips curve cuts the horizontal axis at Y^* (and at U^*). This is how Phillips drew his original curve.

The Phillips curve is *not* the same as the AS curve. The AS curve has the *price level* on the vertical axis whereas the Phillips curve has the *rate of change of wages* on the vertical axis. How are the two curves related? The economy's location on the Phillips curve indicates how the AS curve is shifting as a result of the existing output gap.

For example, consider an economy that begins at point A in all three diagrams; there is no output gap and wages are therefore stable. Now, suppose a positive aggregate demand shock causes real GDP to increase to Y_1 (and unemployment

---

*Recall that we are assuming productivity to be constant so that changes in wages imply changes in unit labour costs. When productivity is growing, however, recessionary output gaps cause unit labour costs to fall. This only requires wages to be growing more slowly than productivity, not to be actually falling.

The Phillips Curve

The factor-price adjustment process that we have been discussing was popularized many years ago in a famous study of wages and unemployment in the United Kingdom. A.W. Phillips observed that wages tend to fall in periods of high unemployment and rise in periods of low unemployment. The resulting negative relationship between unemployment and the rate of change in wages has been called the *Phillips* curve ever since. *Extensions in Theory 24-1* discusses the Phillips curve and its relationship to the aggregate supply (*AS*) curve.

Inflationary and Recessionary Gaps

Now it should be clear why the output gaps are named as they are. When real GDP exceeds potential GDP, there will normally be rising unit costs, and the *AS* curve will be

to fall to U_1) and thus produces an inflationary gap. The excess demand for labour puts upward pressure on wages and the economy moves along the Phillips curve to point *B*, where wages begin rising. The increase in wages increases unit costs and causes the *AS* curve to shift up. Thus, each point on the Phillips curve determines the rate at which the *AS* curve is shifting. To complete the example, note that as the *AS* curve shifts up, the level of GDP will fall and the inflationary gap will begin to close. The economy moves back along the Phillips curve toward point *A*. When all adjustment is complete, the new equilibrium will be at point *C* in part (iii) of the figure, with output equal to Y^* and the price level and nominal wages higher than initially. On the Phillips curve, the economy will be back at point *A*, where real GDP equals Y^* and wages are constant.

Note that the convex shape of the Phillips curve is not accidental—it reflects the adjustment asymmetry we mentioned in the text. The convexity of the Phillips curve implies that an inflationary gap of a given amount will lead to faster wage increases than an equally sized recessionary gap will lead to wage reductions. In other words, an inflationary gap will cause the *AS* curve to shift up more quickly than a recessionary gap will cause the *AS* curve to shift down.

Finally, you might be wondering what would happen if the Phillips curve were to shift. And what would cause such a shift? As we will see in Chapter 30 when we discuss the phenomenon of sustained inflation, an important cause of shifts of the Phillips curve is changes in firms' and households' *expectations* of future inflation. In this chapter, however, we have assumed that expected inflation is zero. But whether there is expected inflation or not, the Phillips curve embodies the factor-price adjustment process that is the focus of this chapter.

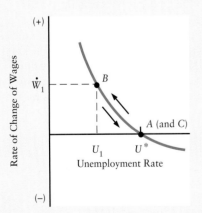

(i) Wage changes and unemployment

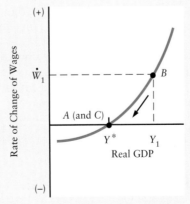

(ii) Wage changes and output

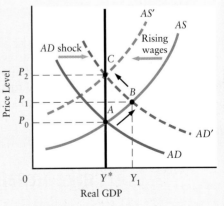

(iii) Aggregate demand and supply

shifting upward. This will in turn push the price level up and create temporary inflation. The larger the excess of real GDP over potential GDP, the greater the inflationary pressure. The term *inflationary gap* emphasizes this salient feature when output exceeds potential output.

When actual output is less than potential output, as we have seen, there will be unemployment of labour and other productive resources. Unit costs will fall slowly, leading to a slow downward shift in the *AS* curve. Hence, the price level will be falling only slowly, so that *unemployment* will be the output gap's most obvious result. The term *recessionary gap* emphasizes this salient feature that high rates of unemployment occur when actual output falls short of potential output.

The induced effects of output gaps on unit costs and the consequent shifts in the *AS* curve play an important role in our analysis of the long-run consequences of aggregate demand and aggregate supply shocks, to which we now turn.

24.2 Demand and Supply Shocks

We can now extend our study to cover the longer-run consequences of aggregate demand and aggregate supply shocks, incorporating changes in factor prices. We need to examine the effects of expansionary and contractionary shocks separately because the behaviour of unit costs is not symmetrical for the two cases. Let's begin with demand shocks.

Expansionary *AD* Shocks

Suppose the economy starts with a stable price level and real GDP equal to potential GDP as shown by the initial equilibrium in part (i) of Figure 24-2. Now suppose that this situation is disturbed by an increase in autonomous expenditure, perhaps caused by an upturn in business confidence and a resulting boom in investment spending. Figure 24-2(i) shows the effects of this aggregate demand shock in raising both the price level and real GDP. The *AD* curve shifts from AD_0 to AD_1, and real GDP rises above potential GDP. An inflationary gap opens up.

We have seen that an inflationary gap leads to increases in wages, which cause unit costs to rise. The *AS* curve shifts up as firms respond to the higher input costs by increasing their output prices. As seen in part (ii) of the figure, the upward shift of the *AS* curve causes a further rise in the price level, but this time the price rise is associated with a *fall* in output.

The cost increases (and the consequent upward shifts of the *AS* curve) continue until the inflationary gap has been removed—that is, until in part (ii) real GDP returns to Y^*. Only then is there no excess demand for labour, and only then do wages and unit costs, and hence the *AS* curve, stabilize.

The adjustment in wages and other factor prices eventually eliminates any boom caused by a demand shock; real GDP returns to its potential level.

Contractionary *AD* Shocks

Suppose again that the economy starts with stable prices and real GDP equal to potential, as shown in part (i) of Figure 24-3. Now assume there is a *decline* in aggregate demand. This negative aggregate demand shock might be a reduction in investment

Practise with Study Guide Chapter 24, Exercises 1 and 2.

FIGURE 24-2   The Adjustment Process Following a Positive Aggregate Demand Shock

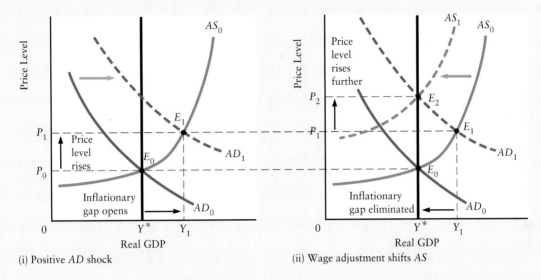

(i) Positive *AD* shock

(ii) Wage adjustment shifts *AS*

A rightward shift of the *AD* curve first raises prices and output along the *AS* curve. It then induces a shift of the *AS* curve that further raises prices but lowers output along the new *AD* curve. In part (i), the economy is in equilibrium at E_0, at its level of potential output, Y^*, and price level P_0. The *AD* curve then shifts from AD_0 to AD_1. This moves equilibrium to E_1, with income Y_1 and price level P_1, and opens up an inflationary gap.

In part (ii), the inflationary gap results in an increase in wages and other factor prices, shifting the *AS* curve upward. As this happens, output falls and the price level rises along AD_1. Eventually, when the *AS* curve has shifted to AS_1, output is back to Y^* and the inflationary gap has been eliminated. However, the price level has risen to P_2. The long-run result of the aggregate demand shock is therefore a higher price level with no change in real GDP.

expenditure, or perhaps a decline in the world demand for Canadian lumber or automobiles.

The first effects of the decline are a fall in output and some downward adjustment of prices, as shown in part (i) of the figure. As real GDP falls below potential, a recessionary gap is created, and unemployment rises. At this point we must analyze two separate cases. The first is where wages fall quickly in response to the excess supply of labour. The second is where wages fall only slowly.

Flexible Wages

Suppose wages (and other factor prices) fell quickly in response to the recessionary gap. The *AS* curve would therefore shift quickly downward as the lower wages led to reduced unit costs.

As shown in part (ii) of Figure 24-3, the economy would move along the new *AD* curve, with falling prices and rising output, until real GDP was quickly restored to potential, Y^*. We conclude that if wages were to fall rapidly whenever there was unemployment, the resulting shift in the *AS* curve would quickly eliminate recessionary gaps.

Flexible wages that fall rapidly during periods of unemployment provide an automatic adjustment mechanism that pushes the economy back toward potential output.

FIGURE 24-3   The Adjustment Process Following a Negative Aggregate Demand Shock

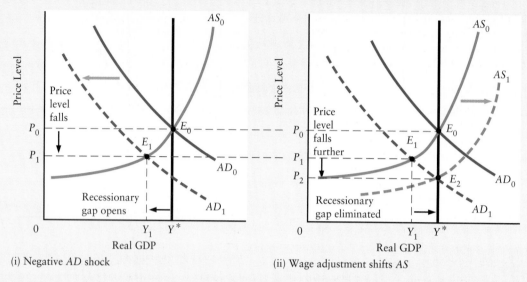

(i) Negative *AD* shock   (ii) Wage adjustment shifts *AS*

A leftward shift of the *AD* curve first lowers the price level and GDP along the *AS* curve and then induces a (possibly slow) shift of the *AS* curve that further lowers prices but raises output along the new *AD* curve. In part (i), the economy is in equilibrium at E_0, at its level of potential output, Y^*, and price level P_0. The *AD* curve then shifts to AD_1, moving equilibrium to E_1, with income Y_1 and price level P_1, and opens up a recessionary gap.

Part (ii) shows the adjustment back to potential output that occurs from the supply side of the economy. The fall in wages shifts the *AS* curve downward. Real GDP rises, and the price level falls further along the new *AD* curve. Eventually, the *AS* curve reaches AS_1, with equilibrium at E_2. The price level stabilizes at P_2 when real GDP returns to Y^*, closing the recessionary gap.

Sticky Wages

Boom conditions, along with labour shortages, do cause wages to rise, shifting the *AS* curve upward. In general, the bigger the inflationary gap, the faster wages will rise and the more quickly the *AS* curve will shift upward. However, as we noted earlier when we encountered the second asymmetry of aggregate supply, the experience of many economies suggests that wages typically do not fall rapidly in response to even large recessionary gaps. It is sometimes said that wages are "sticky" in the downward direction. This does not mean that wages never fall, only that they tend to fall more slowly in a recessionary gap than they rise in an equally sized inflationary gap. When wages are sticky, the analysis is the same as when wages are flexible, and thus Figure 24-3 tells the right story. The only difference is that the *AS* curve shifts more slowly when wages are sticky and thus the recessionary gap remains open for longer. An important implication of sticky wages is that the high unemployment that comes with a recessionary gap may not be quickly eliminated.

If wages are downwardly sticky, the economy's adjustment mechanism is sluggish and thus recessionary gaps are not eliminated quickly.[3]

---

[3] The causes of downward wage stickiness have been hotly debated among macroeconomists for years. We discuss several possible reasons in Chapter 31 when examining the causes of cyclical unemployment.

The weakness of the adjustment mechanism does not mean that recessionary gaps must always be prolonged. Rather, this weakness means that speedy recovery back to potential output must be generated mainly from the demand side. If wages are downwardly sticky and the economy is to avoid a persistent recessionary gap, a quick recovery requires a rightward shift of the AD curve. This sometimes happens when private-sector demand revives. But it also raises the possibility that government *stabilization policy* can be used to accomplish such a rightward shift in the AD curve. This is an important and contentious issue in macroeconomics, one to which we will return often throughout the remainder of this book.

The slow adjustment of wages and prices when output is below potential means that the recessionary effects of negative shocks sometimes persist for long periods.

The difference in the speed of adjustment of wages (and other factor prices) is the important asymmetry in the behaviour of aggregate supply that we noted earlier in this chapter. This asymmetry helps to explain two key facts about the Canadian economy. First, high unemployment can persist for quite long periods without causing decreases in wages and prices of sufficient magnitude to remove the unemployment. An example is the 1991–1995 period when unemployment was high and output was considerably below potential. Second, booms, along with labour shortages and production beyond normal capacity, do not persist for long periods without causing increases in wages and the price level. The periods 1987–1990 and 1999–2001 both displayed output above potential and pressure on wages and prices to rise.

Aggregate Supply Shocks

We have discussed the long-run effects of aggregate demand shocks, and the economy's automatic adjustment mechanism that returns real GDP to its potential level, Y^*. The same adjustment process operates following an aggregate supply shock.

Consider an economy that has a stable price level and real GDP at its potential level, as illustrated by point E_0 in part (i) of Figure 24-4. Suppose there is an increase in the world price of an important input, such as oil. As we have mentioned several times in this book, the OPEC oil shocks of 1973–74 and 1979–80 involved enormous increases in the price of oil and, to date, are surely the best examples that economists have of large negative aggregate supply shocks.

An increase in the price of oil increases unit costs for firms and causes the AS curve to shift upwards. Real GDP falls and the price level increases—this is *stagflation*. The short-run equilibrium is at point E_1 in Figure 24-4. With the opening of a recessionary gap, the economy's adjustment mechanism comes into play, though sticky wages reduce the speed of this adjustment.

The recessionary gap caused by the negative supply shock causes firms to shut down and workers to be laid off. The excess supply of labour (and other factors) eventually pushes wages down and begins to reverse the initial increase in unit costs caused by the increase in the price of oil. This adjustment is shown in part (ii) of the figure. As wages fall, the AS curve shifts back toward its starting point, and real GDP rises back toward its potential level, Y^*. Eventually, the economy returns to its initial point, E_0.

We leave it to the reader to analyze the long-run effects of a positive aggregate supply shock, such as the dramatic reduction in the world price of raw materials that occurred in 1997 and 1998. The logic of the analysis is exactly the same as illustrated in Figure 24-4, except that the initial shift in the AS curve is to the right, creating an inflationary gap.

Exogenous changes in input prices cause the AS curve to shift, creating an output gap. The adjustment mechanism then reverses the initial AS shift and brings the economy back to potential output and the initial price level.

FIGURE 24-4   The Adjustment Process Following a Negative Aggregate Supply Shock

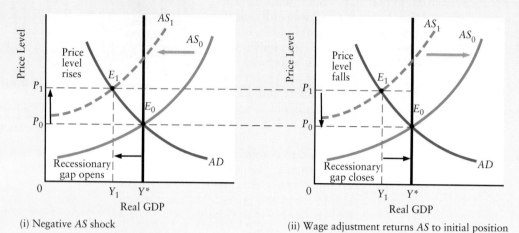

(i) Negative AS shock

(ii) Wage adjustment returns AS to initial position

A negative AS shock caused by an increase in input prices causes real GDP to fall and the price level to rise. The economy's adjustment mechanism then reverses the AS shift and returns the economy to its starting point.

The economy begins at point E_0 in part (i). The increase in the price of oil increases unit costs and causes the AS curve to shift up to AS_1. Real GDP falls to Y_1 and the price level rises to P_1. A recessionary gap is created.

In part (ii), the excess supply of labour associated with the recessionary gap causes wages to fall, possibly slowly. As wages fall, unit costs fall and so the AS curve shifts back down to AS_0. The economy is finally in long-run equilibrium at Y^* and P_0, its starting point.

Economic Shocks and Business Cycles

Aggregate demand and aggregate supply shocks are a major source of fluctuations in real GDP around potential. As we have seen, a positive demand shock, such as an increase in desired investment, will lead to an increase in output and prices. This will be followed by a fall in output and a further increase in prices as the adjustment mechanism restores the economy to long-run equilibrium. Depending on the nature and magnitude of the shock, the adjustment will take many months, maybe even a year or two.

Similarly, a positive supply shock, such as a reduction in the world price of an important input, will cause real GDP to rise and the price level to fall. As the adjustment mechanism comes into play, real GDP will fall back to potential and the price level will rise back to its initial level. As with a demand shock, the full adjustment may take many months.

No matter what the cause of the expansionary shock, the economy will not respond instantaneously. In many industries, it takes weeks or months or even longer to bring new or mothballed capacity into production and to hire and train new workers. Because of these lags in the economy's response, changes in output are spread out over a substantial period of time. An increase in demand or supply may lead to a gradual increase in output that lasts several months. Then, as output does change, the adjustment mechanism comes into play, eventually returning real GDP to its potential level.

Thus, a positive shock—demand or supply—initially leads to an increase in output and then, as the adjustment mechanism begins to operate, is followed by a reduction in output back to potential. Conversely, a negative demand or supply shock initially leads to a reduction in output and then, as the (slower) adjustment mechanism comes into play, is eventually followed by an increase in output back to potential. In both cases, the impact effect of the shock is reversed by the economy's adjustment mechanism. Shocks, therefore, generate *cyclical* movements in real GDP. Such shocks are the fundamental cause of *business cycles*.

Both aggregate demand and aggregate supply are subject to continual random shocks. The economy's adjustment mechanism can convert these shocks into cyclical fluctuations in real GDP.

Figure 24-5 illustrates the central point for both a positive and a negative shock. In this figure, the level of real GDP is plotted on the vertical axis and *time* is shown on the horizontal axis. Even though potential output tends to be steadily growing in reality, we assume for simplicity in this chapter that it is constant, and so the path of Y^* is shown as a horizontal line. In both parts of the figure, t_0 is the time when the shock initially hits the economy and pushes real GDP away from Y^*. Notice that it takes longer for real GDP to return to Y^* following the negative shock, reflecting our assumption of downward wage stickiness.

Long-Run Equilibrium

The economy is in a state of *long-run equilibrium* when factor prices are no longer adjusting to output gaps. As we have seen, wages and other factor prices will be stable only when the level of real GDP is equal to potential output, Y^*. Thus, the economy is in its long-run equilibrium when the short-run equilibrium, as determined by the intersection of the AD and AS curves, is such that $Y = Y^*$.

The value of Y^* depends on real variables such as the labour force, capital stock, and the level of technology, but is independent of nominal variables such as the price level. In other words, the level of output that firms will produce in the long run is independent of the price level. The vertical line above Y^* that we have seen in our diagrams is therefore sometimes called a *long-run aggregate supply curve*—the relationship between the price level and the amount of output supplied by firms *after all factor prices have adjusted to output gaps*. This vertical line is also sometimes called a *Classical aggregate supply curve* because the Classical economists were mainly concerned with the behaviour of the economy in long-run equilibrium.[4]

FIGURE 24-5   Shocks and the Business Cycle

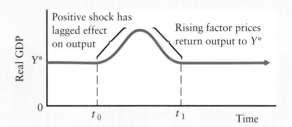

(i) Positive AD or AS shock

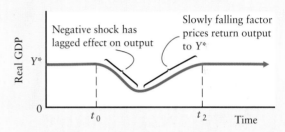

(ii) Negative AD or AS shock

The economy's factor-price adjustment process turns permanent shocks into cyclical movements. Part (i) shows the path of real GDP following a permanent positive AD or AS shock. Output gradually rises above Y^* and creates an inflationary gap. Rising factor prices return output to Y^*. Part (ii) shows the time path of real GDP following a permanent negative AD or AS shock. Output gradually falls below Y^* and creates a recessionary gap. Wages and other factor prices fall slowly, eventually returning output to Y^*. Note that t_2 in part (ii) is later than t_1 in part (i), illustrating that, due to downward wage stickiness, the factor-price adjustment process works more slowly following negative shocks than positive shocks. In both parts of the figure, a permanent shock, combined with the economy's natural adjustment process, results in cyclical movements of real GDP.

---

[4] The Classical school of economic thought began with Adam Smith (1723–1790) and was developed through the work of David Ricardo (1772–1823), Thomas Malthus (1766–1834) and John Stuart Mill (1806–1873). These economists emphasized the long-run behaviour of the economy. Beginning in the middle of the nineteenth century, Neoclassical economists devoted much time and effort to studying short-term fluctuations. *The General Theory of Employment, Interest and Money* (1936), written by John Maynard Keynes (1883–1946), was in a long tradition of the study of short-term fluctuations. Where Keynes differed from the Neoclassical economists was in approaching the issues from a macroeconomic perspective that emphasized fluctuations in real expenditure flows. Each of the economists mentioned in this footnote, along with several others, is discussed in more detail in the timeline at the back of the book.

FIGURE 24-6   Long-Run Equilibrium and Potential Output

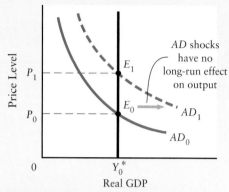

(i) A rise in aggregate demand

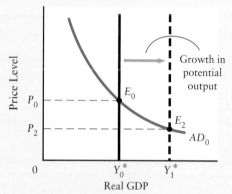

(ii) A rise in potential output

Potential output determines the long-run equilibrium value of real GDP. Given Y^*, aggregate demand determines the long-run equilibrium value of the price level. In both parts of the figure, the initial long-run equilibrium is at E_0, so the price level is P_0 and real GDP is Y_0^*.

In part (i), a shift in the AD curve from AD_0 to AD_1 moves the long-run equilibrium from E_0 to E_1. This raises the price level from P_0 to P_1 but leaves real GDP unchanged at Y_0^* in the long run.

In part (ii), an increase in potential output from Y_0^* to Y_1^* moves the long-run equilibrium from E_0 to E_2. This raises real GDP from Y_0^* to Y_1^* and lowers the price level from P_0 to P_2.

Figure 24-6 shows the long-run equilibrium and price level as determined by the intersection of the AD curve and the vertical Y^* line. Shifts in the AD curve change the price level but not the level of long-run equilibrium output, as shown in part (i). An increase in Y^* changes both output and the price level, as shown in part (ii).

In the long run, real GDP is determined solely by potential output; the role of aggregate demand is only to determine the price level.

Consider the effect of an increase in government purchases in a situation in which the economy begins in long-run equilibrium at E_0 with real GDP equal to Y_0^*. In part (i) of Figure 24-6 it is clear that the long-run effect of an increase in government purchases is to increase the price level but to leave the level of real GDP unchanged at Y_0^*. What the figure does not show, however, is that while the *level* of GDP may be unchanged, the *composition* of GDP has changed.

To see how the composition of GDP is affected by the increase in G, consider what happens as the price level rises from P_0 to P_1 in part (i) of the figure. For a given stock of nominal assets (money and bonds), the rise in the price level reduces the wealth of the private sector and thus reduces household consumption. In addition, for a given exchange rate, the rise in the domestic price level makes Canadian goods more expensive relative to foreign goods, and thus reduces Canada's net exports. (You will recall that these are the two reasons why the AD curve is downward sloping, as we discussed at the beginning of Chapter 23.) Thus, the increase in government purchases, by creating an inflationary gap and forcing up the price level, has "crowded out" some elements of private expenditure—in this case, consumption and net exports.

So, while real GDP is the same at points E_0 and E_1 in part (i) of Figure 24-6, the composition of the GDP is different. Specifically, G is higher at E_1 than it is at E_0; C and NX are lower at E_1 than at E_0.

Why do we care about the composition of GDP? Recall from Chapter 22 that net exports and investment are similar in the sense that they both imply *asset formation* for the domestic economy. Thus, other things being equal, the more of GDP that is used for asset formation, the higher national income will be in the future. Thus, "crowding out" is potentially important if it hinders the economy's prospects for long-run economic growth. In later chapters we will examine a type of crowding out of investment that reduces the economy's long-run growth. In order to do that, however, we must learn some details about money and interest rates, which we examine in Chapters 27 and 28. Until then, our discussion about the composition of GDP is summarized as follows:

In the long run, the level of GDP is given by potential output, Y^*, and is compatible with any price level. However, the *composition* of GDP among consumption, investment, government purchases, and net exports may vary at different price levels.

24.3 **Fiscal Policy and the Business Cycle**

In Chapter 22, we briefly considered the basic concepts of fiscal stabilization policy. In principle, this policy can be used in attempts to stabilize real GDP at or near potential output. In the remainder of this chapter, we look into taxing and spending as tools of fiscal stabilization policy. We will return to more advanced issues of fiscal policy in Chapter 32.

> **Though macroeconomists tend to focus on fluctuations in real GDP when describing business cycles, there is no single "best" measure of the changes in economic activity. For a detailed description of several popular measures of changes in the level of economic activity—including *housing starts, capacity utilization,* and *leading indicators*—look for "Several Measures of Economic Fluctuations in Canada" in the *Additional Topics* section of this book's Companion Website.**
>
> h t t p : / / w w w . p e a r s o n e d . c a / r a g a n

Because increases in government purchases (G) increase aggregate demand and increases in taxation (T) decrease aggregate demand, the *direction* of the required changes in spending and taxation is generally easy to determine once we know the direction of the desired change in real GDP. For example, if output is currently below potential, a desirable fiscal policy will include an increase in G, a decrease in T, or both. However, the *timing, magnitude,* and *mixture* of the changes are more difficult issues.

There is no doubt that the government can exert a major influence on real GDP. Prime examples are the massive increases in military spending during major wars. Canadian federal expenditure during the Second World War rose from 12.2 percent of GDP in 1939 to 41.8 percent in 1944. At the same time, the unemployment rate fell from 11.4 percent to 1.4 percent. Economists agree that the increase in government spending helped to bring about the rise in output and the associated fall in unemployment. More recently, the Canadian government reduced spending and increased taxes in the 1995–98 period as a means of reducing its budget deficit. Many economists agree that these contractionary fiscal policies contributed to the slow growth of Canadian real GDP during this period.

In the heyday of fiscal policy, from about 1945 to about 1970, many economists were convinced that the economy could be stabilized adequately just by varying the size of the government's taxes and expenditures. That day is past. Today, most economists are aware of the many limitations of fiscal policy.

The Basic Theory of Fiscal Stabilization

For information on the Federal Department of Finance, the ministry in charge of fiscal policy, see: www.fin.gc.ca.

A reduction in tax rates or an increase in government purchases will shift the *AD* curve to the right, causing an increase in real GDP. An increase in tax rates or a cut in government expenditure will shift the *AD* curve to the left, causing a decrease in real GDP.

How Fiscal Stabilization Works

A more detailed look at how fiscal stabilization works will help to show some of the complications that arise when implementing fiscal policy.

Practise with Study Guide Chapter 24, Exercise 3.

Closing a Recessionary Gap.   A recessionary gap is shown in Figure 24-7; the economy's short-run equilibrium is at point E_0 with real GDP below Y^*. Such a recessionary gap can be closed in three ways, returning real GDP to Y^*. First, as often happens in practice, private-sector demand recovers and the *AD* curve shifts to the right, as shown in part (ii) of the figure. If such a recovery does not occur rapidly, the economy's adjustment mechanism will come into play. As we discussed earlier in this chapter, the excess supply of factors at E_0 will eventually cause wages and other factor prices to fall, shifting the *AS* curve downward and restoring output to Y^*, as shown in part (i) of the figure. However, as we also discussed, because of the stickiness of wages this process could take a long time. Policymakers may not be prepared to wait the time necessary for the

FIGURE 24-7   The Closing of a Recessionary Gap

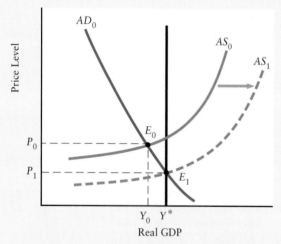 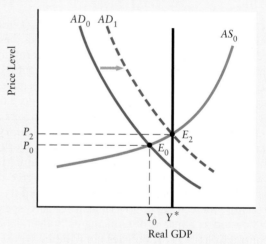

(i) A recessionary gap closed by falling wages and other factor prices

(ii) A recessionary gap closed by fiscal expansion or recovery of private-sector demand

A recessionary gap may be closed by a (slow) downward shift of the *AS* curve or an increase in aggregate demand. Initially, equilibrium is at E_0, with real GDP at Y_0 and the price level at P_0. There is a recessionary gap.

As shown in part (i), the gap might be removed by a shift in the *AS* curve to AS_1, as will eventually happen when wages and other factor prices fall in response to excess supply. The shift in the *AS* curve causes a movement down and to the right along AD_0 to a new equilibrium at E_1, achieving potential output Y^* and lowering the price level to P_1.

As shown in part (ii), the gap might also be removed by a shift of the *AD* curve to AD_1, caused by an expansionary fiscal policy or a recovery of private-sector spending. The shift in the *AD* curve causes a movement up and to the right along AS_0. This movement shifts the equilibrium to E_2, raising output to Y^* and the price level to P_2.

recessionary gap to correct itself. The government can instead use expansionary fiscal policy to shift the AD curve to the right and close the recessionary gap. It would do this by reducing tax rates or increasing the level of government purchases.

The advantage of using fiscal policy rather than allowing the economy's natural adjustment mechanism to operate is that it may substantially shorten what might otherwise be a long recession. One disadvantage is that the use of fiscal policy may stimulate the economy just before private-sector spending recovers on its own. As a result, the economy may overshoot its potential output, and an inflationary gap may open up. In this case, fiscal policy that is intended to promote economic stability can actually cause instability.

Closing an Inflationary Gap.   An inflationary gap is illustrated in Figure 24-8; the economy's short-run equilibrium is at point E_0, with real GDP above Y^*. There are three ways such an inflationary gap may be closed, returning real GDP to Y^*. First, private-sector demand may falter, thus shifting the AD curve to the left. If this does not occur rapidly, the economy's adjustment mechanism will come into play; excess demand for factors will cause wages and other factor prices to rise, shifting the AS curve upward and gradually restoring output to Y^*. Alternatively, the government can use a contractionary fiscal policy to shift the AD curve to the left and close the inflationary gap. The government would do this by increasing tax rates or reducing its level of purchases.

FIGURE 24-8   The Closing of an Inflationary Gap

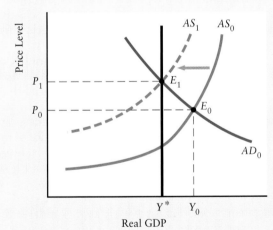

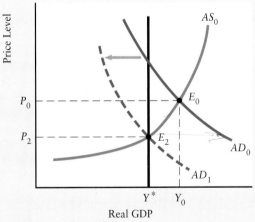

(i) An inflationary gap closed by rising wages and other factor prices

(ii) An inflationary gap closed by contractionary fiscal policy or a reduction in private-sector demand

An inflationary gap may be removed by an upward shift of the AS curve or by a leftward shift of the AD curve. Initially, equilibrium is at E_0, with real GDP at Y_0 and the price level at P_0. There is an inflationary gap.

As shown in part (i), the gap might be removed by a shift in the AS curve to AS_1, as will happen when wages and other factor prices rise in response to the excess demand. The shift in the AS curve causes a movement up and to the left along AD_0. This movement establishes a new equilibrium at E_1, reducing output to its potential level Y^* and raising the price level to P_1.

As shown in part (ii), the gap might also be removed by a shift in the AD curve to AD_1 caused by, for example, a contractionary fiscal policy. The shift in the AD curve causes a movement down and to the left along AS_0. This movement shifts the equilibrium to E_2, lowering income to Y^* and the price level to P_2.

The advantage of using a contractionary fiscal policy to close the inflationary gap is that it avoids the inflationary increase in prices that would otherwise occur. One disadvantage is that if private-sector expenditures fall because of natural causes, real GDP may be pushed below potential, thus opening up a recessionary gap.

This discussion leads to a key proposition:

When the economy's adjustment mechanism is slow to operate, or produces undesirable side effects such as rising prices, there is a potential stabilization role for fiscal policy.

The Paradox of Thrift

An increase in national saving—caused by a reduction in household consumption (C), a reduction in government purchases (G), or an increase in tax revenues (T)—will shift the AD curve to the left and *reduce* the equilibrium level of real GDP in the short run. The contrary case, a decrease in national saving, shifts the AD curve to the right and increases real GDP in the short run. Thus, frugality on the part of individuals, which may seem to be prudent behaviour for each individual taken separately, ends up reducing short-run real GDP. This phenomenon is known as the *paradox of thrift*—the paradox being that what may be good for any individual when viewed in isolation ends up being undesirable for the economy as a whole.

The policy implication of this phenomenon is that a major and persistent recession can be battled by encouraging governments, firms, and households to reduce their saving and therefore increase their spending. In times of unemployment and recession, a greater desire to save will only make things worse. This result goes directly against the idea that we should tighten our belts when times are tough. The notion that it is not only possible but even *desirable* to spend one's way out of a recession touches a sensitive point with people raised on the belief that success is based on hard work and frugality; as a result, the idea often arouses great hostility.

As is discussed in *Lessons From History 24-1*, the implications of the paradox of thrift were not generally understood during the Great Depression of the 1930s. Most governments, faced with depression-induced reductions in tax revenues, reduced their expenditures to balance their budgets. As a result, many economists argue that the fiscal policies at the time actually made things worse. When Milton Friedman (many years later) said, "We are all Keynesians now," he was referring to the general acceptance of the view that the government's budget is much more than just the revenue and expenditure statement of a very large organization. Whether we like it or not, the sheer size of the government's budget inevitably makes it a powerful tool for influencing the economy.

The paradox of thrift applies to shifts in aggregate demand that have been caused by changes in saving (and hence spending) behaviour. That is why it applies only in the short run, when the AD curve plays an important role in the determination of real GDP.

The paradox of thrift does not apply in the long run. Remember that in the long run, aggregate demand does not influence the level of real GDP—output is determined only by the level of potential output, Y^*. In the long run, the more people and government save, the larger is the supply of funds available for investment. As we will see in Chapter 26, this increase in the pool of available funds will reduce interest rates and encourage more investment by firms. The greater rate of investment leads to a higher rate of growth of potential output.

The paradox of thrift—the idea that an increase in saving reduces the level of real GDP—is only true in the short run. In the long run, real GDP is equal to potential output. The increase in saving has the long-run effect of increasing investment and therefore increasing potential output.

Automatic Fiscal Stabilizers

The fiscal policies that we have been discussing are referred to as *discretionary* because the government uses its discretion in changing its purchases (*G*) or tax revenues (*T*) in an attempt to change the level of real GDP. However, even if the government makes no active decisions regarding changes in its purchases or taxation, the government's tax-and-transfer system will act as an *automatic stabilizer* for the economy. Let's see how this works.

When we first introduced government to our macro model in Chapter 22, we made the assumptions that government purchases *(G)* were autonomous with respect to national income but that government net tax revenues *(T)* were positively related to national income. Specifically, we assumed that

$$T = tY$$

where *t* is the net tax rate. This positive relationship between *T* and *Y* has an important implication for the stability of the economy in response to shocks to autonomous expenditure.

For example, consider a shock that increases the short-run level of real GDP. This could be either an aggregate demand or supply shock. As real GDP increases, tax revenues rise and, as there are fewer low-income households and unemployed persons requiring assistance, transfer payments fall. The rise in net tax revenues (taxes minus transfers) dampens the extent to which the rise in national income leads to further induced increases in spending (and then, through the multiplier process, to an increase in real GDP). In other words, the tax-and-transfer system reduces the value of the simple multiplier and thus acts as an **automatic stabilizer** for the economy. In the absence of the tax-and-transfer system, the simple multiplier would be larger and a positive shock would lead to a larger increase in real GDP.

The same is true in the presence of a negative *AD* or *AS* shock. As real GDP declines in response to the shock, government's net tax revenues fall, thus dampening the extent to which the fall in *Y* leads to further induced reductions in spending and output.

Even in the absence of discretionary fiscal stabilization policy, the presence of taxes and transfers that vary with national income provides the economy with an automatic stabilizer.

At the end of Chapter 22 we argued that realistic Canadian values for our model's key parameters are as follows:

* marginal propensity to consume (*MPC*) = 0.8
* net tax rate (*t*) = 0.3
* marginal propensity to import (*m*) = 0.4

The implied value of *z*, the marginal propensity to spend on national income, is therefore

$$z = MPC(1 - t) - m$$
$$= (0.8)(0.7) - 0.4 = 0.16$$

As a result, a realistic value for the simple multiplier in Canada is

$$\text{Simple multiplier} = 1/(1 - z) = 1/0.84 = 1.19$$

The lower is the net tax rate, the larger is the simple multiplier and thus the less stable is real GDP in response to shocks to autonomous spending. For example, if the net tax rate were reduced to 20 percent (*t* = 0.20), the value of *z* would rise to 0.24 and the simple multiplier would rise to 1/(1 − 0.24) = 1/0.76 = 1.31. The larger multiplier implies that a shock to autonomous expenditure would result in a larger total change in GDP—

automatic stabilizers Elements of the tax-and-transfer systems that automatically lessen the magnitude of the fluctuations in national income caused by changes in autonomous expenditures.

LESSONS FROM HISTORY 24-1

Fiscal Policy in the Great Depression

The Great Depression, which is usually dated as beginning with the massive stock-market crash on October 29, 1929, was by far the most dramatic economic event of the twentieth century. As the accompanying figure shows, Canadian real GDP plummeted by almost 30 percent from its peak in 1929 to its low point in 1933. The price level actually *fell* beginning in 1930 and declined by about 20 percent over the next five years. The unemployment rate increased from 3 percent in 1929 to an unparalleled 19.3 percent four years later. To put these numbers in perspective, by today's standards a very serious recession (like the most recent one in 1990–91) sees real GDP fall by 2 percent, the unemployment rate rise to 11 percent, and prices continue rising but perhaps at a slower rate. The economic events of the 1930s certainly deserve to be called the Great Depression!

The Great Depression was not just a catastrophic event that happened exogenously—its depth and duration were made worse by some fundamental mistakes in policy. Failure to understand the implication of the paradox of thrift led many countries to adopt disastrous fiscal policies during the Great Depression. In addition, failure to understand the role of built-in stabilizers has led many observers to conclude, erroneously, that fiscal expansion was tried in the Great Depression but failed. Let us see how these two misperceptions are related.

The Paradox of Thrift in Action

In 1932, Canadian Prime Minister R. B. Bennett said, "We are now faced with the real crisis in the history of Canada. To maintain our credit we must practise the most rigid economy and not spend a single cent." His government that year—at the deepest point in the recession—brought down a budget based on the principle of trying to balance revenues and expenditures, and it included *increases* in tax rates.

In the same year, Franklin Roosevelt was elected U.S. president on a platform of fighting the Great Depression with government policies. In his inaugural address he urged, "Our great primary task is to put people to work. . . . [This task] can be helped by insistence that the federal, state, and local governments act forthwith on the demand that their costs be drastically reduced. . . . "

Across the Atlantic, King George V told the British House of Commons in 1931, "The present condition of the national finances, in the opinion of His Majesty's ministers, calls for the imposition of additional taxation and for the effecting of economies in public expenditure."

As the paradox of thrift predicts, these policies tended to worsen, rather than cure, the Depression.

that is, the economy would be less stable. Therefore, whatever benefits might arise from a reduction in the net tax rate (and we will see later that lower tax rates may tend to increase the economy's long-run growth rate), one drawback is that the tax reduction would lead to the economy being less stable following shocks to autonomous expenditure.

The great advantage of automatic fiscal stabilizers is that they are "automatic." As long as the tax-and-transfer system is in place (and there is no sign of its imminent disappearance!) some stability is provided without anyone having to make active decisions about fiscal policy. As we see next, the sorts of decisions required for successful *discretionary* fiscal policy are not simple, and some attempts to provide stability through discretionary fiscal policy may actually reduce the stability of the economy.

Limitations of Discretionary Fiscal Policy

According to our earlier discussion of fiscal stabilization policy, returning the economy to potential output would appear to be a simple matter of cutting taxes and raising government spending, in some combination. Why do so many economists believe that such policies would be "as likely to harm as help"? Part of the answer is that the execution of discretionary fiscal policy is anything but simple.

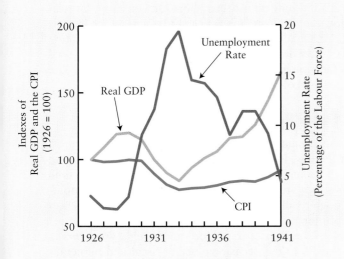

Interpreting the Deficits in the 1930s

Government deficits did increase in the 1930s, but they were not the result of a program of deficit-financed public expenditure. Rather, they were the result of the fall in tax revenues, brought about by the fall in real GDP as the economy sank into depression. The various governments did not advocate programs of massive deficit-financed spending to shift the *AD* curve to the right. Instead, they hoped that a small amount of government spending in addition to numerous policies designed to stabilize prices and to restore confidence would lead to a recovery of private investment expenditure that would substantially shift the *AD* curve. To have expected a massive revival of private investment expenditure as a result of the puny increase in aggregate demand that was instituted by the federal government now seems hopelessly naive.

When we judge these policies from the viewpoint of modern theory, their failure is no mystery. Indeed, Professor E. Cary Brown of MIT, after a careful study, concluded, "Fiscal policy seems to have been an unsuccessful recovery device in the thirties—not because it did not work, but because it was not tried." Once the massive, war-geared expenditure of the 1940s began, output responded sharply and unemployment all but evaporated, as seen clearly in the figure.

The performance of the Canadian and U.S. economies from 1930 to 1945 is well explained by the macroeconomic theory that we have developed in the last few chapters. It is clear that the governments did not effectively use fiscal policy to stabilize their economies. War brought the Depression to an end because war demands made acceptable a level of government expenditure sufficient to remove the recessionary gap. Had the Canadian and American administrations been able to do the same in the early 1930s, it might have ended the waste of the Great Depression many years sooner.

Data in this box are drawn from M.C. Urquhart, *Historical Statistics of Canada*.

Lags

To change fiscal policy requires making changes in taxes and government expenditures. The changes must be agreed on by the cabinet and passed by parliament. The political stakes in such changes are generally very large; taxes and spending are called "bread-and-butter issues" precisely because they affect the economic well-being of almost everyone. Thus, even if economists agreed that the economy would be helped by, say, a tax cut, politicians would likely spend a good deal of time debating *whose* taxes should be cut and by *how much*. The delay between the initial recognition of a recessionary or inflationary gap and the enactment of legislation to change fiscal policy is called a **decision lag**.

Once policy changes are agreed on, there is still an **execution lag**, adding time between the enactment and the implementation of the change. Furthermore, once policies are in place, it will usually take still more time for their economic consequences to be felt. Because of these lags, it is quite possible that by the time a given policy decision has any impact on the economy, circumstances will have changed such that the policy is no longer appropriate.

decision lag
The period of time between perceiving some problem and reaching a decision on what to do about it.

execution lag
The time that it takes to put policies in place after a decision has been made.

Temporary Versus Permanent Policy Changes

To make matters even more frustrating, tax measures that are known to be temporary are generally less effective than measures that are expected to be permanent. If households know that a given tax cut will last only a year, they may recognize that the effect on their long-run consumption possibilities is small and may adjust their short-run consumption relatively little. Thus, the more closely household consumption expenditure is related to lifetime income rather than to current income, the smaller will be the effects on current consumption of tax changes that are known to be of short duration. Or, to use the language that we used when introducing the consumption function in Chapter 21, the more forward-looking are households, the smaller will be the effects of temporary changes in taxes.

The Role of Discretionary Fiscal Policy

fine tuning
The attempt to maintain output at its potential level by means of frequent changes in fiscal or monetary policy.

These difficulties suggest that attempts to use discretionary fiscal policy to "fine tune" the economy are fraught with difficulties. **Fine tuning** refers to the use of fiscal (and monetary) policy to offset virtually all fluctuations in private-sector spending so as to hold real GDP at or near its potential level at all times. However, neither economic nor political science has yet advanced far enough to allow policymakers to undo the consequences of every aggregate demand or supply shock. Nevertheless, many economists still argue that when a recessionary gap is large enough and persists for long enough, *gross tuning* may be appropriate. **Gross tuning** refers to the occasional use of fiscal and monetary policy to remove large and persistent output gaps. Other economists believe that fiscal policy should not be used for economic stabilization under any circumstances. Rather, they would argue, tax and spending behaviour should be the outcome of public choices regarding the long-term size and financing of the public sector and should not be altered for short-term considerations. We return to these debates in Chapter 32.

gross tuning
The use of macroeconomic policy to stabilize the economy such that large deviations from potential output do not persist for extended periods of time.

Fiscal Policy and Growth

Fiscal policy has both short-run and long-run effects on the economy. Its short-run effects, which we have discussed in this chapter, are reflected by shifts in the *AD* curve and changes in the level of GDP. However, the adjustment of factor prices eventually brings real GDP back to Y^*, and so the long-run effects of any given fiscal policy depend on the policy's effects on Y^*. We consider two examples. In both examples, to highlight the difference between the short-run and long-run effects of the policies, we imagine starting in a macroeconomic equilibrium with real GDP equal to Y^*.

Increases in Government Purchases

A fiscal expansion created by an increase in government purchases *(G)* will shift the *AD* curve to the right and increase real GDP in the short run. As factor prices rise in response to the inflationary output gap, output will return back to Y^* but at a higher price level. As we saw earlier in this chapter, the *composition* of GDP will be different at the higher price level even though Y^* may be unchanged. In particular, the increase in *G* has the long-run effect of "crowding out" private spending and reducing the economy's rate of *asset formation*. Reduced asset formation, in turn, leads to a reduced rate of growth of potential output.[5]

---

[5] We continue with the assumption that we first made in Chapter 22 that *G* does not include investment in physical assets. Thus, as the increase in *G* crowds out private-sector investment, the economy's total rate of asset formation declines. In reality, however, government *investment* may crowd out private-sector investment, in which case the effect on the economy's future growth rate depends on the investments in question. We address this issue in more detail in Chapter 32 when we examine government debt and deficits.

Even though an increase in government purchases may have no effect on the *current level* of potential output, the crowding out of private expenditures and reduced asset formation implies that the *growth rate* of potential output may be lower than it would otherwise be.

In this situation, the short-run stimulative benefits of the fiscal expansion need to be weighed against the possible long-run costs of lower growth. If the economy is currently in a deep recession and the economy's natural adjustment process is slow, the gain in short-run economic activity may well outweigh the costs of slower growth. After all, part of Keynes' central message was that the state of the world at potential output is not very interesting to members of a society who are a long way from it.

Reductions in Taxes

A fiscal expansion created by a reduction in taxes is a little more complicated to analyze because there are likely to be longer-term, supply-side effects. The short-run demand-side effects are straightforward. A reduction in the GST rate or in the corporate or personal income-tax rates will increase both investment and consumption spending and shift the *AD* curve to the right. The level of real GDP will rise in the short run. As wages and other factor prices increase, however, the level of output will gradually return to Y^*.

Practise with Study Guide Chapter 24, Exercise 4.

What is the long-run effect of lower taxes on the level of potential output? Lower corporate income-tax rates make investment more profitable to firms, and the stimulative effect on desired investment may offset the "crowding out" associated with the rightward shift of the *AD* curve. If the overall effect on investment is positive, there will tend to be a positive effect on the growth rate of potential output. Lower GST rates and personal income-tax rates may have a similar effect. To the extent that high tax rates discourage work effort, reductions in tax rates will lead to increases in the labour force and consequent increases in the level of potential output.

Reductions in tax rates generate a short-run demand stimulus and may also generate a longer-run increase in the level and growth rate of potential output.

If reduced tax rates *do* lead to a higher growth rate of potential output, there would appear to be no clear tradeoff between the short-run and long-run effects of the fiscal expansion. The economy benefits in the short run from the increase in economic activity and in the long run from the increase in the growth rate. The absence of a tradeoff may, however, be illusory. Even though the growth rate of potential output is higher, the reduced tax revenues lead to fewer resources under the command of government. This means less public spending on many of the things citizens value, such as national parks, public education, and health care.

Another possibility, however, is that the reduction in tax rates leads to such a significant increase in potential output that the government's tax revenues actually increase. (We saw this possibility in Chapter 18 with the Laffer curve, the relationship between tax rates and total tax revenues.) In this case, the tax reduction unleashes such a flood of investment and work effort that the increase in national income is sufficient to more than offset the reduction in tax rates, thus leaving the government able to fund more worthwhile projects than before. This idea is central to what is often called "supply side" economics, as popularized during the early 1980s by advisors to U.S. President Ronald Reagan and British Prime Minister Margaret Thatcher. More recently, the central idea that tax reductions may significantly stimulate economic activity and growth played an important role in the policies of Alberta Premier Ralph Klein and former Ontario Premier Mike Harris, as well as in the proposed tax cut in 2003 by U.S. President George W. Bush.

S U M M A R Y

24.1 Output Gaps and Factor Prices

LO 1 2

- Potential output, Y^*, is the level of real GDP at which all factors of production are being used at their normal rates of utilization.
- The output gap is the difference between potential output and the actual level of real GDP, the latter determined by the intersection of the AD and AS curves.
- An inflationary gap means that Y is greater than Y^*, and hence there is excess demand in factor markets. As a result, wages and other factor prices rise, causing firms' unit costs to rise. The AS curve shifts upward, and the price level rises.

- A recessionary gap means that Y is less than Y^*, and hence there is excess supply in factor markets. Wages and other factor prices fall, but at a slow rate. As firms' unit costs fall, the AS curve gradually shifts downward, eventually returning output to potential.
- The level of potential output, Y^*, acts as an "anchor" for the economy. Given the short-run equilibrium as determined by the AD and AS curves, wages and other factor prices will adjust, shifting the AS curve, until output returns to Y^*.

24.2 Demand and Supply Shocks

LO 3

- Beginning from a position of potential output, an expansionary demand shock creates an inflationary gap, causing wages and other factor prices to rise. Firms' unit costs rise, shifting the AS curve upward and bringing output back to its potential level.
- Beginning from a position of potential output, a contractionary demand shock creates a recessionary gap. Because factor prices tend to be sticky downwards, the automatic adjustment process tends to be slow, and a recessionary gap tends to persist for some time.
- Aggregate supply shocks, such as those caused by changes in the prices of inputs, lead the AS curve to shift, changing real GDP and the price level. But the economy's adjustment mechanism reverses the shift in AS, eventually

bringing the economy back to its initial level of output and prices.
- Demand and supply shocks are important sources of business cycles. As a shock works its way through the economy and the adjustment mechanism comes into play, real GDP will often exhibit a cyclical pattern.
- In the short run, macroeconomic equilibrium is determined by the intersection of the AD and AS curves. In the long run, the economy is in equilibrium only when real GDP is equal to potential output. In the long run, the price level is determined by the intersection of the AD curve and the vertical Y^* curve.
- Shocks to the AD or AS curves can change real GDP in the short run. Only changes in the level of potential output can change output in the long run.

24.3 Fiscal Policy and the Business Cycle

LO 4

- In principle, fiscal policy can be used to stabilize output at Y^*. To remove a recessionary gap, governments can shift AD to the right by cutting taxes or increasing spending. To remove an inflationary gap, governments can pursue the opposite policies.
- In the short run, increases in desired saving on the part of firms, households, and governments lead to reductions in real GDP. This phenomenon is called the paradox of thrift. In the long run, the paradox of thrift does not apply, and increased saving will lead to increased asset formation and economic growth.

- Because government tax and transfer programs tend to reduce the size of the multiplier, they act as automatic stabilizers. When real GDP changes, disposable income changes by less because of taxes and transfers.
- Discretionary fiscal policy is subject to decision lags and execution lags that limit its ability to take effect quickly. Some economists argue that these limitations are so severe that discretionary fiscal policy should never be used for stabilization because it will end up increasing instability. Others argue that the economy's adjustment process works so slowly that discretionary fiscal policy can play a useful role in stabilizing the economy.

- Fiscal policy has different effects in the short and long run. In the short run, a fiscal expansion created by an increase in government purchases (*G*) will increase real GDP. In the long run, the rise in *G* will "crowd out" private spending and reduce the rate of asset formation, thus reducing the growth rate of potential output.

- In the short run, a fiscal expansion created by a reduction in income taxes has a similar effect on real GDP. In the long run, if the tax reduction leads to more investment and work effort, there will be a positive effect on the level and growth rate of potential output.

K E Y   C O N C E P T S

The output gap and factor prices
Inflationary and recessionary gaps
Asymmetry of wage adjustment:
  flexible and sticky wages
The Phillips curve

Short-run versus long-run effects of
  AD and *AS* shocks
Potential output as an "anchor" for
  the economy
Fiscal stabilization policy

The paradox of thrift
Decision lags and execution lags
Automatic stabilizers
Fine tuning and gross tuning

S T U D Y   E X E R C I S E S

1. Fill in the blanks to make the following statements correct.

   a. In our short-run macro model, it is assumed that factor prices are _constant_ and the level of potential output is _____. Changes in real GDP are caused by fluctuations in ___AS___ and ___AD___.

   b. During the macroeconomic adjustment process highlighted in this chapter, the central assumption is that factor prices are _flexible_ and responding to _____. Potential output is assumed to be ___Y*___, and acts as an _anchor_ for real GDP following *AD* or *AS* shocks.

2. Fill in the blanks to make the following statements correct.

   a. When actual GDP is higher than potential GDP, we say that there is a(n) _____ gap. When actual GDP is less than potential GDP we say there is a(n) _____ gap.

   b. An inflationary gap leads to excess demand for labour, which causes wages and thus _____ costs to rise. Firms require higher _____ in order to supply any level of output, and so the *AS* curve shifts _____.

   c. A recessionary gap leads to excess supply of labour, which causes wages and thus _____ costs to fall. Firms reduce _____ for any level of output supplied, and so the *AS* curve shifts _____.

   d. The downward adjustment of wages in response to a recessionary gap is much _____ than the upward adjustment of wages in response to an _____ gap. Economists refer to this phenomenon as _____.

3. Fill in the blanks to make the following statements correct.

   a. Beginning with output equal to potential, suppose there is a sudden increase in demand for Canadian exports. This is a(n) _____ shock to the Canadian economy, which will result in the _____ curve shifting to the _____ and the opening of a(n) _____ gap. Firms' unit costs will start to _____ and the _____ curve will shift _____. Long-run equilibrium will be restored at _____ output and _____ price level.

   b. Beginning with output equal to potential, suppose there is a drop in business confidence and investment falls. This is a(n) _____ shock to the Canadian economy, which shifts the _____ curve to the left and creates a(n) _____ gap. Unit costs will start to _____ and the _____ curve will shift _____. Long-run equilibrium will (slowly) be restored at _____ output and _____ price level.

   c. Beginning with output equal to potential, suppose there is a large and sudden increase in the price of electricity. This is a(n) _____ shock to the Canadian economy, which will result in the

_____ curve shifting _____ and the opening of a(n) _____ gap. If wages are downwardly sticky the economy's _____ mechanism could be very slow and the _____ will persist for a long time.

d. Beginning with output equal to potential, suppose there is a large and sudden decrease in the price of electricity. This is a(n) _____ shock to the Canadian economy, which will result in the _____ curve shifting _____ and the opening of a(n) _____ gap. Unit costs will start to _____ and the _____ curve will shift _____, restoring equilibrium at _____ output and _____ price level.

4. Fill in the blanks to make the following statements correct.

a. In the long run, total output is determined only by _____. In the long run, aggregate demand determines the _____.

b. Permanent increases in real GDP are possible only if _____ is increasing.

c. Suppose illiteracy in Canada were eliminated, and the school dropout rate were reduced to zero. The effect would be a permanent _____ in productivity and a(n) _____ in potential output.

d. A reduction in corporate income tax is likely to make _____ more attractive and thus shift the _____ curve to the right. The result is a(n) _____ in the short-run level of real GDP. In the long run, the greater rate of _____ by firms will lead to a greater rate of growth of _____.

5. The following diagram shows two economies, A and B. Each are in short-run equilibrium at point E, where the AD and AS curves intersect.

a. Explain why in Economy A wages and other factor prices will begin to rise, and why this will increase firms' unit costs.

b. Following your answer in part (a), show the effect on the AS curve. Explain what happens to real GDP and the price level.

c. Explain why in Economy B wages and other factor prices will begin to fall, and why this will decrease firms' unit costs.

d. Following your answer in part (c), show the effect on the AS curve. Explain what happens to real GDP and the price level.

6. The table shows several possible situations for the economy in terms of output gaps and the rate of change of wages. Real GDP is measured in billions of dollars. Assume that potential output is $800 billion.

Situation	Real GDP	Output Gap	Rate of Wage Change	Shift of AS Curve (+/0/−)
A	775	—	−2.0 %	—
B	785	—	−1.2 %	—
C	795	—	−0.2 %	—
D	800	—	0.0 %	—
E	805	—	1.0 %	—
F	815	—	2.4 %	—
G	825	—	4.0 %	—
H	835	—	5.8 %	—

a. Compute the output gap $(Y - Y^*)$ for each situation and fill in the table.

b. Explain why wages rise when output is greater than potential but fall when output is less than potential.

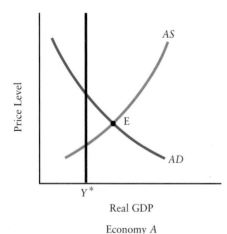

Economy A

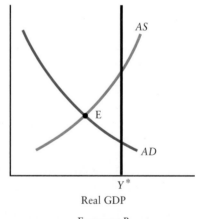

Economy B

c. For each situation, explain whether the economy's *AS* curve is shifting up, shifting down, or is stationary. Fill in the table.

d. Plot the Phillips curve on a scale diagram for this economy. (See *Extensions in Theory 24-1* for a review of the Phillips curve.)

7. Consider an economy that is in equilibrium with output equal to Y^*. There is then a significant reduction in the world's demand for this country's goods.

a. Illustrate the initial equilibrium in a diagram.

b. What kind of shock occurred—aggregate demand or aggregate supply? Show the effects of the shock in your diagram.

c. Explain the process by which the economy will adjust back toward Y^* in the long run. Show this in your diagram.

d. Explain why policymakers may want to use a fiscal expansion to restore output back to Y^* rather than wait for the process you described in part (c). What role does downward wage stickiness play in the policymakers' thinking?

8. Consider an economy that is in equilibrium with output equal to Y^*. There is then a significant reduction in the world price of an important raw material, such as iron ore.

a. Illustrate the initial equilibrium in a diagram.

b. What kind of shock occurred—aggregate demand or aggregate supply? Show the effects of the shock in your diagram.

c. Explain the process by which the economy will adjust back toward Y^* in the long run. Show this in your diagram.

d. Is there a strong case for using a fiscal contraction to return output to Y^*? Explain why or why not.

9. We explained in the chapter how shocks—demand or supply—tend to lead to cyclical fluctuations in real GDP and the price level. The following diagram shows the time paths of real GDP and the price level for an economy that begins at $Y=Y^*$ and is then subjected to a shock that shifts the *AD* curve to the right. We define t^* as the time the shock hits the economy; we define t^{**} to be the time when the economy has adjusted fully and is back in long-run equilibrium.

a. Draw the same types of diagrams for a negative *AD* shock. How does t^{**} for this shock compare to t^{**} for the positive *AD* shock? Explain the shapes of the curves.

b. Draw the same types of diagrams for a positive *AS* shock. Explain the shapes of the curves.

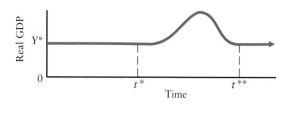

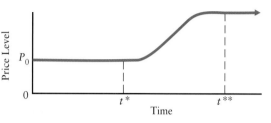

c. Draw the same types of diagrams for a negative *AS* shock. How does t^{**} for this shock compare to t^{**} for the positive *AS* or *AD* shock?

10. In our discussion of fiscal stabilization policy, we explained how income taxes and transfers affected the size of the multiplier. The accompanying diagrams show the initial equilibrium of two hypothetical economies

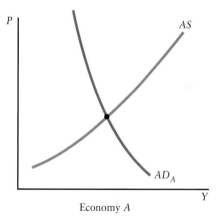

Economy A

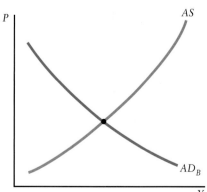

Economy B

that are each about to experience a $10 billion increase in autonomous net exports. Economy A has high (net) tax rates whereas Economy B has low (net) tax rates. Both economies have the same *AS* curve.

a. Explain why Economy A has a lower simple multiplier than Economy B.

b. Explain why the lower simple multiplier in Economy A results in a steeper *AD* curve.

c. Illustrate the shifts in the *AD* curves that result from the increases in net exports. (Hint: you may want to review at this point the relationship between the *AD* curve and the *AE* curve, which we discussed in Chapter 23.)

11. The following diagram shows the *AD*, *AS*, and Y^* curves for an economy. Suppose the economy begins at point *A*. Then the government increases its level of purchases (*G*).

a. Describe the short-run effects of this fiscal expansion. *[handwritten: Price goes up]*

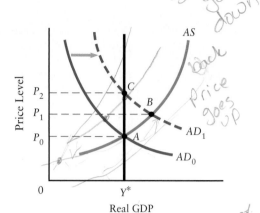

[handwritten: supply goes down, back, price goes up]

[handwritten: Supply goes down or price goes]

b. Describe the adjustment process, and the new long-run equilibrium for the economy.

c. Explain how the *composition* of real GDP has changed from the initial to the new long-run equilibrium.

[handwritten: still operating at y but with a higher price]*

DISCUSSION QUESTIONS

1. Discuss the following two statements in terms of short-run versus long-run outcomes.

a. "Starting from potential output, an increase in government spending can produce more output and employment at the cost of a once-and-for-all rise in the price level."

b. "Increased government spending can never lead to a permanent increase in output."

2. Politicians are sometimes accused of adopting policies that bring "short-term gain at the cost of long-term pain," whereas statesmen offer "short-term pain to buy long-term gain." What policies that shift aggregate demand or aggregate supply curves might come under one or the other of these descriptions?

3. If downward flexibility of money wages would allow the automatic adjustment mechanism to eliminate recessionary gaps quickly, why do workers usually resist wage cuts during times of economic slump?

4. Which of the following would be automatic stabilizers?

a. Employment-insurance payments

b. Cost-of-living escalators in government contracts and pensions

c. Income taxes

d. Free university tuition for unemployed workers after six months of unemployment, provided that they are under 30 years old and have had five or more years of full-time work experience since high school

5. During 1998 and 1999, the Canadian economy was experiencing a sufficiently high rate of growth of real GDP that many economists predicted an increase in inflation. Yet inflation declined slightly. At the same time, world commodity prices continued their decline that began in mid-1997. Explain the behaviour of the Canadian economy—high growth and falling inflation—in terms of aggregate demand and aggregate supply curves. What role, if any, is played by the falling commodity prices? What role is played by the U.S. economy, which at this point was experiencing very strong growth?

6. In 2003, United States President George W. Bush announced a budget proposal to reduce income taxes. He argued that this policy would provide the necessary stimulus to the U.S. economy, which was growing very slowly at the time.

a. Does a reduction in personal income taxes produce a demand-side or a supply-side stimulus to the economy? Explain.

b. Discuss the likely time frame for each possible effect on the U.S. economy. Why did many economic commentators at the time argue that the proposal did not address the *immediate* needs of the U.S. economy?

CHAPTER 25

The Difference Between Short-Run and Long-Run Macroeconomics

LEARNING OBJECTIVES

1. Explain why economists think differently about short-run and long-run changes in macroeconomic variables.

2. Explain why any change in GDP can be decomposed into changes in: factor supply, the utilization rate of factors, and productivity.

3. Show that short-run changes in GDP are mostly caused by changes in factor utilization, whereas long-run changes in GDP are mostly caused by changes in factor supplies and productivity.

4. Recognize that macroeconomic policies will only have a long-run effect on output if they influence factor supplies or productivity.

In Chapters 21, 22, and 23, we developed a model of the economy in the short run—a period of time over which technology and factor supplies are fixed, and wages and other factor prices are constant. In Chapter 24, we saw how the economy evolves, through a process of factor-price adjustment, from its short-run equilibrium to its long-run equilibrium. In the long run, wages and other factor prices have adjusted fully to excess demands or supplies that developed in the short run in response to inflationary or recessionary output gaps. We also saw in Chapter 24 that the level of potential output, Y^*, acts as an "anchor" for the economy. Aggregate demand or supply shocks can lead to short-run deviations of real GDP from Y^*, but the economy's adjustment process ensures that real GDP returns to Y^* in the long run. In the next chapter, we will examine why Y^* grows over periods of many years—a process that we call *long-run economic growth*.

In this chapter, we focus on the distinction between the short run and the long run in macroeconomics, ignoring the details of the adjustment process that gets the economy from one "run" to another. This distinction makes the study of macroeconomics more challenging but, at the same time, more interesting. The distinction becomes especially important when policymakers try to evaluate the desirability of various policies. Different economists will sometimes use different time frames for the evaluation of any given policy. For example, one economist may say that a fiscal expansion is desirable because it will provide stimulus to an economy with unemployment and excess productive capacity; another economist may oppose the policy on the grounds that it will have negative effects on the economy's long-run growth. These two views may be entirely consistent with one another (as we saw at the end of the previous chapter), but the observer is left confused because it is not clear in the debate whether the discussion is about the short run or the long run.

In this chapter, we seek to clarify the distinction between short-run GDP fluctuations and long-run GDP growth. With this distinction firmly in place, we will be ready for the detailed discussion of long-run economic growth in the next chapter.

Practise with Study Guide Chapter 25, Exercise 2.

25.1 **Two Examples**

We begin with two examples of the difference between short-run and long-run macro-economic relationships.

Inflation and Interest Rates in Canada

In the early 1990s, Canada's central bank (the Bank of Canada) embarked on a policy designed to reduce the rate of inflation. For reasons that we will see in detail in Chapters 28 and 29, the Bank's policy was controversial and when his term expired the governor, John Crow, was replaced by his senior deputy governor, Gordon Thiessen. Though Thiessen was committed to following Crow's policy of reducing inflation, he was equally committed to explaining the policy to an often-skeptical public. As we will see, the explanation relies crucially on making the distinction between short-run and long-run macroeconomic relationships.

In April of 1995, Gordon Thiessen was interviewed on CBC Radio. Thiessen was asked about the Bank's policy of reducing inflation, from about 6 percent a few years earlier, and maintaining it since then between 1 percent and 3 percent annually. Thiessen argued that the high nominal interest rates of the past were caused mostly by high inflation. The main reason for this connection between inflation and nominal interest rates is that inflation erodes the value of money. Lenders need to be compensated for the inflation-induced fall in the real value of their money between the time they lend it and the time that they are repaid. This can only be done by charging a nominal interest rate high enough to cover the effects of inflation. Thus, higher inflation pushes up interest rates; lower inflation pushes them down.

At this point, the interviewer had no problem with Thiessen's line of argument, as he easily recalled the time back in 1981 when inflation was at an all-time high of 12 percent and mortgage rates at Canada's banks were an astounding 20 percent! In contrast, by 1995, the rate of inflation was down to just over 2 percent and mortgage rates were only 8 percent. So periods of high inflation did indeed appear to coincide with periods of high interest rates.

Thiessen then started the next part of his argument. He stated that in order to reduce the rate of inflation the Bank of Canada had to reduce the growth rate of the money supply. This action, he admitted, would tighten up credit-market conditions and push up interest rates. Understandably confused at this point, the interviewer asked the inevitable question: How can a policy that raises interest rates be a necessary part of a policy designed to *reduce* both inflation and interest rates?

Thiessen understood the apparent contradiction, but was ready with his answer. He stressed that the key to answering the question is to understand the different short-run and long-run effects of monetary policy. In the short run, a policy by the Bank of Canada to reduce the growth rate of money will make credit more scarce (as we will see in detail in Chapter 28). This greater scarcity of credit causes both nominal and real interest rates to rise. Firms will reduce their investment in new factories, machines, and warehouses, and households will purchase fewer big-ticket items, such as cars, ski vacations, and furniture. Such reductions in expenditure will lead, through the multiplier process that we have already seen, to a reduction in national output. But as firms scale back their production and real GDP falls, workers get laid off and the unemployment rate increases—the economy enters a recession. In short, the Bank of Canada's contractionary monetary policy shifts the *AD* curve to the left and generates a reduction in GDP. When we examine the detailed workings of monetary policy in later chapters, we will see that a monetary policy designed to reduce inflation is usually effective precisely because *it creates a recession.*

So much for the short-run effects of the Bank's policy. Interest rates rise and the economy slows down. How does this reduce the inflation rate? As we saw in Chapter 24, the excess supply of labour that is a key part of the unemployment and recession puts downward pressure on wages. In other words, wages start to increase at a slower rate than before, and maybe even begin to fall. As wage growth declines the pressure on prices to rise also declines. That is, the rate of inflation falls. As inflation falls, and the rate of erosion of money's value falls with it, nominal interest rates will also fall. Thus, as Gordon Thiessen said in the interview, "the best way to get low interest rates is to get low inflation."

The details of monetary policy will be discussed in Chapters 28 and 29, and this argument will be repeated in considerable detail. At that time, we will more clearly see the difference between the short-run and long-run effects of monetary policy. Economists have a special term to reflect this difference. In the long run, economists say that *money is neutral*—meaning that changes in the money supply have no long-run effect on *real* variables such as GDP, employment, and investment but do have an effect on *nominal* variables such as the price level or the rate of inflation. This long-run neutrality of money is another way of stating that changes in the money supply do not change the level of potential output, Y^*. In the short run, however, economists say that *money is not neutral* because changes in the money supply affect real variables. In other words, monetary policy shifts the *AD* curve and generates short-run changes in real GDP. Understanding this difference is crucial to understanding most debates about monetary policy.

Saving and Growth in Japan

By early in 2004, the Japanese economy had been growing slowly, if at all, for over a decade. Japan's economy was stagnant. Many economists argued that an important part of the solution to Japan's economic malaise was for its firms and consumers to spend more. One problem with Japan, they argued, was that its firms and consumers saved "too much." On the other hand, many of these same economists acknowledged that Japan's remarkable economic success in the forty years following the Second World War—high growth rates of real GDP and low unemployment—was to a significant extent due to its high saving rate. But if "too much" saving is an important reason for Japan's recent economic slump, how can high saving be the reason for Japan's economic success over four decades? How can both of these views be correct?

Once again, the key to understanding this apparent contradiction is to recognize that the short-run effect of saving is different from its long-run effect. We saw this distinction in Chapter 24 when we discussed the "paradox of thrift," but it is worth repeating. In the short run, an increase in households' desire to save, perhaps caused by some uncertainty about future economic events, implies a reduction in expenditure. Uncertainty leads firms to spend less on investment goods; households spend less on all sorts of consumer goods. This reduction in expenditure leads, through the usual multiplier process, to a reduction in output. Increased saving in the short run, therefore, can be one reason why an economy such as Japan's enters an economic slump.

The high private saving rate in Japan is one reason that the Japanese economic recovery in the late 1990s was so slow.

But if an increase in firms' and households' saving can cause a recession, how can a high saving rate also explain Japan's many years of healthy economic growth? The answer is that in the long run, over periods of several years or decades, greater saving leads to a larger pool of financial capital. This larger pool of available funds drives down the price of credit—the interest rate—and makes firms' investment projects more profitable. More investment in factories, machines, and warehouses leads to a higher level of potential output, and it is to this higher level of potential output that the economy converges in the long run. This long-run relationship between saving, investment, and growth explains the striking correlation that we will see in the next chapter—countries with high long-run investment rates tend to be countries with high rates of long-run per capita GDP growth.

Economists have special terminology to describe this difference between the short run and the long run. Economists say that national income in the short run is *demand determined*, meaning that increases in demand will lead to increases in output. Thus, an increase in the desire to save, which is a reduction in the desire to spend, leads to less total spending and a reduction in national income. Even though aggregate supply (*AS*) shocks also affect output in the short run (as we saw in Chapters 23 and 24), the term *demand determined* reflects the fact that the position of the aggregate demand (*AD*) curve is important for determining the level of real GDP. In the long run, however, economists say that national income is *supply determined*, meaning that long-run increases in output will be possible only if the level of potential output increases; the position of the *AD* curve has no effect on real GDP in the long run. Increases in potential output require either more factors of production (like labour and capital) or technological change that improves productivity.

A Need to Think Differently

The two examples above suggest that a complete understanding of macroeconomics requires an understanding of both the short run and the long run. Such an understanding, in turn, requires us to think differently about short-run and long-run behaviour. It is one thing to say that macroeconomic variables behave differently over the short run than over the long run; it is quite another to understand *why* this is the case.

In this chapter, we emphasize the distinction between viewing short-run changes in GDP as deviations of output from potential, and long-run changes in GDP as changes in the level of potential output. We introduce a simple method of GDP accounting that clarifies this distinction, and also shows us the various sources of short-run and long-run changes in GDP.

25.2 Accounting for Changes in GDP

The simplest illustration of the distinction between short-run and long-run changes in economic activity is the behaviour of real GDP over time, as shown in Figure 25-1. The figure shows the path of Canadian real GDP and potential GDP, beginning from 1975. Actual GDP is measured by Statistics Canada. Potential GDP, as you may recall from Chapter 19, is the level of output that the economy produces when all factors of production are being utilized at their "normal" rates. But Statistics Canada can't tell us the value of potential GDP because it is not an observed variable—it must be estimated.

The value of potential GDP is estimated by combining three pieces of information: the amounts of available factors of production (like the labour force and the capital stock); an estimate of these factors' "normal" rates of utilization; and an estimate of the factors' productivity.

Figure 25-1 shows two different types of changes in GDP. First, some changes involve departures of actual GDP from potential GDP. For example, notice that actual GDP is equal to potential GDP at point B in 1980. As the Canadian economy then entered a major recession, actual GDP dropped below potential GDP to point C in 1982. An economic recovery then took place, taking actual GDP back to potential GDP at point D in 1986. Such changes in GDP are what economists call short-run changes in GDP—they involve primarily the opening and then closing of an output gap.

The second type of change in GDP involves changes in potential GDP, with little or no change in the output gap. For example, the change in actual GDP from point A in 1976 to point E in 1990 represents entirely a change in potential GDP. We know this because the output gap in both years is zero (that is, in both 1976 and 1990 GDP is equal to potential GDP). Such changes in GDP are what economists call long-run changes in GDP—they involve a change in potential GDP, with little or no change in the output gap.

FIGURE 25-1   Actual and Potential GDP in Canada, 1975–2002

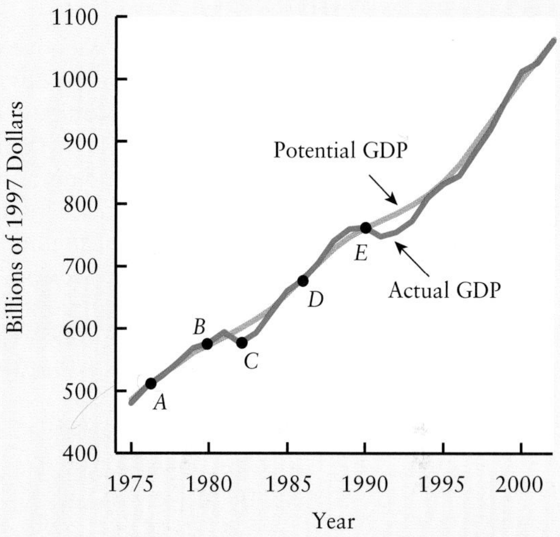

Long-run changes in GDP are reflected by changes in the level of potential GDP. Short-run changes in GDP are shown mostly by changes in the output gap.

(*Source:* Actual GDP: Statistics Canada CANSIM database, Series V3862685. Potential GDP: *Bank of Canada Review,* Spring 2003.)

When studying long-run trends in GDP, economists focus on the change in potential output. When studying short-run fluctuations, economists focus on the change in the output gap.

Practise with Study Guide Chapter 25, Exercise 1.

Figure 25-1 may make us wonder whether short-run changes in GDP have a different cause than long-run changes. After all, as we now know from previous chapters, output is determined in the short run by the *AD* and *AS* curves, but in the long run only by the level of *Y**. To explore the different causes of changes in GDP, we turn to a very simple accounting framework that applies to *all* changes in GDP.

GDP Accounting: The Basic Principle

Suppose we could break down any change in GDP into its component parts. By understanding how each component changes, we can then gain some insights into how short-run changes differ from long-run changes.

To break up GDP into the parts we want to study, we do the following obvious but useful things. First, we write

$$GDP = GDP$$

This is obviously true! Next, we multiply the right-hand side of the equation by F/F, where F is the economy's total available stock of factors. This gives

$$GDP = F \times (GDP/F)$$

Next, we multiply the right-hand side by F_E/F_E, where F_E is the number of the economy's factors that are employed. This gives

$$GDP = F \times (F_E/F) \times (GDP/F_E) \tag{25-1}$$

It may seem like we have done nothing useful since we have simply twice multiplied the right-hand side of an obviously true equation by one. But, in fact, Equation 25-1 is very useful when thinking about the different sources of change in GDP.

First, however, note that Equation 25-1 is written as if we could add together units of labour and land and capital to get a meaningful number for the economy's "available factors." This is not actually possible since different factors are measured in different units. For example, we can't add together six workers and five machines to get a total of 11 factors. In the next section, we will focus on a single factor to avoid this problem. For now, however, our point is simplified by thinking about the economy's total available factors, F, and the number of those factors that are employed, F_E.

To make the discussion less cumbersome, let's name the three components of Equation 25-1.

1. F is the economy's *factor supply;* it is the total amount of all factors of production that the economy currently possesses.

2. F_E/F is the *factor utilization rate*; it is the fraction of the total supply of factors that is actually used or employed at any time.

3. GDP/F_E is a simple measure of *productivity* because it shows the amount of output (GDP) per unit of input employed (F_E).

Note that Equation 25-1 does nothing more than separate any change in GDP into a change in one or more of the three components, F, F_E/F, or GDP/F_E. For example, Canadian GDP increased dramatically in the fifty years between 1950 and 2000. Also, Canadian GDP increased by a few percentage points from 2000 to 2002. In both cases, the increase in GDP was only possible because one or more of three things happened—either the factor supply (F) increased, the factor utilization rate (F_E/F) increased, or the level of productivity (GDP/F_E) increased.

Any change in GDP can be decomposed into a change in factor supply, a change in factor utilization, and a change in productivity.

The usefulness of this accounting exercise becomes clear when we recognize that two of these components, factor supply and productivity, typically change most over long periods of time whereas the third component, factor utilization, changes mostly only over shorter periods. This points us toward a better understanding of the difference between short-run and long-run changes in GDP. We discuss each component in turn.

The Long Run: Factor Supply

There are two main factors of production—labour and capital—that make up the economy's factor supply.

Labour.   The economy's supply of labour can increase for two main reasons. First, population can increase. An increase in population can be caused, in turn, either by greater immigration, an increase in birth rates, or a decrease in the mortality rate. The second way to increase the economy's supply of labour is to increase the fraction of the population that chooses to seek employment. This fraction is called the *labour-force participation rate*. In Canada, the labour-force participation rate is currently about

66 percent. It has increased steadily from the 1960s, due mostly to the increase in the participation rate of married women and the coming-of-age of the baby-boom generation.

No matter how the economy's supply of labour increases, the important point for our purposes is that such changes are mostly *long-run changes*. Population growth, through whatever means, is a very gradual process. Changes in labour-force participation also tend to be gradual. As a result, the economy's supply of labour does not usually change significantly from year to year. Over a period of many years, however, the increase in the supply of labour can be very substantial.

Capital.   The economy's supply of physical capital—machines, factories, and warehouses—increases for one reason. Firms that choose to purchase or build such investment goods today are accumulating physical capital that will be used to produce output in the future. Thus, today's flow of investment expenditure adds to the economy's stock of physical capital.

As is the case for labour, the economy's stock of physical capital changes only very gradually. This is not to be confused with the very dramatic swings in investment that are often observed over the course of the business cycle. The difference is that investment is the *flow* that contributes to the *stock* of capital. But the economy's capital stock is so large compared to the annual flow of investment expenditure that even dramatic swings in the annual level of investment generate almost imperceptible changes in the stock of capital.

Changes in the economy's supply of labour and capital occur only gradually, but over periods of many years the growth is considerable. As a result, changes in factor supply are important for explaining long-run changes in output, but relatively unimportant for explaining short-run changes.

The Long Run: Productivity

The economy's level of productivity is a measure of the amount of output that is produced with a given level of input. In practice, there are several possible measures of productivity, each one measuring something slightly different. Although there is more than one measure of productivity, Equation 25-1 uses the concept of output per employed factor, GDP/F_E. An increase in productivity is called *productivity growth*. Productivity growth is an important source of long-term increases in per capita income and thus in rising living standards.

The economy's level of productivity changes only slowly over time. For example, the average rate of productivity growth in Canada over the past few decades has been about 1.5 percent per year. Such low growth rates do not lead to significant changes in GDP or living standards over short periods of time, but can generate huge improvements in living conditions over many years. For example, you might not notice a 2 percent increase in your income from one year to the next, but you would surely notice the doubling that this annual growth rate would produce if it were sustained over 35 years. [31]

The economy's level of productivity changes only gradually from year to year, but grows substantially over periods of many years. As a result, productivity growth is very important for explaining long-run changes in output, but less important for explaining short-run changes.

The Short Run: Factor Utilization

In Chapters 21 to 23 we examined in detail the behaviour of the economy in the short run. Here we review some of these now-familiar concepts but express them in a way that helps us to understand our central equation decomposing the changes in real GDP.

The factor utilization rate is the last remaining component from our equation. Recall that it is simply the fraction of the total supply of factors that is employed. An immediate question comes to mind: Why would firms ever use fewer factors than are available to them? The answer has to do with how firms respond to changes in the demand for their product. When a firm's sales start dropping off, it must make a choice. It can continue producing at the current rate and let its inventories build up. Or it can reduce its rate of production. For a firm that is interested in maximizing profits, there is a limit to the amount of costly inventories it will be prepared to accumulate. Eventually, a reduction in demand for its product leads the firm to reduce its output and, in turn, reduce its employment of factors. Workers are laid off and equipment and other physical capital is used less intensively.

Similarly, a firm that is faced with a sudden increase in demand for its product has two alternatives. It can continue with its previous rate of production and satisfy the increased demand by letting its inventories run down. Or it can increase its rate of production by hiring more available workers and machines. Since profit-maximizing firms do not want to miss an opportunity to make a profitable sale, as would happen if the stockpile of inventories gets fully depleted, eventually the increase in demand leads them to increase production and hire more factors. Extra workers are hired, existing workers work overtime, and machines and other physical capital are used more intensively.

These responses by firms to changes in demand are only the firms' short-run responses. A low factor utilization rate describes *excess supply* in the factor markets. As we saw in Chapter 24, such a situation of excess supply typically causes downward pressure on wages and other factor prices. This reduction of factor prices, in turn, reduces firms' costs, shifts the *AS* curve downward, and puts downward pressure on product prices. Similarly, in the case of the increase in demand, the situation of a high factor utilization rate describes *excess demand* in factor markets. Such excess demand causes upward pressure on wages and other factor prices. As factor prices rise, firms' costs increase, the *AS* curve shifts upward, and there is upward pressure on the price level. As we saw in Chapter 24, this process of factor-price adjustment in response to output gaps continues until output returns to potential, at which point all factors of production are being used at their "normal" rates of utilization.

The factor utilization rate fluctuates in response to short-run changes in output caused by aggregate demand or aggregate supply shocks. Over time, however, excess supply or excess demand for factors causes an adjustment in factor prices that brings the factor utilization rate back to its "normal" level.

What do we mean by a "normal" factor utilization rate? In Chapter 19 we briefly discussed the idea of the *natural rate of unemployment*. This "natural" or "normal" rate of unemployment is the rate of unemployment against which we compare the actual unemployment rate to judge whether the labour market has excess supply or excess demand. That is, if unemployment is above the natural rate, there is an excess supply of labour; if unemployment is below the natural rate, there is an excess demand for labour. For physical capital, the utilization rate is called the *capacity utilization rate* because the amount of physical capital largely determines the productive *capacity* of a given plant or factory. As with labour, so too is there a "natural" or "normal" capacity utilization rate for capital.

Changes in the factor utilization rate are important for explaining short-run changes in GDP. But after factor prices have fully adjusted, GDP returns to Y^* and the factor utilization rate returns to its "normal" level. As a result, changes in the factor utilization rate are not important for explaining long-run changes in GDP.

GDP Accounting: An Application

We made some strong statements in the previous section regarding short-run versus long-run changes in various economic variables. Are these statements supported by the evidence? In this section, we apply the accounting concept contained in Equation 25-1 to Canadian GDP data to illustrate the basic arguments. Unfortunately, we cannot use *exactly* the same equation because, as we noted then, it is not possible to add units of labour together with units of physical capital. Using exactly the same intuition as earlier, however, we can express the GDP accounting equation in terms of a single factor of production—labour. Letting L be the labour force and E be the level of employment, the new equation is:[1]

$$GDP = L \times (E/L) \times (GDP/E) \qquad (25\text{-}2)$$

The basic interpretation of Equation 25-2 is the same as for Equation 25-1, except now the discussion relates only to labour. The labour force (L) is the supply of labour. The employment rate (E/L) is the fraction of the labour force actually employed (which is equal to one minus the unemployment rate). And the measure of productivity—in this case, labour productivity—is GDP/E.

Figure 25-2 shows the behaviour of these three components for Canada beginning in 1960. Each variable is expressed as an index number, with the value in 1960 set equal to 100. Expressing each variable in this way makes it easy to see each variable's percentage change over the four decades. The first panel in the figure shows the growth of the Canadian labour force. From 1960 to 2002, the index number increased from 100 to 261, an increase of 161 percent. It is clear from the graph that any short-run fluctuations in the Canadian labour force are dwarfed in importance by the long-run upward trend.

Now look at the third panel, showing the growth of Canadian labour productivity. The level of GDP per person employed, expressed as an index number, increases from 100 in 1960 to 179 in 2002, an increase of 79 percent. Like the labour force, the level of labour productivity has its short-run fluctuations, but it is clear that the overriding change—the upward trend—takes place over many years.

Finally, consider the middle panel, showing the Canadian employment rate—the utilization rate of labour. Compared to the other two variables graphed in Figure 25-2, the employment rate shows much more short-run volatility and much less long-run change. The employment rate (expressed as an index number) falls slightly from 100 in 1960 to 98 in 2002, a long-run decrease of only 2 percent. There is very little change over the long run, but considerable changes are occurring over shorter periods of time.

Summing Up

To summarize, we can decompose *any* change in GDP into changes in factor supply, the factor utilization rate, and productivity. But these three components typically contribute to GDP changes over different spans of time. In particular, factor supply and productivity typically change only gradually and hence are important for explaining long-run changes in GDP, but are not usually helpful in explaining short-run changes in GDP. In contrast, the factor utilization rate is quite volatile over short periods of time

---

[1] We get this equation by beginning with GDP = GDP. We then multiply the right-hand side by E/E and then by L/L.

FIGURE 25-2   Three Sources of Changes in GDP

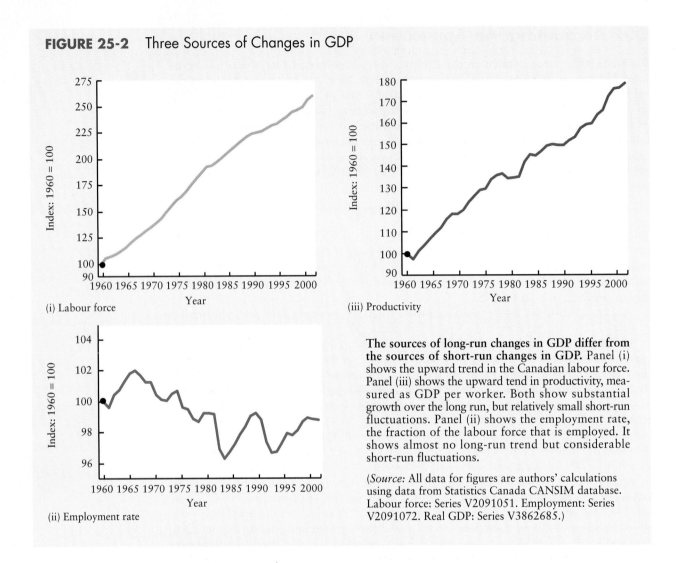

(i) Labour force

(iii) Productivity

(ii) Employment rate

The sources of long-run changes in GDP differ from the sources of short-run changes in GDP. Panel (i) shows the upward trend in the Canadian labour force. Panel (iii) shows the upward tend in productivity, measured as GDP per worker. Both show substantial growth over the long run, but relatively small short-run fluctuations. Panel (ii) shows the employment rate, the fraction of the labour force that is employed. It shows almost no long-run trend but considerable short-run fluctuations.

(*Source:* All data for figures are authors' calculations using data from Statistics Canada CANSIM database. Labour force: Series V2091051. Employment: Series V2091072. Real GDP: Series V3862685.)

but returns to its normal level over several years. Thus, changes in the factor utilization rate are important for explaining short-run changes in GDP but are not of central importance for explaining long-run changes.

25.3 **Policy Implications**

Economists think differently about short-run and long-run macroeconomic relationships. When thinking about short-run fluctuations, economists focus on understanding why actual GDP deviates from potential GDP. As we have seen in previous chapters, such changes in real GDP are caused by aggregate demand and aggregate supply shocks. When thinking about long-run changes in GDP, however, economists focus on understanding why potential GDP changes over time. As we said above, such long-run growth has its source in the growth of factor supplies and productivity. Thus, in understanding long-run growth, economists focus on what causes factor supplies and productivity to change.

When studying short-run fluctuations, economists focus on the deviations of actual output from potential. When studying long-run changes, economists focus on changes in potential output.

Through our development of the macro model in the previous four chapters, we have a good understanding of what causes the *AD* and *AS* curves to shift, and thus a good understanding of the causes of short-run fluctuations in real GDP. Our picture of the short run will be more complete after we discuss monetary policy and interest rates in Chapters 27 and 28, and exchange rates and international trade in Chapter 35.

What we have not yet done, however, is to discuss in detail why potential output grows substantially over long periods of time, thereby improving average living standards from one generation to the next. In the next chapter we explore the issue of long-run economic growth, focusing on the importance of capital accumulation and technological change.

Before we do that, however, it is worth returning to a point that we raised at the beginning of this chapter—that the distinction between the short run and the long run has an important implication for the role and desirability of various macroeconomic policies.

We have discussed in this chapter how changes in demand may cause actual GDP to depart from potential GDP. For example, firms may feel optimistic about the future and increase their investment expenditure, thereby increasing the overall level of demand. Or the government may increase its purchases of goods and services, thus adding to demand. Or foreigners may decide to increase their demand for Canadian goods, thus adding to the overall demand for goods produced by Canadian firms. All of these changes would increase the overall level of demand in the economy and, in the short run, would lead actual GDP to rise above potential GDP. Conversely, any decrease in the demand for goods would, in the short run, cause actual GDP to fall below potential GDP.

In the long run, however, the economy has an adjustment mechanism that tends to return the factor utilization rate to its "normal" level. As we saw in Chapter 24, when actual GDP is above potential GDP, there is an excess demand for factors. This causes factor prices to rise and thereby eliminates the excess demand, bringing actual GDP back to potential. Conversely, when actual GDP is less than potential GDP, there is an excess supply of factors. This causes factor prices to fall and eliminates the excess supply, thereby bringing actual GDP back to potential.

This adjustment process that brings the economy back to the level of potential output in the long run implies a stark result regarding the effects of macroeconomic policy:

Fiscal and monetary policies affect the short-run level of GDP because they alter the level of demand, and thus the position of the *AD* curve. But unless they are able to affect the level of *potential* output, Y^*, they will have no long-run effect on GDP.

Looking Ahead

The discussion in this chapter has focused on one topic—the difference between the short run and the long run in macroeconomics. We have shown that short-run movements in GDP are mostly accounted for by changes in the factor utilization rate, whereas long-run changes in GDP are mostly accounted for by changes in factor supplies and productivity. This difference forces economists to think differently about macroeconomic relationships that exist over a few months as compared to those that exist over several years.

In the previous four chapters we examined in detail the behaviour of the economy in the short run, and the adjustment process that brings the economy from a short-run equilibrium to a long-run equilibrium. We are now ready to take the next step and examine the causes of long-run economic growth.

SUMMARY

25.1 Two Examples

LO 1

- Macroeconomic variables behave differently over the short run than over the long run. One example: a monetary policy designed to reduce inflation and nominal interest rates in the long run requires an *increase* in interest rates in the short run. Another example: an increase in households' or firms' saving rates will reduce the level of output in the short run, but it will increase output in the long run.

- In the short run, there is some adjustment of output and employment, but little adjustment of wages and prices. In the long run, full adjustment of wages and prices takes place.

25.2 Accounting for Changes in GDP

LO 2 3

- All changes in GDP can be accounted for by changes in one or more of the following three variables:
  1. supply of factors
  2. factor utilization rates
  3. factor productivity
- Long-run changes in GDP are caused mostly by changes in factor supplies and factor productivity; the utilization rate of factors does not change significantly over the long run.
- Short-run changes in GDP are caused mostly by changes in the factor utilization rate; factor supplies and productivity have relatively minor short-run fluctuations.

25.3 Policy Implications

LO 4

- When studying short-run fluctuations, economists focus on changes in the output gap and ignore changes in potential output. When studying long-run fluctuations, economists focus on changes in potential output and ignore changes in the output gap.

- Fiscal and monetary policies affect GDP in the short run because they affect the level of demand, and thus the position of the *AD* curve. Unless they are able to affect the level of *potential* output, they will have no long-run effect on GDP.

KEY CONCEPTS

Short-run fluctuations
Long-run trends

Changes in the output gap versus changes in potential output
Accounting for changes in GDP

Factor supplies
Factor utilization rates
Productivity

STUDY EXERCISES

1. Fill in the blanks to make the following statements correct.

   a. Short-run changes in real GDP are caused by _____ and _____ shocks, with little or no change in _____. In the short run, _____ prices and the level of _____ are assumed to be constant.

   b. Long-run trends in GDP involve changes in _____ output. Short-run fluctuations in GDP involve changes in the _____ gap with little or no change in _____.

   c. Any change in GDP is caused by changes in at least one of the following three component parts: _____, _____, and _____.

   d. Long-run changes in GDP are caused mainly by changes in _____ and _____. Short-run changes in GDP are caused mainly by changes in _____.

   e. The economy's adjustment mechanism returns the _____ rate to its "normal" level in the long run.

   f. Fiscal and monetary policies alter the level of output in the short run by causing the _____ curve to shift. There will be a long-run effect on output only if _____ changes.

2. Consider the data below for a hypothetical country.

Year	Real GDP (billions of constant dollars)	Labour Force (millions of people)	Employment (millions of people)
1960	100	1.5	1.4
1965	130	1.6	1.45
1970	175	1.75	1.55
1975	250	1.95	1.65
1980	230	2.15	1.85
1985	265	2.40	2.0
1990	300	2.70	2.2
1995	340	3.0	2.8
2000	375	3.3	3.05

   a. Using the definitions in the chapter, compute the employment rate and the level of productivity (measured as GDP per worker) for each year.

   b. For each 5-year period, compute the percentage change in the labour force, the employment rate, and the level of productivity. Compute the same three things over the entire 40-year period.

   c. Compute the percentage change in real GDP over each 5-year period. Do it also for the entire 40-year period.

   d. Based on Equation 25-2, it can be shown that the percentage change in real GDP is approximately equal to the percentage change in the labour force *plus* the percentage change in the employment rate *plus* the percentage change in the level of productivity. Compare the sum of your answers from part (b) with your answers from part (c). Are they close?

   e. For each 5-year period, what fraction of the percentage change in GDP is accounted for by the change in the employment rate?

   f. Over the entire 40-year period, what fraction of the percentage change in GDP is accounted for by the change in the employment rate?

3. Go to Statistics Canada's website (www.statcan.ca) and look for data on capacity utilization rates in Canadian industries. The capacity utilization rate is the fraction of the capital stock that is utilized or employed. How has this variable changed over the past several decades? Contrast the short-run versus the long-run movements.

4. At the beginning of the chapter we discussed the short-run and long-run effects of an increase in desired saving (as applied to Japan's economy). Based on what you learned in Chapter 24 regarding the economy's adjustment process, use the *AD/AS* model to:

   a. Show the short-run effects of an increase in desired saving (assuming that the economy is initially in a long-run equilibrium with $Y = Y^*$).

   b. Describe the adjustment process that brings the economy to its new long-run equilibrium.

   c. Compare the initial and the new long-run equilibrium. What is the long-run effect of the increase in desired saving?

DISCUSSION QUESTIONS

1. Figure 25-1 shows the path of actual GDP as well as the path of potential GDP. The chapter mentioned that the economy has an adjustment mechanism that brings actual GDP back to potential.

   a. Describe this adjustment process, and how it relates to the concept of market-clearing.

   b. If, following the implementation of some policy, actual GDP eventually returns to potential GDP, does this mean that policy can have no long-run effect on GDP?

Long-Run Economic Growth

The Centre for the Study of Living Standards is an Ottawa-based research institute that studies the determinants of economic growth. Visit its website at www.csls.ca.

Most economists agree that economic growth is the single most powerful engine for generating long-term increases in living standards. What happens to our material living standards over time depends largely on the growth in real GDP in relation to the growth in population—that is, it depends on the growth of real per capita GDP. Growth in real per capita GDP does not necessarily make *everybody* in Canada better off. But it does mean that the *average* standard of living is higher.

What determines the long-run growth rate of per capita GDP in Canada? Is this something that is beyond our control, or are there some government policies that can stimulate economic growth? If there are, what are the costs of such policies, and are the benefits worth the costs?

In this chapter we examine this important issue of economic growth, beginning with some basic concepts and then moving on to explore the costs and benefits of growth. In the remainder of the chapter we consider various theories of economic growth, an area in which much new research is being done. Finally, we examine the idea that there may be *limits to growth* imposed by pollution and resource exhaustion.

26.1 The Nature of Economic Growth

Over the past century, most residents of most countries in the industrialized world have become materially better off decade by decade. Children have typically been substantially better off than their parents were at the same age. Beginning in the mid 1970s, however, the engine of growth faltered. Though growth rates slowed in recent years, they have returned to the levels experienced before the unusually high-growth period following the Second World War. Many economists agree that these lower, but still positive, growth rates may be more sustainable on a long-term basis.

Over the long run, the main cause of rising real GDP is an increasing level of potential output, which, in turn, is due to increases in the supplies of labour and capital, and increases in productivity. As we saw in earlier chapters, government policy can be successful in eliminating a recessionary gap and thereby causing a once-and-for-all increase in real GDP of a few percentage points. But such policy actions cannot raise living standards cumulatively. Substantial and *ongoing* increases in average living standards come from continuing increases in the level of potential output—this is what economists call **economic growth**.

economic growth
Ongoing increases in the level of real potential GDP.

Because economic growth can go on over very long periods, it is a much more powerful method of raising living standards than the removal of recessionary gaps.

Table 26-1 illustrates the cumulative effect of what appear to be very small differences in growth rates. Notice that if one country grows faster than another, the gap in their respective living standards will widen progressively. If, for example, Canada and France start from the same level of income but Canada grows at 3 percent per year while France grows at 2 percent per year, Canada's income will be twice France's in 72 years. [31] You may not think that it matters much whether the economy grows at 2 percent or 3 percent per year, but your children and grandchildren certainly will.

We now examine in more detail the benefits and costs of economic growth.

TABLE 26-1 The Cumulative Effect of Economic Growth

	Annual Growth Rate				
Year	1%	2%	3%	5%	7%
0	100	100	100	100	100
10	111	122	135	165	201
30	135	182	246	448	817
50	165	272	448	1 218	3 312
70	201	406	817	3 312	13 429
100	272	739	2 009	14 841	109 660

Small differences in growth rates make enormous differences in levels of potential GDP over a few decades. Let potential GDP be 100 in year 0. At a growth rate of 3 percent per year, it will be 135 in 10 years, 448 after 50 years, and over 2000 in a century. Notice the difference between 2 percent and 3 percent growth—even small differences in growth rates make big differences in future income levels.

Benefits of Economic Growth

The benefits of economic growth—in particular, increases in income—may appear obvious. It certainly appears that way to the pro-growth author of the open letter in *Applying Economic Concepts 26-1*. But it is important to distinguish between the increases in average living standards that economic growth brings more-or-less automatically, and the reduction in poverty that economic growth makes possible but may still require active policy to make a reality.

Rising Average Living Standards

Economic growth is a powerful means of improving average living standards. A family that is earning $35 000 today can expect an income of about $42 600 within 10 years (in constant dollars) if it experiences a 2 percent annual growth rate in its income. If it has a 4 percent growth rate, its income in 10 years will be $51 800.

A family often finds that an increase in its income can lead to changes in the pattern of its consumption—extra money buys important amenities of life and also allows more saving for the future. Similarly, economic growth that raises average income may change the whole society's consumption patterns. Not only do expanding markets in a rapidly growing country make it profitable to produce more cars, but the government is led to construct more highways and to provide more recreational areas for its affluent and mobile population.

APPLYING ECONOMIC CONCEPTS 26-1

An Open Letter from a Supporter of the "Growth Is Good" School

Dear Ordinary Citizen:

You live in the world's first civilization that is devoted principally to satisfying *your* needs rather than those of a privileged minority. Past civilizations have always been based on leisure and high consumption for a tiny upper class, a reasonable living standard for a small middle class, and hard work with little more than subsistence consumption for the great mass of people.

The continuing Industrial Revolution is based on mass-produced goods for you, the ordinary citizen. It ushered in a period of sustained economic growth that has dramatically raised consumption standards of ordinary citizens. Consider a few examples: travel, live and recorded music, art, good food, universal literacy, inexpensive books, and a genuine chance to be educated. Most important, there is leisure to provide time and energy to enjoy these and thousands of other products of the modern developed economy.

Would any ordinary family seriously prefer to go back to the world of 150 or 500 years ago in its same *relative* social and economic position? Surely the answer is no. However, for those with incomes in the top 1 or 2 percent of the income distribution, economic growth has destroyed much of their privileged consumption position. They must now vie with the masses when they visit the world's beauty spots and be annoyed, while lounging on the terrace of a palatial mansion, by the sound of charter flights carrying ordinary people to inexpensive holidays in faraway places. Many of the rich complain bitterly

about the loss of exclusive rights to luxury consumption, and it is not surprising that they find their intellectual apologists.

Whether they know it or not, the antigrowth economists are not the social revolutionaries they think they are. They say that growth has produced pollution and wasteful consumption of all kinds of frivolous products that add nothing to human happiness. However, the democratic solution to pollution is not to go back to the time when so few people consumed luxuries that pollution was trivial but rather to learn to control the pollution that mass consumption tends to create.

It is only through further growth that the average citizen can enjoy consumption standards (of travel, culture, medical and health care, and so on) now available only to people in the top 25 percent of the income distribution—which includes the intellectuals who earn large royalties from the books they write in which they denounce growth. If you think that extra income confers little real benefit, just ask those in the top 25 percent to trade incomes with average citizens.

Ordinary citizens, do not be deceived by disguised elitist doctrines. Remember that the very rich and the elite have much to gain by stopping growth and even more by rolling it back, but you have everything to gain by letting it go forward.

Onward!

A. N. Optimist

Another example of how economic growth can improve living standards involves environmental protection. In developing countries, most of the resources of the country are devoted to providing basic requirements of life such as food, shelter, and clothing. These countries typically do not have the "luxury" of being concerned about environmental degradation. Some may consider this a short-sighted view, but the fact is that the concerns associated with hunger *today* are much more urgent than the concerns associated with *future* environmental problems. In contrast, richer countries are wealthy enough that they can easily afford to provide the basic requirements of life and devote significant resources to environmental protection. Economic growth provides the higher incomes that often lead to a demand for a cleaner environment, thus leading to higher average living standards that are not directly captured by measures of per capita GDP.

Alleviation of Poverty

Not everyone benefits equally from growth. Many of the poorest are not even in the labour force and hence are unlikely to share in the higher wages that, along with profits, are the primary means by which the gains from growth are distributed. For this reason, even in a growing economy, redistribution policies will be needed if poverty is to be reduced.

A rapid growth rate makes the alleviation of poverty easier politically. If existing income is to be redistributed, someone's standard of living will actually have to be lowered. However, when there is economic growth and when the *increment* in income is redistributed (through active government policy), it is possible to reduce income inequalities without actually having to lower anyone's income. It is much easier for a rapidly growing economy to be generous toward its less fortunate citizens—or neighbours—than it is for a static economy.

Costs of Economic Growth

Applying Economic Concepts 26-2 contains an open letter from an anti-growth advocate who argues that we are caught up in a never-ending search for "more," and as a result are losing sight of the real values that guided our ancestors. You may or may not accept this particular line of argument, but it is important to recognize that economic growth does have some real costs. Let's see what they are.

The Opportunity Cost of Economic Growth

In a world of scarcity, almost nothing is free. Growth requires heavy investment of resources in capital goods, as well as in activities such as education. Often these investments yield no immediate return in terms of goods and services for consumption; thus, they imply that sacrifices are being made by the current generation of consumers.

Practise with Study Guide Chapter 26, Exercise 3.

Economic growth, which promises more goods tomorrow, is achieved by consuming fewer goods today. For the economy as a whole, this sacrifice of current consumption is the primary cost of growth.

An example will suggest the importance of this cost. Suppose a hypothetical economy is operating at potential output and is experiencing growth in real GDP at the rate of 2 percent per year. Its citizens consume 85 percent of the GDP and invest 15 percent. But suppose that if they immediately decrease their consumption to 77 percent of GDP (and increase investment to 23 percent), they will produce more capital and thus shift at once to a 3 percent growth rate. The new rate can be maintained as long as they keep saving and investing 23 percent of real GDP. Should they do it?

Figure 26-1 illustrates the choice in terms of time paths of consumption. With the assumed figures, it takes 10 years for the actual amount of consumption to catch up to what it would have been had no reallocation been made. In the intervening 10 years, a good deal of consumption is lost, and the cumulative losses in consumption must be made up before society can really be said to have broken even. It takes an *additional* nine years before total consumption over the whole period is as large as it would have been if the economy had remained on the 2 percent path. [32] Over a longer period, however, the payoff from the growth policy becomes enormous. Thirty years on, real GDP in the more rapidly growing economy is 21 percent higher than in the slower-growing economy. After fifty years, it is 48 percent higher.

APPLYING ECONOMIC CONCEPTS 26-2

An Open Letter from a Supporter of the "Growth Is Bad" School

Dear Ordinary Citizen:

You live in a world that is being despoiled by a mindless search for ever-higher levels of material consumption at the cost of all other values. Once upon a time, men and women knew how to enjoy creative work and to derive satisfaction from simple activities. Today, the ordinary worker is a mindless cog in an assembly line that turns out more and more goods that the advertisers must work overtime to persuade the worker to consume.

Statisticians count the increasing flow of material output as a triumph of modern civilization. You wake to the hum of your air conditioner, watch the shopping channel while you dress for work, brew your chemically treated decaffeinated coffee, and eat your bread baked from superrefined flour; you climb into your car to sit in vast traffic jams on exhaust-polluted highways.

Television commercials tell you that by consuming more, you are happier, but happiness lies not in increasing consumption but in increasing the ratio of *satisfaction of wants* to *total wants*. Because the more you consume, the more the advertisers persuade you that you want to consume, you are almost certainly less happy than the average citizen in a small town in 1900, whom we can visualize sitting on the family porch, sipping lemonade, and enjoying the antics of the children as they jump rope using pieces of old clothesline.

Today, the landscape is dotted with endless factories that produce the plastic trivia of modern society. They drown you in a cloud of noise, air, and water pollution. The countryside is despoiled by strip mines, petroleum refineries, acid rain, and dangerous nuclear power plants, producing energy that is devoured insatiably by modern factories and motor vehicles. Worse, our precious heritage of natural resources is being rapidly depleted.

Now is the time to stop this madness. We must end this mad rush to produce more and more output, reduce pollution, conserve our natural resources, and seek justice through a more equitable distribution of existing total income.

Many years ago, Thomas Malthus taught us that if we do not limit population voluntarily, nature will do it for us in a cruel and savage manner. Today, the same is true of output: If we do not halt its growth voluntarily, the halt will be imposed on us by a disastrous increase in pollution and a rapid exhaustion of natural resources.

Citizens, awake! Shake off the worship of growth, learn to enjoy the bounty that is yours already, and reject the endless, self-defeating search for increased happiness through ever-increasing consumption.

Upward!

I. Realvalues

If economic growth just means more of the truly "unnecessary" things in life, is it really that worthwhile?

Social Costs of Economic Growth

A growing economy is also a changing economy. Part of growth is accounted for by existing firms expanding and producing more output, hiring more workers, and using more equipment and intermediate goods. But another part of growth is accounted for by existing firms being overtaken and made obsolete by new firms, by old products being made obsolete by new products, and by existing skills being made obsolete by new skills.

FIGURE 26-1   The Opportunity Cost of Economic Growth

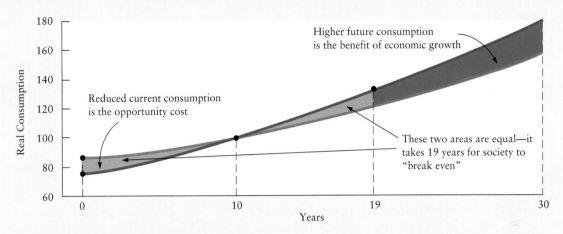

Transferring resources from consumption to investment lowers current consumption but raises future consumption. The example assumes that GDP in year 0 is 100 and that growth of 2 percent per year is possible when consumption equals 85 percent of GDP. The consumption path in this case is shown by the red line, starting at 85 and growing by 2 percent per year. It is further assumed that to achieve a 3 percent growth rate, consumption must fall to 77 percent of GDP. A shift from the red path to the blue path in year 0 decreases consumption for 10 years but increases it thereafter. By year 19 the gains in consumption have made up for the losses from the first 10 years. After 30 years, consumption is 21 percent higher than it would be on the original (red) path.

The process of economic growth renders some machines obsolete and also leaves the skills of some workers partly obsolete.

No matter how well-trained workers are at age 25, in another 25 years many will find that their skills are at least partly obsolete. A high growth rate usually requires rapid adjustments, which can cause much upset and misery to some of the people affected by it.

It is often argued that costs of this kind are a small price to pay for the great benefits that growth can bring. Even if this is true in the aggregate, these personal costs are borne very unevenly. Indeed, many of the people for whom growth is most costly (in terms of lost jobs or lowered incomes) share least in the fruits that growth brings.

Sources of Economic Growth

We know that output is produced by combining the services of various factors of production such as labour, capital, and land. Furthermore, we know that the current state of our knowledge—or technology—limits our ability to get more and more output from a given set of factors of production. This brings us to an important idea that we emphasized in Chapter 25: We can account for growth in real GDP by increases in the *amount* of available factors of production, increases in the *quality* of the available factors of production, or increases in the state of *technology* that determines how much output we are able to get from a given set of factors of production.

The four fundamental determinants of growth of total output are:

1. *Growth in the labour force.* This may be caused by growth in population or by increases in the fraction of the population that chooses to participate in the labour force.

human capital   The set of skills workers acquire through formal education and on-the-job-training.

2. *Growth in human capital.* **Human capital** is the term economists use to refer to the set of skills that workers have. Human capital can increase through either formal education or on-the-job training. Human capital can be thought of as the *quality* of the labour force, but due to its importance we will treat it as a separate factor of production from labour.

3. *Growth in physical capital.* The stock of physical capital (such as factories, machines, transportation, and communications facilities) increases only through the process of investment. We include here improvements in the *quality* of the physical capital.

4. *Technological improvement.* This may be brought about by innovation that introduces new products, new ways of producing existing products, and new forms of business organization.

The various theories of economic growth that we explore in the remainder of this chapter can be viewed as theories of these different sources of growth. For example, some theories emphasize the role of increases in physical capital in explaining growth; others emphasize the role of increases in human capital; still others emphasize the importance of technological improvements. But all theories of economic growth take as a starting point these four fundamental determinants of growth.

26.2 **Established Theories of Economic Growth**

In this section we discuss some of the theories of economic growth that have been used by economists for many years. Despite the appearance of some quite different theories in recent years (which we will see later), these established theories remain relevant and contain important insights about the growth process. Learning these established theories provides a solid basis for examining the newer theories in the next section. We begin with a detailed study of the relationship between saving, investment, and economic growth. We then examine the precise predictions of what economists call the Neoclassical growth theory. For simplicity, we assume in the following discussion that the economy is closed—there is no trade in goods or assets with the rest of the world.

Investment, Saving, and Growth

In previous chapters we saw how changes in desired investment or desired saving led to shifts in the aggregate demand (*AD*) curve and to changes in the short-run equilibrium level of real GDP. The discussion in this chapter focuses instead on the level of output in the long run, after wages and other factor prices have fully adjusted and output has returned to potential output, Y^*.

The theory of economic growth is a long-run theory. It concentrates on the growth of potential output over long periods of time, not on short-run fluctuations of output around potential.

Though we will focus on the long-run behaviour of the economy, we can still use some of the insights we developed in the short-run version of our macro model. Remember back to Chapter 21 when we were building the simplest short-run macro model. The equilibrium level of real GDP was such that desired saving equals desired investment. Recall also that in that chapter we took the real interest rate as given, or exogenous. Thus, taking the real interest rate as given, the condition that saving equals investment determined the equilibrium level of real GDP.

The logic of that equilibrium condition is just as true in the long run. In the long run, with real GDP equal to Y^*, we can use the saving/investment equilibrium condition by turning it "on its head." That is, we can take the level of output as given (at Y^*) and use the condition that desired saving equals desired investment to determine the equilibrium real interest rate. This long-run perspective of our model will tell us a great deal about the relationship between saving, investment, and economic growth.

The Long-Run Connection Between Saving and Investment

Recall that national saving is the sum of private saving and public (government) saving. Desired private saving is the difference between disposable income and desired consumption. With real GDP equal to Y^* in the long run, desired private saving is equal to:

$$\text{Private saving} = Y^* - T - C$$

Public saving is equal to the combined budget surpluses of the federal, provincial, and municipal governments:

$$\text{Public saving} = T - G$$

National saving is therefore equal to:

$$\text{National saving} = NS = Y^* - T - C + (T - G)$$

$$\Rightarrow NS = Y^* - C - G$$

In other words, for a given level of output in the long run, an increase in household consumption or government purchases must imply a reduction in national saving.[1]

Figure 26-2 shows the supply of national saving as a function of the real interest rate. We label the horizontal axis "Loanable Funds," which is measured in dollars. The real interest rate is shown on the vertical axis. The national saving (*NS*) curve is upward sloping because, as we first saw in Chapter 21, an increase in the interest rate leads households to reduce their current consumption, especially on big-ticket items and durable goods such as cars, furniture, and appliances that are often purchased on credit. Note also that the *NS* curve is quite steep, in keeping with empirical evidence suggesting that household consumption responds only modestly to changes in the real interest rate.

Figure 26-2 also shows a downward sloping investment demand curve, *I*. As we first saw in Chapter 21, all components of desired investment (plant and equipment, inventories, and residential investment) are negatively related to the real interest rate because investment is typically financed by borrowing and the real interest rate reflects the cost of borrowing.

---

[1] It appears in our *NS* equation that changes in taxes have no effect on the level of national saving, but this is misleading. Changes in *T* may affect national saving through an *indirect* effect on *C*. For example, as we saw at the end of Chapter 24, a reduction in taxes is likely to lead to an increase in consumption spending and therefore to a reduction in national saving (for given values of Y^* and G).

FIGURE 26-2   The Long-Run Connection Between Saving and Investment

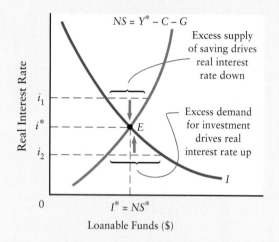

In the long run, the condition that desired national saving equals desired investment determines the equilibrium real interest rate. Investment demand by firms is negatively related to the real interest rate. The supply of national (private plus public) saving is positively related to the real interest rate, since increases in the interest rate lead to a decline in desired consumption (C). Notice that real GDP in this figure is held constant at Y^* since the analysis applies to the long run.

At point E the market for loanable funds clears and the real interest rate is i^*. At this real interest rate, the amount of investment is I^*, which equals the amount of national saving, NS^*.

Our long-run model of saving and investment is now complete. In the short-run model in Chapter 21, the economy is in equilibrium when desired saving equals desired investment. We have modified that setting in only two ways. First, we have added government. Second, and more important, since we are examining the economy in the long run, we are holding real GDP constant at Y^* and letting the equilibrium condition determine the real interest rate in the market for loanable funds.

In the long-run version of our macro model, with real GDP equal to Y^*, the equilibrium interest rate is determined where desired national saving equals desired investment.

In Figure 26-2, equilibrium in the market for loanable funds occurs at interest rate i^* where $NS = I$. Imagine what would happen if the real interest rate were above i^* at i_1. At this high interest rate, the amount of desired saving exceeds the amount of desired investment, and this excess supply of loanable funds pushes down the price of credit—the real interest rate. Conversely, if the interest rate is below i^* at i_2, the quantity of desired investment exceeds the quantity of desired saving, and this excess demand for loanable funds pushes up the real interest rate. Only at point E is the economy in equilibrium, with the real interest rate equal to i^* and desired investment equal to desired saving.

Let's now see how changes in desired saving or desired investment lead to changes in the real interest rate, and what these changes imply for the economy's long-run economic growth.

An Increase in the Supply of National Saving. Suppose the supply of national saving increases, so that the NS curve shifts to the right, as shown in part (i) of Figure 26-3. This increase in the supply of national saving could happen either because household consumption (C) falls or because government purchases (G) fall.[2] A decline in either C or G means that national saving rises *at any real interest rate* and so the NS curve shifts to the right.

The increase in the supply of national saving leads to an excess supply of loanable funds and to a decline in the real interest rate. As the interest rate falls, firms decide to undertake more investment projects and the economy moves from the initial equilibrium E_0 to the new equilibrium E_1. At the new equilibrium, more of the economy's resources are devoted to investment than before, and thus the country's capital stock is rising at a faster rate. The higher rate of investment therefore leads to a higher growth rate of potential output.

[2] We continue in this chapter with a simplifying assumption we made in Chapters 22 and 24—that governments spend on *current* goods and services but do not invest by acquiring physical assets.

FIGURE 26-3   Increases in Desired Investment and Desired National Saving

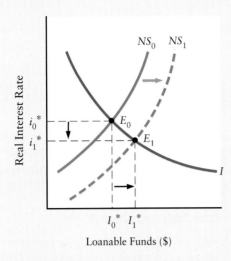

(i) Increase in the supply of saving

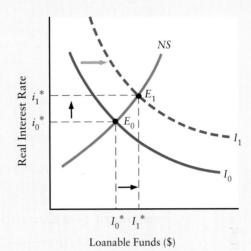

(ii) Increase in the demand for investment

Changes in the supply of national saving or the demand for investment will change the equilibrium real interest rate and the rate of growth of potential output. In part (i), the increase in the supply of national saving pushes down the real interest rate and encourages more investment. In part (ii), the increase in the demand for investment pushes up the real interest rate and encourages more saving. In both cases, there is an increase in the equilibrium amount of investment and the economy moves from E_0 to E_1; this higher rate of capital accumulation leads to an increase in the economy's long-run rate of growth.

In the long run, an increase in the supply of national saving reduces the real interest rate and encourages more investment. The higher rate of investment leads to a higher growth rate of potential output.

An Increase in Investment Demand.   Now suppose that firms' demand for investment increases so that the I curve shifts to the right, as shown in part (ii) of Figure 26-3. The increase in desired investment might be caused by technological improvements that increase the productivity of investment goods or by a government tax incentive aimed at encouraging investment. Whatever its cause, the increase in investment demand creates an excess demand for loanable funds and therefore leads to a rise in the real interest rate. The rise in the interest rate encourages households to reduce their current consumption and increase their desired saving. At the new equilibrium, E_1, both the real interest rate and the amount of investment are higher than at the initial equilibrium. The greater investment means faster growth in the economy's capital stock and therefore a higher rate of growth of potential output.

In the long run, an increase in the demand for investment pushes up the real interest rate and encourages more saving by households. The higher rate of saving (and investment) leads to a higher growth rate of potential output.

Summary. There is a close relationship between saving, investment, and long-run economic growth. We can see this relationship most clearly when studying the market for loanable funds. Let's summarize our results.

1. An increase in the supply of national saving will lead to a fall in the real interest rate and thus to an increase in the amount of investment. This is a shift of the *NS* curve and a movement along the *I* curve.

2. An increase in the demand for investment will lead to a rise in the real interest rate and thus to an increase in the amount of national saving. This is a shift of the *I* curve and a movement along the *NS* curve.

3. A shift in either the *NS* or the *I* curve will lead to a change in the equilibrium real interest rate and to a change in the amount of the economy's resources devoted to investment. An increase in the equilibrium amount of investment implies a greater growth rate of the capital stock and thus a higher growth rate of potential output.

Investment and Growth in Industrialized Countries

We said above that countries with high rates of investment are also countries with high rates of real GDP growth. To provide evidence in support of this claim, Figure 26-4 shows data from the most industrialized countries between 1970 and 1990. Each point in the figure corresponds to a single country and shows that country's annual average investment rate (as a percentage of GDP) plotted against the annual average growth rate in real per capita GDP. What is clear from the figure is a strong positive relationship between investment rates and growth rates, exactly as suggested by our discussion above.

FIGURE 26-4   Cross-Country Investment and Growth Rates

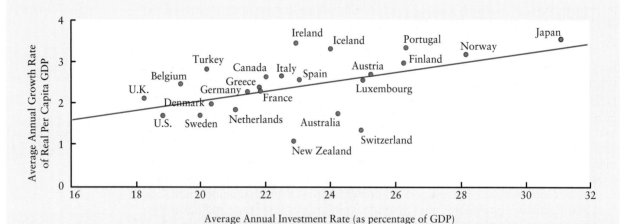

There is a strong positive relationship between a country's investment rate (as a percentage of GDP) and its growth rate of real per capita GDP. For each of the countries, the annual averages for investment rates and per capita GDP growth rates are computed between 1970 and 1990. Each point represents the average values of these variables for a single country over this 20-year period. The line is the "line of best fit" between the growth rates and the investment rates. Countries with high investment rates tend to be countries with high rates of economic growth.

(*Source:* International Monetary Fund.)

Neoclassical Growth Theory

Recall the four fundamental sources of economic growth that we discussed at the beginning of this section. Much of what is referred to as *Neoclassical growth theory* is based on the idea that these four forces of economic growth can be connected by what is called the **aggregate production function.** This is an expression for the relationship between the total amounts of labour (L) and physical capital (K) employed, the quality of labour's human capital (H), the state of technology (T), and the nation's total level of output (GDP). The aggregate production function can be expressed as:

$$GDP = F_T (L, K, H)$$

It is an *aggregate* production function because it relates the economy's *total* output to the *total* amount of the factors that are used to produce that output.[3] (Those who have studied microeconomics will recall that a micro production function, such as is discussed in Chapters 7 and 8, relates the output of *one firm* to the factors of production employed by *that firm*.)

The production function above—indicated by F_T—tells us how much GDP will be produced for given amounts of labour and physical capital employed, given levels of human capital and a given state of technology. Using the notation F_T is a simple way of indicating that the function relating L, K, and H to GDP depends on the state of technology. For a given state of technology (T), changes in either L, K, or H will lead to changes in GDP. Similarly, for given values of L, K, and H, changes in T will lead to changes in GDP. [33]

When discussing economic growth, we focus on the changes in potential output and ignore short-term fluctuations of output around potential. We therefore interpret GDP in the aggregate production function as potential output.

Properties of the Aggregate Production Function

The key aspects of the Neoclassical theory are that the aggregate production function displays *diminishing marginal returns* when either factor is increased on its own and *constant returns to scale* when all factors are increased together (and in the same proportion). To explain the meaning of these concepts more clearly, we will assume for simplicity that technology and human capital are held constant; we therefore focus on the effects of changes in K or L. This is an appropriate simplification when dealing with the Neoclassical theory since early versions of the theory focused on the importance of K and L; changes in technology and human capital played very minor roles.

1. Diminishing Marginal Returns.   To begin, suppose that the labour force grows while the stock of capital remains constant. More and more people go to work using a fixed quantity of capital. The amount that each new unit of input adds to total output is called its *marginal product.* The operation of the **law of diminishing marginal returns** tells us that the employment of additional units of labour will eventually add less to total output than the previous unit. In other words, each additional unit of labour will sooner

---

[3] Natural resources (including land, forests, mineral deposits, etc.) are also important inputs to the production process. We leave them out of this discussion only for simplicity.

aggregate production function
The relation between the total amount of each factor of production employed in the nation and the nation's total GDP.

Hong Kong is an example of an economy that has had very high rates of investment and also very high rates of real GDP growth.

Practise with Study Guide Chapter 26, Exercise 2.

In recent years, the World Bank has emphasized the role of "social capital" in economic growth. See: www.worldbank.org/poverty/scapital.

law of diminishing marginal returns
The hypothesis that if increasing quantities of a variable factor are applied to a given quantity of fixed factors, the marginal product of the variable factor will eventually decrease.

or later produce a diminishing marginal product. A simple production function is shown in Figure 26-5 and the law of diminishing marginal returns is illustrated.

The law of diminishing returns applies to any factor that is varied while the other factors are held constant. Hence, successive amounts of capital added to a fixed supply of labour will also eventually add less and less to GDP.

According to the law of diminishing marginal returns, whenever equal increases of one factor of production are combined with a constant amount of another factor, the increment to total production will eventually decline.

constant returns to scale A situation in which output increases in proportion to the change in all inputs as the scale of production is increased.

2. Constant Returns to Scale.   The other main property of the Neoclassical aggregate production function is that it displays **constant returns to scale.** If the amounts of labour and capital are both changed in equal proportion, total output will also change by that proportion. For example, if L and K both increase by 10 percent, then GDP will also increase by 10 percent. [34]

Economic Growth in the Neoclassical Model

Now that we understand the properties of the aggregate production function, we can examine the predictions of the Neoclassical growth theory. Recall the four fundamental sources of growth:

1. Growth in labour force
2. Growth in human capital
3. Growth in physical capital
4. Technological improvement

What does the Neoclassical theory predict will happen when each of these elements changes? In this section, we focus on the effects of labour-force growth and the accumulation of physical and human capital. In the next section, we focus on technological change.

1. Labour-Force Growth.   Over the long term, we can associate labour-force growth with population growth (although in the short term, the labour force can grow if participation rates rise even though the population remains constant). As more labour is used, more output will be produced. The law of diminishing marginal returns tells us that sooner or later, each additional unit of labour employed will cause smaller and smaller additions to GDP. Eventually, not only will the marginal product of labour be falling, but the average product will fall as well. Beyond that point, although economic growth continues in the sense that total output is growing, living standards are falling in the sense that average GDP *per person* is falling. If we are interested in growth in living standards, we are concerned with increasing real GDP per person.

In the Neoclassical growth model with diminishing marginal returns, increases in population lead to increases in GDP but an eventual decline in living standards.

2. Physical and Human Capital Accumulation.   Consider the accumulation of both physical and human capital. Growth in physical capital occurs whenever there is positive (net) investment in the economy. For example, if Canadian firms produce $100 billion of capital goods this year, and only $20 billion is for the replacement of old, worn-out equipment, then Canada's capital stock increases by $80 billion.

FIGURE 26-5   The Aggregate Production Function and Diminishing Marginal Returns

(1) Units of Labour	(2) Units of Output (GDP)	(3) Average Product of Labour (GDP/L)	(4) Marginal Product of Labour (ΔGDP/ΔL)
1	12.0	12.0	
			5.0
2	17.0	8.5	
			3.8
3	20.8	6.9	
			3.2
4	24.0	6.0	
			2.8
5	26.8	5.4	
			2.6
6	29.4	4.9	
			2.5
7	31.9	4.6	
			2.1
8	34.0	4.2	
			2.0
9	36.0	4.0	
			1.9
10	37.9	3.8	

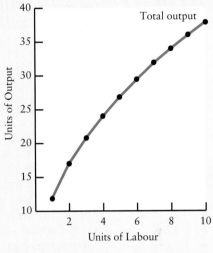

(i) Total output

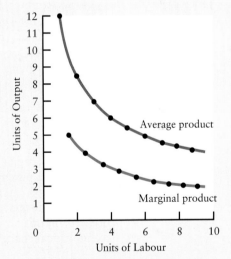

(ii) Marginal and average product of labour

With one input held constant, the marginal and average products of the variable factor eventually decline. We have assumed a hypothetical aggregate production function given by: GDP = 4 $\sqrt{KL}$; we have also assumed that K is constant and equal to 9. Column 2 shows total output as more of the variable factor, labour, is used with a fixed amount of capital. Total output is plotted in part (i) of the figure. Both the average product of labour and the marginal product of labour decline continuously. They are plotted in part (ii) of the figure.

How does human capital accumulate? Human capital has several aspects. One involves improvements in the health and longevity of the population. Of course, these are desired as ends in themselves, but they also have consequences for both the size and the productivity of the labour force. There is no doubt that improvements in the health of workers have increased productivity per worker-hour by cutting down on illness, accidents, and absenteeism. A second aspect of human capital concerns technical training—from learning to operate a machine to learning how to be a scientist. This training depends on the current state of knowledge, and advances in knowledge allow us not only to build more productive physical capital but also to create more effective human capital. Also, the longer a person has been educated, the more adaptable and, hence, the more productive in the long run that person is in the face of new and changing challenges.

The accumulation of capital—either physical or human—affects GDP in a manner similar to population growth. Diminishing marginal returns imply that, eventually, each successive unit of capital will add less to total output than each previous unit of capital.

There is, however, a major contrast with the case of labour-force growth because it is output *per person* that determines living standards, not output per unit of capital. Thus, as the amount of physical or human capital increases, living standards increase because output is rising while the population is constant. However, because the increases in capital are subject to diminishing marginal returns, successive additions to the economy's capital bring smaller and smaller increases in per capita output.

In the Neoclassical model, the law of diminishing marginal returns means that capital accumulation leads to smaller and smaller increases in per capita GDP.

3. Balanced Growth with Constant Technology.   Now consider what happens if labour and capital (both human and physical capital) grow at the same rate. This is what economists call "balanced" growth. In this case, the Neoclassical assumption of constant returns to scale means that GDP grows in proportion to the increases in inputs. For example, if capital and labour increase by 2 percent per year, then GDP also increases by 2 percent per year. As a result, per capita output (GDP/L) remains constant. Thus, balanced growth in labour and capital leads to growth in total GDP but unchanged per capita GDP.

This balanced growth is not, however, the kind of growth that concerns people interested in explaining rising living standards. Since increases in living standards are determined largely by increases in *per capita* output, it is clear that balanced growth is unable to explain *rising* living standards.

If capital and labour grow at the same rate, GDP will increase. But in the Neoclassical growth model with constant returns to scale, such balanced growth will not lead to improvements in living standards.

The Neoclassical growth theory predicts that growth in the labour force leads to declining per capita income, and capital accumulation leads to ever-diminishing growth rates of per capita income. Even increases in labour and capital together cannot explain increases in per capita income. What we observe in many countries around the world, however, is sustained growth in real per capita incomes. How does the Neoclassical theory explain this observation, if not through growth in labour or capital? The answer is technological change, to which we now turn.

The Importance of Technological Change

New knowledge and inventions can contribute markedly to the growth of potential output, even without capital accumulation or labour-force growth. To illustrate this point, suppose that the proportion of a society's resources devoted to the production of capital goods is just sufficient to replace capital as it wears out. If the old capital is merely replaced in the same form, the capital stock will be constant, and there will be no increase in the capacity to produce. However, if there is a growth of knowledge so that as old equipment wears out it is replaced by different and more productive equipment, then productive capacity will be growing.

embodied technical change Technical change that is intrinsic to the particular capital goods in use.

The increase in productive capacity created by installing new and better capital goods is called **embodied technical change**. This term reflects the idea that technological improvements are contained in the new capital goods. Thus, even if the *quantity* of capital may be unchanged, improvements in its *quality* lead to increases in the economy's productive capacity. Embodied technical change has been enormously important through history and continues to be important today. Consider how improvements in the quality of airplanes have revolutionized transportation over the past 50 years, or how improvements in the quality of electronics have revolutionized communications over the same period. Indeed, once you start thinking about embodied technical change, you see many examples of it around you on a daily basis.

Less obvious but nonetheless important are technical changes that are embodied in *human* capital. These are changes that result from a better-educated, more experienced labour force; better management practices and techniques; improved design, marketing, and organization of business activities; and feedback from user experience leading to product improvement.

Many innovations are embodied in either physical or human capital. These innovations cause continual changes in the techniques of production and in the nature of what is produced. Embodied technical change leads to increases in potential output.

Not all technological change is embodied in capital. Examples of *disembodied* technical change include the development of new managerial methods and the development of new materials and production processes; all are examples in which technological improvement allows for more output to be produced from the same capital and labour. However, such disembodied technological changes often get quickly embodied in capital as machines or skills are modified to incorporate the latest developments. Thus distinguishing precisely between embodied and disembodied technological change is often difficult.

We have been discussing the benefits of technological change in terms of raising overall living standards. Ever since the Industrial Revolution, however, some workers have feared the effects of technological change. Technological change, after all, is often responsible for workers losing their jobs as employers replace less efficient labour with more efficient equipment. *Lessons From History 26-1* examines the relationship between technological progress and changes in employment. The main lesson we learn is that technological change over the years has created far more jobs than it has destroyed.

Can We Measure Technological Change?

Technological change is obviously important. You need only look around you at the current products and production methods that did not exist a generation ago, or even 10 years ago, to realize how the advance of technology changes our lives. The development of the Internet is an obvious example of such technological advance. But *how much* does technology change? Unfortunately, technology is not something that is easily measured and so it is very difficult to know just how important it is to the process of economic growth.

In 1957, Robert Solow, an economist at MIT who was awarded the Nobel prize 30 years later for his research on economic growth, attempted to measure the amount of technical change in the United States. He devised a way to infer from the data (under some assumptions about the aggregate production function) how much of the observed growth in real GDP was due to the growth in labour and capital, and how much was due to technical change. His method led to the creation of what is now called the "Solow residual." The Solow residual is the amount of growth in GDP that cannot be accounted for by growth in the labour force or by growth in the capital stock. Since Solow was thinking about changes in GDP as having only three possible sources—changes in capital, changes in labour, and changes in technology—the "residual" was naturally interpreted as a measure of technical change.

LESSONS FROM HISTORY 26-1

Should Workers Be Afraid of Technological Change?

From time immemorial people have observed that technological change destroys particular jobs and have worried that it will destroy jobs in general. Should they worry?

Technological change *does* destroy particular jobs. When water wheels were used to automate the fulling of cloth in twelfth-century Europe, there were riots and protests among the fullers who lost their jobs. A century ago, 50 percent of the labour force in North America and Europe was required to produce the required food. Today, less than 5 percent of the labour force is needed in the high-income countries to feed all their citizens. In other words, out of every 100 jobs that existed in 1900, 50 were in agriculture and 45 of those were destroyed by technological progress over the course of the twentieth century.

Just as technological change destroys some jobs, it also creates many new jobs. The displaced agricultural workers did not join the ranks of the permanently unemployed—although some of the older ones may have, their children did not. Instead they, and their children, took jobs in manufacturing and service industries and helped to produce the mass of new goods and services—such as automobiles, refrigerators, computers, and foreign travel—that have raised living standards over the century.

Worries that technological change will cause general unemployment have been recorded for at least 250 years but, so far at least, there is no sign that those displaced by technological change (or their children) are being forced into the ranks of the permanently unemployed. Over all of recorded history, technological change has created more jobs than it has destroyed.

But how about today? Aren't there good reasons to be more afraid of technological change now than in the past? Modern technologies have two aspects that worry some observers. First, they tend to be *knowledge intensive.* A fairly high degree of literacy and numeracy, as well as familiarity with computers, is needed to work with many of these new technologies. Second, through the process of globalization, unskilled workers in advanced countries have come into competition with unskilled workers everywhere in the world. Both of these forces are decreasing the relative demand for unskilled workers in developed countries and may lead to falling relative wages for unskilled workers in countries like Canada. If labour markets are insufficiently flexible, this change in relative demand may also lead to some structural unemployment.

For these reasons, some people blame the high unemployment rates in Europe (and to a lesser extent, in Canada) on the new technologies. This is hard to reconcile, however, with the fact that the lowest unemployment rates in the industrialized countries are currently being recorded in the United States, the most technologically dynamic of all countries. This suggests that the cause of high European unemployment rates may be not enough technological change and too much government interference in labour markets rather than too much technological change.

See Chapter 26 of www.pearsoned.ca/ragan for an interesting discussion of why the computer revolution has not yet appeared in measurements of productivity growth: Jeremy Leonard, "Computers and Productivity in the Information Economy."

Today, economists do not view the Solow residual as a precise estimate of the amount of technical change. The main reason is that much technical change is known to be embodied in new physical and human capital. Thus, capital accumulation and technological change are inherently connected. For example, imagine a firm that replaces an old 386 PC with the latest Pentium PC. Each PC might be considered one unit of capital, but clearly the Pentium embodies new technology that is completely absent in the old 386. In this case, even though the firm's total capital stock hasn't changed, the process of replacing the old capital with new capital also increased the firm's level of technology. Because capital accumulation and technological advance are so closely linked, Solow's method, which views the two processes as distinct, cannot provide a reliable estimate of technical change. Due to the amount of new technology embodied in new capital equipment, the Solow residual is, at best, an underestimate of the true amount of technical change.

Despite these problems, Solow's method of "growth accounting" and the Solow residual are still widely used by economists in universities and government. The Solow residual often goes by another name—the rate of growth of *total factor productivity (TFP).*

Solow's method of growth accounting is sometimes used to decompose growth rates within a country and to compare these growth rates across countries. For an interesting application of his approach that compares growth in Hong Kong and Singapore, look for "A Growth Tale of Two Cities" in the *Additional Topics* section of this book's Companion Website.

http://www.pearsoned.ca/ragan

26.3 **New Growth Theories**

In recent years, economists have developed new theories of economic growth that go beyond the established theories based on diminishing marginal returns and exogenous technical change. Economic growth is an active area of research in which there is considerable debate over whether new theories are necessary, or whether the established theories do an adequate job of explaining the process of long-term economic growth.

In this section, we give a brief discussion of two strands of this new research—models that emphasize *endogenous technological change* and models based on *increasing marginal returns*.

Endogenous Technological Change

In the Neoclassical model, innovation increases the amount of output producible from a given level of factor inputs. But this innovation is itself unexplained. The Neoclassical model thus views technological change as *exogenous*. It has profound effects on economic variables but it is not itself influenced by economic causes. It just happens.

Yet research by many scholars has established that technological change is responsive to such economic signals as prices and profits; in other words, it is *endogenous* to the economic system. Though much of the earliest work on this issue was done in Europe, the most influential overall single study was by an American, Nathan Rosenberg, whose trailblazing 1982 book *Inside the Black Box: Technology and Economics* argued this case in great detail.

Technological change stems from research and development and from innovating activities that put the results of R&D into practice. These are costly and highly risky activities, undertaken largely by firms and usually in pursuit of profit. It is not surprising, therefore, that these activities respond to economic incentives. If the price of some particular input such as petroleum or skilled labour goes up, R&D and innovating activities will be directed to altering the production function to economize on these inputs. This process is not simply a substitution of less expensive inputs for more expensive ones within the confines of known technologies; rather, it is the *development of new technologies* in response to changes in relative prices.

There are several important implications of this new understanding that, to a great extent, growth is achieved through costly, risky, innovative activity that often occurs in response to economic signals.

Learning by Doing

The pioneering theorist of innovation, Joseph Schumpeter (1883–1950), developed a model in which innovation flowed in one direction, from a pure discovery "upstream," to more applied R&D, then to working machines, and finally to output "downstream."

In contrast, modern research shows that innovation involves a large amount of "learning by doing" at all of its stages. (We discuss this kind of learning in more detail in Chapter 33.) What is learned downstream then modifies what must be done upstream. The best innovation-managing systems encourage such "feedback" from the more applied steps to the purer researchers and from users to designers.

This interaction is illustrated, for example, by the differences that existed for many years between the Japanese automobile manufacturers and their North American competitors in the handling of new models. North American design was traditionally centralized: Design production teams developed the overall design and then instructed their production sections and asked for bids from parts manufacturers to produce according to specified blueprints. As a result, defects in the original design were often not discovered until production was underway, causing many costly delays and rejection of parts already supplied. In contrast, Japanese firms involved their design and production departments and their parts manufacturers in all stages of the design process. Parts manufacturers were not given specific blueprints for production; instead, they were given general specifications and asked to develop their own detailed designs. As they did so, they learned. They then fed information about the problems they were encountering back to the main designers while the general outlines of the new model were not yet finalized. As a result, the Japanese were able to design a new product faster, at less cost, and with far fewer problems than were the North American firms. In recent years, however, the North American automotive firms have adopted many of these Japanese design and production methods.

Knowledge Transfer

The *diffusion* of technological knowledge from those who have it to those who want it is not costless (as it was assumed to be in Schumpeter's model). Firms need research capacity just to adopt the technologies developed by others. Some of the knowledge needed to use a new technology can be learned only through experience by plant managers, technicians, and operators. We often tend to think that once a production process is developed, it can easily be copied by others. In practice, however, the diffusion of new technological knowledge is not so simple.

For example, some economists argue that most industrial technologies require technology-specific organizational skills that cannot be "embodied" in the machines themselves, instruction books, or blueprints. The needed knowledge is *tacit* in the sense that it cannot be taught through books and can only be acquired by experience—much like driving a car or flying an airplane. Acquiring tacit knowledge requires a deliberate process of building up new skills, work practices, knowledge, and experience.

The fact that diffusion is a costly and time-consuming business explains why new technologies take considerable time to diffuse, first through the economy of the originating country and then through the rest of the world. If diffusion were simple and virtually costless, the puzzle would be why technological knowledge and best industrial practices did not diffuse very quickly. As it is, decades can pass before a new technological process is diffused everywhere that it could be employed.

Market Structure and Innovation

Because it is highly risky, innovation is encouraged by strong rivalry among firms and discouraged by monopoly practices. Competition among three or four large firms often produces much innovation, but a single firm, especially if it serves a secure home market protected by trade barriers, seems much less inclined to innovate. The reduction in trade barriers over the past several decades and the increasing globalization of markets as a result of falling transportation and communication costs have increased international competition. Whereas one firm in a national market might have had substantial monopoly power three or four decades ago, today it is more likely to be in intense competition with firms based in other countries. This greater international competition may lead to more innovation.

Shocks and Innovation

One interesting consequence of endogenous technical change is that shocks that would be unambiguously adverse to an economy operating with fixed technology can sometimes provide a spur to innovation that proves a blessing in disguise. A sharp rise in the price of one input can raise costs and lower the value of output per person for some time. But it may lead to a wave of innovations that reduce the need for this expensive input and, as a side effect, greatly raise productivity. One example is the development of fuel-efficient automobiles following large increases in the world price of oil in the 1970s.

Sometimes individual firms will respond differently to the same economic signal. Sometimes those that respond by altering technology will do better than those that concentrate their efforts on substituting within the confines of known technology. For example, in *The Competitive Advantage of Nations,* Harvard economist Michael Porter tells the story of the consumer electronics industry, in which U.S. firms moved their operations abroad to avoid high, rigid labour costs. They continued to use their existing technology and went where labour costs were low enough to make that technology pay. Their Japanese competitors, however, stayed at home. They innovated away most of their labour costs and then built factories in the United States to replace the factories of U.S. firms that had gone abroad!

Increasing Marginal Returns to Investment

We saw earlier that Neoclassical theories of economic growth assume that investment is subject to diminishing marginal returns. New growth theories emphasize the possibility of *historical increasing returns to investment:* As investment in some new area, product, or production technology proceeds through time, each new increment of investment is more productive than previous increments. Economists have noted a number of sources of increasing marginal returns. These fall under the two general categories of *fixed costs* and *knowledge*.

Fixed Costs

There are three reasons why there may be an important fixed-cost component to the amount of investment undertaken in an industry or region.

1. Investment in the early stages of development of a country, province, or town may create new skills and attitudes in the workforce that are then available to all subsequent firms, whose costs are therefore lower than those encountered by the initial

firms. (For those who have studied microeconomics, the early firms are conferring a positive *externality* on those who follow them, as described in Chapter 16.)

2. Each new firm may find the environment more and more favourable to its investment because of the infrastructure that has been created by those who came before.

3. The first investment in a new product will encounter countless production problems that, once overcome, cause fewer problems to subsequent investors.

More generally, many investments require fixed costs, the advantages of which are then available to subsequent firms; hence, the investment costs for "followers" can be substantially less than the investment costs for "pioneers." In short, doing something really new is difficult, whereas making further variations on an accepted and developed new idea becomes progressively easier.

A computer is a private good because if I own it then you cannot also own it. But the knowledge required to build the computer is a public good. And knowledge, unlike traditional factors of production, is not necessarily subject to the law of diminishing returns.

Another important issue concerns the behaviour of customers. When a new product is developed, customers will often resist adopting it, both because they may be conservative and because they know that new products often experience "growing pains." Customers also need time to learn how best to use the new product—they need to do what is called "learning by using."

Slow acceptance of new products by customers is not necessarily irrational. When a sophisticated new product comes on the market, no one is sure if it will be a success, and the first customers to buy it take the risk that the product may subsequently turn out to be a failure. They also incur the costs of learning how to use it effectively. Many potential users take the not unreasonable attitude of letting others try a new product, following only after the product's success has been demonstrated. This makes the early stages of innovation especially costly and risky.

Successive increments of investment associated with an innovation often yield a range of increasing marginal returns as costs that are incurred in earlier investment expenditure provide publicly available knowledge and experience and as customer attitudes and abilities become more receptive to new products.

The implications of these ideas have been the subject of intense study ever since they were first included in modern growth models by Paul Romer of Stanford University.[4] Probably the most important contrast between these new theories and the Neoclassical theory concerns investment and income. In the Neoclassical model, diminishing marginal returns to capital imply a limit to the possible increase of per capita GDP. In the new models, investment alone can hold an economy on a "sustained growth path" in which per capita GDP increases without limit, provided that the investment embodies the results of continual advances in technological knowledge.

Knowledge

An even more fundamental aspect of the new growth theories is the shift from the economics of goods to the economics of *ideas*. Physical goods, such as factories and machines, exist in one place at one time. This has two consequences. First, when physical goods are used by someone, they cannot be used by someone else. Second, if a given labour force is provided with more and more physical objects to use in production, sooner or later diminishing marginal returns will be encountered.

---

[4] As with so many innovations, these new views have many historical antecedents, including a classic article in the 1960s by Nobel Prize winner Kenneth Arrow of Stanford University.

Ideas have different characteristics. Once someone develops ideas, they are available for use by everyone simultaneously. Ideas can be used by one person without reducing their use by others. For example, if one firm uses a truck, another firm cannot use it at the same time; but one firm's use of a revolutionary design for a new suspension system on a truck does not prevent other firms from using that design as well. Ideas are often not subject to the same use restrictions as goods. (For those that have studied microeconomics, some knowledge has aspects that make it a *public good,* as we discussed in Chapter 16.) Ideas are also not necessarily subject to diminishing marginal returns. As our knowledge increases, each increment of new knowledge does not inevitably add less to our productive ability than each previous increment.

New growth theories stress the importance of ideas in producing what is called *knowledge-driven growth.* New knowledge provides the input that allows investment to produce increasing rather than diminishing marginal returns. Because there are no practical limits to human knowledge, there need be no immediate boundaries to finding new ways to produce more output using less of all inputs.

Neoclassical growth theories gave economics the name "the dismal science" by emphasizing diminishing marginal returns under conditions of given technology. The new growth theories are more optimistic because they emphasize the unlimited potential of knowledge-driven technological change.

26.4 **Are There Limits to Growth?**

Many opponents of growth argue that sustained world growth is undesirable; some argue that it is impossible. The idea that economic growth is limited by nature is not new. In the early 1970s, a group called the "Club of Rome" published a book entitled *The Limits to Growth,* which focused on the limits to growth arising from the finite supply of natural resources. Extrapolating from the oil shortages caused by the OPEC cartel, the Club of Rome concluded that industrialized countries faced an imminent absolute limit to growth. Do such limits really exist? We discuss the two issues of resource exhaustion and pollution.

See the United Nations' website for international data on economic development: www.un.org. Click on "Economic and Social Development" and then go to "Statistics."

Resource Exhaustion

The years since the Second World War have seen a rapid acceleration in the consumption of the world's resources, particularly fossil fuels and basic minerals. World population has increased from under 2.5 billion to over 6 billion in that period; this increase alone has intensified the demand for the world's resources. Furthermore, as people attain higher incomes, they consume more resources. Thus, not only are there more people in the world, but many of those people are consuming increasing quantities of resources.

The resources available today could not possibly support all of the world's population at a standard of living equal to that of the average Canadian family—at least, not at the current level of technological development. Our current resources and our present capacity to cope with pollution and environmental degradation are insufficient to accomplish this rise in global living standards with present technology.

Most economists, however, agree that absolute limits to growth, based on the assumptions of constant technology and fixed resources, are not relevant. As emphasized by the new growth theories we discussed in the previous section, technology changes continually, as do the available stocks of resources. For example, 50 years ago, few would have thought that the world could produce enough food to feed its present population of 6 billion people, let alone the 10 billion at which the population is projected to stabilize sometime later this century. Yet significant advances in agricultural methods make this task now seem feasible. Further, while existing resources are being depleted, new ones are constantly being discovered or developed. One example is the development of the Athabaska Tar Sands in Alberta. In the early 1970s, this resource appeared to be far too expensive to develop and therefore an unlikely source of economical oil. Thirty-five years later, after considerable technological improvement, the Tar Sands are only a few years away from ranking among the world's largest reserves of economical petroleum. The general message is this:

Technology is constantly advancing, and many things that seemed impossible a generation ago will be commonplace a generation from now. Such technological advance makes any absolute limits to economic growth less likely.

Yet there is surely cause for some concern. Although many barriers can be overcome by technological advances, such achievements are not instantaneous and are certainly not automatic. There is a critical problem of timing: How soon can we discover and put into practice the knowledge required to solve the problems that are made ever more imminent by the growth in the population, the affluence of the rich nations, and the aspirations of the billions who now live in poverty? There is no guarantee that a whole generation will not be caught in transition between technologies, with enormous social and political consequences.

Pollution

A further problem is how to cope with pollution. Air, water, and soil are polluted by a variety of natural activities and, for billions of years, the environment has coped with these. The earth's natural processes had little trouble coping with the pollution generated by its 1 billion inhabitants in 1800. But the 6 billion people who now exist put such extreme demands on the earth's ecosystems that there are now legitimate concerns about "environmental sustainability." Smoke, sewage, chemical waste, hydrocarbon and greenhouse-gas emissions, spent nuclear fuel, and a host of other pollutants threaten to overwhelm the earth's natural regenerative processes.

Conscious management of pollution was unnecessary when the world's population was 1 billion people, but such management has now become a pressing matter.

Reducing the extent of environmental degradation, however, is different than advocating an "anti-growth" position. To put it differently, there is nothing inconsistent about an economy displaying *both* high rates of economic growth and active environmental protection. As students of microeconomics will recognize, an important part of a policy designed to reduce the extent of environmental degradation is to get polluters (firms or households) to face the full cost of their polluting activities—especially the external costs that their activities impose on society. This often involves levying some form of tax on polluters for every unit of pollution emitted. While such policies, if stringently enforced, will lead to output reductions in specific industries, they need not lead to reductions in the *overall* level of economic activity. And long-run economic growth is related to growth in the *overall* level of economic activity, not to the growth of specific industries.

Furthermore, many technological advances reduce the amount of pollution per unit of output, and also reduce the costs of dealing with whatever pollution remains. Rich, advanced economies such as Canada, the United States, and the European Union create less pollution per dollar of GDP and find it easier to bear the cost of pollution clean-up than do poorer, less technologically advanced economies.

Conclusion

The world faces many problems. Starvation and poverty are the common lot of citizens in many countries and are not unknown even in countries such as Canada and the United States, where average living standards are very high. Growth has raised the average citizens of advanced countries from poverty to plenty in the course of two centuries—a short time in terms of human history. Further growth is needed if people in developing countries are to escape material poverty, and further growth would help advanced countries to deal with many of their pressing economic problems.

Rising population and rising per capita consumption, however, put pressure on the world's natural ecosystems, especially through the many forms of pollution. Further growth must be *sustainable* growth, which must in turn be based on knowledge-driven technological change. Past experience suggests that new technologies will use less of all resources per unit of output. But if they are dramatically to reduce the demands placed on the earth's ecosystems, price and policy incentives will be needed to direct technological change in more "environmentally friendly" ways. Just as present technologies are much less polluting than the technologies of a century ago, the technologies of the future must be made much less polluting than today's.

There is no guarantee that the world will solve the problems of sustainable growth, but there is nothing in modern growth theory and existing evidence to suggest that such an achievement is impossible.

Many of the insights about the determinants of economic growth that we explored in this chapter apply also to economic growth in the developing countries. But the developing countries also have some unique economic and institutional challenges, some which have plagued them for many years. For a detailed discussion, look for "Challenges Facing the Developing Countries" in the *Additional Topics* section of this book's Companion Website.

http://www.pearsoned.ca/ragan

S U M M A R Y

26.1 **The Nature of Economic Growth** ⑩❶❷

- Sustained increases in real GDP are due mainly to economic growth, which continuously pushes the Y^* curve outward, thereby increasing potential output.
- Growth is frequently measured by using rates of change of potential real GDP per person. The cumulative effects of even small differences in growth rates become very large over periods of a decade or more.
- The most important benefit of growth lies in its contribution to the long-run struggle to raise living standards and to escape poverty. Growth also facilitates the redistribution of income among people.

- Growth, though often beneficial, is never costless. The opportunity cost of growth is the diversion of resources from current consumption to capital formation. For individuals who are left behind in a rapidly changing world, the costs are higher and more personal.
- There are four fundamental determinants of growth: increases in the labour force; increases in physical capital; increases in human capital; and improvements in technology.

26.2 **Established Theories of Economic Growth** ⑩❸

- The long-run relationship between saving, investment, and economic growth is most easily observed in the market for loanable funds, in which the interest rate is determined by the equality of desired investment and desired national saving.
- Increases in the supply of national saving will reduce the interest rate and encourage more investment by firms, thus increasing the rate of growth of potential output.
- Increases in the demand for investment will increase the interest rate and encourage an increase in household saving. The higher saving (and investment) in equilibrium leads to a higher growth rate of potential output.
- Neoclassical growth theory assumes an aggregate production function that displays diminishing marginal returns (when one factor is changed in isolation) and constant returns to scale (when all factors are changed in equal proportions).

- In a balanced growth path, the quantity of labour, the quantity of capital, and real GDP all increase at a constant rate. But since per capita output is constant, living standards are not rising.
- Changes in output that cannot be accounted for by changes in the levels of physical and human capital and in the size of the labour force are attributed to changes in what is called total factor productivity (TFP). Although it is sometimes associated with technological change, TFP does not measure all of such change because much of it is embodied in new physical and human capital.
- In the Neoclassical growth model, technological change is assumed to be exogenous—unaffected by the size of the labour force, the size of the capital stock, or the level of economic activity.

26.3 **New Growth Theories** ⑩❹

- Unlike the Neoclassical growth theory, new growth theories emphasize endogenous technological change that responds to market signals such as prices and profits. In particular, shocks that would be adverse in a setting of fixed technology may provide a spur to innovation and result in technological improvements.
- New growth theories also suggest that investment may be subject to *increasing* rather than diminishing marginal

returns. Increasing marginal returns can explain ongoing growth in per capita incomes due to capital accumulation—a phenomenon difficult to explain with the Neoclassical growth model.
- Knowledge is an important input to the production process and, because it is a public good that can be used simultaneously by many, may not be subject to diminishing marginal returns.

26.4 **Are There Limits to Growth?**

- The critical importance of increasing knowledge and new technology to the goal of sustaining growth is highlighted by the great drain on existing natural resources that has resulted from the explosive growth of population and output in recent decades. Without continuing technological change, the present needs and aspirations of the world's population cannot come anywhere close to being met.

- Rising population and rising real incomes place pressure on resources. Technological improvements, however, lead to less resource use per unit of output produced, and also to the discovery and development of new resources.

- The increase in population has similar effects on pollution: The earth's environment could cope naturally with much of human pollution 200 years ago, but the present population is so large that pollution has outstripped nature's coping mechanisms.

K E Y   C O N C E P T S

The cumulative nature of growth
Benefits and costs of growth
The market for loanable funds
Saving, investment, and growth
Neoclassical growth theory

The aggregate production function
Diminishing marginal returns
Constant returns to scale
Balanced growth
Total factor productivity

Endogenous technical change
Increasing marginal returns to investment
The economics of goods and of ideas
Resource depletion and pollution

S T U D Y   E X E R C I S E S

1. Fill in the blanks to make the following statements correct.

   a. Long-run, sustained increases in real GDP are the result of increases in potential output, which we call _____.

   b. Increases in living standards are possible with increases in real _____.

   c. The primary cost of economic growth is the sacrifice of current _____ in exchange for investment that raises future _____.

   d. The four fundamental determinants of growth are
      - _____
      - _____
      - _____
      - _____

2. Fill in the blanks to make the following statements correct.

   a. An increase in the interest rate leads to a(n) _____ in the amount of national saving because households reduce their _____.

   b. An increase in the interest rate leads firms to _____ their amount of desired investment.

   c. In the long run, with output equal to potential, equilibrium in the market for loanable funds determines the interest rate as well as the amount of _____ and _____ in the economy.

   d. Following a shift in either the supply of national saving or the demand for investment, there will be a change in both the equilibrium _____ and the amount of _____ in the economy.

   e. An increase in the amount of the economy's resources devoted to _____ leads to an increase in the growth rate of _____.

3. Fill in the blanks to make the following statements correct.

   a. An important aspect of Neoclassical growth theory is that changes in the supply of one factor, all else held constant, imply eventually _____ marginal returns to that factor.

   b. In Neoclassical growth theory, an increase in the labour force _____ total output and _____ the level of per capita output.

   c. When a new harvesting machine replaces an old harvesting machine on a farm, and is more productive than the old one, we say there has been _____ technical change.

d. Some new growth theories are based on the assumption that technological change is _____ to the economic system; others are based on the possibility that there are _____ marginal returns to investment.

e. Neoclassical growth theories are pessimistic because they emphasize _____ returns with a given state of _____. Modern growth theories are more optimistic because they emphasize the unlimited potential of _____.

4. In the text we said that, over many years, small differences in growth rates can have large effects on the level of income. This question will help you understand this important point. Consider an initial value of real GDP equal to Y_0. If real GDP grows at a rate of g percent annually, after N years real GDP will equal $Y_0(1+g)^N$. Now consider the following table. Let the initial level of GDP in all cases be 100.

Real GDP With Alternative Growth Rates

Year	(1) 1%	(2) 1.5%	(3) 2%	(4) 2.5%	(5) 3%	(6) 3.5%
0	100	100	100	100	100	100
1	—	—	—	—	—	—
3	—	—	—	—	—	—
5	—	—	—	—	—	—
10	—	—	—	—	—	—
20	—	—	—	—	—	—
30	—	—	—	—	—	—
50	—	—	—	—	—	—

a. Using the formula provided above, compute the level of real GDP in column 1 for each year. For example, in Year 1, real GDP will equal $100(1.01)^1 = 101$.

b. Now do the same for the rest of the columns.

c. In Year 20, how much larger (in percentage terms) is real GDP in the 3% growth case compared to the 1.5% growth case?

d. In Year 50, how much larger (in percentage terms) is real GDP in the 3% growth case compared to the 1.5% growth case?

5. The diagram below shows two paths for aggregate consumption. One grows at a rate of 3 percent per year; the other grows at 4 percent per year but begins at a lower level.

a. Suppose the economy jumps from Path 1 to Path 2 in Year 0 because its rate of capital accumulation increases. What is the opportunity cost in this economy for this increase in capital accumulation?

b. Suppose the economy jumps from Path 1 to Path 2 in Year 0 because its rate of R&D expenditures increases. The greater R&D leads to technological improvements that generate the higher growth rate. What is the opportunity cost to this economy for the increase in R&D expenditures?

c. Show in the figure the "breakeven" point for the economy after both of the changes described above. Explain.

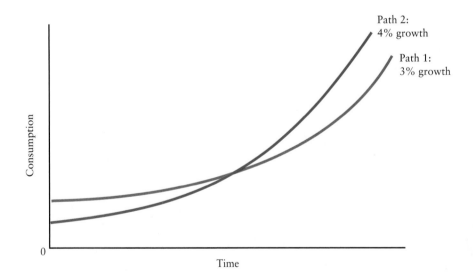

6. Consider an economy in the long run with real GDP equal to the level of potential output, Y^*.

   a. Draw the diagram of the market for loanable funds. Explain the shapes of the investment demand curve and the national saving curve.

   b. Suppose the government pursued a fiscal contraction by reducing the level of government purchases. Explain what would happen to the equilibrium interest rate, the amount of investment in the economy, and the long-run growth rate.

   c. Now suppose the fiscal contraction occurs by increasing taxes. Explain what effect this would have on the interest rate, investment, and long-run growth rate.

7. The Neoclassical growth theory is based on the existence of an aggregate production function—showing the relationship between labour (L), capital (K), technology (T), and real GDP (Y). The table below shows various values for L, K, and T. In all cases, the aggregate production function is assumed to take the following form:

$$Y = T \times \sqrt{KL}$$

Labour (L)	Capital (K)	Technology (T)	Real GDP (Y)
10	20	1	—
15	20	1	—
20	20	1	—
25	20	1	—
10	20	1	—
15	30	1	—
20	40	1	—
25	50	1	—
20	20	1	—
20	20	3	—
20	20	4	—
20	20	5	—

   a. Compute real GDP for each case and complete the table.

   b. In the first part of the table, capital is constant but labour is increasing. What property of the production function is displayed? Explain.

   c. In the second part of the table, capital and labour are increasing by the same proportion. What property of the production function is displayed? Explain.

   d. What type of growth is being shown in the third part of the table?

8. In the early 1970s the Club of Rome, extrapolating from the rates of resource use at the time, predicted that the supply of natural resources (especially oil) would be used up within a few decades. Subsequent events appear to have proven them wrong.

   a. What is predicted to happen to the price of oil (and other natural resources) as population and per capita incomes rise?

   b. Given your answer to part (a), what is the likely response by firms and consumers who use such resources?

   c. Explain why resource exhaustion should, through the workings of the price system, lead to technological developments that reduce the use of the resource.

DISCUSSION QUESTIONS

1. Economic growth is often studied in macroeconomic terms, but in a market economy, who makes the decisions that lead to growth? What kinds of decisions and what kinds of actions cause growth to occur? How might a detailed study of individual markets be relevant to understanding economic growth?

2. Discuss the following quote from a recent newspaper article: "Economics and the environment are not strange bedfellows. Environment-oriented tourism is one creative way to resolve the conflict between our desire for a higher standard of living and the realization that nature cannot absorb everything we throw at it. The growing demand for eco-tourism has placed a premium

on the remaining rain forests, undisturbed flora and fauna, and endangered species of the world."

3. "The case for economic growth is that it gives man greater control over his environment, and consequently increases his freedom." Explain why you agree or disagree with this statement by Nobel laureate W. Arthur Lewis.

4. Dr. David Suzuki, an opponent of further economic growth, has argued that despite the fact that "in the twentieth century the list of scientific and technological achievements has been absolutely dazzling, the costs of such progress are so large that negative economic growth may be right for the future." Policies to achieve this include "rigorous reduction of waste, a questioning and distrustful attitude toward technological progress, and braking demands on the globe's resources." Identify some of the benefits and costs of economic growth, and evaluate Suzuki's position. What government policies would be needed to achieve his ends?

5. In this chapter we discussed four fundamental determinants of growth in real output; increases in the labour force; increases in the stock of physical capital; increases in human capital; and improvements in technology. For each of the four, give an example of a government policy that is likely to increase growth. Discuss also the likely cost associated with each policy. Does one of your proposed policies appear better (in a cost–benefit sense) than the others?

6. The Solow residual has been called a "measure of our ignorance" of the causes of growth. Explain this viewpoint. Is the Solow residual a good measure of technical change?

7. Consider the market for loanable funds and the long-run relationship between saving, investment, and economic growth.

   a. If the government wants to encourage the long-run growth rate, explain why it can directly promote saving *or* investment.

   b. Would one option in (a) be "better" in some way than the other? For example, does it matter that one would have higher interest rates than the other? Explain.

PART TEN

Money, Banking, and Monetary Policy

What is money, and where does it come from? What determines how much money is in the economy? Does the Bank of Canada control interest rates or are these rates determined by market forces? How does the Bank's monetary policy affect real GDP and employment? These are the sorts of questions we address in the next three chapters.

Chapter 27 traces the development of money, from the use of barter in ancient economies to deposit money that is so important today. We will examine the Canadian banking system, from the commercial banks to the Bank of Canada, Canada's central bank. The idea of money creation will then be examined, and we will see that commercial banks do indeed create money. Finally, we will discuss several formal measures of the Canadian money supply.

Chapter 28 begins with a discussion of the demand for money. Here we see why households' and firms' desired holding of money depends on the interest rate. We then examine the concept of monetary equilibrium, and it is here that we consider the Bank of Canada's role in determining interest rates. We also see how changes in the Bank of Canada's policy can affect interest rates, aggregate expenditure, and eventually real GDP and the price level.

In Chapter 29 we focus on monetary policy. We will explore some of the details of how the Bank of Canada's actions influence the commercial banking system. The Bank's policy instruments and policy targets will be discussed, and it is here that we discuss the lags and uncertainty that make the conduct of monetary policy so difficult. Finally, we discuss some of the policy challenges faced by the Bank of Canada over the past few years.

CHAPTER 27

Money and Banking

L LEARNING OBJECTIVES

1. Explain the various functions of money, and how money has evolved over time.

2. Show that modern banking systems include both privately owned commercial banks and government-owned central banks.

3. Explain how commercial banks create money through the process of taking deposits and making loans.

4. List what is included in various measures of the money supply.

In the next three chapters, we look at the role of money and monetary policy. The role of money may seem obvious—money is what people use to buy things. Yet as we shall see, increasing the amount of money circulating in Canada would not make the average Canadian better off in the long run. Although money allows those who have it to buy someone else's output, the total amount of goods and services available for everyone to buy depends on the total output produced, not on the total amount of money that people possess. In short, an increase in the quantity of money will not increase the level of potential real GDP, Y^*. However, most economists agree that changes in the supply of money do have important short-run effects on national income.

We begin by talking in detail about what money is and how it evolved over the centuries to its current form. We then examine the Canadian banking system, which includes a central bank (the Bank of Canada) and many commercial banks. Finally, we explain the process whereby commercial banks "create" money, seemingly out of thin air. This money creation process will play a central role in our discussion of how money influences the level of economic activity, a topic we begin in the next chapter.

27.1 **The Nature of Money**

What exactly is money? In this section, we describe the functions of money and briefly outline its history.

What Is Money?

medium of exchange
Anything that is generally acceptable in return for goods and services sold.

In economics, *money* has usually been defined as any generally accepted medium of exchange. A **medium of exchange** is anything that will be widely accepted in a society in exchange for goods and services. Although its medium-of-exchange role is perhaps its most important one, money also acts as a *store of value* and as a *unit of account*. Different kinds of money vary in the degree of efficiency with which they fulfill these functions. As we shall see, the *money supply* is measured by using different definitions for different purposes.

Money as a Medium of Exchange

If there were no money, goods would have to be exchanged by barter. **Barter** is the system whereby goods and services are exchanged directly with each other. The major difficulty with barter is that each transaction requires a *double coincidence of wants*: anyone who specialized in producing one commodity would have to spend a great deal of time searching for satisfactory transactions. For example, the barber who needs his sink repaired would have to find a plumber who wants a haircut. In a world of many different goods and many different people, the effort required to make transactions would be extreme.

The use of money as a medium of exchange solves this problem. People can sell their output for money and then use the money to buy what they wish from others.

The double coincidence of wants is unnecessary when a medium of exchange is used.

By facilitating transactions, money makes possible the benefits of specialization and the division of labour, which in turn contribute to the efficiency of the economic system. It is not without justification that money has been called one of the great inventions contributing to human freedom and well-being.

To serve as an efficient medium of exchange, money must have a number of characteristics. It must be both easily recognizable and readily acceptable. It must have a high value relative to its weight (otherwise it would be a nuisance to carry around). It must be divisible, because money that comes only in large denominations is useless for transactions having only a small value. It must be reasonably durable (notice that Canadian paper money can easily survive several trips through a washing machine!). Finally, it must be difficult, if not impossible, to counterfeit.

Money as a Store of Value

Money is a convenient means of storing purchasing power; goods may be sold today for money and the money may then be stored until it is needed for some future purchase. To be a satisfactory store of value, however, money must have a relatively stable value. A rise in the price level is also a decrease in the purchasing power of money. When the price level is stable, the purchasing power of a given sum of money is also stable; when the price level is highly variable, so is the purchasing power of money, and the usefulness of money as a store of value is undermined.

Between the early 1970s and the early 1990s, inflation in Canada was high enough and sufficiently variable to diminish money's usefulness as a store of value. Since 1992, inflation has been both low and relatively stable, thus increasing money's role as a store of value. Even Canada's high-inflation experience, however, is very modest compared to that in some other countries, such as Chile in the mid-1970s, Bolivia in the mid-1980s, and Argentina, Romania, and Brazil in the early 1990s. Perhaps the most infamous experience of *hyperinflation* comes from Germany in the early 1920s. This case is discussed in *Lessons From History 27-1*.

Money as a Unit of Account

Money may also be used purely for accounting purposes without having a physical existence of its own. For instance, a government store in a truly communist society might say that everyone had so many "dollars" to use each month. Goods could then be assigned

barter   A system in which goods and services are traded directly for other goods and services.

Practise with Study Guide Chapter 27, Exercise 1.

LESSONS FROM HISTORY 27-1

Hyperinflation

Hyperinflation is generally defined as inflation that exceeds 50 percent per month. At this rate of inflation a chocolate bar that costs $1 on January 1 would cost $129.74 by December 31 of the same year. When prices are rising at such rapid rates, is it possible for money to maintain its usefulness as a medium of exchange or as a store of value? Several examples from history have allowed economists to study the role of money during hyperinflation. This historical record is not entirely reassuring. In a number of instances, prices rose at an ever-accelerating rate until a nation's money ceased to be a satisfactory store of value, even for the short period between receipt and expenditure, and hence ceased also to be useful as a medium of exchange.

The most spectacular example of hyperinflation is the experience of Germany in the period after the First World War. The index shows that a good purchased for one 100-mark note in July 1923 would cost *10 million* 100-mark notes only four months later! Although Germany had experienced substantial inflation during the First World War, averaging more than 30 percent per year, the immediate postwar years of 1920 and 1921 gave no sign of explosive inflation. Indeed, prices were relatively stable until 1922 and 1923 when they exploded. On November 15, 1923, the German mark was officially repudiated, its value wholly destroyed. How could such a dramatic increase in prices happen?

When inflation becomes so high that people lose confidence in the purchasing power of their currency, they rush to spend it. People who have goods become increasingly reluctant to accept the rapidly depreciating money in exchange. The rush to spend money accelerates the increase in prices until people finally become unwilling to accept money on any terms. What was once money ceases to be money. The price system can then be restored only by repudiation of the old monetary unit and its replacement by a new unit.

About a dozen hyperinflations in world history have been documented, among them the collapse of the continental during the American Revolution in 1776, the ruble during the Russian Revolution in 1917, the drachma during and after the German occupation of Greece in the Second World War, the pengö in Hungary in 1945 and 1946, the Chinese national currency from 1946 to 1948, the Bolivian peso in 1984 and 1985, and the Argentinian peso in the early 1990s. Every one of these hyperinflations was accompanied by great increases in the money supply; new money was printed to give governments purchasing power that they could not or would not obtain by taxa-

tion. Further, every one occurred in the midst of a major political upheaval in which grave doubts existed about the stability and the future of the government itself.

Is hyperinflation likely in the absence of civil war, revolution, or collapse of the government? Most economists think not. Further, it is clear that high inflation rates over a period of time do not mean the inevitable or even likely onset of hyperinflation, however serious the distributive and social effects of such rates may be.

During hyperinflation money loses its value so quickly that people cease to accept it as a means of payment. At that point, money may as well be used for wallpaper.

Date	German Wholesale Price Index (1913 = 1)
January 1913	1
January 1920	13
January 1921	14
January 1922	37
July 1922	101
January 1923	2 785
July 1923	74 800
August 1923	944 000
September 1923	23 900 000
October 1923	7 096 000 000
November 1923	750 000 000 000

prices and each consumer's purchases recorded, the consumer being allowed to buy until the allocated supply of dollars was exhausted. These dollars need have no existence other than as entries in the store's books, yet they would serve as a perfectly satisfactory unit of account.

Whether they could also serve as a medium of exchange between individuals depends on whether the store would agree to transfer dollar credits from one customer to another at the customer's request. Canadian banks transfer dollars credited to deposits in this way each time you make a purchase with your ATM card. Thus, a bank deposit can serve as both a unit of account and a medium of exchange. Notice that the use of *dollars* in this context suggests a further sense in which money is a unit of account. People think about values in terms of the monetary unit with which they are familiar.

The Origins of Money

The origins of money go far back in antiquity. Most primitive societies are known to have made some use of it.

Metallic Money

All sorts of commodities have been used as money at one time or another, but gold and silver proved to have great advantages. They were precious because their supplies were relatively limited, and they were in constant demand by the wealthy for ornament and decoration. Hence, these metals tended to have high and stable prices. Further, they were easily recognized, they were divisible into extremely small units, and they did not easily wear out. Thus, precious metals came to circulate as money and to be used in many transactions.

Before the invention of coins, it was necessary to carry the metals in bulk. When a purchase was made, the requisite quantity of the metal was carefully weighed on a scale. The invention of coinage eliminated the need to weigh the metal at each transaction, but it created an important role for an authority, usually a monarch, who made the coins and affixed his or her seal, guaranteeing the amount of precious metal that the coin contained. This was clearly a great convenience, as long as traders knew that they could accept the coin at its "face value." The face value was nothing more than a statement that a certain weight of metal was contained therein.

However, coins often could not be taken at their face value. The practice of clipping a thin slice off the edge of the coin and keeping the valuable metal became common. This, of course, served to undermine the acceptability of coins, even if they were stamped. To get around this problem, the idea arose of minting the coins with a rough edge. The absence of the rough edge would immediately indicate that the coin had been clipped. This practice, called *milling*, survives on Canadian dimes, quarters, and two-dollar coins as an interesting anachronism to remind us that there were days when the market value of the metal in the coin was equal to the face value of the coin.

Not to be outdone by the cunning of their subjects, some rulers were quick to seize the chance of getting something for nothing. The power to mint coins placed rulers in a position to work a very profitable fraud. They often used some suitable occasion—a marriage, an anniversary, an alliance—to remint the coinage. Subjects would be ordered to bring their coins in to the mint to be melted down and coined afresh with a new stamp. Between the melting down and the recoining, however, the rulers had only to toss some further inexpensive base metal in with the molten gold. This *debasing* of the coinage allowed the ruler to earn a handsome profit by minting more new coins than the number of old ones collected, and putting the extras in the royal vault.

The result of debasement was inflation. The subjects had the same number of coins as before and hence could demand the same quantity of goods. When rulers paid their bills, however, the recipients of the extra coins could be expected to spend them. This caused a net increase in demand, which in turn bid up prices. Thus, debasing of the coinage was a common cause of increases in prices.

Gresham's Law.   The early experience of currency debasement led to the observation known as **Gresham's law,** after Sir Thomas Gresham (1519–1579), an adviser to the Elizabethan court, who coined the phrase "bad money drives out good."

Gresham's law
The theory that "bad," or debased, money drives "good," or undebased, money out of circulation.

When Queen Elizabeth I came to the throne of England in the middle of the sixteenth century, the coinage had been severely debased. Seeking to help trade, Elizabeth minted new coins that contained their full face value in gold. However, as fast as she fed these new coins into circulation, they disappeared. Why?

Suppose that you possessed one of these new coins and one of the old ones, each with the same face value, and had to make a purchase. What would you do? You would use the debased coin to make the purchase and keep the undebased one; you part with less gold that way. Suppose that you wanted to obtain a certain amount of gold bullion by melting down the gold coins (as was frequently done). Which coins would you use? You would use new, undebased coins because you would part with less face value that way (it would take more of the debased coins than the new coins to get a given amount of gold bullion). The debased coins (bad money) would thus remain in circulation, and the undebased coins (good money) would disappear—the "bad" money would drive out the "good" money.

Gresham's law predicts that when two types of money are used side by side, the one with the greater intrinsic value will be driven out of circulation.

Gresham's insights have proven helpful in explaining the experience of a number of modern high-inflation economies. For example, in the 1970s, inflation in Chile raised the value of the metallic content in coins above their face value. Coins quickly disappeared from circulation as private citizens sold them to entrepreneurs who melted them down for their metal. Only paper currency remained in circulation and was used even for tiny transactions such as purchasing a pack of matches. Gresham's law is one reason why modern coins, unlike their historical counterparts, are merely tokens that contain a metallic value that is only a small fraction of their face value.

Paper Money

The next important step in the history of money was the evolution of paper currency. Artisans who worked with gold required secure safes, and the public began to deposit gold with these goldsmiths for safekeeping. Goldsmiths would give their depositors receipts promising to hand over the gold on demand. When a depositor wished to make a large purchase, he could go to his goldsmith, reclaim some of his gold, and hand it over to the seller of the goods. If the seller had no immediate need for the gold, he would carry it back to the goldsmith for safekeeping.

If people knew the goldsmith to be reliable, there was no need to go through the cumbersome and risky business of physically transferring the gold. The buyer needed only to transfer the goldsmith's receipt to the seller, who would accept it as long as he was confident that the goldsmith would pay over the gold whenever

The development of paper money, such as this bank note issued by The Montreal Bank over a century ago, was an important step in the evolution of modern, fractional-reserve banking systems. Paper money allowed individuals to avoid the cumbersome transportation of gold when making their daily transactions.

it was needed. If the seller wished to buy a good from a third party, who also knew the goldsmith to be reliable, this transaction could also be effected by passing the goldsmith's receipt from the buyer to the seller. This transferring of paper receipts rather than gold was essentially the invention of paper money.

When it first came into being, paper money represented a promise to pay so much gold on demand. In this case, the promise was made first by goldsmiths and later by banks. Such paper money was *backed* by precious metal and was *convertible on demand* into this metal. In the nineteenth century, private banks commonly issued paper money, called **bank notes,** nominally convertible into gold. As with the goldsmiths, each bank issued its own notes, and these notes were convertible into gold at the issuing bank. Thus, in the nineteenth century, bank notes from many different banks circulated side by side, each of them being backed by gold at the bank that issued them.

bank notes
Paper money issued by commercial banks.

Fractionally Backed Paper Money. Early on, many goldsmiths and banks discovered that it was not necessary to keep one ounce of gold in the vaults for every claim to one ounce circulating as paper money. At any one time, some of the bank's customers would be withdrawing gold, others would be depositing it, and most would be trading in the bank's paper notes without any need or desire to convert them into gold. As a result, the bank was able to issue more money redeemable in gold than the amount of gold that it held in its vaults. This was good business because the money could be invested profitably in interest-earning loans to households and firms. To this day, banks have many more claims outstanding against them than they actually have in reserves available to pay those claims. We say that the currency issued in such a situation is *fractionally backed* by the reserves.

The major problem with a fractionally backed convertible currency was maintaining its convertibility into the precious metal behind it. The imprudent bank that issued too much paper money would find itself unable to redeem its currency in gold when the demand for gold was even slightly higher than usual. It would then have to suspend payments, and all holders of its notes would suddenly find that the notes were worthless. The prudent bank that kept a reasonable relationship between its note issues and its gold reserves would find that it could meet a normal range of demand for gold without any trouble.

If, for whatever reason, the public lost confidence in the banks and demanded redemption of its currency *en masse,* the banks would be unable to honour their pledges. The history of nineteenth- and early-twentieth-century banking on both sides of the Atlantic is full of examples of banks that were ruined by "panics," or sudden runs on their gold reserves. When these happened, the banks' depositors and the holders of their notes would find themselves with worthless pieces of paper.

Fiat Money

As time went on, currency (notes and coins) issued by private banks became less common, and central banks took control of issuing currency. In time, *only* central banks were permitted to issue currency. Originally, the central banks issued currency that was fully convertible into gold. In those days, gold would be brought to the central bank, which would issue currency in the form of "gold certificates" that asserted that the gold was available on demand. The reserves of gold thus set some upper limit on

Paper money used to be backed by the value of gold—meaning that it was redeemable for gold. But now money is not redeemable for anything except itself—people hold it because they know that others will accept it as payment for goods and services.

gold standard
A currency standard whereby a country's currency is convertible into gold at a fixed rate of exchange.

the amount of currency. This practice of backing the currency with gold is known as a **gold standard.**

However, central banks, like private banks before them, could issue more currency than they had in gold because in normal times only a small fraction of the outstanding currency was presented for payment at any one time. Thus, even though the need to maintain convertibility into gold put an upper limit on note issuance, central banks had substantial discretionary control over the quantity of currency outstanding.

During the period between the World Wars (1919–1939), almost all of the countries of the world abandoned the gold standard; their currencies were thus no longer convertible into gold. Money that is not convertible by law into anything valuable derives its value from its acceptability in exchange. Such **fiat money** is widely acceptable because it is declared by government order, or *fiat*, to be legal tender. **Legal tender** is anything that by law must be accepted when offered either for the purchase of goods or services or to discharge a debt.

fiat money   Paper money or coinage that is neither backed by nor convertible into anything else but is decreed by the government to be accepted as legal tender.

legal tender
Anything that by law must be accepted for the purchase of goods and services or in discharge of a debt.

Today, a few countries preserve the fiction that their currency is backed by gold, but no country allows its currency to be converted into gold on demand. Gold backing for Canadian currency was eliminated in 1940, although note issues continued to carry the traditional statement "will pay to the bearer on demand" until 1954. Today's Bank of Canada notes simply say, "This note is legal tender." It is, in other words, fiat money pure and simple.[1]

If fiat money is generally acceptable, it is a medium of exchange. If its purchasing power remains stable, it is a satisfactory store of value. If both of these things are true, it serves as a satisfactory unit of account. Today, almost all currency is fiat money.

Many people are disturbed to learn that present-day paper money is neither backed by nor convertible into anything more valuable—that it consists of nothing but pieces of paper whose value derives from common acceptance and from confidence that it will continue to be accepted in the future. Many people believe that their money should be more "substantial" than this. Yet money is, in fact, nothing more than pieces of paper.

Bank cards like this one are not money. They simply allow consumers to have convenient access to their bank deposits, which are money.

Modern Money: Deposit Money

Early in the twentieth century, private banks lost the authority to issue bank notes, and this authority was reserved for central banks (which we discuss shortly). Yet, as we shall see, they did not lose the power to create *deposit money.*

Today's bank customers frequently deposit coins and paper money with the banks for safekeeping, just as in former times they deposited gold. Such a deposit is recorded as a credit to the customer's account. A customer who wishes to pay a debt may come to the bank and claim the money in dollars and then pay the money to other persons who may themselves redeposit the money in a bank.

As with gold transfers, this is a tedious procedure. It is more convenient to have the bank transfer claims to money on deposit. As soon as cheques, which are

---

[1] See *A History of the Canadian Dollar* (written by James Powell and published by the Bank of Canada) for a detailed and very readable discussion of the evolution of Canadian money.

written instructions to the bank to make a transfer, became widely accepted in payment for commodities and debts, bank deposits became a form of money called *deposit money*. **Deposit money** is defined as money held by the public in the form of deposits in commercial banks that can be withdrawn on demand. Such deposits are called *demand deposits,* the most important of which are chequing accounts. Cheques, unlike bank notes, do not circulate freely from hand to hand; hence cheques themselves are not money. However, a balance in a demand deposit *is* money; the cheque transfers money from one person to another. Because cheques are easily drawn and deposited and are relatively safe from theft, they are widely used. In recent years, the development of debit cards has taken the place of cheques for many transactions. The use of a debit card instantly (electronically) transfers funds from the bank account of the purchaser to the bank account of the seller—it thus has the same effect as a cheque, only faster.

Thus, when commercial banks lost the right to issue notes of their own, the form of bank money changed, but the substance did not. Today, banks have money in their vaults (or on deposit with the central banks), just as they always did. Once it was gold; today it is the legal tender of the times, fiat money. It is true today, just as in the past, that most of the bank's customers are content to pay their bills by passing among themselves the bank's promises to pay money on demand. Only a small proportion of the transactions made by the bank's customers are made in cash.

Bank deposits are money. Today, just as in the past, banks create money by issuing more promises to pay (deposits) than they have cash reserves available to pay out.

deposit money
Money held by the public in the form of demand deposits with commercial banks.

> Any discussion of financial markets and banking systems includes many terms that you may find unfamiliar. For a brief guide to and description of various financial assets, look for "A Quick Introduction to Financial Assets" in the *Additional Topics* section of this book's Companion Website
>
> http://www.pearsoned.ca/ragan

27.2 The Canadian Banking System

Many types of institutions make up a modern banking system such as exists in Canada today. The **central bank** is the government-owned and government-operated institution that serves to control the banking system. Through it, the government's monetary policy is conducted. In Canada, the central bank is the Bank of Canada, often called just the Bank.

Financial intermediaries are privately owned institutions that serve the general public. They are called *intermediaries* because they stand between savers, from whom they accept deposits, and investors, to whom they make loans. For many years, government regulations created a sharp distinction among the various types of financial intermediaries by limiting the types of transactions in which each could engage. The past two decades have seen a sweeping deregulation of the financial system so that many of these traditional distinctions no longer apply. In this book, we use the term *commercial banks* to extend to all financial intermediaries that create deposit money, including chartered banks, trust companies, and credit unions.

central bank   A bank that acts as banker to the commercial banking system and often to the government as well. Usually a government-owned institution that controls the banking system and is the sole money-issuing authority.

David Dodge is the current governor of the Bank of Canada, the offices of which are located on Wellington Street in Ottawa, across the street from the Parliament Buildings.

The Bank of Canada

All advanced free-market economies have, in addition to commercial banks, a central bank. Many of the world's early central banks were private, profit-making institutions that provided services to ordinary banks. Their importance, however, caused them to develop close ties with government. Central banks soon became instruments of the government, though not all of them were publicly owned. The Bank of England (the "Old Lady of Threadneedle Street"), one of the world's oldest and most famous central banks, began to operate as the central bank of England in the seventeenth century, but it was not formally taken over by the government until 1947.

The similarities in the functions performed and the tools used by the world's central banks are much more important than the differences in their organization. Although our attention is given to the operations of the Bank of Canada, its basic functions are similar to those of the Bank of England, the Federal Reserve System in the United States, or the new European Central Bank—which is the sole issuer of the euro.

Organization of the Bank of Canada

The Bank of Canada commenced operations on March 11, 1935. It is a publicly owned corporation; all profits accruing from its operations are remitted to the government of Canada. The responsibility for the Bank's affairs rests with a board of directors composed of the governor, the senior deputy governor, the deputy minister of finance, and 12 directors. The governor is appointed by the directors, with the approval of the federal cabinet, for a seven-year term. Since the Bank's inception, there have been seven governors:

- Graham Towers (1935–54)
- James Coyne (1955–61)
- Louis Rasminsky (1961–73)
- Gerald Bouey (1973–87)
- John Crow (1987–94)
- Gordon Thiessen (1994–2001)
- David Dodge (2001–)

The European Central Bank's website is www.ecb.org.

The organization of the Bank of Canada is designed to keep the operation of monetary policy free from day-to-day political influence. The Bank is not responsible to parliament for its day-to-day behaviour in the way that the department of finance is for the operation of fiscal policy. In this sense, the Bank of Canada has considerable autonomy in the way it carries out monetary policy. Despite this considerable autonomy, however, the Bank of Canada is not completely independent. The *ultimate* responsibility for the Bank's actions rests with the government, since it is the government that must answer to parliament. This system is known as "joint responsibility," and it dates back to 1967.

Under the system of joint responsibility, the governor of the Bank and the minister of finance consult regularly. In the case of fundamental disagreement over policy, the minister of finance has the option of issuing an explicit *directive* to the governor. In such a case (which has not happened since the inception of joint responsibility), the governor would simply carry out the minister's directive (or resign), and the responsibility for monetary policy would rest with the government. In the absence of such a directive, however, responsibility for monetary policy rests with the governor of the Bank.

The system of joint responsibility keeps the conduct of monetary policy free from day-to-day political influence while ensuring that the government retains ultimate responsibility for monetary policy.[2]

Basic Functions of the Bank

A central bank serves four main functions: as a banker for private banks, as a bank for the government, as the regulator of the nation's money supply, and as a supporter of financial markets. The first three functions are reflected in Table 27-1, which shows the balance sheet of the Bank of Canada.

Banker to the Commercial Banks. The central bank accepts deposits from commercial banks and will, on order, transfer them to the account of another bank. In this way, the central bank provides the commercial banks with the equivalent of a chequing account and with a means of settling debts to other banks. The deposits of the commercial banks with the Bank of Canada—also called *reserves*—appear in Table 27-1. In December 2002 the banks had $1.19 billion on reserve at the Bank of Canada. Notice that the cash reserves of the commercial banks deposited with the central bank are liabilities of the central bank, because it promises to pay them on demand.

Historically, one of the earliest services provided by central banks was that of "lender of last resort" to the banking system. Central banks would lend money to private banks that had sound investments (such as government securities) but were in urgent need of cash. If such banks could not obtain ready cash, they might be forced into insolvency,

For information on the Bank of Canada, see its website: www.bank-banque-canada.ca.

TABLE 27-1 Assets and Liabilities of the Bank of Canada, December 2002 (millions of dollars)

Assets		Liabilities	
Government of Canada securities	40 333.1	Notes in circulation	41 146.7
Advances to commercial banks	534.9	Government of Canada deposits	534.6
Foreign-currency assets	678.6	Deposits of commercial banks (reserves)	1 191.3
Other assets	2 412.2	Foreign-currency liabilities	516.2
		Other liabilities and capital	570.0
Total	43 958.8	Total	43 958.8

The balance sheet of the Bank of Canada shows that it serves as banker to the commercial banks and to the Government of Canada and as issuer of our currency; it also suggests the Bank's role as regulator of money markets and the money supply. The principal liabilities of the Bank are the basis of the money supply. Bank of Canada notes are currency, and the deposits of the commercial banks give them the reserves they need to create deposit money. The Bank's holdings of Government of Canada securities arise from its operations designed to regulate the money supply and financial markets.

(*Source: Bank of Canada Annual Report, 2002.*)

---

[2] This system was motivated by the "Coyne Affair" in 1961, during the Conservative government of John Diefenbaker. James Coyne, then governor of the Bank of Canada, disagreed with the minister of finance, Walter Gordon, over the conduct of monetary policy and was eventually forced to resign. Louis Rasminsky then accepted the position as governor of the Bank on the condition that the *Bank of Canada Act* be modified to incorporate the idea of joint responsibility. The *Bank of Canada Act* was so amended in 1967. For a discussion of the early history of the Bank of Canada, see George Watts, *The Bank of Canada: Origins and Early History* (Carleton University Press, 1993).

because they could not meet the demands of their depositors, in spite of their being basically sound. Today's central banks continue to be lenders of last resort.

Banker to the Federal Government.   Governments, too, need to hold their funds in an account into which they can make deposits and on which they can write cheques. The government of Canada keeps some of its chequing deposits at the Bank of Canada. In December 2002, the federal government had $535 million in deposits at the Bank of Canada.

When the government requires more money than it collects in taxes, it needs to borrow, and it does so by issuing government securities (short-term treasury bills or longer-term bonds). Most are sold directly to financial institutions and portfolio managers, but occasionally the Bank of Canada buys some and credits the government's account with a deposit for the amount of the purchase. In December 2002, the Bank of Canada held $40.3 billion in government of Canada securities. These securities are an asset for the Bank of Canada but a liability for the government. (It is largely by earning interest on these securities that the Bank of Canada earns a profit every year—a profit that is eventually remitted to the government.)

We will see in Chapter 29 that the Bank's holdings of government securities and its control over the location of government deposits (switching them between the central bank and the commercial banks) are the primary tools for the conduct of monetary policy.

Regulator of the Money Supply.   One of the most important functions of a central bank is to regulate the *money supply*. Though we have not yet defined the money supply precisely—and there are several different definitions of the money supply that we will encounter—we will see that most measures of the money supply include currency plus deposits held at commercial banks. From Table 27-1, it is clear that the overwhelming proportion of a central bank's liabilities (its promises to pay) are either currency (notes and coins) or the reserves of the commercial banks.[3] These reserves, in turn, underlie the deposits of households and firms—in exactly the same way that the nineteenth-century goldsmith's holdings of gold underlay its issue of notes.

Thus, by changing its liabilities (currency plus reserves), the Bank of Canada can change the money supply. The Bank of Canada can change the levels of its assets and liabilities in many ways and, as its liabilities rise and fall, so does the money supply. In Chapter 29, we will explore in detail how this happens and how the Bank uses this ability to conduct monetary policy.

Regulator and Supporter of Financial Markets.   Central banks usually assume a major responsibility to support the country's financial system and to prevent serious disruption by wide-scale panic and resulting bank failures.

Various institutions—including commercial banks, credit unions, and trust companies—are in the business of borrowing on a short-term basis and lending on a long-term basis. Large, unanticipated increases in interest rates tend to squeeze these institutions. The average rate they earn on their investments rises only slowly as old contracts mature and new ones are made, but they must either pay higher rates to hold on to their deposits or accept wide-scale withdrawals that could easily bring about insolvency. Such dramatic events are relatively rare in the Canadian banking sector, though Canadian banks have failed in the past and it is possible that more may fail in the future. To help keep financial markets operating smoothly, the Bank of Canada is prepared to

---

[3] Currency is a liability for the central bank because holders of currency can take it back to the central bank and redeem it for ... currency! In the days of the gold standard, currency was redeemable for gold. Today, it is just redeemable for itself.

act as a "lender of last resort" to financial institutions that have sound investment portfolios but are in urgent need of cash.

Commercial Banks in Canada

All Canadian banks owned in the private sector are referred to as **commercial banks.** The Canadian banking system is controlled by the provisions of the *Bank Act,* first passed in 1935 and revised several times since. Under the *Bank Act,* charters can be granted to financial institutions to operate as banks and, until 1980, there were only a few chartered banks, most of which were very large and each of which operated under identical regulatory provisions.

The 1980 revisions to the *Bank Act* allowed foreign banks to commence operations in Canada, although the Act severely limited the scale and scope of their activity. Subsequent revisions have removed some of these restrictions and made it easier to obtain new banking charters, but the revisions have maintained the distinction between these newer institutions and banks operating under what are essentially the pre-1980 provisions of the *Bank Act.* The original provisions, in slightly modified form, are now known as Schedule A of the *Bank Act;* the foreign banks and the new, smaller domestic banks operate under Schedules B and C. The term *chartered banks* is usually reserved for the Schedule A banks.

The chartered banks have common attributes: they hold deposits for their customers; they permit certain deposits to be transferred by cheque from an individual account to other accounts held in any bank branch in the country; they make loans to households and firms; they invest in government securities.

Banks are not the only financial institutions in the country. Many other privately owned, profit-seeking institutions, such as trust companies and credit unions, accept savings deposits and grant loans for specific purposes. Finance companies make loans to households for practically any purpose—sometimes at very high interest rates. Department stores and credit-card companies will extend credit so that purchases can be made on a buy-now, pay-later basis.

The chartered banks are subject to federal regulations and until recently were required to hold reserves with the Bank of Canada against their deposit liabilities. Other institutions do not face reserve requirements, but most are subject to various federal and provincial regulations concerning ownership and control and the types of financial activities in which they are allowed to engage. Thus, there are differences among all types of financial institutions, not just between banks and others.

The Canadian chartered banks have historically been such a stable and dominant group that the terms *chartered banks* and the *Canadian banking system* have been considered virtually synonymous. However, events over the past three decades have broken this identification. Especially important have been sweeping changes in the structure and functioning of international financial markets; some of these developments are discussed further in *Applying Economic Concepts 27-1.*

Interbank Activities

Commercial banks have a number of interbank cooperative relationships. For example, banks often share loans. Even the biggest bank cannot meet all the credit needs of a giant corporation, and often a group of banks will offer a "pool loan," agreeing on common terms and dividing the loan up into manageable segments. Another form of interbank cooperation is the bank credit card. Visa and MasterCard are the two most widely used credit cards, and each is operated by a group of banks.

commercial bank
A privately owned, profit-seeking institution that provides a variety of financial services, such as accepting deposits from customers and making loans and other investments.

For information and history of Canada's largest chartered bank, see the Royal Bank's website: www.royalbank.com. Go to "corporate information" and then "history."

APPLYING ECONOMIC CONCEPTS 27-1

The Globalization of Financial Markets

Technological innovations in communication over the past three decades have led to a globalization of the financial service industry. Computers, satellite communication systems, reliable telephones with direct worldwide dialling, fax machines, and the widespread use of the Internet have put people in instantaneous contact anywhere in the world.

As a result of these new technologies, borrowers and lenders can learn about market conditions and then move their funds instantly in search of the best loan rates. Large firms need transaction balances only while banks in their area are open. Once banks close for the day in each centre, the firms will not need these balances until tomorrow's reopening; hence the funds can be moved to another market, where they are used until it closes. They are then moved to yet another market. Funds are thus free to move from London to New York to Tokyo and back to London on a daily rotation. This is a degree of global sophistication that was inconceivable before the advent of the computer, when international communication was much slower and costlier than it now is. To facilitate the movement in and out of various national currencies, increasing amounts of bank deposits are denominated in foreign rather than domestic currencies.

One of the first developments in this movement toward globalization was the growth of the foreign-currency markets in Europe in the 1960s. Initially, the main currency involved was the U.S. dollar, which is why *Eurodollar* markets were the first to develop. Today, the *Eurobond* market is an international market where bonds of various types, denominated in various national currencies, are issued and sold to customers located throughout the world. The customers are mainly public corporations, international organizations, and multinational enterprises. The *Eurocurrency* market is a market for short-term bank deposits and bank loans denominated in various currencies.

The increasing sophistication of information transfer has led to a breakdown of the high degree of specialization that characterized financial markets in earlier decades. When information was difficult to obtain and analyze, an efficient division of labour called for a host of specialist institutions, each with expertise in a narrow range of transactions. As a result of the new developments in communication technology, economies of large scale led to the integration of various financial operations within one firm. For example, in Canada and many other countries, banks will sell you securities (in mutual funds) and, similarly, the mutual-fund companies will now sell you banking services. As the scale of such integrated firms increases, these firms find it easier to extend their operations geographically as well as functionally.

The forces of globalization and Canadian banks' perceived need to achieve larger scale in order to compete successfully against larger foreign-based banks led the four largest Canadian chartered banks to attempt to merge in 1998 (Royal Bank with Bank of Montreal, and CIBC with Toronto-Dominion). The proposed mergers were prevented by the Canadian government, however, on the grounds that they would unduly lessen competition in the Canadian banking industry. Many critics argue that globalization has made the eventual consolidation of Canadian banks all but inevitable. Globalization, they argue, means that governments that are slow to relax their regulations will see their country's financial firms lose ground to fierce international competitors.

Whether Canadian banks will merge, and to what extent the Canadian financial-services industry will be opened up to further international competition, is yet to be determined. But it is clear that the globalization of financial markets is real and is showing no signs of slowing down.

Dramatic reductions in communications costs over the past few decades have meant that financial markets in one country are closely linked to those in the rest of the world.

Probably the most important form of interbank cooperation is cheque clearing and collection, including the clearing of electronic transfers through debit cards. Bank deposits are an effective medium of exchange only because banks accept each other's cheques and allow funds to be transferred electronically when purchases are made with debit cards. If a depositor in the Bank of Montreal writes a cheque to someone who deposits it in TD Canada Trust, the Bank of Montreal now owes money to TD Canada Trust. This creates a need for the banks to present cheques to each other for payment. The same is true for transactions made with bank debit cards.

Millions of such transactions take place in the course of a day, and they result in an enormous sorting and bookkeeping job. Multibank systems make use of a **clearing house** where interbank debts are settled. At the end of the day, all the cheques drawn by the Bank of Montreal's customers and deposited in TD Canada Trust are totalled and set against the total of all the cheques drawn by TD Canada Trust's customers and deposited in the Bank of Montreal. It is necessary only to settle the difference between the two sums. The actual cheques are passed through the clearing house back to the bank on which they were drawn. Both banks are then able to adjust the individual accounts by a set of book entries. A flow of cash between banks is necessary only when there is a net transfer of cash from the customers of one bank to those of another. This flow of cash is accompanied by a daily transfer of deposits held by the commercial banks with the Bank of Canada.

clearing house An institution where interbank indebtedness, arising from the transfer of cheques between banks, is computed and offset and net amounts owing are calculated.

Banks as Profit Seekers

Banks are private firms that seek to make profits. A commercial bank provides a variety of services to its customers: a safe place to store money, the convenience of demand deposits that can be transferred by personal cheque or debit card, a safe and convenient place to earn a modest but guaranteed return on savings, and often financial advice and estate-management services.

Table 27-2 is the combined balance sheet of the chartered banks in Canada. The bulk of a bank's liabilities are deposits owed to its depositors. The principal assets of a bank are the *securities* it owns (including government bonds), which pay interest or dividends, and

Practise with Study Guide Chapter 27, Exercise 2.

TABLE 27-2   Consolidated Balance Sheet of the Canadian Chartered Banks, February 2003 (millions of dollars)

Assets		Liabilities	
Reserves (including deposits with Bank of Canada)	3 622	Demand deposits	100 184
Government of Canada securities	95 583	Savings deposits	380 160
Mortgage and nonmortgage loans	706 985	Time deposits	176 042
Canadian securities (corporate and provincial and municipal governments)	112 496	Government of Canada deposits	1 880
		Foreign-currency liabilities	734 204
Foreign-currency assets	690 609	Shareholders' equity	81 187
Other assets	152 979	Other liabilities	288 617
Total	1 762 274	Total	1 762 274

Reserves are only a tiny fraction of deposit liabilities. If all the commercial banks' customers who held demand deposits tried to withdraw them in cash, the banks could not meet this demand without liquidating almost $100 billion of other assets. This would be impossible without assistance from the Bank of Canada.

(Source: Bank of Canada Review, Spring 2003, Table C3.)

the interest-earning *loans* it makes to individuals and to businesses. A bank loan is a liability to the borrower (who must pay it back) but an asset to the bank.

Commercial banks attract deposits by paying interest to depositors and by providing them with services such as clearing cheques, automated teller machines, debit cards, and the provision of regular monthly statements. Banks earn profits by lending and investing money deposited with them for more than they pay their depositors in terms of interest and other services provided.

Competition for deposits is active among commercial banks and between banks and other financial institutions. Interest paid on deposits, special high-interest certificates of deposit (CDs), advertising, personal solicitation of accounts, giveaway programs for new deposits to existing accounts, and improved services are all forms of competition for funds.

Reserves

Commercial banks keep sufficient cash on hand to be able to meet depositors' day-to-day requirements for cash. However, just as the goldsmiths of long ago discovered that only a fraction of the gold they held was ever withdrawn at any given time, and just as banks of long ago discovered that only a small fraction of convertible bank notes was actually converted, so too do modern bankers know that only a small fraction of their deposits will be withdrawn in cash at any one time.

The reserves needed to assure that depositors can withdraw their deposits on demand will normally be quite small.

bank run A situation in which many depositors rush to withdraw their money, possibly leading to a bank's financial collapse.

In abnormal times, however, nothing short of 100 percent would do the job if the commercial banking system had to stand alone. When a few bank failures cause a general loss of confidence in banks' ability to redeem their deposits, the results can be devastating. Until relatively recently, such an event—or even the rumour of it—could lead to a **bank run** as depositors rushed to withdraw their money. Faced with such a panic, banks would have to close until they had borrowed enough funds or sold enough assets to meet the demand or until the demand subsided. However, banks could not instantly turn their loans into cash because the borrowers would have the money tied up in such things as real estate or business enterprises. Neither could the banks obtain cash by selling their securities to the public because payments would be made by cheques, which would not provide cash to pay off depositors.

The late Jimmy Stewart plays George Bailey in It's a Wonderful Life. *In this scene, Bailey, the owner of a small commercial bank, explains to his panicking customers why they can't all take their money out at the same time. It is a great illustration of a fractional-reserve banking system.*

The difficulty of providing sufficient reserves to meet abnormal situations is alleviated by the central bank. Because it controls the supply of bank reserves, the central bank can provide all the reserves that are needed to meet any abnormal situation. It can do this in two ways. First, it can lend reserves directly to commercial banks on the security of assets that are sound but not easy to liquidate quickly, such as interest-earning residential or commercial mortgages. Second, it can enter the open market and buy all the government securities that commercial banks need to sell. Once the public finds that deposits can be turned into cash, any panic will usually subside and any further drain of cash out of banks will cease.

The possibility of panic withdrawals is also greatly diminished by the provision of deposit insurance, provided in Canada by the Canada Deposit Insurance Corporation (CDIC), a federal Crown corporation. The CDIC guarantees that depositors will get their money back even if a bank fails completely. Most depositors will not rush to withdraw all of their money as long as they are certain they can get it when they need it. Although deposit insurance confers a number of benefits on the operation of the financial system, it has also been subject to considerable criticism in recent years. This is explored in more detail in *Applying Economic Concepts 27-2*.

Target Reserves

We have seen that commercial banks hold reserves in order to meet demands for cash by their depositors. A bank with no access to reserves will be unable to meet these demands and will be forced to suspend payments. This is something that banks must avoid at almost any cost, so that banking panics can be avoided. A bank's **reserve ratio** is the

reserve ratio   The fraction of its deposits that a commercial bank holds as reserves in the form of cash or deposits with the central bank.

APPLYING ECONOMIC CONCEPTS 27-2

Deposit Insurance and the Financial System

Deposit insurance, provided in Canada by the government-owned Canada Deposit Insurance Corporation (CDIC), assures depositors that their funds are secure whatever the fate of the commercial bank holding their deposit. This is a great boon for depositors, but experience has shown that it is a double-edged sword.

The obvious benefit of deposit insurance is that it provides security to depositors. This greater security makes it less likely that a bank panic will start, thereby increasing the stability of the financial system.

On the other hand, deposit insurance creates an incentive for banks to pursue riskier investments than they would if depositors had to worry about losing their deposits should the institution fail. Because of deposit insurance, depositors have no reason to select banks according to the riskiness of their investments. They are free instead to select the bank that pays the highest interest without worrying about the associated risk.

Deposit insurance is thus an example of a government institution that creates a situation whereby "heads the private investor wins, tails the taxpayer loses." Financial institutions take in depositors' insured funds; if the owners place them in risky ventures that pay off, the owners get the profits; if the owners place the funds in ventures that fail often enough to bring down the whole institution, the taxpayers must meet the bill by repaying those who provided the capital (the depositors). Canadian financial institutions have occasionally failed, including

two Western banks in the mid-1980s. When those institutions went under, depositors were repaid by the CDIC. Although the legal ceiling on deposit insurance was then $60 000, deposits in excess of that amount were also repaid, using taxpayer money. This created the precedent that ceilings on deposit insurance were not to be taken seriously. Any amount would likely be repaid. Hence, no investor need worry about the financial probity of the investments made by the institutions in which his or her money was deposited.

Two types of reforms are possible. One type would keep deposit insurance and provide the necessary accompanying regulations. The implications of deposit insurance for the investment behaviour of commercial banks suggest that if deposit insurance is to be maintained, other regulations concerning capital requirements and investment standards need to be applied. In addition, the deposit insurance system might be reformed in order to relate the cost of insurance for a particular institution to the riskiness of its investments.

The other type of reform would take deregulation to its logical conclusion of ending deposit insurance altogether. Many economists believe that if deregulation of financial institutions is regarded as desirable, it should be accompanied by a removal of deposit insurance, so that the people who use the funds will be accountable to those who provide them.

target reserve ratio
The fraction of its deposits that a commercial bank wants to hold as reserves.

fraction of its deposit liabilities that it *actually* holds as reserves, either as cash or as deposits with the central bank. A bank's **target reserve ratio** is the fraction of its deposits it *wishes* to hold as reserves.

In the past, legislation contained in the *Bank Act* required the chartered banks to hold reserves. These requirements were thought necessary to ensure the stability of the banking system. The reserves that the *Bank Act* required the banks to hold were called *required reserves*. Starting in the early 1980s, however, Canadian banks argued that the legal requirement to hold some of their assets as non-interest-bearing reserves placed them at a disadvantage relative to their competitors that were not subject to such requirements. The competitors included both foreign commercial banks and Canadian non-bank financial institutions. Globalization of financial markets had brought domestic banks into direct competition with foreign ones, and continuing deregulation of financial markets had enhanced the competition between banks and nonbank financial institutions. After much deliberation, the government responded to these complaints by phasing out all legal reserve requirements early in the 1990s.

Despite the fact that Canadian banks are no longer legally required to hold reserves against their deposits, the banks' actual reserve ratio is greater than zero. Commercial banks hold some reserves for the simple reason that they want to avoid situations in which they cannot satisfy their depositors' demands for cash. In addition, it is costly to borrow from the Bank of Canada to make up for any shortfall. Look again at Table 27-2. Notice that the banking system's cash reserves of just under $4 billion are less than one-half of 1 percent of its total liabilities of almost $1.8 trillion. If the holders of even 5 percent of deposits demanded cash, the banks would be unable to meet the demand without outside help. Reserves can be as low as they are because the banks know that the Bank of Canada will help them out in time of temporary need. The Canadian banking system is thus a **fractional-reserve system,** with commercial banks holding reserves—either as cash or as deposits at the Bank of Canada—of much less than 100 percent of their deposits.

fractional-reserve system   A banking system in which commercial banks keep only a fraction of their deposits in cash or on deposit with the central bank.

Excess Reserves

Given the expected demands for cash by its depositors, and given the costs associated with borrowing from the central bank to make up for any cash shortfall, each commercial bank sets a target reserve ratio for itself. This target reserve ratio, however, will not be constant over time. During holiday seasons, for example, banks may choose to hold more reserves because they know, based on past experience, that there will be heavy demands for cash.

Commercial banks strive to maintain a target ratio of reserves to deposits. In the past, this target ratio was legally imposed; today it is determined by the banks themselves.

excess reserves
Reserves held by a commercial bank in excess of its target reserves.

At any given time, however, any commercial bank will probably not be exactly at its target level of reserves. Reserves may be slightly above or slightly below the target, but the commercial bank will take actions to restore its actual reserves toward its target level. Any reserves in excess of the target level are called **excess reserves**. As we will see next, a bank can expand or contract its portfolio of loans to adjust its actual reserves toward its target level. Understanding this process is the key to understanding the "creation" of deposit money.

27.3 **Money Creation by the Banking System**

We noted before that the *money supply* refers to both currency and deposits at commercial banks. The fractional-reserve system provides the leverage that permits commercial banks to create new deposits, and thus to create new money. The process is important, so it is worth examining in some detail.

Some Simplifying Assumptions

To focus on the essential aspects of how banks create money, suppose that banks can invest in only one kind of asset—loans—and that there is only one kind of deposit—a demand deposit. Two other assumptions are provisional. When we have developed the basic ideas concerning the banks' creation of money, these assumptions will be relaxed.

1. *Fixed target reserve ratio.* We assume that all banks have the same target reserve ratio, which does not change. In our numerical illustration, we will assume that the target reserve ratio is 20 percent (0.20); that is, for every $5 of deposits the banks wish to hold $1 in cash reserves, investing the rest in new loans.

2. *No cash drain from the banking system.* We also assume that the public holds a fixed amount of the currency in circulation. In particular, we assume that the amount of cash held by the public is *not* a constant ratio of their bank deposits.

The Creation of Deposit Money

A hypothetical balance sheet, showing assets and liabilities, is shown for TD Canada Trust (TD) in Table 27-3. TD has assets of $200 of reserves, held partly as cash on hand and partly as deposits with the central bank, and $900 of loans outstanding to its customers. Its liabilities are $100 to investors who contributed capital to start the bank and $1000 to current depositors. The bank's ratio of reserves to deposits is 0.20 (200/1000), exactly equal to its target reserve ratio.

Practise with Study Guide Chapter 27, Exercise 4.

What Is a New Deposit?

In what follows, we are interested in knowing how the commercial banking system can "create money" when confronted with a new deposit. But what do we mean by a new deposit? By "new," we mean a deposit of cash that is new to the *commercial banking system.* There are three examples.

- First, an individual might immigrate to Canada and bring cash. When that cash is deposited into a commercial bank, it constitutes a new deposit to the (Canadian) banking system.

TABLE 27-3   The Initial Balance Sheet of TD Canada Trust (TD)

Assets ($)		Liabilities ($)	
Reserves (cash and deposits with the central bank)	200	Deposits	1000
Loans	900	Capital	100
	1100		1100

TD Canada Trust has reserves equal to 20 percent of its deposit liabilities. The commercial bank earns money by finding profitable investments for much of the money deposited with it. In this balance sheet, loans are its earning assets.

- Second, an individual who had some cash stashed under his bed (or in a safety deposit box) has now decided to deposit it into an account at a commercial bank.

- Third is the most interesting but also the most complicated example. If the Bank of Canada were to purchase a government security from an individual or from a firm, it would purchase that asset with a cheque drawn on the Bank of Canada. When the individual or firm deposits the cheque with a commercial bank, it would be a new deposit to the commercial banking system.

The important point to keep in mind here is that the *source* of the new deposit is irrelevant to the process of money creation by the commercial banks. In the discussion that follows, we use the example of the Bank of Canada buying government securities from firms or households as a way of generating a new deposit. But this is not crucial. We use this example because, as we shall see in Chapter 29, this is one way that the Bank of Canada conducts its monetary policy. But the general process of money creation we are about to describe applies to *any* new deposit, whatever its source.

TABLE 27-4 TD's Balance Sheet Immediately After a New Deposit of $100

Assets ($)		Liabilities ($)	
Reserves	300	Deposits	1100
Loans	900	Capital	100
	1200		1200

The new deposit raises liabilities and assets by the same amount. Because both cash and deposits rise by $100, the bank's actual reserve ratio, formerly 0.20, increases to 0.27. The bank now has excess reserves of $80.

TABLE 27-5 TD's Balance Sheet After Making a New Loan of $80

Assets ($)		Liabilities ($)	
Reserves	220	Deposits	1100
Loans	980	Capital	100
	1200		1200

TD lends its excess reserves and suffers a cash drain. The bank keeps $20 as a reserve against the initial new deposit of $100. It lends $80 to a customer, who writes a cheque to someone who deals with another bank. When the cheque is cleared, TD suffers an $80 cash drain. Comparing Tables 27-3 and 27-5 shows that the bank has increased its deposit liabilities by the $100 initially deposited and has increased its assets by $20 of cash reserves and $80 of new loans. It has also restored its target reserve ratio of 0.20.

A Single New Deposit

Suppose the Bank of Canada enters the open market and buys $100 worth of Government of Canada bonds from John Smith. The Bank issues a cheque to Smith, who then deposits the $100 cheque into his account at TD Canada Trust. This $100 is a wholly new deposit for the commercial bank, and it results in a revised balance sheet (Table 27-4). As a result of the new deposit, TD's cash assets and deposit liabilities have both increased by $100. More important, TD's ratio of reserves to deposits has increased from 0.20 to 0.27 (300/1100). The bank now has $80 in excess reserves; with $1100 in deposits, its target reserves are only $220.

TD can now lend the $80 in excess reserves that it is holding. As it lends the $80, it increases its loan portfolio by $80 but reduces its cash reserves by the same amount. We say that TD experiences a *cash drain*. Table 27-5 shows TD's balance sheet after this new loan and cash drain. Notice that TD has restored its reserve ratio to 20 percent, its target reserve ratio.

So far, of the $100 initial deposit at TD, $20 is held by TD as reserves against the deposit and $80 has been lent out in the system. As a result, other banks have received new deposits of $80 stemming from the loans made by TD; persons receiving payment from those who borrowed the $80 from TD will have deposited those payments in their own banks. Note that even though the *banking system* suffers no cash drain, TD does suffer a cash drain because most of the $80 goes to other banks and is not redeposited at TD.

The banks that receive deposits from the proceeds of TD's loan are called second-round banks, third-round banks, and so on. In this case, the second-round banks receive new deposits of $80, and when the cheques clear, they have new reserves of $80. Because they desire to hold only $16 in additional reserves to support the new deposits, they have $64 of excess reserves. They now increase their loans by $64. After this money has been spent by the borrowers and has been deposited in other, third-round banks, the balance sheets of the second-round banks will have changed, as in Table 27-6.

The third-round banks now find themselves with $64 of new deposits. Against these they want to hold only $12.80 as reserves, so they have excess reserves of $51.20 that they can immediately lend out. Thus, there begins a long sequence of new deposits, new loans, new deposits, and new loans. These stages are shown in Table 27-7.

The new deposit of $100 to the banking system has led, through the banks' desire to lend their excess reserves, to the creation of new money. After the completion of the process depicted in Table 27-7, the total change in the combined balance sheets of the entire banking system is shown in Table 27-8.

If v is the target reserve ratio, a new deposit to the banking system will increase the total amount of deposits by $1/v$ times the new deposit. [35]

In our example, where $v = 0.2$ and the new deposit equals $100, total deposits in the banking system will eventually increase by $(1/0.2)$ times $100—that is, by $500.

In our example in which there was an initial new deposit of $100, this $100 was also the amount by which reserves increased in the banking system as a whole. This is because the entire amount of new cash eventually ends up in reserves held against a much larger volume of new deposits. Identifying a new deposit as the change in reserves in the banking system permits us to state our central result slightly differently.

With no cash drain from the banking system, a banking system with a target reserve ratio of v can change its deposits by $1/v$ times any change in reserves.

Recalling that the Greek letter delta, Δ, means "the change in," we can express this result in a simple equation. We have

$$\Delta \text{Deposits} = \frac{\Delta \text{Reserves}}{v}$$

The "multiple expansion of deposits" that we have just described applies in reverse to a withdrawal of funds.

TABLE 27-6 Changes in the Balance Sheets of Second-Round Banks

Assets ($)		Liabilities ($)	
Reserves	+16	Deposits	+80
Loans	+64		
	+80		+80

Second-round banks receive cash deposits and expand loans. The second-round banks gain new deposits of $80 as a result of the loan granted by TD. These banks keep 20 percent of the cash that they acquire as their reserve against the new deposit, and they can make new loans using the other 80 percent.

TABLE 27-7 The Sequence of Loans and Deposits After a Single New Deposit of $100

Bank	New Deposits	New Loans	Addition to Reserves
TD	100.00	80.00	20.00
2nd-round bank	80.00	64.00	16.00
3rd-round bank	64.00	51.20	12.80
4th-round bank	51.20	40.96	10.24
5th-round bank	40.96	32.77	8.19
6th-round bank	32.77	26.22	6.55
7th-round bank	26.22	20.98	5.24
8th-round bank	20.98	16.78	4.20
9th-round bank	16.78	13.42	3.36
10th-round bank	13.42	10.74	2.68
Total for first 10 rounds	446.33	357.07	89.26
All remaining rounds	53.67	42.93	10.74
Total for banking system	500.00	400.00	100.00

The banking system as a whole can create deposit money whenever it receives new deposits. The table shows the process of the creation of deposit money on the assumptions that all the loans made by one set of banks end up as deposits in another set of banks (the next-round banks), that the target reserve ratio (v) is 0.20, and that banks always lend out any excess reserves. Although each bank suffers a cash drain whenever it grants a new loan, the system as a whole does not, and in a series of steps it increases deposit money by $1/v$, which, in this example, is five times the amount of any increase in reserves that it obtains.

Deposits of the banking system will fall by $1/v$ times the amount withdrawn from the banking system.

Excess Reserves and Cash Drains

The two simplifying assumptions that were made earlier can now be relaxed.

Excess Reserves

Practise with Study Guide Chapter 27, Exercise 5.

If banks do not choose to lend their excess reserves, the multiple expansion that we discussed will not occur. Go back to Table 27-4. If TD Canada Trust had been content to hold 27 percent of its deposits in reserves, it would have done nothing more. Other things being equal, banks will choose to lend their excess reserves because of the profit motive, but there may be times when they believe that the risk is too great. It is one thing to be offered a good rate of interest on a loan, but if the borrower defaults on the payment of interest and principal, the bank will be the loser. Similarly, if the bank expects interest rates to rise in the future, it may hold off making loans now so that it will have reserves available to make more profitable loans after the interest rate has risen.

Deposit creation does not happen automatically; it depends on the decisions of bankers. If banks do not choose to lend their excess reserves, there will not be an expansion of deposits.

Recall that we have said that the money supply includes both currency and bank deposits. What we have just seen is that the behaviour of commercial banks is crucial to the process of deposit creation. It follows that the money supply is thus at least partly determined by the commercial banks—in response, for example, to changes in national income, interest rates, and expectations of future business conditions.

Cash Drain

Suppose firms and households find it convenient to keep a fixed *fraction* of their deposits in cash instead of a fixed *number* of dollars. In that case, an extra $100 that gets injected into the banking system will not all stay in the banking system. Some fraction will be added to currency in circulation. In such a situation, any multiple expansion of bank deposits will be accompanied by a cash drain to the public. This cash drain will reduce the maximum expansion of bank deposits.

In the case of a cash drain, the relationship between the eventual change in deposits and an injection of cash into the banking system is slightly more complicated. If $X is injected into the system, reserves will ultimately increase by $X. But if c is the ratio of cash to deposits that people want to maintain, the final change in deposits will be given by: [36]

$$\Delta \text{Deposits} = \frac{\Delta \text{Reserves}}{c + v}$$

For example, suppose the Bank of Canada were to enter the open market and purchase $1000 of government securities. As the previous bondholders deposit

TABLE 27-8   Change in the Combined Balance Sheets of All the Banks in the System Following the Multiple Expansion of Deposits

Assets ($)		Liabilities ($)	
Reserves	+100	Deposits	+500
Loans	+400		
	+500		+500

The reserve ratio is returned to 0.20. The entire initial deposit of $100 ends up as reserves of the banking system. Therefore, deposits rise by (1/0.2) times the initial deposit—that is, by $500.

their $1000 into their bank accounts, there is an injection of $1000 into the banking system. If commercial banks' target reserve ratio is 10 percent and there is *no* cash drain, the eventual expansion of deposits will be $10 000 ($\Delta$Deposits = $1000/0.10). But if there is a cash drain of 10 percent, the eventual expansion of deposits will only be $5000 ($\Delta$Deposits = $1000/(0.10 + 0.10)).

The larger is the cash drain from the banking system, the smaller will be the total expansion of deposits created by a change in reserves.

Realistic Expansion of Deposits

So far we have explained the expansion of deposits in the banking system using reserve-deposit and cash-deposit ratios that are easy to work with but unrealistic for Canada. In particular, we have been assuming a reserve-deposit ratio (v) equal to 20 percent, whereas Table 27-2 shows that Canadian commercial banks hold reserves equal to *less than 1 percent* of their deposit liabilities. A realistic value for the cash-deposit ratio in Canada is also approximately 1 percent—indicating that firms and households hold cash outside the banks equal to 1 percent of the value of their bank deposits. Putting these more realistic values for v and c into our equation, we see that a $1 change in reserves generated by a new deposit to the banking system will eventually lead to a total change in deposits equal to $1/(c + v) = $1/(0.01 + 0.01) = $1/(0.02) = $50. Therefore, small changes in the level of reserves can lead, through the commercial banks' process of deposit creation, to very large changes in the total level of deposits.

27.4 **The Money Supply**

Several times in this chapter we have mentioned the *money supply* without ever defining it precisely. But now that you are familiar with the balance sheets of the Bank of Canada and the commercial banking system, and are comfortable with the idea of deposit creation by the commercial banks, we are ready to be more precise about what we mean by the money supply.

The total stock of money in the economy at any moment is called the **money supply** or the *supply of money*. Economists use several alternative definitions for the money supply, most of which are regularly reported in the *Bank of Canada Review*—a quarterly publication of the Bank of Canada. Each definition of the money supply includes the amount of currency in circulation *plus* some types of deposit liabilities of the financial institutions.

money supply   The total quantity of money in an economy at a point in time. Also called the *supply of money.*

Money supply = Currency + Bank deposits

The different definitions vary only by which deposit liabilities are included. We begin by looking at the different kinds of deposits.

Kinds of Deposits

Over the past 20 years or so, banks have evolved a bewildering array of different types of deposits. From our point of view, the most important distinction is between deposits that can be transferred by cheque, called "chequable," and those that cannot, called "nonchequable." Chequable deposits are media of exchange; nonchequable deposits are not.

Until recently, the distinction lay between *demand deposits,* which earned little or no interest but were chequable, and *savings deposits,* which earned a higher interest return but were nonchequable.

Today, however, it is so easy to transfer funds from accounts that are technically nonchequable to other accounts that are chequable that the distinction becomes quite blurred. The deposit that is genuinely tied up for a period of time now takes the form of a **term deposit,** which has a specified withdrawal date, a minimum of 30 days into the future, and which pays a much reduced interest rate in the event of early withdrawal. Term and other nonchequable deposits pay significantly higher interest rates than do chequable deposits.

Nonbank financial institutions such as brokerage firms now offer *money market mutual funds* and *money market deposit accounts.* These accounts earn higher interest and are chequable, although some are subject to minimum withdrawal restrictions and others to prior notice of withdrawal.

The long-standing distinction between money and other highly liquid assets used to be that, narrowly defined, money was a medium of exchange that did not earn interest, whereas other liquid assets earned interest but were not media of exchange. Today, this distinction has almost completely broken down.

term deposit
An interest-earning bank deposit, legally subject to notice before withdrawal (in practice, the notice requirement is not normally enforced).

M1 Currency plus demand deposits.

M2 M1 plus savings deposits at the chartered banks.

M2+ M2 plus deposits held at institutions that are *not* chartered banks.

TABLE 27-9 Three Measures of the Money Supply in Canada, January 2003 (millions of dollars)

Currency	39 247
+ Demand deposits	100 611
= **M1**	**139 858**
+ Personal saving deposits and nonpersonal notice deposits	426 606
= **M2**	**566 464**
+ Deposits at trust and mortgage loan companies, credit unions, and caisses populaires	131 816
+ Money market mutual funds and deposits at other institutions	111 872
= **M2+**	**810 152**

The three widely used measures of the money supply are **M1, M2,** and **M2+.** The narrowest definition, M1, concentrates on what can be used directly as media of exchange, and thus includes only currency and demand deposits. The broader definitions then add in deposits that serve the store-of-value function but can be readily converted to a medium of exchange. M2 is thus M1 plus saving deposits. M2+ is M2 plus deposits at the nonbank financial institutions.

(*Source: Bank of Canada Weekly Financial Statistics,* May 16, 2003.)

Definitions of the Money Supply

Different definitions of the money supply include different types of deposits. The narrowly defined money supply, called **M1,** includes currency and deposits that are themselves usable as media of exchange (such as chequable deposits). A broader definition, **M2,** includes M1 plus savings accounts at the chartered banks. A still broader measure, **M2+,** includes M2 plus the deposits held at the financial institutions that are *not* chartered banks, such as trust companies and credit unions.

M1 concentrates on the medium-of-exchange function of money. M2 and M2+ contain assets that serve the temporary store-of-value function and are in practice quickly convertible into a medium of exchange. Table 27-9 shows the principal elements in these definitions of the money supply. The details of the differences are not important at this stage; what matters is that, broadly defined, money comprises a spectrum of closely related financial assets that their holders regard as highly substitutable for each other.

Near Money and Money Substitutes

Recall our early discussion of money as a medium of exchange and as a store of value. In arriving at empirical measures of money, we must consider some assets that do not perform one or both of these roles perfectly. This brings us to the concepts of *near money* and *money substitutes*.

Assets that adequately fulfill the store-of-value function and are readily converted into a medium of exchange but are not themselves a medium of exchange are sometimes called **near money**. Term deposits are a characteristic form of near money. When you have such a term deposit, you know exactly how much purchasing power you hold (at current prices), and, given modern banking practices, you can turn your deposit into a medium of exchange—cash or a chequing deposit—at a moment's notice (though you may pay a penalty in the form of reduced interest if you withdraw the funds before the end of the specified term).

Why then does everybody not keep his or her money in such deposits instead of in demand deposits or currency? The answer is that the inconvenience of continually shifting money back and forth may outweigh the interest that can be earned. One week's interest on $100 (at 10 percent per year) is only about 20 cents, not enough to cover bus fare to the trust company, the cost of mailing a letter, or the time spent lining up at an automated teller machine. For money that will be needed soon, it would hardly pay to shift it to a term deposit.

Things that serve as media of exchange but are not a store of value are sometimes called **money substitutes**. Credit cards are a prime example. With a credit card, many transactions can be made without either cash or a cheque. The evidence of credit, the credit slip you sign and hand over to the store, is not money, because it cannot be used to make other transactions. The credit card serves the short-run function of a medium of exchange by allowing you to make purchases, even though you have no cash or bank deposit currently in your possession. But this is only temporary; money remains the final medium of exchange for these transactions when the credit account is settled.

Choosing a Measure

Since the eighteenth century, economists have known that the amount of money in circulation is an important economic variable. As theories became more carefully specified in the nineteenth and early twentieth centuries, they included a variable called the "money supply." But for theories to be useful (and especially for the predictions to be testable), we must be able to identify real-world counterparts of these theoretical variables.

The specifics of the definition of money have changed and will continue to change over time. New monetary assets are continually being developed to serve some, if not all, of the functions of money, and they are more or less readily convertible into money. There is no single, timeless definition of money and what is only near money or a money substitute. Indeed, as we have seen, the Bank of Canada uses several definitions of money.

The Role of the Bank of Canada

In this chapter, we have seen that the commercial banking system, when confronted with a new deposit, can create a multiple expansion of bank deposits. This shows how the reserves of the banking system are systematically related to the money supply. We have also had a glimpse of how the Bank of Canada can affect the reserves of the banking system—we will see in Chapter 29 that the Bank of Canada has almost complete control over these reserves. Thus, the Bank of Canada controls reserves, and the commercial banking system turns those reserves into bank deposits.

near money Liquid assets that are easily convertible into money without risk of significant loss of value and can be used as short-term stores of value but are not themselves media of exchange.

Practise with Study Guide Chapter 27, Short-Answer Question 2.

money substitute Something that serves as a medium of exchange but is not a store of value.

Recall that in the previous chapter we examined how in the long run, with real GDP equal to Y^*, the real interest rate was determined by saving and investment. In the next chapter, we return to the short-run version of our macro model (in which Y is no longer assumed to equal Y^*) but add money to that model explicitly. There we will see how the interaction of money demand and money supply determines the equilibrium interest rate in the short run. We will also see how changes in the money market lead to changes in desired aggregate expenditure and real GDP. In Chapter 29 we examine the details of how the Bank of Canada actually conducts its monetary policy, influencing the level of reserves as well as interest rates.

S U M M A R Y

27.1 The Nature of Money

- Money is anything that serves as a medium of exchange, a store of value, and a unit of account.
- Money arose because of the inconvenience of barter, and it developed in stages: from precious metal to metal coinage, to paper money convertible to precious metals, to token coinage and paper money fractionally backed by precious metals, to fiat money, and to deposit money.

27.2 The Canadian Banking System

- The banking system in Canada consists of two main elements: the Bank of Canada (which is the central bank) and the commercial banks.
- The Bank of Canada is a publicly owned corporation that is responsible for the day-to-day conduct of monetary policy. Though the Bank has considerable autonomy in its policy decisions, ultimate responsibility for monetary policy resides with the government.

- Commercial banks are profit-seeking institutions that allow their customers to transfer demand deposits from one bank to another by means of cheques or debit cards. They create money as a by-product of their commercial operations by making or liquidating loans and various other investments.

27.3 Money Creation by the Banking System

- Because most customers are content to pay by cheque or debit card rather than with cash, banks need only small reserves to back their deposit liabilities. It is this *fractional-reserve* aspect of the banking system that enables commercial banks to create deposit money.

- When the banking system receives a new cash deposit, it can create new deposits to some multiple of this amount. For a target reserve ratio of v and a cash–deposit ratio of c, the total change in deposits following an injection of reserves is:

$$\Delta \text{Deposits} = \frac{\Delta \text{Reserves}}{c + v}$$

27.4 **The Money Supply**

LO 4

- The money supply—the stock of money in an economy at a specific moment—can be defined in various ways. M1, the narrowest definition, includes currency and chequable deposits. M2 includes M1 plus savings deposits and smaller term deposits. M2+ includes M2 plus deposits at nonbank financial institutions and money-market mutual funds.

- Near money includes interest-earning assets that are convertible into money on a dollar-for-dollar basis but that are not currently a medium of exchange. Money substitutes are things such as credit cards that serve as a medium of exchange but are not money.

K E Y   C O N C E P T S

Medium of exchange, store of value, and unit of account
Fully backed, fractionally backed, and fiat money

The banking system and the Bank of Canada
Target reserve ratio and excess reserves
The creation of deposit money

Demand and term deposits
The money supply
Near money and money substitutes

S T U D Y   E X E R C I S E S

1. Fill in the blanks to make the following statements correct.

   a. Money serves three functions: _____, _____ and _____.

   b. Suppose children at a summer camp are each given a credit of $20.00 at the snack shop, where purchases are recorded but no cash is exchanged. This is an example of money as a _____ and a _____.

   c. Paper money and coins that are not convertible into anything with intrinsic value, but are declared by the government to be legal tender, are known as _____.

   d. The Bank of Canada has four main functions in the Canadian economy. They are:
   - _____
   - _____
   - _____
   - _____

   e. Canada has a _____-reserve banking system, in which commercial banks keep only a fraction of their total deposits in reserves. A commercial bank has a _____ ratio that governs what it attempts to keep as reserves.

2. Fill in the blanks to make the following statements correct. Answer these questions in the sequence given.

   a. Suppose the Bank of Canada purchases a $1000 bond from Bob's Fishing Supplies, and Bob's deposits its cheque at the CIBC. This is a _____ deposit to the banking system and will allow the commercial banks to _____.

   b. If the CIBC has a target reserve ratio of 5 percent, it will keep _____ dollars as reserves and will lend _____ dollars.

   c. Assuming there is no cash drain from the banking system, the ultimate effect is an _____ in deposits in the banking system of _____ × $1000 = _____.

   d. Suppose the Bank of Canada sells a $1000 bond to Bob's Fishing Supplies, and Bob's pays for that bond with a cheque drawn on its account at the CIBC. This is a _____ of funds from the banking system and will cause the commercial banks to _____.

   e. If the CIBC pays the $1000 from its reserves, its reserve ratio will then be _____ its target rate of 5 percent. If the CIBC keeps its reserves at the new level, its loans must fall by _____ to restore the 5-percent target reserve ratio.

3. Which of the following items can be considered money in the Canadian economy? Explain your answers by discussing the three functions of money—medium of exchange, store of value, and unit of account.

   a. A $100 Bank of Canada note
   b. A Visa credit card
   c. A well-known painting by Robert Bateman
   d. An interest-earning savings account
   e. A U.S. treasury bill payable in three months
   f. A share of Nortel stock

4. The table below shows the balance sheet for the Regal Bank, a hypothetical commercial bank. Assume that the Regal Bank has achieved its target reserve ratio.

Balance Sheet: Regal Bank

Assets		Liabilities	
Reserves	$ 200	Deposits	$4000
Loans	$4200	Capital	$ 400

   a. What is the Regal Bank's target reserve ratio?
   b. What is the value of the owners' investment in the bank?
   c. Suppose that someone makes a new deposit to the Regal Bank of $100. Draw a new balance sheet showing the *immediate* effect of the new deposit. What is the Regal Bank's new reserve ratio?
   d. Suppose instead that someone *withdraws* $100 cash from the Regal Bank. Show the new balance sheet and the new reserve ratio.

5. Consider a new deposit to the Canadian banking system of $1000. Suppose that all commercial banks have a target reserve ratio of 10 percent and there is no cash drain. The following table shows how deposits, reserves, and loans change as the new deposit permits the banks to "create" money.

Round	ΔDeposits	ΔReserves	ΔLoans
First	$1000	$100	$900
Second	—	—	—
Third	—	—	—
Fourth	—	—	—
Fifth	—	—	—

   a. The first round has been completed in the table. Now, recalling that the new loans in the first round become the new deposits in the second round, complete the second round in the table.
   b. Using the same approach, complete the entire table.

   c. You have now completed the first five rounds of the deposit-creation process. What is the total change in deposits *so far* as a result of the single new deposit of $1000?
   d. This deposit-creation process will go on forever, but it will have a *finite* sum. In the text, we showed that the eventual total change in deposits is equal to $1/v$ times the new deposit, where v is the target reserve ratio. What is the eventual total change in deposits in this case?
   e. What is the eventual total change in reserves? What is the eventual change in loans?

6. Consider a withdrawal of $5000 from the Canadian banking system. Suppose that all commercial banks have a target reserve ratio of 8 percent and that there is no cash drain.

   a. Using a table like that shown in the previous question, show the change in deposits, reserves, and loans for the first three "rounds" of activity.
   b. Compute the eventual total change in deposits, reserves, and loans.

7. Consider an individual who immigrates to Canada and deposits $3000 into the Canadian banking system. Suppose that all commercial banks have a target reserve ratio of 10 percent and that individuals choose to hold cash equal to 10 percent of their bank deposits.

   a. In the text, we showed that the eventual total change in deposits is equal to $1/(v+c)$ times the new deposit, where v is the target reserve ratio and c is the ratio of cash to deposits. What is the eventual total change in deposits in this case?
   b. What is the eventual total change in reserves?
   c. What is the eventual total change in loans?

8. Consider an individual who moves from Europe to Canada and brings with him his life savings of $40 000, which he deposits in a Canadian bank. For each of the cases below, compute the overall change in deposits and reserves in the Canadian banking system as a result of this new deposit.

   a. 10 percent target reserve ratio; no cash drain; no excess reserves
   b. 10 percent target reserve ratio; 5 percent cash drain; no excess reserves
   c. 10 percent target reserve ratio; 5 percent cash drain; 5 percent excess reserves

DISCUSSION QUESTIONS

1. A Canadian who receives a U.S. coin has the option of spending it at face value or taking it to the bank and converting it to Canadian money at the going rate of exchange. When the rate of exchange was near par (in the early 1970s), so that $1 Canadian was within 3 cents of U.S.$1, U.S. and Canadian coins circulated side by side, exchanged at face value. Use Gresham's law to predict which coinage disappeared from circulation in Canada when the Canadian dollar fell to U.S.$0.67. Why did a 3-cent differential not produce this result?

2. During hyperinflations in several foreign countries after the Second World War, American cigarettes were sometimes used in place of money. What made them suitable?

3. Suppose that on January 1, 2003, a household had $100 000, which it wished to hold for use one year later. Calculate, using resources available, which of the following would have been the best store of value over that period. Will the best store of value over that period necessarily be the best over the next 24 months?

   a. The (Canadian) dollar
   b. Stocks whose prices moved with the Toronto Stock Exchange (TSX) index
   c. A Government of Canada 5.75 percent bond coming due in 2029
   d. Gold

4. If all depositors tried to turn their deposits into cash at once, they would find that there are not sufficient reserves in the system to allow all of them to do this at the same time. Why then do we not still have panicky runs on the banks? Would it be better for the Bank of Canada to impose a 100 percent reserve requirement? What effect would such a reserve requirement have on the banking system's ability to create money? Would it preclude any possibility of a panic?

5. Compared to a few years ago, credit and bank cards are used extensively today to facilitate purchase of goods and services all over the world. Does this distort the true measure of money in the economy? Should credit and bank cards be incorporated in the definitions of M1 or M2?

CHAPTER 28

Money, Interest Rates, and Economic Activity

LEARNING OBJECTIVES

❶ Explain why the price of a bond is inversely related to the market interest rate.

❷ Describe how the demand for money is related to the interest rate, the price level, and the level of real GDP.

❸ Explain how the interest rate is determined in the short run by the interaction of money demand and money supply.

❹ Explain the monetary transmission mechanism.

❺ Distinguish between the short-run and long-run effects of changes in the money supply.

In Chapter 27, we saw how commercial banks lend their excess reserves to create bank deposits. The banking system transforms a given amount of reserves into the nation's money supply. We concluded by saying that because the Bank of Canada can control the reserves in the banking system, the Bank effectively controls Canada's money supply. What we have not yet discussed, however, is how the Bank of Canada controls the reserves of the banking system. We leave that discussion until the next chapter when we discuss the details of monetary policy. For now, just think of the supply of money as being determined by the Bank of Canada.

In this chapter, we focus on how money affects the economy. Understanding the role of money, however, requires an understanding of the interaction of money supply and money demand. To examine the nature of money demand, we begin by examining how households decide to divide their total holdings of assets between money and interest-earning assets (which here are called "bonds"). Once that is done, we put money supply and money demand together to examine *monetary equilibrium*. Only then can we ask how changes in the supply of money or in the demand for money affect the economy—interest rates, real GDP, and the price level. We begin with a discussion of bond prices and interest rates.

28.1 Understanding Bonds

At any moment, households have a stock of wealth that they hold in many forms. Some of it is money in the bank or in the wallet. Some may be in *treasury bills* and *bonds*, which are IOUs issued by the government or corporations. Some may be in *equity*, meaning ownership shares of a company.

To simplify our discussion, we will group wealth into just two categories, which we call "money" and "bonds." By money we mean all assets that serve as a medium of exchange—that is, paper money, coins, and deposits on which cheques can be drawn. By bonds we mean all other forms of wealth; this includes interest-earning financial assets and claims on real capital (equity). This simplification is useful because it emphasizes the important distinction between interest-earning and non-interest-earning assets. This distinction is central for understanding the demand for money.

Economists often simplify the analysis of financial assets by considering only two types of assets—non-interest-bearing "money" and interest-bearing "bonds."

Before discussing how individuals decide to divide their assets between money and bonds, we need to make sure we understand what bonds are, and how they are priced. This requires an understanding of *present value*.

For readers interested in learning more about the stock market, the market in which equities are traded, look for "A Beginner's Guide to the Stock Market" in the *Additional Topics* section of this book's Companion Website.

http://www.pearsoned.ca/ragan

Present Value and the Interest Rate

A bond is a financial asset that promises to make one or more specified payments at specified dates in the future. The **present value** *(PV)* of any asset refers to the value now of the future payments that the asset offers. Present value depends on the interest rate because when we calculate present value, the interest rate is used to *discount* the future payments. Let's consider two examples to illustrate the concept of present value.

present value (PV) The value now of one or more payments or receipts made in the future; often referred to as *discounted present value.*

A Single Payment One Year Hence

We start with the simplest case. What is the value *now* of a bond that will return a single payment of $100 in one year's time?

Suppose that the interest rate is 5 percent. Now ask how much you would have to lend out at that interest rate today in order to have $100 a year from now. If we use *PV* to stand for this unknown amount, we can write $PV \times (1.05) = \$100$. Thus, $PV = \$100/1.05 = \$95.24$.[1] This tells us that the present value of $100 receivable in one year's time is $95.24; if you lend out $95.24 for one year at 5 percent interest you will get back the $95.24 plus $4.76 in interest, which makes $100.

We can generalize this relationship with a simple equation. If R_1 is the amount we receive one year from now and i is the annual interest rate, the present value is:

$$PV = \frac{R_1}{1 + i}$$

[1] Notice that in this type of formula, the interest rate is expressed as a decimal fraction where, for example, 5 percent is expressed as 0.05, so $1 + i$ equals 1.05.

If the interest rate is 7 percent ($i = 0.07$) and the bond pays $100 in one year ($R_1 = 100), the present value of that bond is $PV = $100/1.07 = 93.46. Notice that, when compared with the previous numerical example, the higher interest rate leads to a lower present value. The future payment of $100 gets discounted at a higher rate and so is now worth less.

A Sequence of Future Payments

Practise with Study Guide Chapter 28, Exercise 1.

Now consider a more complicated case, but one that is actually more realistic. Many bonds promise to make "coupon" payments every year and then return the face value at the end of the term of the loan. For example, imagine a three-year bond that promises to repay the face value of $1000 in three years, but will also pay a 10 percent coupon payment of $100 at the end of each of the three years that the bond is held. How much is this bond worth now? We can compute the present value of this bond by adding together the present values of each of the payments. If the market interest rate is 7 percent, the present value of this bond is:

$$PV = \frac{\$100}{1.07} + \frac{\$100}{(1.07)^2} + \frac{\$1100}{(1.07)^3}$$

The first term is the value today of receiving $100 one year from now. The second term is the value today of receiving the second $100 payment two years from now. Note that we discount this second payment twice—once from Year 2 to Year 1, and once again from Year 1 to now—and thus the denominator shows an interest rate of 7 percent *compounded* for two years. Finally, the third term shows the value today of the $1100 repayment ($1000 of face value plus $100 of coupon payment) three years from now. The present value of this bond is:

$$PV = \$93.46 + \$87.34 + \$897.93$$
$$= \$1078.73$$

In general, any asset that promises to make a sequence of payments into the future of $R_1, R_2, \ldots$ and so on up to R_T has a present value given by:

$$PV = \frac{R_1}{1 + i} + \frac{R_2}{(1 + i)^2} + \ldots + \frac{R_T}{(1 + i)^T}$$

It is useful to try another example. Let's continue with the case in which the bond repays its face value of $1000 three years from now and makes three $100 coupon payments at the end of each year the bond is held. But this time we assume the market interest rate is 9 percent. In this case, the present value of the bond is:

$$PV = \frac{\$100}{1.09} + \frac{\$100}{(1.09)^2} + \frac{\$1100}{(1.09)^3}$$
$$= \$91.74 + \$84.17 + \$849.40$$
$$= \$1025.31$$

Notice that when the market interest rate is 9 percent, the present value of the bond is lower than the present value of the same bond when the market interest rate is 7 percent. The higher interest rate implies that any future payments are discounted at a higher rate and thus have a lower present value.

A General Relationship

There are many types of bonds. Some make no coupon payments but only a single payment (the "face value") at some point in the future. This is the case for short-term government bonds called *treasury bills*. Other bonds, typically longer-term government or corporate bonds, make regular coupon payments as well as a final payment of the bond's face value.

Though there are many types of bonds, they all have one thing in common: they promise to make some payment or sequence of payments in the future. Because bonds make payments in the future, their present value is negatively related to the market interest rate.

The present value of any bond that promises a future payment or sequence of future payments is negatively related to the market interest rate.

Present Value and Market Price

The present value of a bond is important because it establishes the bond's market price.

The present value of a bond is the most someone would be willing to pay now to own the bond's future stream of payments.

To understand this concept, let us return to our example of a bond that promises to pay $100 one year from now. When the interest rate is 5 percent, the present value of this bond is $95.24. To see why this is the maximum that anyone would pay for this bond, suppose that some sellers offer to sell the bond at some other price, say, $98. If, instead of paying this amount for the bond, a potential buyer lends $98 out at 5 percent interest, he or she would have at the end of one year more than the $100 that the bond will produce. (At 5 percent interest, $98 yields $4.90 in interest, which when added to the principal makes $102.90.) Clearly, no well-informed individual would pay $98—or, by the same reasoning, any sum in excess of $95.24—for the bond. Thus, at any price above the bond's present value, the lack of demand will cause the price to fall.

Now suppose that the bond is offered for sale at a price less than $95.24, say, $90. A potential buyer could borrow $90 to buy the bond and would pay $4.50 in interest on the loan. At the end of the year, the bond yields $100. When this is used to repay the $90 loan and the $4.50 in interest, $5.50 is left as profit. Clearly, it would be worthwhile for someone to buy the bond at the price of $90 or, by the same argument, at any price less than $95.24. Thus, at any price below the bond's present value, the abundance of demand will cause the price to rise.

This discussion should make clear that the present value of an asset determines its equilibrium market price. If the market price of any asset is greater than the present value of its income stream, no one will want to buy it, and this excess supply will push down the market price. If the market value is below its present value, there will be a rush to buy it, and this excess demand will push up the market price.

The equilibrium market price of any bond will be the present value of the income stream that it produces.

Interest Rates, Market Prices, and Bond Yields

We now have two relationships that can be put together to tell us about the link between the market interest rate and bond prices. Let's restate these two relationships.

1. The present value of a bond is negatively related to the market interest rate.

2. A bond's equilibrium market price will be equal to its present value.

Putting these two relationships together, we come to a key relationship:

An increase in the market interest rate leads to a fall in the price of any given bond. A decrease in the market interest rate leads to an increase in the price of any given bond.

Remember that a bond is a financial investment for the purchaser. The cost of the investment is the price of the bond, and the return on the investment is the sequence of future payments. Thus, for a given sequence of future payments, a lower bond price implies a higher rate of return on the bond, or a higher *bond yield*.

To illustrate the yield on a bond, consider a simple example of a bond that promises to pay $1000 two years from now. If you purchase this bond for $857.34, your return on your investment will be 8 percent per year because $857.34 compounded for two years at 8 percent will yield $1000 in two years.

$$\$857.34 \, (1.08)^2 = \$1000$$

In other words, your yield on the bond will be 8 percent per year.

Notice that we are making a distinction between the concept of the *yield* on a bond and the *market interest rate*. The bond yield is a function of the sequence of payments and the bond price. The market interest rate is the rate at which you can borrow or lend money in the credit market.

Although they are logically distinct from each other, there is a close relationship between the market interest rate and bond yields. A rise in the market interest rate will lead to a decline in the present value of any bond and thus to a decline in its equilibrium price. As the bond price falls, its yield or rate of return rises. Thus, we see that market interest rates and bond yields tend to move in the same direction.

An increase in the market interest rate will reduce bond prices and increase bond yields. A reduction in the market interest rate will increase bond prices and reduce bond yields. Therefore, market interest rates and bond yields move together.

Because of this close relationship between bond yields and market interest rates, economists discussing the role of money in the macroeconomy typically refer to "the" interest rate—or perhaps to "interest rates" in general—rather than to any specific interest rate among the many different rates corresponding to the many different financial assets. Since these rates all tend to rise or fall together, it is a very useful simplification to refer only to "the" interest rate, meaning the rate of return that can be earned by holding interest-earning assets rather than money.

Bond Riskiness

Sometimes the yields on specific bonds rise or fall even when there is no change in the market interest rate. This occurs when there is a change in the perceived *riskiness* of the bond. If the bond purchasers (lenders) perceive that bond issuers (borrowers) are unlikely to be able to fulfill their future repayment obligations, the expected present value of the bond declines and, as a result, the equilibrium market price for that bond declines. As the market price falls, the yield on that bond rises. Bonds with high yields reflect high-risk investments.

An increase in the riskiness of any bond leads to a decline in its expected present value and thus to a decline in the bond's price. The lower bond price implies a higher bond yield.

It is rare in Canada that government bonds are perceived as risky, but many corporations are sometimes believed to be in precarious financial situations and thus their bonds are perceived to be risky assets. As a result, there are often very high yields (low bond prices) on specific corporate bonds. *Applying Economic Concepts 28-1* discusses the relationship between bond prices, bond yields, riskiness, and *term to maturity* of government and corporate bonds. It will help you understand some of those columns of confusing numbers that appear daily at the back of your favourite newspaper!

28.2 **The Demand for Money**

The amount of money balances that everyone in the economy wishes to hold is called the **demand for money.** Because households and firms are choosing how to divide their given stock of assets between money and bonds, it follows that if we know the demand for money, we also know the demand for bonds. If people wish to hold $1 billion more money, they must also wish to hold $1 billion less of bonds.

demand for money
The total amount of money balances that the public wishes to hold for all purposes.

Reasons for Holding Money

Why do firms and households hold money? There are three reasons. First, households and firms hold money in order to carry out *transactions.* Economists call this the *transactions demand* for money. You carry money in your pocket or keep it in a chequing account in order to have it readily available for your upcoming transactions; it would be very inconvenient to have to sell bonds or withdraw money from your savings account every time you wanted to spend. Similarly, firms are continually making expenditures on intermediate inputs and payments to labour and they keep money available in their chequing accounts to pay these expenses.

A second and related reason firms and households hold money is that they are *uncertain* about when some expenditures will be necessary, and they hold money as a precaution to avoid the problems associated with missing a transaction. This is referred to as the *precautionary demand* for money. For example, you might hold some cash because of the possibility that you might need to take an unplanned taxi ride during a rainstorm; a small business may hold cash because of the possibility that it might need the emergency services of a tradesman, such as a plumber or an electrician.

The third reason for holding money applies more to large businesses and to professional money managers than to individuals because it involves *speculating* about how interest rates are likely to change in the future. Economists call this the *speculative demand* for money. To understand this reason for holding money, recall what we said earlier about the negative relationship between interest rates and bond prices. If interest rates are expected to rise in the future, bond prices will be expected to fall. Whenever bond prices fall, bondholders experience a decline in the value of their bond holdings. The expectation of increases in *future* interest rates will therefore lead to the holding of more money (and fewer bonds) *now* as financial managers adjust their portfolios in order to preserve their values.

APPLYING ECONOMIC CONCEPTS 28-1

Understanding Bond Prices and Bond Yields

Look at the back of the business section of your newspaper and you will find several pages with columns of fine print that list prices for stocks, bonds, precious metals, and mutual funds. We focus here on how to read the section on bonds.

How to Read the Bond Tables

The accompanying table shows nine bond listings just as they appeared in the *Globe and Mail* on March 19, 2003. The five columns are as follows:

1. **Issuer.** This is the issuer of the bond—that is, the borrower of the money. The first seven bonds shown are issued by the government of Canada. The last two are issued by firms whose names you surely recognize.

2. **Coupon.** This is the coupon rate—the annual rate of interest that the bond pays before it matures. For example, a 6 percent coupon rate means that the bondholder (the lender) will receive 6 percent of the face value of the bond every year until the bond matures.

3. **Maturity.** This is when the bond matures and the face value is repaid to the bondholder. All debt obligations are then fulfilled.

4. **Price.** This is the market price of the bond, expressed as the price per $100 of face value. For example, a price

of $104.81 means that for every $100 of face value, the purchaser must pay $104.81. When the price is greater than $100, we say there is a *premium*; when the price is less than $100, we say the bond is selling at a *discount*.

5. **Yield.** This is the rate of return earned by the bondholder if the bond is bought at the *current* price and held to maturity, earning all regular coupon payments.

Bond Prices and Yields

Three general patterns can be seen in the accompanying table. First, for a given issuer and maturity, there is a positive relationship between the bond price and the coupon rate. Rows 1 and 2, for example, show two bonds, both issued by the government of Canada and both maturing on September 1, 2005. The common issuer suggests a common risk of non-repayment (in this case a very low risk). The first bond has a 6 percent coupon whereas the second has a 12.25 percent coupon. Not surprisingly, the higher coupon payments make the second bond a more attractive asset and thus its market price is higher—$119.29 as compared to $104.81. Note, however, that the implied yield on the two bonds is almost identical. If this weren't the case, demand would shift toward the high-yield (low-price) bond, driving down the yield (increasing the price) until the two yields were the same.

The Determinants of Money Demand

We have just seen three general reasons why firms and households hold money. We now want to examine what key macroeconomic variables affect the *amount* of money that is demanded. We focus on three: the interest rate, the level of real GDP, and the price level.

The Interest Rate

No matter what benefits households or firms receive from holding money, there is also a cost. The cost of holding money is the income that *could have been earned* if that wealth were instead held in the form of interest-earning bonds. This is the *opportunity cost* of holding money. An increase in the interest rate leads firms and households to reduce their desired money holdings. Conversely, a reduction in the interest rate means that holding money is less costly and so firms and households will increase their desired money holdings.

Second, for a given bond issuer, there is a positive relationship between the bond yield and the term to maturity. This is shown in the first seven rows, as yields rise from 3.92 percent on bonds maturing in 18 months' time (from the date of the listing) to 5.53 percent on bonds maturing in 26 years' time. This positive relationship is often referred to as the *yield curve* or the *term structure of interest rates*. The higher yields on longer-term bonds reflect what is often called a *term premium*—the higher yield that bondholders must be paid in order to induce them to have their money tied up for longer periods of time.

Third, for a given term to maturity, there is a positive relationship between the bond yield and the perceived riskiness of the bond issuer. Compare rows 5 and 8, for example. Both bonds have very similar (but not identical) maturity dates in 2011, but one is issued by the government of Canada while the other is issued by the Bank of Montreal. Though it is almost impossible for the government of Canada to go

bankrupt and almost inconceivable that it would default on its debt, it is at least possible for the Bank of Montreal to do so. This difference explains the one-percentage-point difference in yields. The same is true between rows 7 and 9 where the 1.2 percentage point yield difference is attributable to the higher likelihood of default by Loblaws than by the Canadian government.

If you run your eyes down the bond tables, you will easily see those corporations viewed by the market as being risky borrowers because the yields on their bonds will be higher—often dramatically so—than the yields on similar-maturity government bonds. For example, in 2003 when Air Canada was experiencing severe financial difficulties, its bonds were selling at such a discount that the implied annual yield was over 30 percent. These very high yields represent a great investment opportunity only if you are prepared to take the associated risk. Beware!

Issuer	Coupon	Maturity	Price	Yield
1. Canada	6.00	Sep 1, 2005	104.81	3.92
2. Canada	12.25	Sep 1, 2005	119.29	3.91
3. Canada	6.00	Jun 1, 2008	106.74	4.53
4. Canada	10.00	Jun 1, 2008	125.18	4.51
5. Canada	6.00	Jun 1, 2011	106.87	4.97
6. Canada	11.25	Jun 1, 2015	154.60	5.16
7. Canada	5.75	Jun 1, 2029	103.00	5.53
8. Bank of Montreal	6.69	Dec 31, 2011	104.42	6.03
9. Loblaws Co.	6.65	Nov 8, 2027	99.19	6.72

Other things being equal, the demand for money is negatively related to the interest rate.[2]

The negative relationship between interest rates and desired money holdings is shown in Figure 28-1, and is drawn as the money demand (M_D) curve. Remember that the decision to hold money is also the decision *not* to hold bonds, and so movements along the M_D curve imply the substitution of assets between money and bonds. For example, as interest rates decline, bonds become a less attractive asset and money becomes more attractive, so firms and households substitute away from bonds and toward money.

---

[2] The opportunity cost of holding money is the interest that could have been earned on bonds—this is the *nominal* interest rate. In the presence of expected inflation, we must distinguish between the *nominal* and *real* interest rates. In this chapter we assume, however, that expected inflation is zero, and so we simply speak of "the" interest rate. We discuss inflation in detail in Chapter 30.

FIGURE 28-1   Money Demand as a Function of the Interest Rate, Real GDP, and the Price Level

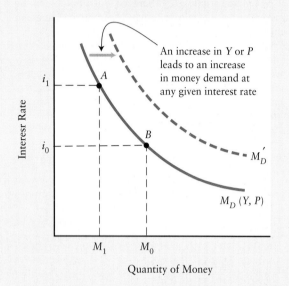

An increase in Y or P leads to an increase in money demand at any given interest rate

The quantity of money demanded is negatively related to the interest rate and positively related to real GDP and the price level. We show the initial money demand curve as $M_D (Y, P)$, indicating that the curve is drawn for given values of Y and P. Increases in Y or P shift the M_D curve to the right; decreases in Y or P shift the M_D curve to the left.

The negative slope of the M_D curve comes from the choice between holding money or holding bonds. A fall in the interest rate from i_1 to i_0 lowers the opportunity cost of holding money because the rate of return on bonds declines. Thus the decision to hold more money (M_0 is greater than M_1) is the "flip side" of the decision to hold fewer bonds.

Let's now see why changes in real GDP and the price level cause the M_D curve to shift.

Real GDP

An important reason for holding money is to make transactions. Not surprisingly, the amount of transactions that firms and households wish to make is positively related to the level of income and production in the economy—that is, to the level of real GDP. This positive relationship between real GDP and desired money holdings is shown in Figure 28-1 by a rightward shift of the M_D curve to M_D'. At any given interest rate, the increase in Y leads to more transactions and thus greater desired money holdings.

An increase in real GDP increases the volume of transactions in the economy and therefore leads to an increase in desired money holding.

The Price Level

An increase in the price level leads to an increase in the *dollar* value of transactions even if there is no change in the *real* value of transactions. That is, as P rises, households and firms will need to hold more money in order to carry out the same real value of transactions. This positive relationship between the price level and desired money holdings is also shown in Figure 28-1 as a rightward shift of the M_D curve to M_D'.

An increase in the price level leads to an increase in desired money holdings.

We can be more precise than just saying that there is a positive relationship between P and desired money holdings. Suppose, for example, that Y and i are constant but that all prices in the economy increase by 10 percent. Since Y is unchanged, the *real* value of desired transactions is also unchanged. Furthermore, since i is unchanged, the opportunity cost of holding money is constant. Therefore, in order to make the same transactions as before, households and firms must not just hold more money than before—they must hold precisely 10 percent more. In other words, if real GDP and the interest rate are constant, the demand for money is *proportional* to the price level.

Money Demand: Summing Up

We have discussed why firms and households hold money and we have examined the relationship between desired money holding and three macroeconomic variables. Since the demand for money reflects firms' and households' preference to hold wealth in the form of a *liquid* asset (money) rather than a less liquid asset (bonds), economists often refer to the money demand function as a *liquidity preference* function. We can summarize our discussion of money demand with the following algebraic statement:

$$M_D = M_D\,(\overset{-}{i},\ \overset{+}{Y},\ \overset{+}{P})$$

This equation says that the amount of money firms and households want to hold at any given time depends on three variables; the sign above each variable indicates whether that variable positively or negatively affects desired money holding. Let's summarize our findings:

1. An increase in the interest rate increases the opportunity cost of holding money and leads to a reduction in the quantity of money demanded.

2. An increase in real GDP increases the volume of transactions and leads to an increase in the quantity of money demanded.

3. An increase in the price level increases the dollar value of a given volume of transactions and leads to an increase in the quantity of money demanded.

Remember that money demand is also related to bond demand. Firms and households must decide at any time how to divide their stock of assets between money and bonds. So our statements here about money demand apply in reverse to the demand for bonds. For example, in Figure 28-1, if the economy moves down the M_D curve from point A to point B as the interest rate falls, firms and households are deciding to hold more money and fewer bonds. The lower interest rate means a lower opportunity cost for holding money and so people choose to hold more; but the lower interest rate equally means that bonds are a less attractive asset and so they choose to hold fewer bonds.

People hold money in order to make transactions. As income rises, the volume of transactions also rises, and so people typically decide to hold more money.

28.3 Monetary Equilibrium and National Income

So far, this chapter has been devoted to understanding bonds and how they relate to the demand for money. In the previous chapter we examined the supply of money. We are now ready to put these two sides of the money market together to see how interest rates are determined. You may recall, however, that we already saw in Chapter 26 a theory of how interest rates are determined. But remember that Chapter 26 was a discussion of long-run economic growth, and real GDP was assumed to be equal to Y^* throughout that discussion. What we do in this chapter and the next is to return to the short-run version of our macro model (in which Y is not assumed to equal Y^*), but make it more complete by adding money and interest rates explicitly. Here we will see how changes in the money market affect interest rates, aggregate expenditure, and the equilibrium level of real GDP in the short run.

We begin by examining the concept of *monetary equilibrium*—this shows how interest rates are determined by the interaction of money demand and money supply. We then explore what economists call the *monetary transmission mechanism*—the fairly involved chain of events that takes us from changes in the interest rate, through to changes in desired aggregate expenditure, to changes in the level of real GDP.

FIGURE 28-2   Monetary Equilibrium

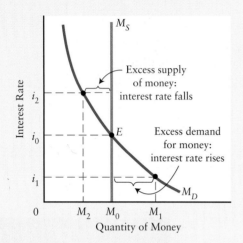

The interest rate rises when there is an excess demand for money and falls when there is an excess supply of money. The fixed quantity of money M_0 is shown by the completely inelastic supply curve M_S. The demand for money is given by M_D; its negative slope indicates that a fall in the rate of interest causes the quantity of money demanded to increase. Monetary equilibrium is at E, with a rate of interest of i_0.

If the interest rate is i_1, there will be an excess demand for money of M_0M_1. Bonds will be offered for sale in an attempt to increase money holdings. This will force the rate of interest up to i_0 (the price of bonds falls), at which point the quantity of money demanded is equal to the fixed available quantity of M_0. If the interest rate is i_2, there will be an excess supply of money M_2M_0. Bonds will be demanded in return for excess money balances. This will force the rate of interest down to i_0 (the price of bonds rises), at which point the quantity of money demanded is equal to the fixed supply of M_0.

monetary equilibrium
A situation in which the demand for money equals the supply of money.

Practise with Study Guide Chapter 28, Exercise 2.

Monetary Equilibrium

Figure 28-2 illustrates the money market. The money supply (M_S) curve is vertical. The money supply increases (M_S shifts to the right) if the central bank increases reserves in the banking system or if the commercial banks decide to lend out a larger fraction of those reserves. The money supply decreases (M_S shifts to the left) if the central bank decreases reserves in the banking system or if the commercial banks decide to reduce lending. The money demand (M_D) curve is downward sloping, indicating that firms and households decide to hold more money if the interest rate falls.

Monetary equilibrium occurs when the quantity of money demanded equals the quantity of money supplied. In Chapter 4, we saw that in a competitive market for some commodity the price will adjust to establish equilibrium. In the market for money, the interest rate is that "price" that adjusts to bring about equilibrium. Let's see how this equilibrium is achieved.

When a single household or firm finds that it is holding a smaller fraction of its wealth in money than it wishes, it can sell some bonds and add the proceeds to its money holdings. Such behaviour by an individual firm or household will have a negligible effect on the economy.

But what happens when *all* of the firms and households in the economy try to add to their money balances? They all try to sell bonds to add to their money balances, but what one person can do, all persons cannot do simultaneously. At any moment, the economy's total supply of money and bonds is fixed. Thus, as everyone tries to sell bonds, an excess supply of bonds develops. But since people are simply trying to switch between a given amount of bonds and money, the excess supply of bonds implies an excess demand for money, as shown at interest rate i_1 in Figure 28-2.

What happens when there is an excess supply of bonds? Like any other good or service, an excess supply causes a fall in the price. As we saw earlier in the chapter, a fall in the price of bonds implies an increase in the interest rate. As the interest rate rises, people economize on money balances because the opportunity cost of holding such balances is rising. Eventually, the interest rate will rise enough that people will no longer be trying to add to their money balances by selling bonds. At that point, there is no longer an excess supply of bonds (or an excess demand for money), and the interest rate will stop rising. The demand for money again equals the supply, as at point E in Figure 28-2.

Suppose now there is more money than firms and households want to hold. That is, there is an excess supply of money, as at interest rate i_2 in Figure 28-2. The excess supply of money implies an excess demand for bonds—people are trying to "get rid of" their excess money balances by acquiring bonds. But when all households try to buy bonds, they bid up the price of bonds, and the interest rate falls. As the interest rate falls, households and firms become willing to hold larger quantities of money. The interest rate falls until firms and households stop trying to convert bonds into money. In other words, it continues until everyone is content to hold the existing supply of money and bonds, as at point *E* in Figure 28-2.

Monetary equilibrium occurs when the rate of interest is such that the quantity of money demanded equals the quantity of money supplied.

The determination of the interest rate depicted in Figure 28-2 is often called the *liquidity preference theory of interest*. This name reflects the fact that a demand to hold money (rather than bonds) is a demand for the more liquid of the two assets—a preference for liquidity.

The Monetary Transmission Mechanism

The mechanism by which changes in the demand for and supply of money affect aggregate demand is called the **monetary transmission mechanism**. It operates in three stages:

1. Changes in the demand for money or the supply of money cause a change in the equilibrium interest rate;

2. The change in the interest rate leads to a change in desired investment expenditure;

3. The change in desired aggregate expenditure leads to a shift in the *AD* curve and thus to short-run changes in real GDP and the price level.

Let's examine these three stages in more detail.

1. Changes in the Interest Rate

The interest rate will change if the equilibrium depicted in Figure 28-2 is disturbed by a change in either the supply of money or the demand for money. For example, as shown in part (i) of Figure 28-3, an increase in the supply of money, with an unchanged money demand curve, creates an excess supply of money at the original interest rate. As we have seen, an excess supply of money leads firms and households to buy bonds, thus driving up the price of bonds and pushing down the interest rate. The original increase in the supply of money could be caused by either the central bank increasing the reserves in the banking system or by the commercial banks lending out a higher fraction of their reserves.

As shown in part (ii) of Figure 28-3, an increase in the demand for money, with an unchanged supply of money, creates an excess demand for money at the original interest rate. Firms and households try to acquire more money by selling their holdings of bonds, which drives down the price of bonds and pushes up the interest rate. The original increase in the demand for money could be caused by an increase in real GDP, an increase in the price level, or an increased preference to hold money rather than bonds, as would happen if there were an increase in the perceived riskiness of bonds.

Changes in either the demand for or the supply of money cause changes in the interest rate.

2. Changes in Desired Investment

The second link in the monetary transmission mechanism relates interest rates to desired investment and consumption expenditure. We saw in Chapter 21 that investment, which includes expenditure on inventory accumulation, residential construction, and business fixed investment, responds to changes in the interest rate. Other things being equal, a decrease in the interest rate makes borrowing cheaper and generates new investment

monetary transmission mechanism The channels by which a change in the demand for or supply of money leads to a shift of the aggregate demand curve.

Practise with Study Guide Chapter 28, Exercise 2.

FIGURE 28-3   Changes in the Equilibrium Interest Rate

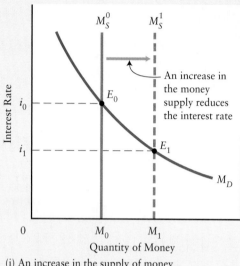

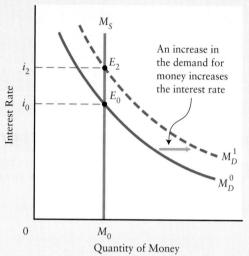

(i) An increase in the supply of money

(ii) An increase in the demand for money

Shifts in the supply of money or in the demand for money cause the equilibrium interest rate to change. In both parts of the figure, the money supply is shown by the vertical curve M_S, and the demand for money is shown by the negatively sloped curve M_D. The initial monetary equilibrium is at E_0, with corresponding interest rate i_0. In part (i), an increase in the money supply causes M_S^0 to shift to M_S^1. The new equilibrium is at E_1, where the interest rate is i_1. In part (ii), an increase in the demand for money causes M_D^0 to shift to M_D^1. The new monetary equilibrium occurs at E_2, and the new equilibrium interest rate is i_2.

expenditure. We also saw that some consumption expenditures, especially big-ticket items like cars and furniture that are often purchased on credit, are negatively related to the interest rate. This negative relationship between desired expenditure and the interest rate is labelled I^D in Figure 28-4, reflecting the fact that investment is the *most* interest-sensitive part of expenditure.

The first two links in the monetary transmission mechanism are shown in Figure 28-4.[3] Although the analysis in Figure 28-4 illustrates a change in the money supply, remember that the process can also be set in motion by a change in the demand for money. In part (i), we see that an increase in the money supply reduces the interest rate. In part (ii), we see that a fall in the interest rate leads to an increase in desired investment expenditure.

An increase in the money supply leads to a fall in the interest rate and an increase in investment expenditure. A decrease in the money supply leads to a rise in the interest rate and a decrease in investment expenditure.

---

[3] In part (i) of Figure 28-4, it is the nominal interest rate—the rate of return on bonds—that affects money demand. In part (ii), however, it is the real interest rate that influences desired investment expenditure. It is therefore worth emphasizing that we are continuing with the assumption that inflation is expected to be zero and so the nominal and real interest rates are the same. This assumption allows us to use the same vertical axis in the two parts of the figure.

FIGURE 28-4 The Effects of Changes in the Money Supply on Investment Expenditure

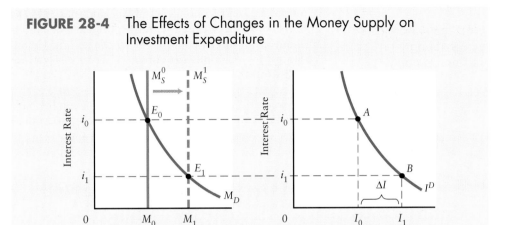

(i) Money demand and supply

(ii) Investment demand

Increases in the money supply reduce the interest rate and increase desired investment expenditure. In part (i), equilibrium in the money market is at E_0, with a quantity of money of M_0 and an interest rate of i_0. The corresponding level of investment expenditure is I_0 (point A) in part (ii). The Bank of Canada then increases the money supply to M_1. This reduces the interest rate to i_1 and increases investment expenditure by ΔI to I_1 (point B).

3. Changes in Aggregate Demand

The third link in the monetary transmission mechanism is from changes in desired expenditure to shifts in the AE function and in the AD curve. This is familiar ground. In Chapter 23, we saw that a shift in the aggregate expenditure curve (caused by something *other than* a change in the price level) leads to a shift in the AD curve. This situation is shown again in Figure 28-5.

An increase in the money supply causes an increase in desired investment and therefore a rightward shift of the AD curve. A decrease in the money supply causes a decrease in desired investment and therefore a leftward shift of the AD curve.

The entire monetary transmission mechanism is summarized in Figure 28-6 for the case of an expansionary monetary shock. An increase in money supply or a decrease in money demand reduces the interest rate, increases desired investment expenditure, and increases aggregate demand.

An Open-Economy Modification

So far, the emphasis in our discussion of the transmission mechanism has been on the effect that a change in the interest rate has on desired investment. In an open economy, however, where financial capital flows easily across borders, the monetary transmission mechanism is a little more complex.

Financial capital is very mobile across international boundaries. Bondholders, either in Canada or abroad, are able to substitute between Canadian bonds, U.S. bonds, German bonds, or bonds from almost any country you can think of. Bonds from different countries are generally not *perfect* substitutes for each other because of varying amounts

FIGURE 28-5   The Effects of Changes in the Money Supply on Aggregate Demand

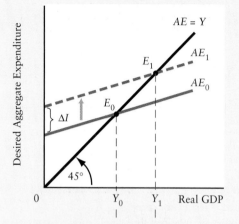

(i) A shift in aggregate expenditure

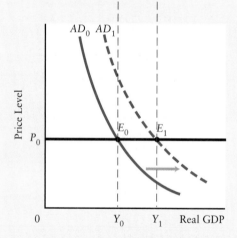

(ii) A shift in aggregate demand

Changes in the money supply cause shifts in the AE and AD functions. In Figure 28-4, an increase in the money supply increased desired investment expenditure by ΔI. In part (i) of this figure, the AE function shifts up by ΔI. At the fixed price level P_0, equilibrium GDP rises from Y_0 to Y_1, as shown by the rightward shift in the curve AD in part (ii).

of political and economic instability, and thus different levels of *risk* associated with the different bonds. But bonds from similar countries—Canada and the United States, for example—are often viewed as very close substitutes.

The ability of bondholders to substitute easily between bonds from different countries implies that monetary disturbances generally lead to international flows of financial capital, which in turn cause changes in exchange rates and changes in exports and imports.

In an open economy with capital mobility, monetary disturbances lead to capital flows, exchange rate changes and changes in net exports.

To understand how capital mobility adds a second channel to the monetary transmission mechanism, consider an example. Suppose the Bank of Canada decides to increase the money supply. As shown in Figure 28-4, the increase in money supply reduces the interest rate and increases desired investment expenditure. This is the first channel of the monetary transmission mechanism. But the story does not end there.

The reduction in Canadian interest rates also makes Canadian bonds less attractive relative to foreign bonds. Canadian and foreign investors alike will sell some of their Canadian bonds and buy more of the high-return foreign bonds. But in order to buy foreign bonds, it is necessary first to exchange Canadian dollars for foreign currency. The increase in the demand for foreign currency causes the Canadian dollar to depreciate relative to other currencies.

An increase in the Canadian money supply reduces Canadian interest rates and leads to a capital outflow. This causes the Canadian dollar to depreciate.

As the Canadian dollar depreciates, however, Canadian goods and services become less expensive relative to those from other countries. As we first saw in Chapter 22, this change in international relative prices causes households and firms—both in Canada and abroad—to substitute away from foreign goods and toward Canadian goods. Imports fall and exports rise.

So the overall effect of the increase in the Canadian money supply is not just a fall in interest rates and an increase in investment. Because of the international mobility of financial capital, the low Canadian interest rates also lead to a capital outflow, a depreciation of the Canadian dollar, and an increase in Canadian net exports. This increase in net exports, of course, *strengthens* the positive effect on aggregate demand already coming from the increase in desired investment.

This complete open-economy monetary transmission mechanism is shown in Figure 28-7. This figure is based on Figure 28-6, but simply adds the second channel of the transmission mechanism that works through capital mobility, exchange rates, and net exports.

In an open economy with capital mobility, an increase in the money supply results in an increase in aggregate demand for two reasons. First, the reduction in interest rates causes an increase in investment. Second, the lower interest rate causes a capital outflow, a currency depreciation, and a rise in net exports.

Our example has been that of a monetary expansion. A monetary contraction would have the opposite effect, but the logic of the mechanism is the same. A reduction in the Canadian money supply would raise Canadian interest rates and reduce desired investment expenditure. The higher Canadian interest rates would attract foreign financial capital as bondholders sell low-return foreign bonds and purchase high-return Canadian bonds. This action would increase the demand for Canadian dollars in the foreign-exchange market and thus cause the Canadian dollar to appreciate. Finally, the appreciation of the Canadian dollar would increase Canadians' imports of foreign goods and reduce Canadian exports to other countries. Canadian net exports would fall.

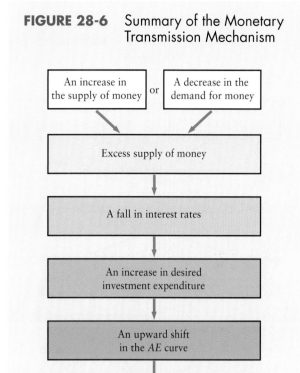

FIGURE 28-6 Summary of the Monetary Transmission Mechanism

The Slope of the *AD* Curve

We can now use the monetary transmission mechanism to add to the explanation of the negative slope of the *AD* curve. In Chapter 23, we mentioned two reasons for the negative slope of the *AD* curve: the change in wealth, and the substitution between domestic and foreign goods, both of which occur when the price level changes. A third effect operates through interest rates.

The third effect is that a rise in the price level raises the money value of transactions. This leads to an increased demand for money, and thus to an increase in the equilibrium interest rate. The rise in the interest rate then reduces desired investment expenditure and so reduces equilibrium national income.

This effect is important because, empirically, the interest rate is the most important link between monetary factors and real expenditure flows. This reason for the negative slope of the *AD* curve is discussed in more detail in the appendix to this chapter.

28.4 **The Strength of Monetary Forces**

In the previous section we saw that a change in the money supply leads to a change in interest rates. The change in interest rates, in turn, leads to changes in investment and, through capital flows and changes in the exchange rate, to changes in net exports. Thus, a change in the money supply leads to a change in desired aggregate expenditure and therefore to a shift in the *AD* curve. From our analysis in Chapter 24, we know that a

FIGURE 28-7 The Open-Economy Monetary Transmission Mechanism

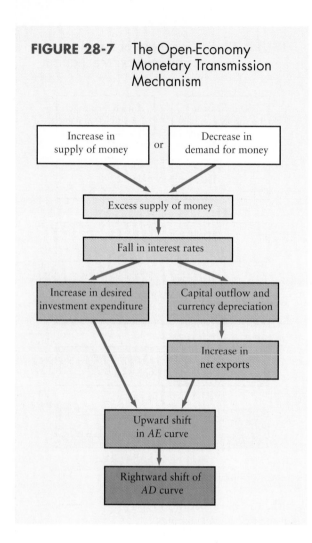

shift in the *AD* curve will lead to different effects in the short run than in the long run. It is in the long run that factor prices will fully adjust to excess demands or excess supplies, and output will return to the level of potential output, *Y**. Let's begin by examining the long-run effects of increases in the money supply, and then turn to an old debate about the strength of monetary forces in the short run.

Long-Run Neutrality of Money

We saw in Chapter 24 that any shock—either to aggregate demand or aggregate supply—that creates an output gap sets in place an adjustment mechanism that will eventually close that gap and return real GDP to its potential level, *Y**. The operation of this adjustment mechanism following an increase in the money supply is illustrated in Figure 28-8.

Although a change in the money supply causes the *AD* curve to shift, it has no effect on the level of real GDP in the long run.

Figure 28-8 shows that the only long-run effect of a shift in the *AD* curve following a change in the money supply is a change in the price level. This result is often referred to as the *neutrality of money*.

In the eighteenth and nineteenth centuries, economists believed that the "money" side of the economy was independent from the "real" side of the economy. This belief was referred to as the *Classical Dichotomy* and embodied the idea of **money neutrality**. The Classical view was that real GDP, employment, investment, and all other real variables in the economy were

money neutrality
The idea that a change in the supply of money has no effect on any real variables but only affects the price level.

determined by real factors, such as the demands and supplies for various goods, which were in turn determined by firms' technologies and consumers' preferences. The Classical economists argued that the creation of additional money, in contrast, would simply raise the price level and have no influence on any real variables. In terms of Figure 28-8, the Classical economists would have argued that by increasing the money supply, the economy would immediately move from E_0 to E_2; there would be no effect on real GDP or employment but the price level would increase.

According to the Classical economists, changes in the supply of money had no effect on real GDP or other real economic variables; the only effect was to change the price level.

Modern economists now see the Classical view as extreme, but recognize that it nonetheless may provide a good description of the economy's long-run equilibrium, after wages and other factor prices have fully adjusted and real GDP has returned to the level of potential output, Y^*. Modern economists' view that the neutrality of money holds in the long run leads them to stress the strong link between changes in the money supply and changes in the price level, at least over long periods of time. Figure 28-9 shows a scatter plot of inflation and money growth for 82 countries over the four decades following the Second World War. Each point in the figure represents the rates of inflation and money supply growth for one country averaged over the 40-year period. The vertical axis measures each country's average annual inflation rate—that is, the average annual rate of increase of the price level. The horizontal axis measures each country's average annual rate of growth of the money supply. As is clear in the figure, there is a positive relationship between money supply growth and inflation, as reflected by the tight bunching of points around the upward-sloping line, the "line of best fit" between money supply growth and inflation. The slope of the line of best fit is 0.97, indicating that two countries that differ in their money growth rates by 10 percent will, on average, differ in their inflation rates by 9.7 percent.

Many modern economists believe that money is neutral in the long run. Long-run neutrality implies that, in the absence of other shocks to the economy, changes in money and changes in the price level are closely linked over long periods of time.

Long-run money neutrality is debatable, however. Though most economists agree that the macroeconomic adjustment process will bring Y back to Y^* in the long run, some economists argue that the value of Y^* is itself influenced by the short-run path of real GDP, and is not determined solely by the longer-run changes in technology and factor supplies that we emphasized in Chapter 26. The hypothesis that the path of real GDP may influence the value of Y^* is known as *hysteresis,* and there is some empirical support for it, especially in some Western European countries.

One possible explanation for hysteresis is the depreciation of human capital that often accompanies prolonged unemployment. Consider a negative shock that reduces real GDP and increases unemployment. If wages and other factor prices are slow to adjust, the unemployment will persist, and some individuals may experience long spells of unemployment. If prolonged lack of work leads these individuals' skills to depreciate, they may eventually become "unemployable," even after the aggregate economy recovers. In this case, the fall in the level of real GDP, if prolonged, will lead to a fall in the level of potential output. (Or equivalently, the rise in the unemployment rate will lead to a rise in the natural rate of unemployment.)

As we said earlier, there is some empirical support for hysteresis, but it is contentious. In Canada, the weight of the empirical evidence is against it, and in favour of the hypothesis that the long-run path of Y^* is independent of the short-run path of real GDP. In

FIGURE 28-8   The Long-Run Neutrality of Money

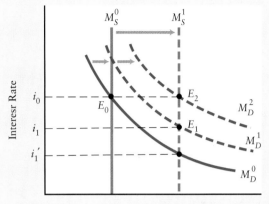

(i) M_D and M_S

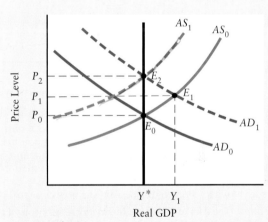

(ii) *AD* and *AS*

The long-run neutrality of money implies that the only long-run effect of an increase in the money supply is a higher price level. The economy is in long-run equilibrium at E_0 in both diagrams, with real GDP equal to Y^* and the price level equal to P_0. An increase in the money supply from M_S^0 to M_S^1 reduces interest rates immediately to i_1' and stimulates aggregate demand, thus shifting the aggregate demand curve from AD_0 to AD_1. As real GDP and the price level increase, the demand for money increases to M_D^1, thus pushing i_1' up to i_1. The point E_1 in part (i) therefore corresponds to E_1 in part (ii). Since real GDP is now above Y^*, wages and other factor prices start to increase, thus shifting the AS curve upward. The adjustment process continues until Y is back to Y^* and the price level has increased to P_2. In the new long-run equilibrium, the higher price level (with unchanged Y^*) has increased money demand to M_D^2, thus restoring the interest rate to its initial level, i_0.

FIGURE 28-9 Inflation and Money Growth Across Many Countries

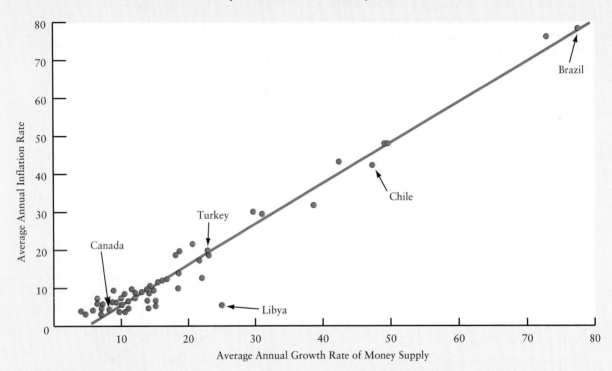

Countries with higher inflation rates tend to be countries with higher rates of growth of the money supply. This figure plots long-run data for many countries. Each point shows the average annual inflation rate and the average annual growth rate of the money supply for a specific country over the post-Second World War period (the precise years vary slightly across countries). For all countries, the inflation data refer to the rate of change of the consumer price index; the money supply data refer to the growth rate of currency. The positive relationship between inflation and money supply growth (with a slope of the best-fit line very close to 1) is consistent with the proposition of long-run money neutrality.

(*Source:* The data are from the International Monetary Fund's *International Financial Statistics,* as compiled by R.J. Barro and R.F. Lucas, in *Macroeconomics,* Irwin 1994.)

the macro model developed and analyzed in this book, it is assumed that Y^* is unaffected by the path of Y, and thus the model generates the prediction of long-run money neutrality. But it should be kept in mind that this particular behaviour of Y^* remains a debatable hypothesis, and should constantly be tested with data.

Short-Run Non-Neutrality of Money

There is less debate regarding the short-run effects of money: A change in the money supply affects the short-run equilibrium level of real GDP. For a given AS curve, the short-run effect of a change in the money supply on real GDP and the price level is determined by the extent of the shift of the AD curve.

How Much Does the *AD* Curve Shift?

The *AD* curve shifts in response to an increase in the money supply. How much the *AD* curve shifts depends on the amount of investment expenditure that is stimulated. The change in investment expenditure in turn depends on the strength of two of the linkages that make up the monetary transmission mechanism: the link between money supply and interest rates, and the link between interest rates and investment. Let's look more closely at these separate parts of the monetary transmission mechanism.

First, consider how much interest rates fall in response to an increase in the money supply. If the M_D curve is steep, a given increase in the money supply will lead to a large reduction in the equilibrium interest rate. A steep M_D curve means that firms' and households' desired money holding is not very sensitive to changes in the interest rate, so interest rates have to fall a lot to get people to be content to hold a larger amount of money. The flatter is the M_D curve, the less interest rates will fall for any given increase in the supply of money.

Second, consider how much investment expenditure increases in response to a fall in interest rates. If the I^D curve is relatively flat, then any given reduction in interest rates will lead to a large increase in firms' desired investment. The steeper is the I^D curve, the less investment will increase for any given reduction in interest rates.

It follows that the size of the shift of the *AD* curve in response to a change in the money supply depends on the shapes of the M_D and I^D curves. The influence of the shapes of the two curves is shown in Figure 28-10 and can be summarized as follows:

1. The steeper the M_D curve, the greater the effect on interest rates of a given change in the money supply.

2. The flatter the I^D curve, the greater the effect on investment expenditure a change in the interest rate will have and hence the larger will be the shift in the *AD* curve.

The combination that produces the largest shift in the *AD* curve for a given change in the money supply is a steep M_D curve and a flat I^D curve. This combination is illustrated in part (i) of Figure 28-10. It accords with the view that monetary policy is relatively effective as a means of influencing real GDP in the short run. The combination that produces the smallest shift in the *AD* curve is a flat M_D curve and a steep I^D curve. This combination is illustrated in part (ii) of Figure 28-10. It accords with the view that monetary policy is relatively ineffective in the short run.

The effectiveness of monetary policy in inducing short-run changes in real GDP depends on the slopes of the M_D and I^D curves. The steeper is the M_D curve, and the flatter is the I^D curve, the more effective is monetary policy.

Keynesians Versus Monetarists

Figure 28-10 characterizes a famous debate among economists during the 1950s and early 1960s. Some economists, following the ideas of John Maynard Keynes, argued that changes in the money supply led to relatively small changes in interest rates and that investment was relatively insensitive to changes in the interest rate. These economists, who called themselves *Keynesians*, concluded that monetary policy was not a very effective method of stimulating aggregate demand—they therefore emphasized the value of using fiscal policy (as Keynes himself had argued during the Great Depression). Another group of economists, led by Milton Friedman, argued that changes in the money supply caused sharp changes in interest rates, which, in turn, led to significant changes in investment

For brief descriptions of the contributions to economics of the Nobel laureates, go to www.nobel.se/economics/laureates/.

FIGURE 28-10 Two Views on the Strength of Monetary Changes

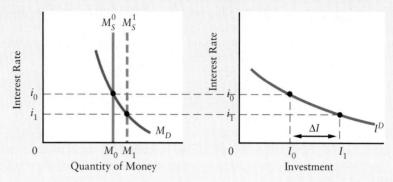

(i) Changes in the money supply effective

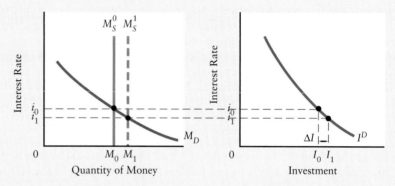

(ii) Changes in the money supply ineffective

The effect of a change in the money supply on aggregate demand depends on the slopes of the M_D and I^D curves. Initially, in parts (i) and (ii), the money supply is M_S^0, and the economy has an interest rate of i_0 and investment expenditure of I_0. The central bank then expands the money supply from M_S^0 to M_S^1. The rate of interest thus falls from i_0 to i_1, as shown in each of the left panels. This causes an increase in investment expenditure of ΔI, from I_0 to I_1, as shown in each of the right panels.

In part (i), the demand for money is insensitive to the interest rate, so the increase in the money supply leads to a large fall in the interest rate. Further, desired investment expenditure is highly interest sensitive, so the large fall in interest rates also leads to a large increase in investment expenditure. Hence, in this case, the change in the money supply will be very effective in stimulating aggregate demand.

In part (ii), the demand for money is more sensitive to the interest rate, so the increase in the money supply leads to only a small fall in the interest rate. Further, desired investment expenditure is much less sensitive to the interest rate, so the small fall in interest rates leads to only a small increase in investment expenditure. Hence, in this case, the change in the money supply will be less effective in stimulating aggregate demand.

Practise with Study Guide Chapter 28, Exercise 4.

expenditure. These economists called themselves *Monetarists* and concluded that monetary policy was a very effective tool for stimulating aggregate demand.[4]

---

[4] Monetarists argued that monetary policy was very effective for stimulating aggregate demand but they *did not* advocate an "activist" monetary policy. One of their concerns was that monetary forces were so strong that an activist monetary policy would destabilize the economy. We address these issues in Chapter 29.

Several decades later, however, this debate between Keynesians and Monetarists is all but over. A great deal of empirical research devoted to uncovering the relationship between interest rates and money demand suggests that money demand is relatively insensitive to changes in the interest rate. That is, the M_D curve is quite steep and, as a result, changes in the money supply cause relatively large changes in interest rates (as argued by the Monetarists). The evidence is much less clear, however, on the slope of the I^D curve. Though the evidence confirms that I^D is clearly downward sloping, there is no consensus on whether the curve is steep or flat. Part of the problem facing researchers is that an important determinant of investment is not observable. Firms' expectations about the future have a significant effect on their investment decisions but this variable is not easily measured by researchers. The unobservability of this variable makes it very difficult to estimate precisely the relationship between interest rates and investment.

What Lies Ahead

In this and the previous chapter we incorporated money into our macro model. You now know what money is and how it is created by the banking system. You also know how the money market determines the interest rate. Finally, you have seen in general terms how monetary disturbances—changes in the demand for or supply of money—affect real GDP and the price level.

What we have not yet discussed is how the Bank of Canada influences the money supply and what factors it must consider when doing so. What are the Bank's objectives? How does it achieve these objectives? With the basics of money now in place, we are ready to discuss the details of monetary policy. We do so in the next chapter.

S U M M A R Y

28.1 **Understanding Bonds**   LO 1

- The present value of any bond that promises to pay some sequence of payments in the future is negatively related to the market interest rate. A bond's present value determines its market price. Thus, there is a negative relationship between the market interest rate and the price of a bond.

- The yield on a bond is the rate of return the bondholder receives, having bought the bond at its purchase price and then receiving the stream of future payments the bond offers. For a given stream of future payments, a lower purchase price implies a higher bond yield.

- An increase in the perceived riskiness of bonds will lead to a reduction in bond prices and thus an increase in bond yields. These changes are associated with investors' adjustment of their portfolios out of bonds and toward money.

28.2 **The Demand for Money**   LO 2

- Households and firms divide their assets between interest-bearing "bonds" and non-interest-bearing "money." They hold money to facilitate both expected and unexpected transactions, and also to protect against the possibility of a decline in bond prices (a rise in interest rates).
- No matter why money is held, the cost of doing so is the interest that could have been earned if bonds were held instead. This is the opportunity cost of holding money.
- Households' and firms' desired money holdings are influenced by three key macroeconomic variables:

1. Increases in the interest rate reduce desired money holdings;
2. Increases in real GDP increase desired money holdings;
3. Increases in the price level increase desired money holdings.

- These relationships are captured in the M_D curve, which is drawn as a negative relationship between interest rates (i) and desired money holding (M_D). Increases in real GDP (Y) or the price level (P) lead to a rightward shift of this M_D curve.

28.3 **Monetary Equilibrium and National Income**   LO 3 4

- In the short run, the interest rate is determined in the money market by the interaction of money supply and money demand. Monetary equilibrium is established when the interest rate is such that the quantity of money supplied is exactly equal to the quantity of money demanded.
- The first stage in the monetary transmission mechanism occurs when the equilibrium interest rate changes. A change in the money supply (coming from the central bank or the commercial banking system) or in the demand for money (coming from a change in Y or P) will lead to a change in the equilibrium interest rate.

- The second stage of the monetary transmission mechanism is that any change in the interest rate leads to a change in desired investment and consumption expenditure. In an open economy with capital mobility, the change in the interest rate leads to capital flows, changes in the exchange rate, and changes in net exports.
- The third stage of the monetary transmission mechanism is that any change in desired investment, consumption, or net exports leads to a shift in the aggregate demand (*AD*) curve, and thus to a change in real GDP and the price level.

28.4 **The Strength of Monetary Forces**   LO 5

- Changes in the money supply have different effects on the economy in the short run than in the long run.
- In the long run, after wages and other factor prices have fully adjusted to any output gaps, real GDP returns to potential output, Y^*. Since the money supply does not influence Y^*, the only long-run effect of changes in the money supply is changes in the price level.

- The neutrality of money is a property of the economy in the long run. There is a strong positive correlation between the rate of money growth and the rate of inflation across countries when viewed over the long run.
- In the short run, the effects of a change in the money supply depend on the shape of the M_D and I^D curves. The steeper is the M_D curve and the flatter is the I^D curve, the more effective changes in the money supply will be in causing short-run changes in real GDP.

K E Y   C O N C E P T S

The interest rate and present value
Interest rates, bond prices, and bond yields
Reasons for holding money

The money demand (M_D) function
Monetary equilibrium
The monetary transmission mechanism
The investment demand (I^D) function

Effects of changes in the money supply
Debate between Keynesians and Monetarists

STUDY EXERCISES

1. Fill in the blanks to make the following statements correct.

   a. Monetary equilibrium occurs when the quantity of _____ equals the quantity of _____. Monetary equilibrium determines the _____.

   b. When there is an excess supply of money, households and firms will attempt to _____ bonds. This action will cause the price of bonds to _____ and the interest rate to _____.

   c. When there is an excess demand for money, households and firms will attempt to _____ bonds. This action will cause the price of bonds to _____ and the interest rate to _____.

   d. The _____ _____ _____ refers to the three stages that link the money market to aggregate demand. The first link is between monetary equilibrium and the _____; the second link is between the _____ and desired _____; the third link is between desired _____ and _____.

   e. Suppose the economy is in equilibrium and then the Bank of Canada increases the money supply. The first effect will be an excess _____ of/for money, which will then lead to a _____ in the interest rate, which will in turn lead to a(n) _____ in desired investment.

   f. Suppose the economy is in equilibrium and the Bank of Canada decreases the money supply. The first effect will be an excess _____ of/for money, which will lead to a _____ in the interest rate, which will in turn lead to a(n) _____ in desired investment.

   g. Through the monetary transmission mechanism, a rightward shift of the AD curve can be caused by a(n) _____ in the money supply; a leftward shift of the AD curve can be caused by a(n) _____ in the money supply.

   h. In an open economy with capital mobility, an increase in the money supply causes interest rates to _____, which leads to a capital outflow. This causes a(n) _____ of the Canadian dollar and thus to a(n) _____ in net exports, which leads the AD curve to shift _____.

2. Fill in the blanks to make the following statements correct.

   a. The concept of long-run neutrality of money tells us that changes in the money supply have no effect on _____ in the long run.

   b. If the demand for money is not very sensitive to changes in the interest rate, then the M_D curve will be relatively _____. An increase in the money supply will lead to a _____ reduction in the interest rate.

   c. If the demand for money is very sensitive to changes in the interest rate, then the M_D curve will be relatively _____. An increase in the money supply will lead to a _____ reduction in the interest rate.

   d. A relatively flat investment demand curve means that a change in the interest rate will have a _____ effect on _____, which leads to a relatively large shift in the _____ curve.

   e. A relatively steep investment demand curve means that a change in the interest rate will have a _____ effect on _____, which leads to a relatively small shift in the _____ curve.

   f. Changes in the money supply will have the largest effect on the position of the AD curve when the M_D curve is _____ and the I^D curve is _____.

3. The following table shows the stream of income produced by several different assets. In each case, P_1, P_2, and P_3 are the payments made by the asset in Years 1, 2, and 3.

Asset	Market Interest Rate (i)	P_1	P_2	P_3	Present Value
Treasury Bill	8%	$1000	$0	$0	—
Bond	7%	$0	$0	$5000	—
Bond	9%	$200	$200	$200	—
Stock	10%	$50	$40	$60	—

   a. For each asset, compute the asset's present value. (Note that the market interest rate, i, is not the same in each situation.)

   b. Explain why the market price for each asset will be the asset's present value.

4. Imagine a bond that promises to make coupon payments of $100 one year from now and $100 two years from now, and to repay the principal of $1000 three years from now. Suppose also that the market interest rate is 8 percent per year, and that no perceived risk is associated with the bond.

a. Compute the present value of this bond.

b. Suppose the bond is being offered for $995. Would you buy the bond at that price? What is the implied yield on the bond at that price? What do you expect to happen to the bond price in the very near future?

c. Suppose the bond is instead being offered at a price of $950. Would you buy the bond at that price? What is the implied bond yield at that price? Do you expect the bond price to change in the near future?

d. If the price of the bond is equal to its computed present value from (a), what is the implied bond yield?

e. Explain why bond yields and the market interest rate tend to move together so that economists can then sensibly speak about "the" interest rate.

5. What motives for holding money—transactions, precautionary, or speculative—do you think explain the following holdings? Explain.

a. Currency in the cash register of the local grocery store at the start of each working day.

b. Money to meet Stelco's bi-weekly payroll deposited in the local bank.

c. A household tries to keep a "buffer" of $1000 in its savings account.

d. An investor sells bonds for cash, which she then deposits in a low-return bank account.

e. You carry $20 in your pocket even though you have no planned expenditures.

6. The diagram below shows the demand for money and the supply of money.

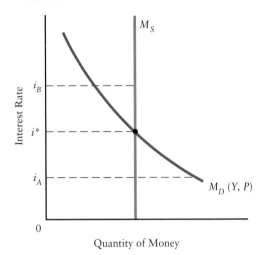

a. Explain why the M_D function is downward sloping.

b. Suppose the interest rate is at i_A. Explain how firms and households attempt to satisfy their excess demand for money. What is the effect of their actions?

c. Suppose the interest rate is at i_B. Explain how firms and households attempt to dispose of their excess supply of money. What is the effect of their actions?

d. Now suppose there is an increase in the transactions demand for money (perhaps because of growth in real GDP). Beginning at i^*, explain what happens in the money market. How is this shown in the diagram?

7. The following diagrams show the determination of monetary equilibrium and the demand for investment. The economy begins with money supply M_S, money demand M_D, and investment demand I^D. The interest rate is i_0 and investment is I_0.

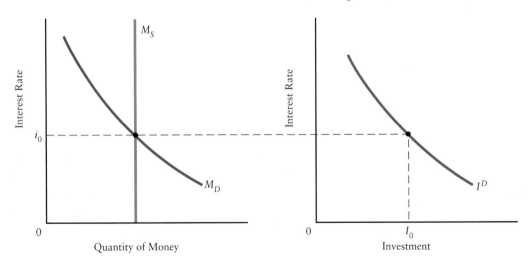

a. Beginning at the initial equilibrium, suppose the Bank of Canada increases the money supply. What happens in the money market and what happens to desired investment expenditure?

b. Beginning in the initial equilibrium, suppose there is a reduction in the demand for money (caused, perhaps, by bonds becoming more attractive to firms and households). What happens in the money market and what happens to desired investment expenditure?

c. Explain why an increase in money supply can have the same effects on desired investment expenditure as a reduction in money demand.

8. In the text we discussed why, in an open economy with international capital mobility, there is a second part to the monetary transmission mechanism. (It may be useful to review Figure 28-7 when answering this question.)

a. Explain why an increase in Canada's money supply makes Canadian bonds less attractive relative to foreign bonds.

b. Explain why Canada's bonds being less attractive leads to a depreciation of the Canadian dollar.

c. Why would such a depreciation of the Canadian dollar lead to an increase in Canada's net exports?

d. Now suppose that the Bank of Canada does not change its policy at all, but the Federal Reserve (the U.S. central bank) increases the U.S. money supply. What is the likely effect on Canada? Explain.

9. In the text we discussed the debate between Keynesians and Monetarists regarding the effectiveness of monetary policy in changing real GDP (see Figure 28-10 to review). Using the same sort of diagram, discuss two conditions in which a change in the money supply would have *no* effect on real GDP.

DISCUSSION QUESTIONS

1. Historically, construction of new houses has been one of the most interest-sensitive categories of aggregate expenditure. Recently, the financial press has carried a number of stories suggesting that because of financial deregulation and innovations in housing finance, this interest sensitivity has apparently decreased. If this is true, what are the implications for monetary policy?

2. Suppose that you alone know that the Bank of Canada is going to engage in policies that will decrease the money supply sharply, starting next month. How might you make profits by purchases or sales of bonds now, with the intention to sell in a few month's time?

3. In the late 1990s, central bankers in Canada and elsewhere (especially the United States) expressed concern about the dramatic increases in stock-market values. In December 1996, U.S. Federal Reserve chairman Alan Greenspan alarmed the markets by referring to investors' "irrational exuberance."

   a. Explain why central bankers might be concerned about "excessive" increases in stock-market values.
   b. Explain how a policy-induced increase in interest rates would affect the stock market.
   c. Suppose prices in the stock market fell sharply for reasons unrelated to domestic interest rates. What would be the likely effect on aggregate demand?

4. In 1997–98, there was a significant recession in the Southeast Asian economies of Malaysia, Indonesia, Thailand, and South Korea.

   a. Explain the likely effects of these events on the demand for Canadian exports. What would be the effect on Canadian aggregate demand?
   b. Suppose the Bank of Canada viewed its monetary policy as being appropriate (for keeping output close to potential) before this "Asian Crisis" occurred. What would you then predict to be the Bank's response to the crisis?

5. In the text we discussed how capital mobility in an open economy added a second part to the transmission mechanism. In this setting, discuss why changes in the Federal Reserve's policy in the United States are carefully watched—and often matched—by the Bank of Canada.

6. After the terrorist attacks of September 11, 2001, stock markets across the world, but especially in North America, fell dramatically. Central banks responded by increasing the money supply and therefore reducing interest rates.

   a. Explain why a sharp fall in stock-market values might be expected to lead to a recession.
   b. After 18 months of expansionary monetary policy, the U.S. economy was still showing no signs of recovery by the middle of 2003. Can you offer an explanation based on the slope of either the M_D or I^D curves?
   c. What else was going on in the world economy in 2003 that might explain why expansionary U.S. monetary policy seemed to be less effective than expected?

Interest Rates and the Slope of the *AD* Curve

The *AD* curve relates the price level to the equilibrium level of real GDP in an economy in which output is demand determined. Its negative slope means that the higher the price level, the lower the equilibrium GDP. In Chapter 23 we explained the slope of the aggregate demand curve by arguing that a change in the price level changed the wealth of firms and households (by changing the real value of money holdings). We also argued that a change in the price level changed the prices of Canadian goods relative to foreign goods, and so affected net exports. What we *did not say* in Chapter 23, however, is that a third reason for a negatively sloped *AD* curve is due to the changes in the interest rate that are caused by the change in the price level. We omitted this argument then for the simple reason that we had not yet introduced the concepts of money demand, money supply, and the determination of interest rates. But we now have the tools in hand to do this.

Let us look at the monetary transmission mechanism in detail. Although the argument contains nothing new, it does require that you follow carefully through several steps.

We start with an initial equilibrium position, corresponding to a given price level P_0. Figure 28A-1 shows the determination of the interest rate by the conditions of monetary equilibrium in part (i); that in turn determines the level of desired investment spending by the investment demand curve in part (ii). Figure 28A-2 shows the *AE* curve, drawn for that level of investment spending, and the determination of equilibrium real GDP in part (i); that level of real GDP is then plotted against the price level to give point *A* on the *AD* curve in part (ii).

A rise in the price level from P_0 to P_1 to P_2 raises the dollar value of transactions and increases the quantity of money demanded at each possible value of the interest rate. As a result, the M_D function shifts

FIGURE 28A-1 Changes in the Price Level: Interest Rates and Investment

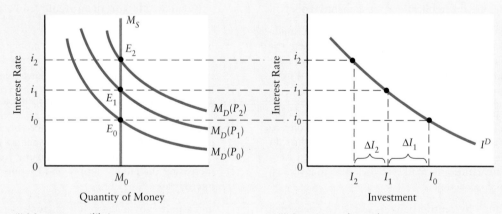

(i) Monetary equilibrium

(ii) Investment demand

Changes in the price level influence the demand for money and hence cause the level of interest rates and desired investment spending to change. In part (i), the money supply is fixed at M_0. Initially, money demand is given by $M_D(P_0)$, equilibrium is at E_0, and the interest rate is i_0. Given that interest rate, desired investment spending is I_0, as shown in part (ii) by the I^D curve.

An increase in the price level from P_0 to P_1 causes an increase in the demand for money, and hence the M_D curve shifts to the right. Monetary equilibrium is at E_1, the interest rate rises to i_1, and desired investment spending falls by ΔI_1 to I_1. A further increase in the price level from P_1 to P_2 causes a further increase in the demand for money. Monetary equilibrium is at E_2, the interest rate rises to i_2, and desired investment spending falls by ΔI_2 to I_2.

upward, raising the equilibrium interest rate and reducing the level of desired investment expenditure. The reduction in investment spending in turn causes the AE curve to shift downward, leading to a reduction in the equilibrium level of national income.

The negative relationship between the price level and equilibrium real GDP shown by the AD curve occurs because, other things being equal, a rise in the price level raises the quantity of money demanded. This increase in money demand pushes up the interest rate, which then reduces investment and equilibrium GDP. Note the qualification "other things being equal." It is important for this process that the money *supply* remain constant. The interest rate rises because the demand for money increases when the price level rises whereas the money supply remains constant.

Practise with Study Guide Chapter 28, Extension Exercise E1.

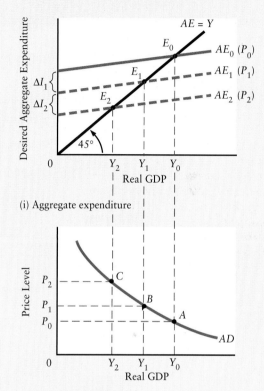

FIGURE 28A-2 Changes in the Price Level: Aggregate Expenditure and Real GDP

(i) Aggregate expenditure

(ii) Aggregate demand

Changes in the price level lead to changes in desired aggregate expenditure and hence in the equilibrium level of real GDP. Equilibrium GDP is determined in part (i). At a given initial price level—hence with an initial level of desired investment spending of I_0 from Figure 28A-1—desired aggregate expenditure is shown by AE_0. Equilibrium is at E_0, and equilibrium real GDP is Y_0. In part (ii), Y_0 is plotted against P_0 to give point A on the AD curve.

An increase in the price level from P_0 to P_1 causes a decrease of ΔI_1 in the level of desired investment spending, as determined in Figure 28A-1 and shown in part (i) here. Thus, the AE curve shifts down to AE_1. Equilibrium is at E_1, and equilibrium real GDP falls to Y_1. In part (ii), the higher price level P_1 is plotted against the lower equilibrium level of income Y_1 as point B on the AD curve.

CHAPTER 29

Monetary Policy in Canada

L LEARNING OBJECTIVES

1 Explain the two methods by which the Bank of Canada can change the level of reserves in the banking system.

2 Explain why the bank rate and the level of reserves cannot be set independently.

3 Differentiate between the Bank's policy targets and its policy instruments.

4 Explain how the Bank's policy of inflation targeting helps to stabilize the economy.

5 Explain why monetary policy affects real GDP and the price level only after long lags.

6 List the main challenges that the Bank of Canada has faced over the past two decades.

In the previous two chapters, we saw how money supply and money demand interact to determine interest rates. Further, we saw how monetary disturbances—changes in either the demand for money or the supply of money—affect interest rates, desired aggregate expenditure, and the level of real GDP.

We also saw how commercial banks, through the process of making loans and new deposits, are able to affect the money supply. But there is still one important piece missing from our analysis. Though we discussed some of the functions of the Bank of Canada in Chapter 27, we have not yet examined how the Bank of Canada influences the level of reserves in the commercial banking system. And it is these reserves that form the basis of commercial-bank lending. Until we have examined the operations of the Bank of Canada in more detail, we do not have a full picture of the determinants of the money supply.

In this chapter, we examine the Bank of Canada's monetary policy—how it sets the level of reserves in the banking system to affect interest rates, the exchange rate, real GDP and, eventually, the price level.

29.1 **The Bank of Canada and the Money Supply**

Deposit money is by far the most important part of the money supply. It accounts for about 65 percent of M1, the narrowest definition of money, and for about 90 percent of M2, the broader measure. As we have seen, commercial banks use their reserves to increase their loans and thereby create deposit money. But the amount of reserves in the banking system is controlled by the Bank of Canada. We now examine how the Bank of Canada alters the level of these reserves.

Open-Market Operations

One tool that the Bank of Canada can use for influencing the supply of money is the purchase or sale of government securities on the open market. These actions are known as **open-market operations.** Just as there are stock markets, there are active and well-organized markets for government securities. Anyone, including you, TD Canada Trust, Ford Motor Company, or the Bank of Canada, can enter this market to buy or sell government securities at whatever price the market establishes. But there is an important difference between the purchase and sale of government securities *among members of the private sector* and *between the central bank and the private sector.* As we shall see, whenever the Bank of Canada is involved in either the purchase or the sale of government securities, the reserves of the entire banking system are altered, and this change affects the money supply.

open-market operations The purchase and sale of government securities on the open market by the central bank.

Open-Market Purchases

Suppose the Bank of Canada buys a $100 000 government bond from the CIBC, which was holding that bond in its asset portfolio. The Bank of Canada receives the bond from the CIBC and credits the CIBC's account at the Bank by $100 000. The CIBC has increased its cash reserves by $100 000.

Table 29-1 shows the balance sheets for the CIBC and for the Bank of Canada, and tracks the immediate effect of this open-market purchase. The Bank of Canada has acquired a new asset in the form of a security and a new liability in the form of a deposit by the CIBC. The CIBC has reduced its bond holdings and increased its reserves by $100 000. It is now in a position to increase its lending and thereby increase deposit money.

When the Bank of Canada buys government bonds on the open market, the reserves of the commercial banks are increased. These banks can then expand deposits, thereby increasing the money supply.

TABLE 29-1 Initial Balance Sheet Changes Caused by an Open-Market Purchase From a Commercial Bank

CIBC		
Assets		Liabilities
Bonds	−$100 000	No change
Reserves	+$100 000	

Bank of Canada		
Assets		Liabilities
Bonds	+$100 000	Commercial Bank Deposits +$100 000

An open-market purchase by the Bank of Canada from a commercial bank leads to an increase in commercial-bank reserves and, eventually, to an increase in the money supply. The Bank of Canada buys a $100 000 bond from the CIBC and credits the CIBC's account at the Bank. For the CIBC this is just a change in the form of its assets, from bonds to cash reserves. The greater reserves lead to increased lending and the creation of deposit money.

Open-Market Sales

Now suppose that the Bank of Canada sells a $100 000 government bond to the CIBC. In this case, the CIBC adds the bond to its asset portfolio and its account at the Bank of Canada is reduced by $100 000. The changes are exactly the opposite to those shown in Table 29-1. The result is that the CIBC's reserves are lower and thus it must reduce its lending (and perhaps call in existing loans) to restore its target reserve ratio. The result will be a reduction in deposits, and thus a reduction in the money supply.

When the Bank of Canada sells government bonds on the open market, the reserves of the commercial banks are decreased. By calling in loans and reducing their lending, commercial banks will reduce deposits and thus reduce the money supply.

If we examine Canadian banking data closely, we find that the reserves in the banking system rarely if ever actually fall. Does this mean that the Bank never conducts a "contractionary" policy? The answer is no. *Applying Economic Concepts 29-1* explains that in a *growing* economy, with a steadily growing demand for money, even a "neutral" monetary policy will see an increasing level of reserves in the banking system. In that setting, a contractionary monetary policy is best described as one that leads to a *reduction in the growth rate* of reserves, rather than an absolute reduction in the level of reserves.

Shifting Government Deposits

In addition to open-market operations, the Bank of Canada has a second general method for changing the level of reserves in the banking system. As the government's *fiscal agent,* the Bank of Canada manages a large amount of government funds. It maintains government accounts on its own books, into which funds are deposited and from which funds are withdrawn. In addition, it manages some government accounts with the commercial banks. Alterations in the amount held in these accounts will affect the reserves of the commercial banks. The process of shifting government accounts from the Bank of Canada to the commercial banks (or in the other direction) is referred to as *cash management.*

Cash management—the shifting of government deposits between the Bank of Canada and the commercial banks—is a major tool used by the Bank of Canada in its day-to-day operations.

Suppose, for example, that the Bank of Canada transfers $100 000 from the government's account at the Bank to the government's account at the CIBC. The transactions involved are illustrated in Table 29-2. From the government's point of view, nothing substantial has changed, since its deposits with one financial institution will have fallen, but its deposits with another have risen by the same amount. However, the

TABLE 29-2 Initial Balance Sheet Changes Caused by a Transfer of Government Deposits from the Bank of Canada to a Commercial Bank

CIBC		
Assets	Liabilities	
Reserves +100 000	Government deposits	+100 000

Bank of Canada		
Assets	Liabilities	
No change	Government deposits	−100 000
	Commercial bank deposits	+100 000

A transfer of government deposits from the Bank of Canada to a commercial bank increases bank reserves and, thus, through an expansion of bank lending, increases the money supply. When the Bank of Canada transfers $100 000 of government deposits to the CIBC, the CIBC's account with the Bank of Canada is credited with a deposit of $100 000. The CIBC's increase in its deposit liabilities to the government is balanced by the increase in its reserves on deposit with the Bank of Canada. Since its deposits and its reserves have increased by the same amount, it has excess reserves and the potential is created for multiple expansion of deposit money.

APPLYING ECONOMIC CONCEPTS 29-1

What Is a "Contractionary" Monetary Policy?

In every year since 1950, real GDP growth and inflation have ensured that nominal national income has risen. As a result, the demand for money has grown. In every year in the period, the nominal money supply has also grown, reflecting the Bank's decision to supply additional reserves to the banking system to meet the growing demand for money. Does this mean that the Bank has never followed a contractionary monetary policy?

The answer is no. When real income growth and inflation result in a continually growing nominal national income, the stance of monetary policy depends upon the rate at which the money supply is allowed to grow *relative to the rate of growth of the demand for money*. A contractionary monetary policy occurs when the growth in the money supply is held below the rate of growth in the demand for money; it does not require a fall in the absolute size of the money supply.

For example, if the nominal demand for money is growing at 4 percent per year, the Bank of Canada can follow a contractionary policy if it limits the rate of growth of the money supply to 2 percent. This would create an excess demand for money, causing interest rates to rise. The higher interest rates, in turn, would feed through the monetary transmission mechanism to slow the growth in spending and, hence, slow the growth in real GDP.

Similarly, an expansionary monetary policy in a growing economy is one for which the growth rate of the money supply exceeds the growth rate of money demand. The excess supply of money then leads to a lower interest rate, an increase in the growth rate of desired spending, and thus a higher growth rate for real GDP.

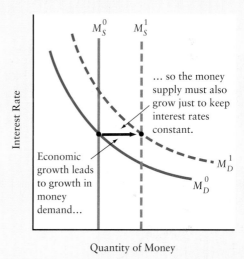

... so the money supply must also grow just to keep interest rates constant.

Economic growth leads to growth in money demand...

CIBC finds that its deposit liabilities and reserves will each have increased by $100 000, and hence its ratio of reserves to deposits will have risen. With an unchanged target reserve ratio, the CIBC will have excess reserves, and thus will begin the process of expanding its loans and creating more deposit money.

A transfer of government deposits from a commercial bank to the Bank of Canada has the opposite effect. The reserves and deposit liabilities of the banking system fall by the same amount, thus driving the actual reserve ratio below the target reserve ratio. Banks will now have insufficient reserves and will begin to call in existing loans and stop making new ones, setting in motion a process of deposit contraction.

When government deposits are transferred between the Bank of Canada and the commercial banks, the reserves of the banking system are changed. Such changes in reserves, through the expansion or contraction of lending, lead to changes in the money supply.

Practise with Study Guide Chapter 29, Exercise 1.

Money Supply or the Interest Rate?

We have now seen how the Bank of Canada can alter the level of reserves in the banking system. Through commercial-bank lending, such changes in reserves lead to changes in the broader money supply. And through the equilibrium of money demand and money supply, the interest rate is then affected.

Note that we have described the mechanics of monetary policy as beginning with a change in reserves and then influencing the interest rate. But many central banks, including the Bank of Canada, actually conduct their policy in the opposite manner—they announce their policy in terms of a desired short-term interest rate and then carry out the necessary open-market operations to make that announced interest rate an equilibrium rate. Figure 29-1 illustrates the money market and shows why these two apparently different approaches to the conduct of monetary policy are really not so different. For any given money demand (M_D) curve, the money supply determines the interest rate. An increase in the money supply leads to a <u>reduction</u> in the equilibrium interest rate. Or, equivalently, we can say that a reduction in the interest rate can only be an equilibrium outcome in the money market if the supply of money increases.

Monetary policy can be viewed from these two different perspectives, but they are really two different sides of the same coin. We can view the central bank as setting the money supply and thus influencing the interest rate, or we can view the central bank as setting the interest rate and then appropriately adjusting the money supply. But for a given negatively sloped money demand curve, interest rates and the money supply cannot be determined independently.

The central bank cannot set the money supply and the interest rate independently. It can set the money supply and let the interest rate adjust, or it can set the interest rate and then adjust the money supply to accommodate the resulting change in desired money holdings.

The Bank of Canada's Approach

The Bank of Canada conducts and announces its monetary policy in terms of setting the interest rate rather than setting the money supply. It does this because specific changes in the interest rate are more meaningful to firms and households than specific changes in the money supply. For example, if we hear that mortgage lending rates at commercial banks have just decreased by one percentage point, most people can readily assess what this means for their plans to buy a new house financed by a mortgage. In contrast, if we hear that the money supply has just increased by $2 billion, it is not clear to most people what this means, or that it will have any effect on interest rates, or by how much.

There is another, more technical, reason why the Bank of Canada conducts its policy by setting the inter-

FIGURE 29-1   The Money Supply and the Interest Rate Are Not Independent

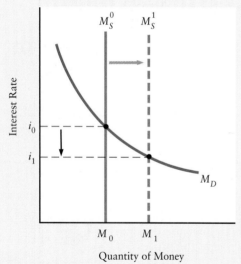

The central bank cannot set the money supply and the interest rate independently. If the central bank sets the money supply, it must then accept whatever adjustment occurs in the interest rate. An increase in the money supply from M_S^0 to M_S^1 leads to a reduction in the interest rate from i_0 to i_1. If the central bank sets the interest rate, it must adjust the money supply to accommodate the change in desired money holdings. A reduction in the interest rate from i_0 to i_1 will lead to an increase in the quantity of money demanded; money supply must be increased from M_S^0 to M_S^1 in order to make i_1 an equilibrium interest rate.

est rate rather than by setting the money supply. As we saw in Chapter 26, there are many measures of the money supply, including M1, M2, M2+, and so on. As innovations in the financial sector lead firms and households to substitute between various types of bank accounts, there will be fluctuations in the demand for the different monetary aggregates, and these changes are often difficult to predict. This "instability" in money demand makes it especially difficult to conduct monetary policy by targeting any particular measure of the money supply and hoping that the intended change in interest rates will follow. It is more straightforward simply to set the interest rate directly. Fluctuations in money demand will still matter; they will affect the amount of open-market operations required to sustain any announced interest rate. But it is far easier to observe fluctuations in the interest rate, and then respond accordingly, than to observe and react to changes in various monetary aggregates (which are usually reported only with considerable lags).

These problems with "instability" of money demand and the appropriate setting of the money supply were experienced by the Bank of Canada in the late 1970s and early 1980s before the Bank adopted its current policy framework. These experiences were important in the development of the Bank's current approach in which the focus of policy is on interest rates directly.

The Bank of Canada communicates its monetary policy by announcing its desired level for short-term interest rates. On eight pre-specified dates throughout the year, the Bank announces its target range for what is called the **overnight interest rate**, the rate at which commercial banks lend to each other for very short periods of time (often just overnight). The interest rate at which the Bank of Canada will lend to commercial banks is called the **bank rate**, and adjusts in lock-step with the Bank's target for the overnight rate. *Applying Economic Concepts 29-2* discusses the setting of the target overnight rate and the bank rate.

29.2 Monetary Policy Targets

The Bank of Canada sets a target range for the overnight interest rate and conducts whatever open-market operations are necessary to ensure that the actual (market-determined) overnight interest rate falls within that target range. Changes in the overnight interest rate then influence longer-term interest rates, as we saw in Chapter 28. From the monetary transmission mechanism, we know how changes in interest rates lead to changes in desired investment expenditure and then to changes in real GDP and the price level. In an open economy, the changes in interest rates will also lead to international flows of financial capital, changes in the exchange rate, and thus to changes in net exports. Both channels of the monetary transmission mechanism work in tandem. An expansionary monetary policy (a decrease in interest rates) leads to increases in both investment and net exports, and thus to an increase in real GDP. A contractionary monetary policy (an increase in interest rates) leads to decreases in both investment and net exports, and thus to a decrease in real GDP. For review, the monetary transmission mechanism is illustrated in Figure 29-2.

Given the long and complex chain of events linking the actions of the Bank of Canada with the eventual changes in real GDP and the price level, it is important for the Bank to make a clear distinction between its *monetary policy instruments* and it *monetary policy targets*. The Bank's **monetary policy instruments** are the tools that it uses to conduct its policy. We described earlier how the Bank of Canada conducts its policy by setting the target range for the overnight rate and then making whatever changes in reserves are necessary to ensure that the actual overnight rate falls within that target

Practise with Study Guide Chapter 29, Exercise 2.

overnight interest rate   The interest rate that commercial banks charge each other for very-short-term loans.

bank rate   The rate of interest at which the Bank of Canada makes loans to commercial banks.

monetary policy instruments   The tools used by the Bank of Canada to conduct its policy.

APPLYING ECONOMIC CONCEPTS 29-2

Monetary Policy and the Bank Rate

Commercial banks in Canada are required to have *non-negative* reserves over a four-week averaging period. For example, if on one day TD Canada Trust has negative reserves of $10 million (meaning that its account at the Bank of Canada is overdrawn by that amount), then on other days within the four-week period the TD must have positive reserves large enough to make the average level of reserves at least zero.

Since borrowing to replenish reserves is costly, commercial banks generally try to avoid this situation by holding larger reserves. When necessary, commercial banks can borrow to replenish their reserves in two ways. They can borrow from other commercial banks (with excess reserves) at the *overnight interest rate*, or they can borrow from the Bank of Canada at the *bank rate*. The overnight rate is a market-determined interest rate. The bank rate, in contrast, is set by the Bank of Canada as the upper end of a 50-basis-point range that the bank announces as its target range for the overnight rate.

By moving the target range up or down, the Bank of Canada signals to the financial markets where it thinks the overnight rate needs to be in order to accomplish its policy goals. Since commercial banks can borrow from the Bank of Canada at the bank rate, they won't be prepared to pay a higher rate to other lenders in the overnight market. Conversely, since commercial banks can lend money to the Bank of Canada (by keeping positive balances there) and earn an interest rate given by the lower end of the desired range, they won't be prepared to lend money for a lower rate to other borrowers in the overnight market. Thus, by announcing this desired range, the Bank of Canada is able to control the range of the overnight rate.

Even though the Bank of Canada conducts its policy by setting the bank rate (or the target range for the overnight rate), our earlier discussion about the importance of the money supply still applies. Whenever the Bank of Canada announces a change in its desired range for the overnight rate it must also alter the money supply by conducting whatever open-market operations are necessary to ensure that the market-determined overnight rate falls within the target range. Interest rates and the money supply are just two different sides of the same coin.

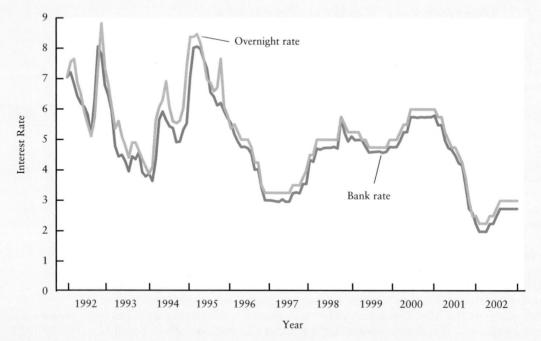

(*Source*: Statistics Canada, CANSIM database, Series V122530. Overnight rate is Series V122514.)

FIGURE 29-2   The Monetary Transmission Mechanism

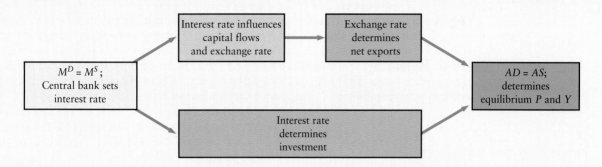

Monetary policy influences aggregate demand through the monetary transmission mechanism. The central bank sets the interest rate and alters the money supply to make this interest rate an equilibrium. The change in interest rates leads, via the monetary transmission mechanism, to changes in desired aggregate expenditure (net exports and investment). Aggregate demand and aggregate supply then determine the price level and the level of real GDP.

range. So we can think of the Bank's policy instrument as either the overnight interest rate or the level of reserves in the banking system—but we know from our earlier discussion that these are just different ways of viewing the same instrument.

The Bank of Canada only has one monetary policy instrument—it sets a target range for the overnight interest rate and then adjusts reserves in the banking system accordingly.

The Bank's **monetary policy targets** are the macroeconomic variables that it seeks to influence. Because the Bank recognizes that the short-run effects of its policies are different from the long-run effects, it has different short-run and long-run objectives.

> **monetary policy targets**   The macroeconomic variables that the Bank of Canada seeks to influence.

Long-Run Target: Inflation

At the end of the previous chapter we reviewed the long-run effects of changes in the supply of money. There we showed that any short-run changes in real GDP caused by a shift in the *AD* curve are reversed in the long run as wages and other factor prices respond to the output gap. The result is what we referred to as the *neutrality of money*—the absence of long-run effects of changes in the money supply on any real variables, such as real GDP, employment, investment, and so on. In contrast, there *is* a long-run effect on the price level. In fact, the *only* long-run effect of a change in the money supply is on the price level.

The evidence in support of long-run money neutrality, some of which we showed at the end of the previous chapter, has led the Bank of Canada and several other central banks (such as those in the United Kingdom, Sweden, and New Zealand) to adopt the view that their ultimate policy target should be the price level or its rate of change, the inflation rate. The adoption of such *inflation targets* does not reflect a lack of interest in the real macroeconomic variables such as output, employment, or real wages; instead, it reflects a recognition that the ultimate effect of monetary policy is only on the price level (or its rate of growth) and thus the targets ought to reflect the limited influence of monetary policy.

The adoption of formal inflation targets by the Bank of Canada (and other central banks) reflects the evidence of long-run money neutrality. The only long-run effects of monetary policy are on the price level and the inflation rate.

The Bank of Canada first adopted its formal inflation targets in 1991 when the annual rate of inflation was almost 6 percent. The targets were expressed as a 2-percentage-point band, in recognition of the fact that modest fluctuations in the inflation rate are inevitable and thus it is unrealistic to expect the Bank to keep the inflation rate at a single, precise value. Beginning in 1992, inflation was to lie within the 3–5 percent range, with the range falling to 2–4 percent by 1993 and to 1–3 percent by the end of 1995, where it remains today. The Bank of Canada conducts its policy with the objective of keeping inflation at or near the midpoint (2 percent) of this target band.

Short-Run Monitoring: The Output Gap

The Bank of Canada recognizes that its monetary policy has real and important effects on the economy in the short run, even though its long-run influence is limited to the price level and the inflation rate. The Bank also recognizes that the long-run effects of its policies only follow after the short-run effects on real GDP are experienced, after which the economy's adjustment process returns real GDP to the level of potential output. As a result, the Bank of Canada closely monitors the level of real GDP in the short run and also the gap between real GDP and Y^*—the output gap.

To understand why the Bank closely monitors the output gap in the short run, consider Figure 29-3, which shows hypothetical time paths for real GDP (Y) and potential output (Y^*) in part (i), and for the rate of inflation with the 1–3 percent target band in part (ii). Until time t_0, the economy is growing with Y equal to Y^* and inflation is more or less constant at the midpoint of the target band. At t_0, a positive shock pushes real GDP above Y^* and opens up an inflationary output gap. Labour and other factors of production are used intensively in order to increase output, and this generates excess demand in factor markets. Wages and other factor prices begin to rise, pushing up firms' costs, and adding to the inflationary pressure. The rate of inflation begins to rise above the midpoint of the target band.

At this point, the Bank of Canada must make a decision. It can choose to leave its policy unchanged, and let the economy's automatic adjustment process operate. The AS curve will

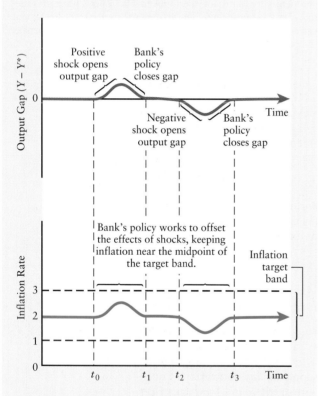

FIGURE 29-3   The Output Gap, Inflation, and Monetary Policy

The Bank of Canada closely monitors the output gap to determine the necessary policy for maintaining inflation near the midpoint of the target band. The economy begins with no output gap and the inflation rate at 2 percent. At time t_0 a positive shock pushes real GDP above Y^* and increases inflationary pressure. The Bank can implement a contractionary monetary policy to close the output gap and reduce inflation back toward 2 percent. At time t_2 a negative shock reduces real GDP below Y^* and reduces inflationary pressure. The Bank can implement an expansionary monetary policy to close the output gap and increase inflation back toward 2 percent.

shift upward and eventually return real GDP to Y^* but only through more inflation. The other choice for the Bank is to attempt to close the output gap by "pulling" real GDP back toward Y^* with a contractionary monetary policy, shifting the AD curve to the left and bringing the rate of inflation back to its starting point near the midpoint of the target band.

The opposite situation can also occur, as shown in the figure at time t_2, when a negative shock pushes real GDP below Y^* and pushes inflation toward the bottom end of the target band. The Bank is again faced with a choice. It can do nothing and let real GDP return (perhaps slowly) to Y^*, but allow inflation to fall even further as the AS curve shifts down during the adjustment process. Or it can try to close the output gap by creating a monetary expansion to shift the AD curve to the right and "pull" real GDP back toward Y^*, raising the rate of inflation back toward the midpoint of the target band.

Output gaps create pressure for the rate of inflation to change. To keep the rate of inflation within its target band, the Bank of Canada closely monitors real GDP in the short run and designs its policy to keep real GDP close to potential output.

Inflation Targeting as a Stabilizing Policy

Figure 29-3 also shows why an inflation-targeting policy helps to stabilize the economy. If the Bank of Canada is committed to keeping the rate of inflation near the midpoint of the target band, positive shocks to the economy that create an inflationary gap and threaten to increase the rate of inflation will be met by a contractionary monetary policy. The Bank will increase interest rates (by reducing reserves in the banking system) and shift the AD curve to the left. This policy will reduce the size of the output gap and push the rate of inflation back down toward the midpoint of the target band. Similarly, if a negative shock to the economy creates a recessionary gap and threatens to reduce the rate of inflation, a central bank committed to its inflation targets will respond with an expansionary monetary policy. In this situation, the Bank of Canada will reduce interest rates (by increasing reserves in the banking system) and shift the AD curve to the right. This policy will reduce the size of the output gap and push the inflation rate back toward the midpoint of the target band.

Inflation targeting is a stabilizing policy. Positive shocks will be met with a contractionary monetary policy; negative shocks will be met with an expansionary monetary policy.

Some economists go so far as to refer to a policy of inflation targeting as an "automatic" stabilizer. But this is an exaggeration, as we can see by recalling our discussion in Chapter 24 of automatic *fiscal* stabilizers, caused by taxes and transfers that vary with the level of national income. The automatic fiscal stabilizers we discussed in Chapter 24 were truly "automatic" in the sense that no group of policymakers had to adjust policy actively—the stabilizers were built right into the tax-and-transfer system. With inflation targeting, however, there must be an active policy decision to keep inflation within the target band, and only then will the Bank's policy adjustments work to stabilize the economy following either positive or negative shocks. But as long as the Bank wants to maintain its set of targets, and have them perceived as being *credible*, then it is committed to carrying out such policy adjustments.

Inflation targets are not as "automatic" a stabilizer as the fiscal stabilizers built into the tax-and-transfer system. But if the central bank is committed to maintaining the credibility of its inflation targets, its policy adjustments will act to stabilize the economy.

Complications in Inflation Targeting

So far, our discussion of inflation targeting makes the conduct of monetary policy seem straightforward. But there are several details that complicate the task considerably. In this section we discuss two technical complications for the conduct of monetary policy, and in the next section we address a more general difficulty.

Volatile Food and Energy Prices

Sometimes the rate of inflation increases for reasons unrelated to a change in the output gap. For example, many commodities whose prices are included in the Consumer Price Index (CPI) are internationally traded goods and their prices are determined in world markets. Oil is an obvious example, as are many fruits and vegetables. When these prices rise suddenly, because of political instability in the Middle East (oil) or because of poor crop conditions in tropical countries (fruits and vegetables), the measured rate of inflation of the Canadian CPI also rises. Yet these price increases have little or nothing to do with the level of excess demand in Canada and thus have little implication for what policy should be followed by the Bank of Canada. By focusing on the rate of inflation of the CPI, the Bank would be misled about the extent of inflationary pressures coming from excess demand in Canada.

For this reason, the Bank of Canada focuses on the "core" rate of inflation. This is the rate of growth of a special price index, one that is constructed by extracting food, energy, and the effects of indirect taxes (such as the GST or excise taxes) from the Consumer Price Index. Figure 29-4 shows the paths of core and CPI inflation since 1992. As is clear from the figure, core inflation is much less volatile than is CPI inflation.

Due to the volatility of food and energy prices that is often unrelated to the level of the output gap in Canada, the Bank of Canada targets the rate of "core" inflation rather than the rate of CPI inflation. Changes in core inflation are a better indicator of Canadian excess demand than are changes in CPI inflation.

Note the sharp divergence between the two inflation rates in 1994. At that time, there were substantial decreases in the excise taxes on cigarettes, and those tax reductions led to a sharp decline in the CPI inflation rate. But this decline in CPI inflation was tax-created rather than caused by the opening of a recessionary output gap, and thus it would have been inappropriate for the Bank of Canada to respond to this decline in inflation by implementing an expansionary monetary policy. Instead, the Bank focused on the core inflation rate that excludes the effect of changes in indirect taxes. The core inflation rate in 1994 was relatively stable and close to the midpoint of the 1–3 percent target band, indicating no need for a change in monetary policy.

The Exchange Rate and Monetary Policy

Practise with Study Guide Chapter 29, Exercise 4.

Given the large amounts of trade that Canadian firms and households do with the rest of the world, it is not surprising that the Bank of Canada pays close attention to movements in the exchange rate, the Canadian-dollar price of one unit of foreign currency. However, because changes in the exchange rate can have several different causes, care must be taken when drawing inferences about the desired change in monetary policy resulting from changes in the exchange rate. As we will see, there is no simple "rule of thumb" for how the Bank should react to a change in the exchange rate. Recall that the Bank's objective is to keep the inflation rate near the midpoint of the 1–3 percent target band, and it does this by responding to changes in the output gap so as to offset changes in infla-

FIGURE 29-4   Canadian CPI and "Core" Inflation, 1992–2002

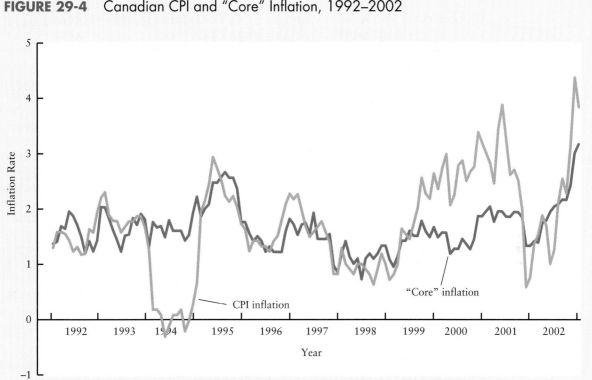

The CPI inflation rate is more volatile than the "core" inflation rate. The core rate of inflation in Canada is the rate of change of a special price index constructed by removing food, energy, and the effects of indirect taxes from the overall Consumer Price Index. For both series shown here, the inflation rate is computed monthly, but is the rate of change in the price index from 12 months earlier.

(*Source:* Statistics Canada, CANSIM database, Series V36397 and V735319.)

tionary pressure. The Bank's appropriate policy response to a change in the exchange rate depends crucially on the *cause* of the change.

Many economic events can lead to changes in the exchange rate. The cause of any change must be known before the appropriate monetary policy response can be determined.

We consider two different examples. In the first, an appreciation of the Canadian dollar leads the Bank to tighten its monetary policy. In the second example, an appreciation of the Canadian dollar leads the Bank to loosen its monetary policy. In both cases, the Bank's actions are consistent with its objective of keeping the inflation rate near the midpoint of the 1–3 percent target band.

For the first example, suppose that the economies of Canada's trading partners are booming and thus demanding more Canadian exports. Foreigners' heightened demand for Canadian goods creates an increase in demand for the Canadian dollar in foreign-exchange markets. The Canadian dollar therefore appreciates. But the increase in demand for Canadian goods also adds directly to Canadian aggregate demand. If this shock persists, it will therefore add to domestic inflationary pressures. In this case, if the Bank notes the appreciation of the dollar (and correctly determines its cause), it can take action to offset the positive demand shock by tightening monetary policy.

The second example involves an increase in demand for Canadian *assets* rather than Canadian goods, and has quite different implications from the first example. Suppose that investors, because of events happening elsewhere in the world, decide to liquidate some of their foreign assets and purchase more Canadian assets instead. In this case, the increase in demand for Canadian assets leads to an increase in demand for the Canadian dollar in foreign-exchange markets. This causes an appreciation of the Canadian dollar. As the dollar appreciates, however, Canadian exports become more expensive to foreigners. There will be a reduction in Canadian net exports and thus a reduction in Canadian aggregate demand. If this shock persists, it will reduce inflationary pressure in Canada. In this case, if the Bank notes the appreciation of the dollar (and correctly determines its cause), it can take action to offset the negative demand shock by loosening monetary policy.

Notice in both examples that the Canadian dollar appreciated as a result of the external shock, but the causes of the appreciation were different. In the first case, there was a positive demand shock to net exports, which then caused the appreciation, which in turn dampened the initial increase in net exports. But the overall effect on the demand for Canadian goods was positive. In the second case, there was a positive shock to the *asset* market, which then caused the appreciation, which in turn reduced the demand for net exports. The overall effect on the demand for Canadian goods was negative. Thus, in the first case, the appropriate response for monetary policy was contractionary, whereas in the second case the appropriate response for monetary policy was expansionary.

Changes in the exchange rate can signal the need for changes in the stance of monetary policy. But care must be taken to identify the cause of the exchange-rate change.

Some financial commentators argue that the Bank of Canada should use its policy to offset changes in the exchange rate. Others argue that the Bank should focus on its inflation targets and not worry so much about changes in the exchange rate.

For a more detailed discussion of how movements in the exchange rate complicate the implementation of monetary policy, look for "Monetary Policy and the Exchange Rate in Canada" in the *Additional Topics* **section of this book's Companion Website.**

http://www.pearsoned.ca/ragan

29.3 Lags in the Conduct of Monetary Policy

In Chapter 28 we encountered one difference between two groups of macroeconomists involved in a debate that was prominent in the 1950s and 1960s. *Monetarists* argued that monetary policy was potentially very powerful in the sense that a given change in the money supply would lead to a substantial change in aggregate demand, whereas *Keynesians* were associated with the view that monetary policy was much less powerful.

This debate had some of its roots in differing interpretations of the causes of the Great Depression, especially as it occurred in the United States amid a large number of commercial-bank failures. Now that you better understand the role of central banks and commercial banks in the determination of the money supply, you can better understand this debate. One interesting part of the debate is why Canada and the United Kingdom had collapses in economic activity similar in magnitude to that in the United States even though they did not suffer the same banking crisis. *Lessons From History 29-1* provides a brief summary of this interesting debate.

The debate between the Monetarists and the Keynesians involved more than just the *size* of the effect of a change in the money supply on national income, however; it also focused on the question of whether active use of monetary policy in an attempt to stabilize output and the price level was likely to be successful, or whether it would instead lead to an increase in fluctuations in those variables. This debate is as important today as it was then, and at its centre is the role of *lags*.

What Are the Lags in Monetary Policy?

Experience has shown that lags in the operation of policy can actually cause stabilization policy to be destabilizing. In Chapter 24, we discussed how decision and implementation lags might limit the extent to which active use of fiscal policy can be relied upon to stabilize the economy. Although both of these sources of lags are much less relevant for monetary policy, the full effects of monetary policy nevertheless occur only after quite long time lags. There are three reasons why a change in monetary policy does not affect the economy instantly.

Deposit Creation Takes Time

Open-market operations or the switching of government deposits affects the reserves of the banks. This process takes place more or less instantly. But the full increase in the money supply occurs only when the commercial banks have granted enough new loans to expand the money supply by the full amount that is possible by existing reserve ratios. This process can take quite a long time.

Changes in Expenditure Take Time

A change in the money supply leads to a change in the interest rate. This, in turn, affects interest-sensitive expenditures. But it takes time for new investment plans to be drawn up, approved, and put into effect. It may take a year or more before the full increase in investment expenditure occurs in response to a fall in interest rates. In an open economy like Canada's, the change in the interest rate also leads to capital flows and a change in the exchange rate. These changes occur very quickly. But the effect on net exports takes more time while purchasers of internationally traded goods and services switch to lower-cost suppliers.

The Multiplier Process Takes Time

Changes in investment and net export expenditures brought about by a change in monetary policy set off the multiplier process that increases national income. This process, too, takes some time to work out. Furthermore, although the end result is fairly predictable, the speed with which the entire expansionary or contractionary process works itself out can vary in ways that are hard to predict. Thus, though the effects of monetary

LESSONS FROM HISTORY 29-1

Two Views on the Role of Money in the Great Depression

In most people's minds, the Great Depression began with the stock market crash of October 1929. In the United States, Canada, and Europe, the decline in economic activity over the next four years was massive. From 1929 to 1933, real output fell by roughly 25 percent, one-quarter of the labour force was unemployed by 1933, the price level fell by over 25 percent, and businesses failed on a massive scale. In the six decades that have followed, no recession has come close to the Great Depression in terms of reduced economic activity, business failures, or unemployment.

The Great Depression has naturally attracted the attention of economists and, especially in the United States, these few years of experience have served as a kind of "retrospective laboratory" in which they have tried to test their theories.

The Basic Facts

The stock market crash of 1929, and other factors associated with a moderate downswing in business activity during the late 1920s, caused the U.S. public (firms and households) to wish to hold more cash and fewer demand deposits. The banking system, however, could not meet this increased demand for liquidity without help from the Federal Reserve

System (the U.S. central bank). As we saw in Chapter 27, because of the fractional-reserve banking system, commercial banks are never able to satisfy from their own reserves a large and sudden demand for cash—their reserves are always only a small fraction of total deposits.

The Federal Reserve had been set up to provide just such emergency assistance to commercial banks that were basically sound but were unable to meet sudden demands by depositors to withdraw cash. However, the Fed refused to extend the necessary help, and successive waves of bank failures followed as a direct result. During each wave, hundreds of banks failed, ruining many depositors and thereby worsening an already severe depression. In the second half of 1931, almost 2000 U.S. banks were forced to suspend operations. One consequence of these failures was a sharp drop in the money supply; by 1933, M2 was 33 percent lower than it had been in 1929.

Competing Explanations

To Monetarists, these facts seem decisive: To them, the fall in the money supply was clearly the major cause of the fall in output and employment that occurred during the Great Depression. Monetarists see the Great Depression as perhaps the single best piece of evidence of the strength of monetary

policy might be reasonably straightforward to predict, the timing of those effects is difficult to predict.

Monetary policy is capable of exerting expansionary and contractionary forces on the economy, but it operates with a time lag that is long and variable.

Economists at the Bank of Canada estimate that it takes between 9 and 12 months for a change in monetary policy to have an effect on real GDP, and a further 9 to 12 months for the policy to have an effect on the price level.

Destabilizing Policy?

To see the significance of lags for the conduct of monetary policy, consider a simple example. To begin, suppose that the lag is known to be exactly 18 months. If on January 1 the Bank of Canada determines that the economy needs a stimulus, it can increase the reserves of the banking system within the day and the money supply can then begin to increase. By the end of that month a significant increase may be registered.

However, because the full effects of this policy take time to work out, the policy may prove to be destabilizing. By October, a substantial inflationary gap may have forces, and the single best lesson of the importance of monetary policy. In their view, the increased cash drain that led to the massive monetary contraction could have been prevented had the Federal Reserve quickly increased the level of reserves in the commercial banking system. In this case, the rise in the monetary base would have offset the increase in the cash drain, so that the money supply (currency plus bank deposits) could be maintained.

Keynesians argue that the fundamental cause of the Great Depression was a reduction in autonomous expenditure. They cite a large decline in housing construction (in response to a glut of housing) and a reduction in consumption driven largely by pessimism caused by the stock market crash. Although Keynesians accept the argument that the Fed's behaviour was perverse, and exacerbated an already bad situation, they do not attribute a pivotal role to the Fed or to the money supply. They see the fall in the money supply as a *result* of the decline in economic activity (through a reduced demand for loans and thus reduced bank lending) rather than as its cause.

Lessons from Canada's Experience

Canada has been used as a "control" in this retrospective laboratory, for the simple reason that Canada had broadly the same magnitude of economic collapse as did the United States, but *did not* have the same magnitude of bank failures. Unfortunately, Canada's experience is not able to resolve the disagreement—both sides of the debate offer explanations of the Canadian experience consistent with their central arguments.

Keynesians look to Canada's experience to support their view that money was not central to the cause of the economic collapse in the United States. They point out that in Canada, where the central bank came to the aid of the banking system, bank failures were much less common during the Great Depression, and as a consequence, the money supply did not shrink drastically as it did in the United States. Thus, their argument is that since Canada did not escape the Great Depression, but it *did* escape the collapse in the money supply, money must not have been the central cause of the U.S. economic collapse.

Monetarists accept the point that Canada did not have a massive reduction in the money supply, but they argue that the economic contraction in the United States (which *was* caused by the collapse in the money supply) spilled over into Canada, largely through a dramatic reduction in demand for Canadian goods. This spillover implies a large decline in autonomous export expenditure for Canada, and thus a decline in Canadian national income. Thus, Monetarists essentially argue that money in the United States was an important contributor to the economic decline in Canada.

For a discussion of these two views, and some attempts to discriminate between them, see Peter Temin, *Did Monetary Forces Cause the Great Depression?* (New York: Norton, 1976). For the classic statement of the Monetarist view, see Milton Friedman and Anna Schwartz, *A Monetary History of the United States 1867–1960* (Princeton: Princeton University Press, 1963).

---

developed because of cyclical forces unrelated to the Bank's monetary policy. However, since the effects of the monetary expansion that was initiated nine months earlier are just beginning to be felt, an expansionary monetary stimulus is adding to the existing inflationary gap.

If the Bank now applies the monetary brakes by contracting the money supply, the full effects of this move will not be felt for another 18 months. By that time, a contraction may have already set in because of the natural cyclical forces of the economy. Thus, the delayed effects of the monetary policy may turn a minor downturn into a major recession.

The long time lags in the effectiveness of monetary policy make monetary fine-tuning difficult; the policy may have a destabilizing effect.

The Bank of Canada recognizes the possibility that if it responds to every shock that influences real GDP, the overall effect of its policy may be to destabilize the economy rather than stabilize it. As a result, it is careful to assess the causes of the shocks that buffet the Canadian economy. It tries to avoid situations in which it responds to short-lived shocks and then must reverse its policy in the near future when the shocks disappear. In general, the Bank responds only to those shocks that are significant in magnitude and persistent in duration.

FIGURE 29-5   Political Difficulties of Forward-Looking Monetary Policy

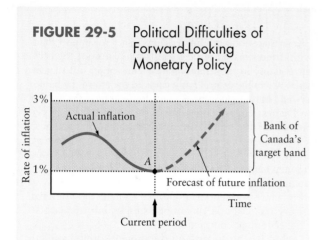

Since monetary policy works only with a considerable time lag, central-bank actions to keep inflation within its target range must be taken in advance of expected future events. Suppose the economy is currently at point *A* with inflation at the lower bound of the target range. If events in the near future are expected to cause inflation to rise sharply, then monetary policy must be tightened immediately to keep inflation within the desired range. The central bank then faces the politically awkward situation of tightening policy at a time when *current* inflation is low.

Political Difficulties

Long lags in the workings of monetary policy also imply political difficulties for the central bank.

Figure 29-5 shows a situation in which the current inflation rate is at the bottom of the Bank's 1–3 percent target band, but the expectation of future events suggests that inflation will be rising sharply. This situation is a typical one faced by the Bank anytime the economy is well into a healthy economic recovery, as was true in the spring of 1997 and also the spring of 2003. In the latter case, the Canadian economy had been growing much more quickly than the U.S. economy, and the future suggested more of the same. Core inflation at the time was still within the target band, but expectations of higher future growth threatened to push core inflation above the 3 percent upper limit.

What is the political problem? Remember that because of the time lags involved, any policy change that occurs today has no effect on real GDP for roughly 9 months and the full effect on the price level (or the rate of inflation) does not occur for 18–24 months. If the economy is at point *A* in Figure 29-5, and inflation is expected to rise in the near future, then monetary policy must be changed *now* in order to counteract this future inflation. But this is politically difficult because the *current* inflation rate is low. The Bank finds itself in the awkward position of advocating a tightening of monetary policy, in order to fight the expectation of future inflation, at a time when the *current* inflation rate suggests no need for tightening. But if the goal is to keep inflation within the target range, such *pre-emptive* monetary policy is necessary because of the unavoidable time lags.

Time lags in monetary policy require that decisions regarding a loosening or tightening of monetary policy be forward-looking. This often creates political difficulties for the central bank.

29.4 **25 Years of Canadian Monetary Policy**

This section describes a few key episodes in recent Canadian monetary history. This is not done to teach history for its own sake, but because the lessons of past experience and past policy mistakes, interpreted through the filter of economic theory, provide our best hope for improving our policy performance in the future.

By 1980, partly as a result of the two OPEC oil shocks, in 1974 and 1979–80, inflation in Canada was over 12 percent. The Bank of Canada (and also the U.S Federal Reserve) embarked on a strict policy of monetary restraint aimed at fighting inflation. Interest rates rose sharply, as shown in Figure 29-6. The result of this aggressive disin-

FIGURE 29-6   Short-Term Interest Rates, Canada and the United States, 1979–2003

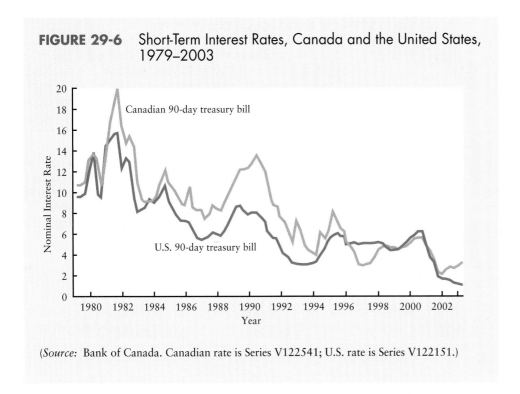

(*Source:* Bank of Canada. Canadian rate is Series V122541; U.S. rate is Series V122151.)

flation policy was, in both countries, the most serious recession since the 1930s. These high interest rates, and the recession they wrought, were more severe than might have been expected from the relatively moderate slowdown in the rate of growth of the money supply induced by the central banks.

An unanticipated surge in the demand for money led to a much tighter monetary policy than the Bank had intended.

In other words, this unplanned tight monetary policy did not occur because money supply fell more than intended, but because money demand increased sharply. With the dramatic fall in inflation and the serious recession, the Bank eased monetary policy in the second half of 1982.

Economic Recovery: 1983–1987

In early 1983, a sustained recovery began, and by mid-1987, real GDP had moved back toward potential. Much of the growth was centred in the export-oriented manufacturing industries in Ontario and Quebec. The first four years of the recovery saw cumulative output growth of 15.7 percent.

The main challenge for monetary policy in this period was to create sufficient liquidity to accommodate the recovery without triggering a return to the high inflation rates that prevailed at the start of the decade.

In other words, the Bank of Canada had to increase the money supply to *accommodate* the recovery-induced increase in money demand *without* increasing the money supply so much that it refueled inflationary pressures.

In spite of much debate and uncertainty, the Bank handled this "re-entry" problem quite well. The Bank allowed a short but rapid burst of growth in the nominal money supply, thus generating the desired increase in real money balances. Once the new level of real balances was achieved, money growth was cut back to a rate consistent with low inflation, allowing for the underlying rate of growth in real income. The trick with this policy was that to avoid triggering expectations of renewed inflation, the Bank had to generate a one-shot increase in the *level* of the money supply without creating the impression that it was raising the long-term *rate of growth* of the money supply.

In late 1983 and early 1984, when growth in monetary aggregates first started to surge, many voiced the fear that the Bank was being overly expansionary and was risking a return to higher inflation. As the re-entry problem came to be more widely understood and as inflationary pressures failed to re-emerge, these criticisms subsided, and the consensus appeared to be that the Bank had done a commendable job of handling the re-entry problem.

Rising Inflation: 1987–1990

By mid-1987, many observers began to worry that Canadian policymakers were too complacent in accepting the 4 percent range that Canadian inflation had settled into. Further, there was concern that inflationary pressures were starting to build—monetary aggregates were growing quickly, real output growth was strong, unemployment was falling, and an inflationary gap was opening.

In 1987, many economists argued that if monetary policy was not tightened, Canada would experience gradually increasing inflation until once again a severe monetary restriction would be necessary.

Inflation slowly crept upward. A monetary restriction designed to reduce inflation would obviously impose costs in the form of lower output and higher unemployment. Was the Bank prepared to inflict such costs, especially given that Canada had emerged from a deep recession only five years earlier?

In January 1988, Bank of Canada Governor John Crow announced that monetary policy would henceforth be guided less by short-term stabilization issues and more by the goal of long-term "price stability." Specifically, he said that "monetary policy should be conducted so as to achieve a pace of monetary expansion that promotes stability in the value of money. This means pursuing a policy aimed at achieving and maintaining stable prices."[1]

Disinflation: 1990–1992

This explicit adoption of price stability as the Bank's only target set off a heated debate about the appropriate stance for monetary policy. The debate was fueled by Crow's decision to give a high profile to his policy by repeatedly articulating and defending it in speeches and public appearances. Some critics said that price stability was unobtainable. Others said the costs of reaching it would be too large in terms of several years of recessionary gaps. Supporters said that the long-term gains from having a stable price level would exceed the costs of getting there.

---

[1] John W. Crow, "The Work of Canadian Monetary Policy," speech given at the University of Alberta, January 18, 1988; reprinted in *Bank of Canada Review,* February 1988.

Despite the Bank's explicit policy of "price stability," the actual inflation rate increased slightly in the years immediately following John Crow's policy announcement, from about 4 percent in 1987 to just over 5 percent in 1990.

The controversy reached new heights when in 1990 the country (and much of the world) entered a sustained recession. Maintaining the policy of tight money with high interest rates seemed perverse to many when the economy was already suffering from too little aggregate demand to sustain potential output.

Furthermore, the high Canadian interest rates attracted foreign funds. Foreigners who wished to buy Canadian bonds needed Canadian dollars, and their demands led to an appreciation of the Canadian dollar. This increased the price of Canadian exports while reducing the price of Canadian imports, putting Canadian export and import-competing industries at a competitive disadvantage, and further increasing the unemployment that had been generated by the worldwide recession.

In spite of heavy political pressure to lower interest rates, and of criticism from many economists who might have supported a move toward price stability in less depressed times, the Bank stood by its tight monetary policy. Indeed, in 1991, it formally announced *inflation-control targets* for the next several years. Beginning in 1992, inflation was to lie within the 3–5 percent range, with the range falling to 2–4 percent by 1993 and to 1–3 percent by the end of 1995.

John Crow was the governor of the Bank of Canada from 1987 to 1994. In 1988 he announced that "price stability" would thenceforth be the Bank of Canada's objective.

The result of this commitment to tight money was an unprecedented differential between Canadian and U.S. interest rates (see Figure 29-6), and a high value of the Canadian dollar, which temporarily hurt the international competitiveness of Canadian goods.

As a result of the tight monetary policy of the Bank, the inflation rate fell sharply, from about 5 percent in 1990 to less than 2 percent in 1992. For 1993 and 1994, inflation hovered around 2 percent. Furthermore, short-term nominal interest rates fell from a high of about 13 percent in 1990 to about 6 percent by the end of 1993. Recall that the nominal interest rate is equal to the real interest rate plus the rate of inflation. So this decline in nominal interest rates was the eventual result of the tight money policy that reduced inflation. The differential between Canadian and U.S. rates also fell and the Canadian dollar depreciated. Figure 29-6 illustrates the story.

Price Stability: 1992–?

The Bank had succeeded in coming close to its target of price stability. Controversy continued, however, on two issues. First, was the result worth the price of a deeper, possibly more prolonged recession than might have occurred if the Bank had been willing to accept 3–4 percent inflation? Second, would the low inflation rate be sustainable once the recovery took the economy back toward potential output? If the inflation rate were to rise to 4 percent during the post-1993 recovery, then the verdict might well be that the cost of temporarily reducing the rate to below 2 percent was not worth the transitory gains.

The debate over the Bank's disinflation policy became centred on Governor John Crow, especially during the federal election campaign of 1993. Some called for the nonrenewal of Crow's term as governor (which would end in 1994), and his replacement with someone more concerned with the costs of disinflation. Others argued that the Bank's policy of "price stability" under Crow's stewardship was the right policy for the times, and

Gordon Thiessen became the governor of the Bank of Canada in 1994 after inflation had hovered around 2 percent for about two years.

that the long-run benefits of low inflation would be worth the costs required to achieve it.[2]

In 1994, the minister of finance appointed Gordon Thiessen, the former senior deputy governor of the Bank, to be the new governor. With some irony, the minister of finance, whose party had been severe critics of Crow's policy while they were in opposition, affirmed the previous monetary policy of the Bank and urged the new governor to maintain the hard-won low inflation rate. The new governor also affirmed the policy of price stability, and extended the formal inflation target of 1 to 3 percent.

For the next five years, the rate of inflation continued to hover between 1 and 2 percent. The main challenge for the Bank in the next few years was to keep inflation low while at the same time encouraging the economy to progress through what was viewed as a fragile economic recovery. Excessive stimulation of the economy would lead to the rise of inflation which would sacrifice the hard-won gains achieved only a few years earlier. On the other hand, insufficient stimulation would itself be an obstacle to economic recovery. By 2002, real GDP in Canada was close to its potential level and core inflation was very close to the midpoint of the 1 to 3 percent target range.

Recent Concerns for Monetary Policy

During the past few years, three issues presented significant challenges to the Bank of Canada and to the conduct of monetary policy. The first was the "Asian Crisis" of 1997–98. The second was the possibility that inflation was "too low." The third was dramatic growth and then subsequent "crashes" in stock-market values.

The Asian Crisis

Beginning in the summer of 1997, the economies of Thailand, Malaysia, Indonesia, and South Korea fell into serious recessions.[3] Since these countries are major importers of raw materials, their recessions led to a large decline in the world's demand for raw materials. As a result, the world price of raw materials fell by an average of about 30 percent in the subsequent year. Since Canada is a major producer and exporter of raw materials, this decline in the demand for raw materials was a negative aggregate demand shock for Canada. The decline in Canada's net exports led to a leftward shift in Canada's *AD* curve.

Working in the opposite direction, however, was the expansionary supply-side effect of lower raw materials prices for the many Canadian manufacturing firms that use raw materials as inputs. Remember from Chapter 23 that reductions in input prices shift the *AS* curve downward and increase real GDP—a positive supply shock.

This positive supply shock was especially important for the United States, a major importer and user of raw materials. The impact of the Asian Crisis on the U.S. economy produced a third effect on Canada as the quickly growing U.S. economy increased its demand for Canadian goods and services.

See Chapter 29 of www.pearsoned.ca/ragan for an interesting discussion of how monetary policy responded to the Asian Crisis: Stephen Poloz, "How Will Central Banks Cope with a Non-Inflationary World?"

---

[2] For a very readable account of Canadian monetary policy from 1988 to 1993, see William Robson and David Laidler, *The Great Canadian Disinflation* (Toronto: C. D. Howe Institute, 1993).

[3] An important part of the cause of these recessions was the sudden collapse of their currencies, which were previously pegged in value to the U.S. dollar. We examine fixed and flexible exchange rates in detail in Chapter 35.

The Asian Crisis therefore produced a complicated combination of forces on the Canadian economy, including

- a negative *AD* effect from the reduction in demand (and thus the prices) for Canadian exports
- a positive *AS* effect from the lower-price inputs for Canadian manufacturing firms
- a positive *AD* effect from the increase in U.S. demand for Canadian goods (caused, in turn, by the positive *AS* effect in the United States)

In the spring of 1997, before the Asian Crisis had begun, the Canadian economy was growing and steadily closing a recessionary gap. The combination of forces created by the Asian Crisis presented problems for the Bank of Canada and for the appropriate direction for monetary policy. Especially difficult was judging the relative strengths of the three separate effects. As it turned out, Canada's recessionary gap continued to shrink as the economy grew steadily. By 1999, the Asian economies were on their way to a healthy recovery.

Is Inflation Too Low?

The second recent problem faced by the Bank was, ironically, caused by its success in reducing inflation and maintaining it at a low level. Canada's inflation rate fell very quickly from 5 percent in 1991 to below 2 percent in 1992. It then remained between 1 and 2 percent for the next seven years. The U.S. Federal Reserve was not as aggressive in its drive to reduce inflation; inflation in the United States did not decline as much or as sharply as in Canada. Interestingly, the Canadian and U.S. economies appeared to perform differently throughout the 1990s. Especially apparent was the difference in unemployment rates between the two countries. From 1985 to 1990, when both economies were growing steadily, the Canadian unemployment rate was just over 2 percentage points higher than the U.S. rate. Beginning in 1991, however, as Canada's sharp disinflation began, the gap increased to 4 percentage points.

Some economists point to the widening gap in unemployment rates as evidence that there are costs associated with very low inflation.[4] These economists argue not only that the process of disinflation involves *temporary* costs in terms of reduced output and higher unemployment, but more controversially that there are *permanent* costs associated with maintaining inflation at very low levels.

That very low inflation may permanently raise unemployment is an argument originally put forward in 1972 by the late James Tobin, an economist from Yale University who was awarded the Nobel Prize in economics in 1981. In Canada, the argument was made by Pierre Fortin of the Université du Québec à Montréal. Central to Tobin's and Fortin's arguments is the importance of downward rigidity in nominal wages—a more extreme version of what we called *wage stickiness* in Chapter 24. Specifically, these economists believe that nominal wages will rise in the presence of excess demand but they will not fall significantly in the presence of excess supply. Why does this wage rigidity lead to higher unemployment when inflation is very low but not when inflation is higher?

Their argument is rather involved, and to understand it we need to proceed carefully. The argument is summarized by the following four points:

- First, the various sectors within the economy are continually being subjected to demand shocks. At any given time, some sectors are expanding while others are

---

[4] In Chapter 31 we discuss some other explanations for why Canada's unemployment rate is higher than the U.S. rate.

contracting. These demand shocks lead to changes in the demand for labour in the various sectors and thus necessitate changes in real wages, rising in expanding sectors and falling in contracting sectors.

- Second, if nominal wages cannot fall because of wage rigidity, then the only way *real* wages can fall is if the price level rises.
- Third, inflation at moderate levels (3–5 percent) is high enough to bring about the necessary drop in real wages in most of the contracting sectors. This is because the pattern of demand shocks across sectors is such that even the sectors with the sharpest contractions require real-wage declines of only 5 percent.
- Finally (and this is the key point), if inflation is very low (1–2 percent), the contracting sectors *cannot* achieve the necessary reduction in real wages through inflation. Firms will instead choose to lay off their workers. Thus, when inflation is very low, the layoffs in the contracting sectors will outnumber the newly hired workers in the expanding sectors. The result is *permanently* higher unemployment.

This view is not shared by all economists. The main point of contention is the cause and extent of the downward rigidity in nominal wages. Many economists believe that while nominal wages may be very slow to fall in response to excess supply, this wage stickiness is largely a result of workers' having lived in an inflationary environment for many years. In such an environment, if prices have been rising at 5, 8, or 10 percent annually, it is easy to understand why workers are reluctant to accept an actual decline in their nominal wages. But as low inflation becomes a more permanent part of the economic environment, workers will naturally come to view occasional reductions in nominal wages as one of the unpleasant but inevitable aspects of economic life. If this is true, the downward rigidity of nominal wages will eventually disappear as Canada's experience with low inflation continues. In this case, real GDP will eventually return to Y^*, unemployment will eventually return to U^*, and low inflation will not involve permanent costs.

This debate is currently unsettled. Much theoretical and empirical research is directed at determining the extent of nominal wage rigidity and how it is related to the overall inflation rate, but it will probably take several years before a consensus emerges on just how important this potential cost of low inflation really is.[5]

The Stock Market

The third problem for monetary policy came from dramatic swings in the stock market. A rising stock market can cause problems for the conduct of monetary policy. From 1994 through 1999, U.S. and Canadian stocks enjoyed unprecedented bull markets. The Dow Jones Industrial Average (an index of U.S. stock prices) increased from about 3500 in mid-1994 to about 11 000 in late 1999, an average annual increase of 26 percent. The Toronto Stock Exchange Index (now called the TSX), increased from roughly 4000 to 8000 over the same period, an average annual increase of 14 percent.

The concern for the Bank of Canada during this time was that the increase in wealth generated by these stock-market gains would stimulate consumption expenditures in what was already a steadily growing economy, thus increasing inflationary pressures. In December of 1996, the chairman of the U.S. Federal Reserve, Alan Greenspan, warned

---

[5] The resurrection of Tobin's ideas is found in G. Akerlof, W. Dickens, and G. Perry, "The Macroeconomics of Low Inflation," *Brookings Papers on Economic Activity*, 1996. The argument for Canada was made by Pierre Fortin in "The Great Canadian Slump," *Canadian Journal of Economics*, 1997. For an assessment of the general argument, see Seamus Hogan, "What Does Downward Nominal-Wage Rigidity Imply for Monetary Policy?" *Canadian Public Policy*, 1998.

market participants about their "irrational exuberance." Bank of Canada Governor Gordon Thiessen made similar remarks in Canada. Both central bankers were trying to dampen expectations in the stock market so that the stock-market gains, and thus the increases in wealth-induced spending, would not significantly contribute to inflationary pressures. But they had to be careful not to have their comments create a "crash" in the market that would have even more dramatic effects in the opposite direction.

As it turned out, the crash happened anyway. In both the United States and Canada, the stock markets had reached such levels that many commentators said it was only a matter of time before participants realized that stock prices no longer reflected the underlying values of the companies, at which point there would be massive selling and an inevitable crash.

Early in 2001 the U.S. economy began to slow down. Fear of an impending recession led to large declines—euphemistically referred to as "corrections"—in stock-market values. When the terrorist attacks in New York and Washington occurred on September 11, 2001, the markets took another dramatic plunge. By late in 2003, stock markets were still far below their pre-crash levels.

Following the stock-market crashes of 2001, the main challenge for monetary policy was to provide enough liquidity to the banking systems to prevent the economy from entering a recession. In both the United States and Canada, the central banks dramatically lowered their key interest rates over a period of several months. By late in 2003, the Canadian economy was growing at a healthy rate and the Bank of Canada had begun tightening its policy by slowly increasing interest rates. Growth in the U.S. economy was much more sluggish, and the U.S. Federal Reserve was slower to increase rates.

Stock markets both captivate and confuse many people. Some view them as nothing more than gambling casinos that could disappear with no real loss for the world; others view them as a vital part of our financial markets, without which our economy would suffer greatly.

> **For a detailed discussion of how stock markets work, and how fluctuations in the stock market are related to fluctuations in the level of economic activity, look for "A Beginner's Guide to the Stock Market" in the *Additional Topics* section of this book's Companion Website.**
>
> h t t p : / / w w w . p e a r s o n e d . c a / r a g a n

S U M M A R Y

29.1 **The Bank of Canada and the Money Supply**

- The Bank of Canada controls the level of reserves in the commercial banking system through open-market operations and by switching government deposits between itself and the chartered banks. Purchases of bonds on the open market or switching government deposits toward the commercial banks increases the reserves of the banking system. Sales on the open market or withdrawing government deposits away from the commercial banks reduces bank reserves.

- The Bank of Canada conducts and announces its policy in terms of changes in the bank rate (which is at the top of its 50-basis-point target range for the overnight interest rate). But the Bank cannot set reserves and the bank rate independently.

29.2 **Monetary Policy Targets**

- The Bank's long-run policy target is the rate of inflation—it attempts to keep the core rate of inflation near the midpoint of its 1–3 percent target band.
- In the short run, the Bank closely monitors the output gap. By tightening its policy during an inflationary gap (and loosening it during a recessionary gap), the Bank can keep the rate of inflation near the midpoint of the target band.

- The policy of inflation targeting helps to stabilize the economy. The Bank responds to positive shocks with a contractionary policy, and responds to negative shocks with an expansionary policy.
- Two technical issues complicate the conduct of monetary policy:
  1. Volatile food and energy prices
  2. Changes in the exchange rate

29.3 **Lags in the Conduct of Monetary Policy**

- Though the Bank can change the reserves of the banking system more or less instantly, it takes time for this change in reserves to be transformed into a change in bank deposits and thus a change in the money supply.
- Once interest rates change in response to a change in the money supply, it takes time for firms and households to change their expenditure. Even once those new

plans are carried out, it takes time for the multiplier process to work its way through the economy, eventually increasing equilibrium national income.

- Long and variable lags in monetary policy lead many economists to argue that the Bank should not try to "fine-tune" the economy. Instead, it should respond only to shocks that are significant in size and persistent in duration.

29.4 **25 Years of Canadian Monetary Policy**

- In the early 1980s, the Bank of Canada embarked on a policy of tight money to reduce inflation. This policy contributed to the severity of the recession.
- A sustained economic recovery occurred from 1983 to 1987. The main challenge for monetary policy during this time was to create sufficient liquidity to accommodate the recovery without triggering a return to the high inflation rates that prevailed at the start of the decade.
- In 1988, when inflation was between 4 and 5 percent, the Bank of Canada announced that monetary policy would henceforth be guided by the long-term goal of "price stability." By 1992, the Bank's tight money policy had reduced inflation to below 2 percent.

- Controversy concerned two issues. First, was the cost in terms of lost output and heavy unemployment worth the benefits of lower inflation? Second, could the low inflation rate be sustained?
- This controversy was partly responsible for the 1994 change in the Bank of Canada's governor, from John Crow to Gordon Thiessen. Despite this administrative change, the stated policy of price stability continued. By 1999, the rate of inflation had been hovering between 1 and 2 percent for about seven years.
- In the past few years, the central challenges faced by the Bank included (1) how to respond to the Asian Crisis, (2) whether very low inflation might involve permanent costs in the form of higher unemployment, and (3) how to respond to dramatic swings in stock-market values.

K E Y   C O N C E P T S

Open-market operations
Shifting government deposits
The bank rate
The overnight rate

Monetary policy targets
Monetary policy instruments
Inflation targeting
Core vs. CPI inflation

The exchange rate and monetary policy
Lags in the effect of monetary policy

STUDY EXERCISES

1. Fill in the blanks to make the following statements correct.

   a. The Bank of Canada can change the reserves in the commercial banking system through _____ and _____.

   b. If the Bank of Canada purchases a bond from the Royal Bank, commercial bank reserves will _____, deposit money will _____, and the money supply will _____.

   c. If the Bank of Canada sells a treasury bill to CIBC, commercial bank reserves will _____, deposit money will _____, and the money supply will _____.

   d. If the Bank of Canada aims to decrease the money supply it can shift government deposits from _____ to _____; if it aims to increase the money supply, it can shift government deposits from _____ to _____.

   e. An increase in the money supply leads to a _____ in interest rates, which leads to a(n) _____ in desired investment and a capital _____ from Canada. The capital flows leads to a(n) _____ of the Canadian dollar and a(n) _____ in net exports. The end result is a(n) _____ in aggregate demand and a _____ shift of the *AD* curve. The equilibrium level of real GDP _____.

2. Fill in the blanks to make the following statements correct.

   a. The long-run policy target for the Bank of Canada is the _____. The current target is to keep the inflation rate between _____ and _____ pecent.

   b. In the short run, the Bank of Canada closely monitors the _____.

   c. It is not possible for the Bank of Canada to independently influence the following two variables: _____ and _____. The Bank of Canada conducts its policy by announcing a change in the _____. It then conducts the necessary _____ in order to make this rate an equilibrium in the money market.

   d. The conduct of monetary policy is made more difficult because of lags. Three reasons for these time lags are :
      - _____
      - _____
      - _____

   e. Economists have estimated that a change in monetary policy has an effect on real GDP after a period of _____ months and an effect on the price level after a period of _____ months.

   f. Because of the long time lags involved in the execution of monetary policy, it is very possible that the policy may in fact have a _____ effect on the economy.

3. Suppose the Bank of Canada enters the open market and sells $100 000 of government securities to a commercial bank. The two balance sheets below are for the *changes* in assets and liabilities for the commercial banks and the Bank of Canada.

Commercial Banks		Bank of Canada	
Assets	Liabilities	Assets	Liabilities
Reserves —	Deposits —	Bonds —	Commercial bank deposits —

   a. What are the immediate effects on assets and liabilities for the commercial banks? Fill in the left-hand table.

   b. What are the changes for the Bank of Canada? Fill in the right-hand table.

   c. Explain in general terms how this open-market sale will affect the total money supply.

4. Suppose the Bank of Canada transfers $100 000 of government deposits from the government's account at the Bank of Canada to the government's account in a commercial bank. The two balance sheets below are for the *changes* in assets and liabilities for commercial banks and the Bank of Canada.

Commercial Banks		Bank of Canada	
Assets	Liabilities	Assets	Liabilities
Reserves —	Deposits —	Bonds —	Commercial bank deposits —
			Government deposits —

   a. What are the immediate effects on assets and liabilities for the commercial banks? Fill in the left-hand table.

   b. What are the changes for the Bank of Canada? Fill in the right-hand table.

   c. Explain in general terms how this transfer of government deposits will affect the total money supply.

5. In the text we stated that the Bank of Canada's long-run policy target is the rate of inflation.

   a. How is this choice of a long-run policy variable related to the idea of long-run money neutrality?
   b. If money were not neutral in the long run, do you think the Bank might choose a different long-run policy variable? Explain.

6. The diagram below shows the demand for money and the supply of money.

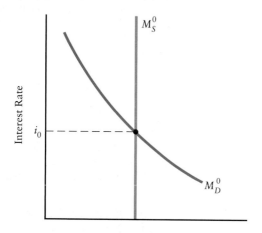

Quantity of Money

   a. Explain (and show in the diagram) why the Bank of Canada cannot independently set the money supply and the interest rate.
   b. Suppose the Bank leaves the money supply unchanged but that the demand for money increases. Show this in the diagram. What happens to interest rates? What happens to investment?
   c. In the situation of part (b), explain why monetary policy has been contractionary even though the Bank did not change the money supply.

7. Milton Friedman was for many years a professor of economics at the University of Chicago, and was the most influential Monetarist of his generation. He is known for accusing the Federal Reserve (the U.S. central bank) of following "an unstable monetary policy," arguing that although the Fed "has given lip service to controlling the quantity of money...it has given its heart to controlling interest rates."

   a. Explain why, if the M_D function were approximately stable, targeting the growth rate in the money supply would produce a "stable" monetary policy. Show this in a diagram.
   b. Explain why, if the M_D function moves suddenly and in unpredictable ways, targeting the money supply produces an "unstable" monetary policy. Show this in a diagram.
   c. The Bank of Canada conducts its policy by setting short-term interest rates. What is the implication for this policy of an "unstable" M_D function?

8. Suppose it is mid-1999 and the stock market has been growing rapidly for the past four years. Some economists argue that the stock market has become "overvalued" and thus a "crash" is imminent.

   a. How does a rising stock market affect aggregate demand? Show this in an *AD/AS* diagram.
   b. For a central bank that is trying to keep real GDP close to potential, explain what challenges are posed by a rapidly rising stock market.
   c. Suppose the stock market "crashes," falling suddenly by 30 percent as it did in 2001. How does this affect aggregate demand? Show this in an *AD/AS* diagram.

DISCUSSION QUESTIONS

1. Describe the tools of monetary policy available to the Bank of Canada, and indicate whether—and if so, how—they might be used for the following purposes:

   a. To create a mild tightening of bank credit
   b. To signal that the Bank of Canada favours a sharp curtailment of bank lending
   c. To permit an expansion of bank credit with existing reserves
   d. To supply banks and the public with a temporary increase of currency for Christmas shopping

2. It is often said that an expansionary monetary policy is like "pushing on a string." What is meant by this statement? How does this contrast with a contractionary monetary policy?

3. In 1988, the Bank of Canada announced that it was committed to achieving "price stability," but it did not commit itself to a particular target growth rate for any monetary aggregate that would be consistent with achieving its price stability target. Why do you think it failed to make such a commitment?

4. In 1993, with 11 percent unemployment, a slow recovery just underway and inflation in the 1 to 2 percent range, the Bank permitted a rapid expansion of M1. Was this inflationary? Why might the Bank have adopted this policy? What is meant by the "re-entry" problem?

5. The term "moral suasion" is generally used to describe attempts by central banks to enlist the cooperation of private financial institutions in the pursuit of some objective of monetary policy. In a country such as Canada, where there are only a few banks, the central bank can easily communicate its view to the commercial banks. Using the balance sheets of the Bank of Canada and the commercial banking system, explain how an attempt by the Bank of Canada to persuade commercial banks to increase their lending would affect bank reserves and total bank deposits. How is this question related to Question 2?

6. Suppose the Canadian economy has real GDP equal to potential and that nothing significant is expected to change in the near future. Then the Canadian dollar suddenly depreciates—apparently permanently—by 5 percent against the U.S. dollar. Explain why the appropriate response of monetary policy depends on the *cause* of the depreciation. In particular, make a distinction between:

   a. A depreciation caused by a reduction in demand for Canadian exports of raw materials; and
   b. A depreciation caused by a reduction in demand for Canadian bonds that are now perceived as less attractive than U.S. bonds.

PART ELEVEN

Macroeconomic Problems

What causes sustained inflation and how can it be reduced? What is the "natural" rate of unemployment, and how is it affected by labour-market policies such as unemployment insurance? Why has the Canadian government so actively pursued policies to reduce the budget deficit? These are the sorts of questions we address in the next three chapters when we explore three key macroeconomic problems. Each chapter may be read independently of the others.

Chapter 30 discusses the causes of inflation. We will see the important distinction between temporary and sustained inflation. We examine the Bank of Canada's role in maintaining a sustained inflation, as well as its role in ending one. We will see here that reducing a sustained inflation is costly, and this explains why policies aimed at fighting inflation are often controversial.

In Chapter 31 we discuss unemployment. Two different theories of cyclical unemployment are considered—New Classical and New Keynesian. We then discuss the natural rate of unemployment—often called the Non-Accelerating Inflation Rate of Unemployment (NAIRU). We examine what determines the NAIRU and why several labour-market policies have the unintended consequence of increasing the NAIRU.

Chapter 32 returns us to the issues of fiscal policy, examining in detail government deficits, surpluses, and government debt. We will see how to judge the stance of fiscal policy, as well as the important connection between government deficits and national saving. We will consider under which conditions government deficits raise interest rates, and what happens as a result.

CHAPTER 30

Inflation

L ## LEARNING OBJECTIVES

1 Explain how wages change in response to both excess demand and inflationary expectations.

2 Show how constant inflation is incorporated into the basic macroeconomic model.

3 Describe how aggregate demand and supply shocks affect inflation and real GDP.

4 Explain how the Bank of Canada may validate demand and supply shocks.

5 Explain the three phases of a disinflation.

6 Describe how the cost of disinflation can be measured by the sacrifice ratio.

If you are a typical reader of this book, you were born in the early or mid-1980s. By the time you were old enough to notice some economic developments going on around you, it was well into the 1990s. By that time, the rate of inflation in Canada was about 2 percent per year. Thus, unless you are older than the typical student taking a course in introductory economics, or you have come to Canada recently from a high-inflation country, inflation has not been a significant phenomenon in your life. It was not so long ago, however, that inflation was considered to be a serious problem in Canada (and many other countries as well).

inflation A rise in the average level of all prices. Often expressed as the annual percentage change in the Consumer Price Index.

Recall from Chapter 19 that **inflation** is a rise in the average level of prices—that is, a rise in the price level. Figure 30-1 shows the rate of CPI inflation in Canada since 1966, and shows what is often called the "twin peaks" of inflation. Rising from the mid-1960s, inflation peaked in 1974 at 11 percent, fell and then peaked again in 1981 at almost 13 percent, and then started its long but bumpy decline to its current level at around 2 percent, the midpoint of the Bank of Canada's official target band.

This very bumpy path for the rate of inflation nicely illustrates one of the reasons that inflation is a problem for the economy. As we mentioned in Chapter 19, economists make the distinction between *anticipated* and *unanticipated* inflation, and we showed why unanticipated inflation is the more serious problem. If firms and workers have difficulty predicting what inflation will be, they have problems determining how wages and prices should be set. The result will be unexpected changes in real wages and relative prices as inflation ends up being different from what was expected. These inflation-induced changes in real wages and relative prices lead to changes in the allocation of resources. As you can well imagine by looking at Figure 30-1, most of the changes in inflation between 1966 and 2002 were sudden and thus difficult to predict. To avoid this uncer-

FIGURE 30-1   Canadian CPI Inflation, 1965–2003

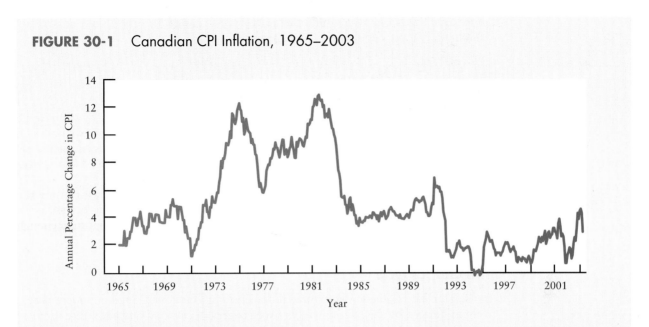

(*Source:* Statistics Canada, CANSIM database, Series V735319.)

tainty in the economy, the Bank of Canada now strives to keep inflation both *low* and *stable*, near the midpoint of the 1–3 percent target band. The result is an environment in which firms, workers and households can much more easily make plans for the future, secure in the knowledge that real wages, real interest rates, and relative prices will not be significantly different because of a volatile inflation rate.

What causes inflation? How can it be eliminated? And why are policies designed to reduce inflation so controversial? These are the central topics of this chapter.

To compute the total inflation from the day of your birth to today, check out the "inflation calculator" at the Bank of Canada's website: www.bankofcanada.ca.

30.1 **Adding Inflation to the Model**

In the previous several chapters we examined the effects of shocks to aggregate demand and aggregate supply. *AD* and *AS* shocks influenced the values of both real GDP and the price level. Following these shocks, the economy's adjustment mechanism always brought the economy back to the potential level of real GDP with a stable price level. In other words, any inflation that we have so far seen in our macroeconomic model was temporary—it only existed while the economy was adjusting toward its long-run equilibrium.

In this chapter we want to understand how a *sustained* inflation can exist, and how we modify our model to account for its presence. After all, even though inflation in Canada is very low, it still appears to be sustained at a rate of about 2 percent per year.

As we will soon see, the key to understanding sustained inflation is to understand the role of *inflation expectations*. When combined with excess demand or excess supply, as reflected by the economy's output gap, such expectations give us a more complete understanding of why wages (and therefore prices) change. Let's begin our analysis by examining in more detail why wages change.

Why Wages Change

In Chapter 24, increases in wages led to increases in unit costs because we maintained the assumption that technology (and thus productivity) was held constant. We continue with that assumption in this chapter. Thus, as wages and other factor prices rise, unit costs increase and the *AS* curve shifts up. Conversely, when wages and other factor prices fall, unit costs fall and the *AS* curve shifts down.

What are the forces that cause wages to change? Two of the main forces are the demand for labour and expectations of future inflation.[1] Much of what we discuss in the case of labour demand was first seen in Chapter 24, but the points are important enough to bear repeating.

The Output Gap

In Chapter 24, we encountered three propositions about how changes in money wages were influenced by the relationship between aggregate demand and aggregate supply:

1. The excess demand for labour that is associated with an inflationary gap puts upward pressure on money wages.

2. The excess supply of labour associated with a recessionary gap puts downward pressure on money wages.

3. The absence of either an inflationary or a recessionary gap means that demand forces do not exert any pressure on money wages.[2]

When real GDP is equal to its potential level (Y^*), the unemployment rate is said to be equal to the NAIRU, which stands for the *non-accelerating inflation rate of unemployment*. The use of this particular name will be explained later in this chapter. Another name sometimes used in place of NAIRU is the *natural rate of unemployment*, but NAIRU is now the more common usage. It is designated by the symbol U^*.

The NAIRU is not zero. Instead, even when output equals potential output, there may be a substantial amount of *frictional* and *structural* unemployment caused, for example, by the movement of people between jobs or between regions. When real output exceeds potential output ($Y > Y^*$), the unemployment rate will be less than the NAIRU ($U < U^*$). When real output is less than potential output ($Y < Y^*$), the unemployment rate will exceed the NAIRU ($U > U^*$).

We have seen that wages react to various pressures of demand. These demand pressures can be stated either in terms of the relationship between actual and potential output or in terms of the relationship between the actual unemployment rate and the NAIRU. When

---

[1] Wages may be affected by other forces that are associated with neither excess demand nor expectations of inflation, such as government guidelines, union power, and employers' optimism. Because there are many such forces that tend to act independently of one another, they may be regarded as random shocks and must be analyzed as separate causes for shifts in the *AS* curve.

[2] As in Chapter 24, we are holding productivity constant in our analysis in this chapter. Otherwise, output gaps would cause changes in wages *relative to productivity*.

$Y > Y^*$ (or $U < U^*$), there is an inflationary gap characterized by excess demand for labour. Wages tend to rise. Conversely, when $Y < Y^*$ (or $U > U^*$), there is a recessionary gap characterized by excess supply of labour. Wages tend to fall.

This relationship between the excess demand or supply of labour and the rate of change of money wages is represented by the Phillips Curve, which we first discussed in Chapter 24.

Expected Inflation

A second force that can influence wages is *expectations* of future inflation. Suppose that both employers and employees expect 3 percent inflation next year. Workers will start negotiations from a base of a 3 percent increase in money wages, which would hold their *real wages* constant. Firms will also be inclined to begin bargaining by conceding at least a 3 percent increase in money wages because they expect that the prices at which they sell their products will rise by 3 percent. Starting from that base, workers may attempt to obtain some desired increase in their real wages. At this point, such factors as profits and bargaining power become important.

The expectation of some specific inflation rate creates pressure for money wages to rise by that rate.

The key point is that money wages can be rising even if no inflationary gap is present. As long as people *expect* prices to rise, their behaviour will put upward pressure on money wages. The central role for the *expectations* of future inflation suggests the importance of examining how firms and workers *form* their expectations. This has been a very active area of research within macroeconomics. *Applying Economic Concepts 30-1* discusses the formation of expectations and explains the important difference between *backward-looking* and *forward-looking* expectations.

Practise with Study Guide Chapter 30, Extension Exercise E1.

Overall Effect

We can now think of changes in money wages as resulting from two different forces:

$$\text{Change in money wages} = \text{Excess-demand effect} + \text{Expectational effect}$$

What happens to wages is the *net* effect of the two forces. Consider two examples. First, suppose that both labour and management expect 3 percent inflation next year and are therefore willing to allow money wages to increase by 3 percent. Doing so would leave *real* wages unchanged. Suppose as well that there is a significant inflationary gap with an associated labour shortage. The demand pressure causes wages to rise by an additional 2 percentage points. The final outcome is that wages rise by 5 percent, the net effect of a 3 percent increase due to expected inflation and a 2 percent increase due to demand forces.

For the second example, assume again that expected inflation is 3 percent, but this time there is a recessionary gap. The associated heavy unemployment exerts downward pressure on wage bargains. Hence, the demand effect now works to dampen wage increases, say, to the extent of 2 percentage points. Wages therefore rise by 1 percent, the net effect of a 3 percent increase due to expected inflation and a 2 percent decrease due to demand forces.

APPLYING ECONOMIC CONCEPTS 30-1
How Do People Form Their Expectations?

The way in which people form their expectations about future inflation may have an important effect on that inflation. Generally, we can distinguish two main patterns: One is to look backward at past experience; the other is to look at current circumstances for a clue as to what may happen in the near future.

The first type of expectations are called *backward-looking*. People look at the past in order to predict what will happen in the future. The simplest possible form of such expectations is to expect the past to be repeated in the future. According to this view, if inflation has been 5 percent over the past year, people will expect it to be 5 percent next year. This expectation, however, is quite naive. Everyone knows that the inflation rate does change, and therefore the past cannot be a perfectly accurate guide to the future.

A less naive version has people revise their expectations in light of the mistakes that they made in estimating inflation in the past. For example, if you thought that this year's inflation rate was going to be 5 percent but it turned out to be only 3 percent, you might revise your estimate of next year's rate down somewhat from 5 percent.

Backward-looking expectations tend to change slowly because some time must pass before a change in the actual rate of inflation provides enough past experience to cause expectations to adjust.

The second main type of expectations are those that look to current conditions to estimate what is likely to happen in the future. One version of this type assumes that people look to the government's current macroeconomic policy to form their expectations of future inflation. They are assumed to understand how the economy works, and they form their expectations by predicting the outcome of the policies now being followed. In an obvious sense, such expectations are *forward-looking*.

A strong version of forward-looking expectations is called **rational expectations**. Rational expectations are not necessarily always correct; rather, the *rational expectations hypothesis* assumes that people make the best possible use of all the available information. One implication is that they will not continue to make persistent, systematic errors when forming their expectations. Thus, if the economic system about which they are forming expectations remains stable, their expectations will be correct *on average*. Sometimes next year's inflation rate will turn out to be above what people expected it to be; at other times, it will turn out to be below what people expected it to be. On average over many years, however, the actual rate will not, according to the rational expectations theory, be consistently under- or overestimated.

Forward-looking expectations can adjust quickly to changes in events. Instead of being based on past inflation rates, expected inflation is based on expected economic conditions and government policies.

Assuming that expectations are solely backward-looking seems overly naive. People do look ahead and assess future possibilities rather than just blindly reacting to what has gone before. Yet the assumption of "fully rational" forward-looking expectations requires workers and firms to have a degree of understanding of the economy that few economists would claim to have. The actual process of wage setting probably combines forward-looking behaviour with expectations based on the experience of the recent past. Depending on the circumstances, expectations will sometimes tend to rely more on past experience and at other times more on present events whose effects are expected to influence the future.

rational expectations
The theory that people understand how the economy works and learn quickly from their mistakes so that even though random errors may be made, systematic and persistent errors are not.

From Wages to Prices

We saw in Chapters 23 and 24 that shifts in the *AS* curve depend on what happens to factor prices. We have just seen that inflationary gaps and expectations of future inflation put pressure on wages to rise and hence cause the *AS* curve to shift upward. Recessionary gaps and expectations of future deflation put pressure on wages to fall and hence cause the *AS* curve to shift downward.

The net effect of the two forces acting on wages—excess demand and inflation expectations—determines what happens to the *AS* curve.

If the net effect of the demand and expectational forces is to raise wages, then the *AS* curve will shift up. This shift will cause the price level to rise—that is, the forces pushing up wages will be *inflationary*. On the other hand, if the net effect of the demand and expectational forces is to reduce wages, the *AS* curve will shift down—the forces reducing wages will be *deflationary*.

Since anything that leads to higher wages will shift the *AS* curve up and lead to higher prices, we can decompose inflation due to wage increases into two component parts: *excess-demand inflation* and *expected inflation*. But because the *AS* curve can also shift for reasons unrelated to changes in wages, we must add a third element. Specifically, we must consider the effect of non-wage supply shocks on the *AS* curve and thus on the price level. The best example of a non-wage supply shock is a change in the prices of raw materials. We can then decompose actual inflation into its three component parts:

$$\begin{array}{c}\text{Actual}\\\text{inflation}\end{array} = \begin{array}{c}\text{Excess-demand}\\\text{inflation}\end{array} + \begin{array}{c}\text{Expected}\\\text{inflation}\end{array} + \begin{array}{c}\text{Supply-shock}\\\text{inflation}\end{array}$$

For example, consider an economy that begins with real GDP equal to potential GDP and expectations of inflation are zero. In this case, the first two terms on the right-hand side are zero. But if an adverse supply shock then occurs, such as a significant increase in the price of imported raw materials, the *AS* curve shifts up and the price level rises. Actual inflation will be positive. As we will see later in the chapter, such supply shocks are not uncommon, and they generate problems for the conduct of monetary policy.

Having discussed the component parts of inflation, we are now in a position to see how constant inflation can be included in our macroeconomic model.

Constant Inflation

Suppose the inflation rate is 3 percent per year and has been 3 percent for several years. This is what we mean by a *constant* inflation. In such a setting, people with backward-looking expectations about inflation will expect the actual level to continue into the future. Furthermore, in the absence of any announcements that the central bank will be attempting to alter its monetary policy, people with forward-looking expectations will expect the actual inflation rate to continue. Thus, for the economy as a whole, the expected rate of inflation will equal the actual rate of inflation.

The Conference Board of Canada conducts a regular survey about people's expectations about inflation. See its website at: www.conferenceboard.ca.

If inflation and monetary policy have been constant for several years, the expected rate of inflation will equal the actual rate of inflation.

Suppose there are no supply shocks (we address these later in the chapter). Since actual inflation equals expected inflation, it immediately follows from the equation above that actual and expected inflation can only be equal if there is *no* excess-demand inflation. This, in turn, implies that there is no inflationary (or recessionary) gap—real GDP must equal its potential level, Y^*.

If expected inflation equals actual inflation, real GDP must be equal to potential GDP.

Figure 30-2 shows a constant inflation in the *AD/AS* diagram. What is causing this inflation? As we will see, such a constant inflation requires both the *expectations* of inflation (which shift the *AS* curve) and the continuing expansion of the money supply by the central bank (which shifts the *AD* curve). Let's see how this works.

Suppose that both workers and employers expect 3 percent inflation over the coming years and that employers are therefore prepared to increase wages by 3 percent per

FIGURE 30-2   Constant Inflation

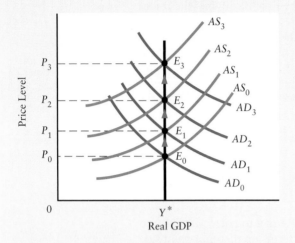

A constant inflation is only possible when $Y = Y^*$. Expectations of a constant rate of inflation cause wages and thus the AS curve to shift upward at a uniform rate from AS_0 to AS_1 to AS_2. Monetary validation is causing the AD curve to shift upward at the same time from AD_0 to AD_1 to AD_2. As a result, real GDP remains at Y^* as the economy moves from equilibrium E_0 to E_1 to E_2 and so on. The constant inflation rate takes the price level from P_0 to P_1 to P_2. Wage costs are rising due to expectations of inflation, and these expectations are being fulfilled.

Practise with Study Guide Chapter 30, Short-Answer Question 2.

year. As wages rise by 3 percent, the AS curve shifts up by that amount. But, in order for 3 percent to be the *actual* rate of inflation, the intersection of the AS and AD curves must be shifting up at the rate of 3 percent. This requires the AD curve to be shifting up at the same 3 percent rate—this AD shift is caused by the growth of the money supply. So in this case there is no excess-demand inflation ($Y = Y^*$), and actual and expected inflation are equal. When the central bank increases the money supply at such a rate that the expectations of inflation end up being correct, it is said to be *validating* the expectations.

Constant inflation with $Y = Y^*$ occurs when the rate of monetary growth, the rate of wage increase, and the expected rate of inflation are all consistent with the actual inflation rate.

The key point about constant inflation is that there is no excess-demand effect operating on wages. Wages rise at the expected rate of inflation. Expansions of the money supply validate those expectations.

30.2 Shocks and Policy Responses

A constant rate of inflation is a special case in our macroeconomic model because the rising price level is not caused by an inflationary output gap. In many cases of inflation, however, inflationary pressure is initially created by an aggregate demand or supply shock. In this section we examine how AS and AD shocks affect inflation and the subsequent effects of the policy responses chosen by the central bank.

Before we do so, however, recall an assumption we made in Chapter 28 when we discussed the long-run effects of monetary policy. In that chapter we assumed the level of potential output to be independent of the path of real GDP. Thus, shocks that led to shifts in the AD or AS curves, and thus led to short-run changes in the level of real GDP, were assumed to have no influence on the level of potential output, Y^*.

We continue with that assumption in this chapter, but note that we can alternatively state the assumption in terms of the NAIRU, U^*. Specifically, we assume that the path of the actual unemployment rate does not affect the value of U^*, which is instead determined by various policy and institutional factors that we explore in detail later in this chapter. As in Chapter 28, the implication of this assumption is that, following AD or AS shocks, the economy's adjustment process eventually returns real GDP and unemployment to their unchanged levels of Y^* and U^*, respectively. As we first noted in Chapter 28, this assumption is controversial. In Western European countries, in particular, there is some empirical evidence to the contrary. But in Canada and the United States the weight of evidence supports the assumption made in this book that Y^* and U^* are independent of the paths of Y and U.

With these assumptions in mind, we now go on to examine the effects of aggregate demand and aggregate supply shocks on inflation.

Demand Shocks

Inflation that is caused by a rightward shift in the *AD* curve is called **demand inflation**. The shift in the *AD* curve could have been caused by a reduction in taxes, by an increase in such autonomous expenditure items as investment, government, and net exports, or by an increase in the money supply.

demand inflation
Inflation arising from excess aggregate demand, that is, when actual GDP exceeds potential GDP.

Major demand-shock inflations occurred in Canada during and after the First and Second World Wars. In these cases, large increases in government expenditure without fully offsetting increases in taxes led to general excess demand. More generally, demand inflation sometimes occurs at the end of a strong upswing, as rising output causes excess demand to develop simultaneously in the markets for labour, intermediate goods, and final output. Demand inflation of this type occurred in Canada in 1989–90 and to a lesser extent in 2002–03.

To begin our study of demand inflation, suppose that an initial long-run equilibrium is disturbed by a rightward shift in the *AD* curve. This shift causes the price level and output to rise. It is important next to distinguish between the case in which the Bank of Canada validates the demand shock and the case in which it does not.

No Monetary Validation

Because the initial rise in *AD* takes output above potential, an inflationary gap opens up. The pressure of excess demand soon causes wages to rise, shifting the *AS* curve upward as shown in Figure 30-3. As long as the Bank of Canada holds the money supply constant, the rise in the price level moves the economy upward and to the left along the new *AD* curve, reducing the inflationary gap. Eventually, the gap is eliminated, and equilibrium is established at a higher but stable price level, with output at its potential level. In this case, the initial period of inflation is followed by further inflation that lasts only until the new equilibrium is reached.

Monetary Validation

Suppose that after the demand shock has created an inflationary gap, the Bank of Canada increases the money supply and therefore validates the demand shock. We illustrate this situation in Figure 30-4.

Two forces are now brought into play. Spurred by the inflationary gap, the increase in wages causes the *AS* curve to shift upward. Fueled by the expansionary monetary policy, however, the *AD* curve shifts to the right. As a result of both of these shifts, the price level rises, but real GDP remains above Y^*. Indeed, if the shift in the *AD* curve *exactly* offsets the shift in the *AS* curve, real GDP and the inflationary gap will remain constant.

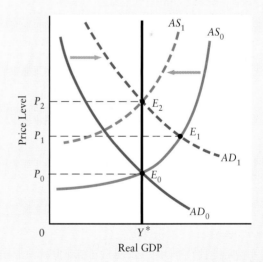

FIGURE 30-3 A Demand Shock with No Validation

A demand shock that is not validated produces temporary inflation, but the economy's adjustment process eventually restores potential GDP and stable prices. The initial long-run equilibrium is at P_0 and Y^*. A positive demand shock shifts AD_0 to AD_1, generating an inflationary gap. The excess demand puts upward pressure on wages, thus shifting AS_0 to AS_1. There is inflation as the economy moves from E_0 to E_1 to E_2, but at E_2 the price level is stable.

FIGURE 30-4   A Demand Shock with Validation

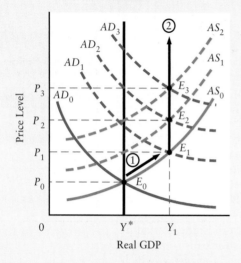

Monetary validation of a positive demand shock causes the *AD* curve to shift further to the right, off-setting the upward shift in the *AS* curve and thereby leaving an inflationary gap despite the ever-rising price level. An initial demand shock shifts equilibrium from E_0 to E_1, taking output to Y_1 and the price level to P_1. The resulting inflationary gap then causes the *AS* curve to shift upward. This time, however, the Bank of Canada validates the demand shock by increasing the money supply. As the money supply is increased, the *AD* curve shifts to the right. By the time the aggregate supply curve has reached AS_1, the aggregate demand curve has reached AD_2. The new equilibrium is at E_2. Output remains constant at Y_1 leaving the inflationary gap constant while the price level rises to P_2.

The persistent inflationary gap continues to push the *AS* curve upward, while the continued monetary validation continues to push the *AD* curve to the right. As long as this monetary validation continues, the economy moves along the vertical path of arrow ②.

Continued validation of a demand shock turns what would have been transitory inflation into sustained inflation fueled by monetary expansion.

Supply Shocks

Any rise in the price level originating from increases in firms' costs that are *not caused by excess demand* in the markets for factors of production is called **supply inflation**.

An example of a supply shock is a rise in the costs of imported raw materials. Another is a rise in domestic wages not due to excess demand in the labour market. The rise in wages may occur, as we saw earlier, because of generally held expectations of future inflation. If both employers and employees expect inflation, money wages are likely to rise in anticipation of that inflation. These shocks cause the *AS* curve to shift upward. Though negative supply shocks are quite common (occurring, for example, every time the prices of raw materials increase), the most significant examples occurred in 1974 and 1979–80 when OPEC restricted the supply of oil and sharply increased world oil prices.[3]

The initial effects of any negative supply shock are that the equilibrium price level rises while equilibrium output falls, as shown in Figure 30-5. As with the case of a demand shock, what happens next depends on how the Bank of Canada reacts. If the Bank responds by increasing the money supply, it validates the supply shock; if it holds the money supply constant, the shock is not validated.

No Monetary Validation

The upward shift in the *AS* curve in Figure 30-5 causes the price level to rise and pushes output below its potential level, opening up a recessionary gap. Pressure mounts for money wages and other factor prices to fall. As wages and other factor prices fall, unit costs will fall. Consequently, the *AS* curve shifts down, increasing equilibrium output while reducing the price level. The *AS* curve will continue to shift, stopping only when real GDP is returned to its potential level and the price level is returned to its initial value of P_0. Thus, the period of inflation accompanying the original supply shock is eventually reversed until the initial long-run equilibrium is re-established.

---

[3] Recall our discussion in Chapter 24 of how many shocks affect *both* the *AD* and *AS* curves. A rise in the price of oil is one example; since some Canadian regions are large oil producers, a rise in the price of oil does represent a positive *AD* shock for Canada. In this discussion we confine ourselves to the effect of the *AS* shift.

A major concern in this case is the speed of the adjustment, which in earlier chapters was referred to as the second asymmetry of aggregate supply. If wages do not fall rapidly in the face of excess supply in the labour market, the adjustment back to potential output can take a long time. For example, suppose the original shock raised firms' costs by 6 percent. To reverse this shock, firms' costs must fall by 6 percent. If money wages fell by only 2 percent per year it would take three years to complete the adjustment.[4]

Whenever wages and other factor prices fall only slowly in the face of excess supply, the recovery to potential output after a non-validated negative supply shock will take a long time.

Concern that such a lengthy adjustment will occur is the motive that often lies behind the strong pressure on the Bank of Canada to validate negative supply shocks.

Monetary Validation

What happens if the money supply is changed in response to a negative supply shock? Suppose the central bank decides to validate the supply shock because it believes that factor prices fall only slowly. The monetary validation shifts the AD curve to the right and causes both the price level and output to rise. As the recessionary gap is eliminated, the price level rises further, rather than falling back to its original value as it did when the supply shock was not validated. These effects are also illustrated in Figure 30-5.

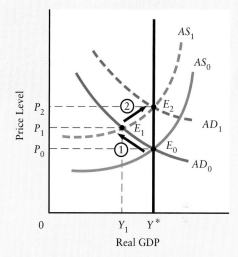

FIGURE 30-5   A Supply Shock With and Without Validation

Adverse supply shocks initially raise prices while lowering output. An adverse supply shock causes the AS curve to shift upward from AS_0 to AS_1, as shown by arrow ①. Equilibrium is established at E_1. If there is no monetary validation, the reduction in factor prices makes the AS curve shift slowly back down to AS_0. If there is monetary validation, the AD curve shifts from AD_0 to AD_1, as shown by arrow ②. Equilibrium is re-established at E_2 with output equal to potential output but with a higher price level, P_2.

Monetary validation of a negative supply shock causes the initial rise in the price level to be followed by a further rise, resulting in a higher price level than would occur if the recessionary gap were relied on to reduce factor prices.

The most dramatic example of a supply-shock inflation came in the wake of the first OPEC oil-price shock. In 1974, the countries who were members of the Organization of Petroleum Exporting Countries (OPEC) agreed to restrict output. Their action caused a dramatic increase in the prices of petroleum and many petroleum-related products such as fertilizer and chemicals. The resulting increase in industrial costs shifted AS curves upward in all industrial countries. At this time, the Bank of Canada validated the supply shock with large increases in the money supply, whereas the Fed (the U.S. central bank) did not. As the theory predicts, Canada experienced a large increase in its price level but almost no recession, and the United States experienced a much smaller increase in its price level but a severe recession.

For information on OPEC, see its website: www.opec.org.

---

[4] Nominal wages rarely fall because there is ongoing productivity growth that offsets the effect on wages of excess supply. But in this chapter we are holding productivity constant so we can focus on the causes and consequences of inflation.

A contract settlement that raises wages for a large number of workers will increase firms' costs and shift the AS curve upward, reducing real GDP.

Is Monetary Validation of Supply Shocks Desirable?

Suppose the central bank validates a negative supply shock and thus prevents what could otherwise be a protracted recession. Expressed in this way, monetary validation sounds like a good policy. Unfortunately, however, there is also a possible cost associated with this policy. The effect of the monetary validation is to extend the period of inflation. If this inflation leads firms and workers to expect *further* inflation, then point E_2 in Figure 30-5 will not be the end of the story. As expectations for further inflation develop, the *AS* curve will continue to shift upward. But if the central bank continues its policy of validation, then the *AD* curve will also continue to shift upward. It may not take long before the economy is in a *wage–price spiral*.

Once started, a wage–price spiral can be halted only if the Bank of Canada stops validating the supply shocks that are causing the inflation. But the longer it waits to do so, the more firmly held will be the *expectations* that it will continue its policy of validating the shocks. These entrenched expectations may cause wages to continue rising even after validation has ceased. Because employers expect prices to rise, they go on granting wage increases. If expectations are entrenched firmly enough, the wage push can continue for quite some time, in spite of the downward pressure caused by the high unemployment associated with the recessionary gap.

Because of this possibility, many economists argue that the wage–price spiral should not be allowed to begin. One way to ensure that it does not begin is to refuse to validate any supply shock whatsoever.

To some economists, caution dictates that no supply shock should ever be validated, in order to avoid a wage–price spiral. Other economists are willing to risk validation in order to avoid the significant, though transitory, recessions that otherwise accompany the supply shock.

Accelerating Inflation

Consider a situation where a demand or supply shock increases real GDP above Y^*. For example, a booming U.S. economy may lead to an increase in demand for Canadian goods, thus shifting Canada's *AD* curve to the right. Or, a reduction in the world price of raw materials may reduce firms' costs and shift the Canadian *AS* curve downward. In both cases, the effect in Canada would be to increase real GDP above Y^*—unemployment is low, businesses are booming, and most people would describe this situation as "good economic times." It may be natural for the Bank of Canada to contemplate sustaining these "good times" by validating the shock. What would be the result of this policy on the rate of inflation?

acceleration hypothesis   The hypothesis that when real GDP is held above potential, the persistent inflationary gap will cause inflation to accelerate.

What happens to the rate of inflation is predicted by the **acceleration hypothesis,** which says that when the central bank engages in whatever rate of monetary expansion is needed to hold the inflationary gap constant, the actual inflation rate will *accelerate*. The Bank of Canada may start by validating 3 percent inflation, but soon 3 percent will become 4 percent and, if the Bank insists on validating 4 percent, the rate will become 5 percent, and so on without limit. The process will only end when the Bank ends its policy of validation.

There are several steps in the reasoning behind this hypothesis. The first concerns the development of inflationary expectations.

Expectational Effects

Recall our earlier discussion in this chapter about how actual inflation can be separated into its component parts of excess demand, expectations, and non-wage supply shocks. It is restated here:

$$\begin{matrix} \text{Actual} \\ \text{inflation} \end{matrix} = \begin{matrix} \text{Excess-demand} \\ \text{inflation} \end{matrix} + \begin{matrix} \text{Expected} \\ \text{inflation} \end{matrix} + \begin{matrix} \text{Supply-shock} \\ \text{inflation} \end{matrix}$$

To illustrate the importance of expectations in accelerating inflation, suppose the inflationary gap creates sufficient excess demand to push up wages by 2 percent per year. As a result, the *AS* curve will also tend to be rising at 2 percent per year.

When inflation has persisted for some time, however, people may come to expect that the inflation will continue. The expectation of 2 percent inflation will tend to push up wages by that amount *in addition to* the demand pressure. As the demand effect on wages is augmented by the expectational effect, the *AS* curve will begin to shift upward more rapidly. When expectations are for a 2 percent inflation and demand pressure is also pushing wages up by 2 percent, the overall effect will be a 4 percent increase in wages. Sooner or later, however, 4 percent inflation will come to be expected, and the expectational effect will rise to 4 percent. This new expectational component of 4 percent, when added to the demand component, will create an inflation rate of 6 percent. And so this cycle will go on. As long as there is a demand effect arising from an inflationary gap and as long as actual inflation is equal to the demand effect plus the expectational effect, the inflation rate cannot stay constant because expectations will always be revised upward toward the actual inflation rate.

More Rapid Monetary Validation Required

The second step in the argument is that if the Bank of Canada still wishes to hold the level of output constant above Y^*, it must increase the rate at which the money supply is growing. This action is necessary because to hold real GDP constant, the *AD* curve must be shifted at an increasingly rapid pace to offset the increasingly rapid shifts in the *AS* curve, which are driven by the continually rising rate of expected inflation.

An Increasing Rate of Inflation

The third step in the argument is that the rate of inflation must now be increasing because of the increasingly rapid upward shifts in both the *AD* and *AS* curves. The rise in the actual inflation rate will in turn cause an increase in the expected inflation rate. This will then cause the actual inflation rate to increase, which will in turn increase the expected inflation rate, and so on. The net result is a *continually increasing rate of inflation.* Now we see the reason for the name NAIRU. At any level of unemployment less than the NAIRU, real GDP is above Y^*, and the inflation rate tends to accelerate. Thus, the NAIRU is the lowest level of sustained unemployment consistent with a *non-accelerating* rate of inflation.

According to the acceleration hypothesis, as long as an inflationary gap persists, expectations of inflation will be rising, which will lead to increases in the actual rate of inflation.

The tendency for inflation to accelerate is discussed further in *Extensions in Theory 30-1*, which examines how expected inflation affects the position of the Phillips curve.

Inflation as a Monetary Phenomenon

A long-standing debate among economists concerns the extent to which inflation is a monetary phenomenon. Does it have purely monetary causes—changes in the demand or the supply of money? Does it have purely monetary consequences—only the price level is affected? One slogan that states an extreme position on this issue was popularized many years ago by Milton Friedman: "Inflation is *everywhere* and *always* a monetary phenomenon." To consider these issues, let us summarize what we have learned already. First, look at the *causes* of inflation:

- *Cause 1:* On the demand side, anything that shifts the *AD* curve to the right will cause the price level to rise.
- *Cause 2:* On the supply side, anything that increases factor prices will shift the *AS* curve upward and cause the price level to rise.

EXTENSIONS IN THEORY 30-1
The Phillips Curve and Accelerating Inflation

As we first saw in Chapter 24, the Phillips curve describes the relationship between unemployment (or output) and the rate of change of wages. The Phillips curve was born in 1958 when Professor A.W. Phillips from the London School of Economics noted a relationship between unemployment and the rate of change of wages over a period of 100 years in the United Kingdom. Phillips was interested in studying the short-run behaviour of an economy subjected to cyclical fluctuations. In the years following Phillips's study, however, some economists treated the Phillips curve as

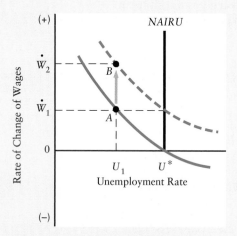

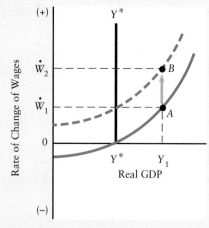

There is no stable tradeoff between inflation and output. To maintain $Y > Y^*$, inflation must be steadily rising.

(i) Wage changes and unemployment

(ii) Wage changes and output

- *Cause 3:* Unless continual monetary expansion occurs, the increases in the price level must eventually come to a halt.

The first two points tell us that a temporary burst of inflation need not be a monetary phenomenon. It need not have monetary causes, and it need not be accompanied by monetary expansion. The third point tells us that *sustained* inflation *must* be a monetary phenomenon. If a rise in prices is to continue indefinitely, it *must* be accompanied by continuing increases in the money supply. This is true regardless of the cause that set the inflation in motion.

Now, let us summarize the *consequences* of inflation, assuming that real GDP was initially at its potential level.

- *Consequence 1:* In the short run, demand-shock inflation tends to be accompanied by an *increase* in real GDP above its potential level.
- *Consequence 2:* In the short run, supply-shock inflation tends to be accompanied by a *decrease* in real GDP below its potential level.
- *Consequence 3:* When all costs and prices are adjusted *fully* (so that real GDP has returned to Y^*), shifts in either the *AD* or *AS* curve leave real GDP unchanged and affect only the price level.

expectations-augmented Phillips curve   The relationship between unemployment and the rate of increase of money wages that arises when the demand and expectations components of inflation are combined.

establishing a long-term tradeoff between inflation and unemployment.

Suppose the government stabilizes output at Y_1 (and hence the unemployment rate at U_1), as shown by points A in the accompanying figures. To do this, it must validate the ensuing wage inflation, which is indicated by $\dot{W}_1$ in the figures. The government thus seems to be able to choose among particular combinations of inflation and unemployment, in which lower levels of unemployment are attained at the cost of higher rates of inflation.

In the 1960s, Phillips curves were fitted to the data for many countries, and governments made decisions about where they wished to be on the tradeoff between inflation and unemployment. Then, in the late 1960s, in country after country, the rate of wage and price inflation associated with any given level of unemployment began to rise. Instead of being stable, the Phillips curves began to shift upward. The explanation lay primarily in the rise of inflation expectations.

It was gradually understood that the original Phillips curve concerned only the influence of demand and left out inflationary expectations. This omission proved important and unfortunate. An increase in expected inflation shows up as an upward shift in the original Phillips curve that was drawn in Chapter 24. The importance of expectations can be shown by drawing what is called an **expectations-augmented Phillips curve**, as shown by the dashed Phillips curve here. The height of the Phillips curves above the axis at Y^* and at U^* show the expected inflation rate. These distances represent the amount that wages will rise when neither excess demand nor excess supply pressures are being felt in labour markets. The actual wage increase is shown by the augmented (dashed) curve, with the increase in wages exceeding expected inflation whenever $Y > Y^*$ ($U < U^*$) and falling short of expected inflation whenever $Y < Y^*$ ($U > U^*$).

Now we can see what was wrong with the idea of a stable inflation–unemployment tradeoff. Targeting a particular output Y_1 or unemployment U_1 in the figures is fine only if no inflation is expected. But getting to Y_1 or U_1 itself requires some inflation ($\dot{W}_1$). And once this rate of inflation comes to be expected, people will demand that much just to hold their own. The Phillips curve will shift upward to the position shown in the figures and the economy will be at points B. Now there is inflation $\dot{W}_2$ because of the combined effects of expectations and excess demand. However, this higher rate is above the expected rate ($\dot{W}_1$). Once this higher rate comes to be expected, the Phillips curve will shift upward once again.

As a result of the combination of excess-demand inflation and expectational inflation, the inflation rate associated with any given positive output gap ($Y > Y^*$ or $U < U^*$) rises over time. This is the phenomenon of accelerating inflation that we discussed in the text.

The shifts in the Phillips curve are such that most economists agree that in the long run, when inflationary expectations have fully adjusted to actual inflation, there is no tradeoff between inflation and unemployment. That is, they believe that the only long-run *equilibrium* is where expected inflation and actual inflation are equal, which occurs only when unemployment is equal to the NAIRU and real GDP is equal to Y^*. In other words, the long-run Phillips curve is a vertical line above U^* (or Y^*).

The first two points tell us that inflation is not, in the short run, a purely monetary phenomenon. The third point tells us that inflation is a purely monetary phenomenon from the point of view of long-run equilibrium.

There is still plenty of room for debate, however, on how long the short run will last. Most economists believe that the short run can be long enough for inflation to have major real effects.

We have now reached three important conclusions:

- *Conclusion 1:* Without monetary validation, demand shocks cause temporary bursts of inflation that are accompanied by inflationary gaps. The gaps are removed as rising factor prices push the *AS* curve upward, returning real GDP to its potential level, but at a higher price level.
- *Conclusion 2:* Without monetary validation, negative supply shocks cause temporary bursts of inflation that are accompanied by recessionary gaps. The gaps are removed as factor prices fall, restoring real GDP to its potential and the price level to its initial level.
- *Conclusion 3:* Only with continuing monetary validation can inflation initiated by either supply or demand shocks continue indefinitely.

To put these conclusions differently, we can modify Friedman's statement slightly to represent the causes of inflation more accurately. While *AD* and *AS* shocks may lead to temporary inflation even in the absence of any actions by the central bank, *sustained* inflation can only occur if there is continual monetary validation by the central bank.

Sustained inflation is everywhere and always a monetary phenomenon.

30.3 **Reducing Inflation**

Suppose an economy has had a sustained rate of inflation for several years. What must the central bank do to reduce the rate of inflation? What are the costs involved in doing so?

The Process of Disinflation

disinflation
A reduction in the rate of inflation.

Disinflation means a reduction in the rate of inflation. In recent years, Canada has had two notable periods of disinflation—in 1981–82 when inflation fell from 12 percent to 4 percent, and in 1990–92 when inflation fell from 5 percent to just over 1 percent.

Reducing the rate of inflation takes time and involves major costs. The process begins when the Bank of Canada stops validating the ongoing inflation. It does this by lowering the rate of growth of the money supply below the rate of growth of money demand, thus creating an excess demand for money. This action forces up interest rates and lowers real aggregate demand, reducing any existing inflationary gap. We will soon see that it is usually necessary for the Bank to go further, creating a substantial recessionary gap that persists until the inflation is eliminated.

The process involves many costs. The recessionary gap hurts all who suffer in recessions, including the unemployed workers and the owners of firms who lose profits and risk bankruptcy. Unemployed resources mean lower output than would otherwise be produced. The temporary rise in interest rates hurts borrowers, including people with mortgages and firms with large loans. Among these groups who are most exposed and may lose their wealth are young households with large mortgages and small firms that have taken on large debts to finance expansions.

Disinflation is thus a classic case of a policy that brings short-term pain for long-term gain. Inevitably, the question arises: Are the future benefits of lower inflation worth the immediate costs of reduced output and higher unemployment?

Reducing sustained inflation quickly incurs high costs for a short period of time; reducing it slowly incurs lower costs but for a longer period of time.

The process of reducing sustained inflation can be divided into three phases. In the first phase, the monetary validation is stopped and the inflationary gap is eliminated. In the second phase, the economy still suffers from declining output and rising prices—stagflation. In the final phase, the economy experiences both increasing output and increasing prices, but the inflation then comes to an end. We now examine these three phases in detail.

The starting point for our analysis is an economy with an inflationary gap $(Y > Y^*)$ and rising inflation.[5]

Practise with Study Guide Chapter 30, Exercise 1.

Phase 1: Removing Monetary Validation

The first phase consists of slowing the rate of monetary expansion, thereby slowing the rate at which the AD curve is shifting upward. The simplest case is when the Bank of Canada adopts a "cold-turkey approach" in which the rate of monetary expansion is cut to zero so that the upward shift in the AD curve is halted abruptly. This halt implies a large and rapid increase in both nominal and real interest rates.

At this point, a controversy often breaks out—as it did in the early 1980s and early 1990s—over the effects that the increase in interest rates has on inflation. One group will point out that the rise in the interest rate increases business costs and that passing on the extra costs through higher prices adds to inflation. They will condemn the Bank's tight monetary policy as inflationary. A second group will argue that the rising interest rate signifies a slowdown in the rate of monetary expansion, without which inflation cannot be curbed.

The first group is correct in pointing out that the rise in interest rates may cause a one-time increase in the price level. The rise in interest costs may shift the AS curve upward, just as a rise in wage costs does. This rise in interest costs, however, has only a *one-time effect* on the price level. The first group is wrong, therefore, in asserting that the Bank's policy of driving up interest rates is contributing to a long-term increase in the rate of inflation.

The second group is correct in saying that the rise in the interest rate is a necessary part of an anti-inflationary policy. As long as the price level continues to rise, the rise in the interest rate reduces desired aggregate expenditure, thus reducing equilibrium real GDP by moving leftward along a fixed AD curve.

Now suppose the Bank resists the pleas to hold down interest rates. It continues with its no-validation policy. The AD curve stops shifting, but under the combined influence of the present inflationary gap and expectations of continued inflation, wages continue to rise. Hence, the AS curve continues to shift upward. Eventually, the inflationary gap will be removed, as shown in part (i) of Figure 30-6.

---

[5] In the simpler case where the economy begins with $Y = Y^*$ and constant inflation, only the second and third phases are relevant.

FIGURE 30-6   Eliminating a Sustained Inflation

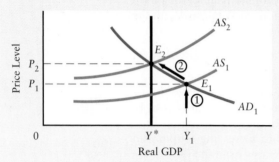

(i) Phase 1: Removing the inflationary gap

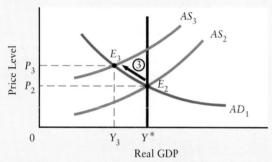

(ii) Phase 2: Stagflation

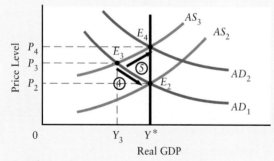

(iii) Phase 3: Recovery

(i) Phase 1: The elimination of a sustained inflation begins with a demand contraction to remove the inflationary gap. The initial position is one where fully validated inflation is taking the economy along the path shown by arrow ①. When the curves reach AS_1 and AD_1, the central bank stops expanding the money supply, thus stabilizing aggregate demand at AD_1. Because of inflation expectations, wages continue to rise, taking the AS curve leftward. The economy moves along arrow ②, with output falling and the price level rising. When aggregate supply reaches AS_2, the inflationary gap is removed, output is Y^*, and the price level is P_2.

(ii) Phase 2: Expectations and wage momentum lead to stagflation, with falling output and continuing inflation. The economy moves along the path shown by arrow ③. The driving force is now the AS curve, which continues to shift because inflation expectations cause wages to continue rising. The recessionary gap grows as output falls. Inflation continues, but at a diminishing rate. If wages stop rising when output has reached Y_3 and the price level has reached P_3, the stagflation phase is over, with equilibrium at E_3.

(iii) Phase 3: After expectations are reversed, recovery takes output to Y^*, and the price level is stabilized. There are two possible scenarios for recovery. In the first, the recessionary gap causes wages to fall (slowly), taking the AS curve back to AS_2 (slowly), as shown by arrow ④. The economy retraces the path originally followed in part (ii) back to E_2. In the second scenario, the central bank increases the money supply sufficiently to shift the AD curve to AD_2. The economy then moves along the path shown by arrow ⑤. This restores output to potential at the cost of further temporary inflation that takes the price level to P_4. Potential output and a stable price level are now achieved.

If demand were the only influence on wages, the story would be ended. At $Y = Y^*$, there would be no upward demand pressure on wages and other factor prices. The AS curve would be stabilized, and real GDP would remain at Y^*.

Phase 2: Stagflation

Governments around the world have often wished that things were really so simple. However, wages depend not only on current excess demand but also on inflation expectations. Once inflation expectations have been established, it is not always easy to get people to revise them downward, even in the face of announced changes in monetary policies. Hence, the *AS* curve continues to shift upward, causing the price level to continue to rise and output to fall. The combination of increased inflation and a reduction in output (or its growth rate) is called **stagflation**. This is phase 2, shown in part (ii) of Figure 30-6.

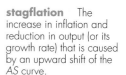

stagflation The increase in inflation and reduction in output (or its growth rate) that is caused by an upward shift of the *AS* curve.

Expectations can cause inflation to persist even after its original causes have been removed. What was initially a demand and expectational inflation due to an inflationary gap becomes a pure expectational inflation.

The ease with which the Bank of Canada can end such an inflation depends on how easy it is to change these expectations of continued inflation. This change is more difficult to the extent that expectations are backward-looking and easier to the extent that expectations are forward-looking.

To the extent that people look mainly to past inflation rates to determine their expectations of the future, they will be slow to change their expectations. As the actual inflation rate falls below the expected rate, a long time will be required for the downward adjustment to take place. The longer a given rate has persisted, the more firmly will people expect that rate to persist.

To the extent that expectations are forward-looking, people will take notice of the Bank's changed behaviour and revise their expectations of future inflation downward in the light of the new monetary policy. If people fully understand the Bank's policies as soon as they are implemented, if they have full confidence that the Bank will stick to its policies, if they know exactly how much time will be required for the Bank's policies to have effect, and if they adjust their expectations exactly in line with this knowledge, there is little need for any recessionary gap to develop. Once the inflationary gap has been removed, expectations will immediately be revised downward, so there will then be no pressure on wages to rise because of either demand or expectational forces. In Figure 30-6, Y would not fall below Y^* because the *AS* curve would stop shifting upward at AS_2. The inflation would be eliminated at almost no cost.

How long inflation persists after the inflationary gap has been removed depends on how quickly expectations of continued inflation are revised downward.

When the *AS* curve does continue to shift upward, causing Y to fall below Y^*, the emerging recessionary gap has two effects. First, unemployment is rising; hence the demand influence on wages becomes negative. Second, as the recession deepens and monetary restraint continues, people begin to revise their expectations of inflation downward. When they have no further expectations of inflation, there are no further increases in wages, and the *AS* curve stops shifting. The stagflation phase is over. Inflation has come to a halt, but a large recessionary gap now exists.

Phase 3: Recovery

The final phase is the return to potential output. When the economy comes to rest at the end of the stagflation, the situation is exactly the same as when the economy is hit by a negative supply shock. The move back to potential output can be accomplished in either of two ways. First, the recessionary gap can be relied on to reduce factor prices, thereby shifting the *AS* curve downward, reducing prices but increasing real GDP. Second, the money supply can be increased to shift the *AD* curve upward, increasing both prices and real GDP. These two possibilities are illustrated in part (iii) of Figure 30-6.

The main cost of disinflation is the reduction in economic activity that is a necessary part of the process. Increases in unemployment and plant closures are typical.

Some economists worry about relying on the *AS* curve to shift downward to return the economy to potential output. Their concern is primarily that it will take too long for prices and wages to fall sufficiently to shift the *AS* curve—though output will eventually return to potential, the long adjustment period will be characterized by high unemployment. These economists have a preference for a monetary expansion to get output back to potential.

Other economists worry about a temporary burst of monetary expansion because they fear that expectations of inflation may be rekindled when the Bank increases the money supply. And, if inflationary expectations *are* revived, the Bank will then be faced with a tough decision—either it must let another recession develop to break these new inflation expectations, or it must validate the inflation to reduce unemployment. In the latter case, the Bank is back where it started, with validated inflation on its hands—and diminished credibility.

sacrifice ratio
The cumulative loss in real GDP, expressed as a percentage of potential output, divided by the percentage-point reduction in the rate of inflation.

The Cost of Disinflation

The foregoing discussion of the process of disinflation makes the cost of disinflation pretty clear:

The cost of disinflation is the cost of the recession that is generated in the process.

As we said earlier, the size and duration of the recession depends to a large extent on how quickly inflation expectations are revised downward as the disinflation continues. If expectations are backward looking and thus slow to adjust to the changes in policy, the recession will be deep and protracted. Conversely, if expectations are forward looking and quick to adjust to changes in policy, the recession may be mild and of short duration.

But *how costly* is the process of disinflation? Economists have derived a simple measure of the cost of disinflation based on the depth and length of the recession and on the amount of disinflation. This measure is called the **sacrifice ratio**, and is defined to be the cumulative loss of real GDP due to a given disinflation (expressed as a percentage of potential GDP) divided by the number of percentage points by which inflation has fallen. For example, the 1990–92 disinflation in Canada reduced inflation by roughly four percentage points. Suppose that the cumulative loss of real GDP due to that disinflation was equal to $80 billion and that potential GDP at the time was equal to $800 billion. The cumulative loss of output would then be 10 percent of potential output. The sacrifice ratio would therefore have been 10/4 = 2.5. The interpretation of this number is that it "costs" 2.5 percent of real GDP for each percentage point of inflation that is reduced.

FIGURE 30-7   The Cost of Disinflation: The Sacrifice Ratio

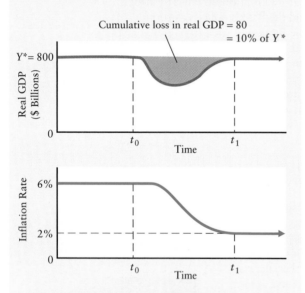

The sacrifice ratio is larger the deeper the recession and the longer it takes real GDP to return to potential. In this example, the economy begins with $Y = Y^*$ and inflation of 6 percent. At t_0, the disinflation begins. A recessionary gap opens up and inflation falls only slowly. By t_1, real GDP has returned to Y^* and inflation has been reduced by 4 percentage points. In this figure, the cumulative loss of real GDP is 10 percent of Y^* and inflation has fallen by 4 percentage points. The sacrifice ratio is therefore 10/4 = 2.5, indicating that it costs 2.5 percent of GDP to reduce inflation by one percentage point.

APPLYING ECONOMIC CONCEPTS 30-2

The Death of Inflation?

With inflation falling rapidly in many countries in the last few years, and with the apparent success in maintaining inflation at very low levels, some economists and policymakers have started asking an inevitable question: Is inflation dead?

Many arguments have been made in defence of the view that inflation is no longer a threat, and they all involve the greater competition that comes from globalization. As we have noted earlier in this book, globalization—the sharp reductions in the cost of transportation and communication in the past two decades—presents domestic firms and workers with greater competition than they would otherwise have. If firms can easily ship their products to various countries quickly and efficiently, domestic firms face greater competition from abroad. Similarly, if firms can easily relocate their factories to produce in lower-cost countries, domestic workers face greater competition from abroad. As a result, domestic firms are less likely to raise prices and domestic workers are less likely to push for wage increases. In short, globalization increases the competitive pressures in the economy, thus reducing the economy's inflationary forces.

Most economists, however, reject this view that the ongoing process of globalization spells an end to inflation. While recognizing that competitive forces may well be enhanced by globalization, most economists argue that such increases in competition will have one-time effects on wages and prices, but will not influence the long-run rate of inflation. (In their view, the increase in competition is best thought of as a one-time increase in the level of Y^*.) Central to this argument, as we have

seen in this chapter, is the view that *sustained* inflation is indeed a monetary phenomenon—that is, sustained inflation is only possible when there is continual growth in the money supply. Thus, though individual demand and supply shocks may affect inflation temporarily, the long-run rate of inflation is ultimately determined by monetary policy.

In this view, inflation is dead only if central banks maintain their current commitment to keeping inflation at very low levels. Any future shocks, followed by monetary validation, could easily tip any individual country—or group of countries—back into an inflationary wage–price spiral.

This book by Roger Bootle argues that the forces of globalization spell the death of inflation. Most central banks disagree.

The numbers in the above example are hypothetical, but typical estimates of the sacrifice ratio for many developed countries range between 2 and 4. Figure 30-7 illustrates the time paths of real GDP and inflation following a disinflation and shows how to compute the sacrifice ratio. Note an important assumption that is implicit whenever measuring the sacrifice ratio in this way. The assumption is that all changes in the path of real GDP are *caused by* the disinflation.

See Chapter 30 of www.pearsoned.ca/ragan for an excellent debate on the death of inflation: John Crow, "The Death of Inflation and Other Metaphors," and Roger Bootle, "The Death of Inflation."

Conclusion

Throughout the history of economics, inflation has been recognized as a harmful phenomenon. The high inflation rates that Canada experienced in the 1970s and early 1980s (see Figure 30-1) were also experienced in many developed countries. In the past 30 years these countries have learned much about the causes of inflation, the policies required to reduce it, and the costs associated with doing so.

In recent years, some commentators have argued that the dangers of inflation have been eliminated, that inflation is now "dead." Central to these arguments is the view that greater international competition through the process of globalization means that the economy is now subject to different rules, specifically that greater competitive forces will keep inflationary pressures at bay. *Applying Economic Concepts 30-2* discusses the alleged death of inflation and argues that one central macroeconomic rule is still present: sustained inflation is still a monetary phenomenon, and therefore inflation can only ever be as dead as central bankers' commitment to maintaining low inflation is alive.

For a discussion of Canada's inflation experience and related policy challenges over the past 30 years, look for "Inflation in Canada" in the *Additional Topics* section of this book's Companion Website.

http://www.pearsoned.ca/ragan

S U M M A R Y

30.1 **Adding Inflation to the Model**

- Sustained price inflation will be accompanied by closely related growth in wages and other factor prices such that the *AS* curve is shifting upward. Factors that influence shifts in the *AS* curve can be divided into two main components: excess demand and expectations. Random supply-side shocks will also exert an influence.
- The influence of excess demand can be expressed in terms of inflationary and recessionary gaps, which relate real output to potential output, or in terms of the difference between the actual rate of unemployment and the NAIRU.

- Expectations of inflation tend to cause wage increases equal to the expected price-level increases. Expectations can be backward-looking, forward-looking, or some combination of the two.
- With a constant rate of inflation, expected inflation will eventually come to equal actual inflation. This implies that there is no demand pressure on inflation—that is, real GDP equals its potential level.
- Constant inflation of X percent per year is shown graphically in the macroeconomic model by the AD and AS curves shifting up by X percent per year, keeping real GDP equal to Y^*.

30.2 **Shocks and Policy Responses** 🅛🅞③④

- The initial effects of positive demand shocks are a rise in the price level and a rise in real GDP. If the inflation is unvalidated, output returns to its potential level while the price level rises further (as the *AS* curve shifts upward). Monetary validation allows demand inflation to proceed without reducing the inflationary gap (*AD* curve continues to shift upward).
- The initial effects of negative supply shocks are a rise in the price level and a fall in real GDP. If inflation is unvalidated, output will slowly return to its potential level as the price level slowly falls to its preshock level (*AS* curve

slowly shifts down). Monetary validation allows supply inflation to continue in spite of a persistent recessionary gap (*AD* curve shifts up with monetary validation).
- If the Bank of Canada tries to keep real GDP constant at some level above Y^*, the actual inflation rate will accelerate. Constant inflation is only possible when there are no demand pressures on inflation—that is, when $Y = Y^*$.
- Aggregate demand and supply shocks have temporary effects on inflation. But *sustained* inflation is a monetary phenomenon.

30.3 **Reducing Inflation** 🅛🅞⑤⑥

- The process of ending a sustained inflation can be divided into three phases.
  1. Phase 1 consists of ending monetary validation and allowing the upward shift in the *AS* curve to remove any inflationary gap that does exist.
  2. In Phase 2, a recessionary gap develops as expectations of further inflation cause the *AS* curve to continue to shift upward even after the inflationary gap is removed.

3. In Phase 3, the economy returns to potential output, sometimes aided by a one-time monetary expansion that raises the *AD* curve to the level consistent with potential output.
- The cost of disinflation is the recession that is created in the process. The sacrifice ratio is a measure of this cost and is calculated as the cumulative loss in real GDP (expressed as a percentage of Y^*) divided by the reduction in inflation.

K E Y   C O N C E P T S

Temporary and sustained inflation
The NAIRU
Forward-looking and backward-looking expectations

Expectational, demand, and supply pressures on inflation
Monetary validation of demand and supply shocks

Expectations-augmented Phillips curve
Accelerating inflation
Ending sustained inflation
Sacrifice ratio

S T U D Y   E X E R C I S E S

1. Fill in the blanks to make the following statements correct.

   a. The term NAIRU stands for the _____.
   b. Unemployment is said to be equal to the NAIRU when GDP is equal to _____.
   c. Changes in money wages result from two different effects: the _____ effect and the _____ effect. Both of these effects cause the _____ curve to shift.

   d. The *AS* curve shifts up when money wages _____ and also shifts up with a negative _____ shock.
   e. Actual inflation can come from any of its three component parts. They are _____, _____, and _____.
   f. If the rate of inflation is constant at 6 percent and actual GDP equals potential GDP, then we can say that the central bank is _____ inflation expectations. That is, the central bank is _____ the

money supply such that the expected and actual inflation rates are equal at _____ percent.

2. Fill in the blanks to make the following statements correct.

   a. Suppose the economy is initially at potential GDP (Y^*) and then there is a sudden increase in the demand for Canadian exports. The AD curve shifts to the _____ and opens a(n) _____ gap.
   b. With an inflationary gap, the economy is operating where GDP is above _____. In an effort to maintain the output gap, the Bank of Canada may choose to validate the inflation by _____ the money supply. The actual inflation rate will _____.
   c. The alternative policy response to an inflationary gap is to not validate the inflation. The _____ curve stops shifting upward. The _____ curve shifts upward due to rising wages caused by _____. Real GDP eventually returns to _____ at a higher _____.
   d. Economists say that sustained inflation is a _____ phenomenon.
   e. Reducing a sustained inflation requires that monetary _____ be stopped. Inflation will persist, however, until _____ of continued inflation are revised downward.
   f. The cost of disinflation is the cost of the _____ that is generated in the process.

3. The table below shows several macroeconomic situations, each with a given amount of excess demand (or supply) for labour and a level of inflation expectations. Both are expressed in percent per year. For example, in Case A excess demand for labour is pushing wages up by 4 percent per year, and expected inflation is pushing wages up by 3 percent per year.

Case	Excess Demand	Inflation Expectations	Total Wage Change	AS Shift
A	+4	+3	—	—
B	+4	0	—	—
C	0	+3	—	—
D	−3	0	—	—
E	−3	+4	—	—

   a. For each case, identify whether there is an inflationary or a recessionary output gap.

   b. For each case, what is the total effect on nominal wages? Fill in the third column.
   c. For each case, in which direction is the AS curve shifting (up or down)? Fill in the last column.

4. This exercise requires you to compute inflationary expectations based on a simple formula, and it will help you to understand why backward-looking expectations adjust slowly to changes in economic events. Suppose that the *actual* inflation rate in year t is denoted Π_t. *Expected* inflation for year $t+1$ is denoted Π^e_{t+1}. Now, suppose that workers and firms form their expectations according to:

$$\Pi^e_{t+1} = \theta\Pi^T + (1-\theta)\Pi_t \qquad \text{(with } 0 < \theta < 1)$$

where Π^T is the central bank's announced *inflation target*. This simple equation says that people's expectations for inflation at $t+1$ are a weighted average of last year's actual inflation rate and the central bank's currently announced target. We will use this equation to see how the size of θ determines the extent to which expectations are backward looking. Consider the table below, which shows the data for a reduction in actual inflation from 10 percent to 2 percent.

Year (t)	Π_t	Π^T	Π^e_{t+1}
1	10	2	—
2	9	2	—
3	6	2	—
4	3	2	—
5	2	2	—
6	2	2	—
7	2	2	—
8	2	2	—

   a. Assume that θ is equal to 0.1. Compute expected inflation for each year and fill in the table.
   b. On a scale diagram, plot the time path of actual inflation, expected inflation, and the inflation target.
   c. Now assume that θ equals 0.9. Repeat parts (a) and (b).
   d. Which value of θ corresponds to more backward-looking expectations? Explain.
   e. Given the different speed of adjustment of inflationary expectations, predict which disinflation is more costly in terms of lost output—the one with $\theta = 0.1$ or with $\theta = 0.9$. Explain.

5. The diagram below shows an *AD/AS* diagram. The economy is in long-run equilibrium with real GDP equal to Y^* and the price level is stable at P_0.

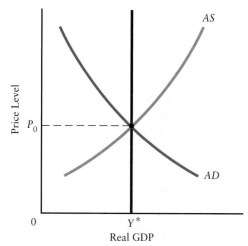

a. Suppose the central bank announces that it will make a one-time increase in the money supply and this will shift the *AD* curve up by 5 percent. Show the likely effect of this announcement on the *AS* curve.
b. Why does the shift of the *AS* curve in part (a) depend on whether workers and firms believe the central bank's announcement?
c. In a new *AD/AS* diagram, show how a sustained and constant inflation of 5 percent is represented.
d. Explain why a constant inflation is only possible when real GDP is equal to Y^*.

6. The diagram below shows an *AD/AS* diagram. Suppose the economy is hit by some positive aggregate demand shock—say an increase in the demand for Canada's exports. This increases real GDP to Y_1.

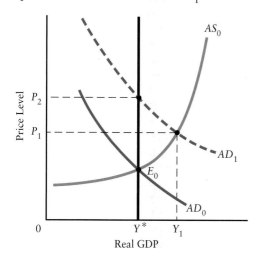

a. Explain what happens if the Bank of Canada does not react to the shock. Show this in the diagram.
b. Now suppose the Bank decides to maintain real GDP at Y_1—that is, it decides to validate the shock. Explain how this is possible, and show it in a diagram.
c. What is the effect on inflation from the policy in part (b)? Is inflation constant or is it rising? Explain.

7. The diagram below shows an *AD/AS* diagram. Suppose the economy is hit by some negative aggregate supply shock—say an increase in wages driven by a major union settlement. This reduces real GDP to Y_1.

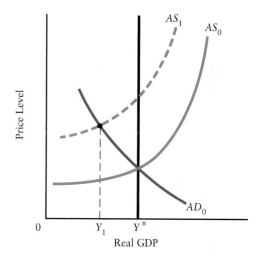

a. Explain what happens if the Bank of Canada does not react to the shock. Show this in the diagram.
b. Now suppose the Bank decides to offset the shock's effect on real GDP—that is, it validates the shock. Explain how this is possible, and show it in a diagram.
c. What danger do many economists see in validating such supply shocks? What is the alternative?

8. The table below shows some data on various disinflations. In each case, assume that potential GDP is equal to $900 billion.

Case	Inflation Reduction	Cumulative GDP Loss	Sacrifice Ratio
A	5 percentage points	$100 billion	—
B	2	30	—
C	6	60	—
D	8	80	—

a. In each case, compute the sacrifice ratio.

b. Explain why the sacrifice ratio can be expected to be smaller when expectations are more forward looking.

c. Explain why the sacrifice ratio can be expected to be smaller when central-bank announcements are more credible.

DISCUSSION QUESTIONS

1. Why might the cost of disinflation vary from one inflationary period to another? Are there reasons to think the cost might be higher the longer inflation has persisted? What might the Bank of Canada do to reduce the cost?

2. What sources of inflation are suggested by each of the following quotations?

   a. A newspaper editorial in Manchester, England: "If American unions were as strong as those in Britain, America's inflationary experience would have been as disastrous as Britain's."

   b. An article in *The Economist:* "Oil price collapse will reduce inflation."

   c. A Canadian newspaper article in October 2002: "Tensions in Iraq fuel an oil-driven inflation."

   d. A newspaper headline in May 1999: "Bank's fast growth of M1 will spur inflation."

3. Discuss the apparent conflict between the following views. Can you suggest how they might be reconciled using aggregate demand and aggregate supply analysis?

   a. "A rise in interest rates is deflationary, because ending entrenched inflation with a tight monetary policy usually requires that interest rates rise steeply."

   b. "A rise in interest rates is inflationary, because interest is a major business cost and, as with other costs, a rise in interest will be passed on by firms in the form of higher prices."

4. What is the relationship between the sacrifice ratio and the central bank's credibility?

   a. Explain why a more credible policy of disinflation reduces the costs of disinflation.

   b. Explain how you think the Bank of Canada might be able to make its disinflation policy more credible.

   c. Can the Bank's policy responses to negative supply shocks influence the credibility it is likely to have when trying to end a sustained inflation? Explain.

5. Suppose you are the governor of the Bank of Canada and that inflation has been high and roughly constant for a number of years. You have two policy choices: you can continue to validate the ongoing inflation; or you can attempt to eliminate the sustained inflation. Outline the issues involved when making this choice. List and explain the costs of ongoing inflation, and also the costs of a potential disinflation. Explain how you make your policy decision.

6. In January 1991, the federal government introduced the Goods and Services Tax (GST). If you were to suppose that the GST was a *new* tax (in fact, it replaced an existing tax), what would be the effect on the *AS* curve? Is the introduction of the GST (or an increase in its rate) inflationary? Does it increase inflation permanently?

7. In the summer of 1999 at a time when U.S. GDP was slightly above potential, a story in *The Globe and Mail* reported that the release of strong employment-growth data for the United States led to a plunge in prices on the U.S. stock market.

   a. Explain why high employment growth would lead people to expect the U.S. central bank to tighten its monetary policy.

   b. Explain why higher U.S. interest rates would lead to lower prices of U.S. stocks.

   c. How would you expect this announcement to affect Canada? (At the time, there was still a small recessionary gap in Canada.)

CHAPTER 31

Unemployment

LEARNING OBJECTIVES

1 Describe how employment and unemployment change over the short and long runs.

2 Explain the difference between the New Classical and New Keynesian views of cyclical unemployment.

3 List the causes of frictional and structural unemployment.

4 Explain the various forces that cause the NAIRU to change.

5 Describe how various policies might be used to reduce unemployment.

When the level of economic activity changes, so do the levels of employment and unemployment. When real GDP increases in the short run, employment usually rises and the unemployment rate falls. Conversely, when real GDP falls in the short run, employment falls and the unemployment rate rises. Figure 31-1 shows the course of unemployment in Canada over the past few decades. It is clear that the unemployment rate follows a cyclical path, rising during recessions and falling during expansions. In addition, the unemployment rate appears to have experienced a long-term increase. What are the sources of these cyclical fluctuations? What are the sources of this long-term increase?

In macroeconomics, economists distinguish between the NAIRU, which you will recall is the unemployment that occurs when real GDP is equal to its potential (Y^*), and *cyclical* unemployment, which is the unemployment associated with fluctuations of real GDP around its potential. We will see in this chapter that short-run fluctuations in unemployment are mainly changes in cyclical unemployment. In contrast, the long-term upward trend in unemployment is due to gradual increases in the NAIRU. Before examining these types of unemployment in detail, we briefly review the Canadian experience with employment and unemployment.

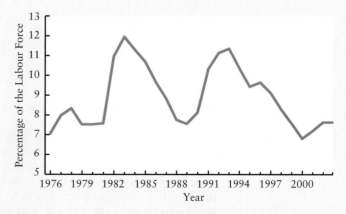

FIGURE 31-1 Canadian Unemployment Rate, 1976–2003

(*Source:* Data from Statistics Canada, annual average of monthly series V2091977.)

31.1 Employment and Unemployment

Look back at Figure 19-4 in Chapter 19, which shows the path of employment and the labour force in Canada since the early 1970s. The most striking feature of part (i) of Figure 19-4 is that, when viewed over the long term, the growth in the labour force has approximately matched the growth in employment. Also notice in part (ii) of Figure 19-4, and also in Figure 31-1, that the unemployment rate displays considerable short-run fluctuations. These two characteristics of the labour force—long-term growth in employment but short-term fluctuations in the unemployment rate—are common to most developed countries.

Over the span of many years, increases in the labour force are more or less matched by increases in employment. Over the short term, however, the unemployment rate fluctuates considerably because changes in the labour force are not exactly matched by changes in employment.

Changes in Employment

The level of employment in Canada has increased dramatically over the past few decades. In 1959, there were approximately 5 million employed Canadians. By 2002, total employment was 15.4 million. The actual level of employment, of course, is determined both by the demand for labour and by the supply of labour. How have the two "sides" of the Canadian labour market been changing?

On the supply side, the labour force has expanded virtually every year since the end of the Second World War. The causes have included a rising population, which boosts entry into the labour force of people born 15 to 25 years previously; increased labour force participation by various groups, especially women; and net immigration of working-age persons.

On the demand side, many existing jobs are eliminated every year, and many new jobs are created. Economic growth causes some sectors of the economy to decline and others to expand. Jobs are lost in the sectors that are contracting and created in sectors that are expanding. Furthermore, even in stable industries, many firms disappear and many new ones are set up. The net increase in employment is the difference between all the jobs that are lost and all those that are created.

In most years, enough new jobs are created both to replace old jobs that have been eliminated and to provide jobs for the growing labour force. The result is a net increase in employment in most years.

Changes in Unemployment

In the early 1980s, worldwide unemployment rose to high levels. The unemployment rate remained high in many advanced industrial countries and only began to come down, and even then very slowly, during the latter half of the decade. Canadian experience reflected these international developments rather closely. From a high of over 12 percent in 1983, the Canadian unemployment rate fell to 7.5 percent in 1989, a point that many economists at the time thought was close to the Canadian NAIRU (see Figure 31-1).

With the onset of another recession in the early 1990s, the unemployment rate then rose through 1990 and 1991, reaching 11.3 percent by 1992. During the next few years, the unemployment rate fell only slowly as the Canadian recovery was weak; by early 1994 the unemployment rate was still above 10 percent. But the speed of the Canadian recovery quickened and unemployment began to drop. By early 2000, after five years of healthy economic recovery, the unemployment rate was 6.8 percent, the lowest it had been in more than 20 years. The world economy and the Canadian economy then began to slow slightly. By early in 2004, the Canadian unemployment rate had increased to 7.5 percent.

During periods of rapid economic growth, the unemployment rate usually falls. During recessions or periods of slow growth, the unemployment rate usually rises.

Flows in the Labour Market

We know that many existing jobs are eliminated every year, as industries contract and firms either shrink or close down altogether. Similarly, new jobs are continually being created, as other industries expand and new firms are born. The focus on the labour market, however, tends to be on the overall level of employment and unemployment rather than on the amount of *job creation* and *job destruction*. This focus can often lead us to the conclusion that few changes are occurring in the labour market when in fact the truth is exactly the opposite.

For example, the Canadian unemployment rate was roughly constant at 9.5 percent from 1995 to 1996. Does this mean no jobs were created during the year? Or that the Canadian labour market was stagnant during this period? No. In fact, workers were finding jobs at the rate of roughly 400 000 *per month*. At the same time, however, other workers were leaving jobs or entering the labour force at roughly the same rate. This tremendous number of flows *out of unemployment* was being approximately matched by the number of flows *into unemployment*. The net result was that total unemployment changed only slightly.

For data on current employment and unemployment in Canada, see Statistics Canada's website: www.statcan.ca. Click on "Canadian Statistics" and then on "Labour."

The level of activity in the labour market is better reflected by the flows into and out of unemployment than by the overall unemployment rate.

By looking at the *gross flows* in the labour market, we are able to see economic activity that is hidden when we just look at the overall level of employment and unemployment (which is determined by *net* flows). Indeed, these gross flows are typically so large that they dwarf the net flows. See *Applying Economic Concepts 31-1* for more discussion of the gross flows in the Canadian labour market, and how these gross-flows data can be used to compute the average length of unemployment spells.

Practise with Study Guide Chapter 31, Additional Multiple-Choice Questions 1–8.

There are a number of problems associated with the measurement of unemployment, including the failure of the official measures to identify *discouraged workers*. For more details on some of the difficulties in interpreting the official unemployment statistics, look for "Problems in Measuring Unemployment" in the *Additional Topics* section of this book's Companion Website.

http://www.pearsoned.ca/ragan

APPLYING ECONOMIC CONCEPTS 31-1

Stocks and Flows in the Canadian Labour Market

In most reports about changes in unemployment, both in Canada and abroad, emphasis is typically on the changes in the *stock* of unemployment—that is, on the number of people who are unemployed at a particular point in time. But as we said in the text, the focus on the stock of unemployment can often hide much activity in the labour market, activity that is revealed by looking at *gross flows* in the labour market.

What Are Labour-Market Flows?

The first figure in this box shows the difference between stocks and flows in the labour market. The blue circles represent the number of individuals at the end of each month (the *stocks)* in each possible "state"—employment (*E*), unemployment (*U*), and *not* in the labour force (*N*). The six red arrows represent the monthly *flows* of individuals between the various states. For example, arrow 1 shows the monthly flow of individuals from *E* to *U*. These individuals begin the month in *E* (employed), leave their jobs sometime during the month, and end the month as unemployed individuals, in *U*. Arrow 3 shows the flow from *N* to *U*—these individuals are new entrants to the labour force during the month and begin their labour-force experience as unemployed individuals.

In the second figure, three series of data are shown for Canada from 1976 to 2003—a period that includes the major recessions of 1981 and 1991. The top line is the stock of unemployment—the actual *number* of people unemployed at a specific point in time (it is not the unemployment *rate*). During the severe recession of the early 1980s, unemployment peaked at approximately 1.7 million people, and then fell during the recovery until 1989. With the onset of the next recession in 1990–1991, unemployment rose again, reaching 1.8 million in early 1992.

The two lower lines show *gross flows* in the labour market. (These flows data are not available for 1997 and 1998, which explains the break in the lines at that point.) The orange line shows the monthly flow into unemployment, corresponding to arrows 1 and 3 in Figure 1. This flow into unemployment represents either:

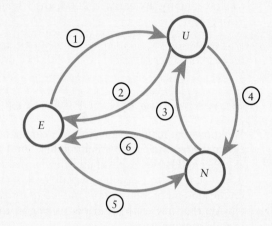

- workers losing jobs through layoffs or plant closure; or
- workers quitting jobs to search for a different job; or
- new entrants to the labour force searching for a job.

Note that the monthly flow into unemployment varies between approximately 300 000 and 500 000 *per month* and also tends to rise and fall together with the overall stock of unemployment.

The green line shows the monthly flow out of unemployment, corresponding to arrows 2 and 4 in Figure 1. This outflow represents either:

- unemployed individuals finding new jobs; or
- unemployed individuals becoming discouraged and leaving the labour force.

Note that the monthly flow out of unemployment is roughly the same size as the monthly inflow (300 000–500 000 per month).

What is the connection between the flows and the stocks in the labour market? Whenever the flows into unemployment exceed the flows out of unemployment, the stock of unemployment rises. Conversely, whenever the flows out of unemployment exceed the flows into unemployment, the stock of unemployment falls.

Using Flows Data

There are two reasons why looking at flows can be very useful when we think about the labour market. First, they show the tremendous amount of activity in the labour market even though the stock of unemployment may not be changing significantly. For example, between 1991 and 1992 the stock of unemployment in Canada varied between 1.4 million and 1.6 million persons. But during that two-year period, roughly 400 000 persons *per month* either became unemployed or ceased being unemployed. This number reflects the massive amount of regular turnover that exists in the Canadian labour market—turnover that is the essence of what economists call *frictional unemployment*.

The second reason why looking at flows is useful is that the relationship between the flows and the stock can tell us something about the amount of time the average unemployed person spends unemployed. If U_S is the stock of unemployment, and U_O is the monthly outflow from unemployment, then one simple estimate of the average duration of an unemployment spell is

$$\text{Average duration of unemployment spell} = \frac{U_S}{U_O}$$

Consider the situation in 1999, at the peak of the most recent business cycle. At that time, the stock of unemployment was approximately 1 million people and the outflow from unemployment was at a rate of approximately 400 000 persons per month. Thus, the average unemployed person in 1999 could expect to leave unemployment in about 2½ months (1 000 000 people/400 000 people per month = 2.5 months). In contrast, in 1992, at the depth of the previous recession, the expected duration of an unemployment spell was over 3½ months (1 600 000/450 000 = 3.6).

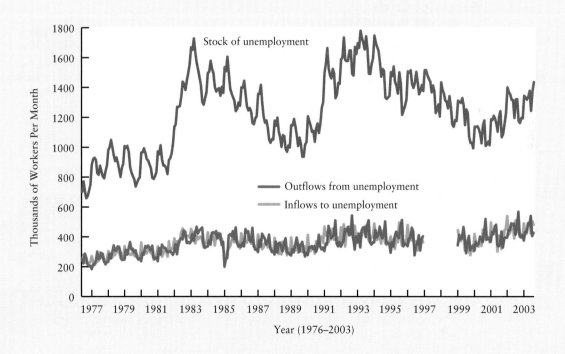

Consequences of Unemployment

Economists view unemployment as a social "bad" just as they view output as a social "good." But this does not mean *all* unemployment is bad, just as we know that all output—such as noise or air pollution—is not good. Indeed, we will see later in this chapter that some unemployment is socially desirable as it reflects the necessary time spent searching to make appropriate matches between firms and workers.

We examine two costs of unemployment. The first is reflected by the loss in output. The second is the harm done to the individuals who are unemployed.

Lost Output

Every person counted as unemployed is willing and able to work but unable to find a job. Hence, the unemployed are valuable resources whose contribution to producing output is wasted. Note that once an unemployed person regains employment, output rises again and this loss goes away. Nothing makes up, however, for the *past* loss that existed while the worker was unemployed. In other words, the loss of output that accompanies unemployment is lost forever. In a world of scarcity with many unsatisfied wants, this loss represents a serious waste of resources.

Personal Costs

For the typical worker in Canada, being unemployed is no longer the disaster that it once was. Most spells of unemployment are short (see *Applying Economic Concepts 31-1* for a simple estimate of the average duration of unemployment spells) and many workers experiencing temporary unemployment have access to the employment insurance program that provides some income during their spell of unemployment. But this does not mean there are no problems associated with unemployment. The effects of long-term unemployment, in terms of the disillusioned who have given up trying to make it within the system and who contribute to social unrest, should be a matter of serious concern to the "haves" as well as the "have-nots." The loss of self-esteem and the dislocation of families that often result from situations of prolonged unemployment are genuine tragedies.

The general case for concern about high unemployment has been eloquently put by Princeton economist Alan Blinder:

> A high-pressure economy provides opportunities, facilitates structural change, encourages inventiveness and innovation, and opens doors for society's underdogs. . . . All these promote the social cohesion and economic progress that make democratic mixed capitalism such a wonderful system when it works well. A low-pressure economy slams the doors shut, breeds a bunker mentality that resists change, stifles productivity growth, and fosters both inequality and mean-spirited public policy. All this makes reducing high unemployment a political, economic, and moral challenge of the highest order.[1]

---

[1] A.S. Blinder, "The Challenge of High Unemployment," *American Economic Review* 78 (1988), 2:1.

31.2 **Cyclical Unemployment**

As we saw in Chapter 19, economists classify unemployment into three types—cyclical, frictional, and structural. The last two together make up the NAIRU, which is the level of unemployment that exists when real GDP equals potential GDP. Thus, our analysis of unemployment occurs in two steps. In this section we discuss **cyclical unemployment,** the difference between the actual level of unemployment and the NAIRU. In the next section we discuss the NAIRU itself, and why it may change over longer periods of time.

People who are cyclically unemployed are normally presumed to be suffering *involuntary unemployment* in that they are willing to work at the going wage rate but are unable to find appropriate jobs. The persistence of cyclical unemployment poses a challenge to economic theory.

cyclical unemployment Unemployment in excess of frictional and structural unemployment; it is due to a shortfall of real GDP below potential GDP.

Why Does Cyclical Unemployment Exist?

To see what is involved in this challenge, suppose the fluctuations in aggregate demand or supply cause real output to fluctuate around its potential level. This fluctuation will cause the demand for labour in each of the economy's labour markets to fluctuate as well, rising in booms and falling in slumps. If all of the labour markets had fully flexible wage rates, wages would fluctuate to keep quantity demanded in each individual market equal to quantity supplied in that market. We would observe cyclical fluctuations in employment and in the wage rate but no changes in the amount of unemployment caused by the regular, natural turnover in the labour market. This behaviour is illustrated in Figure 31-2.

With perfectly flexible wages, employment and real wages would fluctuate but there would be no cyclical unemployment. All unemployment would be either frictional or structural.

The hypothetical situation that we have just described is not what we actually observe. Instead, we observe changes in cyclical unemployment, partly because the changes in wage rates that do occur are insufficient to equate demand and supply, as is shown in Figure 31-3. Unemployment exceeds the NAIRU in slumps and is below it in booms. Although wages do tend to vary over the cycle, the fluctuations are not sufficient to remove all cyclical variations in unemployment. Why is this so?

Two types of explanations have been advanced in recent years. The line of explanation that we consider first is associated with what is called **New Classical economics.** The explanation assumes that labour markets are always in equilibrium in the sense that quantity demanded is continually equated with quantity supplied.

New Classical economics An approach to explaining macroeconomic fluctuations in which fluctuations in economic activity are explained by shocks to technology and tastes rather than to markets that fail to clear.

New Classical Theories[2]

Two major characteristics of New Classical theories are that agents continuously optimize and markets continuously clear. In such theories, there can be no involuntary

---

[2] The label "New Classical" is used because many of the arguments put forward by this group of economists are essentially more detailed and precise versions of arguments that would have been very familiar to the Classical economists, from Adam Smith and David Ricardo to Alfred Marshall.

FIGURE 31-2   Employment and Wages in a New Classical Labour Market

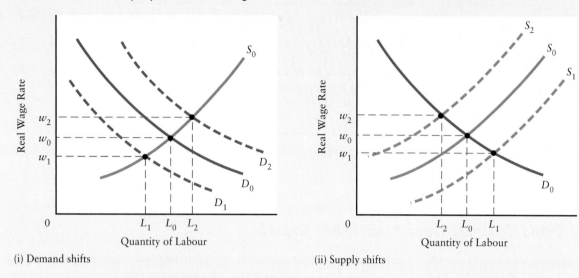

(i) Demand shifts   (ii) Supply shifts

In a New Classical labour market, real wages and employment fluctuate in the same direction when demand fluctuates and in opposite directions when supply fluctuates; in both cases, there is no involuntary unemployment. The figure shows a perfectly competitive market for one type of labour. In part (i), the demand curves D_1, D_0, and D_2 are the demands for this market corresponding to low, medium, and high values for the marginal product of labour. As demand rises from D_1 to D_0 to D_2, real wages rise from w_1 to w_0 to w_2, and employment rises from L_1 to L_0 to L_2. At no time, however, is there any involuntary unemployment. In part (ii), the supply of labour fluctuates from S_1 to S_0 to S_2, and wages fluctuate from w_1 to w_0 to w_2. In this case, wages fall when employment rises, and vice versa, but again there is no involuntary unemployment.

unemployment. These theories then seek to explain unemployment as the outcome of voluntary decisions made by individuals who are choosing to do what they do, including spending some time out of employment.

The New Classical theory explains cyclical fluctuations in employment as having one of two causes. First, as shown in part (i) of Figure 31-2, changes in technology that affect the *marginal product* of labour will lead to changes in the demand for labour, and thus to fluctuations in the level of employment and real wages. Second, as shown in part (ii) of Figure 31-2, changes in the willingness of individuals to work will lead to changes in the supply of labour and thus to fluctuations in the level of employment and real wages. In both cases, however, note that the flexibility of real wages results in a *clearing* of the labour market. In this setting, whatever unemployment exists cannot be involuntary and must be caused by either frictional or structural causes, the two components of the NAIRU.

New Classical theory assumes that labour markets clear. People who are not working are assumed to have voluntarily withdrawn from the labour market for one reason or another. There is no involuntary unemployment.

There are two problems with this New Classical view of labour markets. First, empirical observation is not consistent with the fluctuations in real wages predicted by New Classical theory. In Canada and other developed economies, employment tends to be quite volatile over the business cycle whereas real wages tend to be relatively constant. The second problem is that the New Classical theory predicts *no* involuntary unemployment whatsoever, a prediction that many economists argue is unsupported by most empirical observation. (Many unemployed workers who are nonetheless actively searching for a job would be shocked to find out that some economists view them as *voluntarily* unemployed!)

Extensions in Theory 31-1 examines New Classical theory in more detail, and explains why most economists, though rejecting its explanations of the economy in the short run, believe that it contains valuable insights about the economy's long-run behaviour.

New Keynesian Theories[3]

Many economists find the New Classical explanations implausible. They believe that people correctly read market signals but react in ways that do not cause markets to clear at all times. These economists—who refer to themselves as New Keynesians—believe that many people are involuntarily unemployed in the sense that *they would accept an offer of work in jobs for which they are trained, at the going wage rate, if such an offer were made.* These economists concentrate their efforts on explaining why wages do not quickly adjust to eliminate involuntary unemployment. If wages do not respond quickly to shifts in supply and demand in the labour market, quantity supplied and quantity demanded may *not* be equated for extended periods of time. Labour markets will then display unemployment during recessions and excess demand during booms, as shown in Figure 31-3.

New Keynesian theories start with the everyday observation that wages do not change every time demand or supply shifts. When unemployed workers are looking for jobs, they do not knock on employers'

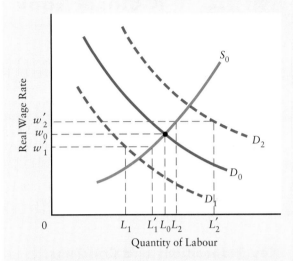

FIGURE 31-3 Unemployment and Sticky Wages in a New Keynesian Labour Market

When the wage rate does not change enough to equate quantity demanded with quantity supplied, there will be unemployment in slumps and labour shortages in booms. When demand is at its normal level D_0, the market is cleared with wage rate w_0, employment is L_0, and there is no involuntary unemployment. In a recession, demand falls to D_1, but the wage only falls to w_1'. As a result, L_1 of labour is demanded and L_1' is supplied. Employment is determined by the quantity demanded at L_1. The remainder of the supply for which there is no demand, L_1L_1', is involuntarily unemployed. In a boom, demand rises to D_2, but the wage rate rises only to w_2'. As a result, the quantity demanded is L_2', whereas only L_2 is supplied. Employment rises to L_2, which is the amount supplied. The rest of the demand cannot be satisfied, making excess demand for labour of L_2L_2'.

doors and offer to work at lower wages than are being paid to current workers; instead, they answer want ads and hope to get the jobs offered but are often disappointed. Nor do employers, seeing an excess of applicants for the few jobs that are available, go to the current workers and reduce their wages until there is no one who is looking for a job; instead, they pick and choose until they fill their needs and then hang a sign saying "No Help Wanted."

---

[3] The label "New Keynesian" is used because many of the arguments put forward by these economists are closely related to the ideas put forward by John Maynard Keynes in *The General Theory of Employment, Interest and Money* (1936).

EXTENSIONS IN THEORY 31-1

A Closer Look at New Classical Theory

New Classical theory attempts to explain cyclical fluctuations in the context of models in which wages and prices adjust very quickly to shocks. These models contrast sharply with the models we have discussed in this book in which fluctuations in output arise largely because wages and prices adjust gradually to shocks. In such models, if wages and prices were able to adjust instantly to all shocks, output would always be equal to potential output—there would never be inflationary or recessionary gaps. The extreme flexibility of wages and prices is therefore a distinguishing feature of New Classical macro theory.

Key Propositions and Criticisms

The view of the business cycle found in New Classical models is that short-run fluctuations in real GDP are caused by fluctuations in potential output, Y^*. In this view, unemployment is always equal to the NAIRU, and it is the NAIRU itself that fluctuates. Thus, the explanation of cyclical fluctuations that arises in New Classical models is based on the role of supply shocks originating from sources such as oil price changes, technical progress, and changes in tastes.

The New Classical approach is controversial. The major claims in its favour include:

1. It has been able to explain the recent behaviour of the economy quite well statistically, while downplaying the role for aggregate demand fluctuations in the business cycle.

2. It suggests that an integrated approach to understanding cycles and growth may be appropriate, as both reflect forces that affect the level of potential output. The distinction it makes is that some shocks are temporary (and hence have cyclical effects) whereas others are permanent (and therefore affect the economy's long-term growth).

3. It provides valuable insights into how shocks, regardless of their origin, spread over time to the different sectors of the economy. By abstracting from monetary issues, and instead focusing only on those *real* factors that influence the level of potential output, it is possible to address more details concerning technology and household choice involving intertemporal tradeoffs between consumption, labour supply, and leisure.

Critics of the New Classical approach focus on some implausible results and express concern about its assumptions of individuals' behaviour. More important, they are skeptical about a model in which monetary issues are completely ignored. For example, they point out that New Classical models are unable to provide insights into the short-term correlation between money and output that is at the heart of the traditional macro model and for which a considerable amount of empirical evidence exists, in Canada as well as many other countries. Furthermore, New Classical models are unable to provide insights into empirical regularities involving nominal variables, such as prices that apparently vary less than quantities and nominal prices that vary procyclically.

Policy Implications

Because the New Classical approach gives no role to aggregate demand in influencing business cycles, it provides no role for stabilization operating through monetary and fiscal policies. Indeed, the models predict that the use of such demand-management policies can be *harmful*.

The basis for this prediction is the proposition that cycles represent *efficient* responses to the shocks that are hitting the economy. Policymakers may mistakenly interpret cyclical fluctuations as deviations from potential output caused by shifts in either the *AD* or *AS* curves. The policymakers may try to stabilize output and thereby distort the maximizing decisions made by households and firms. This distortion will in turn cause the responses to the real shocks (as opposed to nominal, monetary shocks) to be inefficient.

Although a small minority of economists espouse New Classical models as complete or even reasonable descriptions of the business cycle, and hence only a minority take seriously the strict implications for policy, many accept the view that real supply-side disturbances can play an important role in business cycles. Moreover, since the New Classical approach emphasizes the importance of markets always clearing in response to changes in technology or other shocks, many economists who view New Classical models as a poor description of the economy in the short run believe that many of the New Classical insights are invaluable when thinking about the behaviour of the economy in the long run.

Long-Term Employment Relationships

One set of theories explains the familiar observations made in the preceding paragraph as results of the advantages to both workers and employers of relatively long-term and stable employment relationships. Workers want job security in the face of fluctuating demand. Employers want workers who understand the firm's organization, production, and marketing plans. Under these circumstances, both parties care about things in addition to the wage rate, and wages are somewhat insensitive to fluctuations in current economic conditions. Wages are, in effect, regular payments to workers over an extended employment relationship rather than a device for fine-tuning the current supplies of and demands for labour. Given this situation, the tendency is for employers to "smooth" the income of employees by paying a steady wage and letting profits and employment fluctuate to absorb the effects of temporary increases and decreases in demand for the firm's product.

A number of labour-market institutions work to achieve these results. For example, many long-term contracts provide for a schedule of wages over a period of several years. Similarly, fringe benefits, such as pensions and health care, tend to bind workers to particular employers. Another example is pay that rises with years of service. This helps to bind the employee to the company, whereas seniority rules for layoffs bind the employer to the long-term worker.

In labour markets in which long-term relationships are important (as is the case in many labour markets), the wage rate does not fluctuate to clear the market continuously.

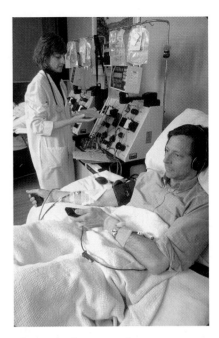

The quick adjustment of wages to excess demands and supplies is not a characteristic of labour markets in which employees and firms have long-term relationships, such as in the health-care sector.

Because wages are thus insulated from short-term fluctuations in demand and supply, any market clearing that occurs does so through fluctuations in the volume of employment rather than in wages. Of course, wages must respond to permanent shifts in market conditions—for example, the permanent and unexpected decline in the demand for the output of a particular industry.

Long-term employment relationships are important in the Canadian economy. According to a recent Statistics Canada survey of full-time workers, the average time spent with the same employer—what is referred to as *job tenure*—is just under nine years. Further, over half of the workers have been with their employer for six years or longer.

Menu Costs and Wage Contracts

A typical large manufacturing firm sells hundreds of differentiated products and employs hundreds of different types of labour. Changing prices and wages in response to every minor fluctuation in demand is a costly and time-consuming activity. Many firms therefore find it optimal to keep their price lists (*menus*) constant for significant periods of time. Since manufacturing firms are often operating in imperfectly competitive markets, they have some discretion over price. Hence, firms often react to small changes in demand by holding prices constant and responding with changes in output and employment. If many firms behave this way, output and employment will respond to changes in aggregate demand. In other words, the amount of involuntary unemployment will fluctuate over the business cycle.

The Canadian evidence is consistent with the existence of sluggish price adjustment by firms, especially those in manufacturing industries. This, of course, is where Keynesian economics came in with an assumption of price stickiness. The New Keynesian literature attempts to model such sticky prices as resulting from firms' optimal response to adjustment costs.

Wages tend to be inflexible in the short term because wage rates are generally set only occasionally. Wages are often set on an annual basis; in some unionized contracts wages are set for up to three years. Such inflexibility of wages implies that changes in aggregate demand and supply will tend to cause changes in the amount of involuntary unemployment.

Efficiency Wages

The idea of *efficiency wages* forms the core of another strand of New Keynesian thinking about why wages do not quickly adjust to clear labour markets. For any of a number of reasons, employers may find that they get more output per dollar of wages paid—that is, a more *efficient* workforce—when they pay labour somewhat more than the minimum amount that would induce workers to work for them.

Suppose it is costly for employers to monitor workers' performance on the job, so that some workers will be able to shirk duties with a low probability of being caught. Given prevailing labour-market institutions, it is generally impossible for employers to levy fines on employees for shirking on the job since the employees could just leave their jobs rather than pay the fines. So firms may instead choose to pay a wage premium— an efficiency wage—to the workers, in excess of the wage that the workers will get elsewhere in the labour market. With such a wage premium, workers will be reluctant to shirk because, if they get caught and laid off, they will then lose this wage premium.

How does this relate to involuntary unemployment? The wage premium paid to prevent workers from shirking means that the quantity of labour supplied may exceed the quantity demanded by firms, thereby creating involuntary unemployment. Wages do not fall to clear the labour market because firms would rather pay a high wage to motivated workers than a lower wage to workers who would then shirk their duties. The result is involuntary unemployment for some workers.

Efficiency-wage theory predicts that firms may find it profitable to pay high enough wages so that working is a clearly superior alternative to being laid off. Involuntary unemployment results.

Union Bargaining

The final New Keynesian theory to be considered assumes that those already employed ("insiders") have more say in wage bargaining than those currently not employed ("outsiders"). Employed workers are often represented by a union, which negotiates the wage rate with firms. The union will generally represent the interests of the insiders but will not necessarily reflect the interests of the outsiders. Insiders will naturally wish to bid up wages even though to do so will harm the employment prospects of the outsiders. Hence this theory generates an outcome to the bargaining process between firms and unions in which the wage is set higher than the market-clearing level, just as with efficiency wages. The consequence is involuntary unemployment.

In addition to explaining the existence of involuntary unemployment, this theory adds one important insight regarding international differences in unemployment. In some countries unions bargain at the level of the firm; in others they bargain at the level of the whole industry or the whole economy. Where bargaining is decentralized, as in

Canada and the United States, the union can push for higher wages for the insiders without worrying about the effects on outsiders or on the rest of the economy. However, where bargaining is centralized, as in much of Western Europe, the effects on the rest of the economy become internalized into the bargaining process, because union negotiators are bargaining on behalf of all workers (and all potential workers), rather than just the current group of insiders.

This theory leads to the following predictions. Decentralized bargaining with strong unions will lead to higher than market-clearing wages, and higher unemployment as the outsiders are excluded from jobs. In contrast, centralized bargaining will produce an outcome closer to the market-clearing outcome (because outsider concerns are voiced), so unemployment will be low. In situations where unionization is low or unions are weak, the outcome will be close to the market-clearing outcome. This analysis may explain why unemployment is relatively high in EU countries (where unions are strong and bargaining is decentralized), lower in Scandinavia (where unions are also strong but bargaining is centralized), and even lower in Canada and the United States (where unions are relatively weak and the extent of unionization is much lower).

In labour markets with powerful unions, wages are set in a bargaining process. If unions act in the interests of the current "insiders," wages will be high and involuntary unemployment will exist. If unions act in the interests of both "insiders" and "outsiders," wages and involuntary unemployment will both be lower.

Convergence of Theories?

We have examined two classes of theories of cyclical unemployment. In the New Classical theories, wages and prices adjust instantly to clear markets and so real GDP is always equal to potential GDP. Unemployment fluctuates, but it is always equal to the NAIRU, U^*. Using the terminology we introduced earlier, there is no *cyclical* unemployment in New Classical models because unemployment always equals U^*. In contrast, New Keynesian models emphasize the gradual adjustment of wages and prices and thus the existence of periods in which real GDP is either above or below potential GDP. In these models, unemployment fluctuates around the value of U^*—that is, U does not always equal U^*. Cyclical unemployment fluctuates over the business cycle. Table 31-1 provides a summary of the key assumptions and predictions of these two classes of theories.

Note, however, that the sharp contrast between New Classical and New Keynesian models applies only to the short-run behaviour of the economy. It is in the short run that the extent of wage and price flexibility distinguishes these two classes of models. In the long run, even the staunchest New Keynesians accept the proposition that wages and prices adjust to eliminate output gaps and thus return real GDP to its potential level and the unemployment rate to the NAIRU (U^*).

Both New Classical and New Keynesians agree that in the long run wage and price flexibility brings the unemployment rate back to U^*.

Let's restate the difference between New Keynesian and New Classical models another way. In New Keynesian models there is a meaningful difference between the short run and the long run that is determined by the degree of wage and price flexibility. In New Classical models, however, wages and prices adjust instantly, so there is no similar distinction between the short run and the long run. But, since *both* classes of models agree that wages and prices are flexible in the long run, they have the same predictions regarding the long-run effects of policy.

TABLE 31-1 Summary of New Classical and New Keynesian Theories

	New Classical Theory	New Keynesian Theory
Key Assumptions		
Market clearing	Wages and price are perfectly flexible; all markets are continuously clearing.	Wages and prices are slow to adjust; markets are not continuously clearing.
Key Predictions		
Unemployment	U is always equal to U^*. There is no cyclical or involuntary unemployment; all unemployment is voluntary.	U often deviates from U^*. Unemployment has both voluntary and involuntary components.
Role of AD shocks	AD shocks do not cause changes in output because the AS curve adjusts instantly to bring Y back to Y^*.	AD shocks cause changes in output because the AS curve adjusts only gradually to bring Y back to Y^*.
Changes in Y^* and U^*	Shocks to technology and preferences lead to changes in both Y^* and U^*.	Shocks to technology and preferences lead to changes in both Y^* and U^*.

For example, New Keynesians argue that a monetary expansion will raise real GDP above Y^* and reduce U below the NAIRU. In the long run, however, output will return to Y^*, U will return to U^*, and the only long-run effect of the monetary expansion will be a higher price level. New Classical economists agree on this predicted long-run effect, but they argue that the short-run real effects on output and unemployment will either be absent or of much shorter duration since wages and prices adjust very quickly.

New Keynesians and New Classical economists agree that the actual unemployment rate is equal to the NAIRU in the long run. Our next job is to understand why the NAIRU changes. We turn to this topic now.

31.3 The NAIRU

The NAIRU is composed of frictional and structural unemployment. Our interest is in why the NAIRU changes over time and in the extent that economic policy can affect the NAIRU.

Frictional Unemployment

frictional unemployment
Unemployment caused by the time that is taken for labour to move from one job to another.

As we saw in Chapter 19, **frictional unemployment** results from the normal turnover of labour. An important source of frictional unemployment is young people who enter the labour force and look for jobs. Another source is people who leave their jobs. Some may quit because they are dissatisfied with the type of work or their working conditions; others may be fired. Whatever the reason, they must search for new jobs, which takes time. Persons who are unemployed while searching for jobs are said to be frictionally unemployed or in *search unemployment*.

The normal turnover of labour causes frictional unemployment to persist, even if the economy is at potential output.

How "voluntary" is frictional unemployment? Some of it is clearly voluntary. For example, a worker may know of an available job but may not accept it so she can search for a better one. Some of it is also involuntary, as when a worker gets laid off and cannot find *any* job offer for a period of weeks, even though he may be actively searching. *Extensions in Theory 31-2*, which discusses search unemployment in more detail, shows that the distinction between voluntary and involuntary unemployment is not always as clear as it might at first seem.

Structural Unemployment

Structural adjustments in the economy can cause unemployment. When the pattern of demand for goods changes, the pattern of the demand for labour changes. Until labour adjusts fully, structural unemployment develops. **Structural unemployment** is caused by a mismatch between the structure of the labour force—in terms of skills, occupations, industries, or geographical locations—and the structure of the demand for labour.

structural unemployment
Unemployment due to a mismatch between characteristics required by available jobs and characteristics possessed by the unemployed labour force.

EXTENSIONS IN THEORY 31-2
Voluntary Versus Involuntary Unemployment

Frictional unemployment is *involuntary* if the job seeker has not yet found a job for which his or her training and experience are suitable. Frictional unemployment is *voluntary* if the unemployed person is aware of available jobs for which he or she is suited but is searching for better options. But how should we classify an unemployed person who refuses to accept a job at a lower skill level than the one for which she is qualified? What if she turns down a job for which she is trained because she hopes to get a higher wage offer for a similar job from another employer?

In one sense, people in search unemployment are voluntarily unemployed because they could almost always find *some* job, no matter how poorly paid or inappropriate to their training; in another sense, they are involuntarily unemployed because they have not yet succeeded in finding the job for which they feel they are suited at a rate of pay that they believe is attainable.

Workers do not have perfect knowledge of all available jobs and rates of pay, and they may be able to gain information only by searching the market. Facing this uncertainty, they may find it sensible to refuse a first job offer, for the offer may prove to be a poor one in light of further market information. But too much search—for example, holding off while being supported by others in the hope of finding a job better than a job for which one is really suited—is an economic waste. Thus, search unemployment is a grey area: Some of it is useful, and some of it is wasteful.

Some search unemployment is desirable because it gives unemployed people time to find an available job that makes the best use of their skills. How long it pays for people to remain in search unemployment depends on the economic costs of being employed. By lowering the costs of being unemployed, employment insurance tends to increase the amount of search unemployment. This may or may not increase economic efficiency, depending on whether or not it induces people to search beyond the point at which they acquire new and valuable information about the labour market.

Natural Causes

Changes that accompany economic growth shift the structure of the demand for labour. Demand rises in such expanding areas as British Columbia's Lower Mainland or Ontario's Ottawa Valley and falls in declining areas such as Newfoundland and Labrador and parts of Quebec. Demand rises for workers with certain skills, such as computer programming and electronics engineering, and falls for workers with other skills, such as stenography, assembly line work, and middle management. To meet changing demands, the structure of the labour force must change. Some existing workers can retrain and some new entrants can acquire fresh skills, but the transition is often difficult, especially for already experienced workers whose skills become economically obsolete.

Increases in international competition can also cause structural unemployment. As the geographical distribution of world production changes, so does the composition of production and of labour demand in any one country. Labour adapts to such shifts by changing jobs, skills, and locations, but until the transition is complete, structural unemployment exists.

Structural unemployment will increase if there is either an increase in the pace at which the structure of the demand for labour is changing or a decrease in the pace at which labour is adapting to these changes.

Following the Canada–U.S. Free Trade Agreement in 1989 and the North American Free Trade Agreement (NAFTA) in 1994, there were significant shifts of economic activity within Canada. The textiles industry, much of which was located in Quebec, contracted; at the same time there was an expansion of the high-tech industry, much of which was located in the Ottawa Valley. The types of workers released from the textiles industry, however, were not exactly what was required in the expanding high-tech industry. This mismatch in skills and locations contributed to structural unemployment during the early 1990s.

Policy Causes

Government policies can influence the speed with which labour markets adapt to changes. Some countries, including Canada, have adopted policies that *discourage* movement among regions, industries, and occupations. These policies (which may be desirable for other reasons) tend to *raise* structural unemployment rather than lower it.

Policies that discourage firms from replacing labour with machines may protect employment over the short term. However, if such policies lead to the decline of an industry because it cannot compete effectively with innovative foreign competitors, more serious structural unemployment can result in the long run.

Employment insurance also contributes to structural unemployment, for at least two reasons. First, the Canadian employment insurance (EI) system ties workers' benefits to the regional unemployment rate in such a way that unemployed workers can collect EI benefits for more weeks in regions where unemployment is high than where it is low. The EI system therefore encourages unemployed workers to remain in high-unemployment regions rather than encouraging them to move to regions where employment prospects are more favourable.

Second, workers are only eligible for employment insurance if they have worked for a given number of weeks in the previous year—this is known as the *entrance requirement*. In some cases, however, these entrance requirements are very low and thus seasonal workers are encouraged to work for a few months and then collect employment insurance and wait for the next season, rather than finding other jobs during the off season.

The Frictional–Structural Distinction

As with many distinctions, the one between frictional and structural unemployment is not precise. In a sense, structural unemployment is really long-term frictional unemployment. Consider, for example, what would happen if there were an increase in world demand for Canadian-made car parts but at the same time a decline in world demand for Canadian-assembled cars. This change would require labour to move from one sector (the car-assembly sector) to another (the car-parts manufacturing sector). If the reallocation were to occur quickly, we call the unemployment *frictional*; if the reallocation were to occur slowly, we call the unemployment *structural*.

The major characteristic of both frictional and structural unemployment is that there are as many unfilled vacancies as there are unemployed persons.

In the case of pure frictional unemployment, the job vacancy and the searcher are matched—the only problem is that the searcher has not yet located the vacancy. In the case of structural unemployment, the job vacancy and the searcher are mismatched in one or more relevant characteristics, such as occupation, industry, location, or skill requirements.

In practice, structural and frictional unemployment cannot be separated. But the two of them, taken together, *can* be separated from cyclical unemployment. Specifically, when real GDP is at its potential level, the *only* unemployment (by definition) is the NAIRU, which comprises frictional and structural unemployment. For example, most economists agree that real GDP in Canada was approximately equal to potential GDP in late 1999. At that time, the unemployment rate was about 7 percent, and thus the NAIRU was approximately 7 percent. In contrast, seven years earlier in 1992, when the economy was at the depth of its most recent recession, the unemployment rate was 11.5 percent. To the extent that the underlying frictions and structural change in the economy were unchanged between 1992 and 1999, we can conclude that in 1992, 4.5 percentage points of the actual unemployment rate were due to cyclical factors and the rest was due to frictional and structural factors.

For information on Canada's Employment Insurance program, see the website for Human Resources Development Canada: www.hrdc-drhc.gc.ca.

Why Does the NAIRU Change?

Structural unemployment can increase because the pace of change accelerates or the pace of adjustment to change slows down. An increase in the rate of growth, for example, usually speeds up the rate at which the structure of the demand for labour is changing. The adaptation of labour to the changing structure of demand may be slowed by such diverse factors as a decline in education and new regulations that make it harder for workers in a given occupation to take new jobs in other areas or occupations. Any of these changes will cause the NAIRU to rise. Changes in the opposite direction will cause the NAIRU to fall.

Demographic Shifts

Because people usually try several jobs before settling into one for a longer period of time, young or inexperienced workers have higher unemployment rates than experienced workers. The proportion of inexperienced workers in the labour force rose significantly as the baby boom generation of the 1950s entered the labour force in the 1970s and 1980s. Because birthrates were low in the 1960s, some demographically induced fall in this type of unemployment occurred during the 1990s.

Young workers have higher unemployment rates than do older workers. As the share of younger workers in the labour force decreases, so will the economy's NAIRU.

During the 1960s and 1970s women tended to have higher unemployment rates than men. Since this was true at all points of the business cycle, the higher unemployment was higher frictional and structural unemployment. Thus, when female labour-force participation rates increased dramatically in the 1960s and 1970s, the NAIRU naturally increased. In recent years, however, female unemployment rates have dropped below the rates for men, and so continued increases in female participation will, if anything, tend to decrease the NAIRU.

Greater labour-force participation by groups with high unemployment rates increases the level of NAIRU.

See Figure 31-4 for Canadian unemployment rates for various demographic groups in 2002. Notice especially the significantly higher unemployment rates for youth of both sexes. These data form the basis for the often-heard view that while overall unemployment may be at acceptable levels, youth unemployment may be a serious problem.

FIGURE 31-4   Unemployment Rates by Demographic Groups, 2002

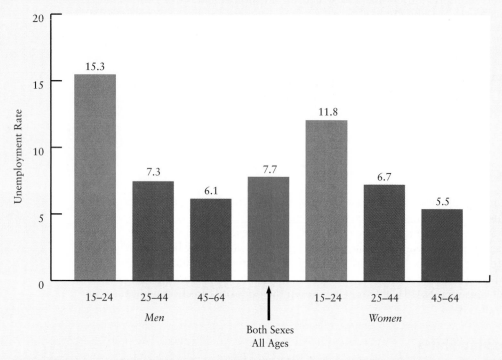

Unemployment is unevenly spread among different groups in the labour force. In 2002, when the overall unemployment rate was 7.7 percent, the unemployment rates for youths (of both sexes) was considerably higher.

(*Source:* These data are available on Statistics Canada's website: www.statcan.ca. Go to "Canadian Statistics" and click on "Labour, employment and unemployment." Then go to "Labour force, employed, and unemployed" and click on "Labour force characteristics by age and sex.")

Hysteresis

Some models of unemployment show that the size of the NAIRU can be influenced by the size of the actual current rate of unemployment. Such models get their name from the Greek word *hysteresis,* meaning "lagged effect."

One mechanism that can lead to hysteresis arises from the importance of experience and on-the-job training. Suppose a recession causes a significant group of new entrants to the labour force to encounter unusual difficulty obtaining their first jobs. As a result, this unlucky group will be slow to acquire the important skills that workers generally learn in their first jobs. When demand increases again, this group of workers will be at a disadvantage relative to workers with normal histories of experience, and the unlucky group may have unemployment rates that will be higher than average. Hence, the NAIRU will be higher than it would have been had there been no recession.

Another force that can cause such effects is emphasized by commentators in Western Europe, which has a more heavily unionized labour force than does either Canada or the United States. In times of high unemployment, people who are currently employed ("insiders") may use their bargaining power to ensure that their own status is maintained and prevent new entrants to the labour force ("outsiders") from competing effectively. In an *insider–outsider* model of this type, a period of prolonged, high unemployment—whatever its initial cause—will tend to become "locked in." If outsiders are denied access to the labour market, their unemployment will fail to exert downward pressure on wages, and the NAIRU will tend to rise.

Globalization and Structural Change

The amount of resources being moved between industries and regions increased in the mid-1970s and this process is continuing into the current decade. In part, this is the result of the increasing integration of the Canadian economy with the rest of the world and the globalization of world markets. Most economists argue that this integration has been beneficial overall, for reasons we discuss in Chapters 33 and 34. One less fortunate consequence, however, is that Canadian labour markets are increasingly affected by changes in demand and supply conditions anywhere in the world—changes that require adjustments throughout the world's trading nations. Although evidence is difficult to obtain, some observers argue that the increasing pace and the changing nature of technological change since the mid-1970s has contributed to an increase in the level of structural unemployment.

Policy and Labour-Market Flexibility

We mentioned briefly above how policies can affect structural unemployment and thus affect the NAIRU. It is worthwhile emphasizing again the important role that government policy can have on the NAIRU.

One important cause of unemployment is *inflexibility* in the labour market. If wages are inflexible, shocks to labour demand or supply can cause unemployment. If workers are unable or unwilling to move between regions or between industries, changes in the structure of the economy can cause unemployment. If it is costly for firms to hire workers, firms will find other ways of increasing output (such as switching to more capital-intensive methods of production). In general, since the economy is always being buffetted by shocks of one sort or another, the less flexible is the labour market, the higher unemployment will be.

Any government policy that reduces labour-market flexibility is likely to increase the NAIRU.

See Chapter 31 of www.pearsoned.ca/ragan for a debate on the effects of mandated job security: Seamus Hogan, "Should Governments Mandate Job Security?" and Marc Van Audenrode, "A Partial Defence of Job Security Provisions."

Consider employment insurance (EI) as an example of a policy that reduces labour-market flexibility. EI provides income support to eligible unemployed workers and thus reduces the costs to the worker of being unemployed. This income support will typically lead the worker to search longer for a new job and thus increase the unemployment rate. This longer search may be desirable since by reducing the cost of unemployment the worker is able to conduct a thorough search for a job that is an appropriate match for his or her specific skills. On the other hand, if the EI system is so generous that workers have little incentive to accept reasonable jobs—instead holding out for the "perfect" job—then the increase in unemployment generated by the EI system will be undesirable.

In general, however, the basic message should be clear. The more generous is the employment insurance system, the less motivated unemployed workers will be to accept a new job quickly. This reduction in labour-market flexibility will increase the NAIRU.

A second example concerns policies designed to increase job security for workers. In most Western European countries, firms that lay off workers are required either to give several months' notice before doing so or, in lieu of such notice, are required to make severance payments equal to several months' worth of pay. In Italy, for example, a worker who has been with the firm for 10 years is guaranteed either 20 months' notice before termination or a severance payment equal to 20 months' worth of pay.

Such job-security provisions reduce the flexibility of firms. But this inflexibility on the part of the firms is passed on to workers. Any policy that forces the firm to incur large costs for laying off workers is likely to lead the same firm to be very hesitant about hiring workers in the first place. Given this reduction in labour-market flexibility, such policies are likely to increase the NAIRU.

See Chapter 31 of www.pearsoned.ca/ragan for a discussion of the likely effects of France's recent policy of shortening the length of the workweek: Jan Olters, "Some Doubts About France's 35-Hour Week."

Such mandated job security is relatively rare in Canada and the United States. Its rarity contributes to the general belief among economists that North American labour markets are much more flexible than those in Europe. Many economists see this as the most important explanation for why unemployment rates in Canada and the United States are significantly below the unemployment rates in Europe, and have been for over two decades.

31.4 Reducing Unemployment

As the Canadian economy grew steadily from 1993 to 1999, the unemployment rate dropped from 11.3 percent to 7 percent. Unemployment in the United States declined by a similar amount, as the U.S. economy was also experiencing steady economic growth. In both cases, most economists viewed the decline in unemployment as a desirable reduction in *cyclical* unemployment.

Despite the reduction in Canada's unemployment rate in the late 1990s, however, many economists have been puzzled at the growing unemployment *gap* between Canada and the United States. Beginning in the early 1980s, the Canadian unemployment rate increased relative to the U.S. rate. By the late 1990s, the gap was approximately four percentage points. In 2000–2003, as growth in the Canadian economy surpassed that in the United States, the gap closed slightly. What is the cause of the gap? *Applying Economic*

Concepts 31-2 examines this issue and concludes that an important part of the answer lies in how the unemployed are counted in the two countries.

In the remainder of this chapter we briefly examine what can be done to reduce unemployment. Other things being equal, all governments would like to reduce unemployment. The questions are "Can it be done?" and "If so, at what cost?"

Practise with Study Guide Chapter 31, Exercise 2.

Cyclical Unemployment

We do not need to say much more about cyclical unemployment because its control is the subject of stabilization policy, which we have studied in several earlier chapters. A major recession that occurs because of natural causes can be countered by monetary and fiscal policies to reduce cyclical unemployment.

There is room for debate, however, about *how much* the government can and should do in this respect. Advocates of stabilization policy call for expansionary fiscal and monetary policies to reduce unemployment (and increase output) during recessionary gaps, at least when they last for sustained periods of time. Advocates of a hands-off approach say that normal market adjustments can be relied on to remove recessionary gaps and that government policy, no matter how well intentioned, will only make things worse. They call for setting simple rules for monetary and fiscal policy that would make discretionary stabilization policy impossible.

Whatever may be argued in principle, however, policymakers have not yet agreed to abandon stabilization measures in practice.

Frictional Unemployment

The turnover that causes frictional unemployment is an inevitable part of the functioning of the economy. Some frictional unemployment is a natural part of the learning process for young workers. New entrants to the labour force (many of whom are young) have to try several jobs to see which is most suitable, and this leads to a high turnover rate among the young and hence high frictional unemployment.

To the extent that frictional unemployment is caused by ignorance regarding where the appropriate jobs are, increasing the knowledge of workers about market opportunities may help. But such measures have a cost, and that cost has to be balanced against the benefits.

Employment insurance is one method of helping people cope with unemployment. It has reduced significantly the human costs of the bouts with unemployment that are inevitable in a changing society. Nothing, however, is without cost. Although employment insurance alleviates the suffering caused by some kinds of unemployment, it also contributes to search unemployment, as we have already observed.

Supporters of employment insurance emphasize its benefits. Critics emphasize its costs. As with any policy, a rational assessment of the value of employment insurance requires a balancing of its undoubted benefits against its undoubted costs. Many Canadians believe that when this calculation is made, the benefits greatly exceed the costs, although many also recognize the scope for reform of certain aspects of the program.

Many provisions have been added over the years to the employment insurance scheme to focus it more on people in general need and to reduce its effect of raising the unemployment rate. For example, workers must be actively seeking employment in order to be eligible for EI. Also, workers who voluntarily quit their jobs (without cause) are not eligible to collect EI. Finally, a system of *experience rating* has recently been

APPLYING ECONOMIC CONCEPTS 31-2

The Canada–U.S. Unemployment Gap

In recent years economists have been examining changes in the gap between the Canadian and U.S. unemployment rates. As the accompanying figure shows, the last year in which the two countries had the same unemployment rate was 1981. Since then the Canadian unemployment rate has exceeded the U.S. rate by an average of two percentage points in the 1980s and by almost four percentage points in the 1990s. What is the cause of this gap? Does the gap reflect a more poorly functioning Canadian economy?

Craig Riddell from the University of British Columbia and David Card from the University of California at Berkeley have shown that an important part of the explanation lies in the difference between *unemployment* and *non-participation* in the labour force. In short, a randomly selected non-working individual in each country is more likely to be considered unemployed in Canada but out of the labour force in the United States. This difference naturally increases the Canadian unemployment rate relative to that in the United States. Let's look at this in more detail.

Decomposing the Unemployment Rate

It is helpful first to define some terms. We will use the following symbols to represent the important labour-market variables:

U = number of persons who are unemployed

LF = number of persons in the labour force

POP = number of persons in the working-age population

N = number of persons in the working-age population who are *not* working

Recall that the unemployment rate is simply the fraction of the labour force that is unemployed, U/LF. We can write this differently as

$$U/LF = (U/N) \times (N/POP) \times (POP/LF)$$

It should be clear that this equation always holds since we could cancel the Ns and the POPs to get simply U/LF = U/LF. But this longer equation allows us to see that any change in the unemployment rate *must be* due to a change in one (or more) of these three separate variables. What are these three variables?

An individual can be non-employed either by being out of the labour force or by being in the labour force but unemployed. The ratio U/N is simply the fraction of the total non-working persons who are classified as unemployed. Clearly, a rise in U/N, other things being equal, raises the unemployment rate. The second variable, N/POP, is the fraction of the working-age population that is *not* working. This is 1 minus the country's *employment rate*. A reduction in the employment rate, other things being equal, means a rise in N/POP and thus an increase in the unemployment rate. The third variable, POP/LF, is simply the inverse of the labour-force participation rate. A fall in the participation rate, other things being equal, means a rise in POP/LF and thus an increase in the unemployment rate.

Growing Labour-Force Attachment in Canada

Card and Riddell argue that the U/N ratio is the key variable for explaining the Canada–U.S. unemployment gap. They refer to U/N as a measure of *labour-force attachment*— since the non-working individuals who are classified as unemployed are "attached" to the labour force.

Card and Riddell find that between 1981 and 1998, fully two-thirds of the Canada–U.S. unemployment gap is explained by an increase in the Canadian U/N ratio relative to that in the United States. One-quarter of the gap is accounted for by a lower employment rate (higher N/POP) and less than 10 percent of the gap is explained by lower labour-force participation (higher POP/LF).

To put it differently, the principal cause of the rising Canada–U.S. unemployment gap appears to be a change in

proposed to distribute the costs more in proportion to the benefits. In the absence of experience rating all firms pay the same EI tax; this implicitly subsidizes those firms who create the most unemployment and taxes most heavily those firms who create the least unemployment. Under experience rating, firms with histories of sizable layoffs pay more than those with lower layoff numbers.

the way that non-employed Canadians spend their time relative to their U.S. counterparts. When not working, Canadians in the past two decades have become more likely to continue searching for jobs, and thus to be officially counted among the unemployed. In contrast, non-working Americans have become relatively more likely to be counted among the non-participants.

Causes of the Greater Attachment

Two main reasons are offered for why Canadians appear to have a greater attachment to the labour force. First, there are slight but significant differences in how the unemployed are classified in the two countries. In order to be considered unemployed in the United States, individuals must be "actively" searching for work. In contrast, Canadians must only be "passively" looking for work. For example, an individual who *only* reads the help-wanted ads in the newspaper would be classified as unemployed in Canada but as out of the labour force in the United States. This difference alone, although it sounds like a minor point, appears to explain one-quarter of the unemployment gap.

Card and Riddell suggest that the greater generosity and availability of the Canadian employment-insurance system is also very important for explaining why Canadians have a greater attachment to the labour force. The greater generosity obviously improves the insurance value of the program for those workers who may lose their jobs. But by reducing the costs associated with being unemployed, it also results in longer job search and higher measured unemployment (for a given level of employment).

Is It a Problem?

In order to know whether a rise in unemployment is undesirable, we must know why the increase occurred. To the extent that the higher Canadian unemployment rate is due to poorer employment growth in Canada, this may represent a problem. Some economists argue that tight fiscal and monetary policies, especially in the 1990s, are largely responsible for the rise in the N/POP ratio in Canada relative to that in the United States.

But the findings by Card and Riddell are that the clear majority of the unemployment gap is due to a rise in labour-force attachment (U/N) in Canada. Is this a problem? As Riddell says, "The implications for individuals' welfare of a rise in unemployment that is not associated with a decline in employment are much less obvious." The greater labour-force attachment arising from the different classification of similar workers is obviously not a problem for individual well-being. However, the greater labour-force attachment arising from a more generous EI system may be a problem. As we said earlier in this chapter, an overly generous EI system may encourage unemployed workers to search *too much*, holding out for the "perfect" job match rather than accepting a merely "good" job offer.

This box is based on Craig Riddell, "Canadian Labour-Market Performance in International Perspective," *Canadian Journal of Economics*, November 1999.

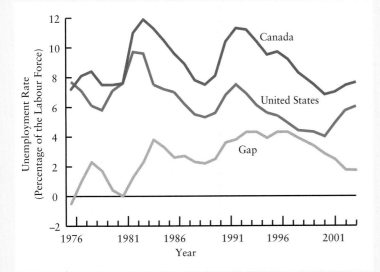

Structural Unemployment

The reallocation of labour among occupations, industries, skill categories, and regions that gives rise to structural unemployment is an inevitable part of a market economy. Much of this required reallocation is driven by technological change, which occurs in different ways and at different paces in various parts of the economy. Ever since the beginning of the Industrial Revolution in the late eighteenth century, workers have resisted the introduction of new techniques that replace the older techniques at which they were skilled. Such resistance is understandable. New techniques often destroy the value of the knowledge and experience of workers skilled in the displaced techniques. Older workers may not even get a chance to start over with the new technique. Employers may prefer to hire younger persons who will learn the new skills faster than older workers who are set in their ways of thinking. But, from society's point of view, new techniques are beneficial because they are a major source of economic growth. From the point of view of the workers they displace, new techniques can be an unmitigated disaster.

There are two basic approaches to reducing structural unemployment: Try to arrest the changes that the economy experiences or accept the changes and try to speed up the adjustments. Throughout history, labour and management have advocated both approaches and governments have tried them both.

Resisting Change

Over the long term, policies aimed at maintaining employment levels in declining industries run into increasing difficulties. Agreements to hire unneeded workers raise costs and can hasten the decline of an industry threatened by competitive products. An industry that is declining because of economic change becomes an increasingly large burden on the public purse as economic forces become less and less favourable to its success. Sooner or later, public support is withdrawn, followed by a precipitous decline.

As we assess these remedies for structural unemployment, it is important to realize that although they are not viable in the long run for the entire economy, they may be the best alternatives for the affected workers during their lifetimes.

There is often a genuine conflict between the private interest of workers threatened by structural unemployment, whose interests lie in preserving existing jobs, and the social interest served by reallocating resources to where they are most valuable.

Assisting Adjustment

A second general approach to dealing with structural change is to accept the decline of specific industries and the loss of specific jobs that go with them and to try to reduce the cost of adjustment for the workers affected. A number of policies have been introduced in Canada to ease the adjustment to changing economic conditions.

One such policy is publicly subsidized education and retraining schemes. The public involvement is motivated largely by imperfections in capital markets that make it difficult for workers to borrow funds for education, training, or retraining. A major component of labour-market policies is a system of loans and subsidies for higher education.

Another policy is motivated by the difficulty in obtaining good information about current and future job prospects. In recent years, the development of the Internet has greatly improved the flow of this type of information. Human Resources Development Canada (HRDC), for example, operates two Internet-based services to speed up and improve the quality of matches between firms and workers. The HRDC National Job Bank allows workers to search various regions of the country for jobs of specific types. The Electronic Labour Exchange allows firms (or workers) to specify certain characteristics and skills and then match these characteristics with workers (or firms) on the "other side" of the labour market.

Policies to increase retraining and to improve the flow of labour-market information will tend to reduce the amount of structural unemployment.

To learn more about the National Job Bank or the Electronic Labour Exchange, see HRDC's website: www.hrdc-drhc-gc.ca.

Conclusion

Over the years, unemployment has been regarded in many different ways. Harsh critics see it as proof that the market system is badly flawed. Reformers regard it as a necessary evil of the market system and a suitable object for government policy to reduce its incidence and its harmful effects. Others see it as overblown in importance and believe that it does not reflect any real inability of workers to obtain jobs if they really want to work.

Most government policy has followed a middle route. Fiscal and monetary policies have sought to reduce at least the most persistent of recessionary gaps, and a host of labour-market policies have sought to reduce the incidence of frictional and structural unemployment. Such social policies as employment insurance have sought to reduce the sting of unemployment for the many who were thought to suffer from it for reasons beyond their control.

As global economic competition becomes more severe and as new knowledge-driven methods of production spread, the ability to adjust to economic change will become increasingly important. Countries that succeed in the global marketplace, while also managing to maintain humane social welfare systems, will be those that best learn how to cooperate with change. This will mean avoiding economic policies that inhibit change while adopting social policies that reduce the human cost of adjusting to change. This is an enormous challenge for future Canadian economic and social policies.

For a widely used international job-match website, go to www.monster.com.

S U M M A R Y

31.1 Employment and Unemployment

- Canadian employment and the Canadian labour force increased along a strong upward trend throughout the twentieth century. The unemployment rate has fluctuated significantly; over the past thirty years it has also shown a slight upward trend.
- Looking only at the level of employment or unemployment misses a tremendous amount of activity in the labour market as individuals flow from unemployment to employment or from employment to unemployment. In recent years in Canada, approximately 400 000 people *per month* flowed between employment and unemployment. This level of gross flows reflects the turnover that is a normal part of any labour market.

- It is useful to distinguish among several types of unemployment: cyclical unemployment, which is associated with output gaps; frictional unemployment, which is caused by the length of time it takes to find a first job and to move from job to job as a result of normal labour turnover; and structural unemployment, which is caused by the need to reallocate resources among occupations, regions, and industries as the structure of demand and supply changes.
- Together, frictional unemployment and structural unemployment make up the NAIRU. The actual unemployment rate is equal to the NAIRU when real GDP is equal to Y^*.

31.2 **Cyclical Unemployment**

- There is a long-standing debate among economists regarding the causes of cyclical unemployment.
- New Classical theories look to explanations that allow the labour market to be cleared continuously by perfectly flexible wages and prices. Such theories can explain cyclical variations in employment but do not predict the existence of involuntary unemployment.
- New Keynesian theories have focused on the long-term nature of employer–worker relationships in which wages tend to respond only a little, and employment tends to

respond a lot, to changes in the demand and supply of labour. More recent New Keynesian theories have examined the possibility that it may be efficient for employers to pay wages that are above the level that would clear the labour market (efficiency wages).

- This debate only applies to the short-run behaviour of the economy. Both classes of models, for example, predict that in the long run, monetary expansions or contractions affect only the price level, and do not affect output, employment, or unemployment.

31.3 **The NAIRU**

- The NAIRU will always be positive because it takes time for labour to move between jobs both in normal turnover (frictional unemployment) and in response to changes in the structure of the demand for labour (structural unemployment).
- Because different workers have different sets of skills and because different firms require workers with different sets of skills, some unemployment—resulting from workers searching for appropriate job matches with employers—is socially desirable.

- Anything that increases the rate of turnover in the labour market, or the pace of structural change in the economy, will likely increase the NAIRU.
- Employment insurance also increases the NAIRU by encouraging workers to continue searching for an appropriate job. Policies that mandate job security increase the costs to firms of laying off workers. This makes them reluctant to hire workers in the first place and thus increases the NAIRU.

31.4 **Reducing Unemployment**

- Cyclical unemployment can be reduced by using monetary or fiscal policies to close recessionary gaps.
- Frictional and structural unemployment can be reduced by making it easier to move between jobs and by raising the cost of staying unemployed (e.g., by reducing employment insurance benefits).

- In a growing, changing economy populated by people who wish to change jobs for many reasons, it is neither possible nor desirable to reduce unemployment to zero.

KEY CONCEPTS

Gross flows in the labour market
Cyclical, frictional, and structural unemployment
New Classical and New Keynesian theories of unemployment

Long-term employment relationships
Efficiency wages
Hysteresis
The components of the NAIRU

Determinants of the size of the NAIRU
Policies to reduce the NAIRU
Labour-market flexibility

STUDY EXERCISES

1. Fill in the blanks to make the following statements correct.

   a. The overall unemployment rate in Canada is not a good indicator of the level of *activity* in the labour market because _____.

   b. *Gross* flows in the labour market are much _____ than *net* flows in the labour market.

   c. In a typical month in Canada, _____ workers flow in each direction between unemployment and employment.

   d. Cyclical unemployment exists when real GDP is _____ than potential GDP. When real GDP is equal to potential GDP, then all unemployment is either _____ or _____.

   e. New Classical theories assume that the labour market always _____ with flexible _____ and that any unemployment that does exist is _____.

   f. New Keynesian theories do not assume that the wage rate _____ to clear the market. A recessionary gap can persist and result in unemployment that is _____.

   g. The New Classical and New Keynesian theories both assume that, in the long run, wages and prices _____ and the unemployment rate will revert to the _____, as any _____ gap is closed.

2. Fill in the blanks to make the following statements correct.

   a. The NAIRU is composed of _____ unemployment and _____ unemployment. The NAIRU is always _____ than zero.

   b. If there are 1000 loggers in British Columbia who are unemployed, and 1000 vacant positions for call-centre operators in New Brunswick, we say that this unemployment is _____.

   c. Suppose the NAIRU in June 2003 was 6.5 percent. If the actual unemployment rate was 7.6 percent, we can conclude that _____ percentage points are due to _____ factors and the remaining _____ percentage points are due to _____ and _____ factors.

   d. Suppose the government increased the number of weeks that an unemployed worker can collect employment-insurance benefits from 12 weeks to 16 weeks. The NAIRU is likely to _____ because of an increase in the amount of _____ unemployment.

   e. Countries with greater labour-market flexibility are likely to have _____ unemployment rates than countries where mandated job security is common.

   f. Cyclical unemployment can be reduced by closing a _____ gap using _____ and _____ policies.

3. The following table shows the pattern of real GDP, potential GDP, and the unemployment rate for several years in Cycleland.

Year	Real GDP (billions of dollars)	Potential GDP (billions of dollars)	Unemployment Rate (%)
1994	790	740	6.3
1995	800	760	6.5
1996	780	780	6.8
1997	750	800	8.2
1998	765	810	8.4
1999	790	830	8.4
2000	815	850	8.0
2001	845	870	7.5
2002	875	890	7.2
2003	900	900	6.8
2004	930	920	6.7

   a. On a scale diagram, draw the path of real GDP and potential GDP (with time on the horizontal axis).

   b. On a separate diagram (below the first one) show the path of the unemployment rate.

   c. For which years is it possible to determine the value of NAIRU?

   d. Does the NAIRU change over the 10-year period? Provide one reason (based on the text) that NAIRU could increase.

4. The diagram on the next page shows a simple *AD/AS* diagram. The economy begins at E_0 with real GDP equal to Y^*.

   a. At E_0, the unemployment rate is 8%. What type of unemployment is this?

   b. A positive aggregate demand shock now shifts the *AD* curve to *AD'*. At E_1 the unemployment rate is only 6.5%. Is there cyclical unemployment at E_1?

   c. Describe the economy's adjustment process to E_2.

   d. What is the unemployment rate at E_2?

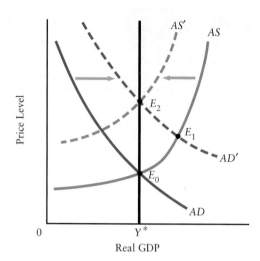

5. The diagram below shows a simple *AD/AS* diagram. The economy begins at E_0 with real GDP equal to potential GDP.

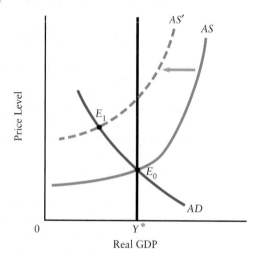

a. At E_0, the unemployment rate is 6%. What type of unemployment is this?

b. A negative aggregate supply shock now shifts the *AS* curve to *AS'*. At E_1 the unemployment rate is 7.5% Is there cyclical unemployment at E_1? How much?

c. If monetary and fiscal policy do not react to the shock, describe the economy's adjustment process to its long-run equilibrium.

d. What is the unemployment rate at the economy's long-run equilibrium? Explain.

6. The diagram below shows a perfectly competitive labour market. The initial equilibrium is with wage w^* and employment L^*.

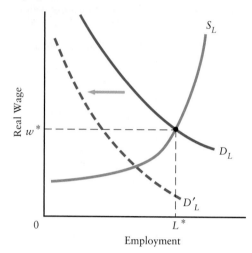

a. Suppose the demand for labour decreases to D'_L. If wages are perfectly flexible, what is the effect on wages and employment? Show this in the diagram.

b. Is there any involuntary unemployment in part (a) after the shock?

c. Now suppose wages can only adjust half as much as in part (a)—that is, wages are sticky. What is the effect on wages and employment in this case? Show this in the diagram.

d. Is there any involuntary unemployment in part (c) after the shock? How much?

7. Consider an economy that begins with real GDP equal to potential. There is then a sudden increase in the prices of raw materials, which shifts the *AS* curve upwards.

a. Draw the initial long-run equilibrium in an *AD/AS* diagram.

b. Now show the immediate effect of the supply shock in your diagram.

c. Suppose that wages and prices in this economy adjust instantly to shocks. Describe what happens to unemployment in this economy. Explain.

d. If wages and prices adjust only slowly to shocks, what happens to unemployment? Explain.

e. Explain why the key difference between New Keynesian and New Classical theories of unemployment involves the degree of wage and price flexibility.

8. The table on the next page shows the percentage of the labour force accounted for by youths (15–24 years old) and older workers (25 years and older) over several years. Suppose that, due to their lower skills and greater

turnover, youths have a higher unemployment rate than older workers (see Figure 31-4).

Year	Percentage of Labour Force	
	Youths	Older Workers
1	20	80
2	21	79
3	22	78
4	23	77
5	25	75
6	27	73
7	29	71
8	31	69

a. Suppose that in Year 1 real GDP is equal to potential GDP, and the unemployment rate among older workers is 6% but is 14% among youths. What is the economy's NAIRU?
b. Now suppose that for the next eight years real GDP remains equal to potential. Compute the value of NAIRU for each year.
c. Explain why NAIRU rises even though output is always equal to potential.

DISCUSSION QUESTIONS

1. Interpret the following statements from newspapers in terms of types of unemployment.
   a. "Recession hits local factory; 2000 laid off."
   b. "Of course, I could take a job as a dishwasher, but I'm trying to find something that makes use of my high school education," says a local teenager in our survey of the unemployed.
   c. "Retraining is the best reaction to the increased use of robots."
   d. "Uneven upturn: Signs of recovery in Alberta, but Ontario is still in recession."

2. Discuss the following views. Is it possible that both views are right? Explain.
   a. "Canadian workers should resist automation, which is destroying their jobs," says a labour leader.
   b. "Given the fierce foreign competition faced by Canadian firms, it's a case of automate or die," says an industrialist.

3. "No one needs to be out of work if he or she really wants a job; just look at the Help Wanted signs in many fast-food businesses and retail shops." Does the existence of the unfilled vacancies suggested in the quotation imply that there need be no cyclical unemployment as long as workers are not excessively fussy about the kinds of jobs they will take?

4. What differences in approach toward the problem of unemployment are suggested by the following facts?
   a. In the 1960s and 1970s, Britain spent billions of dollars on subsidizing firms that would otherwise have gone out of business in order to protect the jobs of the employees.
   b. Sweden has been a pioneer in spending large sums to retrain and to relocate displaced workers.

5. Advocates of discretionary fiscal policy often argue that the government can reduce unemployment by increasing spending on such things as highways, bridges, sewer systems, and so on. What do you think of such a policy to "create jobs"? Is such a policy equally likely to create jobs during a recession as when the economy is already operating at potential output? Explain.

6. Consider two hypothetical countries. In Country A, 20 percent of the labour force is unemployed for half the year and employed for the other half; the remaining 80 percent of the labour force is never unemployed. In Country B, 100 percent of the labour force is unemployed for 10 percent of the year and employed for the other 90 percent of the year. Note that both countries have an overall unemployment rate of 10 percent. Discuss which of these countries seems to have the more serious unemployment problem, and explain why.

7. There is a great deal of debate over the appropriate level of generosity for Canada's employment insurance program.
   a. Explain what problem can be caused by having an EI system that is too generous.
   b. Explain what problem can be caused by having an EI system that is not generous enough.
   c. If EI generosity were reduced and the NAIRU declined as a result, is this necessarily a desirable outcome?

CHAPTER 32

Government Debt and Deficits

1 Explain how the government's annual budget deficit (or surplus) is related to its stock of debt.

2 Explain the meaning of the cyclically adjusted budget deficit, and how it can be used to measure the stance of fiscal policy.

3 Define Ricardian Equivalence.

4 Explain how deficits crowd out investment and net exports.

5 Explain why a high stock of debt may hamper monetary and fiscal policy.

6 Discuss several different proposals for balancing the budget.

Until the late 1990s, no single measure associated with the government was the focus of more attention and controversy than the size of the government budget deficit. Some people argued that the deficit was an economic time bomb, waiting to explode and cause serious harm to our living standards. Others argued that the only real danger posed by deficits was from the dramatic policy changes proposed to eliminate them. By 2004, after two decades of debate about the budget deficit, the focus had shifted to what the governments—federal and provincial—should do with their actual and projected budget surpluses. Just as debates once raged over the harmful effects of high government budget deficits, debates currently rage about whether governments that are facing budget surpluses should increase spending, reduce taxes, or use the surpluses to reduce the outstanding stock of government debt.

In this chapter, we examine various issues surrounding government debt, deficits, and surpluses. We begin by considering the simple arithmetic of government budgets. This tells us how the deficit or surplus in any given year is related to the outstanding stock of debt. We then explore why deficits and debt matter for the performance of the economy—as well as what changes we can expect over the near future if Canadian governments are successful in maintaining either balanced budgets or budget surpluses.

32.1 **Facts and Definitions**

There is a simple relationship between the government's expenditures, its tax revenues, and its borrowing. This relationship is summarized in what economists call the government's *budget constraint*.

The Government's Budget Constraint

As is true for any individual's expenditures, government expenditures must be financed either by income or by borrowing. The difference between individuals and governments, however, is that governments typically do not earn income by selling products or labour services; instead, they earn income by levying taxes. Thus, all government expenditure must be financed either by tax revenues or by borrowing. This point is illustrated by the following simple equation, which is called the government's *budget constraint:*

$$\text{Government expenditure} = \text{Tax revenue} + \text{Borrowing}$$

We divide government expenditure into two categories. The first is purchases of goods and services, G. The second is the interest payments on the outstanding stock of debt; this is referred to as **debt-service payments** and is denoted $i \times D$, where i is the interest rate and D is the stock of government debt. A third category of government spending is *transfers* to individuals and firms (such as employment-insurance benefits and industrial subsidies) but, as we did in earlier chapters, we include transfers as part of T, which is the government's *net tax revenue* (tax revenue minus transfers). The government's budget constraint can therefore be rewritten as

$$G + i \times D = T + \text{Borrowing}$$

or, subtracting T from both sides,

$$(G + i \times D) - T = \text{Borrowing}$$

This equation simply says that any excess of total government spending over net tax revenues must be financed by government borrowing.

The government's annual **budget deficit** is the excess of total government expenditure over net tax revenues in a given year. From the budget constraint above, this annual deficit is exactly the same as the amount borrowed by the government during the year. Since the government borrows by issuing bonds and selling them to lenders, borrowing by the government increases the government's outstanding stock of debt. Since D is the outstanding stock of government debt, ΔD is the *change* in the stock of debt during the course of the year. The budget deficit can therefore be written as

$$\text{Budget deficit} = \Delta D = (G + i \times D) - T$$

The government's annual budget deficit is the excess of total expenditure over net tax revenues in a given year. It is also equal to the change in the stock of government debt during the year.

Notice two points about budget deficits. First, a change in the size of the deficit requires a change in the level of expenditures *relative* to the level of net tax revenues. For a given level of net tax revenues, a smaller deficit can come about only through a reduction in government expenditures; conversely, for a given level of expenditures, a smaller deficit requires an increase in net tax revenues. Second, since the deficit is equal to the amount of new government borrowing, the stock of **government debt** will rise whenever the budget deficit is positive. Even a drastic reduction in the size of the annual budget deficit is therefore not sufficient to reduce the outstanding stock of

debt-service payments Payments that represent the interest owed on a current stock of debt.

budget deficit Any shortfall of current revenue below current expenditure.

government debt The outstanding stock of financial liabilities for the government, equal to the accumulation of past budget deficits.

budget surplus Any excess of current revenue over current expenditure.

government debt; the stock of debt will fall only if the budget deficit becomes *negative*. In this case, there is said to be a **budget surplus.**

A budget deficit increases the stock of debt; a budget surplus reduces it.

The Primary Budget Deficit

Government expenditure comprises purchases of goods and services (G), and debt-service payments ($i \times D$). Since at any point in time the outstanding stock of government debt—determined by *past* government borrowing—cannot be influenced by current government policy, the debt-service component of total expenditures is beyond the control of the government. In contrast, the other components of the government's budget are said to be *discretionary* because the government can choose to change the levels of G or T. To capture the part of the total budget deficit that is attributable to discretionary expenditures and revenues, the government's **primary budget deficit** is defined as the difference between the total budget deficit and the debt-service payments:

primary budget deficit The difference between the government's overall budget deficit and its debt-service payments.

$$
\begin{aligned}
\text{Primary budget deficit} &= \text{Total budget deficit} - \text{Debt-service payments} \\
&= (G + i \times D - T) - i \times D \\
&= G - T
\end{aligned}
$$

The government's primary budget deficit shows the extent to which net tax revenues are able to finance the *discretionary* part of total expenditure. Another name for discretionary expenditure is the government's *program spending*.

It is possible that the government has an overall budget deficit but a *primary* budget surplus, indicating that net tax revenues more than cover program spending but are insufficient to fully cover debt-service payments as well. For example, in the 1996–1997 fiscal year, the federal government had an overall budget deficit of $13.7 billion while debt-service payments were $45.2 billion. There was thus a primary budget *surplus* in that year of $31.5 billion—that is, total net tax revenues exceeded program expenditures by $31.5 billion. By the next fiscal year, the federal government had eliminated the deficit and actually had an overall budget surplus of $3.2 billion. Debt-service payments were $44 billion, so the primary budget surplus was $47.2 billion. In very recent years the situation has been the same: the overall budget was close to balanced but there was a significant primary budget surplus.

The primary budget deficit is the difference between the overall budget deficit and the level of debt-service payments. In recent years, the federal government has had a primary budget surplus, indicating that tax revenues were more than sufficient to cover program expenditures.

For an illustration of the government's budget constraint, and of the distinction between overall budget deficits and primary budget deficits, see Figure 32-1. This distinction becomes very important when we examine changes in the debt-to-GDP ratio later in the chapter.

FIGURE 32-1   An Illustration of the Government's Budget Constraint

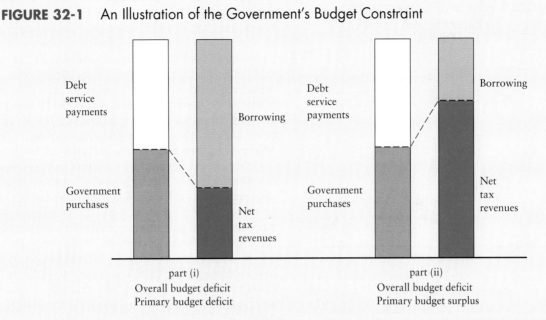

part (i)
Overall budget deficit
Primary budget deficit

part (ii)
Overall budget deficit
Primary budget surplus

The sum of all expenditures by government must be financed either by tax collection or by borrowing. The deficit is the difference between total expenditures and net tax revenue; it is also equal to the total level of borrowing. In both parts of the figure, the government's budget constraint is illustrated by the fact that the two bars are the same height, showing that total expenditures must be equal to net tax revenues plus borrowing. In both parts there is an overall budget deficit because net tax revenues are not sufficient to finance total expenditures (and so there is positive borrowing). In part (i), net taxes are not even enough to cover government purchases, and so there is a primary budget deficit. In part (ii), net taxes are more than enough to cover government purchases, and so there is a primary budget surplus (even though there is an overall budget deficit).

Deficits and Debt in Canada

Federal Government

In a growing economy, many macroeconomic variables such as the levels of government expenditure and tax revenue tend also to grow. As a result, rather than looking at the absolute size of the government deficit or debt, economists focus on government debt and deficits in relation to the overall size of the economy. Some budget deficits that would be unmanageable in a small country like New Zealand might be quite acceptable for a larger country like Canada, and trivial for a huge economy like the United States. Similarly, a government budget deficit that seemed crushing in Canada in 1904 might appear trivial in 2004 because the size of the Canadian economy is many times larger now than it was then.

For the most recent federal budget
forecasts, see the website for the
Department of Finance: www.fin.gc.ca.

The path of federal budget deficits since 1962 is shown in Figure 32-2. The top panel shows total federal spending and total federal tax revenues as percentages of GDP. The bottom panel shows the total federal deficit as a percentage of GDP. Large and persistent deficits began in the mid-1970s and lasted until the mid-1990s.

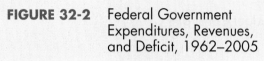

FIGURE 32-2   Federal Government Expenditures, Revenues, and Deficit, 1962–2005

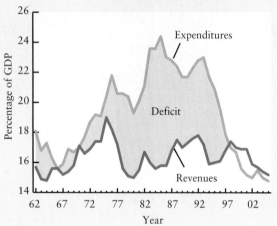

(i) Revenues and expenditures

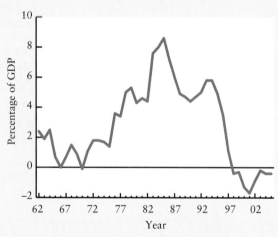

(ii) The budget deficit

The federal budget was in deficit every year between 1971 and 1997, but since 1998 there have been small budget surpluses. Part (i) shows revenues and expenditures as a percentage of GDP. Part (ii) shows the budget deficit (or surplus) as a percentage of GDP. In both parts of the figure, the values shown for 2003–05 are forecasts made at the time of the 2003 federal budget.

(*Source:* Department of Finance *Fiscal Reference Tables* and *2003 Budget*. Reproduced with the permission of the Minister of Public Works and Government Services Canada, 2003. See the Department of Finance website to access these documents: www.fin.gc.ca.)

The substantial increase in the budget deficit in the early 1980s reflects the combined effects of the severe recession in 1982, some mild discretionary fiscal expansion, and increased interest payments on the government's debt. This last element was due in part to the higher real interest rates in the early 1980s and the accumulation of the deficits in the late 1970s that added to the stock of government debt. The effects of a strong economic recovery in the late 1980s, combined with active measures on the part of the federal government, then resulted in a reduction in the deficit. By 1989, at the beginning of a significant economic downturn, the deficit was just under 5 percent of GDP. The recession of 1991 again pushed up the deficit, but by then the large stock of federal government debt made the federal government reluctant to let the deficit rise considerably. As a result, by 1993, two years into a slow economic recovery, the federal budget deficit had increased only to 5.8 percent of GDP. As the recovery progressed further, and the federal government continued its policy of reducing the deficit, the deficit fell rapidly until finally being eliminated in the 1997–98 fiscal year. In the past six years, the federal government has had small surpluses.

As we saw in the previous section, a deficit implies that the stock of government debt is rising. Thus, the persistent deficits that began in the 1970s have their counterpart in a steadily rising stock of government debt. Figure 32-3 shows the path of Canadian federal government debt since 1940. At the beginning of the Second World War, the stock of federal debt was equal to about 45 percent of GDP. The enormous increase in the debt-to-GDP ratio over the next five years reflects wartime borrowing used to finance military expenditures. From 1946 to 1974, however, there was a continual decline in the debt-to-GDP ratio. The economy was growing quickly during this period. But equally important was that the federal government in the postwar years typically ran significant budget surpluses. These two factors explain the dramatic decline in the debt-to-GDP ratio between 1946 and 1974.

By 1974 the federal debt was only 14 percent of GDP. The large and persistent budget deficits beginning in the mid-1970s, however, along with a general slowdown in the rate of economic growth, led to a significant upward trend in the debt-to-GDP ratio. The ratio climbed steadily from 1979 to 1996 when it peaked at over 69 percent of GDP. Then, with the significant reductions in the deficit beginning in 1996, the debt-to-GDP ratio began to fall. By 2002 the federal government's stock of debt was just below 47 percent of GDP, and was projected to fall below 40 percent by 2005.

Provincial Governments

Canada is relatively special among developed countries in the sense that its provincial governments are responsible for a significant fraction of total government revenues and expenditures. In many countries, sizable regional governments either do not exist, as in New Zealand, or are often required to run balanced budgets, as is the case for about two-thirds of the 50 states in the United States. In contrast, the size of Canadian provincial governments—measured by their spending and taxing powers relative to that of the federal government—means that an examination of government debt and deficits in Canada would not be complete without paying attention to the provincial governments' fiscal positions.

For example, in the 2002–03 fiscal year, the federal government had $193 billion of tax revenues, representing 16.2 percent of GDP. In the same year, the combined provincial and territorial governments had more tax revenues—a total of $247 billion, or 20.8 percent of GDP.

When examining the size and effects of budget deficits or surpluses, it is important to consider all levels of government—federal, provincial, and municipal.

During the 1970s, the provincial governments were running budget deficits and so the stock of provincial government debt was increasing. But the deficits were small enough for the debt not to be growing relative to GDP. During the 1980s and early 1990s, however, provincial deficits grew dramatically. The provincial debt grew from roughly 4 percent of GDP in 1980 to 20 percent in 1993. Since then, most provincial governments have reduced or eliminated their deficits, and some are operating small surpluses.

An International Perspective

Figure 32-4 shows how the size of government debt in Canada compares with that in the other major developed economies.[1] Canada's debt (combining all levels of government) is slightly above average among the G7 countries. The two high-debt countries are Japan and Italy. Italy, with a debt-to-GDP ratio of almost

The Canadian government ran very large budget deficits to finance Canada's participation in the Second World War. As a result, Canada's debt increased to 110 percent of GDP by 1946.

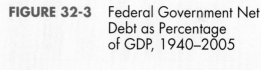

FIGURE 32-3   Federal Government Net Debt as Percentage of GDP, 1940–2005

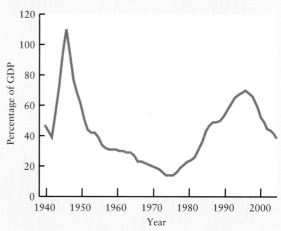

The federal government's debt-to-GDP ratio fell dramatically after the Second World War and continued falling until 1975. It then increased markedly for the next two decades. In the late 1990s when government deficits were reduced and the economy was in a healthy recovery, the debt-to-GDP ratio began to fall. The data for 2003–05 are forecasts made at the time of the 2003 federal budget.

(*Source:* Statistics Canada, CANSIM database, Series V151548, and authors' calculations.)

---

[1] These data are not directly comparable with those in Figure 32-3 for two reasons. First, Figure 32-4 shows the debt of all levels of government combined, whereas Figure 32-3 shows just federal government debt. Second, Figure 32-4 shows *gross* debt whereas Figure 32-3 shows *net* debt. Gross debt is higher than net debt in Canada because some federal debt is held as an asset by provincial governments.

FIGURE 32-4   Consolidated Government Gross Debt, G7 Countries, 2001

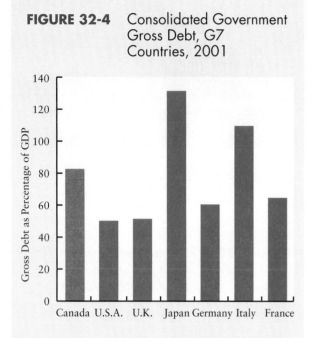

Canada's government debt is slightly above average by the standards of the richest developed countries. The debt-to-GDP ratios shown here are for the year 2001. The data are for all levels of government combined.

(*Source:* These data are available on the website for the Organization for Economic Cooperation and Development (OECD): www.oecd.org.)

fiscal policy The use of the government's tax and spending policies in an effort to influence the level of GDP.

For macroeconomic data that are comparable across countries, see the OECD's website: www.oecd.org.

110 percent, has been a high-debt country for many years. Japan, in contrast, has only recently become a high-debt country. In the late 1990s, in an attempt to stimulate its stagnant economy, Japan increased its government spending considerably. As a result of the fiscal expansion and a significant recession, Japan's debt-to-GDP ratio increased by 40 percentage points between 1995 and 2000.

32.2 **Some Analytical Issues**

In the next section we discuss some potential effects of budget deficits and surpluses on the aggregate economy. Before doing this, however, we must examine some basic analytical issues: deficits and the stance of fiscal policy; changes in the debt-to-GDP ratio; and the relationship between government deficits and national saving.

The Stance of Fiscal Policy

In Chapters 22 and 24 we examined **fiscal policy,** which is the use of government spending and tax polices to alter real GDP. We noted there that changes in expenditure and taxation normally lead to changes in the government's budget deficit or surplus. Thus, it is tempting to view changes in the government's budget deficit as the result of changes in fiscal policy. For example, we could interpret a decrease in the deficit as indicating a contractionary fiscal policy, since the fall in the deficit is associated with either a reduction in government expenditures or an increase in tax revenue (or both). Was the dramatic fall in the Canadian federal budget deficit between 1995 and 1999 *purely* the result of fiscal policy?

No. In general, only some changes in the deficit are due to discretionary changes in the government's expenditure or taxation policies. Other changes have nothing to do with explicit changes in policy, but instead are the result of changes in the level of economic activity that are outside the influence of government policy. If our goal is to judge the stance of fiscal policy, however, it is only the changes in the deficit *caused by changes in policy* that are relevant.

The Budget Deficit Function

To see why the budget deficit can rise or fall even when there is no change in fiscal policy, recall the equation defining the government's budget deficit.

$$\text{Budget deficit} = (G + i \times D) - T$$

The level of net taxes (taxes minus transfers) typically depends on the level of national income, even with unchanged policy. For example, as income rises the level of revenue raised through income taxation also rises. Furthermore, as income rises there are typically fewer transfers (such as welfare or employment insurance) made to the private sector. Thus, net taxes, T, increase when national income increases. In contrast, the level of government purchases and debt-service payments can be viewed as more or less independent of the level of national income, at least over short periods of time. Thus, with no changes in expenditure or taxation policies, the budget deficit will tend to increase in recessions and fall in booms. That is, there is a negative relationship between national income and the government's budget deficit.

For a given spending and taxing policy, the budget deficit rises as real GDP falls, and falls as real GDP rises.

Figure 32-5 plots this basic relationship, which is called the **budget deficit function.** When the government determines its expenditure and taxation polices, it determines the *position* of the budget deficit function. A more expansionary fiscal policy shifts the budget deficit function up. A more contractionary fiscal policy shifts the budget deficit function down. In contrast, a change in the level of real GDP in the absence of any policy change will represent a *movement along* the budget deficit function. Thus, for a given set of policies, the budget deficit will decrease when Y rises and increase when Y falls.

budget deficit function   A relationship that plots the government's budget deficit as a function of the level of real GDP.

cyclically adjusted deficit (CAD)   An estimate of what the government budget deficit would be if real GDP were at its potential level.

Fiscal policy determines the position of the budget deficit function. Changes in real GDP lead to movements along a given budget deficit function.

The Cyclically Adjusted Deficit

Given the problem of using the budget deficit to gauge the stance of fiscal policy, economists define the **cyclically adjusted deficit** (CAD) as the budget deficit that would exist with the current set of policies if real GDP were equal to potential GDP, Y^*. This is also called the *structural budget deficit* or the *full-employment budget deficit*. This is shown in Figure 32-6. All changes in the cyclically adjusted deficit reflect changes in the stance of fiscal policy, because they come only from shifts in the budget deficit function.

Figure 32-7 shows the cyclically adjusted deficit in Canada, and plots it together with the actual budget deficit. Both are expressed as percentages of GDP and represent the combined budget deficits of all levels of government. Unlike the actual budget deficit, which can be precisely measured, the cyclically adjusted deficit can only be estimated. The reason is that its value depends on the value of potential GDP, Y^*, which itself is not directly observable and hence must be estimated. Note from Figure 32-7 that the actual deficit is larger than the cyclically adjusted deficit during times of recessionary gaps such as 1981–1985 and 1990–1997. This relationship reflects the fact that during these periods actual GDP is less than poten-

FIGURE 32-5   The Budget Deficit Function

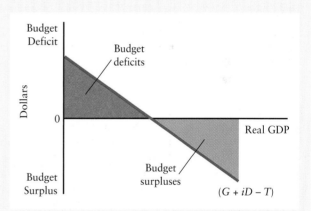

For given government purchases and debt-service payments, there is a negative relationship between real GDP and the government budget deficit. G and iD are independent of the level of real GDP. In contrast, a rise in real GDP leads to higher tax revenues and lower transfers, and thus to higher net tax revenue, T. Thus, the budget deficit falls as real GDP increases. Therefore, even with unchanged fiscal policies, changes in real GDP will lead to changes in the budget deficit.

An expansionary fiscal policy implies an increase in spending or a reduction in taxes *at any level of real GDP*, and thus an upward shift of the budget deficit function. A contractionary fiscal policy shifts the budget deficit function down.

FIGURE 32-6   The Cyclically Adjusted Budget Deficit

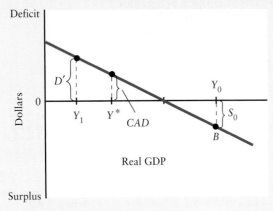

(i) Change in the measured deficit

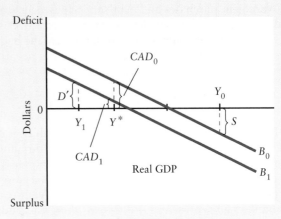

(ii) Change in the cyclically adjusted deficit

The cyclically adjusted deficit is the deficit that would exist if real GDP were equal to Y^*. The budget deficit function is labelled B. In part (i), the cyclically adjusted deficit (CAD) is a deficit. At a sufficiently high income Y_0, the actual budget would be in surplus by an amount S_0. At output lower than Y^*, such as Y_1, the actual budget would be in deficit by D', more than the amount of the CAD. Along the curve in part (i), fiscal policy is unchanged. The deficit (and surplus) changes only because real GDP changes.

Part (ii) shows how the actual deficit (or surplus) might move in a different direction from the CAD. Suppose the economy starts at Y_0, with fiscal policy given by B_0. If fiscal policy is made more restrictive, through some combination of higher taxes and lower government purchases, the budget deficit function shifts to B_1. At the same time, if output should fall to Y_1, the budget surplus of S will turn into a deficit of D'. By looking at the actual budget balance, one would see the budget move from surplus to deficit, suggesting, incorrectly, that fiscal policy had become more stimulative. Focusing on the CAD, however, the level of budget balance at Y^* makes it clear that B_1 is more restrictive than B_0; that is, the CAD is smaller with the fiscal policy given by B_1 than that given by B_0.

Practise with Study Guide Chapter 32, Exercise 2.

tial GDP and thus actual tax revenues are *less than they would be if output were equal to potential.* Conversely, the actual budget deficit is less than the cyclically adjusted deficit during periods of inflationary gaps, such as 1986–1990, reflecting the fact that during these periods actual GDP is greater than potential and thus tax revenues are *greater than they would be if output were equal to potential.* In those years where the actual deficit is approximately equal to the cyclically adjusted deficit, such as 1985, 1990, and 1999, real GDP is approximately equal to potential.

The stance of fiscal policy is shown by the *changes* in the cyclically adjusted deficit. For example, the dramatic rise in the cyclically adjusted deficit from 1981 to 1985 reveals a considerable fiscal expansion; the decline from 1985 through 1987 reveals a fiscal contraction. From 1987 to 1993, the path of the cyclically adjusted deficit suggests that the stance of fiscal policy was roughly constant. Since 1993, the decline in the cyclically adjusted deficit reflects a very considerable fiscal contraction.

The stance of fiscal policy—that is, whether fiscal policy is expansionary or contractionary—is determined by changes in the cyclically adjusted deficit.

The Debt-to-GDP Ratio

In order to gauge the importance of government deficits and debt they should be considered relative to the size of the economy. This is why economists often discuss the federal government's debt-to-GDP ratio rather than the absolute amount of government debt. Here we examine the link between the overall budget deficit, the primary budget deficit, and changes in the debt-to-GDP ratio.

Changes in the Debt-to-GDP Ratio

With a little algebra, it is possible to write a simple expression that relates the government's primary budget deficit to the change in the debt-to-GDP ratio. (To see the complete derivation of this equation, see *Extensions in Theory 32-1*.) The equation is:

$$\Delta d = x + (r - g) \times d$$

where d is the debt-to-GDP ratio, x is the government's *primary* budget deficit as a percentage of GDP, r is the real interest rate on government bonds, g is the growth rate of real GDP, and Δd is the *change* in the debt-to-GDP ratio.

This simple equation shows two separate forces that tend to increase the debt-to-GDP ratio. First, if the real interest rate exceeds the growth rate of real GDP (if r exceeds g), the debt-to-GDP ratio will rise, and Δd will be positive. Second, if the government has a *primary* budget deficit (if x is positive), the debt-to-GDP ratio will rise.

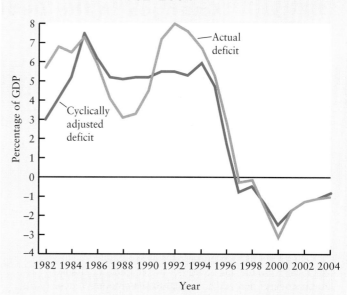

FIGURE 32-7   The Actual and Cyclically Adjusted Deficit, Combined Government, 1982–2004

The difference between the actual budget deficit and the cyclically adjusted budget deficit reveals the level of output compared to potential. The changes in the cyclically adjusted deficit show changes in the stance of fiscal policy. The actual budget deficit is above the cyclically adjusted budget deficit when output is below potential; the actual deficit is less than the cyclically adjusted deficit when output is above potential. An increase in the cyclically adjusted deficit reveals a fiscal expansion; a decrease reveals a fiscal contraction. The values for 2003 and 2004 are forecasts.

(*Source: OECD Economic Outlook*, June 2003.)

Real Interest Rates.   It is the *real* interest rate, and not the nominal interest rate, that is important for determining the change in the debt-to-GDP ratio. Many commentators argue that high nominal interest rates are largely responsible for increasing the government's debt-service requirements and thus pushing up the deficit and debt. But this view is only partly correct. Although it is the nominal interest rate that determines how a given stock of debt will accumulate over time, this view misses the point that it is the accumulation of the *real* stock of debt that matters in terms of the government's *real* financial liabilities. Although high nominal interest rates increase the government's debt-service requirements, the accompanying high inflation reduces the real value of the government's debt. The accumulation of the government's stock of *real* debt therefore depends on the difference between the nominal interest rate and the rate of inflation. This difference is simply the real interest rate, r. It follows, therefore, that changes in the

EXTENSIONS IN THEORY 32-1

Changes in the Debt-to-GDP Ratio

This box derives the simple equation in the text describing the change in the debt-to-GDP ratio. Let d be the debt-to-GDP ratio and let Δd be the amount by which d changes annually. Since d is a ratio, its change over time depends on the change in the numerator relative to the change in the denominator. That is, the debt-to-GDP ratio will increase if the stock of debt grows more quickly than GDP; it will decrease if the stock of debt grows less quickly than GDP. Representing the *percentage change* in d as $\Delta d/d$, we have*

$$\frac{\Delta d}{d} = \frac{\Delta D}{D} - \frac{\Delta GDP}{GDP}$$

Think about each of these terms separately. As you will recall from the first section of this chapter, the change in the stock of debt, ΔD, is equal to the amount of new government borrowing—that is, it is equal to the budget deficit. From the government's budget constraint, the deficit is equal to $(G + i \times D - T)$. The second term in the equation above is the growth rate of nominal GDP. Note that the growth rate of nominal GDP depends on both the rate of growth of real output and the rate of inflation. If we let g be the rate of growth of *real* GDP and π be the rate of inflation, then $g + \pi$ is the growth rate of nominal GDP.

_____

*For any variable X that is equal to the ratio of two other variables, Y/Z, the percentage change in X is closely approximated by the percentage change in Y minus the percentage change in Z. The lower are the rates of change of Y and Z, the better is this approximation.

We therefore rewrite the previous expression to get

$$\frac{\Delta d}{d} = \frac{G - T + i \times D}{D} - (g + \pi)$$

Now we multiply both sides by d to get an expression for the absolute change in the debt-to-GDP ratio:

$$\Delta d = \frac{G - T + i \times D}{D} \times d - (g + \pi) \times d$$

Since d is equal to D/GDP, it follows that d/D is equal to $1/GDP$. Our equation can thus be simplified:

$$\Delta d = \frac{G - T + i \times D}{GDP} - (g + \pi) \times d$$

Now recall that $(G - T)$ is the primary budget deficit. Let x be this primary budget deficit *as a percentage of GDP* and express the debt-service payments also as a percentage of GDP. This gives

$$\Delta d = x + i \times d - (g + \pi) \times d$$

Finally, recall that the real interest rate is equal to the nominal interest rate minus the rate of inflation,

$$r = i - \pi$$

We now combine terms to get

$$\Delta d = x + (r - g) \times d$$

which is the equation shown in the text.

debt-to-GDP ratio (which is a *real* variable) depend on the difference between the real interest rate, r, and the growth rate of real GDP, g.

The Primary Deficit.   If our focus is to be on the debt-to-GDP ratio, rather than on the absolute size of the debt, then tracking the behaviour of the overall budget deficit may be misleading. Suppose that $r = g$ and thus the second term in the equation above is zero. Further, suppose that the government is running a small primary budget surplus, so that total tax revenues more than cover program spending. In this case, the primary surplus (x is negative) implies that the debt-to-GDP ratio is *falling;* but it is entirely possible that the overall budget deficit is positive, revealing simply that the debt-service payments exceed the primary surplus.

Practise with Study Guide Chapter 32, Exercise 3.

Stabilizing the Debt-to-GDP Ratio

Suppose the government's goal is to prevent further increases in the debt-to-GDP ratio. If the real interest rate on government bonds exceeds the growth rate of real GDP—a reasonable description of the Canadian economy over the past two decades—then a government with a positive stock of outstanding debt *must* run a primary surplus in order to stabilize the debt-to-GDP ratio. Furthermore, the larger is the real interest rate relative to the growth rate of GDP, the larger is the primary surplus required to stabilize the debt-to-GDP ratio.

To see this, let x^* be the value of the primary budget deficit that is consistent with a stable debt-to-GDP ratio—that is, x^* is the value of x such that Δd equals zero. From our equation above, setting Δd equal to zero results in

$$x^* = -(r - g) \times d$$

This equation shows the basic point that if the debt-to-GDP ratio is being pushed up by a real interest rate that exceeds the real growth rate of GDP, then a stable debt-to-GDP ratio is only possible with a negative value of x—that is, a primary budget surplus.

If the real interest rate on government bonds exceeds the growth rate of real GDP, stabilizing the debt-to-GDP ratio requires a primary budget surplus.

For an illustration of this central point, consider some of the numbers facing the federal minister of finance at the time of the February 2003 budget. The real interest rate on government debt was about 4 percent while the real growth rate of the economy was about 3 percent. Given the existing debt-to-GDP ratio of about 0.5, these data implied a value of x^* equal to $-(0.040 - 0.03) \times (0.50) = -0.005$. Thus, the federal government would have had to run a primary surplus of about 0.5 percent of GDP in order to keep the debt-to-GDP ratio constant. As it turned out, the actual primary surplus in 2003 was much bigger than necessary to stabilize the debt-to-GDP ratio. The primary surplus was about 4 percent of GDP, so the debt-to-GDP ratio declined.

The simple equation we discussed in the previous section can be used to identify the various causes of the accumulation of Canada's federal debt, and also to illustrate some useful policy lessons regarding debt reduction. For more details, look for "What Caused the Build-Up of Canada's Public Debt?" in the *Additional Topics* section of this book's Companion Website.

h t t p : / / w w w . p e a r s o n e d . c a / r a g a n

Government Deficits and National Saving

As we will see in the next section, the effects of government deficits on real GDP and interest rates depend in large part on the relationship between government deficits and national saving. We therefore examine this important issue now.

Defining Terms

As we saw in Chapter 21, private saving is the difference between disposable income and consumption. And as we saw in Chapter 22, government saving is the difference between government tax revenues and government purchases. That is, government saving is equal to the budget surplus.[2] National saving is the sum of government saving and private saving:

$$\text{National saving} = \text{Private saving} + \text{Government saving}$$

Since government saving is equal to the budget surplus, an increase in the budget deficit is a reduction in government saving.

$$\text{National saving} = \text{Private saving} - \text{Government budget deficit}$$

The effect of budget deficits on the level of national saving thus depends on the link between budget deficits and private saving. For example, suppose that the government budget deficit increases by $1 billion. If this *reduction* in government saving leads to an *increase* in private saving by exactly $1 billion, there will be no change in national saving. On the other hand, if private saving rises by less than $1 billion, national saving will fall as a result of the increase in the budget deficit.

What is the link between the government deficit and the level of private saving? The answer lies in recognizing that—eventually—all government expenditures must be financed by taxes. Earlier in the chapter we said that expenditures during any given year could be financed either by tax revenues or by borrowing. But money borrowed in one year must *eventually* be repaid. Thus, government borrowing today means higher taxes in the future to repay that debt.

Government debt is a postponed tax liability. An increase in the budget deficit today must be matched by an increase in taxes at some point in the future.

The link between government deficits and private saving then rests on the extent to which the current population of taxpayers recognizes the requirement for higher future taxes when the government increases its current borrowing. For example, if the government decides to reduce taxes this year by $5 billion and issue $5 billion in new bonds, do the taxpayers recognize that those bonds will need to be repaid with higher taxes ($5 billion plus interest) in the future?

Ricardian Equivalence

Ricardian Equivalence   The proposition that the method of financing government spending (taxes or borrowing) has no effect on national saving because private saving will just offset any government dissaving.

The link between government deficits and private saving is associated with the idea of **Ricardian Equivalence,** named after the Classical economist David Ricardo (1772–1823), and brought back to prominence among modern-day economists through the work of Robert Barro, currently at Harvard University. The central proposition of Ricardian Equivalence is that consumers recognize government borrowing as a future tax liability and thus they view taxes as *equivalent* to government borrowing in terms of the effect on their own wealth. Therefore, a reduction in taxes and an increase in borrowing (or the reverse case) does not affect the wealth of the private sector and thus does not affect their consumption behaviour.

---

[2] We continue with the simplifying assumption made in earlier chapters that governments do not save by investing in physical assets such as bridges, roads, and dams. The implication is that government saving is exactly equal to the budget surplus. Later in the chapter we relax this assumption when examining the effects of budget deficits on the economy's total investment.

An example to help you understand the basic idea of Ricardian Equivalence is illustrated in Figure 32-8. Suppose the government plans to have steadily growing purchases (G) and also knows that its net tax revenues will increase as the economy grows, though fluctuating over the course of the business cycle. Over time, the path of government purchases is financed by the path of net tax revenue. (In other words, the *present value* of the path of G is equal to the present value of the path of T.) The government now decides to reduce current taxes by $5 billion and thus decides to increase its current borrowing by $5 billion. If current taxpayers recognize that an increase in government borrowing of $5 billion today represents an increase in their future taxes of $5 billion (plus interest), the current generation of taxpayers will not feel any more or less wealthy as a result of the reduction in current taxes, and consequently will not change their level of current expenditure on goods and services. If their consumption is unchanged and their disposable income is higher by $5 billion, their current saving must increase by the full amount of the reduction in government saving. Thus, "Ricardian" consumers faced with a change in the government budget deficit will adjust their private saving so as to keep national saving constant.

Now suppose that current taxpayers *do* perceive an increase in their wealth when their current taxes are reduced. There are several reasons why this might be so. One possibility is that individuals might be short-sighted and thus tend to place more emphasis on current tax reductions than on tax increases in the distant future. This would certainly be true if today's generation of taxpayers knew that the future tax increases would have to be paid by other people. Another possibility is that there may be a great

FIGURE 32-8   A Tax Reduction and Ricardian Equivalence

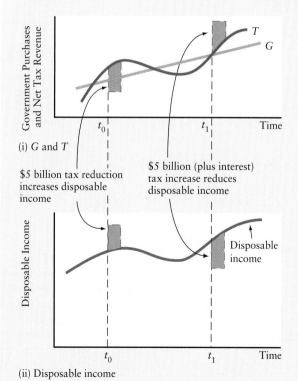

(i) G and T

$5 billion tax reduction increases disposable income

$5 billion (plus interest) tax increase reduces disposable income

Disposable income

(ii) Disposable income

For a given path of government expenditures, a reduction in taxes today must be matched with an increase in future taxes. Ricardian consumers will not feel wealthier as a result. Part (i) shows the initial path of government taxes and expenditures. Part (ii) shows the initial path of disposable income for the private sector.

If the government reduces taxes by $5 billion in year t_0, the deficit will be increased by that amount. Disposable income at t_0 will also increase by $5 billion. But in some future year, say t_1, the government will need to raise taxes by $5 billion (plus interest) to repay that debt. When this happens, the deficit will fall but so will disposable income. Ricardian consumers recognize that there is no change in their lifetime wealth and hence they do not spend more at t_0 when their disposable income rises. Non-Ricardian consumers do not foresee the tax increase at t_1 and thus *do* feel wealthier at t_0—they will increase their consumption at t_0.

deal of uncertainty about the government's future spending plans so that it is unclear whether the current tax reduction will be offset by future tax increases or matched by future expenditure reductions. Whatever the reason, suppose that the current generation *feels* wealthier as a result of the reduction in current taxes. We then expect them to increase their current expenditures on goods and services. As a result of the higher expenditures, private saving of such "non-Ricardian" individuals will therefore increase by less than the reduction in government saving, leading to an overall reduction in national saving.

"Ricardian" consumers will not feel wealthier as a result of government borrowing because they recognize the increase in their future tax liabilities. "Non-Ricardian" consumers do not recognize this future liability and thus feel wealthier when the government borrows.

Whether taxpayers recognize the future tax liabilities associated with government deficits is ultimately an empirical question. Most evidence suggests that Ricardian Equivalence does not hold completely. That is, the evidence suggests that an increase in the government deficit by $5 billion will be associated with an increase in private saving by less than $5 billion and thus a fall in national saving.

Most evidence suggests that an increase in the government deficit leads to a decrease in the level of national saving.

32.3 The Effects of Government Debt and Deficits

Let's now examine why we should care about the size of the government deficit or surplus. We begin with the important idea that deficits *crowd out* private-sector activity and thereby harm future generations. The opposite idea is equally important—that budget surpluses *crowd in* private-sector activity and are therefore beneficial to future generations. In this section, we pose the issue as the effects of budget deficits. At the end of the section we review the arguments by discussing the effects of budget surpluses.

Do Deficits Crowd Out Private Activity?

It is useful to make the distinction between closed and open economies. We consider the two cases separately.

Investment in Closed Economies

We know from Chapter 26, in which we examined the relationship between saving and investment, that in a closed economy saving must exactly equal investment. The only way that a closed economy can save is to accumulate physical capital. Suppose in a closed economy there is an increase in the budget deficit brought about by a reduction in taxes. What is the effect on domestic investment? As we saw in the previous section, the answer to this question depends on the degree to which taxpayers are Ricardian—that is, on the degree to which current taxpayers recognize that today's deficit must be financed by higher future taxes. If taxpayers are not purely Ricardian, private saving will rise by

Practise with Study Guide Chapter 32, Extension Exercise E1.

less than the fall in government saving. This response implies a decrease in the supply of national saving. As we saw in Chapter 26, the decrease in the supply of national saving will lead to an excess demand for loanable funds and thus to an increase in the interest rate. As the real interest rate increases, those components of aggregate demand that are sensitive to the interest rate—investment in particular—will fall. The result is what is called the **crowding out** of domestic investment; it is shown in Figure 32-9.

If a government budget deficit leads to a reduction in national saving and a rise in the interest rate, the result will be a crowding out of private investment.

Net Exports in Open Economies

The effect of budget deficits in an open economy is a little different. Consider once again the possibility that the Canadian government reduces taxes and increases its budget deficit. Furthermore, suppose taxpayers are not purely Ricardian so that private saving rises by less than the fall in government saving. What is the effect of such a fall in national saving in an open economy like Canada's? As real interest rates rise in Canada, foreigners are attracted to the higher-yield Canadian assets and thus foreign financial capital flows into Canada. But since Canadian dollars are required in order to buy Canadian interest-earning assets, this capital inflow increases the demand for Canadian dollars and thus leads to an appreciation of the Canadian dollar.

This appreciation makes Canadian goods more expensive relative to foreign goods, inducing an increase in imports and a reduction in exports, thereby reducing Canada's net exports. In an open economy like Canada's, therefore, a rise in the government deficit leads to an appreciation of the currency and to a crowding out of net exports.

In an open economy, instead of driving up interest rates sufficiently to crowd out private investment, the government budget deficit attracts foreign financial capital and appreciates the domestic currency. The result is a crowding out of net exports.

The Long-Term Burden of the Debt

In a closed economy, a rise in the government deficit pushes up interest rates and crowds out domestic investment. In an open economy a rise in the government deficit appreciates the currency and crowds

FIGURE 32-9   The Crowding Out of Investment

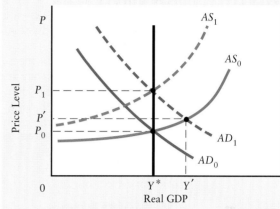

(i) Aggregate demand and supply

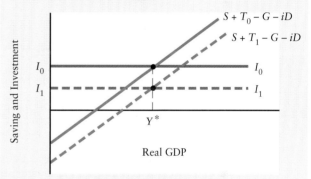

(ii) Saving and investment

For a closed economy whose real GDP equals potential, an increase in the budget deficit will cause a reduction in national saving and investment. Consider a closed economy that is in long-run equilibrium at Y^* and P_0 in part (i). The same equilibrium is shown in part (ii) as saving equal to investment at Y^* and I_0. Suppose the government reduces its taxes from T_0 to T_1, thus increasing the budget deficit. This raises desired aggregate expenditure (and lowers desired national saving) at all levels of income. In part (i), the new short-run equilibrium is at Y' and P'. The adjustment mechanism will then cause factor prices to rise, shifting the AS curve from AS_0 to AS_1. The new long-run equilibrium will be at Y^* and P_1.

The effect of this change on saving and investment can be seen in part (ii). At the new long-run equilibrium, real income is unchanged at Y^*, but the price level is higher. The demand for money has therefore increased, causing a rise in interest rates. These higher interest rates will reduce desired investment expenditure, shown in the figure as a reduction from I_0 to I_1.

crowding out
The offsetting reduction in private expenditure caused by the rise in interest rates that follows an expansionary fiscal policy.

out net exports. Despite the apparent differences in these two effects, they both imply a *long-term burden of government debt.*

The overall effect of the increase in the government deficit in a closed economy is a rise in the real interest rate and a fall in the level of domestic investment. But less current investment means a lower rate of capital accumulation and thus a lower rate of growth of potential output. This reduction in the growth rate is the long-term burden of government borrowing.

The overall effect of the increase in the government deficit in an open economy is an appreciation of the currency and a reduction in net exports. Recall from Chapter 22, however, that such a reduction in net exports implies a reduction in the country's *national asset formation.* Instead of having a smaller future capital stock as a result of the government's budget deficit, the country has an unchanged capital stock but *less of it is owned by domestic residents.* This reduced ownership lowers the domestic residents' future stream of income because payments must be paid to the foreign owners of the domestic capital stock. This reduction in the future stream of income for domestic residents is the long-term burden of the public debt in an open economy.

In both open and closed economies, the long-term burden of public debt takes the form of a lower future growth rate of income and consumption.

Does Government Debt Harm Future Generations?

The previous discussion reveals an important aspect of the costs of government debt and deficits:

Government deficits generate a redistribution of resources away from future generations toward the current generation.

After all, the government deficits are being used to finance goods and services that are provided to the current generation, but that will be financed by taxes levied on future generations.

This last sentence suggests that current government deficits are always financing goods and services that are provided to the current generation. Is this really true? Some government spending is on goods and services that will continue to be used well into the future. For example, if the government increases its current borrowing to finance the building of bridges or the expansion of highways, future generations will receive some of the benefits of this government spending. And, given that future generations will reap the benefits of some of these projects, it may be appropriate that future generations pay some of the taxes required to finance such projects.

Whether current government deficits impose a burden on future generations depends on the nature of the government goods and services being financed by the deficit. At one extreme, the government borrowing may finance a project that generates a return only to future generations, and thus the future generations may not be made worse off by today's budget deficit. An example might be the government's financing of long-term medical research projects that generate a return only in the distant future. Another example is the government's financing of a new highway. At the other extreme, the government deficit may finance some government program that benefits only the current generation, and thus the future generations are inappropriately saddled with the future tax bill. An example might be the government's financing of cultural or sporting events that benefit the current generation but produce little or no benefits for future generations.

Budget deficits used to finance investment projects may not harm future generations because the future generations will benefit from the investment.

The concern that deficits may be inappropriately placing a financial burden on future generations has led some economists to advocate the idea of *capital budgeting* by the government. Under this scheme, the government would essentially classify each of its expenditures as either consumption or investment; the former would be spending that mostly benefits the current generation while the latter would be spending that mostly benefits future generations.

With capital budgeting, government deficits could be used to minimize the undesirable redistributions of income between generations. For example, the government might be committed to borrowing no more in any given year than the expenditures classified as investments. In this way, future generations would receive benefits from current government spending that are approximately equivalent to the future taxes they will pay.

Does Government Debt Hamper Economic Policy?

The costs imposed on future generations by government debt are very real. Unfortunately, the fact that these costs sometimes occur in the very distant future often leads us to ignore their importance. But other costs associated with the presence of government debt are more immediately apparent. In particular, government debt may make the conduct of monetary and fiscal policy more difficult.

Monetary Policy

To see how a large stock of government debt can hamper the conduct of monetary policy, consider a country that has a high debt-to-GDP ratio and that has a real interest rate above the growth rate of GDP. As we saw previously, the debt-to-GDP ratio will continue to grow in this situation unless the government starts running significant primary budget *surpluses*. But such primary surpluses require either increases in taxation or reductions in program spending, both of which are politically unpopular. If such primary surpluses look unlikely to be achieved in the near future, both foreign and domestic creditors may come to expect the government to put pressure on the central bank to purchase—or *monetize*—an increasing portion of its deficit. Such monetization means that the money supply is increasing and will eventually be reflected in higher inflation. Any ensuing inflation would thus erode the real value of the bonds held by creditors. Such fears of future debt monetization will lead to expectations of future inflation and thus will put upward pressure on nominal interest rates and on some prices and wages. Thus, even in the absence of any actions by the central bank to increase the rate of growth of the money supply, a large government debt may lead to the *expectation* of future inflation, thus hampering the task of the central bank in keeping inflation and inflationary expectations low.

In December 1995, before the federal government had been successful in reducing its large annual budget deficits and thus slowing the rise of the debt-to-GDP ratio, the governor of the Bank of Canada at the time, Gordon Thiessen, appeared before the House of Commons Standing Committee on Public Accounts. His comments to that committee expressed this view that high levels of government debt generate concerns on the part of creditors.

> *. . . We would probably all agree . . . that our society needs to sort out its views about acceptable levels of taxation and the size of government, and those views can influence the amount of debt our society can afford to carry. However, when you reach a high debt-to-GDP ratio, what is sustainable is also very much influenced by the willingness of investors in financial markets to hold your debt.*

I do not mean to imply that financial markets might suddenly decide to stop lending to Canadian governments. What happens, as recent experience has shown, is that at very high levels of debt, there may be an increasing nervousness among lenders so that they would only continue to hold Canadian government debt at much higher interest rates.[3]

Fiscal Policy

In Chapter 22 we saw that fiscal policy could potentially be used to stabilize aggregate demand and thereby stabilize real GDP. For example, in a recession the government might reduce tax rates or increase spending to stimulate aggregate demand; in a booming economy, the government might reduce spending or increase tax rates to reduce inflationary pressures. Having cyclically-adjusted budget deficits in recessions and cyclically-adjusted budget surpluses in booms is one way of implementing *counter-cyclical fiscal policy.*

How does the presence of government debt affect the government's ability to conduct such counter-cyclical fiscal policy? Perhaps the easiest way to answer this question is to recall the equation that describes the change in the debt-to-GDP ratio:

$$\Delta d = x + (r - g) \times d$$

This equation shows that the *change* in the debt-to-GDP ratio (Δd) depends on the *level* of the debt-to-GDP ratio (d). For example, if the real interest rate exceeds the growth rate of real GDP, so that $r - g$ is positive, the increase in the debt-to-GDP ratio (Δd) will be higher if d is already high than if it is low (for any given value of x).

With this relationship in mind, consider the dilemma faced during a recession by a government that is considering an expansionary fiscal policy. Such an expansionary fiscal policy would increase the primary budget deficit and therefore increase x. On the one hand, the short-run benefits of a fiscal expansion in terms of raising the level of real GDP seem clear; on the other hand, the same government may be wary of taking actions that lead to large increases in the debt-to-GDP ratio.

If the stock of outstanding government debt is small relative to the size of the economy, the government has a great deal of flexibility in conducting counter-cyclical fiscal policy. The small value of d implies that d will be rising only slowly in the absence of a primary deficit. Thus, there may well be room for the government to increase the primary deficit—either by increasing program spending or by reducing tax rates—without generating a large increase in the debt-to-GDP ratio. But the government has significantly less flexibility if the stock of outstanding government debt is already very large. In this case, the high value of d means that even in the absence of a primary budget deficit, d will be increasing quickly. Thus, any increase in the primary deficit brought about by the counter-cyclical fiscal policy runs the danger of generating increases in the debt-to-GDP ratio that may be viewed by creditors as unsustainable. As the previous quote from Gordon Thiessen suggests, such perceptions of unsustainability may lead to an increase in the real interest rate on government debt, which exacerbates the problem by driving d up even faster.

The idea that a large and rising stock of government debt could "tie the hands" of the government in times when it would otherwise want to conduct counter-cyclical fiscal policy was brought to the fore of Canadian economic policy by the late Douglas

---

[3] Comments by Gordon Thiessen in the *Bank of Canada Review*, Winter 1995–1996.

Purvis of Queen's University (and a coauthor on this textbook for many years). Purvis argued in the mid-1980s that Canadian government deficits must be brought under control quickly so that the debt would not accumulate to the point where the government would have no room left for fiscal stabilization policy. These warnings were not heeded. By the onset of the next recession in 1990, the federal government had added roughly $200 billion to the stock of debt and, predictably, the government felt unable to use discretionary fiscal policy to reduce some of the effects of the recession.

The Current Debate

We have been discussing the effects of government debt and deficits on the economy. As we saw earlier, government deficits were an important part of the Canadian economic environment for over 20 years from the early 1970s to the mid-1990s. But by 1998, after several years of devoted deficit fighting, the federal government had its first surplus in over 20 years, and most of the provinces had also eliminated their budget deficits.

For the next several years, the federal government had modest budget surpluses. This period was also one of rapid economic growth. The combination of the surpluses and the fast-growing economy led to a dramatic decline in the debt-to-GDP ratio. From its peak of almost 70 percent in 1996, the debt-to-GDP ratio fell below 50 percent in 2001 and was projected to fall below 40 percent by 2005.

During this period of modest surpluses and a fast-growing economy, a debate naturally arose over the appropriate fiscal policy for the government to follow. Some people argued the need to restore spending in health care, education, and other social programs to the levels that existed in 1995, before the federal government reduced their transfer payments to the provinces. Others argued the need to reduce income-tax rates, in part to stem an alleged "brain drain"—the exodus of highly trained workers—from Canada to the United States. A third group advocated delaying any spending increases or tax reductions until after a few years of budget surpluses could make a noticeable reduction in the stock of government debt. The Liberal government of Jean Chrétien adopted a policy that combined elements of all three views. In the federal budgets of 2000 and 2001, substantial tax reductions were introduced, to be phased in over the following five years. In the 2003 budget, a considerable increase in federal spending was announced, much of which was directed at health care (and was transferred to the provincial governments). Finally, following the practice established by Paul Martin when he was finance minister from 1993 to 2002, the federal government continued to set aside substantial "contingency funds" to be used only in the event of sudden, unforeseen interest rate hikes or other fiscal "disasters." If they are not used for such disasters, these contingency funds must (by law) be used to reduce the stock of government debt.

From 1998 to 2003, the Canadian government's fiscal policy struck a balance between increased spending, lower taxes, and reductions in the stock of government debt.

Speculation About Future Budget Surpluses

Many observers have noted that recent federal finance ministers have developed a habit of using pessimistic forecasts when predicting the future path of government revenues and expenditures. The result during the 1996–2003 period was that the actual budget deficit was usually smaller—or the actual budget surplus was larger—than what was forecast one or two years earlier.

Prime Minister Paul Martin was the federal finance minister from 1993 to 2002. During this period, the federal government's budget improved from a deficit equal to 6 percent of GDP to a surplus of 1 percent of GDP.

In the federal budget of February 2003, the minister of finance, John Manley, projected a balanced budget for the next three years. Most economists, however, predicted annual surpluses of $5–8 billion as a more likely outcome. What will be the effect on the Canadian economy if there is a series of budget surpluses?

To analyze the economic effects of budget surpluses, we need only to reverse the arguments that we have developed in this chapter. After all, an increase in the budget surplus is just the same as a reduction in the budget deficit. But it will be useful to review and summarize these arguments. If the Canadian federal and provincial governments succeed in running budget surpluses over the next few years, our economic theory tells us we should start to see the following things:

- Assuming that consumers are *not* fully Ricardian, the rise in the government budget surplus will raise the level of national saving.
- The rise in national saving will create an excess supply of loanable funds, thus putting downward pressure on interest rates. The result will be a "crowding in" of investment.
- The lower interest rates will lead to less capital inflow and thus the Canadian dollar will depreciate, leading to a rise in Canada's net exports.
- As the surpluses continue, the stock of government debt will be falling. Combined with a growing economy, this will make the debt-to-GDP ratio fall relatively sharply.
- The lower debt-to-GDP ratio will reduce bondholders' fears of future monetization and thus reduce inflation expectations.
- The lower debt-to-GDP ratio will restore the government's flexibility to use counter-cyclical fiscal policy if the economy enters another recession.

32.4 **Balanced Budgets**

As we have seen in this chapter, government budget deficits contribute to aggregate demand and thus have the potential to be used as an integral part of a fiscal policy designed to stabilize real GDP. However, we have also seen that government budget deficits crowd out private economic activity and impose a long-term burden, either through a reduced stock of physical capital or through greater foreign indebtedness. A tradeoff therefore appears to exist between the desirable short-run stabilizing role of deficits and the undesirable long-run costs of government debt. This tradeoff has been the source of much debate. Here we examine some possible solutions involving different concepts of a balanced budget.

Before going on, however, note that not everyone agrees that the accumulation of government debt represents a problem. One argument often seen in the popular press is that debt itself is not a problem—the problem is that the debt is held by foreigners rather than by domestic residents. Foreign ownership of the debt is alleged to be undesirable because interest payments are made to foreigners, reducing the income available for Canadians. Such claims have even led to the proposal that the Canadian government issue new "Canada-only" bonds to Canadians and then use the newly raised funds to redeem foreign-held government debt. *Applying Economic Concepts 32-1* explains why such a policy would be unlikely to change Canadian national income.

We now go on to examine different concepts of balanced budgets.

See Chapter 32 of www.pearsoned.ca/ragan for an interview with Paul Martin in which he discusses some of the political difficulties of reducing the budget deficit: "Regaining Canada's Fiscal Levers."

APPLYING ECONOMIC CONCEPTS 32-1

Is Foreign-Held Debt a Problem?

In 2003 about one-quarter of the federal government's debt was held outside of Canada. Thus, of the $37 billion in interest payments made on the government debt in 2003, roughly $9 billion was paid to foreigners. This fact has led many commentators in the popular press to suggest that Canada "reclaim" its national debt and keep these "lost" interest payments. These observers seem to believe that if more of the Canadian government debt were held within Canada, then Canada would be a richer country.

How do we "reclaim" the debt? The federal government simply has to issue new debt to Canadians and use the proceeds of this borrowing to redeem existing debt held by foreigners. By so doing, the fraction of government debt held by Canadians would be increased and the fraction held by foreigners decreased. Advocates of this proposal argue that the result would be higher Canadian income in the long run as fewer interest payments are sent to foreign creditors.

Proponents of this view fail to recognize the importance of an *integrated* world capital market and the fact that government bonds are only one type of asset held by creditors. Suppose the federal government issued $1 billion of new "Canadians-only" bonds to Canadians and used the proceeds to redeem an equal amount of existing foreign-held federal government debt. Two questions must be addressed: (1) What would make Canadians buy such bonds? and (2) What would happen to Canada's net foreign indebtedness as a result? We deal with these two issues in turn.

In order to convince Canadians to buy $1 billion worth of these new bonds, these same Canadians must somehow be convinced to divert $1 billion from some other use. For example, they could give up $1 billion worth of consumption to buy these bonds or they could sell $1 billion worth of their holdings of private corporate bonds to buy these new government bonds. In the first case, the reduction in consumption implies an increase in private saving. But it is difficult to see why Canadians would be prepared to increase their private saving simply in response to a change in the ownership of the federal government debt. One thing that might convince them to increase their saving is if these new bonds offered a rate of return greater than that of other assets available on the market. But, in this case, it is hard to see how the

federal government could improve its fiscal position by issuing new high-interest-rate bonds to raise funds used to redeem existing lower-interest-rate bonds.

Suppose, then, that these new "Canadians-only" bonds are *not* successful in increasing the amount of total private saving. Instead, the issuance of these bonds simply leads some Canadians to sell $1 billion of their holdings of private corporate debt so they can purchase the new bonds. The government then takes the $1 billion raised by the selling of the new bonds and redeems $1 billion worth of foreign-held debt. The total amount of government debt is unchanged, but less of the government debt is held by foreigners. The story does not end there, however. Recall that Canadians were able to buy these new government bonds only by selling off some of their current holdings of private corporate debt. But with an unchanged pool of Canadian savings, these corporate bonds *must* be bought by foreigners. Thus, total private corporate debt is unchanged, but *more* of it is held by foreigners. While it is true that the federal government has $1 billion less foreign-held debt, the private sector has $1 billion *more* foreign-held debt. And, though the government will now be making fewer interest payments to foreign creditors, the Canadian economy as a whole—the private plus public sectors—will be making the same interest payments to foreigners as before. Thus, the issuing of "Canadians-only" bonds, and the reduction in foreign-held government debt, has no effect on the stream of income available to domestic residents.

Is there some way for the Canadian economy to reduce its foreign indebtedness? Yes, but with a highly integrated global capital market like the one that exists today, schemes like Canadians-only bonds will not work. The only way that the Canadian economy can reduce its indebtedness to foreign creditors is to increase its national saving rate. This requires either an increase in private saving or an increase in public saving (that is, a reduction in the government's budget deficit), or both. Thus, if the Canadian budget surpluses continue over the next few years, we should observe a gradual decline in Canadian foreign indebtedness.

Annually Balanced Budgets

Practise with Study Guide Chapter 32, Extension Exercise E2.

Much current rhetoric of fiscal restraint calls for the government budget to be balanced every year. Though there has clearly been a significant move toward deficit reduction in Canada over the past few years, both federally and among the provinces, little emphasis has been placed on the idea that governments should be constrained to balance their budgets *every year.*

Balancing the budget on an annual basis would be extremely difficult to achieve. The reason is that a significant portion of the government budget is beyond the short-term control of the government, and a further large amount is hard to change quickly. For example, the entire debt-service component of government expenditures is determined by past borrowing and thus cannot be altered by the current government. In addition, as we saw in our discussion of the cyclically adjusted deficit, changes in real GDP that are beyond the control of the government lead to significant changes in tax revenues (and transfer payments) and thus generate significant changes in the budget deficit.

Even if it were possible for the government to control its path of spending and revenues perfectly on a year-to-year basis, it would probably be *undesirable* to balance the budget every year. We saw above that government tax revenues (net of transfers) tend to fall in recessions and rise in booms. In contrast, the level of government purchases is more or less independent of the level of real GDP. As a result, fiscal policy contains a built-in stabilizer as we first saw in Chapter 24; in recessions, the increase in the budget deficit stimulates aggregate demand whereas in booms the budget surplus reduces aggregate demand.

But things would be very different with an annually balanced budget. With a balanced budget, government expenditures would be *forced* to adjust to the changing level of tax revenues. In a recession, when tax revenues naturally decline, a balanced budget would require either a *reduction* in government expenditures or an *increase* in tax rates, thus generating a major *destabilizing* force on real GDP. Similarly, as tax revenues naturally rise in an economic boom, the balanced budget would require either an increase in government expenditures or a reduction in taxes, thus risking an overheating of the economy.

An annually balanced budget would accentuate the swings in real GDP.

Cyclically Balanced Budgets

One alternative to the extreme policy of requiring an annually balanced budget is to require that the government budget be balanced over the course of a full economic cycle. Budget deficits would be permitted in recessions as long as they were matched by surpluses in booms. In this way, the built-in stabilizers could still perform their important role, but there would be no persistent build-up of government debt. In principle, this is a desirable treatment of the tradeoff between the short-run benefits of deficits and the long-run costs of debt.

Despite its appeal, the idea of cyclically balanced budgets has its problems as well. Perhaps the most important problem with a cyclically balanced budget is an operational one. In order to have a law that requires the budget to be balanced over the business cycle, it is necessary to be able to *define* the cycle unambiguously. But there will always be disagreement about what stage of the cycle the economy is currently in, and thus there will be disagreement as to whether the current government should be increasing or reducing its deficit. Compounding this problem is the fact that politicians will have a stake in the identification of the cycle. Those who favour increased deficits will argue that this year is an unusually bad year and thus an increase in the deficit is justified; deficit "hawks," in contrast, will always tend to find this year to be unusually good, and thus a time to run budget surpluses.

Though a budget balanced over the course of the business cycle is in principle a desirable means of reconciling short-term stabilization with long-term prudence, the business cycle may not be well enough defined to make a formal policy of this type operational.

A second problem is largely political. Suppose one government runs large deficits for a few years and then gets replaced in an election. Would the succeeding government then be bound to run budget surpluses? What one government commits itself to in one year does not necessarily restrict what it (or its successor) does in the next year. This problem leads many in the U.S. to suggest a Constitutional Amendment to deal with deficits; once the Constitution is altered, any government is bound by it until, through a very lengthy process, it is changed again.

Allowing for Growth

A further problem with any policy that requires a balanced budget—whether over one year or over the business cycle—is that the emphasis is naturally on the overall budget deficit. But, as we saw earlier in this chapter, what determines the change in the debt-to-GDP ratio is the growth of the debt *relative* to the growth of the economy. With a growing economy, it is possible to have positive overall budget deficits—and thus a growing debt—and still have a falling debt-to-GDP ratio. Thus, to the extent that the debt-to-GDP ratio is the relevant gauge of a country's debt problem, focus should be placed on the debt-to-GDP ratio rather than on the budget deficit itself.

Some economists view a stable (or falling) debt-to-GDP ratio as the appropriate indicator of fiscal prudence. Their view permits a deficit such that the stock of debt grows no faster than GDP.

By this standard, the budgets of the last few years have been "prudent" because they have led to a growth rate in the stock of debt smaller than the growth rate of real GDP, and thus a reduction in the debt-to-GDP ratio. For example, in 1996, the debt-to-GDP ratio reached its recent maximum of 70 percent. Significant fiscal contractions, combined with healthy economic growth, led to a decline in the debt-to-GDP ratio to below 50 percent by 2001. Given the forecasts of balanced budgets (or even small surpluses) from 2003 to 2006, even moderate economic growth of 2 percent per year would lead the debt-to-GDP ratio to fall below 40 percent by 2005.

For some forecasts and analysis of the government's fiscal options, see the Royal Bank's website: www.royal-bank.ca. Go to "corporate information" and then "economics."

S U M M A R Y

32.1 **Facts and Definitions**

- The government's budget deficit is equal to total government expenditure minus total government revenue. Since the government must borrow to finance any shortfall in its revenues, the annual deficit is equal to the annual increase in the stock of government debt. Whenever the deficit is positive, the stock of government debt is growing.
- The primary budget deficit is equal to the excess of the government's program spending over total tax revenues.

The difference between the total budget deficit and the primary deficit is the debt-service payments.

- In 1975, the Canadian federal government net debt was 14 percent of GDP. Large and persistent budget deficits beginning in the 1970s increased the stock of debt so that by 1996 the federal government net debt was equal to 70 percent of GDP. By 2003, after several years of fiscal contraction, the budget was balanced and the debt was 50 percent of GDP.

32.2 **Some Analytical Issues**

- Since taxes (net of transfers) tend to rise when real GDP rises, the overall budget deficit tends to rise during recessions and fall during booms. This tendency makes the budget deficit a poor measure of the stance of fiscal policy.
- The cyclically adjusted deficit is the budget deficit that would exist with the current set of fiscal policies if real GDP were equal to potential GDP. Changes in the cyclically adjusted deficit reflect changes in the stance of fiscal policy.
- The change in the debt-to-GDP ratio from one year to the next is given by

$$\Delta d = x + (r - g) \times d$$

where d is the debt-to-GDP ratio, x is the primary deficit as a percentage of GDP, r is the real interest rate on government bonds, and g is the growth rate of real GDP. If r exceeds g, then a primary surplus is required to stabilize the debt-to-GDP ratio.

- National saving equals government saving plus private saving. An increase in the government budget deficit represents a fall in government saving. The link between budget deficits and private saving depends on the extent to which taxpayers recognize the future tax liabilities associated with current government deficits.
- If taxpayers are non-Ricardian, as most evidence suggests, an increase in the budget deficit will lead to a smaller increase in private saving, and thus to a fall in national saving.

32.3 **The Effects of Government Debt and Deficits**

- In a closed economy, an increase in the budget deficit leads to a reduction in national saving and a rise in real interest rates. This increase in interest rates reduces the amount of investment and leads to a reduction in the growth rate of potential output.
- In an open economy, an increase in the budget deficit initially pushes up real interest rates. The higher interest rate attracts foreign financial capital and appreciates the currency. As the currency appreciates, there is a reduction in net exports. The capital inflow implies an increase in the country's net foreign indebtedness.
- In either open or closed economies, the long-term burden of government debt is a redistribution of resources

away from future generations and toward current generations.

- A large debt-to-GDP ratio may lead creditors to expect increases in inflation, as the government attempts to finance deficits through the creation of money. Such increases in inflationary expectations hamper the conduct of monetary policy.
- A large debt-to-GDP ratio also limits the extent to which the government can conduct counter-cyclical fiscal policy without risking large increases in the debt-to-GDP ratio that may be viewed by creditors as unsustainable.

32.4 **Balanced Budgets**

- Since tax revenues (net of transfers) naturally rise as real GDP increases, a policy to balance the budget on an annual basis forces either expenditures to rise or tax rates to fall during booms. This produces destabilizing fiscal policy.
- Cyclically balanced budgets, in principle, permit the short-run benefits of deficits to be realized without incurring the long-run costs of debt accumulation. Implementation of this policy is difficult, however, since the precise identification of the business cycle is very controversial.
- In a growing economy, it is more sensible to focus on changes in the debt-to-GDP ratio than on balancing the budget over some specific horizon.

K E Y   C O N C E P T S

Government's budget constraint
Primary budget deficit
The relationship between deficits and the national debt
Debt-service payments

Debt-to-GDP ratio
National, government, and private saving
Ricardian Equivalence
Crowding out of investment

Crowding out of net exports
Long-term burden of the debt
Annually balanced budget
Cyclically balanced budget

S T U D Y   E X E R C I S E S

1. Fill in the blanks to make the following statements correct.

   a. The government's budget constraint shows that government expenditures must be equal to the sum of _____ and _____.

   b. The government's annual budget deficit is the excess of total _____ over total _____ in a given year.

   c. If the government's total budget deficit is $20 billion and its debt-service payments are $18 billion, then its _____ is $2 billion. If the total budget deficit is $20 billion and its debt-service payments are $26 billion, then its _____ is $6 billion.

   d. In recent years, Canada has had a series of _____ and the debt-to-GDP ratio has been _____.

2. Fill in the blanks to make the following statements correct.

   a. When there is no change in the government's fiscal policy it is still possible for the budget deficit to fall because _____.

   b. For a given set of fiscal policies, the budget deficit _____ as real GDP rises and _____ as real GDP falls.

   c. The cyclically adjusted deficit is the budget deficit that would exist if real GDP equalled _____ and the government's _____ were at their current levels.

   d. Suppose the real interest rate is 2 percent and the growth rate of real GDP is 1.5 percent. If the government wants to stabilize the debt-to-GDP ratio, then it is necessary to have a _____.

   e. Suppose a tax reduction leads to an increase in the government deficit by $8.5 billion. If all consumers in Canada were "Ricardian," then private saving would _____ by _____ billion. If all consumers in Canada were only somewhat "Ricardian," then private saving would _____ by _____ billion.

3. Fill in the blanks to make the following statements correct.

   a. In a closed economy, when the government borrows to finance the deficit, interest rates will _____ and some private investment will be _____.

   b. In an open economy, when the government borrows to finance the deficit, interest rates will _____, the Canadian dollar will _____, and net exports will _____.

   c. The long-term burden of government debt is the reduced _____ for future generations.

   d. Suppose a law was passed that required the government to balance its budget each year. Fiscal policy would then have a _____ effect.

e. A cyclically balanced budget is difficult to implement because it is difficult to identify the _____.

4. The table below shows government spending data over eight years in Debtland. All figures are in billions of dollars. The symbols used are as defined in the text.

	(1)	(2)	(3)	(4)	(5)	(6)
					Primary	Stock
				Budget	Budget	of
Year	G	T	iD	Deficit	Deficit	Debt
1999	175	175	25	—	—	—
2000	180	180	26	—	—	—
2001	185	185	27	—	—	—
2002	188	190	26	—	—	—
2003	185	195	25	—	—	—
2004	185	200	24	—	—	—
2005	180	205	23	—	—	—
2006	175	210	22	—	—	—

a. Compute Debtland's budget deficit in each year and complete column 4 in the table. (Since we are computing the deficit, a negative number indicates a surplus.)
b. Compute Debtland's primary budget deficit in each year and complete column 5 in the table.
c. Suppose the initial stock of debt (in 1998) was $400 billion. Noting that the deficit in 1999 adds to the existing stock of debt, what is the stock of debt by the end of 1999?
d. Compute the stock of debt for each year and complete column 6 in the table.
e. Suppose you know that Debtland's debt-to-GDP ratio was the same in 2006 as in 1998. By what percentage did GDP grow between 1998 and 2006?

5. The figure below shows the budget deficit function for a country.

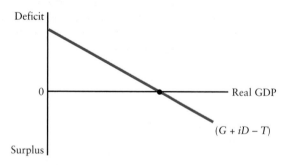

a. Explain why the budget deficit function is downward sloping.

b. If the government increases its level of purchases (G), what happens to the budget deficit at any level of real GDP? Show this in the diagram.
c. If the government increases its level of net tax revenues (T), what happens to the deficit at any level of real GDP? Show this in the diagram.
d. Explain why a rise in the actual budget deficit does not necessarily reflect an expansionary fiscal policy. How would a fiscal expansion appear in the diagram? A fiscal contraction?

6. The U.S. government was slightly ahead of the Canadian government in reducing its budget deficit. The following table shows the actual budget deficit and the cyclically adjusted deficit (both as a percentage of GDP) for the United States from 1989 to 1997.

Year	Actual Deficit	CAD
1989	2.8	2.9
1990	3.9	3.2
1991	4.6	3.4
1992	4.7	3.7
1993	3.9	3.7
1994	3.0	2.8
1995	2.3	2.6
1996	1.4	1.6
1997	0.3	1.0

a. On a scale diagram (with the year on the horizontal axis) graph the actual deficit and the cyclically adjusted deficit.
b. Identify the periods when U.S. fiscal policy was expansionary.
c. Identify the periods when U.S. fiscal policy was contractionary.
d. Look back at Figure 32-7. How does the stance of U.S. fiscal policy compare with Canada's?

7. The following table shows hypothetical data from 1999 to 2005 that can be used to compute the change in the debt-to-GDP ratio. The symbols used are defined in the text.

Year	(1) x	(2) r	(3) g	(4) d	(5) Δd
1999	0.03	0.045	0.025	0.70	—
2000	0.02	0.04	0.025	—	—
2001	0.01	0.035	0.025	—	—
2002	0.00	0.035	0.025	—	—
2003	−0.01	0.03	0.025	—	—
2004	−0.02	0.03	0.025	—	—
2005	−0.03	0.025	0.025	—	—

a. Remember from the text that the change in the debt-to-GDP ratio (Δd) during a year is given by $\Delta d = x + (r-g)d$. Compute Δd for 1999.

b. Column 4 is the debt-to-GDP ratio. Note that d in 2000 is equal to d from 1999 plus Δd in 1999. Compute d in 2000.

c. Using the same method, compute d and Δd for each year, and complete columns 4 and 5.

d. Plot d in a scale diagram with the year on the horizontal axis. What discretionary variable was most responsible for the observed decline in d?

e. Note that as the primary deficit (x) falls between 1999 and 2005, there is also a downward trend in the real interest rate. Can you offer an explanation for this?

8. The diagram below shows an *AD/AS* diagram. The economy begins at E_0 with output equal to Y^*. Suppose the government in this closed economy increases G and finances it by running a deficit (borrowing). The *AD* curve shifts to the right.

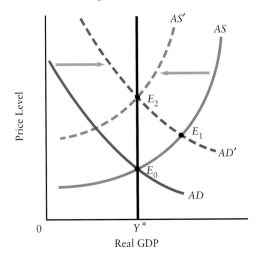

a. How does the interest rate at E_1 compare with that at E_0? Explain.

b. Given your answer to part (a), how does investment at E_1 compare to investment at E_0?

c. Explain the economy's adjustment toward E_2. What happens to the interest rate and investment?

d. What is the long-run effect of the fiscal expansion? How would this be reflected in the diagram?

9. The diagram below shows an *AD/AS* diagram. The economy begins at E_0 with output equal to Y^*. Suppose the government in this closed economy decreases its budget deficit by increasing T (and keeping G unchanged), thus causing the *AD* curve to shift to the left.

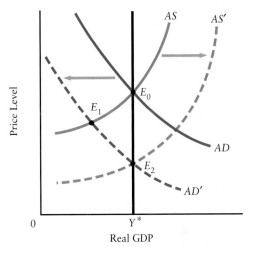

a. How does the interest rate at E_1 compare with that at E_0? Explain.

b. Given your answer to part (a), how does investment at E_1 compare to investment at E_0?

c. Explain the economy's adjustment toward E_2. What happens to the interest rate and investment?

d. What is the long-run effect of the government deficit? How would this be reflected in the diagram?

e. Comparing the short-run and the long-run effects of this policy, what dilemma does the government face in reducing its deficit?

DISCUSSION QUESTIONS

1. Evaluate each of the following proposals to "control the deficit" in order to avoid the long-run burden of the debt.
   a. Maintain a zero cyclically adjusted deficit.
   b. Keep the debt-to-GDP ratio constant.
   c. Limit government borrowing in each year to some fixed percentage of national income in that year.

2. Judith Maxwell, former chairperson of the now disbanded Economic Council of Canada, warned in 1991 that "when interest rates are higher than the economic growth rate, the ratio of debt to GDP acquires dangerous upward momentum." Discuss why this is so. How does the primary deficit enter the analysis?

3. In the federal budget of 1995, the minister of finance announced some significant expenditure reductions that would reduce the deficit. In the budget of 1996, he announced no new expenditure cuts yet still predicted the deficit would fall. Explain how these statements by the minister of finance should be interpreted.

4. Prime Minister Paul Martin was the federal minister of finance from 1993 to 2002 and is credited with reducing Canada's budget deficit during that period. He stressed the importance of using very conservative forecasts for economic growth. Explain the role of forecasts, and why Martin chose to use conservative ones.

5. In the text we discussed the effects of government budget deficits. In the past 15 years, however, the Canadian federal deficit has fallen markedly, from 5 percent of GDP in 1989 (the peak of the business cycle) to a *surplus* of 0.5 percent of GDP in 2003 (close to a peak in the business cycle). Discuss the likely short-term and long-term effects that you would expect to follow such a sustained *reduction* in the deficit.

6. A government official recently exclaimed, "The prime minister's policies are working! Lower interest rates combined with staunch fiscal policy have reduced the deficit significantly." What do interest rates have to do with government spending and taxes when it comes to deficit management?

PART TWELVE

Canada in the Global Economy

Does a country always benefit from free trade? If so, why do many people appear to believe the opposite? How is Canada's exchange rate determined? Should Canada maintain a flexible exchange rate or should it peg the value of its currency to the U.S. dollar? These are the sorts of questions you will be able to answer after reading the final three chapters of this book.*

Chapter 33 explores the gains from trade, and how these gains are based on the important concept of comparative advantage. We discuss the reasons why a country might have a comparative advantage in a particular product, and how some government policies can have the effect of changing a country's pattern of comparative advantage. We will also examine a country's terms of trade, the relative prices at which a country trades with the rest of the world.

In Chapter 34, the focus is on trade policy. We explore the case for free trade as well as the case for protection (we also examine some common but fallacious arguments for protection). We then discuss some methods of protection, such as tariffs, quotas, and nontariff barriers. The chapter then examines current trade policy in Canada, with an emphasis on the North American Free Trade Agreement.

Chapter 35 discusses the exchange rate and the balance of payments. We examine the foreign-exchange market and why the balance of payments accounts are always in balance. The important distinction between fixed exchange rates and flexible exchange rates will be discussed in detail, and we will explore the kinds of events that lead to an appreciation or a depreciation of the Canadian dollar. Finally, we explore three "hot" policy debates, including the cases for and against Canada's adopting a fixed exchange rate.

---

*Chapter 35 does not appear in *Microeconomics*.

CHAPTER 33

The Gains from International Trade

L *LEARNING OBJECTIVES*

1 Explain why the gains from trade depend on the pattern of comparative advantage.

2 Describe how factor endowments and climate can influence a country's comparative advantage.

3 Explain the law of one price.

4 Explain why countries export some goods and import other goods.

Canadian consumers buy cars from Germany, Germans take holidays in Italy, Italians buy spices from Africa, Africans import oil from Kuwait, Kuwaitis buy Japanese cameras, and the Japanese buy Canadian lumber. *International trade* refers to the exchange of goods and services that takes place across international boundaries.

The founders of modern economics were concerned with foreign trade problems. The great eighteenth-century British philosopher and economist David Hume (1711–1776), one of the first to work out the theory of the price system, developed his concepts mainly in terms of prices in foreign trade. Adam Smith (1723–1790), in *The Wealth of Nations*, attacked government restriction of international trade. David Ricardo (1772–1823) developed the basic theory of the gains from trade that is studied in this chapter. The repeal of the Corn Laws—tariffs on the importation of grains into the United Kingdom— and the transformation of that country during the nineteenth century from a country of high tariffs to one of complete free trade were to some extent the result of agitation by economists whose theories of the gains from international trade led them to condemn tariffs.

International trade is becoming increasingly important, not just for Canada but for the world as a whole. As Figure 33-1 shows, the volume of world trade has grown much faster than has world real GDP over the past half-century. Since 1950, the world's real GDP has increased by six times, an average annual growth rate of 3.7 percent. Over the same period, however, the volume of world trade has increased by over *21* times, an average annual growth rate of 6.1 percent.

Figure 33-2 shows some data for Canadian trade in 2002. The figure shows the value of Canadian exports and imports in several broad industry groupings. There are three important points to note from the figure. First, international trade is very important for Canada. In 2002, Canada exported $410 billion and imported over $350 billion in goods—if we added trade in services, the values would be even higher; each flow (exports and imports) amounts to approximately 40 percent of GDP. Second, exports and imports are roughly the same size, so that the *volume* of trade is much larger than the *balance* of trade—the value of exports minus the value of imports. Third, in most of the

FIGURE 33-1   The Growth in World
Trade, 1950–2001

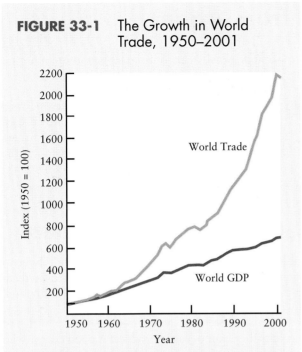

The volume of world trade has grown much faster than
world GDP over the past 50 years. The figure shows
the growth of real GDP and the volume of trade since
1950. Both are expressed as index numbers, set equal
to 100 in 1950. Real world GDP has increased six times
since 1950; world trade volume has increased 21 times.

(*Source:* World Trade Organization website:
www.wto.org. Go to "Resources" and select "Trade
Statistics." Then click on "All Tables and Charts" and go
to "Selected Long-Term Trends." Choose Table 11.1.)

FIGURE 33-2   Canadian Exports and
Imports of Goods by
Industry, 2002

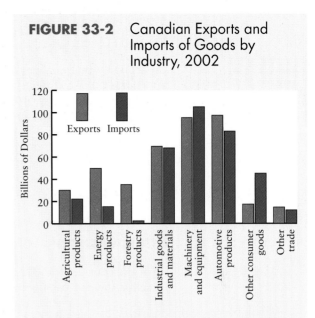

Canada exports and imports large volumes of goods in
most industries. The data show the value of goods
exported and imported by industry in 2002 (trade in
services is not shown). The total value of goods
exported was $410.6 billion; the total value of goods
imported was $356.1 billion.

(*Source:* These data are available on Statistics Canada's
website: www.statcan.ca. Go to "Canadian Statistics"
and click on "International trade.")

industry groupings there are significant amounts of both imports and exports. Such
intra-industry trade will be discussed later in the chapter. Canada does not just export
resource products and import manufactured goods; it also imports many resource products and exports many manufactured goods.

In this chapter, we inquire into the gains to living standards that result from international trade. We find that the source of the gains from trade lies in differing cost conditions among geographical regions. World income is maximized when countries specialize
in the products in which they have the lowest opportunity costs of production. These costs
are partly determined by natural endowments (geographical and climatic conditions),
partly by public policy, and partly by historical accident.

For information on world trade, see the
World Trade Organization's website:
www.wto.org

Canada trades with many countries, but most of our trade is
with the United States, and the fraction of our total trade with
the United States has been increasing in recent years. For more
information on the location of Canada's trade, look for "Who
Are Canada's Trading Partners?" in the *Additional Topics* section
of this book's Companion Website.

http://www.pearsoned.ca/ragan

33.1 **The Gains from Trade**

open economy
An economy that engages in international trade.

closed economy
An economy that has no foreign trade.

An economy that engages in international trade is called an **open economy;** one that does not is called a **closed economy.** A situation in which a country does no foreign trade is called one of *autarky.*

The benefits of trade are easiest to visualize by considering the differences between a world with trade and a world without it. Although politicians often regard foreign trade differently from domestic trade, economists from Adam Smith on have argued that the causes and consequences of international trade are simply an extension of the principles governing domestic trade. What are the benefits of trade among individuals, among groups, among regions, or among countries?

Interpersonal, Interregional, and International Trade

To begin, consider trade among individuals. Without trade, each person would have to be self-sufficient: each would have to produce all the food, clothing, shelter, medical services, entertainment, and luxuries that he or she consumed. A world of individual self-sufficiency would be a world with extremely low living standards.

Trade among individuals allows people to specialize in activities they can do well and to buy from others the goods and services they cannot easily produce. A good doctor who is a bad carpenter can provide medical services not only for her own family but also for an excellent carpenter without the training or the ability to practise medicine. Thus, trade and specialization are intimately connected.

Without trade, everyone must be self-sufficient; with trade, people can specialize in what they do well and satisfy other needs by trading.

The same principle applies to regions. Without interregional trade, each region would be forced to be self-sufficient. With trade, each region can specialize in producing products for which it has some natural or acquired advantage. Plains regions can specialize in growing grain, mountain regions in mining and forest products, and regions with abundant power in manufacturing. Cool regions can produce wheat and other crops that thrive in temperate climates, and hot regions can grow such tropical crops as bananas, sugarcane, and coffee. The living standards of the inhabitants of all regions will be higher when each region specializes in products in which it has some natural or acquired advantage and obtains other products by trade than when all regions seek to be self-sufficient.

This same basic principle also applies to nations. A national boundary seldom delimits an area that is naturally self-sufficient. Nations, like regions and individuals, can gain from specialization. More of some goods are produced domestically than residents wish to consume, while residents would like to consume more of other goods than is produced domestically. International trade is necessary to achieve the gains that international specialization makes possible.

With trade, each individual, region, or nation is able to concentrate on producing goods and services that it produces efficiently while trading to obtain goods and services that it does not produce efficiently.

gains from trade
The increased output due to the specialization according to comparative advantage that is made possible by trade.

Specialization and trade go hand in hand because there is no incentive to achieve the gains from specialization without being able to trade the goods produced for goods desired. Economists use the term **gains from trade** to embrace the results of both.

We will examine two sources of the gains from trade. The first is differences among regions of the world in climate and resource endowment that lead to advantages in producing certain goods and disadvantages in producing others. These gains occur even though each country's costs of production are unchanged by the existence of trade. The second source is the reduction in each country's costs of production that results from the greater scale of production that specialization brings.

The Gains from Trade with Constant Costs

In order to focus on differences in countries' conditions of production, suppose each country's average costs of production are constant. We will use an example below involving only two countries and two products, but the general principles apply as well to the case of many countries and many products.

Practise with Study Guide Chapter 33, Exercise 1.

Absolute Advantage

One region is said to have an **absolute advantage** over another in the production of good X when an equal quantity of resources can produce more X in the first region than in the second. Or, to put it differently, one country has an absolute advantage in the production of good X if it takes fewer resources to produce one unit of good X there than in another country. Table 33-1 shows an example. The two "countries" are Canada and the European Union (EU) and the two goods are wheat and cloth. The table shows the *absolute cost* of producing one unit of wheat and one unit of cloth in each country. The absolute cost is the dollar cost of the labour, capital, and other resources required to produce the goods. Thus, the country that can produce a specific good with fewer resources can produce it at a lower absolute cost.

In Table 33-1, the absolute resource cost for both wheat and cloth is less in Canada than in the EU. Canada is therefore said to have an *absolute advantage* over the EU in the production of both wheat and cloth. Canada has an absolute advantage over the EU in producing these goods because it is a more efficient producer—it takes less labour and other resources to produce the goods in Canada than in the EU.

The situation in Table 33-1 is hypothetical, but it is encountered often in the real world. Some countries, because they have access to cheap natural resources or better-trained workers or more sophisticated capital equipment, are low-cost producers for a wide range of products. Does this mean that high-cost countries stand no chance of being successful producers in a globalized world of international trade? Will the low-cost countries produce everything, leaving nothing to be done by high-cost countries? The answer is no. As we will see immediately, the gains from international trade do not depend on the pattern of absolute advantage.

absolute advantage
The situation that exists when one country can produce some commodity at lower absolute cost than another country.

TABLE 33-1   Absolute Costs and Absolute Advantage

	Wheat (kilograms)	Cloth (metres)
Canada	$1 per kilogram	$5 per metre
EU	$3 per kilogram	$6 per metre

Absolute advantage reflects the differences in absolute costs of producing goods between countries. The numbers show the dollar cost of the resources necessary for producing wheat and cloth in Canada and the EU. Note that Canada is a lower-cost producer than the EU for both wheat and cloth. Canada is therefore said to have an absolute advantage in the production of both goods.

Comparative Advantage

The great English economist David Ricardo (1722–1823) was the first to provide an explanation of the pattern of international trade in a world in which countries had different costs. His theory of *comparative advantage* is still accepted by economists as a valid

comparative advantage   The situation that exists when a country can produce a good with less forgone output of other goods than can another country.

statement of the gains from international trade. A country is said to have a **comparative advantage** in the production of good X if the cost *in terms of forgone output of other goods* is lower in that country than in another. Thus, the pattern of comparative advantage is based on *opportunity costs* rather than absolute costs. Table 33-2 illustrates the pattern of comparative advantage in the Canada–EU example. The opportunity cost in Canada for one kilogram of wheat is computed by determining how much cloth must be given up in Canada in order to produce an additional kilogram of wheat. From Table 33-1, the absolute costs of wheat and cloth were $1 per kilogram and $5 per metre, respectively. Thus, in order to produce one extra kilogram of wheat, Canada must use resources that could have produced one-fifth of a metre of cloth. So the opportunity cost of one kilogram of wheat is 0.2 metres of cloth. By exactly the same reasoning, the opportunity cost of one metre of cloth in Canada is 5.0 kilograms of wheat.

Even though a country may have an absolute advantage in all goods (as Canada does in Table 33-1), it *cannot* have a comparative advantage in all goods. Similarly, even though a country may be inefficient in absolute terms and thus have no absolute advantage in any goods (as is the case for the EU in Table 33-1) it *must* have a comparative advantage in some good. In Table 33-2, Canada has a comparative advantage in the production of wheat because Canada must give up less cloth to produce one kilogram of wheat than must be given up in the EU. Similarly, the EU has a comparative advantage in the production of cloth because the EU must give up less wheat in order to produce one metre of cloth than must be given up in Canada.

The gains from specialization and trade depend on the pattern of comparative, not absolute, advantage.

In our example, total world wheat production can be increased if Canada devotes more resources to the production of wheat and fewer resources to the production of cloth—that is, if it *specializes* in wheat production. Similarly, total world cloth production can be increased if the EU devotes more resources to the production of cloth and fewer to wheat—if it specializes in cloth production. Such reallocations of resources increase total world output because each country is specializing in the production of the good in which it has the lowest opportunity cost. The gains from specialization along the lines of comparative advantage are shown in Table 33-3.

TABLE 33-2   Opportunity Costs and Comparative Advantage

	Wheat (kilograms)	Cloth (metres)
Canada	0.2 m of cloth	5.0 kg of wheat
EU	0.5 m of cloth	2.0 kg of wheat

Comparative advantages reflect opportunity costs that differ between countries. The first column shows the opportunity cost of a kilogram of wheat in terms of the amount of cloth that must be given up. The second column shows the opportunity cost of a metre of cloth in terms of the amount of wheat that must be given up. Canada has a comparative advantage in wheat production because it has a lower opportunity cost for wheat than does the EU. The EU has a comparative advantage in cloth because its opportunity cost for cloth is lower than that in Canada.

TABLE 33-3   The Gains from Specialization

	Changes from each country producing more units of the product in which it has the lower opportunity cost	
	Wheat (kilograms)	Cloth (metres)
Canada	+5.0	−1.0
EU	−4.0	+2.0
Total	+1.0	+1.0

Whenever opportunity costs differ between countries, specialization can increase the production of both products. These calculations show that there are gains from specialization given the opportunity costs of Table 33-2. To produce five more kilograms of wheat, Canada must sacrifice 1.0 m of cloth. To produce two more metres of cloth, the EU must sacrifice 4.0 kg of wheat. Making both changes increases world production of both wheat and cloth.

World output increases if countries specialize in the production of the goods in which they have a comparative advantage.

Not *any* pattern of specialization, however, is beneficial for the world. In our example, if Canada were to specialize in cloth and the EU in wheat, total world output would *fall.* To see this, note that in order to produce one extra metre of cloth in Canada, 5.0 kilograms of wheat must be sacrificed (see Table 33-2). Similarly, in order to produce four extra kilograms of wheat in the EU, two metres of cloth must be sacrificed. Thus, if each country produced these additional units of the "wrong" good, total world output of wheat would fall by one kilogram and total output of cloth would fall by one metre.

Specialization of production *against* the pattern of comparative advantage leads to a decline in total world output.

We have discussed comparative advantage in terms of opportunity costs. We can also illustrate it by considering the two countries' production possibilities boundaries. Recall the connection between a country's production possibilities boundary and the opportunity costs of production. The slope of the production possibilities boundary indicates the opportunity costs. The existence of different opportunity costs across countries implies comparative advantages that can lead to gains from trade. Figure 33-3 illustrates how two countries can both gain from trade when they have different opportunity costs in production and those opportunity costs are independent of the level of production. An alternative diagrammatic illustration of the gains from trade appears in *Extensions in Theory 33-1* where the production possibilities boundary is concave (which means that the opportunity cost for each good is higher when more of that good is being produced).

Practise with Study Guide Chapter 33, Exercise 4.

FIGURE 33-3 The Gains from Trade with Constant Opportunity Costs

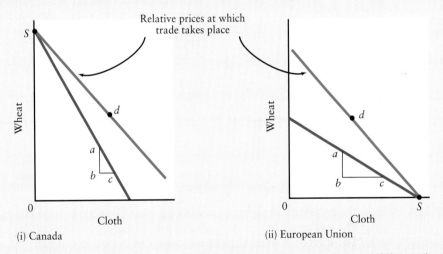

International trade leads to specialization in production and increased consumption possibilities. The purple lines in parts (i) and (ii) represent the production possibilities boundaries for Canada and the EU, respectively. In the absence of any international trade these also represent each country's consumption possibilities.

The difference in the slopes of the production possibilities boundaries reflects differences in comparative advantage, as shown in Table 33-2. In each part the opportunity cost of increasing production of wheat by the same amount (measured by the distance *ba*) is the amount by which the production of cloth must be reduced (measured by the distance *bc*). The relatively steep production possibilities boundary for Canada thus indicates that the opportunity cost of producing wheat in Canada is less than that in the European Union.

If trade is possible at some relative prices between the two countries' opportunity costs of production, each country will specialize in the production of the good in which it has a comparative advantage. In each part of the figure, production occurs at *S* (for specialization); Canada produces only wheat, and the EU produces only cloth.

Consumption possibilities are given by the green line that passes through *S* and has a slope equal to the with-trade relative prices. Consumption possibilities are increased in both countries; consumption may occur at some point such as *d* that involves a combination of wheat and cloth that was not obtainable in the absence of trade.

EXTENSIONS IN THEORY 33-1

The Gains From Trade More Generally

Examining the gains from trade is relatively easy in the case where each country's production possibilities boundary is a straight line. What happens in the more realistic case where the production possibilities boundary is concave? As this box shows, the same basic principles of the gains from trade apply to this more complex case.

International trade leads to an expansion of the set of goods that can be consumed in the economy in two ways:

1. By allowing the bundle of goods consumed to differ from the bundle produced; and,

2. By permitting a profitable change in the pattern of production.

Without international trade, the bundle of goods produced is the bundle consumed. With international trade, the consumption and production bundles can be altered independently to reflect the relative values placed on goods by international markets.

Fixed Production

In each part of the figure, the purple curve is the economy's production possibilities boundary. In the absence of inter-national trade, the economy must consume the same bundle of goods that it produces. Thus, the production possibilities boundary is also the consumption possibilities boundary. Suppose the economy produces and consumes at point a, with x_1 of good X and y_1 of good Y, as in part (i) of the figure.

Next suppose that with production point a, good Y can be exchanged for good X internationally. The consumption possibilities are now shown by the line tt drawn through point a. The slope of tt indicates the quantity of Y that exchanges for a unit of X on the international market.

Although production is fixed at point a, consumption can now be anywhere on the line tt. For example, the consumption point could be at b. This could be achieved by exporting y_2y_1 units of Y and importing x_1x_2 units of X. Because point b (and all others on line tt to the right of a) lies outside the production possibilities boundary, there are potential gains from trade. Consumers are no longer limited by their own country's production possibilities. Let us suppose that they prefer point b to point a. They have achieved a gain from trade by being allowed to exchange some of their production of good Y for some quantity of good X and thus to consume more of good X than is produced at home.

Practise with Study Guide Chapter 33, Extension Exercise E1.

The conclusions about the gains from trade arising from international differences in opportunity costs are summarized below.

1. Country A has a comparative advantage over Country B in producing a product when the opportunity cost of production in Country A is lower. This implies, however, that it has a comparative *dis*advantage in the other product.

2. Opportunity costs depend on the relative costs of producing two products, not on absolute costs.

3. When opportunity costs are the same in all countries, there is no comparative advantage and there is no possibility of gains from specialization and trade.

4. When opportunity costs differ in any two countries and both countries are producing both products, it is always possible to increase production of both products by a suitable reallocation of resources within each country.

Variable Production

There is a further opportunity for the expansion of the country's consumption possibilities: With trade, the production bundle may be altered in response to international prices. The country may produce the bundle of goods that is most valuable in world markets. That is represented by the bundle *d* in part (ii). The consumption possibilities boundary is shifted to the line *t′t′* by changing production from *a* to *d* and thereby increasing the country's degree of specialization in good *Y*. For every point on the original consumption possibilities boundary *tt*, there are points on the new boundary *t′t′* that allow more consumption of both goods—for example, compare points *b* and *f*. Notice also that, except at the zero-trade point *d*, the new consumption possibilities boundary lies *everywhere above the production possibilities curve*.

The benefits of moving from a no-trade position, such as point *a*, to a trading position such as points *b* or *f* are the *gains from trade* to the country. When the production of good *Y* is increased and the production of good *X* decreased, the country is able to move to a point such as *f* by producing more of good *Y*, in which the country has a comparative advantage, and trading the additional production for good *X*.

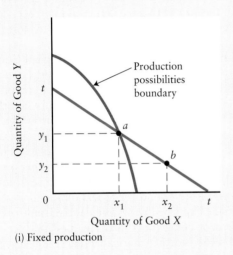

(i) Fixed production

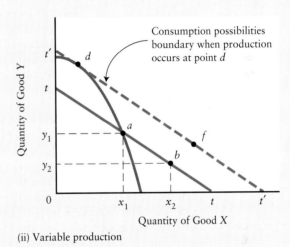

(ii) Variable production

The Gains from Trade with Variable Costs

So far, we have assumed that opportunity costs are the same whatever the scale of output, and we have seen that there are gains from specialization and trade as long as there are interregional differences in opportunity costs. If costs vary with the level of output, or as experience is acquired via specialization, *additional* gains are possible.

Scale and Imperfect Competition

Production costs generally fall as the scale of output increases. The larger the scale of operations, the more efficiently large-scale machinery can be used and the more a detailed division of tasks among workers is possible. Small countries (such as Switzerland, Belgium, and Israel) whose domestic markets are not large enough to exploit economies of scale would find it prohibitively expensive to become self-sufficient by producing a little bit of everything at very high cost.

Wine is a good example of an industry in which there is much intra-industry trade. Canada, for example, imports wine from many countries but also exports Canadian-made wine to the same countries.

Trade allows small countries to specialize and produce a few products at high enough levels of output to reap the available economies of scale.

Very large countries, such as the United States, have markets large enough to allow the production of most items at home at a scale of output great enough to obtain the available economies of scale. For them, the gains from trade arise mainly from specializing in products in which they have a comparative advantage. Yet, even for such countries, a broadening of their markets permits achieving scale economies in subproduct lines, such as specialty steels or certain lines of clothing.

One of the important lessons learned from patterns of world trade since the Second World War has concerned imperfect competition and product differentiation. Virtually all of today's manufactured consumer goods are produced in a vast array of differentiated product lines. In some industries, many firms produce this array; in others, only a few firms produce the entire array. In either case, they do not exhaust all available economies of scale. Thus, an increase in the size of the market, even in an economy as large as the United States, may allow the exploitation of some previously unexploited scale economies in individual product lines.

These possibilities were first dramatically illustrated when the European Common Market (now known as the European Union) was set up in the late 1950s. Economists had expected that specialization would occur according to the theory of comparative advantage, with one country specializing in cars, another in refrigerators, another in fashion and clothing, another in shoes, and so on. This is not the way it worked out. Instead, much of the vast growth of trade was in *intra-industry* trade—that is, trade of goods or services within the same broad industry. Today, one can buy French, English, Italian, and German fashion goods, cars, shoes, appliances, and a host of other products in London, Paris, Berlin, and Rome. Ships loaded with Swedish furniture bound for London pass ships loaded with English furniture bound for Stockholm, and so on.

The same increase in intra-industry trade happened with Canada–U.S. trade over successive rounds of tariff cuts, the most recent being the 1989 Canada–U.S. Free Trade Agreement, and its 1994 expansion into the North American Free Trade Agreement (NAFTA) which included Mexico. In several broad industrial groups, including automotive products, machinery, textiles, and forestry products, both imports and exports increased in each country. What free trade in Europe and North America did was to allow a proliferation of differentiated products, with different countries each specializing in different subproduct lines. Consumers have shown by their expenditures that they value this enormous increase in the range of choice among differentiated products.

Learning by Doing

The discussion so far has assumed that costs vary with the *level* of output. But they may also vary with the *accumulated experience* in producing a product over time.

Early economists placed great importance on a concept that is now called **learning by doing.** They believed that as countries gained experience in particular tasks, workers and managers would become more efficient in performing them. As people acquire expertise, costs tend to fall. There is substantial evidence that such learning by doing does occur. It is particularly important in many of today's knowledge-intensive high-tech industries.

The distinction between this phenomenon and the gains from economies of scale is illustrated in Figure 33-4. It is one more example of the difference between a movement along a curve and a shift of the curve.

The opportunity for learning by doing has an important implication: Policymakers need not accept *current* comparative advantages as given. Through such means as edu-

learning by doing
The reduction in unit costs that often results as workers learn through repeatedly performing the same tasks. It causes a downward shift in the average cost curve.

cation and tax incentives, they can seek to develop new comparative advantages.[1] Moreover, countries cannot complacently assume that their existing comparative advantages will persist. Misguided education policies, the wrong tax incentives, or policies that discourage risk taking can lead to the rapid erosion of a country's comparative advantage in particular products.

Sources of Comparative Advantage

We have seen that comparative advantage is the source of the gains from trade. But why do comparative advantages exist? Since a country's comparative advantage depends on its opportunity costs, we could also ask: Why do different countries have different opportunity costs?

Different Factor Endowments

The traditional answer to this question was provided early in the twentieth century by two Swedish economists, Eli Heckscher and Bertil Ohlin. Ohlin was subsequently awarded the Nobel Prize in economics for his work in the theory of international trade. Their explanation for international differences in opportunity costs is now incorporated in the Heckscher–Ohlin model. According to their theory, the international cost differences that form the basis for comparative advantage arise because factor endowments differ across countries. This is often called the *factor endowment theory of comparative advantage.*

To see how this theory works, consider the prices for various types of goods in countries *in the absence of trade.* A country that is well endowed with fertile land but has a small population (like Canada) will find that land is cheap but labour is expensive. It will therefore produce land-intensive agricultural goods cheaply and labour-intensive goods, such as machine tools, only at high cost. The reverse will be true for a second country that is small in size but possesses abundant and efficient labour (like Japan). As a result, the first country will have a comparative advantage in agricultural production and the second in goods that use much labour and little land.

FIGURE 33-4   Gains from Trade Due to Scale and Learning Effects

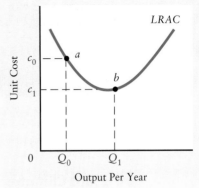

(i) Economies of scale

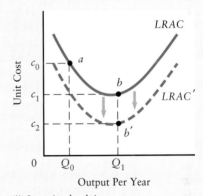

(ii) Learning by doing

Specialization may lead to gains from trade by permitting economies of larger-scale output, by leading to downward shifts of cost curves, or both. Consider a country that wishes to consume the quantity Q_0. Suppose that it can produce that quantity at an average cost per unit of c_0. Suppose further that the country has a comparative advantage in producing this product and can export the quantity $Q_0 Q_1$ if it produces Q_1. This may lead to cost savings in two ways.

As shown in part (i), the increased level of production of Q_1 compared to Q_0 permits it to *move along* its cost curve from a to b, thereby reducing costs per unit to c_1. This is an economy of scale.

As shown in part (ii), as workers and management become more experienced, they may be able to produce at lower costs. This is learning by doing. The downward *shift* of the cost curve lowers the cost of producing every unit of output. At output Q_1, costs per unit fall to c_2. The movement from a to b' incorporates both economies of scale and learning by doing.

---

[1] They can also foolishly use such policies to develop industries in which they do not have and will never achieve comparative advantages.

Canada is extremely well endowed with forests. It is no surprise, therefore, that it has a comparative advantage in a whole range of forestry products.

According to the Heckscher–Ohlin theory, countries have comparative advantages in the production of goods that use intensively the factors of production with which they are abundantly endowed.

For example, Canada is abundantly endowed with forests relative to most other countries. According to the Hecksher–Ohlin theory, Canada has a comparative advantage in goods that use forest products intensively, such as newsprint, paper, raw lumber, and wooden furniture. In contrast, relative to most other countries, Canada is sparsely endowed with labour. Thus, Canada has a comparative disadvantage in goods that use labour intensively, such as cotton or many other textile products.

Different Climates

The factor endowment theory has considerable power to explain comparative advantage but it does not provide the whole explanation. One additional influence comes from all those natural factors that can be called *climate* in the broadest sense. If you combine land, labour, and capital in the same way in Nicaragua and in Iceland, you will not get the same output of most agricultural goods. Sunshine, rainfall, and average temperature also matter. If you seek to work with wool or cotton in dry climates, you will get different results than when you work in damp climates. (You can, of course, artificially create any climate you wish in a factory, but it costs money to create what is freely provided elsewhere.)

Climate affects comparative advantage.

Of course, if we consider "warm weather" a factor of production, then we could simply say that countries like Nicaragua are better endowed with that factor than countries like Iceland. In this sense, explanations of comparative advantage based on different climates are really just a special case of explanations based on factor endowments.

Acquired Comparative Advantage

Today it is clear that many comparative advantages are *acquired*. Further, they can change. Thus, comparative advantage should be viewed as being *dynamic* rather than static. New industries are seen to depend more on human capital than on fixed physical capital or natural resources. The skills of a computer designer, a videogame programmer, or a sound mix technician are acquired by education and on-the-job training. Natural endowments of energy and raw materials cannot account for Silicon Valley's leadership in computer technology, for Canada's prominence in communications technology, for Taiwan's excellence in electronics, or for Switzerland's prominence in private banking. When countries find their former dominance (based on comparative advantage) in such smokestack industries as cars and steel declining, their firms need not sit idly by. Instead, they can begin to adapt by developing new areas of comparative advantage.

Contrasts

This modern view is in sharp contrast with the traditional assumption that cost structures based largely on a country's natural endowments lead to a given pattern of international comparative advantage. The traditional view suggests that a government interested in maximizing its citizens' material standard of living should encourage specialization of production in goods for which it currently has a comparative advantage. If all countries follow this advice, each will be specialized in a relatively narrow range of distinct products. The British will produce engineering products, Canadians will be producers of resource-based primary products, Americans will be farmers and factory workers, Central Americans will be banana and coffee growers, and so on.

There are surely elements of truth in both extreme views. It would be unwise to neglect resource endowments, climate, culture, social patterns, and institutional arrangements. But it would also be unwise to assume that all of them were innate and immutable.

To some extent, these views are reconciled by the theory of human capital, which is a topic we discussed in Chapter 14 in *Microeconomics*. Comparative advantages that depend on human capital are consistent with traditional Heckscher–Ohlin theory. The difference is that this type of capital is acquired through conscious decisions relating to such matters as education and technical training.

33.2 **The Determination of Trade Patterns**

Comparative advantage has been the central concept in our discussion about the sources of the gains from trade. If Canada has a comparative advantage in lumber and Italy has a comparative advantage in shoes, then the total output of lumber and shoes could be increased if Canada specialized in the production of lumber and Italy specialized in the production of shoes. With such patterns of specialization, Canada would naturally export lumber to Italy and Italy would export shoes to Canada.

It is one thing to discuss the potential gains from trade if countries specialized in the production of particular goods and exported these to other countries. But do *actual* trade patterns occur along the lines of comparative advantage? In this section of the chapter we use a simple demand-and-supply model to examine why Canada exports some products and imports others. We will see that comparative advantage, whether natural or acquired, plays a central role in determining actual trade patterns.

For data on Canadian trade by industry and by country, see Statistics Canada's website: www.statcan.ca. Go to "Canadian Statistics" and then "Trade."

There are some products, such as coffee and mangoes, that Canada does not produce (and will probably never produce). Any domestic consumption of these products must therefore be satisfied by imports from other countries. At the other extreme, there are some products, such as nickel or potash, of which Canada is one of the world's major suppliers, and demand in the rest of the world must be satisfied partly by exports from Canada. There are also some products, such as houses, that are so expensive to transport that every country produces approximately what it consumes.

Our interest in this section is in the many intermediate cases in which Canada is only one of many producers of an internationally traded product, as with beef, oil, copper, wheat, lumber, and newsprint. Will Canada be an exporter or an importer of such products? And what is the role played by comparative advantage?

The Law of One Price

Whether Canada imports or exports a product for which it is only one of many producers depends to a great extent on the product's price. This brings us to what economists call the *law of one price*.

The law of one price states that when a product that can be cheaply transported is traded throughout the entire world, it will tend to have a single worldwide price.

Many basic products—such as copper wire, steel pipe, iron ore, and computer RAM chips—fall within this category. The world price for each good is the price that equates the quantity demanded worldwide with the quantity supplied worldwide. The world price of an internationally traded product may be influenced greatly, or only slightly, by the demand and supply coming from any one country. The extent of one country's influence will depend on how important its quantities demanded and supplied are in relation to the worldwide totals.

The simplest case for us to study arises when the country, which we will take to be Canada, accounts for only a small part of the total worldwide demand and supply. In this case, Canada does not itself produce enough to influence the world price significantly. Similarly, Canadian purchases are too small a proportion of worldwide demand to affect the world price in any significant way. Producers and consumers in Canada thus face a world price that they cannot influence by their own actions.

Notice that in this case, the price that rules in the Canadian market must be the world price (adjusted for the exchange rate between the Canadian dollar and the foreign currency). The law of one price says that this must be so. What would happen if the Canadian domestic price diverged from the world price? If the Canadian price were below the world price, no supplier would sell in the Canadian market because more money could be made by selling abroad. The absence of supply to the Canadian market would thus drive up the Canadian price. Conversely, if the Canadian domestic price were above the worldwide price, no buyer would buy from a Canadian seller because money could be saved by buying abroad. The absence of demand on the Canadian market would thus drive down the Canadian price.

Practise with Study Guide Chapter 33, Exercise 5.

The Pattern of Foreign Trade

Let us now see what determines the pattern of international trade in such circumstances.

An Exported Product

To determine the pattern of Canadian trade, we first show the Canadian domestic demand and supply curves for some product, say, lumber. This is done in Figure 33-5. The intersection of these two curves tells us what the price and quantity would be *if there were no foreign trade*. Now compare this no-trade price with the world price of that product.[2] If the world price is higher, the actual price in Canada will exceed the no-trade price. In this situation there will be an excess of Canadian supply over Canadian demand. Domestic producers want to sell Q_2 units of lumber but domestic consumers want to buy only Q_1 units. If Canada were a closed economy, such excess supply would drive the price down to p_d. But in an open economy with a world price of p_w, this excess supply gets exported to Canada's trading partners.

Countries export products whose world price exceeds the price that would exist domestically if there were no foreign trade.

Export Development Canada is a Crown corporation devoted to improving Canada's export prospects. For information about Canada's exports, check out its website: www.edc.ca.

---

[2] If the world price is stated in terms of some foreign currency (as it often is), the price must be converted into Canadian dollars using the current exchange rate between the foreign currency and Canadian dollars.

What is the role of comparative advantage in this analysis? We have said that Canada will export lumber if the world price exceeds Canada's no-trade price. Note that in a competitive market the price of the product reflects the product's marginal cost, which in turn reflects the opportunity cost of producing the product. That Canada's no-trade price for lumber is lower than the world price reflects the fact that the opportunity cost of producing lumber in Canada is less than the opportunity cost of producing it in the rest of the world. Thus, by exporting goods that have a low no-trade price, Canada is exporting the goods for which it has a comparative advantage.

Countries export the goods for which they are low-cost producers. That is, they export goods for which they have a comparative advantage.

An Imported Product

Now consider some other product—for example, computer RAM chips. Once again, look first at the domestic demand and supply curves, shown this time in Figure 33-6. The intersection of these curves determines the no-trade price that would rule if there were no foreign trade. The world price of RAM chips is below the Canadian no-trade price so that, at the price ruling in Canada, domestic demand is larger and domestic supply is smaller than if the no-trade price had ruled. The excess of domestic demand over domestic supply is met by imports.

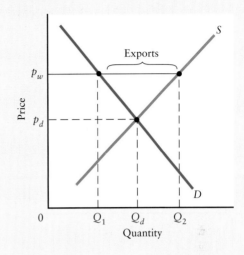

FIGURE 33-5   An Exported Good

Exports occur whenever there is excess supply domestically at the world price. The domestic demand and supply curves are D and S, respectively. The domestic price in the absence of foreign trade is p_d, with Q_d produced and consumed domestically. The world price of p_w is higher than p_d. At p_w, Q_1 is demanded while Q_2 is supplied domestically. The excess of the domestic supply over the domestic demand is exported.

Countries import products whose world price is less than the price that would exist domestically if there were no foreign trade.

Again, this analysis can be restated in terms of comparative advantage. The high Canadian no-trade price of RAM chips reflects the fact that RAM chips are more costly to produce in Canada than elsewhere in the world. This high cost means that Canada has a comparative disadvantage in RAM chips. So Canada imports goods for which it has a comparative disadvantage.

Countries import the goods for which they are high-cost producers. That is, they import goods for which they have a comparative disadvantage.

Is Comparative Advantage Obsolete?

In the debate preceding the signing of both the Canada–U.S. Free Trade Agreement and the North American Free Trade Agreement (NAFTA), some opponents argued that the agreements relied on an outdated view of the gains from trade based on comparative advantage. The theory of comparative advantage was said to be obsolete.

In spite of such assertions, comparative advantage remains an important economic concept. At any one time—because comparative advantage is reflected in international relative prices, and these relative prices determine what goods a country will import and what it will export—the operation of the price system will result in trade that

FIGURE 33-6   An Imported Good

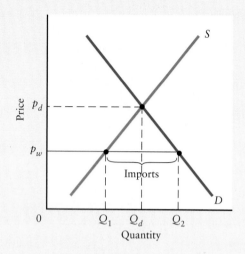

Imports occur whenever there is excess demand domestically at the world price. The domestic demand and supply curves are D and S, respectively. The domestic price in the absence of foreign trade is p_d, with Q_d produced and consumed domestically. The world price of p_w is less than p_d. At the world price Q_2 is demanded, whereas Q_1 is supplied domestically. The excess of domestic demand over domestic supply is satisfied through imports.

follows the current pattern of comparative advantage. For example, if Canadian costs of producing steel are particularly low relative to other Canadian costs, Canada's price of steel will be low by international standards, and steel will be a Canadian export (which it is). If Canada's costs of producing textiles are particularly high relative to other Canadian costs, Canada's price of textiles will be high by international standards, and Canada will import textiles (which it does). Thus, there is no reason to change the view that Ricardo long ago expounded: *Current comparative advantage is a major determinant of trade under free-market conditions.*

What has changed, however, is economists' views about the *determinants* of comparative advantage. It now seems that current comparative advantage may be more open to change by private entrepreneurial activities and by government policy than used to be thought. Thus, what is obsolete is the belief that a country's current pattern of comparative advantage, and hence its current pattern of imports and exports, must be accepted as given and unchangeable.

The theory that comparative advantage determines trade flows is not obsolete, but the theory that comparative advantage is completely determined by forces beyond the reach of public policy has been discredited.

It is one thing to observe that it is *possible* for governments to influence a country's pattern of comparative advantage. It is quite another to conclude that it is *advisable* for them to try. The case in support of a specific government intervention requires that (1) there is scope for governments to improve on the results achieved by the free market, (2) the costs of the intervention be less than the value of the improvement to be achieved, and (3) governments will actually be able to carry out the required interventionist policies (without, for example, being sidetracked by considerations of electoral advantage).

The Terms of Trade

We have seen that world production can be increased when countries specialize in the production of the products for which they have a comparative advantage and then trade with one another. We now ask: How will these gains from specialization and trade be shared among countries? The division of the gain depends on what is called the **terms of trade,** which relate to the quantity of imported goods that can be obtained per unit of goods exported. They are measured by the ratio of the price of exports to the price of imports.

A rise in the price of imported goods, with the price of exports unchanged, indicates a *fall in the terms of trade;* it will now take more exports to buy the same quantity of imports. Similarly, a rise in the price of exported goods, with the price of imports unchanged, indicates a *rise in the terms of trade;* it will now take fewer exports to buy the same quantity of imports. Thus, the ratio of these prices measures the amount of imports that can be obtained per unit of goods exported.

terms of trade
The ratio of the average price of a country's exports to the average price of its imports, both averages usually being measured by index numbers.

The terms of trade can be illustrated along with the country's production possibilities boundary, as shown in Figure 33-7. The figure shows the hypothetical case in which Canada produces wheat and cloth. As we saw earlier, the slope of Canada's production possibilities boundary shows the relative opportunity costs of producing the two goods in Canada. A steep production possibilities boundary indicates that only a small amount of cloth must be given up to get more wheat; thus cloth is relatively costly and wheat is relatively cheap. A flatter production possibilities boundary indicates that a larger amount of cloth must be given up to get more wheat; thus cloth is relatively cheap and wheat is relatively expensive. Thus, the slope of the production possibilities boundary in Figure 33-7 shows the relative price of cloth (in terms of wheat) that Canada faces in the absence of international trade.

If, through international trade, Canada has access to different relative prices, Canada will be led to specialize in the production of one good or the other. In Figure 33-7, we show a case in which the relative price of cloth is lower when trade occurs than when Canada does not trade. Faced with a lower relative price of cloth, Canada ends up specializing in the production of the relatively high-priced product (wheat), and importing the relatively low-priced product (cloth). This point of specialization is point S in Figure 33-7.

The *blue* lines in the figure show alternative values for Canada's terms of trade. A rise in the terms of trade indicates a decrease in the price of imports relative to the price of exports—that is, a fall in the relative price of cloth (or a rise in the relative price of wheat). This increase in the terms of trade is shown as an upward rotation of the blue line from T_0 to T_1. A reduction in the terms of trade is shown as a downward rotation in the blue line, from T_1 to T_0.

It should be clear from Figure 33-7 why changes in the terms of trade are important. Suppose the international relative prices are initially given by T_0. Canada specializes in the production of wheat (point S) but consumes at some point like A where it finances imports of cloth with exports of wheat. Now suppose there is a shift in world demand toward wheat and away from cloth, and this leads to an increase in the relative price of wheat. The terms of trade increase to T_1 and, with unchanged production at point S, Canada can now afford to consume at a point like B where consumption of both wheat and cloth has increased.

A rise in a country's terms of trade is beneficial because it expands the country's consumption possibilities.

Conversely, a reduction in the price of a country's exports (relative to the price of its imports) is harmful for a country. In Figure 33-7, this is shown as a change of the terms of trade from T_1 to T_0. Even though production may remain unchanged, the range of goods available to be consumed falls, and this reduction in consumption possibilities leads to an overall loss of welfare.

FIGURE 33-7   A Change in the Terms of Trade

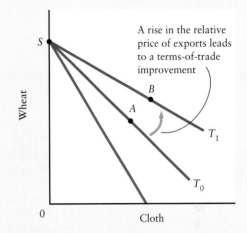

Changes in the terms of trade lead to changes in a country's consumption possibilities. The hypothetical production possibilities boundary is shown for Canada. At relative prices T_0, Canada specializes in the production of wheat, producing at point S, but is able to consume at a point like A. It pays for its imports of cloth with its exports of wheat. If the price of wheat rises relative to the price of cloth, production remains at S but the line T_1 shows Canada's new consumption possibilities. Consumption can now take place at a point like B where consumption of both wheat and cloth has increased. The increase in the terms of trade makes Canada better off because of the increase in consumption possibilities.

Practise with Study Guide Chapter 33, Exercise 3.

How do we measure the terms of trade in real economies? Because international trade involves many countries and many products, we cannot use the simple ratio of the prices of two goods as in Figure 33-7. The basic principle, however, is the same. A country's terms of trade are computed as an index number:

$$\text{Terms of trade} = \frac{\text{Index of export prices}}{\text{Index of import prices}} \times 100$$

A rise in the index is referred to as a *favourable* change in a country's terms of trade (sometimes called a terms of trade *improvement*). A decrease in the index of the terms of trade is called an *unfavourable* change (or a terms of trade *deterioration*). For example, the sharp rise in oil prices in the 1970s led to large unfavourable shifts in the terms of trade of oil-importing countries. When oil prices fell sharply in the mid-1980s, the terms of trade of oil-importing countries changed favourably. The converse was true for oil-exporting countries.

Canada's terms of trade since 1961 are shown in Figure 33-8. As is clear, the terms of trade are quite variable, reflecting frequent changes in the relative prices of different products. Note the dramatic increase (improvement) in Canada's terms of trade in the early 1970s, reflecting the large increase in oil prices caused by OPEC's output restrictions. Since Canada is a net exporter of oil, its terms of trade improve when the price of oil increases.

FIGURE 33-8   Canada's Terms of Trade, 1961–2003

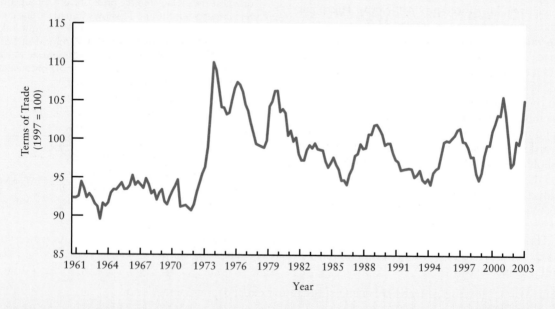

Canada's terms of trade have been quite variable over the past 40 years. The data shown are Canada's terms of trade—the ratio of an index of Canadian export prices to an index of Canadian import prices. As the relative prices of lumber, oil, wheat, electronic equipment, textiles, fruit, and other products change, the terms of trade naturally change.

(Source: Statistics Canada, CANSIM database, Series V1997754 and V1997751 and authors' calculations.)

S U M M A R Y

33.1 The Gains from Trade

- Country A has an absolute advantage over Country B in the production of a specific product when the absolute resource cost of the product is less in Country A than in Country B.
- Country A has a comparative advantage over Country B in the production of a specific good if the forgone output of other goods is less in Country A than in Country B.
- Comparative advantage occurs whenever countries have different opportunity costs of producing particular goods. World production of all products can be increased if each country transfers resources into the production of the products for which it has a comparative advantage.
- The most important proposition in the theory of the gains from trade is that trade allows all countries to obtain the goods for which they do not have a comparative advantage at a lower opportunity cost than they would face if they were to produce all products for themselves; spe-

cialization and trade therefore allow all countries to have more of all products than they could have if they tried to be self-sufficient.
- As well as gaining the advantages of specialization arising from comparative advantage, a nation that engages in trade and specialization may realize the benefits of economies of large-scale production and of learning by doing.
- Classical theory regarded comparative advantage as largely determined by natural resource endowments that are difficult to change. Economists now believe that some comparative advantages can be acquired and consequently can be changed. A country may, in this view, influence its role in world production and trade. Successful intervention leads to a country's acquiring a comparative advantage; unsuccessful intervention fails to develop such an advantage.

33.2 The Determination of Trade Patterns

- The law of one price says that internationally traded goods that are inexpensive to transport must sell at the same price in all countries. Economists call this the world price.
- Countries will export a good when the world price exceeds the price that would exist in the country if there were no trade. The low no-trade price reflects a low opportunity cost and thus a comparative advantage in that good. Thus, countries export goods for which they have a comparative advantage.
- Countries will import a good when the world price is less than the price that would exist in the country if there

were no trade. The high no-trade price reflects a high opportunity cost and thus a comparative disadvantage in that good. Thus, countries import goods for which they have a comparative disadvantage.
- The terms of trade refer to the ratio of the prices of goods exported to the prices of those imported. The terms of trade determine the quantity of imports that can be obtained per unit of exports.
- A favourable change in the terms of trade—a rise in export prices relative to import prices—is beneficial for a country because it expands its consumption possibilities.

K E Y   C O N C E P T S

Interpersonal, interregional, and international specialization

Absolute advantage and comparative advantage

Opportunity cost and comparative advantage

The gains from trade: specialization, scale economies, and learning by doing

The sources of comparative advantage

Factor endowments

Acquired comparative advantage

The law of one price

The terms of trade

STUDY EXERCISES

1. Fill in the blanks to make the following statements correct.

   a. A nation that engages in international trade is able to specialize in producing goods that it produces _____ and trade to obtain goods that it does not produce _____.

   b. The "gains from trade" refers to the increased _____ due to specialization and trade.

   c. Suppose Argentina can produce one kilogram of beef for $2.50 and Brazil can produce one kilogram of beef for $2.90. Argentina is said to have a(n) _____ in beef production over Brazil. The gains from trade do *not* depend on _____.

   d. Comparative advantage is based on _____ rather than absolute costs.

   e. It is possible for a country to have a comparative advantage in some good and a(n) _____ in none.

   f. If all countries specialize in the production of goods for which they have a comparative advantage, then world output will _____.

   g. If opportunity costs are the same in all countries, there is no _____ and no possibility of _____.

2. Fill in the blanks to make the following statements correct.

   a. A product such as coffee beans is easily transported and traded around the world. The law of _____ tells us that it will tend to have _____ worldwide price.

   b. If the domestic price of copper wire in Canada (in the absence of trade) is $20 per unit and the world price is $24 per unit, then Canada will have an excess _____ which it will then _____. The opportunity cost of producing copper wire in Canada is _____ than the opportunity cost of producing it in the rest of the world.

   c. Canada will import goods for which it has an excess _____ at the world price. In the absence of trade, the _____ price of these goods would be less than the _____ price.

   d. A rise in Canada's terms of trade means that the average price of Canada's _____ has risen compared to the average price of Canada's _____. This change is referred to as a terms of trade _____.

   e. The terms of trade determine the quantity of _____ that can be obtained per unit of _____.

3. The following diagram shows the production possibilities boundary for Arcticland, a country that produces two goods, ice and fish. Labour is the only factor of production.

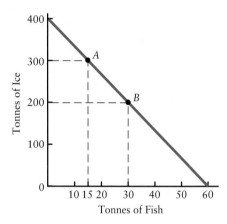

   a. Beginning at any point on Arcticland's production possibilities boundary, what is the opportunity cost of producing 10 more tonnes of fish?

   b. Beginning at any point on Arcticland's production possibilities boundary, what is the opportunity cost of producing 100 more tonnes of ice?

4. The following table shows the production of wheat and corn in Brazil and Mexico. Assume that both countries have one million acres of arable land.

	Brazil	Mexico
Wheat	90 bushels per acre	50 bushels per acre
Corn	30 bushels per acre	20 bushels per acre

   a. Which country has the absolute advantage in wheat? In corn? Explain.

   b. Which country has the comparative advantage in wheat? In corn? Explain.

   c. Explain why one country can have an absolute advantage in both goods but cannot have a comparative advantage in both goods.

   d. On a scale diagram with wheat on the horizontal axis and corn on the vertical axis, draw each country's production possibilities boundary.

   e. What is shown by the slope of each country's production possibilities boundary? Be as precise as possible.

5. The following diagrams show the production possibilities boundaries for Canada and France, both of which produce two goods, wine and lumber.

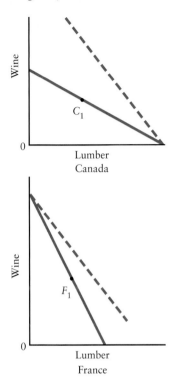

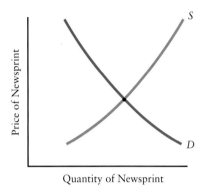

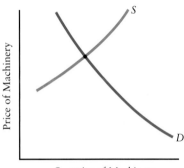

a. Which country has the comparative advantage in lumber? Explain.
b. Which country has the comparative advantage in wine? Explain.
c. Suppose Canada and France are initially not trading with each other and are producing at points C_1 and F_1, respectively. Suppose when trade is introduced, the free-trade relative prices are shown by the dashed line. Which combination of goods will each country now produce?
d. In this case, what will be the pattern of trade for each country?

6. The diagrams below show the Canadian markets for newsprint and machinery, which we assume to be competitive.

a. Suppose there is no international trade. What would be the equilibrium price and quantity in the Canadian newsprint and machinery markets?
b. Now suppose Canada is open to trade with the rest of the world. If the world price of newsprint is higher than the price of newsprint from part (a), what will happen to the levels of domestic production and consumption? Explain.

c. If the world price of machinery is lower than the price of machinery from part (a), what happens to the levels of domestic consumption and production? Explain.

7. The table below shows indexes for the prices of imports and exports over several years for a hypothetical country.

Year	Import Prices	Export Prices	Terms of Trade
1998	90	110	—
1999	95	87	—
2000	98	83	—
2001	100	100	—
2002	102	105	—
2003	100	112	—
2004	103	118	—

a. Compute the terms of trade in each year for this country and fill in the table.
b. In which years do the terms of trade improve?
c. In which years do the terms of trade deteriorate?
d. Explain why a terms of trade "improvement" is good for the country.

8. For each of the following events, explain the likely effect on Canada's terms of trade. Your existing knowledge of Canada's imports and exports should be adequate to answer this question.

   a. A hurricane damages much of Brazil's coffee crop.
   b. OPEC countries succeed in significantly restricting the world supply of oil.
   c. Several new large copper mines come into production in Chile.
   d. A major recession in Southeast Asia reduces the world demand for pork.

DISCUSSION QUESTIONS

1. Adam Smith saw a close connection between the wealth of a nation and its willingness "freely to engage" in foreign trade. What is the connection?

2. One critic of the North American Free Trade Agreement argued that "it can't be in our interest to sign this deal; Mexico gains too much from it." What does the theory of the gains from trade have to say about that criticism?

3. One product innovation that appears imminent is the electric car. However, development costs are high and economies of scale and learning by doing are both likely to be operative. As a result, there will be a substantial competitive advantage for those who develop a marketable product early. What implications might this have for government policies toward North American automobile manufacturers' activities in this area? Should the Canadian or U.S. governments encourage joint efforts by Chrysler, Ford, and GM, even if this appears to lessen competition between them?

4. Studies of Canadian trade patterns have shown that industries with high wages are among the largest and fastest-growing export sectors. One example is the computer software industry. Does this finding contradict the principle of comparative advantage?

5. Predict what each of the following events would do to the terms of trade of the importing country and the exporting country, other things being equal.

   a. A blight destroys a large part of the coffee beans produced in the world.
   b. The Koreans cut the price of the steel they sell to Canada.
   c. General inflation of 4 percent occurs around the world.
   d. Violation of OPEC output quotas leads to a sharp fall in the price of oil.

6. Are there always benefits to specialization and trade? When are the benefits greatest? Under what situations are there *no* benefits from specialization and trade?

CHAPTER 34

Trade Policy

LEARNING OBJECTIVES

L

1 Describe the various situations in which a country may rationally choose to protect some industries.

2 List the most common fallacious arguments in favour of protection.

3 Explain the effects of a tariff or quota on imported goods.

4 Explain why trade-remedy laws are sometimes just thinly disguised protection.

5 Distinguish between trade creation and trade diversion.

6 List the main features of the North American Free Trade Agreement.

Conducting business in a foreign country is not always easy. Differences in language, in local laws and customs, and in currency often complicate transactions. Our concern in this chapter, however, is not with these complications but with government policy toward international trade, which is called **trade policy**. At one extreme is a policy of free trade—that is, an absence of any form of government interference with the free flow of international trade. Any departure from free trade designed to protect domestic industries from foreign competition is called **protectionism.**

We begin by briefly restating the case for free trade and then go on to study various valid and invalid arguments that are commonly advanced for some degree of protection. We then explore some of the methods commonly used to restrict trade, such as tariffs and quotas. Finally, we examine the many modern institutions designed to foster freer trade on either a global or a regional basis. Of central importance to Canada is the North American Free Trade Agreement (NAFTA).

trade policy
A government's policy involving restrictions placed on international trade.

protectionism Any government policy that interferes with free trade in order to give some protection to domestic industries against foreign competition.

34.1 **Free Trade or Protection?**

Today, most governments accept the proposition that a relatively free flow of international trade is desirable for the health of their individual economies. But heated debates still occur over trade policy. Should a country permit the completely free flow of international trade, or should it sometimes seek to protect its local producers from foreign competition? If some protection is desired, should it be achieved by tariffs or by nontariff barriers? **Tariffs** are taxes designed to raise the price of foreign goods. **Nontariff barriers (NTBs)** are devices other than tariffs designed to reduce the flow of imports; examples are quotas and customs procedures that are deliberately more cumbersome than necessary.

tariff A tax applied on imports of goods or services.

nontariff barriers (NTBs) Restrictions other than tariffs designed to reduce the flow of imported goods or services.

The Case for Free Trade

The case for free trade was presented in Chapter 33. Comparative advantages arise whenever countries have different opportunity costs. Free trade encourages all countries to specialize in producing products in which they have a comparative advantage. This pattern of specialization maximizes world production and hence maximizes average world living standards (as measured by the world's per capita GDP).

Free trade does not necessarily make *everyone* better off than they would be in its absence. For example, reducing an existing tariff often results in individual groups receiving a smaller share of a larger world output so that they lose even though the average person gains. If we ask whether it is *possible* for free trade to improve everyone's living standards, the answer is yes because the larger total value of output that free trade generates could, at least in principle, be divided up in such a way that every individual is better off. If we ask whether free trade always does so in practice, however, the answer is, not necessarily.

Free trade makes the country as a whole better off, even though it may not make every individual in the country better off.

Given that all countries can be better off by specializing in those goods in which they have a comparative advantage, it is puzzling that most countries of the world continue in some way to restrict the flow of trade. Why do tariffs and other barriers to trade continue to exist two centuries after Adam Smith and David Ricardo stated the case for free trade? Is there a valid case for some protection?

The Case for Protection

Two kinds of arguments for protection are commonly offered. The first concerns national objectives *other than* maximizing total income; the second concerns the desire to increase one country's national income, possibly at the expense of the national incomes of other countries.

Objectives Other than Maximizing National Income

A country's national income may be maximized with free trade and yet it may still be rational to oppose free trade because of other policy objectives.

Countries whose economies are based on the production of only a few goods face risks from fluctuations in world prices. For this reason, protection to promote diversification may be viewed as desirable.

Advantages of Diversification.   For a very small country, specializing in the production of only a few products—though dictated by comparative advantage—might involve risks that the country does not wish to take. One such risk is that technological advances may render its basic product obsolete. Another risk, especially for countries specialized in producing a small range of agricultural products, is that swings in world prices lead to large swings in national income. Everyone understands these risks, but there is debate about what governments can do about it. The pro-tariff argument is that the government can encourage a more diversified economy by protecting industries that otherwise could not compete. Opponents argue that governments, being naturally influenced by political motives, are poor judges of which industries can be protected in order to produce diversification at a reasonable cost.

Protection of Specific Groups.   Although specialization according to comparative advantage will maximize per capita GDP over the whole economy, some specific groups may have higher incomes under protection than under free trade. Of particular interest in Canada and the United States has been the effect that greater international trade has on the incomes of unskilled workers.

Consider the ratio of skilled workers to unskilled workers. There are plenty of both types throughout the world. Compared to much of the rest of the world, however, Canada has more skilled and fewer unskilled people. When trade is expanded because of a reduction in tariffs, Canada will tend to export goods made by its abundant skilled workers and import goods made by unskilled workers. (This is the basic prediction of the *factor endowment theory* of comparative advantage that we discussed in Chapter 33.) Because Canada is now exporting more goods made by skilled labour, the domestic demand for such labour rises. Because Canada is now importing more goods made by unskilled labour, the domestic demand for such labour falls. This specialization according to comparative advantage raises average Canadian living standards, but it will also tend to raise the wages of skilled Canadian workers relative to the wages of unskilled Canadian workers.

If increasing trade has these effects, then reducing trade by raising trade barriers can have the opposite effects. Raising trade barriers may raise the incomes of unskilled Canadian workers, giving them a larger share of a smaller total GDP. The conclusion is that trade restrictions can improve the earnings of one group whenever the restrictions increase the demand for that group's services. This is done, however, at the expense of a reduction in *overall* national income and hence the country's average living standards.

This analysis is important because it reveals both the grain of truth and the dangers that lie behind the resistance to trade liberalization (i.e., freer trade) on the part of some labour groups and some organizations whose main concern is with the poor.

Social and distributional concerns may lead to the rational adoption of protectionist policies. But the cost of such protection is a reduction in the country's average living standards.

Economists cannot say that it is irrational for a society to sacrifice some income to achieve broader social goals. But economists can do three things when presented with such arguments for adopting protectionist measures. First, they can ask if the proposed measures really do achieve the ends suggested. Second, they can calculate the cost of the measures in terms of lowered average living standards. Third, they can see if there are alternative means of achieving the stated goals at lower cost in terms of lost national income.

Maximizing National Income

Next we consider several arguments for the use of tariffs when the objective is to maximize a country's national income.

To Improve the Terms of Trade.   Tariffs can be used to change the terms of trade in favour of a country that makes up a large fraction of the world demand for some product that it imports. By restricting its demand for that product through a tariff, it can force down the price that foreign exporters receive for that product. The price paid by domestic consumers will probably rise but as long as the increase is less than the tariff, foreign suppliers will receive less per unit. For example, a 20 percent U.S. tariff on the import of Canadian softwood lumber might raise the price paid by U.S. consumers by 12 percent and lower the price received by Canadian suppliers by 8 percent (the difference between the two prices being received by the U.S. treasury). This reduction in the price received by

Practise with Study Guide Chapter 34, Extension Exercise E1.

the foreign suppliers of a U.S. import is a terms-of-trade improvement for the United States (and a terms-of-trade deterioration for Canada).

Note that not all countries can improve their terms of trade by levying tariffs on imported goods. A *necessary* condition is that the importing country has *market power*, in other words, that it is a large importer of the good in question, so that its restrictive trade policies lead to a decline in the world price of its imports. Small countries, like Canada, are not large enough importers of any good to have a significant effect on world prices. For small countries, therefore, tariffs cannot improve their terms of trade.

Large countries can improve their terms of trade by levying tariffs on some imported goods; small countries cannot.

infant industry argument   The argument that new domestic industries with potential for economies of scale or learning by doing need to be protected from competition from established, low-cost foreign producers so that they can grow large enough to achieve costs as low as those of foreign producers.

To Protect Infant Industries.   The oldest valid argument for protection as a means of raising living standards concerns economies of scale. It is usually called the **infant industry argument.** An infant industry is nothing more than a new, small industry. If such an industry has large economies of scale, costs will be high when the industry is small but will fall as the industry grows. In such industries, the country first in the field has a tremendous advantage. A developing country may find that in the early stages of development, its industries are unable to compete with established foreign rivals. A trade restriction may protect these industries from foreign competition while they grow up. When they are large enough, they will be able to produce as cheaply as foreign rivals and thus be able to compete without protection.

Most of the now industrialized countries developed their industries initially under quite heavy tariff protection. (In Canada's case, the National Policy of 1876 established a high tariff wall behind which many Canadian industries developed and thrived for many years.) Once the industrial sector was well developed, these countries moved to reduce their levels of protection, thus moving a long way toward freer trade. Electronics in Taiwan, automobiles in Japan, commercial aircraft in Europe (specifically the consortium of European governments that created Airbus), and shipbuilding in South Korea are all examples in which protection of infant industries was successful. In each case, the national industry, protected by its home government, developed into a major player in the global marketplace.

One practical problem with this argument for protection is that some infants "never grow up." Once the young firm gets used to operating in a protected environment, it may resist having that protection disappear, even though all economies of scale may have been achieved. This is as much a political problem as an economic one. Political leaders must therefore be careful before offering protection to infant industries because they must recognize the political difficulties involved in removing that protection in the future.

To Encourage Learning by Doing.   Learning by doing, which we discussed in Chapter 33, suggests that the pattern of comparative advantage can be changed. If a country learns enough by producing products for which it currently has a comparative *dis*advantage, it may gain in the long run by specializing in those products, developing a comparative advantage as the learning process lowers their costs.

Learning by doing is an example of what in Chapter 33 we called *dynamic* comparative advantage. The success over the past four decades of such newly industrializing countries (NICs) as Hong Kong, South Korea, Singapore, Taiwan, Indonesia, and Thailand seemed to many observers to be based on acquired skills and government policies that created favourable business conditions. These successes gave rise to the theory that comparative advantages can change and that they can be developed by suitable government policies, which can, however, take many forms other than restricting trade.

Some countries have succeeded in developing strong comparative advantages in targeted industries, but others have failed. One reason such policies sometimes fail is that protecting local industries from foreign competition may make the industries unadaptive and complacent. Another reason is the difficulty of identifying the industries that will be able to succeed in the long run. All too often, the protected infant grows up to be a weakling requiring permanent protection for its continued existence, or else the rate of learning is slower than for similar industries in countries that do not provide protection from the chill winds of international competition. In these instances, the anticipated comparative advantage never materializes. The NICs mentioned above avoided these problems by insisting that the protected industries serve the export market. If they could not succeed within a few years in the tough world of international competition, they lost their domestic support.

To Earn Economic Profits.   Another argument for tariffs or other trade restrictions is to help create an advantage in producing or marketing some new product that is expected to generate economic profits. To the extent that all lines of production earn normal profits, there is no reason to produce goods other than ones for which a country has a comparative advantage. Some goods, however, are produced in industries containing a few large firms where economies of scale provide a natural barrier to entry. Firms in these industries can earn economic profits (that is, greater than normal profits) even over long periods of time. If protection of the domestic market can increase the chance that one of the protected domestic firms will become established and thus earn high profits, the protection may pay off. This is the general idea behind the concept of *strategic trade policy.*

Opponents of strategic trade policy argue that it is nothing more than a modern version of age-old and faulty justifications for tariff protection. Once all countries try to be strategic, they will all waste vast sums trying to break into industries in which there is no room for most of them. Domestic consumers would benefit most, they say, if their governments let other countries engage in this game. Consumers could then buy the cheap, subsidized foreign products and export traditional nonsubsidized products in return. The opponents of strategic trade policy also argue that democratic governments that enter the game of picking and backing winners are likely to make more bad choices than good ones. One bad choice, with all of its massive development costs written off, would require that many good choices also be made in order to make the equivalent in profits that would allow taxpayers to break even overall.

An ongoing dispute between Canada and Brazil illustrates how strategic trade policy is often difficult to distinguish from pure protection. The world's two major producers of regional jets are Bombardier, based in Montreal, and Embraer SA, based in Brazil. For several years, each company has accused its competitor's government of using illegal subsidies to help the domestic company sell jets in world markets. Brazil's Pro-Ex program provides Embraer's customers with low-interest loans with which to purchase Embraer's jets. The Canadian government's Technology Partnerships program subsidizes research and development activities in high-tech aerospace and defence companies. As the leading Canadian aerospace company, Bombardier benefits significantly from this program.

In 1999, the World Trade Organization (WTO) ruled that both the Brazilian and Canadian governments were using illegal subsidy programs to support their aerospace firms. Both countries, however, naturally view their respective programs as necessary responses to the other country's subsidization. Many economists believe that an agreement to eliminate both programs would leave a "level playing field" while saving Brazilian and Canadian taxpayers a considerable amount of money. By 2003, after much discussion

For a list and discussion of many ongoing trade disputes, see the WTO's website: www.wto.org.

and debate, this issue remained unresolved. Both countries continue to support their respective aerospace firms and both sets of taxpayers continue to foot the bill.

The Importance of Competition

In today's world, a country's products must stand up to international competition if they are to survive. Over time, this requirement demands that they hold their own in competition for successful innovations. Over even so short a period as a few years, firms that do not develop new products and new production methods fall seriously behind their competitors in many industries. Protection, by reducing competition from foreign firms, reduces the incentive for industries to fight to succeed internationally. If any one country adopts high tariffs unilaterally, its domestic industries will become less competitive. Secure in its home market because of the tariff wall, its protected industries are likely to become less and less competitive in the international market. As the gap between domestic and foreign industries widens, any tariff wall will provide less and less protection. Eventually, the domestic industries will succumb to the foreign competition. Meanwhile, domestic living standards will fall relative to foreign ones as an increasing productivity gap opens between domestic protected industries and foreign, internationally oriented ones.

Although restrictive trade policies have sometimes been pursued following a rational assessment of the approximate cost, such policies are often pursued for political objectives or on fallacious economic grounds, with little appreciation of the actual costs involved.

Fallacious Arguments for Protection

We have seen that free trade is generally beneficial for a country overall even though it does not necessarily make every person better off. We have also seen that there are some situations in which there are valid arguments for restricting trade. For every valid argument, however, there are many fallacious arguments—many of these are based, directly or indirectly, on the misconception that in every transaction there is a winner and a loser. Here we review a few arguments that are frequently advanced in political debates concerning international trade.

Keep the Money at Home

This argument says that if I buy a foreign good, I have the good and the foreigner has the money, whereas if I buy the same good locally, I have the good and our country has the money, too. This argument is based on a common misconception. It assumes that domestic money actually goes abroad physically when imports are purchased and that trade flows only in one direction. But when Canadian importers purchase Japanese goods, they do not send dollars abroad. They (or their financial agents) buy Japanese yen and use them to pay the Japanese manufacturers. They purchase the yen on the foreign-exchange market by giving up dollars to someone who wishes to use them for expenditure in Canada. Even if the money did go abroad physically—that is, if a Japanese firm accepted a shipload of Canadian $100 bills—it would be because that firm (or someone to whom it could sell the dollars) wanted them to spend in the only country where they are legal tender—Canada.

Canadian currency, or any other national currency, ultimately does no one any good except as purchasing power. It would be miraculous if Canadian money could be exported in return for real goods. After all, the Bank of Canada has the power to create as much new Canadian money as it wishes (at almost zero direct cost). It is only because Canadian money can buy Canadian products and Canadian assets that others want it.

Protect Against Low-Wage Foreign Labour

This argument says that the products of low-wage countries will drive Canadian products from the market, and the high Canadian standard of living will be dragged down to that of its poorer trading partners. For example, if Canada imports cotton shirts from China, higher-cost Canadian textile firms may go out of business and Canadian workers may be laid off. Arguments of this sort have swayed many voters over the years.

As a prelude to considering this argument, think what the argument would imply if taken out of the international context and put into a local one, where the same principles govern the gains from trade. Is it really impossible for a rich person to gain by trading with a poor person? Would the local millionaire be better off if she did all her own typing, gardening, and cooking? No one believes that a rich person gains nothing by trading with those who are less rich.

Why, then, must a rich group of people lose when they trade with a poor group? "Well," some may say, "the poor group will price its goods too cheaply." Does anyone believe that consumers lose from buying in discount houses or supermarkets just because the prices are lower there than at the old-fashioned corner store? Consumers gain when they can buy the same goods at a lower price. If Chinese, Mexican, or Malaysian firms pay low wages and sell their goods cheaply, workers in those countries may suffer, but Canadians will gain by obtaining imports at a low cost in terms of the goods that must be exported in return. The cheaper our imports are, the better off we are in terms of the goods and services available for domestic consumption.

As we said earlier in this chapter, *some* Canadians may be better off if Canada places high tariffs on the import of Chinese goods. In particular, if the Chinese goods compete with goods made by unskilled Canadian workers, then those unskilled workers will be better off if a Canadian tariff protects their firms and thus their jobs. But Canadian income overall—that is, average per capita real income—will be higher when there is free trade.

See Chapter 34 of www.pearsoned.ca/ragan for an interview with MIT's Paul Krugman, who explains why countries do not "compete" against each other: Paul Krugman, "Fresh Thoughts from a Saltwater Economist."

Exports Are Good; Imports Are Bad

Exports create domestic income; imports create income for foreigners. Thus, other things being equal, exports tend to increase our total GDP, and imports tend to reduce it. Surely, then, it is desirable to encourage exports by subsidizing them and to discourage imports by taxing them. This is an appealing argument, but it is incorrect.

Exports raise GDP by adding to the value of domestic output and income, but they do not add to the value of domestic consumption. The standard of living in a country depends on the level of consumption, not on the level of income. In other words, income is not of much use except that it provides the means for consumption.

If exports really were "good" and imports really were "bad," then a fully employed economy that managed to increase exports without a corresponding increase in imports ought to be better off. Such a change, however, would result in a reduction in current standards of living because when more goods are sent abroad but no more are brought in from abroad, the total goods available for domestic consumption must fall.

The living standards of a country depend on the goods and services consumed in that country. The importance of exports is that they provide the resources required to purchase imports, either now or in the future.

Create Domestic Jobs

It is sometimes said that an economy with substantial unemployment, such as Canada during much of the 1990s, provides an exception to the case for freer trade. Suppose that tariffs or import quotas cut the imports of Japanese cars, Korean textiles, German kitchen equipment, and Polish vodka. Surely, the argument goes, this will create more employment in Canadian industries producing similar products. This may be true but it will also *reduce* employment in other industries.

The Japanese, Koreans, Germans, and Poles can buy from Canada only if they earn Canadian dollars by selling their domestically produced goods and services to Canada (or by borrowing dollars from Canada).[1] The decline in their sales of cars, textiles, kitchen equipment, and vodka will decrease their purchases of Canadian lumber, cars, software, banking services, and holidays. Jobs will be lost in Canadian export industries and gained in industries that formerly faced competition from imports. The major long-term effect is that the same amount of total employment in Canada will merely be redistributed among industries. In the process, living standards will be reduced because employment expands in inefficient import-competing industries and contracts in efficient exporting industries.

A country that imposes tariffs in an attempt to create domestic jobs risks starting a "trade war" with its trading partners. Such a trade war can easily leave every country worse off, as world output (and thus income) falls significantly. An income-reducing trade war followed the onset of the Great Depression in 1929 as many countries increased tariffs to protect their domestic industries in an attempt to stimulate domestic production and employment. Most economists agree that this trade war made the Great Depression worse than it otherwise would have been.

Several fallacious arguments for protection often appear in political debate. These arguments suffer from a misunderstanding of the sources of gains from trade or from the misbelief that protection can increase total employment.

34.2 Methods of Protection

We now go on to explore the various tools that governments use to provide protection to domestic industries.

Two main types of protectionist policy are illustrated in Figure 34-1. Both cause the price of the imported good to rise and its quantity demanded to fall. They differ, however, in how they achieve these results. The caption to the figure analyzes these two types of policy.

Tariffs

A tariff, also called an *import duty*, is a tax on imported goods. For example, consider a Canadian firm that wants to import cotton T-shirts from India at $5 per shirt. If the

---

[1]They can also get dollars by selling to other countries and then using their currencies to buy Canadian dollars. But this intermediate step only complicates the transaction; it does not change its fundamental nature. Other countries must have earned the dollars by selling goods to Canada or borrowing from Canada.

Canadian government levies a 20 percent tariff on imported cotton shirts, the Canadian firm pays $5 to the Indian exporter *plus* $1 (20 percent of $5) in import duties to the Canada Customs and Revenue Agency. The immediate effect of a tariff is therefore to increase the domestic price of the T-shirt to $6. This price increase has important implications for domestic consumers as well as domestic producers. The effect of a tariff is shown in Figure 34-1.

The initial effect of the tariff is to raise the domestic price of the imported product above its world price by the amount of the tariff. Imports fall. As a result, foreign producers sell less and must transfer resources to other lines of production. The price received on domestically produced units rises, as does the quantity produced domestically. On both counts, domestic producers earn more. However, the cost of producing the extra production at home exceeds the price at which it could be purchased on the world market. Thus, the benefit to domestic producers comes at the expense of domestic consumers. Indeed, domestic consumers lose on two counts: First, they consume less of the product because its price rises, and second, they pay a higher price for the amount that they do consume. This extra spending ends up in two places: The extra that is paid on all units produced at home goes to domestic producers, and the extra that is paid on units still imported goes to the government as tariff revenue.

The overall loss to the domestic economy from levying a tariff is best seen in terms of the changes in consumer and producer surplus. Before the tariff, consumer surplus was equal to the entire area below the demand curve and above the price line at p_w. After the tariff, the price increase leads to less consumption and less consumer surplus. The loss of consumer surplus is the sum of the areas ①, ②, ③, and ④ in Figure 34-1. As domestic producers respond to the higher domestic price by increasing their production and sales, they earn more producer surplus, equal to area ①. Finally, the taxpayers gain the tariff revenue equal to area ③. This is simply a redistribution of surplus away from consumers toward taxpayers. In summary:

Loss of consumer surplus = ① + ② + ③ + ④
Gain of producer surplus = ①
Gain of tariff revenue   = ③
—————————————————————————————
Net loss in surplus   = ② + ④

The overall effect of the tariff is therefore to create a deadweight loss to the domestic economy equal to areas ② plus ④. Domestic consumers are worse off, while domestic firms and taxpayers are better off. But the net effect is a loss of surplus for the economy. This is the overall cost of levying a tariff.

A tariff imposes costs on domestic consumers, generates benefits for domestic producers, and generates revenue for the government. But the overall net effect is negative; a tariff generates a deadweight loss for the economy.

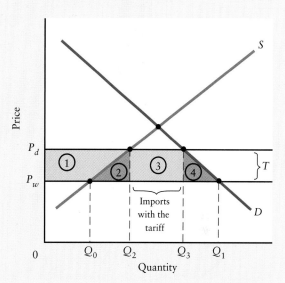

FIGURE 34-1   The Deadweight Loss of a Tariff

A tariff imposes a deadweight loss for the importing country. Before the tariff, the price in the domestic economy is the world price, p_w. Imports are Q_0Q_1. With a tariff of $\$T$ per unit, the domestic price rises to p_d. Domestic consumption falls to Q_3, and consumer surplus falls by areas ① + ② + ③ + ④. Domestic production rises to Q_2 and producer surplus increases by area ①. Imports fall to Q_2Q_3 and the government collects tariff revenue equal to area ③. The sum of areas ② and ④ represents the deadweight loss of the tariff.

Practise with Study Guide Chapter 34, Exercise 1.

Quotas and Voluntary Export Restrictions (VERs)

import quota A limit set by the government on the quantity of a foreign commodity that may be shipped into that country in a given time period.

voluntary export restriction (VER) An agreement by an exporting country to limit the amount of a good exported to another country.

The second type of protectionist policy directly restricts the quantity of an imported product. A common example is the **import quota**, by which the importing country sets a maximum of the quantity of some product that may be imported each year. Another measure is the **voluntary export restriction (VER)**, an agreement by an exporting country to limit the amount of a product that it sells to the importing country.

Figure 34-2 shows that a quantity restriction and a tariff have similar effects on domestic consumers and producers—they both raise domestic prices, increase domestic production, and reduce domestic consumption. But a direct quantity restriction is actually *worse* than a tariff for the importing country because the effect of the quantity restriction is to raise the price received by the foreign suppliers of the good. In contrast, a tariff leaves the foreign suppliers' price unchanged and instead generates tariff revenue for the government of the importing country.

Import quotas and voluntary export restrictions (VERs) impose larger deadweight losses on the importing country than do tariffs that lead to the same level of imports.

Canada, the United States, and the European Union have used VERs extensively, and the EU makes frequent use of import quotas. Japan has been pressured into negotiating several VERs with Canada, the United States, and the EU in order to limit sales of some of the Japanese goods that have had the most success in international competition. For example, in 1983, the United States and Canada negotiated VERs whereby the Japanese government agreed to restrict total sales of Japanese cars to these two countries for three years. When the agreements ran out in 1986, the Japanese continued to restrict their automobile sales by unilateral voluntary action. Japan's readiness to restrict its exports to North America partly reflects the high profits that Japanese automobile producers were making under the system of VERs, as explained in Figure 34-2. In recent years, such VERs have become less important because Japan's major automobile producers, Honda and Toyota, both have established manufacturing plants in Canada.

Tariffs Versus Quotas?

The ongoing dispute between Canada and the United States over Canadian softwood lumber exports illustrates an important distinction between tariffs and quotas. This trade dispute is examined in more detail later in the chapter, but for now suffice it to say that the United States has protected its softwood lumber industry in recent years in two ways:

FIGURE 34-2   The Deadweight Loss of an Import Quota

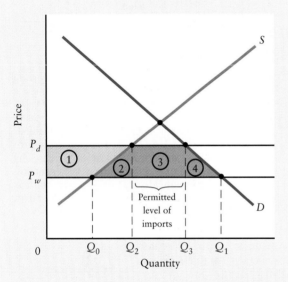

An import quota drives up the domestic price and imposes a deadweight loss on the importing country. With free trade, the domestic price is the world price, p_w. Imports are Q_0Q_1. If imports are restricted to only Q_2Q_3 (either through quotas or VERs), the domestic price must rise to the point where the restricted level of imports just satisfies the domestic excess demand. The rise in price and reduction in consumption reduces consumer surplus by areas ① + ② + ③ + ④. Domestic producers increase their output as the domestic price rises, and producer surplus increases by area ①. Area ③ does *not* accrue to the domestic economy; instead this area represents extra producer surplus for the *foreign* firms that export their product to this country. The net effect of the quota or VER is a deadweight loss of areas ② + ③ + ④. Import quotas are therefore worse than tariffs for the importing country.

- by imposing tariffs on imports of Canadian softwood lumber
- by pressuring Canadian governments to place export quotas on Canadian softwood lumber shipments to the United States.

Analysis of Figures 34-1 and 34-2 reveals that the choice between tariffs and quotas matters greatly for Canadian producers.

In the case of a U.S. tariff on imported Canadian softwood lumber, Figure 34-1 illustrates the U.S. market. An import tariff raises the domestic price for U.S. lumber users and also increases the profits of U.S. lumber producers. Canadian lumber producers are harmed because there is less demand for their product at the unchanged world price. Area ③ in the figure represents U.S. tariff revenue collected on the imports of Canadian lumber—revenue that accrues to the United States.

Figure 34-2 illustrates the U.S. market for softwood lumber in the case in which a quota is placed on the level of Canadian exports (U.S. imports). As with the tariff, the restricted supply of Canadian lumber to the U.S. market drives up the price to U.S. users and also raises profits for U.S. producers. But with a quota there is an important difference: the higher price in the U.S. market is received by the Canadian lumber producers, as shown by area ③ in the figure.

Therefore, while a tariff and quota may lead to the same reduced volume of exports, the tariff permits some surplus to be captured by the importing country whereas the quota allows some surplus to be captured by the exporting country (area ③ in both cases). In the U.S.–Canadian softwood lumber dispute, both tariffs and quotas have been used. And while both systems are to be preferred *overall* by a system of free trade, Canada has an interest in imposing quotas on Canadian lumber exporters rather than having the same export reduction accomplished by a U.S. tariff.

Trade-Remedy Laws and Nontariff Barriers

As tariffs in many countries were lowered over the years since the Second World War, countries that wished to protect domestic industries began using, and often abusing, a series of trade restrictions that came to be known as nontariff barriers (NTBs). The original purpose of some of these barriers was to remedy certain legitimate problems that arise in international trade and, for this reason, they are often called *trade-remedy laws*. All too often, however, such laws are misused to become potent means of simple protection.

Dumping

Selling a product in a foreign country at a lower price than in the domestic market is known as **dumping**. For example, if U.S.-made cars are sold for less in Canada than they are sold for in the United States, the U.S. automobile firms are said to be *dumping*. Dumping is a form of price discrimination studied in the theory of monopoly. Most governments have antidumping duties designed to protect their own industries against what is viewed as unfair foreign pricing practices.

dumping The practice of selling a commodity at a lower price in the export market than in the domestic market for reasons unrelated to differences in costs of servicing the two markets.

Dumping, if it lasts indefinitely, can be a gift to the receiving country. Its consumers get goods from abroad at lower prices than they otherwise would.

Dumping is more often a temporary measure, designed to get rid of unwanted surpluses, or a predatory attempt to drive competitors out of business. In either case, domestic producers complain about unfair foreign competition. In both cases, it is accepted international practice to levy antidumping duties on foreign imports. These duties are designed to eliminate the discriminatory elements in their prices.

Unfortunately, antidumping laws have been evolving over the past three decades in ways that allow antidumping duties to become barriers to trade and competition rather than to provide redress for unfair trading practices.

Several features of the antidumping system that is now in place in many countries make it highly protectionist. First, any price discrimination between national markets is classified as dumping and is subject to penalties. Thus prices in the producer's domestic market become, in effect, minimum prices below which no sales can be made in foreign markets, whatever the nature of demand in the domestic and foreign markets. Second, following a change in the U.S. law in the early 1970s, many countries' laws now calculate the "margin of dumping" as the difference between the price that is charged in that country's market and the foreign producer's average cost. Thus when there is a global slump in some industry so that the profit-maximizing price for all producers is below average cost, foreign producers can be convicted of dumping. This gives domestic producers enormous protection whenever the market price falls temporarily below average cost. Third, law in the United States (but not in all other countries) places the onus of proof on the accused. Facing a charge of dumping, a foreign producer must prove within the short time allowed for such a defence that the charge is unfounded. Fourth, U.S. antidumping duties are imposed with no time limit, so they often persist long after foreign firms have altered the prices that gave rise to them.

Antidumping laws were first designed to permit countries to respond to predatory pricing by foreign firms. More recently, they have been used to protect domestic firms against any foreign competition.

Governments have often been persuaded that low-price competition from foreign firms is "unfair" competition, and have levied antidumping duties on the imported goods. A recent example in Canada was an alleged case of dumping by Gerber, a U.S.-based producer of jarred baby food. In 1997, Heinz, the only Canadian producer, claimed that Gerber was pricing its products in Canada below costs, causing Heinz to lose sales. Heinz pushed for antidumping duties to be imposed on Gerber imports, and in 1998 the Canadian government agreed and imposed a 69 percent duty on Gerber imports. This duty was high enough to cause Gerber to reconsider the value of selling in the Canadian market. Later in the same year, however, consumer groups and the federal Competition Bureau argued that the very high duties on Gerber's products effectively left Heinz as a monopolist in the Canadian market. They finally convinced a reluctant Canadian government to repeal the duty so that consumers could benefit from the competition between Gerber and Heinz.

Countervailing Duties

Countervailing duties, which are commonly used by the U.S. government but much less so elsewhere, provide another case in which a trade-remedy law can become a covert method of protection. The countervailing duty is designed to act as a means of creating a "level playing field" on which fair international competition can take place. Privately owned domestic firms rightly complain that they cannot compete against the seemingly bottomless purses of foreign governments. Subsidized foreign exports can be sold indefinitely at prices that would produce losses in the absence of the subsidy. The original object of countervailing duties was to counteract the effect on price of the presence of such foreign subsidies.

If a domestic firm suspects the existence of such a subsidy and registers a complaint, its government is required to make an investigation. For a countervailing duty to be levied, the investigation must determine, first, that the foreign subsidy to the specific industry in question does exist and, second, that it is large enough to cause significant injury to competing domestic firms.

There is no doubt that countervailing duties have sometimes been used to counteract the effects of unfair competition that are caused by foreign subsidies. Many governments complain, however, that countervailing duties are often used as thinly disguised protection. At the early stages of the development of countervailing duties, only subsidies whose prime effect was to distort trade were possible objects of countervailing duties. Even then, however, the existence of equivalent domestic subsidies was not taken into account when decisions were made to put countervailing duties on subsidized imports. Thus the United States levies some countervailing duties against foreign goods even though the foreign subsidy is less than the domestic subsidy. This does not create a level playing field.

Canada's supply-management programs such as those in the dairy industry have been a perpetual source of friction in international trade negotiations.

Over time, the type of subsidy that is subject to countervailing duties has evolved until almost any government program that affects industry now risks becoming the object of a countervailing duty. Because all governments, including most U.S. state governments, have programs that provide direct or indirect assistance to industry, the potential for the use of countervailing duties as thinly disguised trade barriers is enormous.

The most well-known example in Canada of a U.S. countervailing duty is the one currently imposed on U.S. imports of Canadian softwood lumber. The U.S. justification for the duty is that Canadian provincial governments allegedly provide a subsidy to domestic lumber producers by charging artificially low *stumpage fees*—the fees paid by the companies to cut trees on Crown land. The Canada–U.S. softwood lumber dispute has been going on for years and will probably continue for several more. We discuss the dispute in more detail later in the chapter.

34.3 Current Trade Policy

In the remainder of the chapter, we discuss trade policy in practice. We start with the many international agreements that govern current trade policies and then look in a little more detail at the NAFTA.

Before 1947, any country was free to impose tariffs on its imports. However, when one country increased its tariffs, the action often triggered retaliatory actions by its trading partners. The 1930s saw a high-water mark of world protectionism as each country sought to raise its employment and output by raising its tariffs. The end result was lowered efficiency, less trade, but no more employment or income. Since the end of the Second World War, much effort has been devoted to reducing tariff barriers, both on a multilateral and on a regional basis.

The GATT and the WTO

One of the most notable achievements of the post-Second World War era was the creation of the General Agreement on Tariffs and Trade (GATT) in 1947. The GATT has since been replaced by the World Trade Organization (WTO). The principle of the GATT was that each member country agreed not to make unilateral tariff increases. This prevented the outbreak of "tariff wars" in which countries raised tariffs to protect particular domestic industries and to retaliate against other countries' tariff increases.

The Uruguay Round

The Uruguay Round—the final round of trade agreements under GATT—was completed in 1994 after years of negotiations. It reduced world tariffs by about 40 percent. A significant failure of these negotiations was the absence of an agreement to liberalize trade in agricultural goods. The European Union and Canada both resisted an agreement in this area. The EU has a scheme called the Common Agricultural Policy (CAP) that provides general support for most of its agricultural products, many of which are exported. The EU's position as a subsidized net exporter causes major harm to agricultural producers in developing countries whose governments are too poor to compete with the EU in a subsidy war. Canada, which has free trade in many agricultural commodities, was concerned about maintaining its supply management over a number of industries including poultry, eggs, and dairy products. These schemes are administered by the provinces who restrict domestic production and thus push domestic prices well above world levels. The federal government made such high domestic prices possible by imposing quotas on imports of these products at the national level.

Canada, the EU, and a number of other countries that lavishly protect some or all of their domestic agricultural producers were finally forced to agree to a plan to end all import quotas on agricultural products. In a process called "tariffication," these quotas have been replaced by "tariff equivalents"—tariffs that restrict trade by the same amount as the quotas did. Canadian tariff equivalents are as high as several hundred percent in some products, showing just how restrictive the Canadian policy is. The hope among countries that are pushing for freer trade in agricultural commodities is that pressure will build to reduce these very high tariffs over the next few decades.

Despite the failure to achieve free trade in agricultural products, the Uruguay Round is generally viewed as a success. Perhaps its most significant achievement was the creation of the World Trade Organization (WTO) to replace the GATT. An important part of the WTO is its formal dispute-settlement mechanism. This mechanism allows countries to take cases of alleged trade violations—such as illegal subsidies or tariffs—to the WTO for a formal ruling, and also obliges member countries to follow the ruling. The WTO's dispute-settlement mechanism is thus a significant step toward a "rules based" global trading system.

International trade negotiations sometimes generate considerable grass-roots opposition. There is some opposition to the reduction of tariffs in developed countries, and some controversy regarding the appropriate way to address the concerns of developing countries.

The Doha Round

Agriculture also plays a central role in the current round of trade negotiations, which began in Doha, Qatar, in 2000. Many issues will be discussed and negotiated in the period before the 2005 deadline, ranging from competition policy to antidumping and from environmental policies to electronic commerce. But one of the most contentious issues is agriculture. The WTO member governments claim to be committed to reducing export subsidies and other forms of government support to agriculture. Movements in this direction will naturally cause political friction within the developed economies that currently protect and support their agricultural producers, especially the United States and the European Union, which provide (by far) the most support to their farmers. A failure to reduce agricultural support in the developed countries, however, will increase the political frictions that already exist between developed and developing nations. For the many developing countries who have natural comparative advantages in agricultural products and who cannot afford to compete in a "subsidy war" with the developed countries, the liberalization of trade in agricultural products is crucial. They see the Doha round as central to their economic development.

> **Many countries, including Canada, provide generous financial support to their farmers and livestock producers. For some international comparisons of the generosity of agricultural subsidies, and for how these policies affect the ongoing WTO negotiations, look for "Farm Subsidies and the World Trade Organization" in the *Additional Topics* section of this book's Companion Website.**
>
> h t t p : / / w w w . p e a r s o n e d . c a / r a g a n

Protests About the WTO

Despite the successes of the WTO, it does have its critics. In December 1999, trade ministers from the WTO member countries met in Seattle to set the agenda for what would become the Doha Round of trade negotiations. The Seattle meetings were delayed and interrupted by massive protests from environmental and labour groups, among others, who argued that the WTO's process of negotiating trade agreements pays insufficient attention to environmental and labour standards, especially in the developing countries. Many WTO officials and trade ministers, including those from the developing countries, recognized the importance of environmental and labour issues but questioned the wisdom of formally including these concerns in trade agreements. Reaching agreement on trade issues among the 134 member countries of the WTO is difficult enough—it would be almost impossible if the issues were bundled with the even more contentious environmental and labour issues. The result would be an overall agreement that achieved very little in terms of either trade liberalization, environmental protection, or establishing labour standards. Instead, many trade officials argued that the existing International Labour Organization should be strengthened and a separate international organization like the WTO should be created to promote environmental issues. These organizations could then push ahead to achieve in their respective domains the same success that the GATT achieved over 50 years of negotiations.

Some of the protesters against the WTO process argue that paying greater attention to environmental and labour issues will improve the living standards in developing countries, where such standards typically fall far behind those in developed economies. One of the interesting ironies of the negotiations, however, is that the governments of the developing countries are among the strongest *opponents* of including environmental and labour issues in trade negotiations. They feel that developed countries would use stringent environmental and labour standards as a means of preventing imports from developing countries, thus protecting their own industries.

As it turned out, the work programme for the Doha Round includes very little on environmental issues and nothing on labour standards. Apparently, the view of the Doha negotiators was that many trade issues could usefully be discussed without getting embroiled in the very contentious but important environmental and labour issues. Perhaps the *next* round of WTO talks will include these broader issues.

In any event, it seems a safe bet that these tensions between trade policy and environmental/labour policies will continue. At some point, further progress on trade liberalization will require that environmental and labour issues be addressed. Either domestic political pressures will push individual member countries to insist that these issues be included within the WTO negotiations, or other organizations like the WTO will be

For more information on the WTO, see its website at www.wto.org.

developed and/or strengthened to address the concerns. Whatever approach is followed, it appears that these will surely continue to be hot policy issues in the twenty-first century.

Regional Trade Agreements

Regional agreements seek to liberalize trade over a much smaller group of countries than the WTO membership. Three standard forms of regional trade-liberalizing agreements are *free trade areas, customs unions,* and *common markets.*

free trade area (FTA)
An agreement among two or more countries to abolish tariffs on all or most of the trade among themselves while each remains free to set its own tariffs against other countries.

A **free trade area** (**FTA**) is the least comprehensive of the three. It allows for tariff-free trade among the member countries, but it leaves each member free to levy its own trade policy with respect to other countries. As a result, members must maintain customs points at their common borders to make sure that imports into the free trade area do not all enter through the member that is levying the lowest tariff on each item. They must also agree on *rules of origin* to establish when a good is made in a member country and hence is able to pass tariff-free across their borders, and when it is imported from outside the FTA and hence is subject to tariffs when it crosses borders within the FTA. The three countries in North America formed a free-trade area when they created the NAFTA in 1994. In 2003, the United States signed bilateral FTAs with Chile and Singapore.

customs union
A group of countries who agree to have free trade among themselves and a common set of barriers against imports from the rest of the world.

A **customs union** is a free trade area in which the member countries agree to establish a common trade policy with the rest of the world. Because they have a common trade policy, the members need neither customs controls on goods moving among themselves nor rules of origin. Once a good has entered any member country it has met the common rules and regulations and paid the common tariff and so it may henceforth be treated the same as a good that is produced within the union. An example of a customs union is Mercosur, an agreement linking Argentina, Brazil, Paraguay, and Uruguay.

common market
A customs union with the added provision that factors of production can move freely among the members.

A **common market** is a customs union that also has free movement of labour and capital among its members. The European Union is by far the most successful example of a common market. Indeed, the EU is now moving toward a full e*conomic union* in which all economic policies in the member countries are harmonized. The adoption of the euro as the common currency of 11 EU countries in 1999 was a significant step in this direction.

Trade Creation and Trade Diversion

A major effect of regional trade liberalization is to reallocate resources. Economists divide these effects into two categories: *trade creation* and *trade diversion.* These concepts were first developed by Jacob Viner, a Canadian-born economist who taught at the University of Chicago and Princeton University and was a leading economic theorist in the first half of the twentieth century.

trade creation
A consequence of reduced trade barriers among a set of countries whereby trade within the group is increased and trade with the rest of the world remains roughly constant.

Trade creation occurs when producers in one member country find that they can export to another member country as a result of the elimination of the tariffs. For example, when the North American Free Trade Agreement (NAFTA) eliminated most cross-border tariffs among Mexico, Canada, and the United States, some U.S. firms found that they could undersell their Canadian competitors in some product lines, and some Canadian firms found that they could undersell their U.S. competitors in other product lines. As a result, specialization occurred, and new international trade developed. This trade, which is based on (natural or acquired) comparative advantage, is illustrated in Table 34-1.

Trade creation represents efficient specialization according to comparative advantage.

Trade diversion occurs when exporters in one member country *replace* foreign exporters as suppliers to another member country. For example, trade diversion occurs when U.S. firms find that they can undersell competitors from the rest of the world in the Canadian market, not because they are the cheapest source of supply, but because their tariff-free prices under NAFTA are lower than the tariff-burdened prices of imports from other countries. This effect is a gain to U.S. firms and Canadian consumers of the product. U.S. firms get new business and therefore they clearly gain. Canadian consumers buy the product at a lower tariff-free price from the U.S. producer than they used to pay to the third-country producer (with a tariff), and so they are also better off. But Canada as a whole is worse off as a result of the trade diversion. Canada is now buying the product from a U.S. producer at a higher price with no tariff. Previous to the agreement, it was buying from a third-country producer at a lower price (and collecting tariff revenue). Table 34-1 also illustrates trade diversion.

From the global perspective, trade diversion represents an inefficient use of resources.

trade diversion
A consequence of reduced trade barriers among a set of countries whereby trade within the group replaces trade that used to take place with countries outside the group.

The History of Free Trade Areas

The first important free trade area in the modern era was the European Free Trade Association (EFTA). It was formed in 1960 by a group of European countries that were unwilling to join the European Common Market (the forerunner of the European Union) because of its all-embracing character. Not wanting to be left out of the gains from trade, they formed an association whose sole purpose was tariff removal. First, they removed all tariffs on trade among themselves. Then each country signed a free-trade-area agreement with the EU. This made the EU–EFTA market the largest tariff-free market in the world (over 300 million people). In recent years almost all of the EFTA countries have entered the EU.

Australia and New Zealand have also entered into an association that removes restrictions on trade in goods and services between their two countries. The countries of Latin America have been experimenting with free trade areas for many decades. Most earlier attempts failed but, in the past few years, more durable FTAs seem to have been formed, the most successful of which is Mercosur, which includes Argentina, Brazil, Uruguay, and Paraguay. Whether these will remain stand-alone agreements or evolve into a broader continental agreement remains to be seen.

In 1989, a sweeping agreement between Canada and the United States instituted free trade on almost all goods and most nongovernment services and covered what is the world's largest flow of international trade between any two countries. In 1994, this agreement was extended into the North American Free Trade Agreement (NAFTA) by renegotiating the Canada–U.S. agreement to include Mexico. Provision is made within

TABLE 34-1   Trade Creation and Trade Diversion

Producing Country	Price in Canada Without Tariffs (dollars)	Price in Canada with a 10 Percent Tariff (dollars)
Trade creation		
Canada	40.00	40.00
United States	37.00	40.70
Trade diversion		
Taiwan	20.00	22.00
United States	21.50	23.65

Regional tariff reductions can cause trade creation and trade diversion. The table gives two cases. In the first case, a U.S. good, which could be sold for $37.00 in Canada, has its price increased to $40.70 by a 10 percent Canadian tariff. The Canadian industry, which can sell the good for $40.00 with or without a tariff on imports, is protected against the more efficient U.S. producer. When the tariff is removed by the NAFTA, the U.S. good wins the market by selling at $37.00. Trade is created between Canada and the United States by eliminating the inefficient Canadian production.

In the second case, Taiwan can undersell the U.S. in the Canadian market for another product when neither is subject to a tariff (column 1) and when both are subject to a 10 percent tariff (column 2). But after the NAFTA, the U.S. good enters Canada tariff-free and sells for $21.50, whereas the Taiwanese good, which is still subject to the Canadian tariff, continues to sell for $22.00. The U.S. good wins the market, and Canadian trade is diverted from Taiwan to the U.S. even though Taiwan is the lower-cost supplier (excluding the tariff).

the NAFTA for the accession of other countries with the hope that it may eventually evolve into an agreement linking all countries of the western hemisphere.

In 1998, the negotiations for the Free Trade Area of the Americas (FTAA) were formally launched in Santiago, Chile. These negotiations will take many years and will involve discussions of rules of origin, environmental concerns, the treatment of foreign direct investment, agricultural policy, and how best to integrate the many regional agreements into a single comprehensive agreement. Only time will reveal the eventual outcome of these negotiations.

The North American Free Trade Agreement

The NAFTA dates from 1994 and is an extension of the 1989 Canada–U.S. Free Trade Agreement (FTA). It is a free trade area and not a customs union; each country retains its own external trade policy, and rules of origin are needed to determine when a good is made within the NAFTA and thus allowed to move freely among the members.

National Treatment

The fundamental principle that guides the NAFTA is the principle of *national treatment*. The principle of national treatment is that countries are free to establish any laws they wish and that these can differ as much as desired among member countries, with the sole proviso that these laws must not discriminate on the basis of nationality. Canada can have tough environmental laws or standards for particular goods, but it must enforce these equally on Canadian, Mexican, and U.S. firms and on domestically produced and imported goods. The idea of national treatment is to allow a maximum of policy independence while preventing national policies from being used as trade barriers.

Other Major Provisions

There are several other major provisions in NAFTA. First, all tariffs on trade between the United States and Canada were eliminated by 1999. Canada–Mexico and Mexico–U.S. tariffs are to be phased out by 2010. Also, a number of nontariff barriers are eliminated or restricted.

Second, the agreement guarantees national treatment to foreign investment once it enters a country while permitting each country to screen a substantial amount of inbound foreign investment before it enters.

Third, all existing measures that restrict trade and investment that are not explicitly removed by the agreement are "grandfathered," a term referring to the continuation of a practice that predates the agreement and would have been prohibited by the terms of the agreement were it not specifically exempted. This is probably the single most important departure from free trade under the NAFTA. Under it, a large collection of restrictive measures in each of the three countries are given indefinite life. An alternative would have been to "sunset" all of these provisions by negotiating dates at which each would be eliminated. From the point of view of long-term trade liberalization, even a 50-year extension would have been preferable to an indefinite exemption.

Fourth, a few goods remain subject to serious nontariff trade restrictions. In Canada, the main examples are supply-managed agricultural products, beer, textiles, and the cultural industries. Restrictions for the Canadian supply-managed agricultural products may be short-lived because of their tariffication under the Uruguay round of GATT.

Textile restriction in both the United States and Canada comes under the Multifiber Agreement, which is being phased out over a 15-year period under the Uruguay round. In the United States, textiles, shipping between U.S. ports, and banking were shielded from free trade in good and services.

Fifth, trade in most nongovernmental services is liberalized by giving service firms the right of establishment in all member countries and the privilege of national treatment. There is also a limited opening of the markets in financial services to entry from firms based in the NAFTA countries.

Finally, a significant minority of government procurement is opened to cross-border bids.

For information about NAFTA, go to the website for the NAFTA Secretariat: www.nafta-sec-alena.org.

Dispute Settlement

From Canada's point of view, by far the biggest setback in the negotiations for the Canada–U.S. FTA was the failure to obtain agreement on a common regime for countervailing and antidumping duties. In view of that failure, no significant attempt was made to deal with this issue in the NAFTA negotiations. The U.S. Congress has been unwilling to abandon the unilateral use of these powerful weapons.

In the absence of such a multilateral regime, a dispute-settlement mechanism was put in place. Under it, the domestic determinations that are required for the levying of antidumping and countervailing duties are subject to review by a panel of Canadians, Americans, and Mexicans. This international review replaces appeal through the domestic courts. Panels are empowered to uphold the domestic determinations or refer the decision to the domestic authority—which in effect is a binding order for a new investigation. The referral can be repeated until the panel is satisfied that the domestic laws have been correctly and fairly applied.

The establishment of the dispute-settlement mechanism in NAFTA was pathbreaking: For the first time in its history, the United States agreed to submit the administration of its domestic laws to *binding* scrutiny by an international panel that often contains a majority of foreigners.

Results

The Canada–U.S. FTA aroused a great debate in Canada. Indeed, the Canadian federal election of 1988 was fought almost entirely on the issue of free trade. Supporters looked for major increases in the security of existing trade from U.S. protectionist attacks and for a growth of new trade. Detractors predicted a flight of firms to the U.S., the loss of Canadian competitiveness, and even the loss of Canada's political independence.

By and large, however, both the Canada–U.S. FTA and NAFTA agreements worked out just about as expected by their supporters. Industry restructured in the direction of greater export orientation in all three countries, and trade creation occurred. The flow of trade among the three countries increased markedly. This trend is particularly true between Canada and the United States. As the theory of trade predicts, specialization occurred in many areas, resulting in more U.S. imports of some product lines from Canada and more U.S. exports of other goods to Canada. In 1988, before the Canada–U.S. FTA took effect, Canada exported $85 billion in goods to the United States, and imported $74 billion from the United States. By 2002, the value of Canada–U.S. trade had almost quadrupled—Canadian exports of goods to the United States had increased to $348 billion and imports from the United States had increased to $255 billion. (Note that these figures exclude trade in services; with services included, the increase in Canada–U.S. trade between 1988 and 2002 would be even larger.)

See Chapter 34 of www.pearsoned.ca/ragan for an interesting discussion of the results of FTA and NAFTA: Richard Lipsey, "Free Trade—Real Results Versus Unreal Expectations."

APPLYING ECONOMIC CONCEPTS 34-1

Canadian Wine: A Free-Trade Success Story

Before the Canada–U.S. FTA was signed in 1989, great fears were expressed over the fate of the Canadian wine industry, located mainly in Ontario and British Columbia. It was heavily tariff protected and, with a few notable exceptions, concentrated mainly on cheap, low-quality products. Contrary to most people's expectations, rather than being decimated, the industry now produces a wide variety of high-quality products, some of which have won international competitions in Europe.

The nature of the pre-FTA protection largely explains the dramatic turnaround of the Canadian wine industry once the FTA took effect. First, Canadian wine producers were protected by high tariffs on imported wine, but were at the same time required by law to produce wine using only domestically grown grapes. The domestic grape growers, however, produced varieties of grapes not conducive to the production of high-quality wines, and with a captive domestic market, they had little incentive to change their behaviour. Thus Canadian wine producers concentrated their efforts on "hiding" the attributes of poor-quality grapes rather than enhancing the attributes of high-quality grapes. The result was low-quality wine.

The second important aspect of the protection was that the high Canadian tariff was levied on a per unit rather than on an *ad valorem* basis. For example, the tariff was expressed as so many dollars per litre rather than as a specific percentage of the price. Charging a tariff by the litre gave most protection to the low quality wines with low value per litre. The higher the per-litre value of the wine, the lower the percentage tariff protection. For example, a $5-per-litre tariff would have the following effects. A low-quality imported wine valued at $5 per litre would have its price raised to $10, a 100 percent increase in price, whereas a higher quality imported wine valued at $25 per litre would have its price increased to $30, only a 20 percent increase in price.

Responding to these incentives, the Canadian industry concentrated on low-quality wines. The market for these wines was protected by the nearly prohibitive tariffs on competing low-quality imports, and also by the high prices charged for high-quality imports. In addition, protection was provided by many hidden charges that the various provincial governments' liquor monopolies levied in order to protect local producers.

When the tariff was removed under the FTA, the incentives were to move up-market, producing much more value per acre of land. Fortunately, much of the Canadian wine-growing land in the Okanagan Valley in BC and the Niagara Peninsula in Ontario is well-suited for growing the grapes required for good wines. Within a very few years, and with some government assistance to grape growers to make the transition from low-quality to high-quality grapes, Canadian wines were competing effectively with imported products in the medium-quality range. BC and Ontario wines do not yet reach the quality of major French wines in the $40–$70 (per bottle) range but they compete very effectively in quality with wines in the $10–$25 range, and sometimes even higher up the quality scale.

The success of the wine industry is a fine example of how tariffs can distort incentives and push an industry into a structure that makes it dependent on the tariff. Looking at the pre-FTA industry, very few people suspected that it would be able to survive, let alone produce a world-class product.

Prior to the FTA, the nature of protection encouraged the production of low-quality grapes and wine in Canada. The reduction in tariffs brought about by the FTA led to a successful restructuring of the Canadian wine industry.

It is hard to say how much trade diversion there has been and will be in the future. The greatest potential for trade diversion is with Mexico, which competes in the U.S. and Canadian markets with a large number of products produced in other low-wage countries. Southeast Asian exporters to the United States and Canada have been worried that Mexico would capture some of their markets by virtue of having tariff-free access denied to their goods. Most estimates predict, however, that trade creation will dominate over trade diversion.

Most transitional difficulties were initially felt in each country's import-competing industries, just as theory predicts. An agreement such as the NAFTA brings its advantages by encouraging a movement of resources out of protected but inefficient import-competing industries, which decline, and into efficient export industries, which expand because they have better access to the markets of other member countries. Southern Ontario and parts of Quebec had major problems as some traditional exports fell and resources had to be moved to sectors where trade was expanding. By the late 1990s, however, eight years after the agreement, Southern Ontario was booming again and its most profitable sectors were those that exported to the United States.

See Chapter 34 of www.pearsoned.ca/ragan for an interview with former Prime Minister Brian Mulroney on the political aspects of FTA and NAFTA: "Standing Firm on Free Trade."

There were also some pleasant surprises resulting from free trade. Two Canadian industries that many economists expected to suffer from the FTA and NAFTA were wine-making and textiles. Yet both of these industries prospered as Canadian firms improved quality, productivity, and benefited from increased access to the huge U.S. market. *Applying Economic Concepts 34-1* discusses the success of the Canadian wine industry after the tariffs on wine were eliminated.

Finally, the dispute-settlement mechanism seems to have worked well. A large number of disputes have arisen and have been referred to panels. Panel members have usually reacted as professionals rather than as nationals. Most cases have been decided on their merits; allegations that decisions were reached on national rather than professional grounds have been rare.

See the website for the Department of Foreign Affairs and International Trade for information on the dispute-settlement mechanism: www.dfait-maeic.gc.ca.

With over $600 billion annually in two-way trade between Canada and the United States, however, it is inevitable that some disputes arise. *Applying Economic Concepts 34-2* discusses three of the most contentious trade disputes that still disturb the generally tranquil state of Canada–U.S. trade.

Companion Website

After many years of successful trade liberalization in goods and services, attention is beginning to swing toward the liberalization of trade in *assets*. For a discussion of a recent attempt to establish a widespread agreement concerning investment, and of the accompanying political obstacles, look for "Will the World Achieve Freer Trade in Assets?" in the *Additional Topics* section of this book's Companion Website.

http://www.pearsoned.ca/ragan

APPLYING ECONOMIC CONCEPTS 34-2

Headline Trade Disputes Between Canada and the United States

The flow of goods and services across the Canada–U.S. border is the largest flow of trade between any two countries. In 2002, approximately $700 billion worth of goods and services crossed this border. Although more than 95 percent of this trade passes between the two countries without dispute or hindrance, some items have been beset by persistent disputes. Here is a brief discussion of three of the most contentious areas in U.S.–Canadian trade.

Softwood Lumber

Canada exports large amounts of softwood lumber to the United States. U.S. producers have persistently claimed that Canadian provincial government policies provide a concealed subsidy that should be evened out with a countervailing duty. The main bone of contention is *stumpage,* which is the royalty that governments charge the logging companies for cutting timber on government-owned land. In the United States, stumpage fees are set by open auction. In Canada, the fees are set in private negotiations between logging companies and the government. U.S. critics argue that the much lower Canadian stumpage fees that emerge from this negotiation process are a subsidy from the government to the lumber industry. Canadians argue that the higher U.S. stumpage fees reflect the higher services that U.S. governments provide to their lumber companies by way of infrastructure that Canadian lumber companies must provide for themselves.

Just before the Canada–U.S. FTA was finalized, the Canadian government imposed an export tax on lumber going to the United States, to forestall the imposition of a U.S. countervailing duty. When this tax expired, the United States imposed a countervailing duty. Two dispute-settlement panels found in Canada's favour, but largely on the grounds of narrow technicalities. In 1996, the Canada–U.S. Softwood Lumber Agreement was signed. This agreement restricted the volume of duty-free exports of Canadian softwood lumber to the United States until 2001, with the Canadian government imposing export taxes on any exports that exceeded the limit. When that agreement expired, the U.S. government imposed a countervailing duty of 27 percent, which naturally alarmed Canadian softwood lumber producers whose livelihood relies on open access to the huge U.S. market. The dispute was taken to the World Trade Organization for resolution. In 2003, the WTO agreed with the U.S. claim that the Canadian stumpage fees embody a subsidy to Canadian producers and thus a U.S. countervailing duty is appropriate. But the WTO disagreed with the method the Americans used to arrive at the 27 percent duty. Not surprisingly, both sides interpreted the ruling as a partial victory. As this book went to press in the fall of 2003, the Americans were re-computing the level of their countervailing duty. Look for the next WTO ruling, after which the debate will surely continue.

Supply-Managed Agricultural Industries

Several of the Canadian provinces use supply-management systems to support farm incomes. Such systems typically involve issuing quotas to farmers to restrict output. The result of such quotas is to substantially raise the prices paid by Canadian consumers. For years, the Canadian government had supported these policies by imposing import quotas on the managed products, without which their prices would be driven down to world levels. The Canadian government successfully negotiated exemptions for these quotas under the Canada–U.S. FTA. In the Uruguay round of GATT negotiations, despite spirited resistance, the Canadian government was forced to agree to "tariffication" of these quotas. The United States then took the position that although the quotas had been exempt under the FTA, their tariff equivalents were not. After all, the U.S. argued, all tariffs without exception are to be removed by 1999 under the FTA. However, a legal ruling determined that the Canadian tariffs need not disappear. So the current situation is that the Canadian tariffs remain and the U.S. interests continue to argue for their elimination.

Cultural Industries

Canada has always sought to support its magazines, book sellers, film distributors, and other cultural industries from U.S. competition. Although there was never any pressure to prevent governments on both sides of the border from subsidizing the performing arts, such as music and drama, protection of the cultural industries more widely defined was a serious bone of contention during the FTA negotiations. In the end, Canada got exemption for all of its broadly defined cultural industries.

In the mid-1990s, the Canadian government became concerned over the presence of Canadian editions of U.S. split-run magazines. These magazines, such as *Time* and *Sports Illustrated*, contain mostly U.S. content but also include a few pages of Canadian editorial content. Because the fixed costs of the magazine are covered by the U.S. sales of the magazine, the Canadian advertising rates can be lower than those of Canadian-based magazines. The Canadian government and Canadian magazine publishers argued that the presence of such split-run magazines would make it more difficult for Canadian magazines to sell advertising space, thus putting them in an untenable financial position. Failure of Canadian magazines would then damage an important part of Canadian culture. In 1995, the Canadian government imposed an 80 percent tax on advertising expenditures in the Canadian editions of U.S. split-run magazines.

The U.S. government and U.S. magazine publishers argued that the Canadian government's attempts to protect Canadian culture by protecting its magazines were nothing more than simple trade protection. On this basis, they saw no difference between aid to Canadian magazines and aid to textiles firms or the aerospace industry. The United States brought its complaint to the World Trade Organization and, in 1997, the WTO ruled against Canada—that is, it ruled that Canada's tax on split-run advertising contravened international trade agreements.

The Canadian government then attempted to write new legislation that would be consistent with WTO rules but would still have the effect of preventing the U.S. split-run magazines. This prompted the United States to threaten the imposition of duties on a whole range of Canadian exports if the Canadian government did not drop its attempts to prevent the split-runs. Finally, in 1999, the Canadian and U.S. governments reached an agreement to provide limited access to the Canadian market for the U.S.-based split-run magazines.

S U M M A R Y

34.1 Free Trade or Protection?   LO❶❷

- The case for free trade is that world output of all products can be higher under free trade than when protectionism restricts regional specialization.
- Trade protection may be advocated to promote economic diversification or to provide protection for specific groups. The cost of such protection is lower average living standards.
- Protection can also be urged on the grounds that it may lead to higher living standards for the protectionist country than would a policy of free trade. Such a result might come about by using a monopoly position to influence the terms of trade or by developing a dynamic compara-

tive advantage by allowing inexperienced or uneconomically small industries to become efficient enough to compete with foreign industries.
- Some fallacious protectionist arguments are that (a) mutually advantageous trade is impossible because one trader's gain must always be the other's loss; (b) buying abroad sends our money abroad, while buying at home keeps our money at home; (c) our high-paid workers must be protected against the competition from low-paid foreign workers; and (d) imports are to be discouraged because they lower national income and cause unemployment.

34.2 Methods of Protection   LO❸❹

- A tariff raises the domestic price of the imported product and leads to a reduction in the level of imports. Domestic consumers lose and domestic producers gain. The overall effect of a tariff is a deadweight loss for the importing country.
- A quota (or voluntary export restriction) restricts the amount of imports and thus drives up the domestic price of the good. Domestic consumers lose and domestic producers gain. The overall effect is a *larger* deadweight loss

than with a tariff because rather than the importing country collecting tariff revenue, foreign producers benefit from a higher price.
- As tariff barriers have been reduced over the years, they have been replaced in part by nontariff barriers. The two most important are antidumping and countervailing duties, which, although providing legitimate restraints on unfair trading practices, are often used as serious nontariff barriers to trade.

34.3 Current Trade Policy   LO❺❻

- The General Agreement on Tariffs and Trade (GATT), under which countries agreed to reduce trade barriers through multilateral negotiations and not to raise them unilaterally, has greatly reduced world tariffs since its inception in 1947.
- The World Trade Organization (WTO) was created in 1995 as the successor to GATT. It has 134 member countries and contains a formal dispute-settlement mechanism.
- Regional trade-liberalizing agreements such as free trade areas and common markets bring efficiency gains through trade creation and efficiency losses through trade diversion.

- The North American Free Trade Agreement (NAFTA) is the world's largest and most successful free trade area, and the European Union is the world's largest and most successful common market.
- NAFTA is based on the principle of "national treatment." This allows Canada, the United States, and Mexico to implement whatever social, economic, or environmental policies they choose providing that such policies treat foreign and domestic firms (and their products) equally.

K E Y   C O N C E P T S

Free trade and protectionism
Tariffs and import quotas
Voluntary export restrictions (VERs)
Countervailing and antidumping duties

The General Agreement on Tariffs and
   Trade (GATT)
The World Trade Organization (WTO)
Common markets, customs unions,
   and free trade areas

Trade creation and trade diversion
Nontariff barriers
The North American Free Trade
   Agreement (NAFTA)

S T U D Y   E X E R C I S E S

1. Fill in the blanks to make the following statements correct.

   a. The _____ argument provided the rationale for Canada's National Policy of 1876. A high tariff wall allowed many Canadian industries to develop where they may not have been able to compete otherwise.

   b. Advertisements that encourage us to "buy Canadian" are promoting a _____ argument for protection. The reason is that money spent on imported goods must ultimately be spent on _____ goods and services anyway.

   c. Fallacious arguments for protection usually come from a misunderstanding of the gains from _____ or from the misbelief that protection can increase total _____.

2. Fill in the blanks to make the following statements correct.

   a. A tariff imposed on the import of leather shoes will cause an _____ in the domestic price. Total quantity sold of leather shoes in Canada will _____. Domestic (Canadian) production of leather shoes will _____ and the quantity of shoes imported will _____.

   b. The beneficiaries of the tariff described above are _____ because they receive a higher price for the same good and _____ because they receive tariff revenue. The parties that are clearly worse off are _____ because they now pay a higher price for the same good, and _____ because they sell less in the Canadian market.

   c. The overall effect of a tariff on the importing country is a(n) _____ in welfare. The tariff creates a _____ loss for the economy.

   d. Suppose an import quota restricted the import of leather shoes into Canada to 20 000 pairs per year when the free trade imported amount was 40 000 pairs. The domestic price will _____, total quantity sold in Canada will _____, and domestic production will _____.

   e. The beneficiaries of the quota described above are _____ and _____ because they both receive a higher price in the Canadian market. The party that is clearly worse off is _____ because they are now paying a higher price.

   f. The overall effect of an import quota on the importing country is a(n) _____ in welfare. The quota imposes a(n) _____ loss for the economy.

3. Fill in the blanks to make the following statements correct.

   a. A regional trade agreement such as NAFTA, or a common market such as the European Union, allows for _____, whereby trade within the group of member countries is increased.

   b. A regional trade agreement such as NAFTA, or a common market such as the European Union, also results in _____, whereby trade within the group of member countries replaces trade previously done with other _____.

   c. The fundamental principle that guides NAFTA is the principle of _____, which means that any member country can implement the policies of its choosing, as long as _____ and _____ firms are treated equally.

4. Canada produces steel domestically and also imports it from abroad. Assume that the world market for steel is competitive and that Canada is a small producer, unable to affect the world price. Since Canada imports steel, we know that in the absence of trade, the Canadian equilibrium price would exceed the world price.

   a. Draw a diagram showing the Canadian market for steel, with imports at the world price.

   b. Explain why the imposition of a tariff on imported steel will increase the price of steel in Canada.

   c. Who benefits and who is harmed by such a tariff? Show these effects in your diagram.

5. The diagram below shows the Canadian market for leather shoes, which we assume to be competitive. The world price is p_w. If the Canadian government imposes a tariff of t dollars per unit, the domestic price then rises to $p_w + t$.

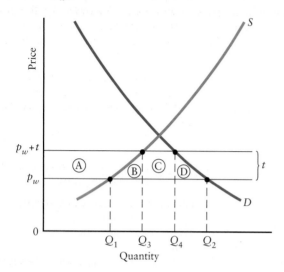

a. What quantity of leather shoes is imported before the tariff is imposed? After the tariff?
b. What is the effect of the tariff on the Canadian production of shoes? Which areas in the diagram show the increase in domestic producer surplus?
c. Which areas in the diagram show the reduction in domestic consumer surplus as a result of the higher Canadian price?
d. The Canadian government earns tariff revenue on the imported shoes. Which area in the diagram shows this tariff revenue?

6. Use the diagram from Question 5 to analyze the effects of imposing an import quota instead of a tariff to protect domestic shoe producers. Draw the diagram as in Question 5 and answer the following questions.

a. Explain why an import quota of Q_3Q_4 raises the domestic price to $p_w + t$.
b. With import quotas, the Canadian government earns no tariff revenue. Who gets this money now?
c. Is the import quota better or worse than the tariff for Canada as a whole? Explain.

7. Under pressure from the Canadian and U.S. governments in the early 1980s, Japanese automobile producers agreed to restrict their exports to the North American market. After the formal agreement ended, the Japanese producers decided unilaterally to continue restricting their exports. Carefully review Figure 34-2 and then answer the following questions.

a. Explain why such Voluntary Export Restrictions (VERs) are "voluntary."
b. Explain why an agreement to export only 100 000 cars to North America is better for the Japanese producers than a North American tariff that results in the same volume of Japanese exports.
c. Who is paying for these benefits to the Japanese producers?

8. Go to Statistics Canada's website: www.statcan.ca. Go to "Canadian Statistics" and then "international trade," and answer the following questions.

a. For the most recent year shown, what was the value of Canada's exports to the United States? To the European Union?
b. For the same year, what was the value of Canada's imports from the United States? From the European Union?
c. Compute what economists call the "volume of trade" (the sum of exports and imports) between Canada and the United States. How has the volume of trade grown over the past five years? Has trade grown faster than national income?

9. The table below shows the prices *in Canada* of cotton towels produced in the United States, Canada, and Malaysia. All cotton towels are identical.

Producing Country	Canadian Price (in $) Without Tariff	Canadian Price (in $) With 20% Tariff
Canada	4.75	4.75
United States	4.50	5.40
Malaysia	4.00	4.80

a. Suppose Canada imposes a 20 percent tariff on imported towels from any country. Assuming that Canadians purchase only the lowest-price towels, from which country will Canada buy its towels?
b. Now suppose Canada eliminates tariffs on towels from all countries. Which towels will Canada now buy?
c. Canada and the United States now negotiate a free-trade agreement that eliminates all tariffs between the two countries, but Canada maintains the 20 percent tariff on other countries. Which towels now get imported into Canada?
d. Which of the situations described above is called trade creation and which is called trade diversion?

DISCUSSION QUESTIONS

1. Some Canadians opposed Canada's entry into NAFTA on the grounds that Canadian firms could not compete with the goods produced by cheap Mexican labour. Comment on the following points in relation to the above worries:

   a. "Mexicans are the most expensive cheap labour I have ever encountered"—statement by the owner of a Canadian firm that is moving back to Canada from Mexico.

   b. The theory of the gains from trade says that a high-productivity, high-wage country can gain from trading with a low-wage, low-productivity country.

   c. Technological change is rapidly reducing labour costs as a proportion of total costs in many products; in many industries that use high-tech production methods this proportion is already well below 20 percent.

2. Should Canada and the United States trade with countries with poor human rights records? If trade with China is severely restricted because of its lack of respect for human rights, who will be the gainers and who the losers? Argue the cases that this policy will help, and that it will hinder, human rights progress in China.

3. Import quotas and voluntary export restrictions are often used instead of tariffs. What real difference, if any, is there between quotas, voluntary export restrictions (VERs), and tariffs? Explain why lobbyists for some import-competing industries (cheese, milk, shoes) support import quotas while lobbyists for others (pizza manufacturers, soft drink manufacturers, retail stores) oppose them. Would you expect labour unions to support or oppose quotas?

4. Over the past several years, many foreign automobile producers have built production and assembly facilities in Canada and in the United States. What are some advantages and disadvantages associated with shifting production from, for example, Japan to Canada? Will these cars still be considered "imports"? What is beginning to happen to the definitions of "foreign made" and "domestic made"?

5. Consider a mythical country called Forestland, which exports a large amount of lumber to a nearby country called Houseland. The lumber industry in Houseland has convinced its federal government that it is being harmed by the low prices being charged by the lumber producers in Forestland. You are an advisor to the government in Forestland. Explain who gains and who loses from each of the following policies.

   a. Houseland imposes a tariff on lumber imports from Forestland

   b. Forestland imposes a tax on each unit of lumber exported to Houseland

   c. Forestland agrees to restrict its exports of lumber to Houseland

   d. Which policy is likely to garner the most political support in Houseland? In Forestland?

6. In March 1999, the Canadian government imposed antidumping duties of up to 43 percent on hot-rolled steel imports from France, Russia, Slovakia, and Romania. The allegation was that these countries were dumping steel into the Canadian market.

   a. Who benefits from such alleged dumping? Who is harmed?

   b. Who benefits from the imposition of the antidumping duties? Who is harmed?

   c. Is Canada as a whole made better off by the imposition of the duties? Explain.

Exchange Rates and the Balance of Payments

LEARNING OBJECTIVES

1. Describe the components of Canada's balance of payments and explain why the balance of payments accounts always balance.

2. Describe the demand for and the supply of foreign currency.

3. Explain the various factors that cause changes in the exchange rate.

4. Explain why a current account deficit is not necessarily undesirable.

5. Summarize the theory of purchasing power parity, and explain its limitations.

6. Describe how flexible exchange rates can dampen the effects of external shocks on output and employment.

In 1973, it cost only 96 Canadian cents to purchase one U.S. dollar. By 2004, the Canadian dollar had depreciated so much that it then cost over $1.35 Canadian to purchase one U.S. dollar. This 30-year depreciation of the Canadian dollar was neither smooth nor steady. During the late 1980s, the Canadian dollar appreciated by over 10 percent; during the late 1990s, it depreciated just as much; and in 2003, it appreciated again by over 10 percent. What explains the long-run depreciation of the Canadian dollar? And what explains the sometime dramatic movements in the exchange rate over shorter periods of time?

In this chapter we examine why the exchange rate changes, and what these changes imply for the economy. We examine the important difference between *flexible* and *fixed* exchange rates, and the Bank of Canada's role under each system. The discussion will bring together material on three topics studied elsewhere in this book: the theory of supply and demand (Chapter 3), the nature of money (Chapter 27), and international trade (Chapter 33).

We begin, however, by examining a country's balance of payments—the record of transactions in goods, services, and assets with the rest of the world. After introducing terms, we see why the balance of payments is defined in such a way that it *always* balances.

balance of payments accounts A summary record of a country's transactions with the rest of the world, including the buying and selling of goods, services, and assets.

35.1 **The Balance of Payments**

Statistics Canada carefully documents transactions between Canada and the rest of the world. The record of such transactions is made in the **balance of payments accounts.**

For computing Canada's balance of payments, each transaction, such as the exports or imports of goods, or the international purchase or sales of assets, is classified according to whether the transaction generates a *payment* or a *receipt* for Canada.

Table 35-1 shows the major items in the Canadian balance of payments accounts for 2002. Transactions that represent a receipt for Canada, such as the sale of a product or asset to foreigners, are recorded in the balance of payments accounts as a *credit* item. Transactions that represent a payment for Canada, such as the purchase of a product or asset from foreigners, are recorded as a *debit* item.

There are three main categories to the balance of payments: the *current account*, the *capital account*, and the *official financing account*. We examine each account in turn.

The Current Account

The **current account** records transactions arising from trade in goods and services. It also includes net investment income that residents of one country earn from assets issued to them by foreigners. The current account is divided into two main sections.

The first section, called the **trade account**, records payments and receipts arising from the import and export of goods, such as computers and cars, and services, such as legal or architectural services. (Tourism constitutes a large part of the trade in services.) Canadian imports of goods and services require a payment to foreigners and thus are entered as debit items on the trade account; Canadian exports of goods and services generate a receipt to Canada and thus are recorded as credit items.

The second section, called the **capital-service account,** records the payments and receipts that represent income on assets. When Canadians pay income to the foreign owners of Canadian-located assets, this requires a payment to foreigners and thus is entered as a debit item. Income Canadians receive that is earned from their assets located abroad is a receipt from foreigners and thus enters as a credit item.

As shown in Table 35-1, Canadian exports of goods and services were $472 billion in 2002, and Canadian imports of goods and services were $423 billion. The trade account had a surplus of $49 billion—in other words, in 2002 Canada sold $49 billion more worth of goods and services to the world than it bought from the world. But in terms of the capital-service account, things were the other way

TABLE 35-1 Canadian Balance of Payments, 2002 (billions of dollars)

CURRENT ACCOUNT	
Trade Account	
Merchandise exports	+414.3
Service exports	+58.3
Merchandise imports	−356.5
Service imports	−66.7
Trade balance	+49.4
Capital-Service Account	
Net investment income (including unilateral transfers)	−26.2
Current Account balance	+23.2
CAPITAL ACCOUNT	
Net change in Canadian investments abroad [capital outflow (−)]	−81.8
Net change in foreign investments in Canada [capital inflow (+)]	+68.5
Capital Account balance	−13.3
OFFICIAL FINANCING ACCOUNT	
Changes in reserves [increases (−)]	+0.3
Statistical Discrepancy	−10.2
Official Financing balance	−9.9
Balance of Payments	0.0

The overall balance of payments always balances, but the individual components do not have to. In 2002, Canada had an overall trade surplus (including trade in goods and services) of $49.4 billion. There was a deficit of $26.2 billion on the capital-service account. There was thus a $23.2 billion surplus on the current account. There was a deficit on the capital account because the trading of assets internationally resulted in a net outflow of capital. The capital plus current account surplus is what is sometimes referred to as the balance of payments, and in 2002, there was an overall surplus of just $9.9 billion. This is exactly offset by the official financing balance plus the statistical discrepancy. The statistical discrepancy entry compensates for the inability to measure some items accurately.

(*Source:* Statistics Canada webpage: www.statcan.ca. Go to "Canadian Statistics" and click on "Economic conditions" and then "National accounts.")

current account
The part of the balance of payments accounts that records payments and receipts arising from trade in goods and services and from interest and dividends that are earned by capital owned in one country and invested in another.

trade account   In the balance of payments, this account records exports and imports of goods and services.

capital-service account   In the balance of payments, this account records the payments and receipts that represent income on assets (such as interest and dividends).

capital account
The part of the balance of payments accounts that records payments and receipts arising from the import and export of long-term and short-term financial capital.

direct investment
Nonresident investment in the form of a takeover or capital investment in a domestic branch plant or subsidiary corporation in which the investor has voting control. Also called *foreign direct investment.*

portfolio investment
Foreign investment in bonds or a minority holding of shares that does not involve legal control.

official financing account   In the balance of payments, this account records the central bank's purchases and sales of foreign-currency reserves.

around. The table shows that Canadians paid $26 billion more to foreigners in investment income than they received from foreigners. The current account balance (the sum of the trade and capital-service accounts) had a surplus of $23.2 billion.

The Capital Account

The second main division in the balance of payments is the **capital account,** which records international transactions in assets. The purchase of foreign assets by Canadians is treated just like the purchase of foreign goods. Since purchasing a foreign asset requires a payment from Canadians to foreigners, it is entered as a debit item in the Canadian capital account. Note that when Canadians purchase foreign assets, financial capital is leaving Canada and going abroad, and so this is called a *capital outflow.*

The sale of Canadian assets to foreigners is treated just like the sale of Canadian goods to foreigners. Since selling a Canadian asset abroad generates a receipt for Canada, it is entered as a credit item in the Canadian capital account. Note that when Canadians sell assets to foreigners, financial capital is entering Canada from abroad, and so this is called a *capital inflow.*

As shown in Table 35-1, in 2002, Canadians increased their holdings of assets abroad by $81.8 billion, resulting in a capital outflow of that amount. At the same time, foreigners increased their holdings of assets in Canada by $68.5 billion, resulting in a capital inflow of that amount. The net capital outflow resulted in a deficit in the capital account of $13.3 billion.

Though not shown in Table 35-1, the capital account is divided into *direct investment* and *portfolio investment.* **Direct investment** (also called *foreign direct investment*) relates to changes in foreign ownership of domestic firms and domestic ownership of foreign firms. One form of direct investment in Canada is capital investment in a branch plant or a subsidiary corporation in Canada in which the investor has voting control. Another form is a takeover, in which a controlling interest in a firm, previously controlled by residents, is acquired by foreigners. **Portfolio investment** is investment in bonds or a minority holding of shares that does not involve legal control.

The Official Financing Account

The final section in the balance of payments represents transactions in the official reserves that are held by the central bank and is called the **official financing account** or sometimes the *official settlements account.* The central banks of most countries, including Canada, hold financial reserves in the form of gold, foreign currencies, and bonds denominated in foreign currencies. (Check back to the Bank of Canada's balance sheet in Chapter 27 to see how large these reserves are in a typical year.)

The Bank of Canada can intervene in the market for foreign currency to influence the Canadian dollar's exchange rate. For example, to prevent the Canadian dollar from depreciating, the Bank of Canada must purchase Canadian dollars and sell foreign currency. It can do so only if it holds reserves of foreign currency. When the Bank of Canada wishes to stop the Canadian dollar from appreciating, it enters the market and sells dollars. In this case, the Bank purchases foreign currency, which it then adds to its reserves.

Since foreign currency is an asset for the Bank of Canada, it follows that when the Bank of Canada enters the foreign-exchange market to buy or sell foreign currency, it is simply buying or selling an asset. In the balance of payments, we deal with that transaction in the same way we deal with other asset transactions. Specifically, when the Bank purchases foreign currency (and sells Canadian dollars) this transaction represents the purchase of an asset from abroad, and thus it enters as a debit item in the balance of payments. Conversely, when the Bank sells foreign currency (and purchases Canadian dollars), this transaction represents the sale of an asset to foreigners, and thus it enters as a credit item in the balance of payments.

Table 35-1 shows that in 2002 the Bank of Canada *decreased* its reserves of foreign exchange by only $0.3 billion; it therefore sold more foreign exchange during the year than it bought.

For balance of payments statistics for many countries, see the IMF's website: www.imf.org.

The Meaning of Payments, Balances, and Imbalances

We first examine why the overall balance of payments *always* balances. We then explore what is meant by the often-used terms "balance of payments deficit" or "balance of payments surplus."

The Balance of Payments Must Balance

The balance of payments accounts are based on the important idea of *double-entry bookkeeping*. Since any transaction involves something being sold and something being received, each transaction has two entries in the balance of payments. The value of the good or asset that is *sold* appears as a credit item in the balance of payments accounts. The value of the good or asset that is *received* in the transaction appears as a debit item in the balance of payments accounts. Since the dollar value of what is sold obviously equals the dollar value of what is received, these two entries clearly offset each other. Thus the balance of payments must always balance. In some cases, the different entries will appear on different accounts; in other cases both entries will appear on the same account. Some examples will help to illustrate how this works.

Suppose a Canadian software company sells computer software to a customer in Germany for $1 million. The sale of the software is an export of a good for Canada and thus enters as a credit item in Canada's current account. In return, the Canadian firm receives $1 million cash, which we suppose the firm deposits in a bank account. The creation of this $1 million deposit is essentially a "purchase" of assets (the bank deposit) for Canada and appears as a debit item in Canada's capital account. Thus, as a result of this transaction, the $1 million credit on the current account is offset by the $1 million debit on the capital account. The balance of payments, as always, is in balance.

Now consider a wealthy Canadian investor who sells a Canadian government bond to a Swiss citizen for $5 million. The sale of the bond appears as a credit item in Canada's capital account. In return, suppose the Canadian investor receives the $5 million cash directly into his Swiss bank account. This is the accumulation of an asset for Canada and thus appears as a debit item in Canada's capital account. Thus, as a result of this transaction, the $5 million credit on the capital account is offset by the $5 million debit on the capital account. The current account is not affected by this transaction. And, as always, the balance of payments is in balance.

Double-entry bookkeeping in the balance of payments means that any transaction leads to both a credit item and an equal-value debit item. The balance of payments must therefore always balance.

This accounting result is important. It is not based on assumptions about behaviour or any other theoretical reasoning—it is an *accounting identity*. Many people nonetheless find the idea of double-entry bookkeeping confusing. *Applying Economic Concepts 35-1* discusses an individual student's balance of payments with the rest of the world, and illustrates why any individual's balance of payments must always balance.

APPLYING ECONOMIC CONCEPTS 35-1

A Student's Balance of Payments with the Rest of the World

Many students find a country's balance of payments confusing, especially the idea that the balance of payments *must always* balance. Why, they often ask, can't Canada export more goods and services to the world than it imports, and at the same time have a net sale of assets to the rest of the world? The connection between the current-account transactions and the capital-account transactions is not always obvious.

Perhaps the easiest way to see this connection is to consider an individual's "balance of payments" with the rest of the world. Of course, most individuals would not normally compute their balance of payments, but by doing so we can recognize the everyday concepts involved and also see the necessary connection between any individual's "current account" and "capital account." The reason why Canada's balance of payments must always balance is exactly the same reason why an individual's balance of payments must always balance.

The table shows the balance of payments for Stefan, a university student. Stefan is fortunate in several respects. First, his parents are able to provide some of the funds needed to

Stefan's Balance of Payments	
Current Account (Income and Expenditure)	
Labour income ("exports")	+$10 000
Purchase of goods and services ("imports")	−$17 000
Interest income	+$ 500
Transfers (from his parents)	+$10 000
Current Account Balance	+ $3 500
Capital Account (Changes in Assets)	
(− denotes an increase)	
Financial Assets	
Purchase of Canada Savings Bonds	−$1 500
Change in Savings Account Deposits	−$2 000
Capital Account Balance	−$3 500
BALANCE OF PAYMENTS	$0

The Relationships Among Various Balances

Two important implications follow directly from our observation that the overall payments must balance:

1. The terms *balance of payments deficit* and *balance of payments surplus* must refer to the balance on some part of the payments accounts. The terms make no sense if they are applied to the overall balance of payments.

2. A deficit on any one part of the accounts implies an offsetting surplus on the rest of the accounts.

We now consider two important applications of these statements. The first application concerns the balance on the official financing account and the combined balance on the current plus capital accounts; the second concerns the separate balances on current and capital accounts. Keep in mind that we use the word *overall* when referring to the balance of payments *including the official financing account.*

Official Financing and the Rest of the Accounts.   We know that the term "balance of payments deficit" does not strictly make sense since the balance of payments must always balance overall. But such a term is nonetheless often used in the press and even by some economists. What does this mean? Most often the term is used carelessly—a balance of payments deficit is mentioned when what is actually meant is a current account deficit.

finance his education. Second, he has a summer job that pays well. Third, he was given some Canada Savings Bonds when he was born that provide him with some interest income every year.

The top part of the table shows Stefan's income and expenditures for a single year. This is his current account. The bottom part shows the change in Stefan's assets over the same year. This is his capital account. (Note that, for Stefan as well as for any country, the capital account does not show the overall stock of assets—it only shows the *changes* in the stock of assets during the year.)

Let's begin with his current account. Stefan has a good summer job that earns him $10 000 after taxes. This $10 000 represents Stefan's "exports" to the rest of the world—he earns this income by selling his labour services to a tree-planting company. Over the year, however, he spends $17 000 on tuition, books, clothes, beer, pizza, photocopying, and other goods and services. These are Stefan's "imports" from the rest of the world. Stefan clearly has a "trade deficit" equal to $7000—he "imports" more than he "exports."

There are two other sources of income shown in Stefan's current account. First, he earns $500 in interest income. Second, his parents give him $10 000 to help pay for his education—a *transfer* in the terminology of balance of payments accounting. The interest income and transfer together make up Stefan's "capital-service account"—Stefan has a surplus of $10 500.

Stefan's overall current account shows a surplus of $3500. This means he receives $3500 more in total income than he spends on goods and services. But where does this $3500 go?

Now let's consider Stefan's capital account, the bottom part of the table. The $3500 surplus on current account *must* end up as increases in Stefan's assets. He increases his holdings of Canada Savings Bonds by $1500 and increases his savings-account deposits by $2000. In both cases he is purchasing assets—he buys a bond and he also "buys" a bank deposit. Since Stefan must make a payment to purchase these assets, they appear as a debit item in his capital account. Stefan's capital account balance is a deficit of $3500.

Finally, note that Stefan's current account and capital account *must* sum to zero. There is no way around this fact. Any surplus of income over expenditures (on current account) must show up as an increase in his assets (or a decrease in his debts) on capital account. Conversely, any excess of expenditures over income must be financed by reducing his assets (or by increasing his debts). Stefan's balance of payments *must* balance.

What is true for Stefan is true for any individual and also true for any accounting unit you choose to consider. Saskatoon's balance of payments with the rest of the world must balance. Saskatchewan's balance of payments with the rest of the world must balance. Western Canada's balance of payments with the rest of the world must balance. And so must Canada's, and any other country's.

There are also occasions when people speak of a country as having a balance of payments deficit or surplus when they are actually referring to the balance of all accounts *excluding* official financing—that is, to the combined balance on current and capital accounts.

For example, consider a situation in which Canada has a current account deficit of $20 billion—Canada is buying $20 billion more in goods and services from the rest of the world than it is selling to the world. At the same time, suppose the capital account surplus is only $15 billion—Canada is selling $15 billion more in assets to the rest of the world than it is buying in return. In this case, some people would say that Canada has a "balance of payments deficit" of $5 billion. But what is really true is that the current plus capital accounts together have a deficit of $5 billion. This is only possible, of course, if the official financing account has a surplus of $5 billion. Thus, the Bank of Canada, on the official financing account, is selling $5 billion of foreign currency reserves (and in return receiving $5 billion in Canadian dollars). The $5 billion surplus on the official financing account is exactly "financing" the "balance of payments deficit."

A "balance of payments deficit" refers to a situation in which the Bank of Canada is selling foreign currency. A "balance of payments surplus" refers to a situation in which the Bank of Canada is buying foreign currency. In both cases, as always, the balance of payments is actually in balance.

The Bank of Canada holds millions of dollars' worth of gold as
part of its official reserves.

The Current and Capital Account Balances.   Suppose the Bank of Canada does not engage in any foreign-exchange transactions. The official financing account is thus zero. Now any deficit or surplus on the current account must be matched exactly by an equal and opposite surplus or deficit on the capital account.

For example, if Canada has a current account deficit of $10 billion, there *must* be a capital account surplus of $10 billion. The intuition is straightforward. If Canada has a $10 billion deficit on current account, it is importing more goods and services (including debt service) than it is exporting. But how does it finance these "extra" imports? Some individual or firm or government in Canada must sell some Canadian assets to (or borrow from) some individual or firm or government in the rest of the world—that is, Canada must have a capital account surplus.

Similarly, suppose Canada has a current account surplus of $10 billion, reflecting more earnings from exports than expenditures on imports. What does Canada do with the "extra" earnings? It must acquire some assets from the rest of the world—that is, Canada must have a capital account deficit.

If the central bank does not change its holdings of foreign-currency reserves, the current account and capital account must sum to zero.

This brings us to the end of our discussion of the balance of payments. Keep in mind that this is just an exercise in accounting. Though at times you may find it difficult to keep the various credits and debits in the various accounts straight in your mind, remember that the structure of the accounting system is quite simple. Here is a brief review:

Practise with Study Guide Chapter 35,
Short-Answer Question 1.

1. The current account shows all transactions in goods and services between Canada and the rest of the world (including investment income and transfers).

2. The capital account shows all transactions in assets between Canada and the rest of the world.

3. The official financing account shows the change in the Bank of Canada's holding of foreign-currency reserves (including gold).

4. All transactions involving a payment from Canada appear as a debit item. All transactions involving a receipt to Canada appear as a credit item.

5. The balance of payments—the sum of the current account, capital account, and official financing account—must always be zero.

We now go on to explore how exchange rates are determined in the foreign-exchange market. We will see that a knowledge of the various categories in the balance of payments will help in our understanding of why changes in exchange rates occur.

35.2 The Foreign-Exchange Market

Money is vital in any sophisticated economy that relies on specialization and trade. Yet money as we know it is a *national* matter. If you live in Argentina, you earn pesos and spend pesos; if you operate a business in Austria, you borrow euros and pay your workers in euros. The currency of a country is acceptable within the border of that country, but usually it will not be accepted by firms and households in another country. Just try buying your next pair of jeans in Canada with British pounds sterling or Japanese yen.

Trade between countries normally requires the exchange of the currency of one country for that of another.

The exchange of one currency for another is called a *foreign-exchange transaction*. The **exchange rate** is the rate at which one currency exchanges for another. In Canada's case, the exchange rate is the Canadian-dollar price of one unit of foreign currency. For example, in September 2003, the price of one U.S. dollar was 1.38 Canadian dollars. Thus, the Canada–U.S. exchange rate was 1.38.

We could just as easily define the exchange rate in the opposite way. We could define it as the number of units of foreign currency that could be purchased with one Canadian dollar. In our example from September 2003, the exchange rate between the Canadian and U.S. dollars would then be 1/1.38 = 0.724. One Canadian dollar would purchase 72.4 U.S. cents.

In this book, however, we *always* define the exchange rate in the way Canadian economists usually do—as the Canadian-dollar price of one unit of foreign currency. This definition makes it clear that foreign currency, like any good or service, has a price expressed in Canadian dollars. In this case, the price of the "good" has a special name—the exchange rate.

An **appreciation** of the Canadian dollar means that it takes fewer Canadian dollars to purchase one unit of foreign currency. For example, if the Canadian dollar appreciates against the U.S. dollar from 1.38 to 1.31, it takes 7 fewer Canadian cents to purchase one U.S. dollar. Thus, an appreciation of the Canadian dollar implies a *fall* in the exchange rate. Conversely, a **depreciation** of the Canadian dollar means that it takes more Canadian dollars to purchase one unit of foreign currency. Thus, a depreciation of the Canadian dollar means a *rise* in the exchange rate.

An appreciation of the Canadian dollar is a fall in the exchange rate; a depreciation of the Canadian dollar is a rise in the exchange rate.

We now go on to build a simple model of the foreign-exchange market. This will allow us to analyze the determinants of the exchange rate. To keep things simple, we use an example involving trade between Canada and Europe, and thus we examine the determination of the exchange rate between the two currencies, the Canadian dollar and the euro. But, in this example, Europe is just a shorthand for "the rest of the world" and the euro is just a shorthand for "all other currencies." (It would be more natural to think in terms of Canada–U.S. trade since 80 percent of Canadian trade is with the United States, but this quickly becomes confusing because both countries' currencies are called the dollar.)

Because dollars are traded for euros in the foreign-exchange market, it follows that a demand for euros implies a supply of dollars and that a supply of euros implies a demand for dollars.

For this reason, a theory of the exchange rate between dollars and euros can deal either with the demand and supply of dollars or with the demand and supply of euros; both need not be considered. We will concentrate on the demand, supply, and price of euros. Thus, the market we will be considering (in general terms) is the foreign-exchange market—the "product" is foreign exchange (euros in our case) and the "price" is the exchange rate (the Canadian-dollar price of euros).

We develop our example in terms of the demand and supply analysis first encountered in Chapter 3. To do so, we need only to recall that in the market for foreign exchange, transactions that generate a receipt for Canada in its balance of payments represent a *supply* of foreign exchange. Foreign exchange is being supplied by the

exchange rate
The number of units of domestic currency required to purchase one unit of foreign currency.

appreciation   A fall in the exchange rate—it takes fewer units of domestic currency to purchase one unit of foreign currency.

depreciation   A rise in the exchange rate—it takes more units of domestic currency to purchase one unit of foreign currency.

foreigners who purchase Canadian goods or assets. Conversely, transactions that are a payment from Canada in the balance of payments represent a *demand* for foreign exchange. Foreign exchange is being demanded by the Canadians who are purchasing foreign goods or assets.

We begin by focusing only on the demand and supply of foreign exchange arising from the current and capital accounts. Later we turn to the important role of official financing by the Bank of Canada. But, for now, suppose the Bank of Canada makes no transactions in the foreign-exchange market.

The Supply of Foreign Exchange

Whenever foreigners purchase Canadian goods, services, or assets, they supply foreign currency to the foreign-exchange market and demand, in return, Canadian dollars with which to pay for their purchases. Thus, the supply of foreign exchange arises from Canada's sales of goods, services, and assets to the rest of the world.

Canadian Exports

One important source of supply of foreign exchange is foreigners who wish to buy Canadian-made goods and services. A Japanese importer of lumber is such a purchaser; an Austrian couple planning a vacation in Canada is another; the Russian government seeking to buy Canadian steel is a third. All are sources of supply of foreign exchange, arising out of international trade. Each potential buyer wants to sell its own currency in exchange for Canadian dollars that it can then use to purchase Canadian goods and services.

Capital Inflows

A second source of supply of foreign exchange comes from foreigners who wish to purchase Canadian assets, such as government or corporate bonds, or plant and equipment currently located in Canada. To buy Canadian assets, holders of foreign currencies must first sell their foreign currency and buy Canadian dollars. In recent years, foreign households and firms have invested tens of billions of dollars in Canadian securities and real estate. This has required the conversion of foreign currencies into Canadian dollars. The resulting transactions are called *long-term capital flows.*

In Chapter 29 we discussed how the Bank of Canada's efforts to reduce inflation in the early 1990s pushed Canadian interest rates well above those in other countries. With the increase in Canadian rates, floods of "foreign money" came into Canada to buy short-term treasury bills, certificates of deposit, and other securities. The buyers were seeking a high return on their liquid assets, but first these buyers had to convert their U.S. dollars, yen, guilder, marks, and francs into Canadian dollars in the foreign-exchange market. When people sell financial assets in one country for foreign exchange that they then use to buy short-term financial assets in another country, the transactions are called *short-term capital flows.*

Reserve Currency

Firms, banks, and governments often accumulate and hold foreign-exchange reserves, just as individuals maintain savings accounts. These reserves may be in several different currencies. For example, the government of Nigeria may decide to increase its reserve holdings of Canadian dollars and reduce its reserve holdings of euros; if it does so, it will be a supplier of euros (and a demander of Canadian dollars) in foreign-exchange markets.

The Total Supply of Foreign Exchange

The supply of foreign exchange (or the demand for Canadian dollars) by holders of foreign currencies is the sum of the supplies for all of the purposes just discussed—for purchases of Canadian exports, for capital inflow to Canada and for the purchase of Canadian dollars to add to currency reserves.

Furthermore, because people, firms, and governments in all countries purchase goods and assets from many other countries, the demand for any one currency will be the aggregate demand of individuals, firms, and governments in a number of different countries. Thus, the total supply of foreign exchange (or the demand for Canadian dollars) may include Germans who are offering euros, Japanese who are offering yen, Argentinians who are offering pesos, and so on. For simplicity, however, we go back to our two-country example and use only Canada and Europe.

The Supply Curve for Foreign Exchange

The supply of foreign exchange on the foreign-exchange market is represented by a positively sloped curve, such as the one shown in Figure 35-1. This figure plots the Canadian-dollar price of euros (the exchange rate) on the vertical axis and the quantity of euros on the horizontal axis. Moving up the vertical scale, more dollars are needed to purchase one euro—the dollar is depreciating. Moving down the vertical scale, fewer dollars are needed to purchase one euro—the dollar is appreciating.

Why is the supply curve for foreign exchange positively sloped? Consider the supply of foreign exchange derived from foreign purchases of Canadian exports. If the Canadian dollar depreciates, it takes fewer euros to purchase one Canadian dollar. Thus, for a given Canadian-dollar price of the product the euro price has fallen. European consumers will therefore buy more of the cheaper Canadian goods and will thus supply more foreign exchange for this purpose. In the opposite case, when the dollar appreciates, the euro price of Canadian exports rises. European consumers will buy fewer Canadian goods and thus supply less foreign exchange.[1]

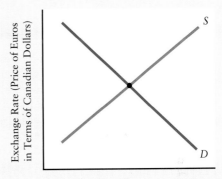

FIGURE 35-1 The Foreign-Exchange Market

Quantity of Foreign Currency (Euros)

The demand for foreign exchange is negatively sloped, and the supply of foreign exchange is positively sloped, when plotted against the exchange rate, measured as the Canadian-dollar price of one unit of foreign currency. The demand for foreign exchange is given by the negatively sloped blue line D. It represents the sum of transactions on both current and capital accounts that require payments to foreigners.

The supply of foreign exchange is given by the positively sloped red line S. It represents the sum of transactions on both current and capital accounts that represent receipts from foreigners.

---

[1] We have assumed here that the foreign price elasticity of demand for Canadian exports is greater than 1, so that a price change leads to a proportionately larger change in quantity demanded. This is a common assumption in the analysis of international trade. In the case of Canada (and other small countries) it is common to go further and make the "small open economy" assumption—that the country faces *given world prices* for both its exports and imports. In this case, the foreign price elasticity of demand for exports is infinite.

Similar considerations affect other sources of supply of foreign exchange. When the Canadian dollar depreciates (a higher exchange rate), Canadian assets and securities become attractive purchases, and the quantity purchased will rise. With this rise, the amount of foreign exchange supplied to pay for the purchases will increase.

The supply curve for foreign exchange is positively sloped when it is plotted against the exchange rate; a depreciation of the Canadian dollar (a rise in the exchange rate) increases the quantity of foreign exchange supplied.

The Demand for Foreign Exchange

The demand for foreign exchange arises from all international transactions that represent a payment in Canada's balance of payments. What sorts of international transactions generate a demand for foreign exchange (and a supply of Canadian dollars)? Canadians seeking to purchase foreign products will be supplying Canadian dollars and demanding foreign exchange for this purpose. Canadians may also seek to purchase foreign assets. If they do, they will supply Canadian dollars and demand foreign exchange. Similarly, a country with reserves of Canadian dollars may decide to sell them in order to demand some other currency.

The Demand Curve for Foreign Exchange

When the Canadian dollar depreciates, the Canadian-dollar price of European goods rises. Because it takes more dollars to buy the same European good, Canadians will buy fewer of the now more expensive European goods. The amount of foreign exchange being demanded by Canadians in order to pay for imported European goods will fall.[2] In the opposite case, when the Canadian dollar appreciates, European goods become cheaper, more are sold, and more dollars are spent on them. Thus, more foreign exchange will be demanded to pay for the extra imports. This same argument applies in exactly the same way to the purchases of foreign assets. Figure 35-1 shows the demand curve for foreign exchange.

The demand curve for foreign exchange is negatively sloped when it is plotted against the exchange rate; an appreciation of the Canadian dollar (a fall in the exchange rate) increases the quantity of foreign exchange demanded.

35.3 The Determination of Exchange Rates

The demand and supply curves in Figure 35-1 do not include official financing transactions (the demands for or supplies of foreign exchange by the Bank of Canada). To com-

---

[2] As long as the price elasticity of demand for imports is greater than 1, the fall in the volume of imports will exceed the rise in price, and hence fewer dollars will be spent on them. This condition (and the one in the previous footnote) is related to a famous long-standing issue in international economics, called the *Marshall–Lerner condition*. In what follows, we take the standard approach of assuming that both the price elasticity of demand for imports and the price elasticity of the demand for Canadian exports exceeds 1. This guarantees that the slopes of the curves are as shown in Figure 35-1.

plete our analysis, we must incorporate the role of official financing transactions. We need to consider three important cases:

1. When the central bank makes no transactions in the foreign-exchange market, the exchange rate is determined by the equality between the supply of and demand for foreign exchange arising from the capital and current accounts. In this situation there is said to be a purely **flexible exchange rate.**

2. When the central bank intervenes in the foreign-exchange market to "fix" the exchange rate at a particular value, there is said to be a **fixed exchange rate** or *pegged exchange rate.*

3. Between these two "pure" systems is a variety of possible intermediate cases, including the *adjustable peg* and the *managed float.* In the **adjustable peg system,** central banks fix specific values for their exchange rates, but they explicitly recognize that circumstances may arise in which they will change that value. In a **managed float,** the central bank seeks to have some stabilizing influence on the exchange rate but does not try to fix it at some publicly announced value.

Most countries today operate a mostly flexible exchange rate. It is mostly market determined but the central bank sometimes intervenes to offset short-run fluctuations. There are, however, some important exceptions. The countries of the European Union (EU), for example, had a system of fixed exchange rates (relative to each other's currencies) between 1979 and 1999. In 1999 the EU introduced a common currency—the euro—that was adopted by most of the EU member countries (an important exception being the United Kingdom). Thus, they now have fixed exchange rates relative to each other (since they have the same currency) but have a flexible exchange rate (with some short-term interventions) relative to countries outside the EU. The United States, Japan, the United Kingdom, Australia, and most other major industrialized countries have flexible exchange rates with relatively small amounts of foreign-exchange intervention by their central banks.

Canada used flexible exchange rates (with limited intervention) throughout most of the period following the Second World War. Even when most countries pegged their currencies to the U.S. dollar under the Bretton Woods system, Canada had a flexible exchange rate. Later in the chapter we examine the issues involved in choosing between a flexible and fixed exchange-rate system. For now, let's explore how the various systems operate.

flexible exchange rate An exchange rate that is left free to be determined by the forces of demand and supply on the free market, with no intervention by central banks.

fixed exchange rate An exchange rate that is maintained within a small range around its publicly stated par value by the intervention in the foreign-exchange market by a country's central bank.

adjustable peg system A system in which exchange rates are fixed in the short term but are occasionally changed in response to changes in economic events.

managed float A situation in which the central bank intervenes in the foreign-exchange market to smooth out some of the large, short-term fluctuations in a country's exchange rate, while still leaving the market to determine the exchange rate in the longer term.

Flexible Exchange Rates

Consider an exchange rate that is set in a freely competitive market, with no intervention by the central bank. Like any competitive price, the exchange rate fluctuates according to the conditions of demand and supply.

Suppose the current exchange rate is so high (say, e_1 in Figure 35-2) that the quantity of foreign exchange supplied exceeds the quantity demanded. There is thus an abundance of foreign exchange and a shortage of Canadian dollars. This excess supply of foreign exchange, just as in our analysis in Chapter 3, will cause the price of foreign exchange (the exchange rate) to fall. As the exchange rate falls—an appreciation of the Canadian dollar— the euro price of Canadian goods rises, and this leads to a reduction in the quantity of foreign exchange supplied. Also, as the exchange rate falls, the Canadian-dollar price of European goods falls, and this fall leads to an

In 1999, 11 countries of the European Union adopted a common currency— the euro. Late in 2003, the exchange rate was 0.89 euros per U.S. dollar, or 0.65 euros per Canadian dollar.

FIGURE 35-2 Fixed and Flexible Exchange Rates

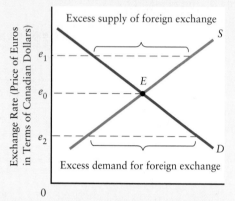

In the absence of central bank intervention, the exchange rate adjusts to clear the foreign-exchange market. The demand for and supply of foreign exchange are as in Figure 35-1. If official financing is zero, there is a flexible exchange rate. It will adjust to equate the demand and supply of foreign exchange; this occurs at E with an exchange rate of e_0.

If the exchange rate is higher than that, say at e_1, the supply of foreign exchange will exceed the demand. The exchange rate will fall (the dollar will appreciate) until it reaches e_0, where balance is achieved at E. If the exchange rate is below e_0, say at e_2, the demand for foreign exchange will exceed the supply. The exchange rate will rise (the dollar will depreciate) until it reaches e_0, where balance is achieved at E.

The central bank can fix the exchange rate by using its official financing transactions to meet the excess demands or supplies that arise at the fixed value of the exchange rate. For example, if it chooses to fix the exchange rate at e_1, there will be an excess supply of foreign exchange. The central bank will purchase foreign exchange (and sell dollars) to meet the excess supply. Alternatively, if the central bank chooses to fix the exchange rate at e_2, there will be an excess demand for foreign exchange. The central bank will sell foreign exchange (and buy dollars) to meet the excess demand.

increase in the quantity of foreign exchange demanded. Thus, the excess supply of foreign exchange leads to a fall in the exchange rate, which in turn reduces the amount of excess supply. Where the two curves intersect, quantity demanded equals quantity supplied, and the exchange rate is at its equilibrium value.

What happens when the exchange rate is below its equilibrium value, such as at e_2 in Figure 35-2? The quantity of foreign exchange demanded will exceed the quantity supplied. With foreign exchange in excess demand, its price will naturally rise, and as it does the amount of excess demand will be reduced until equilibrium is re-established.

A foreign-exchange market is like other competitive markets in that the forces of demand and supply lead to an equilibrium price at which quantity demanded equals quantity supplied.

Recall that we have been assuming that there is no official financing by the central bank, so that demand and supply in the foreign-exchange market represent transactions only on the current or capital account. We now consider a system of fixed exchange rates in which official financing plays a central role in the analysis.

Fixed Exchange Rates

When the central bank fixes the exchange rate at a particular value, the current account and the capital account do not necessarily sum to zero. The balance on the official financing account has to be whatever is necessary to offset the excess demand or supply of foreign exchange that arises. This is also shown in Figure 35-2.

The gold standard that operated for much of the nineteenth century and the early part of the twentieth century was a fixed exchange-rate system. The Bretton Woods system, established by international agreement in 1944 and operated until the early 1970s, was a fixed exchange-rate system that provided for circumstances under which exchange rates could be adjusted. It was thus an adjustable peg system; the International Monetary Fund (IMF) has its origins in the Bretton Woods system, and one of its principal tasks was approving and monitoring exchange-rate changes. The European Exchange Rate Mechanism (ERM), which existed from 1979 to 1999, was also a fixed exchange-rate system for the countries in the European Union; their exchange rates were fixed to each other but floated as a block against the U.S. dollar and other currencies. As mentioned earlier, this system of separate currencies with fixed exchange rates was replaced in 1999 when most of the countries of the EU adopted a common currency—the euro.

For information on the European Central Bank, see its website: www.ecb.int.

Applying Economic Concepts 35-2 examines how a fixed exchange-rate system operates. It shows why a central bank that chooses to fix its exchange rate must give up some control of its foreign-exchange reserves. This presents some problems, as it did for Thailand in the summer of 1997, at the beginning of the 1997–1998 Asian Crisis.

We now go on to study the workings of a flexible exchange-rate system, the system used in Canada and most major countries.

Changes in Flexible Exchange Rates

What causes exchange rates to vary? The simplest answer to this question is changes in demand or supply in the foreign-exchange market. Anything that shifts the demand curve for foreign exchange to the right or the supply curve for foreign exchange to the left leads to a rise in the exchange rate—a depreciation of the Canadian dollar. Conversely, anything that shifts the demand curve for foreign exchange to the left or the supply curve for foreign exchange to the right leads to a fall in the exchange rate—an appreciation of the Canadian dollar. These points are nothing more than a restatement of the laws of supply and demand, applied now to the market for foreign exchange; they are illustrated in Figure 35-3.

What causes the shifts in demand and supply that lead to changes in exchange rates? There are many causes, some transitory and some persistent. Let's look at several of the most important ones.

FIGURE 35-3   Changes in Exchange Rates

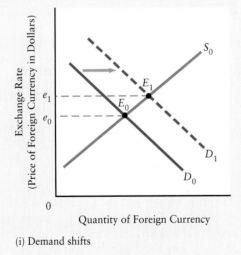

(i) Demand shifts

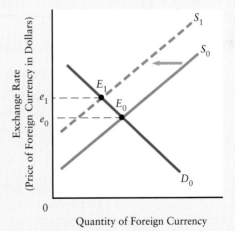

(ii) Supply shifts

An increase in the demand for foreign exchange or a decrease in the supply will cause the dollar to depreciate (the exchange rate to rise); a decrease in the demand or an increase in supply will cause the dollar to appreciate (the exchange rate to fall). The initial demand and supply curves are D_0 and S_0. Equilibrium is at E_0 with an exchange rate of e_0. An increase in the demand for foreign exchange from D_0 to D_1 in part (i), or a decrease in the supply of foreign exchange from S_0 to S_1 in part (ii), will cause the dollar to depreciate. In both parts, the new equilibrium is at E_1, and the dollar depreciation is shown by the rise in the exchange rate from e_0 to e_1. Conversely, a decrease in the demand for foreign exchange or an increase in the supply of foreign exchange will cause the dollar to appreciate.

APPLYING ECONOMIC CONCEPTS 35-2

Managing Fixed Exchange Rates

This box provides some details on how a central bank operates a regime of fixed exchange rates. Though Canada has a flexible exchange rate (with only occasional foreign-exchange intervention by the Bank of Canada), we will imagine a situation in which the Bank of Canada pegs the Canadian–U.S. exchange rate.

Suppose the Bank of Canada fixed the exchange rate between the narrow limits of, say, C$1.47 to C$1.53 to the U.S. dollar. The Bank then stabilizes the exchange rate in the face of seasonal, cyclical, and other fluctuations in demand and supply, entering the market to prevent the rate from going outside the permitted band. At the price of $1.47, the Bank offers to buy any amount of U.S. dollars; at the price of $1.53, the Bank offers to sell any amount of U.S. dollars. When the Bank buys U.S. dollars, its foreign-exchange reserves rise; when it sells U.S. dollars, its foreign-exchange reserves fall.

We make the following observations:

1. If the demand curve cuts the supply curve in the range 1.47 to 1.53, as D_0 does in the accompanying figure, the Bank need not intervene in the market.

2. If the demand curve shifts to D_1, the Bank must sell U.S. dollars from its reserves to the extent of Q_4Q_1 in order to prevent the price of U.S. dollars from rising above 1.53.

3. If the demand curve shifts to D_2, the Bank must buy U.S. dollars to the extent of Q_2Q_3 in order to prevent the price of U.S. dollars from falling below 1.47.

If, on average, the demand and supply curves intersect in the range 1.47 to 1.53, the Bank's foreign-exchange reserves will be relatively stable, with the Bank buying U.S. dollars when the demand is abnormally low and selling them when the demand is abnormally high. Over a long period, however, the average level of reserves will be fairly stable.

If conditions change, the Bank's foreign-exchange reserves will rise or fall more or less continuously. For example, suppose the average level of demand becomes D_1, with fluctuations on either side of this level. The average drain on the Bank's foreign-exchange reserves will then be Q_4Q_1 *per period*. But this situation cannot continue indefinitely because the Bank only has a limited amount of foreign-exchange

Practise with Study Guide Chapter 35, Exercise 2.

A Supply-Side Increase in the Domestic Price of Exports

Suppose some event on the supply side of the paper market results in an increase in the Canadian-dollar price of Canadian paper. For example, the government may impose a new pollution tax on paper producers. What this will do to the supply of foreign exchange depends on the price elasticity of foreign demand for the Canadian product. If foreign demand for Canadian paper is elastic, perhaps because other countries supply the same product in world markets, the total amount spent on Canadian paper will decrease and hence less foreign exchange will be supplied to purchase Canadian paper. Thus, the supply curve for foreign exchange will shift to the left and the Canadian dollar will depreciate. This is illustrated in part (ii) of Figure 35-3. If the demand is inelastic (say, because Canada is the only country that produces this particular kind of paper), then more will be spent, the supply of foreign exchange to pay the bigger bill will shift the supply curve to the right, and the Canadian dollar will appreciate.

A Rise in the Foreign Price of Imports

Suppose the euro price of European automobiles increases sharply. Suppose also that Canadian consumers have an elastic demand for European cars because they can easily switch to Canadian-made substitutes. Consequently, they spend fewer euros for European automobiles than they did before and hence demand less foreign exchange. The demand

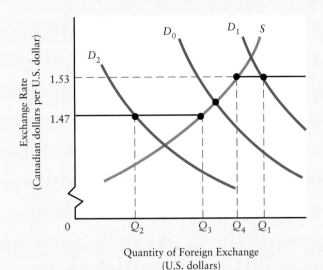

Exchange Rate
(Canadian dollars per U.S. dollar)

D_2 D_0 D_1 S

1.53

1.47

0   Q_2 Q_3 Q_4 Q_1

Quantity of Foreign Exchange
(U.S. dollars)

reserves. In this situation, the Bank has two alternatives: It can change the fixed exchange rate so that the band of permissible prices straddles the new equilibrium price, or it can try to shift the curves so that the intersection is in the band 1.47 to 1.53. To accomplish this goal, it must restrict demand for foreign exchange: It can impose import quotas and foreign-travel restrictions, or it can seek to increase the supply of U.S. dollars by encouraging Canadian exports.

Thailand in 1997 provides an example of an exchange rate fixed at a level that led to a persistent excess demand for foreign exchange. Thailand's central bank had fixed the value of its currency, the baht, to the U.S. dollar. When an excess demand for foreign currency developed in Thailand, the central bank began to deplete its stock of foreign-exchange reserves as it purchased the baht in an attempt to support its external value. By July of 1997, however, the central bank's stock of foreign-exchange reserves had been depleted to such an extent that it could no longer fix the exchange rate. With an excess demand for foreign exchange and a central bank that could no longer fix the exchange rate, depreciation was the natural result. The baht depreciated dramatically and Thailand then moved away from a fixed exchange-rate system. This event is generally viewed as the beginning of the 1997–1998 Asian Crisis during which several countries, including Malaysia, Indonesia, and South Korea, experienced similar declines in their foreign-exchange reserves and were forced to abandon their fixed exchange rates.

Practise with Study Guide Chapter 35, Exercise 5.

curve for foreign exchange shifts to the left, and the Canadian dollar will appreciate. If the demand for European cars were inelastic, total spending on them would rise, and the demand for foreign exchange would shift to the right, leading to a depreciation of the Canadian dollar. This is illustrated in part (i) of Figure 35-3.

Changes in Overall Price Levels

Suppose that instead of a change in the price of a specific export, such as cars or paper, there is a change in *all* prices because of general inflation. We consider separate cases, each corresponding to a different pattern of Canadian relative to foreign inflation.

Equal Inflation in Both Countries.   Suppose inflation is running at 5 percent in both Canada and Europe. In this case, the euro prices of European goods and the dollar prices of Canadian goods both rise by 5 percent. At the *existing* exchange rate, the dollar prices of European goods and the euro prices of Canadian goods will each rise by 5 percent, and hence the relative prices of imports and domestically produced goods will be unchanged in both countries. Since there is no reason to expect a change in either country's demand for imports at the original exchange rate, the inflation in the two countries leaves the equilibrium exchange rate unchanged.

Inflation in Only One Country.   What will happen if there is inflation in Canada while the price level remains stable in Europe? The dollar price of Canadian goods will rise, and they will become more expensive in Europe. This increase will cause the quantity of Canadian exports, and therefore the amount of foreign exchange supplied by European importers, to decrease. Thus, the supply curve for foreign exchange shifts to the left.

At the same time, European goods in Canada will have an unchanged Canadian-dollar price, while the price of Canadian goods sold in Canada will increase because of the inflation. Thus, European goods will be more attractive compared with Canadian goods (because they have become relatively cheaper), and thus more European goods will be bought in Canada. At any exchange rate, the amount of foreign exchange demanded to purchase imports will rise. Thus, the demand curve for foreign exchange shifts to the right.

Canadian inflation that is unmatched in Europe will therefore cause the supply curve for foreign exchange to shift to the left and the demand curve for foreign exchange to shift to the right. As a result, the equilibrium exchange rate *must* rise—there is a depreciation of the Canadian dollar relative to the euro.

Inflation at Unequal Rates.   The two foregoing examples are, of course, just limiting cases of a more general situation in which the rate of inflation is different in the two countries. The arguments can readily be extended when we realize that it is the *relative* inflation in two countries that determines whether home goods or foreign goods look more or less attractive. If country A's inflation rate is higher than country B's, country A's exports are becoming relatively expensive in B's markets while imports from B are becoming relatively cheap in A's markets. This causes the price of A's currency to fall—A's currency depreciates relative to B's.

Other things being equal, if Canada has higher inflation than other countries, the Canadian dollar will be depreciating relative to other currencies. If Canada has lower inflation than other countries, the Canadian dollar will be appreciating.

Capital Movements

Capital flows can exert strong influences on exchange rates. For example, an increased desire by Canadians to purchase European assets (a capital export for Canada) will shift the demand curve for foreign exchange to the right, and the dollar will depreciate.

A movement of financial capital has the effect of appreciating the currency of the capital-importing country and depreciating the currency of the capital-exporting country.

This statement is true for all capital movements, short-term or long-term. Because the motives that lead to large capital movements are likely to be different in the short and long terms, however, it is worth considering each separately.

Short-Term Capital Movements.   An important motive for short-term capital flows is a change in interest rates. International traders hold transactions balances just as do domestic traders. These balances are often lent out on a short-term basis rather than being left idle. Naturally, the holders of these balances will tend to lend them, other things being equal, in markets where interest rates are highest. Thus, if one country's short-term interest rate rises above the rates in other countries (say, because that country undertakes a contractionary monetary policy), there will tend to be a large inflow of short-term capital into that country in an effort to take advantage of the high rate. This inflow of financial capital will increase the demand for the domestic currency and cause it to appreciate. If the short-term interest rate should fall in one country (say, because of a monetary expansion in that country), there will tend to be a shift in capital away from that country and its currency will tend to depreciate. We saw this basic relationship between interest rates, capital flows, and the exchange rate in Chapter 28 when we discussed the monetary transmission mechanism in an open economy.

Changes in Canadian monetary policy lead to changes in interest rates and thus to international flows of financial capital. A contractionary monetary policy in Canada will lead to a rise in Canadian interest rates, a capital inflow, and an appreciation of the Canadian dollar. An expansionary monetary policy in Canada will lead to a reduction in Canadian interest rates, a capital outflow, and a depreciation of the Canadian dollar.

A second motive for short-term capital movements is speculation about the *future value* of a country's exchange rate. If foreigners expect the Canadian dollar to appreciate in the near future, they will rush to buy assets that pay off in Canadian dollars, such as Canadian stocks or bonds; if they expect the Canadian dollar to depreciate in the near future, they will be reluctant to buy or to hold Canadian securities.

Long-Term Capital Movements.   Long-term capital movements are largely influenced by long-term expectations about another country's profit opportunities and the long-run value of its currency. A French firm would be more willing to purchase a Canadian factory if it expected that the dollar profits would buy more euros in future years than the profits from investment in a French factory. This could happen if the Canadian firm earned greater profits than the French firm, with exchange rates remaining unchanged. It could also happen if the profits were the same but the French firm expected the Canadian dollar to appreciate relative to the euro.

Structural Changes

An economy can undergo structural changes that alter the equilibrium exchange rate. *Structural change* is an all-purpose term for a change in cost structures, the invention of new products, changes in preferences between products, or anything else that affects the pattern of comparative advantage. Consider three examples.

Suppose the reluctance of firms in one country to adopt technological innovations results in that country's products not improving as rapidly as those produced in other countries. Consumers' demand (at fixed prices) will shift slowly away from the first country's products and toward those of its foreign competitors. This shift will cause a gradual depreciation in the first country's currency because fewer people want to buy that country's goods and thus fewer people want to buy that country's currency.

A second example relates to the discovery of valuable mineral resources. Prominent examples are the development of natural gas in The Netherlands in the early 1960s, the development of North Sea oil in the United Kingdom in the 1970s, and the recent discovery of large diamond mines in the Northwest Territories. If firms in one country make such a discovery and begin selling these resources to the rest of the world, the foreign purchasers must supply their foreign currency in order to purchase the currency of the exporting country. The result is an appreciation of the currency of the exporting country.

Anything that leads to changes in the pattern of trade, such as changes in costs or changes in demand, will generally lead to changes in exchange rates.

A final example relates to changes in demand for a country's exports. For many countries, including Canada, the prices of the goods that it sells to other countries are determined in world markets. Examples include commodities such as oil, copper, pulp, lumber, wheat, coffee, cocoa, zinc, tin, aluminum, and gold. Changes in the world demand for or supply of these commodities typically have significant effects on exchange rates. For example, if there is a reduction in the world demand for these products there will be an accompanying reduction in demand for the currencies of those countries that export these products. Their currencies will depreciate. Similarly, increases in the world price of these commodities will lead to appreciations of the currencies in countries that export them. For this reason, the Canadian dollar is often referred to as a "commodity currency" because there is a strong correlation between changes in world commodity prices and changes in the Canadian exchange rate.

The Volatility of Exchange Rates

We have discussed several variables that can lead to changes in the exchange rate, including changes in relative prices, changes in interest rates, and changes in the pattern of trade. Since these variables are changing at different times by different amounts and often in different directions, it should not be surprising that exchange rates are constantly changing. Indeed, exchange rates are one of the most volatile of all macroeconomic variables. One reason for this volatility that we have not yet discussed is that foreign-exchange traders, when they are deciding whether to buy or sell foreign currency, respond to all sorts of "news" that they think will influence economic conditions, both currently and in the future. Since such news is constantly becoming available, the exchange rate is continuously changing as this new information leads traders to change their demand and supply decisions. *Applying Economic Concepts 35-3* discusses in more detail how news affects the volatility of exchange rates.

Economists have long noticed that exchange rates tend to be more volatile than any of the variables we have been discussing. For a brief discussion of a famous theory in which the expectations of future exchange-rate changes plays a central role, look for "Expectations and Exchange-Rate Overshooting" in the *Additional Topics* section of this book's Companion Website.

http://www.pearsoned.ca/ragan

35.4 **Three Policy Issues**

This chapter has so far explained how the balance of payments accounts are constructed and how exchange rates are determined. It is now time to use this knowledge to explore some important and interesting policy issues. We examine three policy issues that are commonly discussed in the popular press. As we will see, these discussions are not always as well-informed as they could be. We pose the three policy issues as questions:

1. Is a current account deficit bad for Canada?

2. Is there a "correct" value for the Canadian dollar?

3. Should Canada fix its exchange rate with the U.S. dollar?

APPLYING ECONOMIC CONCEPTS 35-3
News and the Exchange Rate

Foreign-exchange markets are different from markets for consumer goods in that the vast bulk of trading takes place between professional foreign-exchange traders working for banks, mutual-fund companies, and pension funds. These traders do not meet each other face to face. Rather, they do their transactions over the telephone, and the other party to the transaction could be anywhere in the world. The structure of this market has one interesting implication: exchange rates respond to news. Let's see why this is and what this means.

Deals done by the professional traders are all on a large scale, typically involving sums no smaller than $1 million and often very much larger. Each trader tends to specialize in trades between a small number of currencies, say the Canadian and the U.S. dollars, or the U.S. dollar and the Japanese yen. But the traders for all currencies for each bank sit close together in a trading room so they can hear what is going on in the other markets. When a big news event breaks, anywhere in the world, this will be shouted out simultaneously to all traders in the room.

Each trader is also faced with several computer screens and many buttons that connect him or her quickly by telephone to other traders. Speed of transaction can be very important if you are dealing with large amounts of money in a market that is continuously changing the prices quoted. The most recent price quotes from around the world appear on the screens. However, contracts are agreed over the telephone (and are recorded in case of a disagreement) and the paperwork follows within two days.

As exchange rates are closely related to expectations and to interest rates, the foreign-exchange traders have to keep an eye on all major news events affecting the economic environment. Since all the players in the foreign-exchange markets are professionals, they are well-informed, not just about what has happened but also about forecasts of what is likely to happen. Accordingly, the exchange rate at any point in time reflects not just history but also current expectations of future events.

As soon as some future event comes to be expected—such as the central bank's plans to tighten monetary policy—it will be reflected in the current exchange rate. Events expected to happen soon will be given more weight than those events expected to happen in the more distant future. The fact that expectations of future events get incorporated quickly into the exchange rate has an interesting implication: the only component in today's news that will cause the exchange rate to change is what was *not expected* to happen. Economists attribute the unforecastable component of news to a random error. It is random in the sense that it has no detectable pattern and it is unrelated to the information available before it happened.

Some events are clearly unforecastable, like an earthquake in Japan or a head of state having a heart attack. Others are the production of economic statistics for which forecasts have generally been published. In the latter case it is the deviation of announced figures from their forecast value that tends to move exchange rates.

Exchange rates are therefore moved by news. And since news is random and unpredictable, changes in exchange rates will tend to be random. Some people, observing the volatility of exchange rates, conclude that foreign-exchange markets are inefficient. However, with well-informed professional traders who have forward-looking expectations, new information is rapidly transmitted into prices. The volatility of exchange rates, therefore, largely reflects the volatility of relevant, but unexpected, events around the world.

Current news events, the announcements made by public officials, and the expectation of future events play a large role in determining whether currency traders decide to buy or sell foreign exchange. The frequency and randomness of news releases partly explain why exchange rates tend to be so volatile.

Current Account Deficits

Figure 35-4 shows the path of Canada's current account balance (as a percentage of GDP) since 1961. In most years, Canada has a significant trade surplus since it exports more goods and services to the world than it imports. But because it makes more investment payments (both interest and dividends) to foreigners than it receives from foreigners, it has a deficit on the capital-service portion of the current account. Thus in typical years Canada has a current account deficit of 2 or 3 percent of GDP. In the past few years, however, Canada's trade surplus has increased by more than the capital-service deficit, and the result has been a significant turnaround in the current account balance. In 2002, Canada had a current account surplus of almost 2 percent of GDP.

As we have learned, Canada's balance of payments must always balance, so any current account deficit is matched by a capital account surplus of the same size (the balance on the official financing account is usually very small). This capital account surplus means that Canada sells more assets to the rest of the world—both bonds and equity—than it buys from the rest of the world.

Is it undesirable for Canada to have a current account deficit and, therefore, a capital account surplus? It is certainly common for TV anchors to report negatively upon a rise in the current account deficit and positively upon its decline. But are current account deficits really a problem? Should we be celebrating Canada's recent current account surpluses? We address this issue in three parts.

FIGURE 35-4   Canada's Current Account Balance, 1961–2002

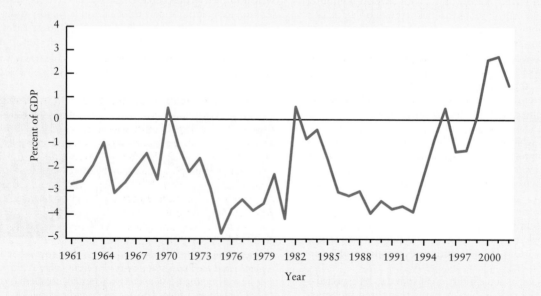

(*Source:* Statistics Canada, CANSIM database, Series V113713 expressed as a percentage of nominal GDP.)

Mercantilism

Many people argue that a current account deficit is undesirable because it means that Canada is buying more goods and services from the world than it is selling to the world. Central to this view is the belief that exports are "good" and imports are "bad." We discussed this belief, and argued why it was incorrect, in Chapter 34 when we explored some of the fallacious arguments for trade protection.

As a carryover from a long-discredited eighteenth-century doctrine called *mercantilism*, a current account surplus is sometimes called a "favourable balance," and a current account deficit is sometimes called an "unfavourable balance." Mercantilists, both ancient and modern, believe that a country's gains from trade arise only from having a "favourable" balance of trade—that is, by exporting more goods and services than it imports. But this belief misses the central point of comparative advantage that we explored in Chapter 33—that countries gain from trade because trade allows each country to specialize in the production of those products in which its opportunity costs are low. The gains from trade have *nothing* to do with whether there is a trade deficit or a trade surplus.

Lessons From History 35-1 discusses the doctrine of mercantilism. The lesson to be learned is that the gains from trade depend on the *volume* of trade (imports plus exports) rather than the *balance* of trade. There is nothing inherently bad about having a current account deficit.

LESSONS FROM HISTORY 35-1

Mercantilism, Then and Now

Media commentators, politicians, and much of the general public often appear to believe that a nation should secure a current account surplus. They appear to believe that the benefits derived from international trade are measured by the size of that surplus.

This view is related to the *exploitation doctrine* of international trade: One country's surplus is another country's deficit. Hence, one country's gain, judged by its surplus, must be another country's loss, judged by its deficit.

People who hold such views today are echoing an ancient economic doctrine called *mercantilism*. The mercantilists were a group of economists who preceded Adam Smith. They judged the success of trade by the size of the trade balance. In many cases, this doctrine made sense in terms of their objective, which was to use international trade as a means of building up the political and military power of the state, rather than as a means of raising the living standards of its citizens. A current account surplus allowed the nation (then and now) to acquire assets. (In those days, the assets took the form of gold. Today, they are mostly claims on the currencies of other countries.) These assets could then be used to pay armies, to purchase weapons from abroad, and to finance colonial expansions.

If the objective is to promote the welfare and living standards of ordinary citizens, however, the mercantilist focus on the balance of trade makes no sense. The principle of comparative advantage shows that average living standards are maximized by having individuals, regions, and countries specialize in the things they produce comparatively best and then trading to obtain the things they produce comparatively worst. The more specialization there is, the more trade occurs.

For the country as a whole, therefore, the gains from trade are to be judged by the *volume* of trade rather than by the *balance* of trade. A situation in which there is a large volume of trade even though each country has a zero balance of trade can thus be regarded as satisfactory. Furthermore, a change in policy that results in an equal increase in both exports and imports will generate gains because it allows for specialization according to comparative advantage, even though it causes no change in either country's trade balance.

International Borrowing

If Canada has a current account deficit, it also has a capital account surplus. It is a net seller of assets to the rest of the world. These assets are either bonds, in which case Canadians are borrowing from foreigners, or they are shares in firms (equities) in which case Canadians are selling their capital stock to foreigners.

It follows that the question "Should Canada have a current account deficit?" is the same as the question "Should Canadians be net sellers of assets to foreigners?" It is not immediately clear that the answer to this question should be no. It is true that by selling bonds to foreigners, Canadians increase their indebtedness to foreigners and will eventually have to redeem the bonds as well as pay interest. And by selling income-earning equities to foreigners, Canadians give up a stream of income that they would otherwise have. But, in both cases, they get a lump sum of funds that can be used for any type of consumption or investment. Is it obviously "better" to have a lower debt or a higher future income stream than to have a lump sum of funds right now? If it were better, no family would ever borrow money to buy a house or a car, and no firm would ever borrow money to build a factory.

A country that has a current account deficit is either borrowing from the rest of the world or selling its ownership of some of its capital stock to the rest of the world. This is not necessarily undesirable.

To argue that it is undesirable for Canada to have a current account deficit is to argue that Canadians as a whole should not borrow from (or sell physical assets to) the rest of the world. But surely the wisdom of borrowing depends on *why* Canadians are borrowing. It is therefore important to know *why* there is a current account deficit.

Causes of Current Account Deficits

There are several possible causes of a current account deficit. This can be seen most clearly by recalling some national-income accounting from Chapter 20. Recall that GDP is equal to the sum of actual consumption, investment, government purchases and net exports,

$$GDP = C_a + I_a + G_a + NX_a$$

where the subscript "*a*" denotes *actual* expenditure rather than desired expenditure. Next, note that GNP is equal to GDP plus the net investment income received from abroad, which we call *R*.

$$GNP = GDP + R = C_a + I_a + G_a + NX_a + R$$

Note that the current account balance is simply the trade balance, NX_a, plus the net investment income, *R*. We denote the actual current account balance CA_a. If CA_a is positive, there is a current account surplus; if CA_a is negative, there is a current account deficit. The equation now becomes

$$GNP = C_a + I_a + G_a + CA_a \qquad (35\text{-}1)$$

Now consider how a given amount of GNP that accrues to households can be spent. There are only three ways to dispose of income. It can be consumed, saved, or paid in taxes. That is,

$$GNP = C_a + S_a + T_a \qquad (35\text{-}2)$$

By equating Equations 35-1 and 35-2, and by omitting the "a" subscripts for simplicity, we derive an interesting relationship between national saving, investment, and the current account balance:

$$C + I + G + CA = C + S + T$$
$$\Rightarrow CA = S + (T - G) - I$$

This equation says that the current account balance in any year is exactly equal to the excess of national saving, $S + (T - G)$, over domestic investment I. If Canadians (and their governments) decide to save more than is needed to finance the amount of domestic investment, where do the excess funds go? They are used to acquire foreign assets, and thus Canada has a current account surplus ($CA > 0$). In contrast, if Canadians do not save enough to finance the amount of domestic investment, the balance must be financed by foreign funds. Thus, Canada has a current account deficit ($CA < 0$). Finally, we can re-arrange this equation very slightly to get

$$CA = (S - I) + (T - G) \qquad (35\text{-}3)$$

which says that the current account balance is equal to the excess of private saving over investment plus the government budget surplus.

Equation 35-3 shows three separate reasons for any given increase in the current account deficit (a fall in CA). First, a reduction in private saving, other things being equal, will lead to a rise in the current account deficit. Second, a rise in domestic investment, other things being equal, will increase the current account deficit. Finally, other things being equal, a rise in the government's budget deficit (a fall in the budget surplus) will raise the current account deficit. This third case is often referred to as a situation of *twin deficits*. That is, a rise in the government's budget deficit will also have the effect (if S and I remain constant) of increasing the current account deficit.

An increase in the level of investment, a decrease in the level of saving, and an increase in the government's budget deficit are all possible causes of an increase in a country's current account deficit.

In the end, it makes little sense to discuss the desirability of a change in the current account deficit without first knowing the *cause* of the change. Knowing the cause is crucial to knowing whether the change in the current account deficit is undesirable. The following two examples illustrate this important point.

First, suppose investment opportunities in Canada are very promising and, as a result, there is an increase in the level of investment. Most people would consider such an investment boom desirable because it would increase current output and employment and, by increasing the country's capital stock, it would also increase the level of potential output in the future. But as is clear from Equation 35-3, the immediate effect of the rise in Canadian investment is an increase in the Canadian current account deficit. The

A boom in domestic investment, other things being equal, will lead to an increase in the current account deficit. But there is little that is undesirable about this situation!

current account deficit increases because, in the absence of increased domestic saving, the increase in domestic investment can only take place if it is financed by a capital inflow from other countries. This capital inflow represents a rise in Canada's current account deficit. In this case, however, it would be difficult to argue that the increase in Canada's current account deficit is undesirable as it simply reflects a boom in domestic business opportunities.

For a second example, suppose the domestic economy begins to slow and households and firms are pessimistic about the future. In such a situation, we expect households to increase their saving and firms to reduce their investment, thus increasing the value of $(S - I)$. As the economy slows we would also expect the government's tax revenues to fall, thus decreasing the value of $(T - G)$. But it is easy to imagine a situation where the first effect dominates the second effect, thus leading to an increase in the current account surplus. Is the increase in Canada's current account surplus desirable? Most people would probably agree that the onset of a recession as described above is surely undesirable, involving a loss of output and employment.

A country's current account deficit can increase for a number of reasons. Whether the rise in the current account deficit is desirable depends on its underlying cause. A rise in the current account deficit may reflect a positive economic development; a decline in the current account deficit may reflect a negative economic development.

Is There a "Correct" Value for the Canadian Dollar?

From the summer of 1997 to the end of 1999, the external value of the Canadian dollar fell from about 72 to 65 U.S. cents. It was common to hear financial commentators discuss how the Canadian dollar was "undervalued." Opposite statements were heard a few years earlier in 1991 when, as a result of high Canadian interest rates caused by a significant monetary contraction, foreign financial capital flowed into Canada and the Canadian dollar appreciated enormously (its external value increased to about 90 U.S. cents). At that time many financial commentators argued that the Canadian dollar was "overvalued." In both cases, the observers appeared to believe that there was some "correct" value for the Canadian dollar. Is there?

As we saw in the previous section, a country that chooses to use a flexible exchange rate has its exchange rate determined by competitive forces in the foreign-exchange market. In Canada, and other countries as well, fluctuations in exchange rates have many causes. Some changes may be good for Canada, such as a worldwide shortage of wheat that drives up the world price of wheat, a major Canadian export. Others may be bad for Canada, such as the discovery of new copper mines in Chile that drives down the price of copper, also a major Canadian export. But the various supply and demand forces are coming together in the foreign-exchange market to determine the equilibrium value of the exchange rate. Changes in this value may reflect positive or negative events for Canada, but it makes little sense to think of this equilibrium value as being either too high or too low.

With a flexible exchange rate, the market determines the value of the exchange rate. With respect to the forces of demand and supply, the equilibrium exchange rate is the "correct" exchange rate.

In saying that the current equilibrium exchange rate is the "correct" rate in no way suggests that it will necessarily be the correct exchange rate in the future. Indeed, foreign-exchange markets are so large, with so many participants in so many countries, each responding to a slightly different set of events and expectations, that the equilibrium exchange rate is constantly changing. In other words, as various forces lead to frequent changes in the demand for and supply of the Canadian dollar in foreign-exchange markets, the "correct" value of the Canadian exchange rate is constantly changing.

Some economists accept that the current exchange rate, as determined by the foreign-exchange market, is indeed the correct rate, but they make a distinction between the immediate value of the exchange rate and its long-run value. These economists argue that, whereas various shocks may cause the exchange rate to rise or fall in the short run, there does exist some "fundamental" level to which it will return. This brings us to the theory of *purchasing power parity*.

Purchasing Power Parity

The theory of **purchasing power parity (PPP)** holds that over the long term, the value of the exchange rate between two currencies depends on the two currencies' relative purchasing power. The theory holds that a currency will tend to have the same purchasing power when it is spent in its home country as it would have if it were converted to foreign exchange and spent in the foreign country. Another way to say the same thing is that the price of *identical baskets of goods* should be the same in the two countries when the price is expressed in the same currency. If we let P_C and P_E be the price levels in Canada and Europe, respectively, and let e be the price of euros in terms of Canadian dollars (the exchange rate), then the theory of purchasing power parity predicts the following equality in the long run:

$$P_C = e \times P_E \qquad (35\text{-}4)$$

This equation simply says that if a basket of goods costs 1000 euros in Europe and the exchange rate is 1.4 (that is, 1.4 Canadian dollars per euro), then that same basket of goods should cost 1400 dollars in Canada (1.4 × 1000 = 1400).

According to the theory of purchasing power parity, the exchange rate between two countries' currencies is determined by the relative price levels in the two countries.

The idea behind PPP is a simple one. Suppose that Equation 35-4 did *not* hold—specifically, suppose that P_C was greater than $e \times P_E$, so that Canadian-dollar prices in Canada exceeded the Canadian-dollar prices of the same goods in Europe. In this case, people would increase their purchases of European goods and reduce their purchases of Canadian goods. These actions would have the effect of depreciating the Canadian dollar (a rise in e); this depreciation would continue until the equality was re-established.

The *PPP exchange rate* is the value of the exchange rate that makes Equation 35-4 hold. That is, the PPP exchange rate (between the Canadian dollar and the euro) is defined to be

$$e^{PPP} \equiv P_C/P_E \qquad (35\text{-}5)$$

Note that the PPP exchange rate is itself not constant. If inflation is higher in Canada than in Europe, for example, P_C will be rising faster than P_E and so the PPP exchange rate will be rising. Conversely, if inflation is lower in Canada than in Europe, P_C will be rising more slowly than P_E and the PPP exchange rate will be falling.

A Caveat About PPP

Should we expect the *actual* exchange rate to equal the PPP exchange rate? The theory of purchasing power parity predicts that if the actual exchange rate (e) does not equal the PPP exchange rate (e^{PPP}), then demands and supplies of Canadian and European goods

purchasing power parity (PPP)   The theory that over the long term, the exchange rate between two currencies adjusts to reflect relative price levels (relative purchasing power).

Practise with Study Guide Chapter 35, Exercise 4.

For *The Economist's* Big Mac Index that uses the idea of PPP, see its website: www.economist.com.

will change until $e = e^{PPP}$. Thus, the theory of PPP predicts that the actual exchange rate will eventually equal the PPP exchange rate.

Figure 35-5 shows the path of the actual Canadian–U.S. exchange rate and the PPP exchange rate over the past 20 years. It is clear from the figure that there are long periods of time over which the actual exchange rate deviates significantly from the PPP exchange rate. Indeed, looking at this figure it is difficult to see much support at all for the central prediction of the theory that the actual exchange rate will equal the PPP exchange rate. Why is this the case? Is there something wrong with the theory of purchasing power parity?

Recall from Equation 35-4 that P_C and P_E were defined as the prices of *identical baskets of goods* in Canada and Europe, respectively. Given that the goods are the same, the argument that the prices should (eventually) be equated across the two countries is sensible—if the prices are not equated across the two countries, there would be an incentive to purchase in the cheaper country rather than in the more expensive country, and this would lead to changes in the exchange rate until Equation 35-4 *did* hold.

One problem, however, when we apply the theory of purchasing power parity to *national price indices,* such as the Consumer Price Index or the Implicit GDP Deflator, is that the two baskets of goods are typically *not* the same—for two reasons.

FIGURE 35-5 Actual and PPP Exchange Rates, 1981–2001

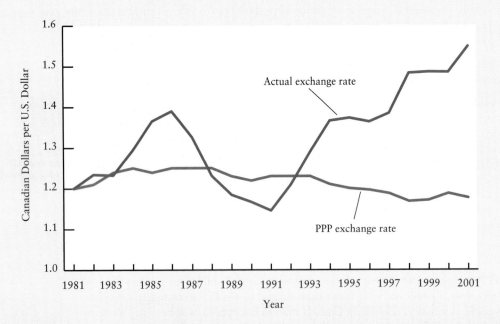

The actual exchange rate deviates from the PPP exchange rate for extended periods. The Canada–U.S. PPP exchange rate is the ratio of Canadian to U.S. price indices. Since these two price indices have moved closely together since 1981 (similar paths for inflation), the PPP exchange rate has not changed significantly. In contrast, the actual Canada–U.S. exchange rate has fluctuated dramatically and shows little or no tendency to track the PPP exchange rate.

(*Source: Bank of Canada Review,* Fall 2002.)

Different Countries Produce Different Goods.   Suppose we apply the theory of PPP to the Canada–Europe exchange rate and we use the GDP deflators from the two countries as the measures of prices. Recall from Chapter 20 that the GDP deflator is an index of prices *of the goods produced within the country.* But Canada and Europe clearly produce very different goods. The price of forest products will have a large weight in the Canadian GDP deflator, but less weight in the European GDP deflator; in contrast, the price of wine will have a much larger weight in the European GDP deflator than in the Canadian GDP deflator.

The implication of these differences for the theory of PPP is important. As long as changes in the *relative* prices of goods occur, such as a change in the price of forest products relative to wine, then P_C (the Canadian GDP deflator) will change relative to P_E (the European GDP deflator) *even though the prices of individual goods might be equated across the two countries.* Thus, differences in the structure of the price indices between two countries mean that using a PPP exchange rate computed on the basis of Equation 35-5 will be misleading. In other words, in the presence of changing relative prices, there is no reason to expect the actual exchange rate to equal the PPP exchange rate as defined in Equation 35-5.

Nontraded Goods Are Important.   The previous discussion emphasized that the *baskets* of goods across two countries might differ even though the products in the baskets were the same. But even if Canada and Europe produced exactly the same range of goods, so that the various weights in the GDP deflators were the same, there is another reason why the basket of goods in Canada differs from the basket of goods in Europe. Some of the goods produced in Canada are *nontraded goods,* such as haircuts and restaurant meals. Nontraded goods are also produced in Europe. But, since nontraded goods cannot be traded (by definition), there is nothing that will force their prices to be equal across the two countries. If haircuts are more expensive in Paris than in Toronto (as they are), we do not expect people to shift their consumption of haircuts away from Paris toward Toronto, and thus we should not expect the actual exchange rate to move to make Equation 35-4 hold.

The conclusion of this discussion is that we must be very careful in selecting the price indices we use when we apply the theory of purchasing power parity. We know that countries have different patterns of production and thus have different structures to their national price indices. Thus, in the presence of changes in relative prices of various products, the national price indices can change in ways that will not lead to changes in the exchange rate. Similarly, the presence of nontraded goods implies that some differences in prices across countries will not lead to changes in the location of demand and thus changes in the exchange rate.

Changes in relative prices and the presence of nontraded goods imply that purchasing power parity need not hold—not even as a long-run proposition.

Should Canada Have a Fixed Exchange Rate?

In recent years, some economists have suggested that Canada peg the value of its currency to the U.S. dollar. Advocates of a fixed Canadian exchange rate see this policy as a means of avoiding the significant fluctuations in the Canadian exchange rate that would otherwise occur—fluctuations such as the 15 percent appreciation that occurred between 1989 and 1991, the 10 percent depreciation that occurred between 1997 and 1998 and the 18 percent appreciation that occurred in 2003. They argue that exchange-rate fluctuations generate uncertainty for importers and exporters and thus increase the costs associated with trade.

Others have gone further in suggesting that Canada actually abandon its currency altogether and simply adopt the U.S. dollar. They point to the European Union, which introduced the euro as its common currency in 1999. If a common currency is acceptable to most of Europe, why should Canada and the United States be any different? Note that if Canada and the United States were to share a common currency, the exchange rate between the two countries would, of course, be fixed.

These are contentious suggestions that have attracted a great deal of public attention in recent years. We examine this issue by comparing the main benefits of flexible and fixed exchange rates. Whereas flexible exchange rates dampen the effects on output and employment from external shocks to the economy, fixed exchange rates reduce the uncertainty faced by traders. The benefits and costs of having a common currency between two regions is examined in *Extensions in Theory 35-1*, which explains the theory of "optimal currency areas."

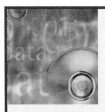

EXTENSIONS IN THEORY 35-1
Optimal Currency Areas

In 1961, Canadian economist Robert Mundell, now at Columbia University, developed the theory of "optimal currency areas." In 1999 he was awarded the Nobel Prize in economics, partly for this work. He examined the conditions under which it is optimal for two countries to have a common currency, and the conditions under which the countries would be better off maintaining separate currencies with a flexible exchange rate. Mundell's conclusions can be summarized as follows.

1. Other things being equal, the more the two countries trade with one another, the larger are the benefits from having a common currency (and the lower are the benefits from having separate currencies with a flexible exchange rate).

2. Other things being equal, the less correlated are the two countries' terms of trade, the smaller are the benefits from having a common currency (and the larger are the benefits from having separate currencies with a flexible exchange rate).

The Basic Theory

The accompanying diagram illustrates the situation that Mundell describes. Our example is that of Canada and the United States. The green arrows represent the trade of goods, services, and assets between the two countries. The red arrows represent the various shocks to each country's terms of trade. Mundell's central result is that, other things being equal, the more important the green arrows are, the better it is to have a common currency. On the other hand, the "less similar"

each country's red arrows are, the worse it is to have a common currency. By "less similar" we mean that the changes in one country's terms of trade are different, or occur at different times, than the changes in the other country's terms of trade.

To understand Mundell's arguments, we must understand how the green and red arrows relate to the costs and benefits of having a common currency (rather than separate currencies with a flexible exchange rate).

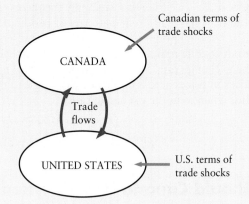

The main benefit of the two regions having a common currency is that importers and exporters in each country can save on the costs associated with having a flexible (and perhaps volatile) exchange rate. There are two types of costs. The first is the *uncertainty* that is generated by having a volatile exchange rate. The more uncertainty there is surrounding the price of foreign currency, the less likely are firms

Flexible Exchange Rates as "Shock Absorbers"

For most of the years following the Second World War, Canada has used a flexible exchange rate. Even when most other major countries chose to peg the value of their currencies to the U.S. dollar (and to gold) under the Bretton Woods system, Canada usually chose a flexible exchange rate (there were a few short periods in which Canada fixed its exchange rate). For all of its history Canada's economy has been dependent on the export of resource-based products, the prices of which are determined in world markets and are often highly variable from year to year. Changes in these prices constitute changes in Canada's terms of trade and, as we saw earlier in this chapter, changes in a country's terms of trade are an important reason why exchange rates are so variable.

That the exchange rate adjusts in response to shocks is actually the main advantage of a flexible (rather than fixed) exchange rate. A flexible exchange rate acts as a

See Chapter 35 of www.pearsoned.ca/ragan for a debate on the appropriate exchange rate regime for Canada: Pierre Fortin, "What Can We Do About Exchange Rates that Move Too Much?" and William Robson, "Resisting the Lure of Fixed Exchange Rates."

to enter contracts that involve foreign exchange. This reduction in trade leads to a reduction in the gains from trade. The second cost is the *transaction cost* of converting one currency into another. With separate currencies someone (either the importer or the exporter) must spend the time and resources necessary to convert currencies for every transaction between the two countries. Given that such costs are incurred every time goods are traded, it follows that the greater is the volume of trade between the two regions, the greater are the benefits (that is, the costs avoided) from having a common currency.

The main benefit from each country's maintaining a separate currency with a flexible exchange rate is that the exchange rate can act as a "shock absorber," dampening the effects on the country's output and employment from shocks to its terms of trade. For example, consider what would happen if there were a reduction in the world price of copper. Copper is a major Canadian export but a U.S. import. When the price of copper falls due to a reduction in world copper demand, Canada's terms of trade deteriorate but the U.S. terms of trade improve. The fall in the price of copper leads to a contraction in the Canadian copper industry. If Canada shares a common currency with the United States, the result of the shock will simply be a reduction in output and employment in Canada's copper industry. The contraction in that sector will eventually reduce wages, and the economy will eventually return to potential output. But the adjustment may be long and painful.

In contrast, if Canada and the United States have separate currencies, the reduction in the world price of copper will tend to depreciate the Canadian dollar relative to the U.S. dollar. The Canadian copper industry will still be in recession, for there has been a reduction in demand for its products, but the overall Canadian downturn will be dampened by the depreciation of the Canadian dollar. In other words, even though the copper industry is in recession, other sectors of the Canadian economy will actually *expand* as a result of the currency depreciation because their products are now more competitive in world markets. The overall result is

that, with a separate currency and flexible exchange rate, the deterioration in Canada's terms of trade leads to a less severe Canadian recession than if Canada shared a currency with the United States.

Mundell said that two countries constitute an *optimal currency area* if by adopting a common currency the two countries together save more in uncertainty and transactions costs than they incur by sacrificing the output-dampening effects of a flexible exchange rate.

What Is the Optimal Currency Area?

Some economists have recently advocated that Canada adopt the U.S. dollar as its currency. Do they believe that Canada and the United States constitute an optimal currency area? Probably not, but that is also not quite the right policy question. The provinces and territories of Canada already use a common currency even though they may not satisfy Mundell's condition for being an optimal currency area. Similarly, the U.S. states use a common currency and may not constitute an optimal currency area. Thus, the relevant policy question from Canada's perspective is whether Canada and the United States together form a *better* currency area than Canada by itself.

Some economists think this is probably true. They point to the massive and growing volume of trade between the two countries as the best reason for Canada and the United States to share a currency. Other economists stress the importance of exchange rates as shock absorbers. They point to the 1997–1998 decline in world commodity prices as an ideal example of a situation in which Canada benefited from having a flexible exchange rate. Canada's resource sector contracted sharply in response to this shock. Especially hard hit was British Columbia's forestry industry. But the depreciation of the Canadian dollar (by roughly 10 percent against the U.S. dollar) led to expansions in manufacturing industries in Ontario and Quebec that significantly reduced the overall effect of the shock.

"shock absorber," dampening the effects on the country's output and employment from external shocks. To understand how this happens, consider a simple example.

Suppose a reduction in world demand leads to a reduction in the world price of newsprint, a major Canadian export. When world demand for newsprint declines, there is a reduction in demand for Canadian exports and an accompanying reduction in demand for Canadian dollars (or a reduction in the supply of foreign exchange) in the foreign-exchange market. The effect on Canadian real GDP is shown in part (ii) of Figure 35-6 by the leftward shift of the AD curve. The effect in the foreign-exchange market is shown in part (i) by the leftward shift of the supply curve for foreign exchange. Consider the effect of this shock in two different situations. In the first, the Bank of Canada maintains a fixed exchange rate; in the second the Bank of Canada allows the exchange rate to be freely determined by demand and supply.

If the Bank of Canada fixes the exchange rate at e_0, the reduction in the supply of foreign exchange from S_0 to S_1 leads to an excess demand for foreign currency. To keep the exchange rate fixed at e_0, the Bank must sell sufficient foreign-exchange reserves to satisfy the excess demand. But the negative shock to aggregate demand still occurs and thus output and employment in Canada fall, as shown in part (ii) of Figure 35-6.

FIGURE 35-6   Flexible Exchange Rates as a Shock Absorber

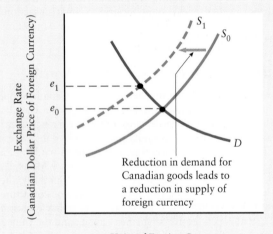

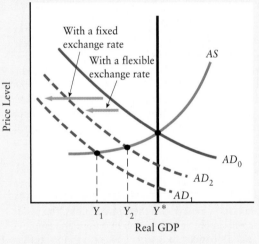

(i) Foreign-exchange market

(ii) AD and AS

Flexible exchange rates adjust to terms of trade shocks and thus dampen the effect on output and employment. The economy begins with the exchange rate equal to e_0 in part (i) and GDP equal to Y^* in part (ii). A reduction in the world's demand for Canadian exports causes a reduction in the supply of foreign exchange, shifting S_0 to S_1 in part (i).

With a fixed exchange rate, the Bank of Canada maintains the exchange rate at e_0, satisfying the excess demand for foreign exchange by selling its foreign-currency reserves. The reduction in the demand for Canada's exports is a negative aggregate demand shock. AD_0 shifts to the left to AD_1 in part (ii), causing GDP to fall to Y_1. The recessionary gap eventually pushes wages down, the AS curve shifts downward over time, and the economy moves along AD_1 to Y^*. The adjustment, however, may be protracted.

With a flexible exchange rate, the Bank of Canada allows the Canadian dollar to depreciate. The exchange rate rises to e_1 in part (i). The reduction in demand for Canadian exports still causes the AD curve to shift to the left in part (ii), but the shift is dampened by the depreciation of the dollar, which makes Canadian products more competitive in world markets. The AD curve shifts only to AD_2 and so GDP falls only to Y_2. There is still a recession, but smaller than in the case with a fixed exchange rate.

Canadian wages will eventually fall and the *AS* curve will eventually shift downward, returning real GDP to the level of potential output. But the closing of the recessionary gap may be slow and painful.

If Canada instead has a flexible exchange rate, the reduction in the world price of newsprint will lead to a reduction in the supply of foreign exchange and thus to a depreciation of the Canadian dollar. The exchange rate will increase from e_0 to e_1. The *AD* curve will shift to the left, reducing Canada's GDP, just as in the fixed-exchange-rate case. The newsprint industry will still be in recession, for there has been a reduction in demand for its products. But the overall Canadian downturn will be dampened by the depreciation of the Canadian dollar. Other exporting sectors of the Canadian economy will actually *expand* as a result of the depreciation because their products are now more competitive in world markets. Thus, as shown in part (ii) of Figure 35-6, the leftward shift of the *AD* curve will not be as large as in the case of the fixed exchange rate. The overall result is that, with a flexible exchange rate, the deterioration in Canada's terms of trade leads to a less severe Canadian recession than if Canada had a fixed exchange rate.

One of the advantages of flexible exchange rates is that, in response to shocks to the terms of trade, the exchange rate can act as a shock absorber, dampening the effects of the shock on output and employment.

The Asian Crisis of 1997–1998 provides an excellent example of how Canada's flexible exchange rate dampened the effects of a negative external shock. When the Asian countries of Malaysia, Indonesia, Thailand, and South Korea experienced their large recessions in 1997 and 1998, their demand for many raw materials declined sharply. As they are major users of raw materials, the effect was felt on world markets. The average prices of raw materials fell by roughly 30 percent from the summer of 1997 to the end of 1998. Many of these raw materials, of course, are important exports for Canada, and so the decline in their world prices implied a terms of trade deterioration for Canada.

Especially hard hit was British Columbia's forestry sector, in which output fell dramatically in many paper and lumber mills due to the lack of sales in Asia. As expected, there was also a significant depreciation of the Canadian dollar, just as described in Figure 35-6. But as the Canadian dollar depreciated, the Canadian manufacturing sector, concentrated mainly in Ontario and Quebec, was given a large boost. The 10 percent depreciation of the Canadian dollar meant that Canadian machinery, furniture, telecommunications equipment, and a whole range of other products were now more competitive in world markets. Thus, the boom in the Central Canadian manufacturing sector offset to some extent the significant recession that was going on in British Columbia. If Canada had had a fixed exchange rate, the 10 percent depreciation would not have occurred. But the initial shock from the Asian Crisis would still have taken place. The net result would have been lower output and higher unemployment than actually occurred.

Note that having a fixed exchange rate does not prevent a country from being subjected to shocks from the rest of the world. Many advocates of fixed exchange rates, however, seem to think that by fixing the value of a country's currency, the country is shielding itself from undesirable fluctuations. But shocks to a country's terms of trade will always occur. As long as there are changes in the demand for and supply of various products around the world, there will also be changes in a country's terms of trade. What Figure 35-6 shows, however, is that by fixing the exchange rate and thus avoiding the fluctuations in the value of the currency, the effects of the shock merely show up as increased volatility in output and employment.

A country will always experience shocks in its terms of trade. A flexible exchange rate absorbs some of the shock, reducing the effect on output and employment. A fixed exchange rate simply redistributes the effect of the shock—the exchange rate is smoother but output and employment are more volatile.

Trade, Transactions Costs, and Uncertainty

See Chapter 35 of www.pearsoned.ca/ragan for an interview with Milton Friedman on the desirability of flexible exchange rates: "Confirmed Convictions."

Despite the benefits of international trade, there are costs involved in exporting and importing goods and services. The *transactions costs* of international trade involve the costs associated with converting one currency to another, as must be done either by the importer or the exporter of the product that is traded. For example, if you have an import–export business in Canada and want to import some bicycles from Japan, you will probably have to purchase Japanese yen at a bank or foreign-exchange dealer and, with those yen, pay the Japanese seller for the bicycles. Even if the Japanese seller accepts Canadian dollars for the bicycles, and this often is the case, he will be required to convert those Canadian dollars into yen before he can use that money in Japan to pay his workers or pay for other costs of production.

The greater is the volume of trade between two countries, the higher are the aggregate transactions costs associated with international trade.

Such transactions costs exist even if trade takes place between two countries with fixed exchange rates. For example, if Canada pegged the value of the Canadian dollar to the U.S. dollar, any trade between the two countries would still require the costly conversion of one currency to the other. Thus, the existence of transactions costs cannot be used as an argument in favour of fixed exchange rates and against flexible exchange rates. As long as there are two currencies, the transactions costs must be borne by one party or the other. These transactions costs could only be avoided if the two countries shared a common currency. *Extensions in Theory 35-1* examines the theory of "optimal currency areas" in which these transactions costs play a central role.

Many economists believe, however, that the volatility of flexible exchange rates generates another type of cost for importers and exporters. Specifically, the unpredictability of the exchange rate leads to *uncertainty* about the profitability of any specific international transaction. Such uncertainty, given risk-averse firms, can be expected to lead to a smaller volume of international trade and thus to fewer benefits from such trade.

For example, suppose a Canadian appliance manufacturer enters into a contract to purchase a specified amount of steel from a Japanese producer for a specified yen price in one year's time. In this case, the Japanese producer bears no *foreign-exchange risk* because the price is specified in yen. But the Canadian appliance manufacturer bears considerable risk. If the yen depreciates relative to the dollar over the coming year, fewer Canadian dollars will be required to pay for the steel. But if the yen appreciates relative to the dollar over the coming year, more Canadian dollars will be required to pay for the steel. The Canadian buyer therefore faces a risk in terms of the Canadian-dollar cost of the steel. If the firm is *risk averse*, meaning simply that it would be prepared to pay a cost to avoid the risk, the presence of the risk may lead to fewer international transactions of this type. Perhaps to avoid the foreign-exchange risk, the Canadian buyer will decide instead to buy Canadian-made steel, even though it may be slightly more expensive or not quite the right type that is needed.

If the presence of foreign-exchange risk leads to less international trade, there will be a reduction in the gains from trade.

Practise with Study Guide Chapter 35, Extension Exercise E1.

Many of the people who advocate Canada's move to a fixed exchange rate point to the avoidance of this foreign-exchange risk as the main benefit. They argue that if the Canadian dollar were pegged in value to the U.S. dollar, both importers and exporters would face less uncertainty on the most important part of their trade—that between Canada and the United States. With the greater certainty, they argue, would come greater trade flows and thus an increase in the overall gains from trade.

But many economists disagree. While accepting the basic argument regarding the risks created by flexible (and volatile) exchange rates, they note that importers and exporters already have the means to avoid this uncertainty. In particular, traders can participate in *forward markets* in which they can buy or sell foreign exchange *in the future* at prices specified today. For example, the Canadian appliance manufacturer could enter into a contract to purchase the required amount of yen in one year's time at a price of 100 yen per Canadian dollar. In this case, no matter what happened to the yen–dollar exchange rate in the intervening year, the uncertainty regarding the Canadian-dollar price of the steel would be entirely eliminated.

Summing Up

So, should Canada give up its flexible exchange rate and instead peg the value of the Canadian dollar to the U.S. dollar? Advocates of this policy emphasize the foreign-exchange risk faced by importers and exporters, and the gains from increased trade that would result from a fixed exchange rate. Opponents to the policy emphasize the shock-absorption benefits from a flexible exchange rate, and the greater volatility in output and employment that Canada would have if it were to fix its exchange rate.

This debate will surely go on for a while, partly because it is difficult to quantify the costs and benefits of a flexible exchange rate. Economists on both sides of the debate understand and accept the logic of the arguments from the other side. But researchers have so far been unable to determine how much of a shock is absorbed by a flexible exchange rate, and thus to estimate how much more volatile output and employment would be with a fixed exchange rate. Similarly, it is very difficult to estimate just how much more trade would take place if the foreign-exchange risk faced by traders were eliminated by means of a fixed exchange rate. Without convincing empirical evidence supporting the move to a fixed exchange rate, however, the status quo will probably remain. It is probably safe to assume that Canada will continue to have a flexible exchange rate, at least for the next several years.

S U M M A R Y

35.1 The Balance of Payments ⓛ⓵

- Actual transactions among Canadian firms, households, and governments and those in the rest of the world are reported in the balance of payments accounts. In these accounts, any transaction that represents a receipt for Canada (Canadians sell goods or assets to foreigners) is recorded as a credit item. Any transaction that represents a payment from Canada (Canadians purchase goods or assets from foreigners) is recorded as a debit item.
- If all transactions are recorded in the balance of payments, the sum of all credit items necessarily equals the sum of all debit items. Thus, the balance of payments must always balance.

- Categories in the balance of payments accounts are the trade account, the capital-service account, the current account (which is equal to the trade account plus the capital-service account), the capital account, and the official financing account.
- When a country is said to have a "balance of payments deficit" (or surplus), what is meant is that the sum of current and capital accounts is a deficit (or surplus). That is, it excludes the transactions on the official financing account. If official financing is zero, a balance on current account must be matched by a balance on capital account of equal magnitude but opposite sign.

35.2 **The Foreign-Exchange Market**

- The exchange rate between the Canadian dollar and some foreign currency is defined to be the number of Canadian dollars required to purchase one unit of the foreign currency. A rise in the exchange rate is a depreciation of the Canadian dollar; a fall in the exchange rate is an appreciation of the Canadian dollar.
- The supply of foreign exchange (or the demand for Canadian dollars) arises from Canadian exports of goods and services, capital flows into Canada, and the desire of foreign banks, firms, and governments to use Canadian dollars as part of their reserves.
- The demand for foreign exchange (or the supply of Canadian dollars to purchase foreign currencies) arises from Canadian imports of goods and services, capital

flows from Canada, and the desire of holders of Canadian dollars to decrease the size of their holdings.
- A depreciation of the Canadian dollar lowers the foreign price of Canadian exports and increases the amount of foreign exchange supplied (to purchase Canadian exports). Thus, the supply curve for foreign exchange is positively sloped when plotted against the exchange rate.
- A depreciation of the Canadian dollar raises the dollar price of imports from abroad and hence lowers the amount of foreign exchange demanded to purchase foreign goods. Thus, the demand curve for foreign exchange is negatively sloped when plotted against the exchange rate.

35.3 **The Determination of Exchange Rates**

- When the central bank does not intervene in the foreign exchange market, there is a flexible exchange rate. Under fixed exchange rates, the central bank intervenes in the foreign-exchange market to maintain the exchange rate at an announced value. To do this, the central bank must hold sufficient stocks of foreign-exchange reserves.
- Under a flexible, or floating, exchange rate, the exchange rate is determined by supply of and demand for the currency.

- The Canadian dollar will appreciate in foreign-exchange markets if there is an increase in the supply of foreign exchange (an increase in the demand for Canadian dollars) or if there is a reduction in the demand for foreign exchange (a reduction in the supply of Canadian dollars). The opposite changes will lead to a depreciation of the Canadian dollar.
- Changes in the exchange rate are caused by changes in such things as the rate of inflation in different countries, capital movements, structural conditions, and expectations about the future exchange rate.

35.4 **Three Policy Issues**

- The view that current account deficits are undesirable is usually based on the mercantilist notion that exports are "good" and imports are "bad." But the gains from trade have nothing to do with the balance of trade—they depend on the volume of trade.
- From national income accounting, the current account surplus is given by

$$CA = (S - I) + (T - G)$$

An increase in investment, a decrease in saving, and an increase in the government budget deficit can each be the cause of a rise in the current account deficit.
- With a flexible exchange rate, supply and demand in the foreign-exchange market determine the "correct" value of the exchange rate. But this "correct" value is constantly changing as market conditions vary.
- The theory of purchasing power parity (PPP) predicts that exchange rates will adjust so that the purchasing

power of a given currency is the same in different countries. That is, the prices of identical baskets of goods will be equated in different countries (when expressed in the same currency).
- If price indices from different countries are used as the basis for computing the PPP exchange rate, differences in the structure of price indices across countries, together with the presence of nontraded goods, can be responsible for persistent deviations of the actual exchange rate from this measure of the PPP exchange rate.
- An important benefit of a flexible exchange rate is that it acts as a shock absorber, dampening the effects on output and employment from shocks to a country's terms of trade.
- An important benefit of fixed exchange rates is that it reduces transactions costs and foreign-exchange risk faced by importers and exporters.

e. Explain how a flexible exchange rate acts as a shock absorber, insulating the economy from both positive and negative shocks.

8. Every few months, *The Economist* publishes its "Big Mac Index." Using the current exchange rates, it compares the U.S.-dollar price of Big Macs in several countries. It then concludes that countries in which the Big Mac is cheaper (in U.S. dollars) than in the United States have "undervalued" currencies. Similarly, countries with Big Macs more expensive than in the United States have "overvalued" currencies. The table below shows the domestic-currency prices of Big Macs in various countries. It also shows the exchange rate, expressed as the number of units of domestic currency needed to purchase one U.S. dollar.

Country	Domestic Currency Price	Exchange Rate	U.S. Dollar Price
Canada	$2.75 (Cdn.)	1.52	$ —
Australia	$3.50 (Aus.)	1.85	$ —
U.S.A.	$2.25	1.00	$ —
Japan	375 yen	125	$ —
France	3.6 euros	1.15	$ —
U.K.	1.50 pounds	0.80	$ —

a. For each country, use the exchange rate provided to convert the domestic-currency price to the U.S.-dollar price.
b. By the logic used in *The Economist*, which currencies are overvalued and which are undervalued relative to the U.S. dollar?
c. Are Big Macs traded goods? If not, does this present a problem for *The Economist*? Explain.
d. Which of the following goods do you think would be a better candidate for this exercise? Explain your choice.
   (i) cement
   (ii) diamonds
   (iii) fresh fruit
   (iv) computer RAM chips

9. A former Canadian prime minister once suggested that Canada should try to have balanced trade, industry by industry.

a. Do you think this makes sense? Explain.
b. How about the idea of balanced trade, country by country? Explain whether this makes sense.

DISCUSSION QUESTIONS

1. What is the probable effect of each of the following on the exchange rate of a country, other things being equal?

   a. The quantity of oil imports is greatly decreased, but the value of imported oil is higher due to price increases.
   b. The country's inflation rate falls well below that of its trading partners.
   c. Rising labour costs of the country's manufacturers lead to a worsening ability to compete in world markets.
   d. The government greatly expands its gifts of food and machinery to developing countries.
   e. A major boom occurs with rising employment.
   f. The central bank raises interest rates sharply.
   g. More domestic oil is discovered and developed.

2. Canada's trade surplus with the United States (or the U.S. trade deficit with Canada) is the cause of considerable concern to some U.S. politicians. Many economists, however, argue that U.S. policymakers should not be concerned with reducing the U.S. trade deficit with Canada primarily because there is no reason to expect a balance between any two countries. Comment on the need for policies to address the U.S. trade deficit with Canada.

3. Outline the reasoning behind the following recent newspaper headline: "Loonie strengthens as Bank of Canada raises rates."

4. "Under a flexible exchange rate system, no country need suffer unemployment, for if its prices are low enough, there will be more than enough demand to keep its factories and farms fully occupied." The evidence suggests that flexible exchange rates have not generally eliminated unemployment. Can you explain why? Can changing exchange rates ever cure unemployment?

5. A recent letter to *The Globe and Mail* said that "the economy of this once wonderful country is in the sewer and the politicians keep on tinkering, not knowing how to fix

it." The letter proposed a 20 percent depreciation of the Canadian dollar, and argued that the immediate effects would be (among other things):

- a dramatic rise in exports
- a dramatic fall in imports
- a large net inflow of new foreign investment

What do you think of the proposal? What would the Bank of Canada have to do to achieve a 20 percent depreciation of the Canadian dollar? If such a depreciation were to take place, is it possible for it to have the effects claimed by the author of the letter? Explain.

6. Many commentators are perplexed when they observe a depreciation of the Canadian dollar but not a reduction in the Canadian current account deficit. Explain why there is not a precise relationship between the value of the dollar and the current account balance. Give one example of an event that would give rise to each of the following:

a. Appreciation of the Canadian dollar and a fall in Canada's current account surplus.
b. Depreciation of the Canadian dollar and a fall in Canada's current account surplus.

Challenges Facing the Developing Countries

LEARNING OBJECTIVES

1 Describe the extent of world income inequality.

2 Explain some of the main challenges facing developing countries.

3 Define the view of development known as the "Washington Consensus."

4 Outline the current debates about development policies.

Companion
Website

The chapter Challenges Facing the Developing Countries can be found on the Companion Website at **www.pearsoned.ca/ragan**.

Mathematical Notes

1. Because one cannot divide by zero, the ratio $\Delta Y / \Delta X$ cannot be evaluated when $\Delta X = 0$. However, as ΔX *approaches* zero, the ratio $\Delta Y / \Delta X$ increases without limit:

$$\lim_{\Delta X \to 0} \frac{\Delta Y}{\Delta X} = \infty$$

Therefore, we say that the slope of a vertical line (when $\Delta X = 0$ for any ΔY) is equal to infinity. (p. 40)

2. Many variables affect the quantity demanded. Using functional notation, the argument of the next several pages of the text can be anticipated. Let Q^D represent the quantity of a commodity demanded and

$$T, \overline{Y}, N, \hat{Y}, p, p_j$$

represent, respectively, tastes, average household income, population, income distribution, the commodity's own price, and the price of the jth other commodity.

The demand function is

$$Q^D = D(T, \overline{Y}, N, \hat{Y}, p, p_j), \qquad j = 1, 2, \ldots, n$$

The demand schedule or curve is given by

$$Q^D = d(p) \Big|_{T, \overline{Y}, N, \hat{Y}, p_j}$$

where the notation means that the variables to the right of the vertical line are held constant.

This function is correctly described as the demand function with respect to price, all other variables being held constant. This function, often written concisely as $Q^D = d(p)$, shifts in response to changes in other variables. Consider average income: if, as is usually hypothesized, $\partial Q^D / \partial \overline{Y} > 0$, then increases in average income shift $Q^D = d(p)$ rightward and decreases in average income shift $Q^D = d(p)$ leftward. Changes in other variables likewise shift this function in the direction implied by the relationship of that variable to the quantity demanded. (p. 51)

3. Quantity demanded is a simple and straightforward but frequently misunderstood concept in everyday use, but it has a clear mathematical meaning. It refers to the dependent variable in the demand function from note 2:

$$Q^D = D(T, \overline{Y}, N, \hat{Y}, p, p_j)$$

It takes on a specific value whenever a specific value is assigned to each of the independent variables. The value of Q^D changes whenever the value of any independent variable is changed. Q^D could change, for example, as a result of a change in any one price, in average income, in the distribution of income, in tastes, or in population. It could also change as a result of the net effect of changes in all of the independent variables occurring at once.

Some textbooks reserve the term *change in quantity demanded* for a movement along a demand curve, that is, a change in Q^D as a result *only* of a change in p. They then use other words for a change in Q^D caused by a change in the other variables in the demand function. This usage is potentially confusing because it gives the single variable Q^D more than one name.

Our usage, which corresponds to that in more advanced treatments, avoids this confusion. We call Q^D quantity demanded and refer to any change in Q^D as a *change in quantity demanded*. In this usage it is correct to say that a movement along a demand curve is a change in quantity demanded, but it is incorrect to say that a change in quantity demanded can occur *only because of* a movement along a demand curve (because Q^D can change for other reasons, for example, a *ceteris paribus* change in average household income). (p. 58)

4. Similar to the way we treated quantity demanded in note 2, let Q^S represent the quantity of a commodity supplied and

$$C, X, p, w_i$$

represent, respectively, producers' goals, technology, the product's price, and the price of the ith input.

The supply function is

$$Q^S = S(C, X, p, w_i), \qquad i = 1, 2, \ldots, m$$

The supply schedule or curve is given by

$$Q^S = s(p) \Big|_{C, X, w_i}$$

This is the supply function with respect to price, all other variables being held constant. This function, often written concisely as $Q^S = s(p)$, shifts in response to changes in other variables. (p. 59)

5. Equilibrium occurs where $Q^D = Q^S$. For *specified values of all other variables*, this requires that

$$d(p) = s(p) \qquad [5.1]$$

Equation 5.1 defines an equilibrium value of *p*; hence, although *p* is an *independent* or *exogenous* variable in each of the supply and demand functions, it is an *endogenous* variable in the economic model that imposes the equilibrium condition expressed in Equation 5.1. Price is endogenous because it is assumed to adjust to bring about equality between quantity demanded and quantity supplied. Equilibrium quantity, also an endogenous variable, is determined by substituting the equilibrium price into either $d(p)$ or $s(p)$.

Graphically, Equation 5.1 is satisfied only at the point where the demand and supply curves intersect. Thus, supply and demand curves are said to determine the equilibrium values of the endogenous variables, price and quantity. A shift in any of the independent variables held constant in the *d* and *s* functions will shift the demand or supply curves and lead to different equilibrium values for price and quantity. (p. 65)

6. The axis reversal arose in the following way. Alfred Marshall (1842–1924) theorized in terms of "demand price" and "supply price," these being the prices that would lead to a given quantity being demanded or supplied. Thus,

$$p^D = d(Q) \qquad [6.1]$$
$$p^S = s(Q) \qquad [6.2]$$

and the condition of equilibrium is

$$d(Q) = s(Q)$$

When graphing the behavioural relationships expressed in Equations 6.1 and 6.2, Marshall naturally put the independent variable, *Q*, on the horizontal axis.

Leon Walras (1834–1910), whose formulation of the working of a competitive market has become the accepted one, focused on quantity demanded and quantity supplied *at a given price*. Thus,

$$Q^D = d(p)$$
$$Q^S = s(p)$$

and the condition of equilibrium is

$$d(p) = s(p)$$

Walras did not use graphical representation. Had he done so, he would surely have placed *p* (his independent variable) on the horizontal axis.

Marshall, among his other influences on later generations of economists, was the great popularizer of graphical analysis in economics. Today, we use his graphs, even for Walras's analysis. The axis reversal is thus one of those historical accidents that seem odd to people who did not live through the "perfectly natural" sequence of steps that produced it. (p. 65)

7. The definition in the text uses finite changes and is called *arc elasticity*. The parallel definition using derivatives is

$$\eta = \frac{dQ}{dp} \cdot \frac{p}{Q}$$

and is called *point elasticity*. Further discussion appears in the Appendix to Chapter 4. (p. 79)

8. The propositions in the text are proved as follows. Letting *TE* stand for total expenditure, we can write

$$TE = p \cdot Q$$

It follows that the change in total expenditure is

$$dTE = Q \cdot dp + p \cdot dQ \qquad [8.1]$$

Multiplying and dividing both terms on the right-hand side of Equation 8.1 by $p \cdot Q$ yields

$$dTE = \left[\frac{dp}{p} + \frac{dQ}{Q} \right] \cdot (p \cdot Q)$$

Because *dp* and *dQ* are opposite in sign as we move along the demand curve, *dTE* will have the same sign as the term in brackets on the right-hand side that dominates—that is, on which percentage change is largest.

A second way of arranging Equation 8.1 is to divide both sides by dp to get

$$\frac{dTE}{dp} = Q + p \cdot \frac{dQ}{dp} \qquad [8.2]$$

From the definition of point elasticity in note 7, however,

$$Q \cdot \eta = p \cdot \frac{dQ}{dp} \qquad [8.3]$$

which we can substitute into Equation 8.1 to obtain

$$\frac{dTE}{dp} = Q + Q \cdot \eta = Q \cdot (1 + \eta) \qquad [8.4]$$

Because η is a negative number, the sign of the right-hand side of Equation 8.4 is negative if the absolute value of η exceeds unity (elastic demand) and positive if it is less than unity (inelastic demand).

Total expenditure is maximized when dTE/dp is equal to zero. As can be seen from Equation 8.4, this occurs when elasticity is equal to -1. (p. 82)

9. The distinction made between an incremental change and a marginal change is the distinction for the function $Y = Y(X)$ between $\Delta Y/\Delta X$ and the derivative dY/dX. The latter is the limit of the former as ΔX approaches zero. We shall meet this distinction repeatedly—in this chapter in reference to marginal and incremental *utility* and in later chapters with respect to such concepts as marginal and incremental *product, cost,* and *revenue.* Where Y is a function of more than one variable—for example, $Y = f(X,Z)$—the marginal relationship between Y and X is the partial derivative $\partial Y/\partial X$ rather than the total derivative, dY/dX. (p. 125)

10. The hypothesis of diminishing marginal utility requires that we can measure utility of consumption by a function

$$U = U(X_1, X_2, \ldots, X_n)$$

where $X_1, \ldots, X_n$ are quantities of the n goods consumed by a household. It really embodies two utility hypotheses: first,

$$\partial U/\partial X_i > 0$$

which says that the consumer can get more utility by increasing consumption of the commodity; second,

$$\partial^2 U/\partial X_i^2 < 0$$

which says that the utility of *additional* consumption of some good declines as the amount of that good consumed increases. (p. 125)

11. Because the slope of the indifference curve is negative, it is the absolute value of the slope that declines as one moves downward to the right along the curve. The algebraic value, of course, increases. The phrase *diminishing marginal rate of substitution* thus refers to the absolute, not the algebraic, value of the slope. (p. 145)

12. The relationship between the slope of the budget line and relative prices can be seen as follows. In the two-good example, a change in expenditure (ΔE) is given by the equation

$$\Delta E = p_C \cdot \Delta C + p_F \cdot \Delta F \qquad [12.1]$$

Expenditure is constant for all combinations of F and C that lie on the same budget line. Thus, along such a line we have $\Delta E = 0$. This implies

$$p_C \cdot \Delta C + p_F \cdot \Delta F = 0 \qquad [12.2]$$

and thus

$$\Delta C/\Delta F = -p_F/p_C \qquad [12.3]$$

The ratio $\Delta C/\Delta F$ is the slope of the budget line. It is negative because, with a fixed budget, one must consume less C in order to consume more F. In other words, Equation 12.3 says that the negative of the slope of the budget line is the ratio of the absolute prices (i.e., the relative price). Although prices do not show directly in Figure 6A-3, they are implicit in the budget line: Its slope depends solely on the relative price, while its position, given a fixed money income, depends on the absolute prices of the two goods. (p. 147)

13. *Marginal product,* as defined in the text, is really *incremental* product. More advanced treatments distinguish between this notion and marginal product as the limit of the ratio as ΔL approaches zero. Marginal product thus measures the rate at which total product is changing as one factor is varied and

is the partial derivative of the total product with respect to the variable factor. In symbols,

$$MP = \frac{\partial TP}{\partial L}$$

(p. 162)

14. We have referred specifically both to diminishing *marginal* product and to diminishing *average* product. In most cases, eventually diminishing marginal product implies eventually diminishing average product. This is, however, not necessary, as the accompanying figure shows.

    In this case, marginal product diminishes after v units of the variable factor are employed. Because marginal product falls toward, but never quite reaches, a value of m, average product rises continually toward, but never quite reaches, the same value. (p. 165)

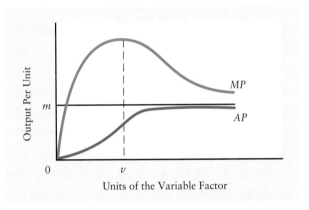

Units of the Variable Factor

15. Let Q be the quantity of output and L the quantity of the variable factor. In the short run,

$$TP = Q = f(L) \qquad [15.1]$$

We now define

$$AP = \frac{Q}{L} = \frac{f(L)}{L} \qquad [15.2]$$

$$MP = \frac{dQ}{dL} \qquad [15.3]$$

We are concerned with the relationship between AP and MP. Where average product is rising, at a maximum, or falling is determined by its derivative with respect to L:

$$\frac{d(Q/L)}{dL} = \frac{L \cdot (dQ/dL) - Q}{L^2} \qquad [15.4]$$

This may be rewritten

$$\frac{1}{L} \cdot \left[\frac{dQ}{dL} - \frac{Q}{L} \right] = \frac{1}{L} \cdot (MP - AP) \qquad [15.5]$$

Clearly, when MP is greater than AP, the expression in Equation 15.5 is positive and thus AP is rising. When MP is less than AP, AP is falling. When they are equal, AP is neither rising nor falling. (p. 166)

16. The text defines *incremental cost*. Strictly, marginal cost is the rate of change of total cost with respect to output, Q. Thus,

$$MC = \frac{dTC}{dQ}$$

From the definitions, $TC = TFC + TVC$. Fixed costs are not a function of output. Thus, we may write $TC = Z + f(Q)$, where $f(Q)$ is total variable costs and Z is a constant. From this we see that $MC = df(Q)/dQ$. MC is thus independent of the size of the fixed costs. (p. 167)

17. This point is easily seen if a little algebra is used:

$$AVC = \frac{TVC}{Q}$$

but note that $TVC = L \cdot w$ and $Q = AP \cdot L$, where L is the quantity of the variable factor used and w is its cost per unit. Therefore,

$$AVC = \frac{L \cdot w}{AP \cdot L} = \frac{w}{AP}$$

Because w is a constant, it follows that AVC and AP vary inversely with each other, and when AP is at its maximum value, AVC must be at its minimum value. (p. 170)

18. A little elementary calculus will prove the point:

$$MC = \frac{dTC}{dQ} = \frac{dTVC}{dQ} = \frac{d(L \cdot w)}{dQ}$$

If w does not vary with output,

$$MC = \frac{dL}{dQ} \cdot w$$

However, referring to note 15 (Equation 15.3), we see that

$$\frac{dL}{dQ} = \frac{1}{MP}$$

Thus,

$$MC = \frac{w}{MP}$$

Because w is fixed, MC varies negatively with MP. When MP is at a maximum, MC is at a minimum. (p. 170)

19. Strictly speaking, the marginal rate of substitution refers to the slope of the tangent to the isoquant at a particular point, whereas the calculations in Table 8A-1 refer to the average rate of substitution between two distinct points on the isoquant. Assume a production function

$$Q = Q(K,L) \qquad [19.1]$$

Isoquants are given by the function

$$K = I(L,\overline{Q}) \qquad [19.2]$$

derived from Equation 19.1 by expressing K as an explicit function of L and Q. A single isoquant relates to a particular level of output, $\overline{Q}$. Define Q_K and Q_L as an alternative, more compact notation for $\partial Q/\partial K$ and $\partial Q/\partial L$, the marginal products of capital and labour. Also, let Q_{KK} and Q_{LL} stand for $\partial^2 Q/\partial K^2$ and $\partial^2 Q/\partial L^2$, respectively. To obtain the slope of the isoquant, totally differentiate Equation 19.1 to obtain

$$dQ = \ Q_K \cdot dK + Q_L \cdot dL$$

Then, because we are moving along a single isoquant, set $dQ = 0$ to obtain

$$\frac{dK}{dL} = - \ \frac{Q_L}{Q_K} = MRS$$

Diminishing marginal productivity implies $Q_{LL} < 0$ and $Q_{KK} < 0$, and hence, as we move down the isoquant of Figure 8A-1, Q_K is rising and Q_L is falling, so the absolute value of MRS is diminishing. This is called the *hypothesis of a diminishing marginal rate of substitution*. (p. 198)

20. Formally, the problem is to choose K and L in order to maximize

$$Q = Q(K,L)$$

subject to the constraint

$$p_K \cdot K + p_L \cdot L = C$$

To do this, form the Lagrangean,

$$\mathcal{L} = Q(K, L) - \lambda(p_K \cdot K + p_L \cdot L - C)$$

where λ is called the Lagrange multiplier.

The first-order conditions for this maximization problem are

$$Q_K = \lambda \cdot p_K \qquad [20.1]$$
$$Q_L = \lambda \cdot p_L \qquad [20.2]$$
$$p_K \cdot K + p_L \cdot L = C \qquad [20.3]$$

Dividing Equation 20.1 by Equation 20.2 yields

$$\frac{Q_K}{Q_L} = \frac{p_K}{p_L}$$

That is, the ratio of the marginal products, which is -1 times the MRS, is equal to the ratio of the factor prices, which is -1 times the slope of the isocost line. (p. 201)

21. Marginal revenue is mathematically the derivative of total revenue with respect to output, dTR/dQ. Incremental revenue is $\Delta TR/\Delta Q$. However, the term *marginal revenue* is used loosely to refer to both concepts. (p. 209)

22. For notes 22 through 24, it is helpful first to define some terms. Let

$$\pi_n = TR_n - TC_n$$

where π_n is the profit when Q_n units are sold.

If the firm is maximizing its profits by producing Q_n units, it is necessary that its profits be at least as large as the profits at output zero. That is,

$$\pi_n \geq \pi_0 \qquad [22.1]$$

The condition says that profits from producing must be greater than profits from not producing. Condition 22.1 can be rewritten as

$$TR_n - TVC_n - TFC_n$$
$$\geq TR_0 - TVC_0 - TFC_0 \qquad [22.2]$$

However, note that by definition

$$TR_0 = 0 \qquad [22.3]$$

$$TVC_0 = 0 \qquad [22.4]$$

$$TFC_n = TFC_0 = Z \qquad [22.5]$$

where Z is a constant. By substituting Equations 22.3, 22.4, and 22.5 into Condition 22.2, we get

$$TR_n - TVC_n \geq 0$$

from which we obtain

$$TR_n \geq TVC_n$$

This proves Rule 1.

On a per-unit basis, it becomes

$$\frac{TR_n}{Q_n} \geq \frac{TVC_n}{Q_n} \qquad [22.6]$$

where Q_n is the number of units produced.

Because $TR_n = Q_n \cdot p_n$, where p_n is the price when n units are sold, Condition 22.6 may be rewritten as

$$p_n \geq AVC_n$$

(p. 210)

23. Using elementary calculus, we may prove Rule 2.

$$\pi_n = TR_n - TC_n$$

each of which is a function of output Q. To maximize π, it is necessary that

$$\frac{d\pi}{dQ} = 0 \qquad [23.1]$$

and that

$$\frac{d^2\pi}{dQ^2} < 0 \qquad [23.2]$$

From the definitions,

$$\frac{d\pi}{dQ} = \frac{dTR}{dQ} - \frac{dTC}{dQ} = MR - MC \quad [23.3]$$

From Equations 23.1 and 23.3, a necessary condition for attaining maximum π is $MR - MC = 0$, or $MR = MC$, as is required by Rule 2. (p. 211)

24. To prove that for a negatively sloped demand curve, marginal revenue is less than price, let $p = p(Q)$. Then

$$TR = p \cdot Q = p(Q) \cdot Q$$

$$MR = \frac{dTR}{dQ} = Q \cdot \frac{dp}{dQ} + p$$

For a negatively sloped demand curve, dp/dQ is negative, and thus MR is less than price for positive values of Q. (p. 233)

25. The equation for a downward-sloping straight-line demand curve with price on the vertical axis is

$$p = a - b \cdot Q$$

where $-b$ is the slope of the demand curve. Total revenue is price times quantity:

$$TR = p \cdot Q = a \cdot Q - b \cdot Q^2$$

Marginal revenue is

$$MR = \frac{dTR}{dQ} = a - 2 \cdot b \cdot Q$$

Thus, the MR curve and the demand curve are both straight lines, and the (absolute value of the) slope of the MR curve $(2b)$ is twice that of the demand curve (b). (p. 234)

26. The marginal revenue produced by the factor involves two elements: first, the additional output that an extra unit of the factor produces and, second, the change in price of the product that the extra output causes. Let Q be output, R revenue, and L the number of units of the variable factor hired. The contribution to revenue of additional labour is $\partial R/\partial L$. This, in turn, depends on the contribution of the extra labour to output $\partial Q/\partial L$ (the marginal product of the factor) and $\partial R/\partial Q$ (the firm's marginal revenue from the extra output). Thus,

$$\frac{\partial R}{\partial L} = \frac{\partial Q}{\partial L} \cdot \frac{\partial R}{\partial Q}$$

We define the left-hand side as marginal revenue product, MRP. Thus,

$$MRP = MP \cdot MR$$

(p. 316)

27. The proposition that the marginal labour cost is above the average labour cost when the average is rising is essentially the same proposition proved in note 15. Nevertheless, let us do it again, using elementary calculus.

The quantity of labour supplied depends on the wage rate: $L^s = f(w)$. Total labour cost along the supply curve is $w \cdot L^s$. The average cost of labour is $(w \cdot L^s) / L^s = w$. The marginal cost of labour is

$$\frac{d(w \cdot L^s)}{dL^s} = w + L^s \cdot \frac{dw}{dL^s}$$

Rewrite this as

$$MC = AC + L^s \cdot \frac{dw}{dL^s}$$

As long as the supply curve slopes upward, $dw/dL^s > 0$; therefore, $MC > AC$. (p. 349)

28. In the text, we define MPC as an incremental ratio. For mathematical treatment, it is sometimes convenient to define all marginal concepts as derivatives: $MPC = dC/dY_D$, $MPS = dS/dY_D$, and so on. (p. 523)

29. The basic relationship is

$$Y_D = C + S$$

Dividing through by Y_D yields

$$\frac{Y_D}{Y_D} = \frac{C}{Y_D} + \frac{S}{Y_D}$$

and thus

$$1 = APC + APS$$

Next, take the first difference of the basic relationship to get

$$\Delta Y_D = \Delta C + \Delta S$$

Dividing through by ΔY_D gives

$$\frac{\Delta Y_D}{\Delta Y_D} = \frac{\Delta C}{\Delta Y_D} + \frac{\Delta S}{\Delta Y_D}$$

and thus
$$1 = MPC + MPS$$

(p. 524)

30. The total expenditure over all rounds is the sum of an infinite series. If we let A stand for autonomous expenditure and z for the marginal propensity to spend, the change in autonomous expenditure is ΔA in the first round, $z \cdot \Delta A$ in the second, $z^2 \cdot \Delta A$ in the third, and so on. This can be written as

$$\Delta A \cdot (1 + z + z^2 + \ldots + z^n)$$

If z is less than 1, the series in parentheses converges to $1/(1 - z)$ as n approaches infinity. The total change in expenditure is thus $\Delta A/(1 - z)$. In the example in the box, $z = 0.80$; therefore, the change in total expenditure is

$$\frac{\Delta A}{1 - z} = \frac{\Delta A}{0.2} = 5 \cdot \Delta A$$

(p. 539)

31. This is based on what is called the "rule of 72." Any sum growing at the rate of X percent per year will double in approximately $72/X$ years. For two sums growing at the rates of X percent and Y percent per year, the *difference* between the two sums will double in approximately $72/(X - Y)$ years. (pp. 631, 639)

32. The time taken to break even is a function of the *difference* in growth rates, not their *levels*. Thus, if 4 percent and 5 percent or 5 percent and 6 percent had been used in the example, it still would have taken the same number of years. To see this quickly, recognize that we are interested in the ratio of two exponential growth paths:

$$\frac{e^{r_1 t}}{e^{r_2 t}} = e^{(r_1 - r_2)t}$$

(p. 641)

33. A simple example of a production function is $GDP = z(LK)^{1/2}$. This equation says that to find the amount of GDP produced, multiply the amount of labour by the amount of capital, take the square root, and multiply the result by the constant z. This production function has positive but diminishing marginal returns to either factor. This can be seen by evaluating the first and second partial derivatives and showing the first derivatives to be positive and the second derivatives to be negative.

For example,

$$\frac{\partial GDP}{\partial K} = \frac{z \cdot L^{1/2}}{2 \cdot K^{1/2}} > 0$$

and

$$\frac{\partial^2 GDP}{\partial K^2} = -\frac{z \cdot L^{1/2}}{4 \cdot K^{3/2}} < 0$$

(p. 649)

34. The production function GDP $= z(LK)^{1/2}$ displays contant returns to scale. To see this, multiply both L and K by the same constant, θ, and see that this multiplies the whole value of GDP by θ:

$$z(\theta L \cdot \theta K)^{1/2} = z(\theta^2 \cdot LK)^{1/2} = \theta z(LK)^{1/2} = \theta \cdot \text{GDP}$$

(p. 650)

35. This is easily proved. The banking system wants sufficient deposits (D) to establish the target ratio (v) of deposits to reserves (R). This gives $R/D = v$. Any change in D of size ΔD has to be accompanied by a change in R of ΔR of sufficient size to restore v. Thus, $\Delta R/\Delta D = v$, so $\Delta D = \Delta R/v$ and $\Delta D/\Delta R = 1/v$. This can be shown also in terms of the deposits created by the sequence in Table 27-7. Let v be the reserve ratio and $e = 1 - v$ be the excess reserves per dollar of new deposits. If X dollars are initially deposited in the system, the successive rounds of new deposits will be X, eX, $e^2 X$, $e^3 X$, ... The series

$$X + eX + e^2 X + e^3 X + \ldots$$
$$= X \cdot [1 + e + e^2 + e^3 + \ldots]$$

has a limit of $X \cdot \dfrac{1}{1 - e}$

$$= X \cdot \dfrac{1}{1 - (1 - v)} = \dfrac{X}{v}$$

This is the total new deposits created by an injection of X of new reserves into the banking system. For example, when $v = 0.20$, an injection of \$100 into the system will lead to an overall increase in deposits of \$500. (p. 687)

36. Suppose that the public wishes to hold a fraction, c, of deposits in cash, C. Now suppose that X dollars are injected into the system. Ultimately, this money will be held either as reserves by the banking system or as cash by the public. Thus, we have

$$\Delta C + \Delta R = X$$

From the banking system's reserve behaviour, we have $\Delta R = v \cdot \Delta D$, and from the public's cash behaviour, we have $\Delta C = c \cdot \Delta D$. Substituting into the above equation, we get the result that

$$\Delta D = \dfrac{X}{v + c}$$

From this we can also relate the change in reserves and the change in cash holdings to the initial injection:

$$\Delta R = \dfrac{v}{v + c} \cdot X$$

$$\Delta C = \dfrac{c}{v + c} \cdot X$$

For example, when $v = 0.20$ and $c = 0.05$, an injection of \$100 will lead to an increase in reserves of \$80, an increase in cash in the hands of the public of \$20, and an increase in deposits of \$400. (p. 688)

Time Line of Great Economists

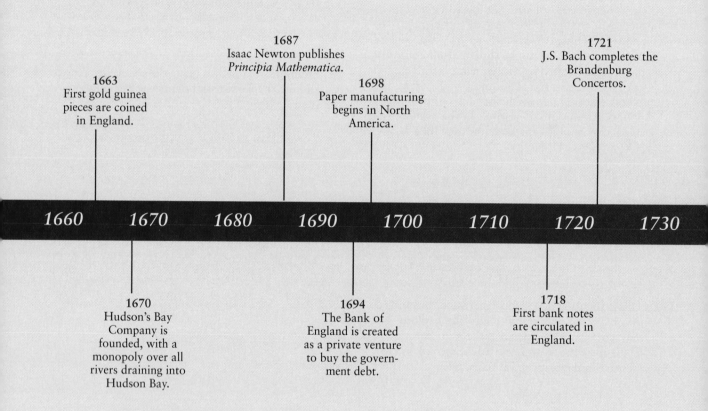

1663
First gold guinea
pieces are coined
in England.

1687
Isaac Newton publishes
Principia Mathematica.

1698
Paper manufacturing
begins in North
America.

1721
J.S. Bach completes the
Brandenburg
Concertos.

1660   1670   1680   1690   1700   1710   1720   1730

1670
Hudson's Bay
Company is
founded, with a
monopoly over all
rivers draining into
Hudson Bay.

1694
The Bank of
England is created
as a private venture
to buy the govern-
ment debt.

1718
First bank notes
are circulated in
England.

ADAM SMITH (1723–1790)

Adam Smith was born in 1723 in the small Scottish town of Kirkcaldy. He is perhaps the single most influential figure in the development of modern economics, and even those who have never studied economics know of his most famous work, *The Wealth of Nations*, and of the terms *laissez faire* and the *invisible hand*, both attributable to Smith. He was able to describe the workings of the capitalist market economy, the division of labour in production, the role of money, free trade, and the nature of economic growth. Even today, the breadth of his scholarship is considered astounding.

Smith was raised by his mother, as his father had died before his birth. His intellectual promise was discovered early, and at age 14 Smith was sent to study at Glasgow and then at Oxford. He then returned to an appointment as professor of moral philosophy at University of Glasgow, where he became one of the leading philosophers of his day. He lectured on natural theology, ethics, jurisprudence, and political economy to students who travelled from as far away as Russia to hear his lectures.

In 1759, Smith published *The Theory of Moral Sentiments*, in which he attempted to identify the origins of moral judgment. In this early work, Smith writes of the motivation of self-interest and of the morality that keeps it in check. After its publication, Smith left his post at the University of Glasgow to embark on a European tour as the tutor to a young aristocrat, the Duke of Buccleuch, with whom he travelled for two years. In exchange for this assignment Smith was provided with a salary for the remainder of his life. He returned to the small town of his birth and spent the next 10 years alone, writing his most famous work.

An Inquiry into the Nature and Causes of the Wealth of Nations was published in 1776. His contributions in this book (generally known as *The Wealth of Nations*) were revolutionary, and the text became the foundation of much of modern economics. It continues to be reprinted today. Smith rejected the notion that a country's supply of gold and silver was the measure of its wealth—rather, it was the real incomes of the people that determined national wealth. Growth in the real incomes of the country's citizens—that is, economic growth—would result from specialization in production, the division of labour, and the use of money to facilitate trade. Smith provided a framework for analyzing the questions of income growth, value, and distribution.

Smith's work marked the beginning of what is called the Classical period in economic thought, which continued for the next 75 years. This school of thought was centred on the principles of natural liberty (laissez faire) and the importance of economic growth as a means of bettering the conditions of human existence.

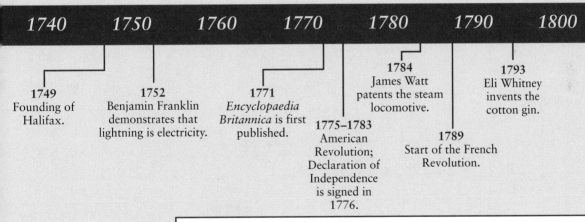

1740 1750 1760 1770 1780 1790 1800

1749 Founding of Halifax.

1752 Benjamin Franklin demonstrates that lightning is electricity.

1771 *Encyclopaedia Britannica* is first published.

1775–1783 American Revolution; Declaration of Independence is signed in 1776.

1784 James Watt patents the steam locomotive.

1789 Start of the French Revolution.

1793 Eli Whitney invents the cotton gin.

THOMAS MALTHUS (1766–1834)

Thomas Malthus was born into a reasonably well-to-do English family. He was educated at Cambridge and from 1805 until his death he held the first British professorship of political economy in the East India Company's college at Haileybury. In 1798 he published *An Essay on the Principle of Population as It Affects the Future Improvement of Society*, which was revised many times in subsequent years until finally he published *A Summary View of the Principle of Population* in 1830.

It is these essays on population for which Malthus is best known. His first proposition was that population, when unchecked, would increase in a geometric progression such that the population would double every 25 years. His second proposition was that the means of subsistence (i.e. the food supply) cannot possibly increase faster than in arithmetic progression (increasing by a given number of units every year). The result would be population growth eventually outstripping food production, and thus abject poverty and suffering for the majority of people in every society.

Malthus's population theory had tremendous intellectual influence at the time and became an integral part of the Classical theory of income distribution. However, it is no longer taken as a good description of current or past trends.

D A V I D   R I C A R D O   *(1772–1823)*

David Ricardo was born in London to parents who had immigrated from the Netherlands. Ricardo's father was very successful in money markets, and Ricardo himself had earned enough money on the stock exchange that he was very wealthy before he was 30. He had little formal education, but after reading Adam Smith's *The Wealth of Nations* in 1799, he chose to divide his time between studying and writing about political economy and increasing his own personal wealth.

Ricardo's place in the history of economics was assured by his achievement in constructing an abstract model of how capitalism worked. He built an analytic "system" using deductive reasoning that characterizes economic theorizing to the present day. The three critical principles in Ricardo's system were (1) the theory of rent, (2) Thomas Malthus's population principle, and (3) the wages-fund doctrine. Ricardo published *The Principles of Political Economy and Taxation* in 1817, which dominated Classical economics for the following half-century.

Ricardo also contributed the concept of comparative advantage to the study of international trade. Ricardo's theories regarding the gains from trade had some influence on the repeal of the British Corn Laws in 1846—tariffs on the importation of grains into Great Britain—and the subsequent transformation of that country during the nineteenth century from a country of high tarrifs to one of completely free trade.

1814
British forces burn
Washington, D.C., in the
War of 1812.

1831
The first horse-
drawn buses
appear in
New York.

1837
Victoria becomes
Queen of England
(until 1901).
Rebellions in
Upper and Lower
Canada.

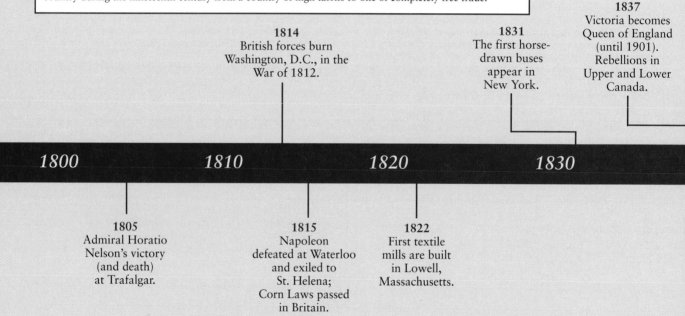

1800   **1810**   **1820**   **1830**

1805
Admiral Horatio
Nelson's victory
(and death)
at Trafalgar.

1815
Napoleon
defeated at Waterloo
and exiled to
St. Helena;
Corn Laws passed
in Britain.

1822
First textile
mills are built
in Lowell,
Massachusetts.

J O H N   S T U A R T   M I L L   *(1806–1873)*

John Stuart Mill, born in London, was the son of James Mill, a prominent British historian, economist, and philosopher. By age 12 he was acquainted with the major economics works of the day, and at 13 he was correcting the proofs of his father's book, *Elements of Political Economy*. J. S. Mill spent most of his life working at the East India Company—his extraordinarily prolific writing career was conducted entirely as an aside. In 1848 he published his *Principles of Political Economy*, which updated the principles found in Adam Smith's *The Wealth of Nations* and which remained the basic textbook for students of economics until the end of the nineteenth century. In *Principles*, Mill made an important contribution to the economics discipline by distinguishing between the economics of production and of distribution. He pointed out that economic laws had nothing to do with the distribution of wealth, which was a societal matter, but had everything to do with production.

Previous to Mill's *Principles* was his *System of Logic* (1843), which was the century's most influential text on logic and the theory of knowledge. His essays on ethics, contemporary culture, and freedom of speech, such as *Utilitarianism* and *On Liberty*, are still widely studied today.

KARL MARX (1818–1883)

Karl Marx was born in Trier, Germany (then part of Prussia), and studied law, history, and philosophy at the universities of Bonn, Berlin, and Jena. Marx travelled between Prussia, Paris, and Brussels, working at various jobs until finally settling in London in 1849, where he lived the remainder of his life. Most of his time was spent in the mainly unpaid pursuits of writing and studying economics in the library of the British Museum. Marx's contributions to economics are intricately bound to his views of history and society. *The Communist Manifesto* was published with Friedrich Engels in 1848, his *Critique of Political Economy* in 1859, and in 1867 the first volume of *Das Kapital*. (The remaining volumes, edited by Engels, were published after Marx's death.)

For Marx, capitalism was a stage in an evolutionary process from a primitive agricultural economy toward an inevitable elimination of private property and the class structure. Marx's "labour theory of value," whereby the quantity of labour used in the manufacture of a product determined its value, held the central place in his economic thought. He believed that the worker provided "surplus value" to the capitalist. The capitalist would then use the profit arising from this surplus value to reinvest in plant and machinery. Through time, more would be spent for plant and machinery than for wages, which would lead to lower profits (since profits arose only from the surplus value from labour) and a resulting squeeze in the real income of workers. Marx believed that in the capitalists' effort to maintain profits in this unstable system, there would emerge a "reserve army of the unemployed." The resulting class conflict would become increasingly acute until revolution by the workers would overthrow capitalism.

1859
Charles Darwin publishes *On the Origin of Species.*

1867
British North America Act establishes the Dominion of Canada. Alfred Nobel invents dynamite.

1846
Britain repeals the Corn Laws.

1840

1850

1860

1870

1844
Electric telegraph opens between Washington and Baltimore.

1861–1865
The U.S. Civil War; Abraham Lincoln is assassinated in 1865.

1869
Opening of the Suez Canal.

1840
Act of Union unites Upper and Lower Canada.

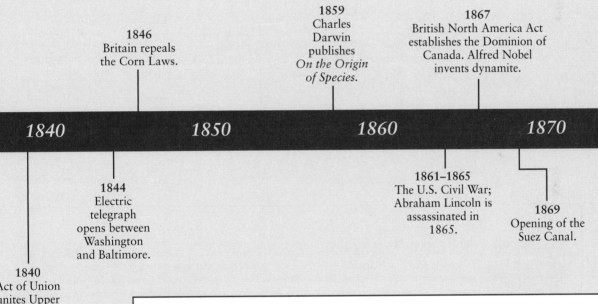

LEON WALRAS (1834–1910)

Leon Walras was born in France, the son of an economist. After being trained inauspiciously in engineering and performing poorly in mathematics, Walras spent some time pursuing other endeavors, such as novel writing and working for the railway. Eventually he promised his father he would study economics, and by 1870 he was given a professorship in economics in the Faculty of Law at the University of Lausanne in Switzerland. Once there, Walras began the feverish activity that eventually led to his important contributions to economic theory.

In the 1870s, Walras was one of three economists to put forward the marginal utility theory of value (simultaneously with William Stanley Jevons of England and Carl Menger of Austria). Further, he constructed a mathematical model of general equilibrium using a system of simultaneous equations that he used to argue that equilibrium prices and quantities are uniquely determined. Central to general equilibrium analysis is the notion that the prices and quantities of all commodities are determined simultaneously because the whole system is interdependent. Walras's most important work was *Elements of Pure Economics,* published in 1874. In addition to all of Walras's other accomplishments in economics (and despite his early poor performance in mathematics!), we today regard him as the founder of mathematical economics.

Leon Walras and Alfred Marshall are regarded by many economists to be the two most important economic theorists who ever lived. Much of the framework of economic theory studied today is either Walrasian or Marshallian in character.

CARL MENGER (1840–1921)

Carl Menger was born in Galicia (then part of Austria), and he came from a family of Austrian civil servants and army officers. After studying law in Prague and Vienna, he turned to economics and in 1871 published *Grundsatze der Volkswirtschaftslehre* (translated as *Principles of Economics*), for which he became famous. He held a professorship at the University of Vienna until 1903. Menger was the founder of a school of thought known as the "Austrian School," which effectively displaced the German historical method on the continent and which survives today as an alternative to mainstream Neoclassical economics.

Menger was one of three economists in the 1870s who independently put forward a theory of value based on marginal utility. Prior to what economists now call the "marginal revolution," value was thought to be derived solely from the inputs of labour and capital. Menger developed the marginal utility theory of value, in which the value of any good is determined by individuals' subjective evaluations of that good. According to Menger, a good has some value if it has the ability to satisfy some human want or desire, and *utility* is the capacity of the good to do so. Menger went on to develop the idea that the individual will maximize total utility at the point where the last unit of each good consumed provides equal utility—that is, where marginal utilities are equal.

Menger's emphasis on the marginal utility theory of value led him to focus on consumption rather than production as the determinant of price. Menger focused only on the demand for goods and largely ignored the supply. It would remain for Alfred Marshall and Leon Walras to combine demand and supply for a more complete picture of price determination.

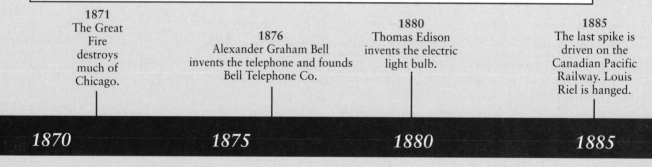

1871
The Great Fire destroys much of Chicago.

1876
Alexander Graham Bell invents the telephone and founds Bell Telephone Co.

1880
Thomas Edison invents the electric light bulb.

1885
The last spike is driven on the Canadian Pacific Railway. Louis Riel is hanged.

1870   *1875*   *1880*   *1885*

ALFRED MARSHALL (1842–1924)

Alfred Marshall was born in Clapham, England, the son of a bank cashier, and was descended from a long line of clerics. Marshall's father, despite intense effort, was unable to steer the young Marshall into the church. Instead, Marshall followed his passion for mathematics at Cambridge and chose economics as a field of study after reading J. S. Mill's *Principles of Political Economy*. His career was then spent mainly at Cambridge, where he taught economics to John Maynard Keynes, Arthur Pigou, Joan Robinson, and countless other British theorists in the "Cambridge tradition." His *Principles of Economics,* published in 1890, replaced Mill's *Principles* as the dominant economics textbook of English-speaking universities.

Marshall institutionalized modern marginal analysis, the basic concepts of supply and demand, and perhaps most importantly the notion of economic equilibrium resulting from the interaction of supply and demand. He also pioneered partial equilibrium analysis—examining the forces of supply and demand in a particular market provided that all other influences can be excluded, *ceteris paribus.*

Although many of the ideas had been put forward by previous writers, Marshall was able to synthesize the previous analyses of utility and cost and present a thorough and complete statement of the laws of demand and supply. Marshall refined and developed microeconomic theory to such a degree that much of what he wrote would be familiar to students of this textbook today.

It is also interesting to note that although Alfred Marshall and Leon Walras were simultaneously expanding the frontiers of economic theory, there was almost no communication between the two men. Though Marshall chose partial equilibrium analysis as the appropriate method for dealing with selected markets in a complex world, he did acknowledge the correctness of Walras's general equilibrium system. Walras, on the other hand, was adamant (and sometimes rude) in his opposition to the methods that Marshall was putting forward. History has shown that both the partial and the general equilibrium approaches to economic analysis are required for understanding the functioning of the economy.

THORSTEIN VEBLEN (1857–1929)

Thorstein Veblen was born on a farm in Wisconsin to Norwegian parents. He received his Ph.D. in philosophy from Yale University, after which he returned to his father's farm because he was unable to secure an academic position. For seven years he remained there, reading voraciously on economics and other social sciences. Eventually, he took academic positions at the University of Chicago, Stanford University, the University of Missouri, and the New School for Social Research (in New York). Veblen was the founder of "institutional economics," the only uniquely North American school of economic thought.

In 1899, Veblen published *The Theory of the Leisure Class,* in which he sought to apply Charles Darwin's evolutionism to the study of modern economic life. He examined problems in the social institutions of the day, and savagely criticized Classical and Neoclassical economic analysis. Although Veblen failed to shift the path of mainstream economic analysis, he did contribute the idea of the importance of long-run institutional studies as a useful complement to short-run price theory analysis. He also reminded the profession that economics is a *social* science, and not merely a branch of mathematics.

Veblen remains most famous today for his idea of "conspicuous consumption." He observed that some commodities were consumed not for their intrinsic qualities but because they carried snob appeal. He suggested that the more expensive such a commodity became, the greater might be its ability to confer status on its purchaser.

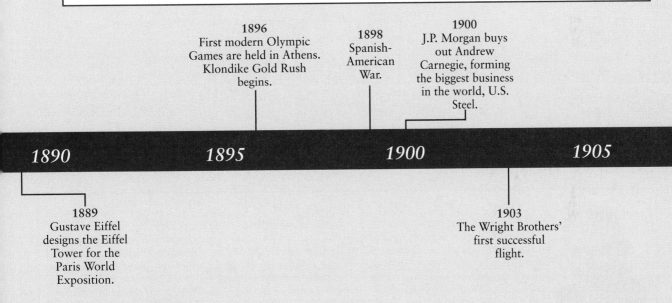

1896 First modern Olympic Games are held in Athens. Klondike Gold Rush begins.

1898 Spanish-American War.

1900 J.P. Morgan buys out Andrew Carnegie, forming the biggest business in the world, U.S. Steel.

1890 **1895** **1900** **1905**

1889 Gustave Eiffel designs the Eiffel Tower for the Paris World Exposition.

1903 The Wright Brothers' first successful flight.

VILFREDO PARETO (1848–1923)

Vilfredo Pareto was an Italian, born in Paris, and was trained to be an engineer. Though he actually practiced as an engineer, he would later succeed Leon Walras to the Chair of Economics in the Faculty of Law at the University of Lausanne.

Pareto built upon the system of general equilibrium that Walras had developed. In his *Cours d'économie politique* (1897) and his *Manuel d'économie politique* (1906) Pareto set forth the foundations of modern welfare economics. He showed that theories of consumer behaviour and exchange could be constructed on assumptions of ordinal utility, rather than cardinal utility, eliminating the need to compare one person's utility with another's. Using the indifference curve analysis developed by F. Y. Edgeworth, Pareto was able to demonstrate that total welfare could be increased by an exchange if one person could be made better off without anyone else becoming worse off. Pareto applied this analysis to consumption and exchange, as well as to production. Pareto's contributions in this area are remembered in economists' references to *Pareto optimality* and *Pareto efficiency.*

JOSEPH SCHUMPETER (1883–1950)

Joseph Schumpeter was born in Triesch, Moravia (now in the Czech Republic). He was a university professor and later a Minister of Finance in Austria. In 1932, he emigrated to the United States to avoid the rise to power of Adolf Hitler. He spent his remaining years at Harvard University.

Schumpeter, a pioneering theorist of innovation, emphasized the role of the entrepreneur in economic development. The existence of the entrepreneur meant continuous innovation and waves of adaptation to changing technology. He is best known for his theory of "creative destruction," where the prospect of monopoly profits provides owners the incentive to finance inventions and innovations. One monopoly can replace another with superior technology or a superior product, thereby circumventing the entry barriers of a monopolized industry. He criticized mainstream economists for emphasizing the static (allocative) efficiency of perfect competition—a market structure that would, if it could ever be achieved, retard technological change and economic growth.

Schumpeter's best known works are *The Theory of Economic Development* (1911), *Business Cycles* (1939), and *Capitalism, Socialism and Democracy* (1943).

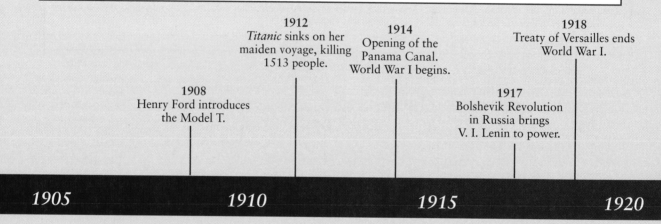

1912
Titanic sinks on her maiden voyage, killing 1513 people.

1914
Opening of the Panama Canal. World War I begins.

1918
Treaty of Versailles ends World War I.

1908
Henry Ford introduces the Model T.

1917
Bolshevik Revolution in Russia brings V. I. Lenin to power.

1905   *1910*   *1915*   *1920*

JOHN MAYNARD KEYNES (1883–1946)

John Maynard Keynes was born in Cambridge, England. His parents were both intellectuals, and his father, John Neville Keynes, was a famous logician and writer on economic methodology. The young Keynes was educated at Eton and then at Kings College, Cambridge, where he was a student of Alfred Marshall and Arthur Pigou. His career included appointments to the Treasury in Britain during both World Wars I and II, a leading role in the establishment of the International Monetary Fund (through discussions at Bretton Woods, New Hampshire, in 1944), and editorship of the *Economic Journal* from 1911 to 1945, all in addition to his academic position at Kings College.

Keynes published extensively during his life but his most influential work, *The General Theory of Employment, Interest, and Money,* appeared in 1936. This book was published in the midst of the Great Depression when the output of goods and services had fallen drastically, unemployment was intolerably high, and it had become clear to many that the market would not self-adjust to achieve potential output within an acceptable period of time. Fluctuations in economic activity were familiar at this point, but the failure of the economy to recover rapidly from this depression was unprecedented. Neoclassical economists held that during a downturn both wages and the interest rate would fall low enough to induce investment and employment and cause an expansion. They believed that the persistent unemployment during the 1930s was caused by inflexible wages and they recommended that workers be convinced to accept wage cuts.

Keynes believed that this policy, though perhaps correct for a single industry, was not correct for the entire economy. Widespread wage cuts would reduce the consumption portion of aggregate demand, which would offset any increase in employment. Keynes argued that unemployment could be cured only by manipulating aggregate demand, whereby increased demand (through government expenditure) would increase the price level, reduce real wages, and thereby stimulate employment.

Keynes's views found acceptance after the publication of his *General Theory* and had a profound effect on government policy around the world, particularly in the 1940s, 1950s, and 1960s. As we know from this textbook, Keynes's name is attached to much of macroeconomics, from much of the basic theory to the Keynesian short-run aggregate supply curve and the Keynesian consumption function. His contributions to economics go well beyond what can be mentioned in a few paragraphs—for, in effect, he laid the foundations for modern macroeconomics.

EDWARD CHAMBERLIN *(1899–1967)*

Edward Chamberlin was born in La Conner, Washington, and received his Ph.D. from Harvard University in 1927. He became a full professor at Harvard in 1937 and stayed there until his retirement in 1966. He published *The Theory of Monopolistic Competition* in 1933.

Before Chamberlin's book (which appeared more or less simultaneously with Joan Robinson's *The Economics of Imperfect Competition*), the models of perfect competition and monopoly had been fairly well worked out. Though economists were aware of a middle ground between these two market structures and some analysis of duopoly (two sellers) had been presented, it was Chamberlin and Robinson who closely examined this problem of imperfect markets.

Chamberlin's main contribution was explaining the importance of product differentiation for firms in market structures between perfect competition and monopoly. Chamberlin saw that though there may be a large number of firms in the market (the competitive element), each firm created for itself a unique product or advantage that gave it some control over price (the monopoly element). Specifically, he identified items such as copyrights, trademarks, brand names, and location as monopoly elements behind a product. Though Alfred Marshall regarded price as the only variable in question, Chamberlin saw both price and the product itself as variables under control of the firm in monopolistically competitive markets.

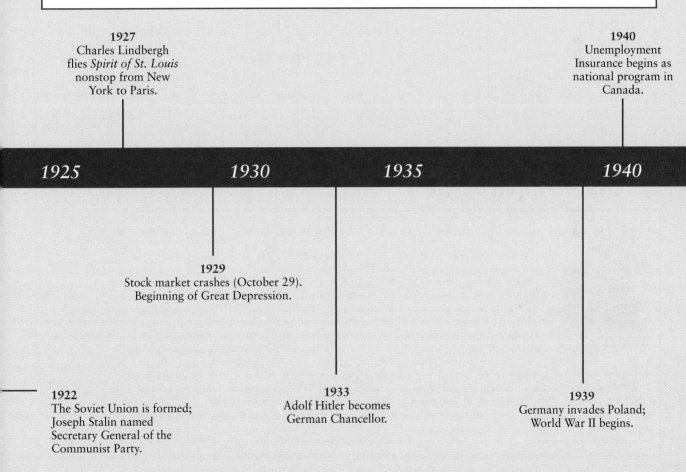

1927
Charles Lindbergh flies *Spirit of St. Louis* nonstop from New York to Paris.

1940
Unemployment Insurance begins as national program in Canada.

1925   *1930*   *1935*   *1940*

1929
Stock market crashes (October 29). Beginning of Great Depression.

1922
The Soviet Union is formed; Joseph Stalin named Secretary General of the Communist Party.

1933
Adolf Hitler becomes German Chancellor.

1939
Germany invades Poland; World War II begins.

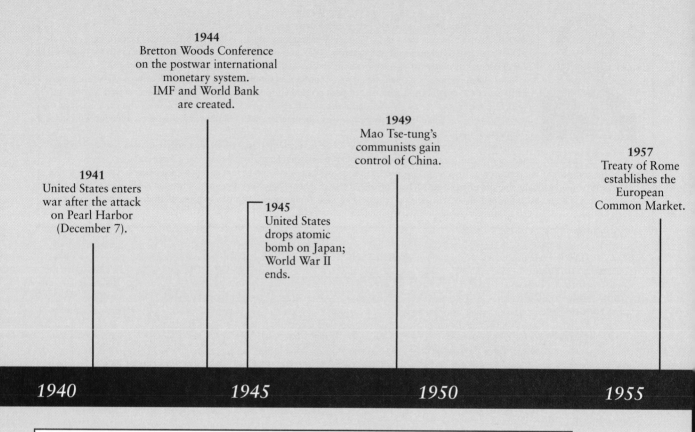

1944
Bretton Woods Conference
on the postwar international
monetary system.
IMF and World Bank
are created.

1949
Mao Tse-tung's
communists gain
control of China.

1957
Treaty of Rome
establishes the
European
Common Market.

1941
United States enters
war after the attack
on Pearl Harbor
(December 7).

1945
United States
drops atomic
bomb on Japan;
World War II
ends.

1940   *1945*   *1950*   *1955*

1959
Fidel Castro
overthrows
Fulgencio Batista
in Cuba.

FRIEDRICH AUGUST VON HAYEK *(1899–1992)*

Friedrich von Hayek was born in Vienna and studied at the University of Vienna, where he was trained in the Austrian tradition of economics (a school of thought originating with Carl Menger). He held academic positions at the London School of Economics and the University of Chicago. He returned to Europe in 1962 to the University of Freiburg in what was then West Germany and the University of Salzburg in Austria. He was awarded the Nobel Prize in Economics in 1974.

Hayek contributed new ideas and theories in many different areas of economics, but he is perhaps best known for his general conception of economics as a "coordination problem." His observation of market economies suggested that the relative prices determined in free markets provided the signals that allowed the actions of all decision makers to mesh—even though there was no formal planning taking place to coordinate these actions. He emphasized this "spontaneous order" at work in the economy as the subject matter for economics. The role of knowledge and information in the market process became central to Hayek, an idea that has grown in importance to the economics profession over the years.

Hayek's theory of business cycles provided an example of the breakdown of this coordination. A monetary disturbance (e.g., an increase in the money supply) would distort the signals (relative prices) by artificially raising the return to certain types of economic activity. When the disturbance disappeared, the boom caused by these distorted signals would be followed by a slump. Although Hayek's business-cycle theory was eclipsed by the Keynesian revolution, his emphasis on economics as a coordination problem has had a major influence on contemporary economic thought.

Hayek was also prominent in advocating the virtues of free markets as contributing to human freedom in the broad sense as well as to economic efficiency in the narrow sense. His *The Road to Serfdom* (1944) sounded an alarm about the political and economic implications of the then-growing belief in the virtues of central planning. His *Constitution of Liberty* (1960) is a much deeper philosophical analysis of the forces, economic and otherwise, that contribute to the liberty of the individual.

Credits

Photo Credits

Chapter 1 p. 3: Photo courtesy of the Adam Smith Institute, London, UK; p. 6: CP/Lionel Cironneau; p. 9: Getty Images/Stone/Daniel Bosler; p. 15: Photo Disc Inc.

Chapter 2 p. 28: © Jose Luis Pelaez, Inc./CORBIS/Magmaphoto.com; p. 32: Dick Hemingway.

Chapter 3 p. 52: Getty Images/Stone/Chris McCooey; p. 59: Saskatchewan Travel; p. 63: "These materials have been reproduced with the permission of eBay Inc." Copyright © eBay Inc. All rights reserved; p. 70: CP/Jacques Boissinot.

Chapter 4 p. 81: Imperial Oil Limited; p. 93: Dick Hemingway.

Chapter 19 p. 480: Shark Images Photography/Marko Shark; p. 490: Canadian Pacific.

Chapter 20 p. 506: Toyota Manufacturing Canada Inc.; p. 511: FPG International LLC/Michael Goldman; p. 512: AP Wide WorldPhoto.

Chapter 21 p. 523: Dick Hemingway; p. 528: Al Harvey/The Slide Farm.

Chapter 22 p. 563: Ontario Ministry of Tourism and Recreation.

Chapter 23 p. 574: Photo Edit/Myrleen Ferguson; p. 581: British Columbia Forest Service/Ray Wormald Photo.

Chapter 24 p. 600: Index Stock Imagery Inc./Jeff Greenberg; p. 601: Photolibrary.com; p. 607: Impact Visuals Photos & Graphics, Inc. Dona Binder.

Chapter 25 p. 628: © CORBIS/Digital Stock Images/MAGMA.

Chapter 26 p. 642: AP/Wide World Photos; p. 649: Photo Disc Inc.; p. 658: Photo Disc Inc.

Chapter 27 p. 672: Bank of Montreal Archives; p. 673: Getty/Stone Allstock; p. 674: Dick Hemingway; p. 676 (top and bottom): CP/Jonathon Hayward; p. 680: Getty/Stone/Alan Klehr; p. 682: Zuma Press.

Chapter 28 p. 697 (right): Bob Carroll; p. 697 (left): Dick Hemingway; p. 705: Dick Hemingway.

Chapter 29 p. 743: CP/Tom Hanson; p. 744: CP/Fred Chartrand.

Chapter 30 p. 764: CP/Ryan Remiorz; p. 771: Photo Disc Inc.; p. 773: Published by Nicholas Brealey Publishing, 1996, 1997.

Chapter 31 p. 789: Gary Conne/PhotoEdit; p. 796: Myrleen Ferguson Cate/PhotoEdit.

Chapter 32 p. 813: NAC/Donald I. Grant/PA115568; p. 824: Photo Disc Inc.; p. 828: AP/Jane Hwang.

Chapter 33 p. 845: Photo Disc Inc.; p. 848: British Columbia Forest Service/R.J. Challenger Photo.

Chapter 34 p. 860: SuperStock, Inc/Ping Amranand; p.871: Agriculture Quebec; p. 872: © Christopher J. Morris/ CORBIS/MagmaPhoto.com; p. 878: Courtesy of the Wine Council of Ontario.

Chapter 35 p. 892: CP Archive/Uniphoto; p. 897: Getty/ Stone/Luc Hautecoeur; p. 905: GettyImages Inc. – Taxi; p. 909: © Royalty Free/CORBIS/MAGMA.

Figure Credits

Figure 19-1; Tables 20-1, 20-2, 35-1: http://www.statcan.ca/english/Pgdb/econom.htm#nat.
Figure 19-4: http://www.statcan.ca/english/Pgdb/econom.htm#pri.
Figure 31-4: http://statcan.ca/english/Pgdb/labor20a.htm.
Figure 33-2: http://statcan.ca/english/Pgdb/intern.htm.

Index

Key terms and their page references are in boldface.